THE
SOCIOLOGISTS
OF
THE CHAIR

THE
SOCIOLOGISTS
OF
THE CHAIR

A Radical Analysis of the Formative

Years of North American Sociology

(1883–1922)

HERMAN SCHWENDINGER

&

JULIA R. SCHWENDINGER

Basic Books, Inc., *Publishers*

NEW YORK

For our comrade

ANATOLE SHAFFER

who dreamed about and struggled for
a democratic socialist society

From the moment when a subordinate class becomes really independent and dominant, calling into being a new type of State, the need arises concretely of building a new intellectual and moral order, i.e., a new type of society, and hence the need to elaborate the most universal concepts, the most refined and decisive ideological weapons.

ANTONIO GRAMSCI, *Prison Notebooks*

The task of social science now is to raise self-consciousness to the second degree, to find out the causes, the mode of functioning and the consequences of the adoption of ideologies, so as to submit them to rational criticism.

JOAN ROBINSON, *Freedom and Necessity*

ACKNOWLEDGMENTS

Many people have contributed their time and thoughts to this work in its final form. We are grateful to the following persons: Joanne Brown, Arlene Daniels, Linda Feldman, Steve Feldman, Janice Frankel, Ann Goolsby, Bill Gum, Marsha Hill, John Horton, Betty Knox, Mari Malvey, David Matza, Sheldon Messinger, Margie Moffet, Linda Peechee, Leslie Reid, Leni Schwendinger, Joseph Schwendinger, Lloyd Street, and Paul Takagi. We particularly appreciated the final typing and editorial assistance given by Ronnie London Carbone, Dan Carroll, Lynn Cooper, Eliot Currie, Suzie Dod, Gene Grabiner, Virginia Engquist Grabiner, Mike Hannigan, June Kress, Tommie Milord, Anthony Platt, Robert J. Schwendinger, Greg Shank, Richard Speiglman, Alan Sutter, Iris Topel, Joseph Weis, Dovie White, Martin Williams, Patricia Williams, and Sue Wilson. Many of these people gave their time in a voluntary and most generous fashion. Their supportive efforts symbolized a spirit of human solidarity which runs counter to the way cynics have described the modern urban society.

Another person whom we thank is Lena Siegel, our "mother in residence." Her contribution was less direct—she made life comfortable around us, keeping the table and larder filled while we concentrated on the book for lengthy stretches of time.

These friends, colleagues, clerical workers, relatives, and students vary greatly in their political beliefs. Because of this, it is important to emphasize that we alone are responsible for the political opinions expressed in this work.

H.S./J.R.S.

CONTENTS

xi

Contents

BOOK II

THE TRANSITIONAL FIGURES

BOOK III

CONSOLIDATION AND OPPRESSION

Contents

xiv

Contents

GENERAL INTRODUCTION

The Sociologists of the Chair is a study of the relationship between the newly emerging science of sociology and a particular phase in the development of liberalism. The formative years of American sociology are bounded by the publication of Lester Ward's *Dynamic Sociology* in 1883 and William Ogburn's *Social Change* in 1922. During these years, an elite group of American sociologists made profound contributions to one aspect of a changing liberal tradition. These contributions were added to the already existent body of literature created by other liberal intellectuals in Europe and America. At that time, laissez-faire liberalism was reconstituted and a new mode of thought, corporate liberalism, emerged as the dominant liberal ideology.

Origins of the Phrase "Sociologists of the Chair"

Parallel corporate-liberal developments occurred throughout the Western world. For example, in the 1870s a group of German political economists, some of whom became advisers to Chancellor Bismarck, suggested that the reconciliation of industrial conflicts could succeed only through direct intervention of the state in economic life. Although they were liberals, the German political economists were called *"socialists* of the chair" because more conservative intellectuals felt that state regulation of economic affairs represented a form of creeping *socialism*. The German political economists were also called "socialists of the *chair"* because they were employed primarily in *academic* institutions. The word "chair," in this context, refers to a professorship or other position of authority in a university.

In this work, the phrase "sociologists of the chair" has been adapted from the German usage to characterize the leading early American sociologists for two major reasons. First, a number of these Americans studied in Germany and their writings were profoundly influenced by the "socialists of the chair." Second, the phrase "sociologists of the chair" clearly denotes the fact that American sociology has been essentially an academic enterprise. American sociology did not emerge, like Marxian sociology, outside of the academy.

This volume argues that any attempt to explain the development of sociology in the United States must take into account the university as a prime generator of the liberal ideology and the functions of that ideology on the operations of the university and American life. The academy, with few exceptions, has been and continues to be a major instrument for developing and sustaining liberal ideology in the United States. Liberalism, in this view, does not

xvii

merely function as an influential *external* source of sociological ideas. Academic life is organized generally around liberal precepts, and academics, among others, *make liberalism what it is.*

During the formative years, liberal scholars made substantial modifications in legal, philosophical, and social scientific assumptions and doctrines. These modifications laid the analytic foundations for the modern bourgeois social sciences and professional schools in American institutions of higher learning. These liberals also developed assumptions and doctrines for the development of technocratic relationships in all the major institutions in the United States.

Varieties of Liberalism

Liberalism is defined by Theodorson and Theodorson (1969:203) as "an ideological orientation based on a belief in the importance of the freedom and welfare of the individual, and the possibility of social progress and the improvement of the quality of life through change and innovation in social organization." Although this definition appears in *A Modern Dictionary of Sociology,* it is neither sociological nor a reflection of political reality. Liberalism is far more than a neatly circumscribed set of social doctrines and a general belief in social improvement.

Analytically, liberalism refers to a comprehensive world view composed of economic, political, legal, philosophical, and ethical ideas. Sociologically, liberalism has become the dominant world view of advanced capitalist societies; it is imposed by ruling class institutions on the population at large. Although liberal ideas and doctrines are initially formulated by diverse intellectuals, the persons who command these institutions determine the selection of ideas and doctrines which constitute liberalism. Common liberal ideas, such as the belief in "progress" or "individual welfare," impart an illusory sense of ethical and logical consistency to liberal ideology as a whole. However, like all comprehensive world views, liberalism does not signify a monolithic body of empirical assumptions and consistent social, political, and economic doctrines.

Three long-term variations in liberal thought are related to American sociology. These variations are designated *classical* liberalism, *laissez-faire* liberalism, and *corporate* liberalism. Classical liberal notions were primarily produced by Western European scholars during the seventeenth and eighteenth centuries. These centuries represent the end of the precapitalist period although they overlap the rise of industrial capitalism in Great Britain. Laissez-faire liberalism drew upon British and French mercantile ideas; nevertheless, it expanded vigorously in Great Britain and the United States during the rise and consolidation of nineteenth-century industrial capitalism. Corporate liberalism, however, emerged throughout the Western world toward the end of the nineteenth century and provided new definitions of social reality under monopoly capitalism.

Corporate liberals argued that without political regulation of economic life, capitalism would be destroyed by class conflicts involving militant labor unions and socialist movements on the one hand, and gigantic monopolies or monopoly trusts on the other. They also argued that laissez-faire liberal doctrines had to be revised substantially because they opposed the expansion of the capitalist state. Additional corporate-liberal conceptions made liberalism politically viable in the face of changing political realities. This volume will focus on the relationships between early sociological ideas and this long-term development of liberalism. Consequently, these corporate-liberal conceptions will be "held constant" and the works of intellectual precursors will be examined where they bear on these conceptions.

The discussion of the historical precursors of these ideas, in Book I, is based on selections from a highly varied population of writers. These writers included nonliberals because at each new stage of liberal development, intellectuals reconstitute the standards which influence the selection of preexisting ideas, and the ongoing integration of these ideas into liberal thought. For instance, laissez-faire liberals felt that the French physiocrats had contributed to the doctrine of free trade even though the physiocrats had focused on an agrarian rather than an industrial free trade policy. Corporate liberals used Comte's ideas to fashion their own liberal doctrines even though he had been antagonistic to certain liberal ideas during his own lifetime.

Principles for Selecting Contents

This volume is concerned mainly, but not exclusively, with the writings of leading North American sociologists. Around this central focus, the volume broadly distinguishes three major divisions. The first division, Book I, discusses the historical precursors and the material foundations of leading sociological writings in the United States. Book II concentrates primarily on the earliest transitional writings by the founders of American sociology. Book III deals with the period in which the leading sociological ideas were elaborated, systematized, and consolidated. Generally, the three books distinguish events occurring at three sequential periods of time. The last book departs somewhat from this general scheme and also discusses early writings on women, the relation between academic sociology and the American university, and the issue of academic freedom.

It is impossible to describe the writings of all the historical precursors of early American sociology. The number of precursors is actually indeterminate. Consequently, only a handful of the most important representatives will be discussed in Book I. These persons and their ideas are selected in order to highlight the character of liberalism as a *whole* as well as the qualitatively new integration of liberal ideas forged by early *corporate* liberals toward the end of the nineteenth century.

In the present study, identification of a person's contribution to liberalism is based first and foremost on an examination of the general contents of liberalism, and not on the writings of any single individual. For example, John Locke's contribution to classical liberalism lies in a *selected* number of influential ideas expressed in his writings. Liberalism cannot be reduced to Lockean ideas, nor should the host of liberals who contributed to liberalism be personified by Locke. The complex theories of Hobbes, Bentham and Adam Smith were also rich in ideas, but only those adopted into corporate liberalism will be considered significant in this study.

It should be assumed that many of the intellectuals who contributed to liberalism were influenced by nonliberal ideologies. Hobbes' relation to the development of classical liberalism is based on his concept of how humans behave under conditions of scarcity and his secular interpretation of the origins of the state. The fact that his conception of the state was also organized around feudal absolutist standards does not minimize his contribution to liberalism. It merely indicates that his ideas were expressed in transitional forms.

Similar considerations bear on the analysis of the dual relation between Bentham and classical liberal and laissez-faire liberal modes of thought. Bentham generalized preexisting developments in philosophical hedonism and utilitarianism. His formalization of these generalizations represented a high point in the development of classical liberalism and simultaneously laid the foundation for the development of laissez-faire liberalism.

Malthus provides another illustration of the complexities involved in the development of liberal thought. Laissez-faire liberalism was organized around doctrines which pertained to industrial relations and worldwide markets (e.g., free labor, free trade, and the gold standard). At first glance, these doctrines appear to be far removed from Malthus, who was an apologist for the great English landowners. But Malthus' relation to the development of laissez-faire liberalism was based on his attitudes toward free labor and his emphasis on the self-regulating forces of competition, rather than his doctrinaire defense of a landowning class.

Finally, corporate liberalism was partly generated and is being regenerated by a few writers who have called themselves socialists.[1] But the relationship between their writings and corporate liberalism is not based on political self-identities. It is based on their contributions to the assumptions and doctrines which characterize corporate liberalism. Corporate liberalism exists independently of any single scholar. If a theoretical study of corporate liberalism holds this ideology "constant" in order to distinguish it apart from other modes of thought, then the specific ideas expressed by individual writers may vary considerably or not at all, depending on the specific person or writings in question.

This methodological perspective underlies Book II. That book selects and emphasizes *the general trends* within leading American sociological thought which contributed to the development of corporate liberalism. Some variations among early American sociologists will be described. But this variation remains within the range of the assumptions and doctrines which characterize liberal thought as a whole and corporate liberalism in particular.

A Marxian Perspective

Certain radical principles also structure the analysis of the development of liberalism in this volume. But the word "radical" needs some clarification because it has been used loosely by modern sociologists. Some sociologists, for example, consider themselves radical simply because they have departed from the current fashion in scholarly thought, rhetoric, or methodology.[2] Others regard the mere expression of moral objections to political, economic, or social policies to be sufficient for classifying themselves as radical scientists. Still others maintain that any critical standpoint toward social institutions clearly identifies them as radicals even though this perspective often leads to nothing more significant than the espousal of technocratic reforms. In fact, some sociologists who define themselves as radicals sound their clarion calls for "radical changes" and "structural transformation" only in the very last paragraph, if not the last sentence, of their articles. Usually, their ringing phrases are so vague that only the most naive or uncritical readers can think they really know what is meant by them.

Individual sociologists continue to use the word "radical" in a moral, apolitical, technocratic, or deliberately ambiguous sense. However, none of the foregoing delimitations are adequate for classifying scientists who represent authentically radical traditions in the United States. Furthermore, in the present work, the word "radical" is not confined to Marxian socialist traditions. The history of the United States is replete with abolitionist, feminist, populist, and labor movements which have supported truly radical, egalitarian and democratic traditions. There are many radicals today who have adapted these traditions to present conditions and who militantly oppose oppressive institutions in our society.

On the other hand, we are equally convinced that Karl Marx and Frederick Engels founded a revolutionary social science which is essential for understanding the fundamental sources of oppression in our society. This science not only seeks to understand the world but to change it. Equipped with an explicit recognition of the dynamic relations between theory and practice, Marxists have been concerned with analyzing the related evolutionary and revolutionary changes taking place throughout the world. Today, these changes have developed into rapidly changing worldwide conditions marked by monopoly capitalism, monopoly-state capitalism, modern imperialism, national liberation movements, socialist revolutions, and transitional socialist societies.

The Marxian historical perspective is called "the materialist conception of history." This approach to social change was generated by the material and ideological conditions accompanying the rise of nineteenth-century industrial capitalism in Europe. Just prior to the formative years of American sociology, Engels (1882) wrote about the class nature of these conditions. He stated, for example, that with the emergence of *class conflicts* during the epoch of capitalism, some nineteenth-century intellectuals gradually became aware

. . . that all past history, with the exception of primitive conditions, was the history of class struggles, that these warring classes of society are always the products of the conditions of production and exchange, in a word, of the economic conditions of their time; that therefore, the economic structure of society always forms the real basis from which, in the last analysis, is to be explained the whole superstructure of legal and political institutions, as well as of religious, philosophical, and other conceptions of each historical period. [*ibid.:*163]

This awareness was crystallized in the writings of Karl Marx, whose works mark the birth of historical materialism.

There are many differences in the application of Marx's ideas and analytic strategy by twentieth-century Marxists, who are of course living in a world that has changed greatly since their mentor's lifetime. Whatever their differences, however, Marxists continue to modify, extend, and discover new social relationships which characterize political economies as a whole. Conceptions of forces and relations of production, of social classes and ideology, are still utilized as significant determinants of long-term trends throughout the world. Social conditions are still given fundamental weight in the determination of social consciousness. Other analytic assumptions characterize Marxian writings today and have influenced this volume on the early development of American sociology.

In this volume Marxist assumptions are used to identify the relations between liberalism and capitalism. For example, liberal thought mediates and rationalizes exploitation, domestic and international imperialism, and social inequalities which are organized around the capitalist division of labor in the family, corporation, and civil bureaucracy. The analysis of liberalism, therefore, requires the identification of the capitalist conditions which have led to the development of this ideology as well as the reciprocal effects on the further development of these conditions. Hobbes' concept of the egoistic man is liberal not merely because it assumes that men are naturally selfish and will compete with each other whenever they are confronted with a condition of scarcity. It is liberal because it is a hegemonic conception which maintains and mediates capitalist relationships. The forms of selfish behavior which have continued to be classified by this conception are seen as expressions of a natural law which cannot be fundamentally altered by human institutions. The hegemonic use of egoism limits the possibilities of human existence insofar as working-class people have been convinced that because of "selfish human nature" bourgeois inequalities will continue to exist for all time.

Ideological Functions of Formal Mystifications

During the formative years, the intellectuals who contributed heavily to theoretical developments were general theorists like Lester Ward; their work usually represented abstract attempts to understand the nature of social order and social change, everywhere and always. Their writings stamped them as intellectuals' intellectuals. The products of their labor provided analytic methods, analytic categories, basic assumptions about the nature of man, woman, and society, and an ensemble of mechanisms considered fruitful to theorists interested in delimited areas of social behavior.

Although these hegemonic intellectuals formulated specific theories about social relationships, the uniqueness of their contribution to the development of sociology lay in their ability, first, to distinguish various trends in social thought; second, to abstract common theoretical categories and generalizations; and third, to reconceptualize and formalize their meanings on a more abstract level. These men were also adept at reflecting on the implicit analytic strategies by which theorists arrived at their explanations. But after distinguishing these categories, they reconceptualized them in order to make them explicitly available to other scholars.

The formal classification and restatement of substantive categories was then applied to new areas of inquiry, and their most abstract formulations generated new theories by the mere addition of variant abstractions to the original body of theories. However, this process of theory building did not proceed on the basis of systematic confirmation of the original source theories; theory building by the contemplation of the preexisting theories resulted in the preservation of social myths. The accumulation of diverse expressions of these myths, moreover, reinforced the belief that these mystifications were in fact "objective" representations of social reality. The highly abstract and formal character of the source theories, which anchored these expressions, also appeared to place them beyond "patriotism" and "parochialism," that is, beyond any prejudicial bias.

In this volume, the analysis of this complex process of theoretical development will facilitate identification of some of the most abstract categories of liberal sociological thought. The further identification of the ideological functions of these categories will encourage the reader to move beyond the radical criticism of *each* liberal category or *each* liberal theory or *each* liberal school of thought as an entity unto itself. By the end of this volume, the reader will become familiar with categories, generalizations, and analytic strategies that identify whole *families* of liberal theories and liberal schools of thought.

Anticipated Criticism of Marxist Realism

This volume repeatedly utilizes such substantive terms as "sexism," "racism," "national chauvinism," "imperialism," and "exploitation" in order to identify the ideological functions of sociological writings. These words, moreover, simultaneously express analytic and moral standpoints of the authors.

These moral and analytic usages may startle and inflame academics who are naive members of a liberal culture—naive because they actually believe that established sociological categories enable them to deal with social reality in an "objective" and "value-free" manner. These "ethnocentric" academics denounce terms like "exploitation" and "imperialism" as being "epithets" or "political rhetoric" rather than scientific categories. The category of "corporate liberalism" is often regarded as an arbitrary moral category. The irony underlying this criticism is that *realistic* categories like sexism and imperialism are denounced as ideological and not analytic, while *formal* liberal mystifications are regarded as analytic and not ideological.[3]

A critical analysis of "bourgeois reason" points to the underlying connections between this liberal mode of thought and such relationships as racism, sexism, economic exploitation, imperialism, and political oppression. Liberal scholars frequently become angry with these references and object to the never-ending use of these "odious" relationships as *major* reference points in Marxist evaluations of liberal works. This sort of counterattack is sometimes made by academics who justify their indignation by pointing out that their liberal colleagues have repeatedly *professed* good rather than bad intentions. Sociologists frequently represent their own works as examples of humanistic attempts to inquire into the nature of social life.

We will not ignore the stated intentions of the men who founded academic sociology in the United States. But a scholar's stated intentions may be highly misleading. Consequently, this work will consider what the early sociologists *said* they were doing—or what they said their colleagues *ought* to be doing and compare it with what they, in fact, *were* doing. In this process, our analytic attention will focus on the mutually reinforcing relationship between the existing forms of social oppression and the actual contents of sociological writings at the time. Political repression, for example, will be regarded as the primary factor in the maintenance of liberal hegemony within academic institutions in the United States. Liberal scholarship never would have dominated the field of sociology, then or now, in the absence of politically repressive conditions.

Academics might also attack as unjustifiable the use of categories like "sexism" and "racism" to describe early sociological writings, because these categories symbolize judgements of the past in terms of present "left political standards." Such standard criticisms can be met with the following observations. First, historians have *always* interpreted the past on the basis of ideological standards which are tacitly embodied in modern psychological, sociological, and political categories.[4] No historian, in fact, can transcend the analytic and ethical standards which are implicit in his world view and which structure the selection and evaluation of the meanings of past events. To self-consciously interpret past trends of thought in terms of their contribution to contemporary social and political concerns represents the highest form of sociological inquiry.

Second, such criticisms avoid coming to grips with the ideological and material contradictions *actually* existing during the formative years. From the very beginning of those years, militant demands for racial, sexual, national, and economic equality were being raised by social movements and political organizations. Intellectuals in these movements and organizations created their own ideas about the possibilities of human existence. Because of this development the early sociologists were not "men of their times" in the myopic sense that liberal scholars use this phrase. They were the products of historical conditions which were being opposed by other persons in their own lifetimes. These sociologists were also active agents who helped create these conditions, and their energetic activities in this regard involved the selection of ideological notions from among the widely ranging theories of sexual, racial, economic, and national inequalities, which were actually available to them. In this context, references to their *racist* attitudes, their *sexist* perspectives, and their *imperialistic* biases illuminate their decision-making processes. These references appear to be an imposition of modern "left standards" only to those scholars who may believe that distinguishing features of oppressive social relations and ideas were first invented by Marxist scholars in the sixties.

Finally, such criticisms are "unhistorical"; they ignore the historical connections between the formative years and the modern period. In contrast, the present work treats early sociological writings as expressions of relationships that were grounded in past, present and future developments. These early writings are viewed as part of long-term ideological and material trends. In this context, the formative writings operate as causes as well as effects, and their reciprocal ties to a changing social context are grasped by a macroscopic theory of historical change.

Marxists have employed their realistic categories in an unceasing critique of ruling ideas in capitalist societies. These historically based critiques have been directed, in particular, at the idealistic myths underlying historical theories organized primarily around "great men," "great ideas," and "great traditions." For example, in his writings about the materialist conception of history, Engels noted that in the previous (eighteenth) century, the scholars of the Enlightenment were dominated by idealistic conceptions of social change. As a consequence, they envisioned a utopian "kingdom of reason" wherein superstition, injustice, privilege, and oppression were to vanish in the face of "eternal truth, eternal justice, equality grounded in nature and the inalienable rights of man." However, "We know today," Engels added in 1872

that this kingdom of reason was nothing more than the idealized kingdom of the bourgeoisie; that eternal justice found its realization in bourgeois justice; that equality reduced itself to bourgeois equality before the law; that bourgeois property was proclaimed as one of the essential rights of man; and that the government of reason, the Social Contract of Rousseau, came into existence and could only come into existence as a bourgeois-democratic republic. [*ibid.*:142]

Our study will show that by the end of the formative years, the leading scholars in American sociology formulated their *own* kingdoms of reason based on principles of equity, tolerance, pluralism, and bourgeois democracy. In charting the nature of these kingdoms, the Americans also employed what they alleged to be "universals" such as synergy and sublimation, conflict and accommodation, social control and cultural lag. Partly because they were markedly ahistorical and extremely general in application, these universal ideas were couched in very formal generalizations. In spite of their formal masks, however, it will be found that they were firmly grounded in liberal doctrines of class harmony and class collaboration. They were also anchored in other tenets of liberalism which justified the corporate-liberal state, social class inequality, the centralization of capital, and modern imperialism. These ahistorical ideas, therefore, were just as much the product of doctrines that justified newly emerging (although much more advanced) capitalist relationships as were the earlier liberal concepts of eternal truth, eternal justice, and natural man.

The New Corporate-Liberal Kingdom
and the Princes of Reason

The repressive conditions affecting academic freedom, the business domination of the universities, and the technocratic goals maintaining the ideological functions of the social sciences in North American universities are discussed in the concluding parts of Book III. These parts focus on the rhetoric of ideological neutrality which became fashionable among sociologists toward the end of the formative years. This rhetoric defined, as the epitome of *scientific* method, the blatantly ideological products of leading sociologists.

American sociologists today are removed by over a half-century from the formative years; yet, the concepts and theories developed during those years are repeatedly used by modern scholars. For example, the now venerable rhetoric of neutrality can be found expressed in a 1970 presidential speech to the American Sociological Association entitled "Sociology and the Distrust of Reason" by Reinhard Bendix. In that speech Bendix defended "reason" by rejecting the so-called romanticism which had become so widespread among radical students. He urged students and colleagues to continue to follow in the footsteps of such liberal princes of reason as Durkheim, Freud, and Weber. But what kinds of substantive theories and scientific doctrines did these men create in the name of reason and rationality? Durkheim's theories underwrote an official morality based on *technocratic* and *imperialist* doctrines; Freud's theories buttressed the *exploitative* and *sexist* conditions in modern societies with the force of natural law; and with regard to the role of the social scientist, Weber (as Bendix [1970:835] is fully aware) espoused an

xxvi

elitist doctrine of ideological neutrality: he felt that social science should be the product of the disinterested pursuit of knowledge by an intellectual aristocracy.

According to Bendix, Weber's conception of the social scientist's "calling" was based on the social tradition of rationalism. This tradition emerged during the period of the Enlightenment in the seventeenth and eighteenth centuries. But how does traditional rationalism actually compare with what Bendix and his contemporaries nurture as "value-free" beliefs? While there are some similarities between Weber's notion and the rationalist tradition, the men of the Enlightenment generally believed that the positive functions of scientific knowledge should be evaluated in terms of their political utility (James F. Becker 1961, 1964). Consequently, radical sociologists, not Weberians, are heirs to this aspect of the Enlightenment.

Radicals, in fact, have initiated events which may finally enable some academic sociologists to justifiably claim that they are also heirs to the humanistic tradition of the Enlightenment. Their claims are not being secured on the basis of humanitarian sounding platitudes, vague references to reason, or the continuing appeals for accommodation to liberal thought and liberal institutions, but rather because these intellectuals have aligned themselves with revolutionary movements. It is virtually impossible, without this alignment, to organize analytic activity on the basis of a comprehensive radical ideology and an uncompromising radical stand on the major political and economic issues which influence the material conditions of oppressed human beings throughout the world.

To conclude, the most significant issues in our time involve the achievement of an end to imperialism, racism, sexism, economic exploitation, and political oppression. Above all, they require the attainment of socialism, which is the only feasible alternative to capitalism. These issues were just as important to the writings produced by outstanding liberal sociologists during the formative years. Consequently, this volume inquires into whether or not sociological writings epitomized the kind of "reason" which actually justified imperialism. Let us ask whether men like Lester F. Ward, Edward Alsworth Ross, and W. I. Thomas were racists. The politically repressive discourse about the professional role of the sociologist by Albion Small, Charles Ellwood, Ulysses G. Weatherly, and Robert E. Park will be examined. Sexism, exploitation, technocratic and antisocialist doctrines will be scrutinized. Our evaluation of sociological writings on the basis of political standards that are open and aboveboard will embody, in practice, the differences between radical and liberal scholarship today.

It will eventually be suggested that social scientists must abandon liberalism if they are really interested in making a contribution, however small, to the common good. Most men and women do make their greatest contribution to the material and spiritual needs of others in their daily work; as a consequence, workaday life bears the greatest brunt of an individual's responsibility to humankind. It is unfortunate, in light of this, to find so many sociologists dissipating lifetimes of exhausting work while laboring under the illusion that their daily conduct is regulated solely by scientific curiosity. The spectacle of sociologists who energetically profess a humanistic outlook while contributing to the oppressive institutions in our society is another example of liberal irrationality.

NOTES

1. Chapter 11 will note that some of the late nineteenth-century German political economists, who contributed to the development of corporate liberalism, called themselves socialists. In the modern period, one finds sociologists such as Lewis Coser considering himself a socialist (Coser 1967). Chapter 71 describes some of Coser's ideas which are corporate liberal rather than socialist.

2. Howard S. Becker goes so far as to state, "Good sociologists produce radical results." He adds by way of clarification, "What I mean by a radical result is one that rises above current orthodoxies, whether they are political, moral, institutional, scientific or whatever. That may or may not go with political radicalism, conventionally defined" (Debro 1970:171).

3. We would like to thank Alan Sutter for noting this irony.

4. This volume describes some of the ideal-type categories which are repeatedly used to organize historical events on the basis of liberal standards (e.g., Nisbet 1966, Bramson 1961, Friedrichs 1970, Gouldner 1970, Bendix 1970).

BOOK I

HISTORICAL
PRECURSORS
AND MATERIAL
FOUNDATIONS

INTRODUCTION TO
BOOK I

THE coming chapters discuss the reciprocal relationship between two emerging phenomena, academic sociology and corporate liberalism. The development of American sociology has been influenced by the development of corporate liberalism. And perhaps more profoundly, the outstanding intellectual contribution of academic sociologists has been the further development and refinement of corporate liberalism. The major trends in American sociology, therefore, will be regarded as *one aspect* of the complex social processes generating and regenerating liberalism. Many of the very basic categories and analytic strategies produced by American sociologists have emerged as an *inherent* part of the liberal ideology.

It will be noted that there are other relationships between the dominant characteristics of academic social science and liberalism. For example, one characteristic is the way in which the production of ideology has become instituted within the university. Since the rise of the modern university, a complex division of labor has been established among academics in a variety of disciplines and professional schools. This division of labor has generated and maintained the production of ideological conceptions. The overwhelming majority of academic social scientists have become specialists whose careers, for the most part, are unwittingly devoted to the cultivation of a liberal metaphysics of normality.

Book I deals with the historical precursors and the material conditions underlying the early development of North American sociology. It will depart greatly from current sociological works which locate the most significant origins of American or Western sociology in early nineteenth-century antiliberal modes of thought. We contend that American sociology was essentially a liberal response to the great conflicts of the times: all other ideologies are insignificant in comparison to liberalism as a determinant of the development of American sociology. The term "insignificant," in this context, refers specifically to the fact that by comparison with liberalism, other ideologies, such as Protestantism, played a minor role in the *integration* of ideas that distinguishes the development of sociology in the United States.

Unless the notion of significance is restricted to the determinants of *integrative* ideas, the search for origins degenerates to the level of decomposing a system of ideas into its elements and to endless wrangling over the relative contribution of historical precursors and to endless debate over which conditions generated each one of these elements.[1] Aside from its futility, this kind of argument is difficult to conduct in relation to American sociologists because they sampled widely among preexisting and contemporary writers. Their selections were not restricted to classical liberal and laissez-faire liberal ideas. Moreover, the variation in content, the magnitude of the number and sources of ideas selected, integrated, or discarded by the pioneering sociologists is so great that diffusionist or "great man" theories of history serve only to cloud the actual events of that time. The American scholars borrowed ideas from German, Austro-Hungarian, French, English, and Belgian scholars, not to mention theologians, economists, philosophers, and historians in their own country. Consequently, it is impossible to regard the foundations of American sociology as limited merely to the works of Maistre, Saint-Simon, Comte, or even Spencer. While these men are important, they represent only the beginnings of a long list of precursors.

On the other hand, certain European writings are not significant for an understanding of early American sociology. For instance, Max Weber, who is important to modern American sociology, had virtually no influence on the leading sociologists during the formative period. The founders, moreover, did not wait upon Weber in order to develop their own reductionist strategies for analyzing macroscopic changes or American natural-social-law conceptions of social relationships. They certainly did not wait upon Weber's technocratic standards and doctrines. In fact, the writings of Weber and the Americans may have differed in some respects, but they were parallel corporate liberal developments.

Unlike their modern, professional counterparts, the early sociologists of the chair did not use Weber's works.[2] The early American sociologists had independently developed ideas which were a part of their own sociological tradition. If we were eclectic in our theoretical approach, or concerned solely with the modern period, we would analyze the reasons why contemporary sociologists use Weber's writings to justify their technocratic biases. Weber's writings are not given priority because this work is concerned with the foundations of American sociology.

The virtual omission of Weber signifies only one of the major *theoretical* differences between this work and the works of other writers in the history of the field. These theoretical differences place an enormous burden on the organization of Book I because they symbolize the degree to which the taken-for-granted knowledge in the field cannot be relied upon for simplifying the varied historical precursors of early American writings. The juxtaposition of background ideas being used here is not readily found in the typical sociology course or textbook. Book I has singled out some of the preexisting ideas and relationships that are essential to understanding the *content* of later sociological writings. The reader cannot expect to fully understand the rationales which have led to our selection of preexisting ideas and relations, until he/she has become acquainted with the writings of the later formative years. Without a large body of taken-for-granted knowledge, it is virtually impossible to establish these rationales by simultaneously juxtaposing earlier and later ideas.

Consequently, Book I generally arranges the discussion of the historical precursors chronologically according to the times in which these persons lived. Thus, the classical liberals and laissez-faire liberals are discussed earlier than the German socialists of the chair because most of them lived and wrote at an earlier period. Book I does deviate from this time sequence in order to distinguish two important trends in analytic thought which overlap each other in time. Both of these trends were primarily created by aristocratic and bourgeois intellectuals, who speculated about the kinds of social mechanisms that would be necessary for stabilizing and integrating social institutions, market relationships, and even entire societies. The first of these trends was organized around categories that were close to the mainstream of economic liberalism: the categories used emphasized the integrative effects of (1) the natural forces of competition and (2) exchange relations based on the pursuit of self interest. The second trend, on the other hand, incorporated categories produced by writers who felt that social order was dependent upon the maintenance of despotic, inegalitarian systems of authority.

Toward the end of Book I the reader is introduced to similarities and differences between the writings by early American sociologists and the writings by classical and laissez-faire liberals. The implicit difficulties in making such a comparative analysis are heightened by the fact that these early American writings have not been regular reading for recent generations of students. Therefore, this volume contains numerous accounts of selected works by early sociologists. This is done in order to enhance the utility of this volume as a basic text and reference work on the history of North American sociology. The reader will find the contents and the section headings within each chapter to be a helpful outline to the volume.

Familiarity with the material in the summaries of early writings is mandatory in order to offset the effects of the overwhelming agreement among modern American sociologists, that early members of the field were overshadowed by Europeans. Alvin Gouldner (1970) and Robert Friedrichs (1970), for example, explain sociological developments beyond the turn of the century by concentrating almost entirely on French, English, and German developments. As a consequence, the spirit of their argument does more than state a position opposed to the contents of this volume. From a dynamic point of view, their works virtually exclude the writings of such American sociologists as Ward, Ross, and Small from a position of importance to modern sociological thought.

This historical evidence weighs heavily against Gouldner and Friedrichs. The intensive examination of early writings in this volume will recognize the international relations involved in the development of sociology. But it will focus on the extraordinary significance, for modern American sociology, of the very general conceptual framework established by *American* writers during the formative years.

The numerous accounts of American sociological writings indicate that what some liberal scholars have heretofore seen as a chaotic body of writings (e.g., Friedrichs 1970:11) was, in fact, an interrelated and highly structured liberal ideology. Aside from whatever additional meanings are gained from the critical accounts, it also becomes obvious that these writings speak very much for themselves. These writings are patently ideological statements. The connection between these writings and an ideological defense of capitalism, imperialism, racism, and sexism, is made explicit by their authors. This connection is plain for all to see because these writings were not obfuscated by the modern technocratic rhetoric of ideological neutrality and the highly standardized and abstracted formal vocabularies which pervade sociological writings *today*. To be sure, early sociologists like Albion Small did favor highly obscurantist usages which masked the ideological foundations of their writings; but these usages were neither systematically employed nor methodically standardized until 1921. Before that time, the ideological contents of leading sociological writings was still very much open and above board. It remains but to pinpoint and name the common ideological relationships.

NOTES

1. For example, see the disagreements between Parsons (1937:307), Gouldner (1958:viii) and Nisbet (1965:28) about the influence of Comte and Saint-Simon on Durkheim.

2. Park and Burgess' (1924) grand theory which was written at the very end of the formative years contains only three (bibliographic) references to Weber. One of these references (Park and Burgess 1924:217 item 12) suggests that they saw Weber as just another "social control" theorist. Weber's economic writings are considered "an attempt to define society as a control organization within the limits of an economic community."

PART ONE
Classical Liberalism

CHAPTER 1

The Natural-Law Tradition

The natural-law tradition contains a number of the most important assumptions utilized by liberal ideologists over the centuries. Because of this, we will first discuss its origins and then we will turn to the ways in which liberals have revised and used this tradition. When this is done, we will point out that the "natural-social-law tradition," which was eventually created by these revisions, is very much in evidence in modern American sociological writings.

Natural Law and Orderly Nature
of the Universe

The ideas which are at the center of the natural-law tradition are primarily utilized for solving the conceptual problem of social integration. Consequently they attempt to answer such questions as: Why do social institutions *persist* over time? What holds society *together?* How is social *order* maintained? Questions of this kind were posed in antiquity and some of their answers were framed on the basis of natural law conceptions.

Natural law, the ancients said, is the law that nature imposes on all living creatures. On this basis, philosophers distinguished *natural justice* from man-made justice, and *natural rights* from socially instituted rights or the arbitrary claims of individuals. Natural law also was considered an expression of an *inherent tendency* for order which was characteristic of all natural relationships and whose fulfillment was *morally appropriate*. Thus natural law had empirical and moral implications which were inseparable from one another.

Natural law can be contrasted with religious law which was directly attributed to a Divine Will. Natural law also differed from precepts of distinctly human origins such as the mandates contained in one or another body of man-made laws. But natural law is more difficult to fathom than either of these alternatives because it located justice and right in the *orderly nature* of the universe itself. With regard to religious law, for example, feudal bishops often told their monarchs that their rule was an expression of the divine right of kings. In some principalities, on the other hand, a monarchy was justified by the (man-made) consensus of an aristocratic electorate. The natural-law philosopher St. Thomas Aquinas, however, indicated that a monarchy was the best possible political regime because it was in accord with the natural and universal order of things. This pervasive order was reflected in the existence of *one ruler* among men, *one ruler* among bees, and *one ruler* in the universe as a whole[1] The relationships between a monarch and a monarchy, a queen bee and her colony of bees, a God and his universe, were perceived as examples of an inherent necessity which has existed for all time throughout the entire cosmos. The inherent necessity of natural law is eloquently exemplified by the effect on the colony when the queen bee is removed. The bee society ceases to function and may indeed cease to exist. The relations between the queen and her colony are necessary prerequisites for the survival of the colony.

Although inherently necessary, natural-law relationships were not considered to be inexorable in every individual case. Instead, these relationships were necessary in the sense that stable and orderly relationships among the living could not exist without them. Individuals, in this view, could choose to live "unnaturally" but this choice would be disastrous because unnatural relationships would eventually degenerate into disorder and chaos. (If men chose to live in a republic rather than a monarchy, for example, it was expected that their political relationships would become unstable and that anarchy would ensue.)

Human beings, therefore, could choose between "natural" and "unnatural" relationships. This freedom of choice enabled the use of natural-law relationships as standards for judging the right and wrong of individual conduct.[2] Consequently, natural law relationships were regarded as more than empirically necessary prerequisites for order; natural law provided standards of justice that often buttressed "well-ordered" societies.[3]

On the other hand, it was also assumed that natural-law relationships were independent of human will and human conventions. During the seventeenth century, republican writers relied on this basic assumption whenever they claimed that monarchies oppressed an individual's right to live naturally. Since, in their eyes, natural law was more valid than aristocratic ("man-made") law, natural-law standards were used to justify the revolutionary overthrow of monarchial regimes.

Classical Antecedents
of Liberal Natural-Law Conceptions

A brief review of very early natural-law thinking will introduce additional assumptions which were relevant to the development of liberal natural-law conceptions. This review will also illustrate the degree to which the basic assumptions mentioned previously had their origins in philosophers of antiquity.

Plato's writings provide an illustration of a very early usage of the classical conceptions of natural law. Book VIII of the *Republic* indicates, for example, that all men are part of nature. Because inherent necessities characterize order everywhere, men, as part of nature, are universally equipped with natural purposes or tendencies toward order. To explain disorder, however, Plato indicated that man is a rational being who is possessed of freedom to act in accordance with his nature. Man may learn to understand human nature and is free to decide to act in conformity or nonconformity with natural law. Man is therefore free to fulfill or not fulfill his natural tendencies toward orderly relationships.

In Plato's writings, the modes of existence that are in conformity with human nature are ideal or good in a very direct, moral sense. Human nature consequently provides men with *moral standards* which are independent of their own social or political conventions. Furthermore, adherence to these natural moral standards is consequential for social and political life; if men fail to understand their nature and neglect to obey the moral implications inherent in nature, then social chaos, anarchy, and tyranny will ensue (Wild 1953:23–24).

Plato's natural-law notions were organized around his images of a utopian society. However, his operative notions of justice in real life were not identical to his conception of natural (utopian) relationships because he believed that men could only *approximate* the standards supplied by nature.[4] Plato's natural modes of existence were limited because they referred only to an *ideal* rather than a concrete form of social existence.

In contrast, Aristotle related natural-law conceptions to the analysis of law and justice in a more usual sense because his philosophy involved the notion of *individual rights*. In Aristotle's writings, natural law offered the grounds on which a person could actually claim a right. His concept of natural rights had direct political implications. For example, Aristotelian thought suggested that the right to worship the gods by sacrifices or to be ruled by a monarch, were natural rights. Because Aristotle claimed that any political society must recognize natural rights if it is to survive, the notion of natural right was used to indicate the *necessary conditions* for the survival of political societies. This interpretation was consistent with the assumption that natural-law relationships were inherently necessary for order.

The Romans also added to the development of the natural-law tradition when they differentiated what was called *jus gentium:* "the law of peoples." The Romans distinguished this law from their *jus civile:* man-made or positive law. They arrived at the "law of the peoples" by identifying commonalities among national, city, and tribal laws. These commonalities appeared to be universal and hence more valid or "natural" than laws varying with different localities and societal groups (Brinton 1963:103).

It was the Stoics, however, who unequivocally transformed "the law of peoples" into "natural law" and provided the latter with a clearly expressed philosophical rationale.[5] The Romans identified certain rules as somehow more "natural" than the formal civil law, but the Stoics had perceived natural law as the *origin* of certain kinds of legal rules. They evaluated these rules to be as good as, if not superior to, rules instituted solely by human beings.

The ancient ideas associated with natural law were reintegrated and elaborated by St. Thomas Aquinas in the thirteenth century. In the Thomist doctrine, natural law, or "naturally just" law, continued to be construed as a set of rules imposed by nature on all living creatures. Although perceived as immutable in principle, it was also conceded that variation in time, place, and types of people could result in different manifestations of these rules. Therefore, natural-law notions were not only used to distinguish socially necessary conditions but also historically relative and socially expedient relationships (Schumpeter 1954:109). With this scheme, St. Thomas (1938:41) argued, for example, that governance by the multitude was inferior to the rule of society by one man. The multitude was reputed to be rent by disagreements; it was incapable of forging the unity necessary for the achievement of the welfare and safety of society. Thus, not only was the "rule of one man" considered to be in *accord with nature* but it was also more *socially expedient* than "the rule of many."

Furthermore, Thomist doctrine held that laws promulgated by legislative bodies were either deductions from natural law or adjustments of its rules under particular conditions. This interpretation consequently maintained the traditional use of natural law as a higher-order moral principle. By deduction from first principles or, by specifying certain conditions, natural law was capable of conversion into practical precepts or guidelines by which other rules could be ethically evaluated.

Summarizing the main ideas in this brief discussion of the historical development of natural law, we can see that first, natural law was construed as a set of rules that nature imposed on living creatures. Second, it became admissible for this set of rules to be associated with historically relative and socially necessary or expedient conditions. Third, it was concluded that no law made by man could violate a rule of natural law. Fourth, natural law was used to designate optimum political regimes (e.g., a monarchy as opposed to a republic). Finally (but by no means the least important from an analytic point of view), natural-law scholars used the concept of natural right to identify socially necessary conditions for the establishment of orderly social relationships.

10

It is of the greatest significance to note that all institutions, good or bad, could ultimately be justified by recourse to natural law. Furthermore, since no law made by man could violate a rule of natural law, human beings could not justifiably institute radical changes in society—or maintain existing social institutions—unless the desired institutions could be shown to conform to natural law.

The Secularization of Natural Law

By the sixteenth and seventeenth centuries, natural-law concepts were adopted and modified by secular scholars. Natural law epitomized the application of reason to the analysis of moral relationships. Later, in the changing interpretations of natural law during the seventeenth- and eighteenth-century Enlightenment, human rationality was partly associated with the awareness of empirical regularities in natural relationships. In this process, the medieval Thomist correspondence between the dictates of reason and social necessity or expedience was retained, but the meaning of natural law came to be associated only or primarily with an empirical and rational, as opposed to theological, analysis.

The contrast between St. Thomas (1226–1274) and Thomas Hobbes (1588–1679) illustrates the secularization of the concept of natural law. St. Thomas had asserted that the force of a divine will was ultimately accountable for both the ethical and the empirical ordering of the universe, of which human relationships are a part. Hobbes, on the other hand, located the *ultimate* origins of human relationships in the nature of man. (It was this nature which justified the advantages of a political community.) Furthermore, St. Thomas had perceived human nature from the standpoint of a medieval theologian: although humans shared certain characteristics with other beasts such as the desires for self-preservation and procreation, their social lives prepared them for higher spiritual ends. Later, Hobbes, in sharp contrast, regarded natural human purposes to be *chiefly* organized around the desire for self-preservation: it was therefore man's earthly characteristics which justified social relationships rather than the natural necessity to move closer to God.

From the beginning of the Enlightenment to the early part of the nineteenth century, intellectuals justified their concepts of human rights on the basis of natural law. The culmination of this trend was represented by such works as Thomas Paine's *Rights of Man*. This trend emphasized the fulfillment of natural rights as a vehicle for social as well as individual well-being. In addition, the concept of natural justice referred increasingly to the good of everyone (the common good) or to standards of equity inherent in social relationships, irrespective of whether these relations involved individual contracts or social institutions existing in the past or present (Schumpeter 1954:109).

Toward the end of the Enlightenment, many definitions of natural right stood in opposition to the laws of existing regimes. However, it should not be inferred that natural rights in this context merely symbolized an ideal state of affairs. The concept of natural right also referred to what *must* be done if political institutions were to survive, as well as to what ought to be done if justice were to be secured. If humans were not granted their natural rights, existing political institutions would inevitably be rent by discord and overthrown; they would be replaced by institutions that were in harmony with natural rights. Social institutions, therefore, could not survive if they did not secure natural rights and, as a consequence, what *ought* to be done, in this context, was firmly wedded to what would *in fact* work out in reality. The concept of natural right was therefore at once a moral standard for judging political institutions and a realistic statement about the prerequisites for the survival of these institutions.

Operative Interpretations of Natural Law

It has been noted that Plato, Aristotle, the Stoics, St. Thomas, and various seventeenth- and eighteenth-century scholars were as one in the belief that the moral rules inherent in natural relationships were applicable to humans everywhere. But the specific natural law doctrines promulgated by these scholars were very different from each other. None of these scholars shared the same opinion about the nature of the moral rules or the nature of human beings. Each one made a very different *operative* interpretation of the axiomatic claim that there exist moral principles inherent in natural relationships.

The operative interpretations of natural-law axioms were dependent, to a large extent, on the ideological standpoint of individual scholars. (St. Thomas' scholastic interpretation, for example, was shaped by his medieval Catholicism.) During the Enlightenment, however, Christianity underwent considerable change in countries like England, and religious principles became reconciled with the new middle-*class* defense of *property* rights. As a consequence, many natural-law liberal scholars did not specifically eschew religious doctrines at that time, but their operative interpretations of the nature of man (which is crucial to the identification of natural law and natural right) changed and became far closer to the views of an atheist like Hobbes than a medieval scholastic like St. Thomas.

An English philosopher and product of this property-oriented class approach, John Locke (1632–1704), formulated a concept of man that figured significantly in the emergence of classical liberalism. Although linked to various religious assumptions about the nature of the universe and moral law, Locke's view of man was similar to Hobbes' insofar as it assumed that the desire for self-preservation was basic to human nature. However, Locke profoundly modified the Hobbesian conception by adding that a natural right to *property* was derived from the natural right to self-preservation. In this context, moreover, the natural right to the acquisition of property was construed as the natural right of *unlimited acquisition* (Strauss 1969:84). On this basis, as we shall see in chapters to come, the concept of natural right was transformed into a natural-law justification for capitalism.

Natural-Law Defense of Social Inequalities

During the Enlightenment, some scholars felt that feudal institutions had been highly unnatural because they were contradictory to human nature. However, these critics of feudalism were not opposed to social *inequality* in forms more "natural" than those prevailing during their lifetime. In other words, it should not be inferred that seventeenth- or eighteenth-century scholars favored egalitarian relationships by virtue of their criticism of feudal inequalities. It is apparent, for example, that in the development of a classical liberal concept of man, social inequalities based upon the private ownership of property were perceived as being natural.

It has been further noted that the concepts of human nature emerging during the Enlightenment were organized around certain universal needs such as self-preservation. At that time it was argued that basic social and political institutions, such as the patriarchal family and the political state, did not exist for supernatural reasons, but because they were necessary for the fulfillment of universal and natural needs. Therefore, various types of socially instituted forms of inequality came to be interpreted as expressions or "functions" of natural purposes or needs which seemed to explain their existence. In this explanatory context, moreover, social inequalities as ultimate expressions of the very nature of man were not left at that; inequalities were also alleged to be *just* because they were natural.

Chapter 24 describes the changing character of the natural-law tradition during the formative years of American sociology. It will also be noted that early sociologists emphasized the negative side of traditional natural law ideas. This emphasis was used whenever they claimed, for example, that whoever attempted to establish economic equality was bound to fail because such equality was *contrary to human nature*. However, some of these men also developed a crucial extension beyond this venerable natural law justification. They asserted that radical social changes would inexorably fail because they were contrary to the inherent *nature of social systems*. Their sociological arguments, furthermore, employed corporate-liberal references to mythical universal social laws, and fallacious universal social properties. Called into play to defend capitalist inequities in the face of socialist movements, these mythical laws and properties limited the historically determined potentialities of human society on the basis of fundamental properties of *social* organization, rather than simply on the earlier natural laws and qualities based on the inherent nature of *individual* men. On the basis of this logic, the early Americans laid the foundations for what will be called the *natural-social-law* tradition. The concept of the natural-social-law tradition will be further clarified in Chapter 24.

NOTES

1. St. Thomas Aquinas (1938:41) stated that "the rule of one man" is in accord with nature and "whoever is in accord with nature is best . . . Even among bees there is one queen [*rex*] and in the whole universe there is one God, Maker and Ruler of all things."

2. A particularly succinct interpretation of natural law, therefore indicates that it is "a law that determines what is right and wrong and has power or is valid by nature, inherently, hence everywhere and always" (Strauss 1969:80).

3. However, given the existence of moral standards, the distinction between what is naturally just or unjust in any *particular* instance cannot be made without an empirical analysis of that instance. The generalizations representing the reoccurring aspects of these instances could, if found, be called "natural laws" in an empirical sense (i.e., they refer to empirical regularities). If they are *empirical* generalizations, furthermore, one may ask whether they are true irrespective of the ethical judgements associated with them.

4. Strauss (1969:81) points out that in Plato's writings, "Political society requires the *dilution* of the perfect and exact right, of natural right proper: of the right in accordance with which the wise would assign to everyone what he deserves according to his virtue and therefore would assign unequal things to unequal people" (our emphasis).

5. John Wild (1953:111) states that "we find in the early Stoic fragments five characteristic doctrines of natural-law philosophy: (1) the world is an order of interdependent tendencies which are the ground of objective moral norms; (2) the human individual possesses a rational nature which he shares with all other rational beings; (3) this nature determines certain tendencies requiring completion, if human life is to be lived; (4) virtue is the rational direction of these tendencies in accordance with nature, towards their proper goal; and (5) such fulfillment is the happy or blessed life."

CHAPTER 2

Liberal-Functionalism among Classical Liberals

The Natural and Normal Society

Before plunging into our discussion of the major features of liberal-functionalism and its relation to natural law, the reader needs to know why this kind of functionalism is a concern of this book. Briefly, liberal-functionalism has structured the perspectives of the majority of liberal scholars who have attempted to explain the extraordinary social instabilities in their societies. For example, in Book II we will note that corporate liberals in Europe and America around the turn of the century firmly believed that industrial societies could not be stabilized unless man's *naturally* egoistic inclinations were kept within legitimate bounds. At that time, liberals largely equated the concept of social normality with social stability, and stability, in turn, was equated with socially instituted control over selfish individual behavior. Depending upon the writer, this control was to be accomplished through one or more institutional forms including governmental commissions, social planning agencies, occupational codes of ethics, and a universal compulsory education. The systematic introduction of the institutional forms by which this social control could take place was viewed as a tacit criterion for evaluating progress in an industrial society.

A definite ideological point of view was gradually developed for defining the essential features of the normal industrial society. At the very least, such an ideological perspective contained ethical rules or standards for distinguishing acceptable (i.e., *normal*) social relationships. These relationships were thought to be essential to basic (i.e., *natural*) human needs, and therefore, like their liberal predecessors, the corporate liberals also considered acceptable capitalist relations as being, in a derivative sense, both natural and normal.

Similar explanations in America today characterize the conventional, functionalist, academic approaches to the study of people and society. These approaches are also generally based on the operation of explicit and implicit ideological standards. Because of these standards, moreover, the long-term effect of functional analysis has been the continual clarification of those human relationships deemed to be ideologically significant by generations of liberals. The natural-law tradition has played an important role in advancing this form of liberal practice. By secularizing this tradition, liberal scholars generated a powerful ideological strategy for explaining any human condition. The historical variants of this strategy will be generally signified in this work by the term "liberal-functionalism."

Liberal-Functionalism Defined

Among classical liberal scholars, functionalist analysis was primarily addressed to the identification of the social conditions which were considered necessary to the *survival* of individuals. Those social conditions considered necessary were identified by the fact that they led to the satisfaction of human needs. The term "liberal-functionalism" will refer, in part, to all the basic assumptions, analytic strategies, and methodological principles which have been customarily used by liberals in identifying these social conditions.

Varying liberal-functional conceptions of man and society are in vogue among liberal scholars at any given time. Not only have these concepts changed greatly over the centuries, but they have been broadened to include references to individual and social relationships necessary for the survival of *social systems* as well as individuals. However, the survival of social systems has also been theoretically anchored in the alleged necessity for gratifying basic human needs.

The concepts of basic human needs or basic social needs in liberal-functionalism continued in the spirit of the natural-law tradition by referring to the minimum *socially necessary* conditions for survival of individuals or social systems. These concepts were also used to refer to the *optimum* ("the best possible") *conditions* necessary for survival. Both of these meanings were eventually incorporated into modern phrases such as "the *functional* prerequisites" of individuals and/or social systems.

Selfish Human Needs Universalized

As indicated, liberal-functionalism is concerned with conditions leading to the satisfaction of basic human needs. However, the ideological nature of this concern depends heavily on what is regarded as the contents of these basic needs. Historically, as we will see, liberal scholars grounded human needs in such notions as selfishness, competition, private property, and individual survival. All of these notions were encompassed in the category of egoism.

To a certain extent, the relationships signified by the liberal notions of basic needs had been expressed prior to the seventeenth century. The medieval scholars, for example, had suggested that the origin of private property was due, in part, to the necessity of avoiding a chaotic struggle for goods, and that the political state was necessary for the enforcement of peace and order. But their ideas were not yet integrated into a very general doctrine asserting that the state must prevent the complete destruction of man because he is a ravenous beast at heart (Schumpeter 1954:119). In the defense of the political state, the old notions of social contract and the selfish nature of man were transformed by Hobbes into a sweeping doctrine which claimed that individuals will attempt to destroy each other in order to achieve their own selfish ends.[1] Given the selfish nature of man, the monarch, state, and law are obeyed because it is not only mutually advantageous but also absolutely necessary that human nature be confined by powerful rulers and institutions.

Hobbes' concept of man was used to justify the monarchy but it also became the single most important and enduring model for the liberal conception of functional imperatives. In part, Hobbes' concept was congenial to liberals because he located the functional preconditions for the political state in the *nature* of man rather than in divine authority. As such, his theory represented the beginnings of the scientific approach to the origins of social institutions. Furthermore, although the selfish conception of man's nature had been familiar among Greek scholars as the Thrasymachean ethic, Hobbes' conception is distinguished from this older view by the fact that he also sought scientific vindication for man's selfishness through an appeal to the laws of nature (Girvetz 1950:29).

As an early materialist, Hobbes subsumed human nature under the general assumption that all reality is constituted by matter in motion. Conduct, he noted, is motivated by the desire to aid the "vital motion" of the organism and to avoid those factors which retard this motion. Establishing the *survival* of the individual organism as an ethical standard, he proposed that every organism seeks its own preservation; whatever maintains its personal preservation is regarded as good and whatever endangers the organism is bad. This ethical view of man, which regards him as self-seeking by his very nature, is called psychological egoism. Man associates with others for no other motives than his own self-interest.

Hobbes' conception of human nature was speculative. It conformed with his materialist view of the sources and objects of knowledge [2] because he contended that an empirical examination of social life would confirm his view of the necessary functions of government. He asserted that the *natural* state of man required the existence of the coercive power of government. On the basis of this premise, he reasoned that without government men would destroy each other; therefore, government was universally necessary for all other forms of social cooperation as well as for the survival of humanity. This reasoning was based on an *egoistic* natural-law conception.

The term "egoism" is used by modern scholars to vaguely suggest any relationship that an individual regards as in his own interest. However, individuals can be self-interested while not conforming to Hobbes' use of the term "egoism." In Hobbes' version, egoism is equated with individual selfishness and mutual destruction. This selfishness and destruction allegedly arise out of the natural inclination of men to destroy, subdue, or compete with each other in order to achieve the *scarce* goods of life. It is the condition of *scarcity* that stimulates this expression of man's egoistic tendencies.

Expansion of Capitalism
and Reification of Market Relationships

Egoism and scarcity became widely regarded as universal human qualities because of the expansion of capitalist modes of production and distribution in feudal societies. These modes had become a significant feature of transitional feudal life long before the Protestant "Spirit of Capitalism" came into being. Capitalist enterprise began to influence the framework of feudal institutions as early as the thirteenth century, and by the fifteenth, large business enterprises, stock and commodity speculation, and "high finance" were firmly established in important commercial centers in Europe (Schumpeter 1954:78). These institutions induced an intense preoccupation with profitable accumulation and a pervasive anxiety that became associated with the early entrepreneurial personality (Origio 1957). Even more significant were the economic changes which followed hard on the heels of these developments. These changes were represented, above all, by the gradual emergence of the landless laborer and the great landowner whose only ties to the land were wages and rents (Tawney 1912). It became clearly apparent that basic modifications in the class organization of feudal life were being generated by the commercialization and consolidation of land.

The influence of commercialization of land was far-reaching: drawing the small landholder into the intense competition for land. This competition drove up rents and land payments because many small farmers attempted to enlarge their farms at their neighbors' expense. This was done by offering higher payments to large landowners who could appropriate the neighbor's land and make it available to the highest bidders (Fisher 1961). Others, faced with the inability to retain the homes and farms occupied by their families for centuries, longed for the past when agricultural products and services had been exchanged instead of payments for rent.[3]

The commercial spirit of the times also affected professions and universities. In Tudor and Stuart England, for example, the qualities necessary for professional success were similar to those required for business—especially for property investment and management. Members of the professions of medicine and law were noted for their involvement in land speculation.[4] Public offices were often treated less as positions of public trust than as "a species of property that could be bought, leased and mortgaged" to persons interested primarily in their personal fortunes (*ibid.:* 12). London became the central social, economic, and political arena for great landowners, merchants, merchant-manufacturers, bankers, and professionals. One contemporary wag observed that the conversation among citizens in the eating places of London "is of nothing but of Statutes, Bonds, Recognizances, Fines, Recoveries, Audits, Subsidies, Inclosures, Liveries, Inditements, Outlaries, Foeffments, Indgments, Commissions, Banderouts, Amercements, and of such horrible matter, that when a Lifetenant dines with his punck [5] in the nexte roome; hee thinkes verily the men are conjuring" (Aydelotte 1913:81).

The businessman's mentality eventually spread "in *all* classes and over all fields of human thought and action" (Schumpeter 1954:79). Influenced by new forms of economic rationality, laical and secular philosophers and scientists borrowed natural-law conceptions from their predecessors—canons, monks, and friars—and eventually replaced God with Nature as the final authority on the propriety of man's selfishness and the righteousness of his established institutions. In this process, a new metaphysics of normality which we have called liberal-functionalism was contrived. This metaphysics included the liberal concepts of egoism and scarcity.

Although egoism and scarcity appear to refer to immutable properties of man and society in capitalist nations, egoism is actually a *reification* of the normative relations in the market economy. Scarcity, furthermore, is *instituted* by this economy. Hobbes' conception of man, therefore, did not actually reflect a universal property inherent in the nature of man. It reflected the business mentality which, with the emergence of capitalism, gradually pervaded all aspects of life. From this perspective, the competition for scarce goods seemed to be a characteristic of all men for all time. In spite of major changes in liberal ideology over the centuries, this concept of man has continued to operate as a main theoretical anchor in liberal analysis. Because of the widespread subscription to the assumptions underlying this model of man, liberal sociology has primarily been a "sociology of scarcity." [6]

18

Egoism Generalized as Pleasure

John Locke claimed that the desire for property was natural to man and an essential part of the concept of human rights. While Hobbes provided the general framework within which liberal-functionalism constructed its images of man, other liberal scholars took pains to locate the functional origins of government in the need to preserve and protect the individual's right to private property. For these classical and laissez-faire liberals, as we shall see, governments arose historically in order to protect and preserve this right, not to mediate between men as generally aggressive animals.

Classical liberals were not merely interested in explaining the origins of the state; they were concerned with the origins of all social institutions as well as of human civilization itself. The achievement of highly general theories of social development, however, was not possible until the nature of egotistical individual desires was perceived in a highly generalized form. An abstract representation of this point of view was formulated when the vast totality of concrete human desires was associated with a single quality: namely, pleasure.

The theory of man that construed all conduct to be motivated by desire for the greatest pleasure was formulated by a number of philosophers. This theory, psychological hedonism, was only a variant of psychological egoism. In subsequent chapters, there are many examples of hedonistic conceptions of man: works by Ward and Freud, for example, contain direct quotations or paraphrasings of Jeremy Bentham's assertion that nature "placed mankind under the governance of two sovereign masters, *pain* and *pleasure*." [7] It is important to note, however, that Bentham identified the empirical existence of pleasure with its status as a moral imperative. He stated that "it is for them (the sovereign masters—pain and pleasure) alone to point out what we *ought* to do, as well as to determine what we *shall* do. On the one hand, the standard of *right and wrong*, on the other, the chain of *causes and effects* are fastened to their throne. They govern us in all we do, in all we say, in all we think . . ." (Bentham 1907:1 our emphasis). In this formulation, the original nature of man includes both moral imperatives and empirical relationships. And it is this direct correspondence between *moral imperatives* and fairly invariant empirical conditions of *human nature,* that is at the core of the liberal concept of natural law.

The Psychological Creed of Classical Liberalism

An intricate psychological creed lies at the center of classical liberalism. This creed, as Harry Girvetz (1950:33) points out, orients its adherents more toward "immutable laws which govern human nature than to the changing institutional setting which constitutes our social environment." Upon examining the components of this creed, Girvetz indicates that its basic axioms can be classified according to whether they refer to egoism, rationalism, quietism, or atomism. We have provided an interpretation of the concept of psychological egoism and its variant, hedonism.

Classical liberalism also presumes that men are basically *rational* even though pleasure, not reason, is the prime mover of human conduct. What distinguishes men from other animals, in this view, is that desires and therefore actions of men are moderated by reason and calculation. (As Bentham noted, "when matters of such importance as pain and pleasure are at stake . . . who is there that does not calculate?") Another important premise underlying the classical liberal psychological creed is *quietism*. If self-interest is the prime mover of conduct, then it can be presumed that the organism remains at rest in the absence of stimulation from desires to obtain pleasure. This aspect of the psychological creed also implies that individuals are in a state of rest when they have fulfilled their desires. In its crudest interpretation, quietism suggests that human activity does not create desires. To the contrary, desires alone create activity. Also, if the term "value," or any other term denoting a preferred state of affairs, such as an "end," "purpose," or "motive," is substituted for desire, then even the maintenance or "continued motion" of a form of human conduct can only be explained as the outcome of subscription to a set of individual values. Without this kind of explanation, a system of structured relationships between individuals would dissolve into disconnected, inert, atomistic entities (*ibid.*:36–41).

The fourth and final psychological dimension is that of *atomism*. In the atomistic approach to man, according to Girvetz, each individual is also perceived as a waxen tablet which passively registers and stores sense impressions gathered in daily experience. Each of these impressions or ideas is combined with others to form complex bundles of impressions according to the laws of association. In this associationist framework, a complex system of ideas which exists in the minds of individuals is derived entirely from the characteristics of its parts, and consequently, each component part is viewed as an independent, homogeneous, and unitary entity. Furthermore, the essential characteristics of each component exist independently of their relation to the other parts, and independently of the general system of components within which it is included. Because of this structural relationship, a system of ideas is merely the mechanical sum of its atomistic parts (*ibid.*:41–45).

Girvetz's four categories are useful in identifying significant parts of classical liberal psychology. It is important to add, however, the observation that each category contains ideas which influence the interpretation of all other categories. For example, in classical liberalism, individuals are generally seen as pleasure-seeking. Therefore, each person cannot be regarded entirely as an entity passively reflecting the impressions of the external world; each person's strong desires define his essential being and explain his compulsion to act. Further, when the individual's reasoning powers are examined from the very moment of birth, it becomes clear that these powers are acquired through experience. At birth the individual does not have the information by which he can rationally moderate his desires because he is, only with respect to reason, a waxen tablet awaiting the impressions of the external world. When the relations between egoism, rationalism, quietism, and atomism are examined, therefore, we find that classical liberalism contains a complex model of man which views reason and desire very differently. It regards them as dual aspects of human individuality having dissimilar origins and playing very distinct analytic roles in a causal explanation. In this explanation, desire, not reason, is the causal variable or the "dynamic agency" of the individual's social conduct. This kind of dualism, used by ancient scholars, was important in the development of liberal conceptions of individual personality.

According to this model of man, the behavior of all individuals is governed by the same dynamic principles. Each person, for example, is driven by both basic needs and attentiveness to the most advantageous way of finding fulfillment. As a result, social relationships come into existence in order to fulfill egoistic desires, but if these means are ineffectual, then the social relations dissolve, and the individual either finds or constructs more expedient instituted relationships to take their place. Social institutions, therefore, in this view are "an arrangement of convenience, whereby faculties operate more effectively and propensities are more likely to find fruition" (*ibid.*:43). Put in the jargon of modern sociological liberal-functionalism, social institutions are analytically evaluated almost entirely in terms of the presence or absence of opportunities for satisfaction of individual desires. Social relationships are therefore viewed as "opportunity structures" or *means* which are rationally assessed by each and every individual. It is as if every member of the human race, possessing free will, is in the marketplace with freedom to choose between various institutions and institutional identities. The modern sociological concept of institutions and class systems as "opportunity structures" is a direct outgrowth of these classical liberal assumptions.

NOTES

1. Rousseau took issue with Hobbes because he felt that society, not human nature, created a state of war of each against all. For an informative discussion of the differences between Hobbes and Rousseau in this respect, see Zeitlin (1968:24–27).
2. For an informative discussion of Hobbes' materialist perspective, see Cornforth (1967:24–29).
3. A contemporary of the period bitterly observed that "as for fynes yt was not a thinge knowne among them a hundred years past . . . nowe the poore tenants that lyved well in that golden world ys taught to singe unto his lord a new song . . . the world ys so altered with ye poore tenants that he standeth in bodylie feare of his greedy neighbor . . ." (Owen 1892–1897, also quoted in Fisher 1961:9).
4. "Of the acquisitiveness and business capacity of lawyers it is needless to comment . . . According to at least one commentary, medical men showed similar qualities; and the fact that Barbon, Petty and Hughe Chamberlayne, three of the biggest speculators of the later seventeenth century, were also doctors certainly suggests some affinity between medicine and money making" (Fisher, 1961:11–12).
5. The term "punck" refers to the "Lifetenant's" (i.e., the lieutenant's) orderly.
6. For an informative discussion of political economy as "a science of scarcity," see Lefebvre (1968). During the formative years, as we shall see in Book II, leading Ameri-

can sociologists were obsessed with the social regulation of the general "conditions of scarcity" which are characteristic of capitalist societies.

7. Quoted in Girvetz (1950:29). Emphasis Bentham's (1907:1).

CHAPTER 3

The Contradiction between the Individual and Society

Social Foundations of Psychological Assumptions

While classical liberalism is clearly grounded in the development of capitalism during the two centuries prior to the great thrust of the industrial revolution, the search for types of changes accounting for specific parts of this world view represents an extremely difficult historical problem. Girvetz (1950:38) has suggested that there may be a relationship between quietist premises and the changing industrial view of man's nature, that is, the new liberal concept of the natural indolence of man. Bentham writes, for example, *"Aversion*—not *desire*—is the emotion—the only true emotion—which *labour* taken by itself, is qualified to produce: of any such emotion as *love* or *desire, ease,* which is the *negative* or *absence* of *labour*—*ease,* not *labour*—is the object." [1] This proposition, which asserts that if a person is confronted with the choice between labor or ease, he will invariably choose the latter, is manifestly untrue. It is true, however, that during the period prior to the industrial revolution, the British working classes had their own sense of time, dignity, and preindustrial values, which defined manufacturing labor as irksome, oppressive, and unrewarding (Thompson 1963). Under these conditions, the only way in which members of the labor forces could be made to work was for them to be driven to work by the threat of hunger and other forms of coercion. There was simply nothing intrinsically satisfying in the laborious tasks confronting them. It is, therefore, possible to interpret the quietistic proposition as the product of the world view of a new industrial middle-class. This view, moreover, generally defined working-class attitudes toward industrial labor as representing the vice of indolence.

What were the foundations of egoistic premises? We have indicated that medieval scholars were aware of the fact that men regulated their market-place activity according to utilitarian considerations. We have also noted that egoism is the reification of market relationships which were instituted by cap-

22

italist modes of production and distribution. In comparing medieval habits of mind with the business mentality that accompanied the emergence of capitalism, R. H. Tawney (1926:61) argued that at least when medieval critics insisted upon "the prevalence of avarice and greed in high places," they also *"called these vices by their right names,* and had not learned to persuade themselves that greed was enterprise and avarice was economy" (our emphasis). In his view, egoistic premises reflected psychological principles and the growing importance of middle-class legitimations of private property and pecuniary incentives. A similar point is made about Benthamism, which, according to Albert V. Dicey, "was fundamentally a middle class creed" (Girvetz 1950:178). It is therefore not surprising that liberal scholars urged their contemporaries to encourage such egotistic characteristics as profitable initiative, and argued against coddling people or undermining the incentive to work. They pointed to greed as a blessing because it was perceived as the mainspring of human action. They also extolled the organization of economic life around the virtue of accumulating wealth while they decried the vice of indolence (*ibid.*).

By equating acquisitiveness with all other human intentions, eighteenth-century egoism and hedonism signified a highly abstract moral vocabulary of motives that was eventually used to claim that private accumulation of wealth was essential to the common good. Selfish intention, therefore, replaced the altruism which had served as an unquestionable ideal for thousands of years. When one adds the dimensions of natural law to this argument and defines self-interest solely in terms of egotistic desires, egotism becomes essential to the survival of mankind. *Selfish desire* in this context is not only defined as good for the individual and society; it becomes the single most important desire from a liberal-functionalist point of view.

The Utilitarian Reconciliation of Individual and Society

The psychological and ethical assumptions underlying the classical liberal-functionalist analysis were fully integrated by the doctrine of utilitarianism. By starting from the innumerable sensations of individual pleasure, Bentham finally arrived at the normative principle of hedonistic utilitarianism, namely, the Greatest Happiness of the Greatest Number. It was argued that if each individual's "happiness" was summed into a grand total, the result would be equivalent to the common good, or the welfare of society. At first glance, this solution appeared to be a rigorous rationale for the definition of social value. However, Bentham's "exact" science of human behavior assumes that qualitative differences in human motives can be reduced to quantitative differences, without violating an objective understanding of the variation in the individual and social relationships under consideration. In order for this premise to be true, one has to agree with Bentham's belief that, with regard to inquiries into human behavior, one desire is similar to another as long as the quantities of pleasure associated with the thought of attainment of these two qualities are the same. Obviously, as a *general* rule, this quantitative relation cannot be taken seriously today.

In developing the utilitarian ethic, moreover, Bentham and other liberals also asserted that each person had a moral obligation to seek the greatest happiness for the greatest number of people in society. Their critics contended that this moral imperative was inconsistent with ethical egoism because the latter placed self-interest as the ultimate moral end. What happens when a person's self-interest conflicts with the interests of most persons in society? Does the individual's interest represent the essence of goodness in his case? This appears to be the hedonists' logical conclusion (albeit not an agreeable one to their critics) because there are no objective criteria for goodness; ultimately, goodness can be reduced to each individual's personal desires. There is a *contradiction* in the liberal reconciliation between man and society.

In all fairness to scholars like Bentham, however, it should be noted that their operative interpretation of an individual's natural self-interest did not admit any contradiction between the individual good and the common good. Invoking principles of natural law, these scholars insisted that all individual human beings were possessed with normal and natural desires. These specific desires had become associated mainly with pleasure rather than pain because members of society generally found them to be socially useful and therefore moral. These desires were considered to have lofty moral purposes and were contrasted with "swinish" purposes which encouraged persons to engage, for example, in irresponsible sexual acts. These acts led to bastardy and social sanctions or other painful consequences such as venereal disease which would outweigh the pleasures of the moment.

Bentham called normal and natural interests the "true interests" and indicated that the masses had acquired false or artificial interests because of the corrupting influence of worldly life. He suggested that the masses had to be helped to recognize their "true interests" by educational means and the judicious expenditure of rewards and punishments. Under the influence of universal education, in particular, man would be encouraged to become a truly *rational* and therefore, *moral* creature.[2]

A conception of a virtuous and enlightened man lay behind this natural-law vision of human rationality; and, this man was highly informed by the Judaic-Christian moral tradition. The humanistic qualities of the enlightened man did not lie in the simple interest of service to mankind. It resided in two important qualities of man. The first was formulated from the specific sets of virtues inherently associated with his natural desires. The second quality was expressed in the optimistic belief that even if man were corrupted by worldly life, or possessed by swinish or selfish desires, he could transcend these desires through enlightened rationality. Most natural-law theorists during the seventeenth and eighteenth centuries differed about whether natural man had selfish or unselfish desires. But their common belief in the optimistic and socially beneficial effects of human reason has been clearly identified with the Enlightenment.

The moral worth of natural-law doctrines can be evaluated according to whether they advanced the concept of human equality, liberty, and dignity within their concrete historic setting. They can be assessed in terms of their role in expanding the understanding of human potentialities. On the one hand, such dominating forms of thought as Lutheranism or Catholicism during these centuries justified human inequality and the sovereign state on the basis of divine will. On the other hand, armed with a conception of naturally unselfish man, some natural-law theorists defied theocratic interpretations by asserting that man was possessed with inalienable rights before the ascendency of the state; no social arrangement could justifiably deprive man of his natural rights. And those who followed, claiming that man's original rights could be fulfilled in a proper society, also courageously challenged prevailing doctrines by asserting that society, not man's original character, transforms him into a corrupt and depraved creature (e.g., Rousseau 1950).

The First Reconstruction of Classical Liberalism

Scholarly writings about the essential nature of human beings sometimes relied on a dualistic conception of man during the eighteenth century. This dualism admitted altruistic as well as egoistic elements in human nature. Hume, under the influence of Shaftesbury (1714) and Hutcheson (1755), perceived that in human nature ". . . there is some benevolence, however small, . . . some particle of the dove kneaded into our frame, along with the elements of the wolf and the serpent" (Hume 1930:109). As a derivative from this universal he created an enlightened moral individual who was compassionate and kind, yet moderately hedonistic. And we have seen that Bentham, who held that the only standard an individual could rely on was his own self-interest, qualified this interpretation by emphasizing reasonable or enlightened self-interest that takes into account the interests, feelings, and reactions of others.

This dualistic (egoistic-altruistic) model of man, however, did not eliminate the contradiction between the individual and society. As long as man was even somewhat egoistic, natural individual selfishness appeared to threaten the common good. Moreover, the spread of industrialism seemed to encourage egoism and suppress altruism. Under industrial conditions, every human relationship appeared to be reduced to matters of personal utility and cash payments.

During the heyday of nineteenth-century industrial capitalism, natural-law assumptions were integrated into the first reconstruction of classical liberalism by laissez-faire theorists. These liberal theorists used natural law to justify the repression of the struggles of working-class movements for human equality, liberty, and dignity. They argued against the expansion of human potentiality by narrowly organizing their theories of the evolution of mankind primarily around the selfish striving for private property. Embodied in laissez-faire liberalism, natural law justified the premise that human progress was assured by selfish striving. Given this assurance, an individual had no obligation to the welfare of mankind which transcended his own pecuniary interests. Within this developed liberal framework, natural law constituted a body of amoral, if not morally reprehensible doctrines.

The nineteenth-century antiliberal critics of the utilitarian doctrines reacted strongly to the moral assumptions underlying these doctrines. They centered their fire on the immoral potential of the utilitarian principles which were used to justify selfish striving. The utilitarians, on their part, had anticipated or responded to this criticism by introducing various qualifications into their interpretations of utilitarianism and hedonism. Bentham and Mills, for example, stressed the *obligatory* character of the common good. Bentham, in addition, felt that the state could actively solve the problems of moral behavior by signifying what was good for the community as a whole. Furthermore, by a calculated application of punishments, legislators could enable individuals to identify their personal interests with those of the community.

Nineteenth-century laissez-faire liberals responded further to the antiliberal criticism of utilitarianism by reaffirming the notion that natural law rather than man-made institutions created the contradiction between the short-run activities of individuals and the general good of society. (Nature rather than human institutions had equipped man with a natural compulsion to seek his immediate pleasure independent of the common good.) The laissez-faire liberals also insisted that in spite of this contradiction, human selfishness contributed to industrial prosperity over the long run. In their view, furthermore, individual avarice created the harsh competitive conditions that shortened the lives of inferior human beings and, as a result, selfish human behavior was gradually creating a generally superior master race throughout the world.

In time, therefore, in spite of the intervening conception of enlightened self-interest, psychological egoism was used to reduce all social values to those based on highly individualistic notions of happiness. These concepts of happiness were eventually interpreted either in terms of the individual's self-interest or, as was often the case with altruism, in terms of the abnegation of self-interest in favor of another person's self-interest. (Some writers postulated a corporate self-interest as the altruistic replacement for individual egoism.) The middle- and upper-class conception of social value or common good, which emerged within this framework, usurped all other social values represented by other classes which existed in society. In spite of the contradiction between the individual and society embodied in utilitarian doctrines, this way of analyzing human behavior rendered plausible as an ultimate normative standard, the "greatest possible balance of good over evil in the universe." Neither God nor the class struggle were explicitly admitted into the grand, superindividualistic domain of the common good.

The Imperatives of Competition,
Private Property, and Equality

What kinds of ideological factors should be considered before all others when evaluating liberal-functionalism? To answer this question, it must be recalled that before the classical liberals, the Christian medieval scholars had taught that all men were equal in the eyes of God as witnessed by the Savior who died for the salvation of all. Hobbes, however, asserted on empirical rather than ethical grounds that human faculties are "equal in the sense that the range of their variations is so narrowly limited as to make complete equality a permissible working hypothesis" (Schumpeter 1954:121). As indicated, liberals began to extend this conception in very limited areas of social and political life during the eighteenth century. Their interpretation of individual equality represented a broadening of the concept of human rights and, therefore, of individual liberty. For instance, Rousseau (1950:306–322) indicated that property could remain private only if it was distributed fairly equally among the members of the population. Otherwise, some individuals would be tempted to accumulate all property in their hands, and society would eventually consist of propertied and propertyless persons. Rousseau also suggested that forms of property which could not be distributed equally should be owned in common.

However, it is important to note that liberals like Bentham who were much more representative of dominant liberal trends did not use the notions of economic equality which influenced Rousseau because these notions conflicted with their own concepts of property rights. Liberal concepts of equality were operatively restricted to legal interpretations which favored the power and status of the growing mercantile and industrial middle class during that time. These interpretations discriminated against rural small producers as well as rural and urban workers. The subsequent rights granted to small farmers and working class people were achieved on the basis of their own political and economic struggles or, as in France, in exchange for their support of bourgeois political aims in the revolutionary struggles against the monarchy.

Eighteenth-century political and economic struggles were spurred by rapidly changing economic relationships. Increasingly, individuals no longer produced their own necessities of life. They did not eat the food they farmed, wear the clothes they spun, or take shelter in the houses they built. Increasingly, basic commodities represented the efforts of countless individuals who, as employees of merchant-imperialists, extracted raw materials, processed, transported, and made the products available to others. Then, as now, these commodities represented the fruits of *social* labor.

In light of these changes in production, the most significant moral core of the naturalistic argument of classical liberalism, was the legitimation of the private expropriation of the labor power which was necessary for the production of commodities. This naturalistic argument justified a new set of impera-

27

tives which asserted, as a higher moral principle, each individual's claim to the fruits of social labor on the basis of his alleged superior or inferior abilities in a competitive market. This new, liberal argument cut both ways. It attacked the legitimacy of distributing wealth on the basis of feudal privilege. It also denounced the new application of communitarian moral principles which claimed that every individual was entitled to an equal share in the fruits of social labor irrespective of his social status.

If we keep in mind that historical analysis is also concerned with the relations of the past and present to the *future* of humankind, then the most significant feature of liberalism is not its conflict with feudal concepts of equity. The significant feature is the liberal's commitment to distribute the fruits of social labor unequally, according to individual ability, political power, or the ownership of property, rather than equally, according to social needs.

NOTES

1. Quoted with emphasis added by Girvetz (1950:38).

2. This point was expressed in Bentham's earlier writings about the "artificial" identification of common interests. For an informative discussion of these writings, see Halevy (1955:17—18).

PART TWO
Laissez-Faire Liberalism: Malthus and Spencer

CHAPTER 4

Thomas Malthus and Free Labor

During the last half of the eighteenth century English life was unalterably changed by the industrial revolution, and in France, in 1789, a one-thousand-year-old history of feudal relationships came to an end with the revolutionary overthrow of the monarchy. These revolutionary economic and political changes reverberated throughout Europe. Radical democratic movements grew rapidly among the European working class populations and threatened the lives and holdings of the wealthy bourgeoisie and the great landowners.

Alarmed by these developments, bourgeois and aristocratic writers focused their attention on the tumultuous economic crises, the violent periodic wars, and the harsh industrial or commercial conditions which seemed to generate working-class radicalism. Simultaneously these writers formulated numerous conservative, if not outright reactionary solutions to contemporary problems. The proposed solutions, however, varied greatly depending upon the writer's personal attitudes toward maintaining feudal institutions, religion and the church, the great landowning class, and the new financial and industrial bourgeoisie.

Two Analytic Trends in Social Thought

In time, several definable analytic trends began to emerge from the writings of these bourgeois and aristocratic intellectuals. Two of these trends can be distinguished for the purposes at hand. The first trend was organized primarily around categories which were fairly close to the mainstream of *economic*

29

liberalism.[1] The second trend, on the other hand, attempted to utilize categories which, to a large extent, had been produced by preexisting writings about the necessary conditions for the maintenance of despotic social and political *systems of authority.*

We will deal with the first of these analytic trends, and discuss the second trend in Part Three. The reader should keep in mind, in both parts, that our discussion will center on developmental trends in *analytic* social thinking rather than on the differences between specific *political* doctrines espoused by individual intellectuals. To be sure, the fact that most of these intellectuals believed in the preservation of private landed, commercial, or industrial property is crucial for understanding why their analytic perspectives were compatible in the first place. However, these general attitudes toward property are not necessarily fully identical with personal political alignments at any given time.

For example, writers who were representative of the first trend included both Thomas Malthus and Herbert Spencer, even though their specific political sympathies varied considerably. Malthus was an apologist for the great English landowners and an intellectual opponent of the industrial bourgeoisie.[2] In contrast, Spencer championed the industrialist and was antagonistic toward landed wealth. Both of these writers, on the other hand, were ideologues who justified the devastating effects of competitive relationships in capitalist societies.

Preview of Coming Chapters

The first analytic trend began just before the turn of the nineteenth century and culminated in social Darwinism during the latter half of the nineteenth century. (Social Darwinists claimed, among other things, that the "natural forces of competition" would create an era of peace and prosperity which would be unparalleled in the history of humankind.) Social Darwinism, moreover, was incorporated into a much more comprehensive ideological perspective called *laissez-faire liberalism.* Whatever their differences, Malthus and Spencer represented critical points in the development of the laissez-faire liberal perspective. In this chapter, the discussion of Malthus' writings will begin to introduce the reader to the political and economic events which influenced Malthus' point of view. The doctrine of free labor will be introduced toward the end of this chapter and that of free trade will be briefly mentioned in the beginning of the next chapter. Spencer's brand of liberal-functionalism will then be discussed. Gradually, as the reader moves through the following chapters, he/she will increasingly encounter various economic concepts dealing with the nature of exchange relationships. These concepts are crucial for understanding laissez-faire liberal sociologists as well as the outstanding liberal theorists in American sociology during the formative years. Let us now turn to the political and economic events that influenced Malthus' writings.

30

Malthus' Attack on Perfectibility
of Man and Society

Malthus' famous essay (which claimed that population growth would always prevent "the future improvement" of society) was written after the French Revolution and during one of the turbulent decades in English history. Ostensibly, this essay originated, according to Malthus, in a discussion with a friend [3] about the nature of avarice. The essay was critically addressed to Condorcet, Godwin, and other more radical thinkers of the Enlightenment. Malthus, upon criticizing these men, opposed the radical belief that it was possible to create a better society in which all members would live in "ease, happiness, and comparative leisure; and feel no anxiety about providing the means of subsistence for themselves and families." Malthus argued that these radicals were grossly mistaken: a society of this sort was impossible to achieve. In his opinion, a *scientific* analysis of social relationships provided conclusive proof that "the perfectibility of the mass of mankind" was a hopeless illusion (Malthus 1914).

To understand Malthus' reaction to the radical doctrines about the perfectibility of man and society, we must turn back the clock for a brief glance at the nature of the vast popular outcry against economic and political conditions in the last decade of the eighteenth century. Toward the end of that century the English workers, proudly convinced of their rights as freeborn men, had organized economic and political societies (e.g., the Corresponding Societies) partly in reaction to the destruction of their preindustrial modes of life. In the process of asserting traditional rights to live as they had in the past, these workers began to adopt, generate, and disseminate radical doctrines.[4] In the 1790s, the depressive economic conditions and the oppressive political regime of George III further stimulated these radical developments.

The French Revolution also influenced the development of radical workingmen's organizations. Several of the leaders of the English workingmen's societies, such as John Thelwall, for example, considered themselves Jacobins. Their Jacobite organizations were characterized by egalitarian and non-bureaucratic relationships and their Jacobite traditions supported self-education, republicanism, internationalism, and a radical, critical perspective towards political and religious institutions (Thompson 1963:183). In fact, long before Marx wrote about how the industrial workers would become class conscious, John Thelwall remarked that a new Socratic spirit will develop "wherever large bodies of [working] men will assemble." Furthermore, he saw the birth of new political relationships in the development of industrial conditions and proclaimed that

Monopoly, and the hideous accumulation of capital in a few hands . . . carry in their own enormity, the seeds of cure. . . . Whatever presses men together . . . though it may generate some vices, is favorable to the diffusion of knowledge, and ultimately promotive of human liberty. Hence, every large workshop and manu-

31

factory is a sort of political society, which no act of parliament can silence and no magistrate disperse. [*Ibid.*:185]

By 1795, the extraordinary numbers being mustered by the radical societies began to become highly visible. At that time, the London Corresponding Society held the largest political meeting in the history of England. James Dugan (1965:30), for example, has observed that

On the eve of the opening of Parliament in October, ... 150,000 people [at the London Corresponding Society meeting] in Islington . . . passed *viva voce* a *Remonstrance to the King* which asked: "Wherefore, in the midst of apparent plenty, are we thus compelled to starve? . . . Parliamentary corruption like a foaming whirlpool swallows the fruits of all our labors."

Shortly thereafter King George himself was mobbed while his carriage made its way through London's streets to Westminster Palace, and a twenty-seven-year-old journeyman printer was hanged for making an attempt on the king's life (*ibid.*:32).

However, no event more dramatically symbolized the economic and political instabilities of the time than the rising in 1796–1797 of the seamen who manned the ships of the British navy. These seamen were among the most oppressed and exploited workers in the British Isles, and according to Captain Horatio Nelson they were "finished at forty-five, double-ruptured, raw with scurvy, and racked with agonizing pain after every meal" (*ibid.*:37). Just prior to the year in which Malthus' essay was first published, these heroic British workers rose against their officers in the Great Mutiny at Spithead and the Nore, in the greatest naval mutiny of all time.[5] At the height of the mutiny, British seamen unfurled "the red jack" (the red flag) from the mainmasts of *more than one hundred* British naval vessels! [6]

The potentialities for change which were inherent in the diffusion of such radical doctrines as those of the Jacobins, did not escape the notice of either governmental officials or conservative intellectuals. The English government had previously become sharply aware of the effects of radical movements among the common people during the most explosive years of the agrarian revolution (Tawney 1912). Consequently, it is not surprising that strong measures were taken to prevent the circulation of these dangerous political ideas.[7] Such works as Thomas Paine's *Rights of Man* were banned.[8] Workingmen's labor organizations and political societies were repressed. The Great Mutiny was utterly *smashed,* the principle seamen hanged and a few hounded all over the world until caught *many years later.* Simultaneously English economists, clergymen, and philosophers justified this savage repression and some, like the parson, Thomas Malthus, also developed pseudoscientific justifications for the terrible forms of poverty, exploitation, and imperialist conflagration that were taking their toll of the English and Irish working classes.

The Theory behind Malthus' Dismal Prophecy

Malthus organized this theoretical justification of the conditions underlying economic crises and imperialist wars, around ecological relationships, demographic trends, and individual moral attitudes.[9] In his "Essay on Population," Malthus (1914:5–11) first claimed that all "plants and irrational animals . . . are impelled by a powerful instinct to the increase of their species." However, this increase was not kept in check among humans by limitations in available land and food. The human species also possesses the instinct to propagate but unlike all other forms of life, Malthus noted, it is capable of doubling the size of its population "every twenty-five years." At this rate it would rapidly outstrip the available food supply and therefore, Malthus believed, unless the population is held in check by certain "natural forces," millions of people all over the world will be "totally unprovided for."

How did Malthus see "natural forces" checking population growth? First, individual "moral restraints" restricted what Malthus considered a "strong inclination" to produce children promiscuously. Malthus observed, however, that individual moral restraint was in itself an insufficient force for limiting the population because it was weakened by a "general corruption of morals, with regard to sex." This corruption was said to poison "the springs of domestic happiness," it weakened "conjugal and parental affection" and the "united exertions and ardor of parents in the care and education of their children." The only way in which the population could be limited under these morally outrageous conditions was by allowing those individuals who engaged in improvident "excesses to be subject to any cause, which in any degree contributes to shorten the natural duration of human life." These causes included, "all unwholesome occupations, severe labor and exposure to the seasons, extreme poverty, bad nursing of children . . . the whole train of common diseases and epidemics, wars, plague and famine" (*ibid.*:13–14). Thus, these persons already identified as at best inferior and at worst downright bad would get what they deserved.

Malthus did not claim that *he,* or his scholarly peers, or the strong arm of the government should subject these improvident individuals to these miserable conditions. Even if he felt that this should be the proper function of an exceedingly moral and responsible citizenry, it was not necessary to carry out this task personally because, according to him, the natural forces of the universe were already busy at work reestablishing the balance between population and food. It was nature with an armament of plagues, wars, and famines, plus a small measure of voluntary sexual self-restraint on the part of individuals, not the economy or the institutions of justice, that would achieve the proper equilibrium (*ibid.*).

Some of the Economic Ideas Underlying Malthus' Theory

Malthus (*ibid.:*15) observed that in the process of righting the human race, nature subjected "lower classes of society to distress" and prevented "any great permanent melioration of their condition." Operating on the basis of an established belief that wages naturally fall when the number of laborers increases in proportion to the amount of wages available at any given time, he indicated that there would be less wages available for distribution to each worker when the population grew larger than the food supply. At the same time, "the price of provisions would . . . tend to rise" since there was a smaller proportion of food in relation to the increased size of the population. Consequently, he asserted that "the laborer must do more work to earn the same as he did before." His increased industriousness, combined with the "plenty" and "cheapness of labor," would encourage other individuals who own or invest in farm holdings to hire additional workingmen "to turn up fresh soil, and to manure and improve more completely what is already in tillage, till ultimately the means of subsistence may become in the same proportion to the population as at the period from which we set out" (*ibid.:*15–16).

In Malthus' theory, the events culminating in misery for large sections of the population finally come to a halt when "farmers and capitalists are growing rich from the real cheapness of labor," and "their increasing capitals enable them to employ a greater number of men" for their own profit (*ibid.:*18). Unfortunately, these highly beneficent effects of the pursuit of selfish pecuniary interests do not last long. As the conditions of life for the improvident masses of humanity become more comfortable, the population, again, begins to rapidly outstrip the existing supply of food and this dismal imbalance initiates a new, destructive phase, in which the never-ending, periodic appearance of war, famines, and epidemics occurs all over again. According to Malthus *(ibid.:*16), this "oscillation" is *inexorable.*

From this point of view, Malthus flatly argued that remedial legislation could not improve the conditions of the poor because it would create more misery than it alleviated. He maintained that he had not merely demonstrated that the poor were morally responsible for their own misery through excessive birth rate, but that poor people would continue to propagate and thereby create a greater imbalance in the population-food ratio if they were aided by such measures as "poor law" legislation. On the basis of this "scientific observation" it could be claimed that there was some justice in the misery to which the masses of poverty-stricken workers were subjected. Because of the morally corrupt "natures" of those most responsible for overpopulating the earth, the "laboring classes" were being punished for their improvident behavior; their poverty was testimony to their outrageous violations of natural law.[10]

Free Labor and the Ideological Functions
of Malthus' Theory

Malthus' theory justified capitalist and feudal wars and poverty or, as in the case of famines and disease, the lack of the kinds of social planning and social conditions which would ameliorate natural calamities. Although it had no basis in fact, Malthus' essay was seized upon by aristocratic and middle-class circles because it refuted radical interpretations of social ills. Other kinds of ideological functions were served by Malthus' theory. As long as poverty was "explained" on the basis of individual moral degeneracy, then educative measures alone, aimed at moral regeneration of working class individuals, could ameliorate their condition. Because of this, the theory provided an empirical justification for the numerous contemporary religious movements which aimed at inculcating the working population with the new industrial discipline. These movements were eventually able to destroy the human characteristics which had sustained the precapitalist leisure and work patterns. In this acculturation process, working men acquired a sense of industrial clock-time and "efficient," "industrious," habit patterns which were geared to the new machine technology (Thompson 1963).

Malthus' theory also played an inadvertent [11] but nevertheless important ideological role in the competition between the great landowners and the merchant-manufacturers for the available labor force. Several factors accounted for this. The first of these was the fact that in feudal England, "poor-relief" usually took the form of food payments which prevented the starvation of periodically unemployed farm laborers and their families. Toward the end of the eighteenth century, however, relief programs had been widely extended by the rural gentry who were attempting to maintain a stable labor force in the countryside, in spite of the growing competition for labor and recurrent economic crises. As a consequence, the movement of labor to the industrial communities was being hampered by the rural relief programs.

Although the large landowners were burdened by added taxes (which were used to support the "poor-relief" programs), their interests were favored somewhat by the existence of a large reservoir of extremely cheap, although sometimes subsidized, labor in the countryside. However, at that time, the new industrial developments in England also required, above all, stable concentrations of a plentiful supply of *free labor* in the developing manufacturing communities. (Free labor is wage labor that is not bound to employers by any other ties than cash payments, such as ties of fealty or dependence on "poor-relief.") Because of this, English liberals increasingly became concerned with undermining the traditional obligations of community members toward the rural poor. By explaining poverty on the basis of the natural forces of the universe, Malthus provided these liberals with the outstanding rationale for abandoning legislative supports for relief programs in rural areas. By 1834, political movements led by English merchants and manufac-

35

turers finally succeeded in repealing the legislation maintaining the last surviving vestiges of "poor-relief" outside of the workhouse or insane asylum.

In conclusion, the 1834 reforms meant that the government would interfere no longer in the determination of labor policies which favored the landowning as opposed to the industrial interests. The governmental affirmation of the liberal policy of free labor permitted the individual industrialist to exert enormous control over the lives of British workingmen. Without relief, landless and unemployed farmers and laborers swarmed to the cities. Working-class men, women, and children were "set free" to either starve or toil in the new commercial and industrial establishments. Their misery, however, was less a function of Malthus' "natural forces of the universe," than of the systematic attempts on the part of legislative representatives of a rising class to destroy existing legislative supports for the poor, and thereby to assure a plentiful supply of cheap labor for factories and warehouses in a rapidly expanding capitalist economy.

NOTES

1. Historically, liberalism has been equated, in particular, with economic writings and customs emerging as early as the sixteenth century. For a comprehensive understanding of economic liberalism, see R. H. Tawney's (1920, 1926) magnificent works.

2. The relation between Malthus' theories and the defense of the landowners will not be discussed in this work. Nor will his "underconsumption" theory of economic relationships be considered. For an excellent analysis of Malthusian doctrines and theories, see Ronald Meek (1971).

3. The "friend" referred to by Malthus was actually his father, a social reformer who believed in the perfectibility of man.

4. Thompson (1963:182) notes that "the history of reform agitation between 1792 and 1796 was (in general terms) the story of the simultaneous default of the middle-class reformers and the rapid 'leftwards' movements of the plebeian Radicals. The experience marked the popular consciousness for fifty years, and throughout this time the dynamic of Radicalism came not from the middle class but the artisans and labourers."

5. For a magnificently detailed account of the great mutiny, see James Dugan (1965).

6. Dugan (1965:38) states: "In this nadir of imperialism, unsuspected by the government, the last defenders of the home islands, the seamen of the grand fleet and the North Sea fleet, went on strike. Their protest is unparalleled in history. In the four main naval bases of England, about half the lower deck of the navy and five thousand marines hauled down the royal standard and the Union Jack and the pendants of admirals of the red, admirals of the white and admirals of the blue. On more than a hundred vessels they raised the red flag of defiance. They swore oaths of extreme fidelity to their cause, deposed his Majesty's officers, and elected their own. They established the first government based on universal suffrage that Britain had ever seen, afloat or ashore."

7. Ronald Meek (1971:3) writes, for example: "Those who feared radical social reform fought back against those who hoped and worked for it. A regime of thought control, terror and physical repression was instituted. The Habeas Corpus Act was suspended; there were many trials for high treason, often with savage sentences; and there was pitiless persecution of those who were suspected of harboring 'democratic' thoughts."

8. Thomas Paine's works were particularly influential at the time. Thompson (1963:167) points out, for example, that "there were Corresponding Society members among the mutineers [who participated in the great mutiny mentioned in the text above]; Richard Parker himself, the unwilling 'Admiral' of the 'Floating Republic' of the Nore, exemplified the role of educated 'quota men' who brought into the fleet the language of *Rights of Man* and some experience in committee organization."

9. In this process, Malthus set an important analytic style for modern discourse concerning the causes of the great problems of our time. Expressed in terms of North American sociology, this style specified population pressure, competition between atomistic individuals, and the "adaptive" characteristics of these individuals, in the formulation of theoretical mechanisms. An important outcome of this analytic influence, as integrated by Spencer, became social Darwinism and was later significantly modified by Ward and others to become reform Darwinism. Ward, Durkheim, and others modified this analytic approach and prepared the groundwork for the use of similar notions by later sociologists (e.g., Riesman 1950).

10. Malthus (1914:1) indicated that his theory accounted "for much of that poverty and misery observable among the lower classes of people of every nation and for those reiterated failures in the efforts of the higher classes to relieve them."

11. Malthus opposed "poor-relief" legislation in order to relieve the tax burdens that these statutes imposed on large landowners. He did not write his essay to strengthen the merchant-capitalists and industrialists.

CHAPTER 5

Liberal-Functionalism in Analogical Disguise

Laissez-Faire! Hands Off!!

The unfolding of the laissez-faire movement for free trade preceded that of free labor. By the eighteenth century, mercantilism had spurred the emergence of powerful groups of merchants and landowners who were interested in free trade primarily in agricultural goods. Chafing under the restrictions of protectionist policies, and unable to trade because of commercial monopolies and patents granted by feudal governments, these groups began to formulate doctrines based upon the concept of noninterference by government in the affairs of business and trade. The slogan "Laissez-faire!" particularly symbolized these doctrines and this concept. In this chapter we will discuss the broadening of the meaning of this slogan to include other social interrelations. We will also examine the nineteenth-century laissez-faire doctrines that justified the necessity of capitalism and the institution of private property.

During the mercantile period, the concept of laissez-faire was generally narrow in meaning. The physiocrats, for example, had advocated free trade doctrines during the second half of the eighteenth century. However, even though the classical liberal economists claimed that the physiocrats had formulated laissez-faire doctrines because they favored free trade generally, physiocratic doctrines called for strong governmental policies, other than tariffs on imports, which would favor and stimulate the commercial distribution of

37

agricultural goods. (The French physiocrats did not call for tariffs because free trade did not conflict with the agrarian price structure in France at that time.) [1] As such the physiocratic doctrine of free trade was a narrow, agrarian interest-group conception which was contained within the broader framework of mercantilism and was therefore oriented towards the attainment of national prosperity through state-regulated commerce. It was actually an expression of the impact of agricultural commercialization within a changing, but nevertheless still feudal, agrarian economy.

As industrialization and commerce progressed, however, merchant-manufacturers and, ultimately, industrial capitalists, grew strong enough to openly confront the landed gentry for control of national policies. Consequently, the laissez-faire doctrines were increasingly broadened to include resistance to all governmental policies hampering the development of the industrial economy. The previous chapter, for example, noted that liberal criticisms of the economic policies of feudal governments were aimed at the elimination of all policies supportive of a relatively immobile agrarian labor force. Simultaneously, governmental policies aimed at ameliorating the conditions of the urban working class also came under attack. However, this laissez-faire stand against governmental intervention into the affairs of industrialists and merchants did not oppose the systematic use of governmental agents and policies for the repression of working-class organizations and movements aimed at protecting the economic welfare of the working class.

Laissez-faire doctrines did not advocate a halt to interference by government in economic affairs in any *absolute* sense. With the destruction of the feudal obligations to the poor, and the reconstruction of the legal system on the basis of the new capitalist property rights, the state systematically interfered in the lives of workingmen in order to protect the property rights of the owners of landed and industrial capital alike. This interference was justified in the name of the newly constituted system of law; as a result, the repressive policies of the liberal state were not defined as "interference" but rather as the "protection" of basic property rights. The laissez-faire liberals declared that the only justifiable functions of the political state were safeguarding the nation from enemies, preventing crime, and protecting private property. But terms such as "crime" and "private property" had already been modified during the precapitalist period in order to support the stability of the nascent capitalist society. [2]

Later, during the *second half* of the nineteenth century, those aspects of the laissez-faire doctrines which applied to notions of free labor were sharply opposed by social reformers, militant labor unions, and socialist movements. This opposition was intensified by the serious administrative and social problems emerging within the great industrial cities. Reforms were needed to prevent massive epidemics in densely packed and infested slum areas, and mass education was required in order to develop a work force capable of utilizing the increasingly complex industrial technology. All of these developments spurred the cry for the expansion of the administrative functions of the state. This call for expansion also conflicted with traditional laissez-faire doctrines. These doctrines had heretofore served capitalism well, justifying those policies which were useful spurs to its industrial development right up to the very last decades of the nineteenth century.

The writings of Herbert Spencer provide an illustration of some of the laissez-faire ideas which accompanied these comprehensive social changes. (These writings also provide an opportunity to acquaint the reader with some of the most important laissez-faire doctrines which were vigorously attacked by the early American sociologists.) The discussion of Spencer's work will show that he modified classical liberal concepts as well as Malthus' theory, in order to justify a much broader interpretation of laissez-faire. In developing his justification, Spencer also enlisted the "natural forces of the universe" to defend British capitalism. But the operation of these laws, Spencer declared contemptuously, did not require "meddling" by the government in order to function properly.

Problems of Social Integration and Social Change

Before we deal directly with Spencer's writings, two important analytic notions dealing with stability and change should be mentioned. Spencer proposed one general solution to the problem of explaining both *social integration* and *social change*. This problem of social integration is confronted by theoretical social scientists whenever they are interested in explaining the *orderly recurrence* or persistence of social systems.[3] The problem of social change, on the other hand, deals with the quantitative or qualitative *transformations* of social systems over time. Stability and change, as we shall see, are interrelated social phenomena.

The sociological giants of the nineteenth century, Auguste Comte, Karl Marx, Frederick Engels, Herbert Spencer, and Emile Durkheim, were all interested in the integrative and changing features of capitalism. Each of these men, furthermore, assumed that society is more than the sum of its parts: it exhibits structural features based on interrelationships between individuals, groups, institutions, nations, and classes. Although widespread, this assumption never united these men because of their disagreements about *which* relations were most important in understanding how a society is integrated and changed. What are the important relations in this regard? The modes of production and the conflicts between the classes? The adaptive qualities of the human race and the competition for the survival of the fittest? Or perhaps the nature of personal goals and the availability of opportunities to achieve these goals in daily life? No questions have stimulated more academic sound and fury than those concerned with plausible answers to the problems of social integration and social change.

Spencer's Structure and Function:
An Instance of Liberal-Functionalism

Spencer explored a brace of analytical trails in search of his own solutions to these problems. The first terminated in his belief that the *orderly* processes governing relations among parts of human society were similar to the processes governing relations among parts of a biological organism. The second culminated in his assertion that the macroscopic *changes* taking place among both biological and social organisms were governed by evolutionary laws of the universe. Let us examine the logical grounds for each of these generalizations in order to clarify Spencer's brand of liberal-functionalism.

Spencer's rationale for the first generalization was straightforward analogy. His initial premise, that society is more than the sum of its parts, drew breath from his observation that a biological organism manifests a general persistence of arrangements. In his words (1873:326), "a society as a whole, considered apart from its living units, represents phenomena of growth, structure and function, analogous to those of growth, structure and function in an animal; and these last are needful keys to the first."

This assertion was grounded in a broad classification scheme [4] that sweepingly included in its purview all aspects of a human society, dividing them according to two major categories: structure and function. Once this scheme was made clear, Spencer equated biological structure with social structure, and the biological functioning of parts of an organism with the social functions of the components of a social structure. Spencer even suggested that the methodological strategy for organizing "the compilations and digests of materials" from all aspects of social life follow the structural and functional strategy which he ascribed to the biologist (Rumney 1966:44).[5]

Spencer's Models Expressed in Biological Analogies

One of the most obvious characteristics associated with Spencerian thought is the frequent use of biological analogies to support the notion of functional integration. Rumney points out that Spencer compared railway and highway systems with vascular systems in animals. Fluctuations in traffic over the rails and roads were likened to pulsations in the circulation of blood. The telegraph lines connecting individuals throughout a nation were considered analogous to the nerve fibers of an animal. Institutions of state, such as legislative bodies, found their parallel in the higher nerve centers of organisms: "Strange as the assertion will be thought," Spencer wrote, "our Houses of Parliament discharge in the social economy functions which are in sundry respects, comparable to those discharged by the cerebral masses in the vertebrate animal" (*ibid.*:50).

Spencer's Models Often Expressed
by Formal Principles

Spencer went beyond the construction of organismic parallels and integrated his structural and functional propositions into an evolutionary theory of social and natural processes that was so general that it purported to represent the "laws of the Cosmos." Included among these "laws" was the assertion that in the course of evolutionary development all matter, including societies or "superorganisms," tends toward a continuously changing state of greater heterogeneity. Social institutions, for example, become more differentiated and complex and this tendency results in the necessity for greater integration of the relationships within them. Thus, highly evolved civilizations exhibit a greater degree of both *differentiation* and *integration* than less evolved ones. Such "tendencies" or "laws" as "the tendency toward heterogeneity," "equilibrium," or "solidarity" are based totally on formal categories which are not concretely specified and which, therefore, do not make *substantive* (i.e., empirical) sense per se. They will generally be referred to as *formal principles* or *formal generalizations*.

Spencer often used these formal generalizations in the place of empirical mechanisms. (A mechanism in this work is broadly defined as the empirical relationships which underlie the specific process by which personal or social relationships are either changed or maintained.) Spencer asserted, for example, that the relationships between various parts of the universe became differentiated because "evolving aggregates" exhibited a "tendency toward heterogeneity." But assertions of this kind often provided no clue about the empirical relationships and concrete processes which were involved in establishing the greater differentiation represented, for example, by distinctive solar systems as opposed to gaseous interstellar masses such as the Crab Nebula.

Spencer's Biological Analogies
and Formal Principles Arbitrary in Certain Respects

The formal "tendencies" toward differentiation and integration were not always used consistently in Spencer's writings. From the very beginning of his work, Spencer applied his biological analogies and general "laws" to past and present societies in an arbitrary manner. In describing a stage in the development of civilizations called the industrial order (modeled after English nineteenth century capitalism), he departed widely from the constant use of the organismic illustrations which were employed for explaining governmental functions in militaristic societies. In militaristic societies, governments were generally likened to the brain of an organism. In the *militaristic order,* government, like a brain, had extensive regulatory and integrative functions. But the "brain" of nations in a higher state of evolutionary development, the *industrial order,* operated differently from the brain of living creatures. This political "brain" was highly atrophied and limited in respect to regulative and integrative functions, when compared to other less developed types of societies. The industrial government appeared "atrophied" by comparison because it did not "interfere" in the economic affairs of businessmen.

The government in an industrial society did perform a few limited integrative functions such as the maintenance of law and order. By contrast, the other institutions in this society (e.g., economic institutions) were alleged to be in a state of constant growth and differentiation. Hence, in spite of his own dual criteria of ever greater differentiation and integration, Spencer considered the industrial society (because of its greater individuation and freedom for human organisms) as the most progressive in all of human history. Thus, Spencer's formal "law" was certainly not applied consistently, for in this case, *less* integration and *greater* differentiation obtain in the higher industrial order, while *high* integration and *low* differentiation mark the lower militaristic order.

In considering these inconsistencies, Jay Rumney (*ibid.:*53) correctly suggests that when Spencer described the industrial order, he also threw his analogous model of the social organism overboard because it was incompatible with his evaluation of the industrial society as the most progressive form of evolutionary development. We would argue further that, because of the careless ease with which Spencer modified his analogy, it is quite possible, in our opinion, that some of his biological analogies and formal generalizations played only a superficial role in their use as models and mechanisms for social theorizing. Parallels between biological and social relations appear to have been constructed primarily as intermediary *illustrations* or *justifications* for theoretical generalizations which were actually *modeled after other kinds of ideas.* Some of his generalizations about the effects of economic competition on the biological "fitness" of individuals derive different parts of the same proposition from social and biological disciplines. However, at times the biological components of their relations do not appear to have been clearly derived from biological theories. Instead, they seem to have been manufactured from whole cloth in accordance with economic presuppositions established by classical political economists. This will be made more explicit in a moment, when we shall suggest that his solution to the problem of social change rested on what might be called *a political economy of cellular relationships* which was reputed to exist within the body of every member of society.

Spencer's Mechanism for the Survival of the Fittest

Spencer, as well as Darwin, formulated theories of natural selection which were influenced by Malthusian doctrines. Spencer, concerned primarily with the evolution of man in society, moved beyond Malthus' pessimistic conclusions about the detrimental effects on man of the inevitability of wars, famines, and epidemics. He paradoxically asserted that the same imbalance in population and food that created these conditions also brought about a moral improvement of man, an increase in human intelligence, and a decrease in the rate of population growth (Spencer 1852). How did all of this come about?

Spencer (*ibid.:*499–501) declared that the forward march of civilization has, in large part, been due to population pressures which compelled man to "abandon predatory habits and to take to agriculture." These pressures have led to the "clearing of the earth's surface," and "forced men into the social state." By making social organization "inevitable," population pressures have brought men into relationships requiring more intelligent adaptations, as well as the greater necessity for development of "social sentiments." Over time, the destructive natural checks on the population eliminate less intelligent and improvident members of the race because they are less adaptive than others. This eventuates in an increase in the average intelligence and moral qualities of the race as a whole.

Equating an increase in intelligence with greater growth of the nervous system, and an increase in fertility with greater growth of the reproductive system, Spencer (*ibid.:*492) proposed that the nervous and reproductive systems of individuals compete for the same fund of "phosphorous," "neurine," and other nutrient elements. His political economy of cellular relationships was like two parties *competing* for the same (scarce) sum of wealth; an acquisition on the part of one party would imply a loss to the other. Because of this inverse relation, an increase in the intellectual status of the race can only take place at the expense of its ability to propagate at previous rates. Therefore, although it was originally responsible for stimulating social organization and human intelligence, population pressure would eventually disappear because of this very development. "The pressure of population, as it gradually finishes its work," Spencer (*ibid.:*501) noted, "must gradually bring itself to an end." And happily, the miseries accompanying population pressure, such as the imbalance between the size of the population and the food supply, would also disappear.

Spencer's optimism did not extend to "inferior" and obviously poverty-stricken human beings. Echoing Malthus, he blandly asserted that there are individuals who have difficulty in "getting a living" because of their "excess in fertility." These individuals are on "the high road to extinction" because they are not stimulated to improve their mental productivity. They will be supplanted, according to Spencer, by individuals who are less stimulated by sexual needs. Indicating further that premature death occurs among individuals who possess the least powers of self-preservation, while those "select" human beings "left behind to continue the race" have superior powers of self-preservation, Spencer justified the early deaths of some of its members on the necessity for the forward moving development of the human species. This was accomplished by expanding his explanation to include all possible individual qualities which may interfere with his functionalist conceptions of the prerequisites for "social survival." He stated (*ibid.:*500) that "whether the dangers to existence be of the kind produced by excess of fertility, or of *any other kind,* it is clear that by the ceaseless exercise of the faculties needed to contend with them [i.e., dangers to existence], and by the *death* of all men who fail to contend with them successfully, there is ensured a constant progress toward a higher degree of skill, intelligence and self-regulation —a better coordination of actions—a more complete life" (our emphasis). From this liberal perspective an industrial order would achieve perfect equilibrium over the long run because the race belonging to that order would eventually evolve into a more adaptable biological type. In time, this superior race would change its social institutions and nations would mirror the perfect nature of man by coexisting in a functional harmony. As we have seen, this utopian achievement was assured by the evolutionary workings of the mechanisms that encouraged "the survival of the fittest."

Although Spencer concluded that some institutions and individuals did not adapt adequately to environmental circumstances and as a consequence, poverty, disease, and other evils came into existence, these maladjusted relations were passing affairs in the evolution of the laissez-faire industrial order. In fact, it has been shown that these social "miseries" were portrayed as having positive effects for the development of mankind because they resulted in the premature death of *inferior* and therefore *worthless* human beings.

NOTES

1. As Joseph A. Schumpeter (1954:231) notes, French agriculture was not interested in protectionism: "There was no danger of large wheat imports as a normal phenomenon, and free trade in agricultural products would have, if anything, increased their prices."

2. After describing the effects on upper class consumption patterns of the extraordinary wealth accumulated during the Georgian period, James Dugan (1965:17) indicates that "to counter crimes of poverty, the Georgians accumulated a system of laws called the Bloody Code, which prescribed death for more than 350 offenses, most of them against property. You could be hanged for stealing an item worth two-pence, for carrying a gun or snare on the squire's land, for fishing in his pond, or for cutting down his tree. Convicts were executed in clusters on Hanging days. If a victim remained alive after the cart pulled away, a compassionate friend or relative might come from the crowd and pull his legs to hasten death."

3. The problem of social integration is sometimes referred to alternatively, as the problem of "order," the problem of "social order," or the problem of "social stability."

4. The term "classification scheme" is used here synonymously with Richard S. Rudner's (1966:32–34) "nontheoretic classification schemata." It is "nontheoretic" because it is based on formal (i.e., sheerly analytic) rather than substantive categories.

5. Because of his development of the concepts structure, function, and immanent purpose (e.g., survival of the race), and through them his formalization of the universal necessities of competition and inequality, Spencer became a significant forerunner of the modern analytic approach to sociological relationships called *structural-functionalism.* Talcott Parsons (1961:x), a leading structural-functionalist, states, for example, that "very much of the framework of a *satisfactory* sociological scheme was already present in Spencer's thinking. It is *not necessary to reject* his general scheme, but rather to *supplement* it. Durkheim's contribution was such a supplement and the same can be said for modern social psychology. They combine with Spencer's to further a process of cumulative development of thinking about human society" (our emphasis).

CHAPTER 6

Exchange, Scarcity, and Economic Man

Spencer and the Concept of Economic Man

We have shown that some of Spencer's ideas were dependent for their credibility on economic liberalism. Like other aspects of the liberal world view, economic liberalism emerged substantially during the transition from feudalism to capitalism. Liberal economic categories developed in Britain alongside of the medieval categories, which positioned individuals according to the rights and duties of their station in life, each station being graded in a hierarchy ranging from lowly villein to divine monarch. By the eighteenth century, commonly used motivational categories, which had been organized with special reference to these feudal definitions, were rapidly disappearing. Lofty terms like "grace," "service," and "fidelity" were increasingly supplanted by mundane economic vocabularies of motive. Human beings, as Adam Smith noted, were being driven by their "propensity to truck, barter and exchange one thing for another."

During the precapitalist mercantile period, commercial activity was often justified by reference to higher ends than private gain. It was defined as service to the commonwealth or as the fulfillment of a religiously sanctioned calling. But with the rise of capitalism, the competitive search for private profit was elevated to the status of a self-evident justification for behavior performed during the greater part of a man's lifetime (Tawney 1926). In this process, liberal philosophers developed an enduring definition of competitive man that located in his egoistic heart the paramount desire for self-preservation. Liberal economists eventually named this definition of man, "homo economicus": the economic man. In the competitive antagonisms generated by his striving for a superior share of the nation's wealth, no more ultimate justification for everyday decisions could be invoked than that of economic survival. Economic survival! Economic self-preservation! How plausible this standard seemed in laissez-faire capitalist societies. Eventually the selfish value of "economic survival" was regarded as the ultimate standard for groups, nations, and even mankind as a whole. Every social system appeared to personify this economic man: fighting selfishly for its own survival!

In Spencer's works, the egoistic concept of man was generalized beyond all imagination. He believed that the origin of virtually every significant social institution was dependent upon egoistic striving. He claimed that the pursuit of private interest produced art, science, language, and industry. According to Spencer, "the very language" of the laws of the land was not "in the remotest degree due to the legislator." Instead, the law had developed inadvertently out of social relationships based on the atomistic and egoistic pursuit of personal satisfactions.

Spencer granted that the state was necessary for preventing the Hobbesian war of all against all. But underneath all political process was the driving force of atomistic self-interest. Social progress, social harmony and human institutions could not endure without the beneficial effects of egoistic striving.

Spencer and the Concept of Integrative Exchange

Spencer also recognized that the pursuit of private gain had often degenerated into open warfare. But he maintained that the growth of trade had created harmonious adjustments among the functionally interdependent parts of society. Trade produces "the healthful activity and due proportioning of those industries, occupations and professions, which maintain and aid the life of a society" (Spencer 1940:200—202). In his view, commercial expansion was replacing warlike, military "compulsion" with free markets based on a harmony of interests and voluntary exchange relations.

Consequently it was not competition in general which was universally integrative in Spencer's theory of industrial relationships; it was voluntary exchange within the "free market" which made possible that "vast elaborate industrial organization by which a great nation is sustained." To recognize and enforce the rights of competing individuals to exchange whatever they had of value, including land, labor, or capital, was to recognize and enforce the conditions which were integrative of all aspects of social life.

But Spencer ignored the degree to which exchange relations in capitalist societies were based on forcible as well as voluntaristic relations. Part Four will point out, for example, that the terms under which "free trade" was carried on between metropolitan and semicolonial or colonial countries were often backed by the force of arms. This force was exerted by imperialist nations or comprador classes.

Further analysis of exchange relations within capitalist societies have also underscored the fact that workers have been forced to exchange their labor services for wages in order to make a living because they do not own the means of production. Moreover, the capital which has been used to expand these means themselves has often been accumulated through the use of piracy, brigandage, genocidal policies and the forcible appropriation of peasant landholdings (Marx 1959:717—754). This capital was not accumulated merely on the basis of voluntary exchange relations.

Finally, the vast edifice of capitalism itself rests on a dialectic which is based in part on that negation of exchange Marx called "exploitation." In the process of production, Marx (*ibid.*:167–230) noted, workers produce surplus value which is appropriated by their employers. This act of appropriation is a negation of exchange because "the capitalist obtains *without exchange,* without equivalent, free of charge, some of the labor time crystallized in value" (Mandel 1970:83).

Consequently some of the most significant forms of exchange in capitalist societies are not based solely (if at all) on voluntaristic relations or relations of equality. And contrary to what Spencer believed, capitalist exchange relations have not proved universally integrative. Instead of the peaceful integration of human relations, the expansion of capitalist forms of exchange has generated violent peasant uprisings, imperialist wars, and class conflicts throughout the world.[1]

The Concepts of Rationality of Exchange, Scarcity Postulate, Economizing Behavior, and Economistic Fallacy

Thus Spencer's writings were partly organized around categories derived from economic liberalism. In subsequent years, liberal social scientists clarified some of the basic assumptions which underlie these categories. Because they repeatedly appear in early American sociological writings, we will briefly describe the basic assumptions, beginning with the notion of "the rationality of exchange."

The notion of exchange in nineteenth-century liberal theories was used in the analysis of competitive market relationships. Many liberal economists at the time falsely assumed that trade throughout history had been organized around exchange in a competitive market characterized by fluctuating prices and private ownership of commodities. Prices, in this kind of market, were partly established through bargaining procedures, and the term *price-making* market has been used by liberal scholars to refer to the relations in this market—relations that, on the whole, are immediately apprehended in daily economic experience.[2] These references have focused in particular on the formal analysis of rules or "rational principles" that guide the kinds of choices people make in their economic activity. These rules are called "logics of rational action" or "logics of rationality"; and the differences between these rules are regarded as variants of the logics of rational action. Generally, these logics are formal descriptions of how individuals decide to use the means at their disposal to obtain their ends.

By defining *rational action* simply as the choice of an appropriate means to an end, i.e., by a formal definition, the standards by which a means is considered appropriate can be determined by an economist through reference to either the laws of nature or the rules of the game (Polanyi 1957:245). In its most abstract sense, a logic of rationality does not refer to the *content* of ei-

47

ther means or ends but rather to the *logical principles* by which means and ends are related (i.e., the logics of means-ends relationships). It is convenient analytically to divorce the substantive content of means and ends from the formal logics by which people combine them in order to understand the different grounds on which choices are made. This simplification enables economists to objectify the various types of rules by which people relate all conceivable means to an enormous variety of human goals.

It has been observed that rational economic activity may be based on the logic of reciprocity such as that found by Malinowski among the Trobriand Islanders (*ibid.*:254–257). Or it might be based on a redistributive principle such as that used in the very ancient kingdom of Egypt, for example, by which the ruling group acquired and stored grain at central storage points and redistributed it as needed. These variant principles of rational action are historically specific and make sense only within the context of specific kinds of institutional relationships at particular places and times.

Thus, comparative analysis of economic activities within different societies indicates that all exchanges are *not* governed by the same rules. For example, there are exchanges wherein people appropriate goods for a price which has been either (1) "set" or (2) "bargained." The exchange of ownership of goods and services at set rates was characteristic of exchange relations in feudal cities where trade was regulated according to "just prices." Just prices were set by guilds, a council of city fathers, or ruling houses. In the countryside, exchanges were governed by ties of fealty in which "just" and predetermined services were required from serfs, feudal retainers, and nobles based on their respective functions related to work or defense of the land.

Exchange at *bargained* prices, on the other hand, is characteristic of price-making markets, i.e., markets regulated by competitively determined prices. This type of exchange assumes a degree of voluntaristic behavior which is exercised through ability of exchangists to adjust prices within certain limits. This voluntarism is evident in the degree to which the individual controls his money because it is simply a means to be used as the owner sees fit within prevailing market conditions. If a person were not able to use his money in alternative ways, his economic behavior would not be characterized as voluntaristic in this context.

Properties that have monetary values, like machines, also have alternative uses, or can be used as collateral for money which provides owners with a large range of possible uses. The power to make choices in the use of a means such as money, or the property it stands for, is customarily referred to as a "right." We often hear of the right to use property as one pleases. Whether it is denoted by terms like "free choice," "no trespassing on private property," "it's a free country" (where freedom is interpreted as the freedom to decide the use of one's property), the right of the individual to appropriate and use property or money as a means for his individual purposes, is a precondition for competitive markets and their fluctuating prices. This right and its preconditions may also have influenced broader conceptions of men as voluntaristic entities. Notions of free will, independent of either laws of nature or God, were heavily dependent for credibility on the expansion of competitive capitalist markets in relatively recent historical time.

Further inquiries into exchange relations have indicated that when individuals are faced with the problem of economizing in a price-making market, they are confronted time and again with the fact that their means are *insufficient* to meet all of their needs. Farmers, managers, and bankers, for example, have limited resources at their disposal, such as specific farm acreage, a fixed number of workers, or a particular amount of money for investment. Moreover, resources can be used in *alternative* ways: different crops could be planted on the acreage; production could be organized on the basis of a single craftsman, teams, or assembly line; or the money could be invested in different kinds of securities. Each one of these alternative uses of the resources have different consequences and, depending upon the cost involved in the employment of *each* use, would yield a greater or lesser profit in light of market prices.

Ultimately, economists formalized and thereby made available a simple but more general description of the innumerable instances in which "economical" choices were made. In order to achieve a very general formulation, however, it is preferable to use such formal terms as "means" instead of such words as "farm acreage," "work forces," or "investment capital." It is also preferable to use terms such as "maximum use value" and "ends" instead of the "most profitable use" and "profits." These abstract terms enable the model of economizing behavior to be easily applied to other social types in addition to farmers, managers, and bankers. Housewives generally economize in food purchases, for example, because they are interested in the welfare of their family members, not in private profits.

Formal terms such as "means," "ends," and "maximum use value" are not only an aid in generalizing, they also enable the economist to classify the very basic assumptions used in analyzing choice behavior in the market. In an economistic analysis, it is usually assumed that when persons make "economical" choices, there is an *insufficiency* (i.e., "a scarcity") of means. Secondly, it is assumed that these means can be used in *alternative* ways. Thirdly, it is also assumed that *a choice is induced* by this insufficiency and, finally, that the choice is made in consideration of ends *ranked in terms of some value* (Polanyi 1957:246). This set of assumptions is called "the scarcity postulate" even though it contains several propositions.

Let us highlight the generality of this sequence of assumptions and actions by applying it to a decision-making process which seems far removed from the competitive marketplace. The illustration will explicate several uses and conclusions of the marketplace analogy. An adolescent, for example, who has saved five dollars to buy a gift for a friend, may find that a particular store offers a variety of gifts. Since the adolescent waited until the very last minute (and cannot afford to shop around), these gifts include the full range of available uses to which the money can be put. Once in the store, the young person

49

is confronted with the problem of choice and the solution to this problem can be described as a specific sequence of actions. First, the shopper realizes that the accumulated money is insufficient to purchase all the gifts the friend might desire. Second, because of this insufficiency, the choice of gifts is restricted to those costing five dollars or less and the gifts are arranged in order of preference. In this case, the order of preference is based on the purchaser's knowledge of the friend's tastes. Third, once this order is established, the "best" choice consists of using the money to obtain the most preferred gift, or gifts, in this order until the five dollars has been exhausted.

This example illustrates a particular, albeit typical, kind of choice behavior, but it does not attempt to illustrate all the ways in which adolescent girls or boys choose gifts. Indeed, persons familiar with adolescents may know full well that it is often difficult to describe their choices in any "rational" manner, much less on economistic grounds. In this example, however, the sequence of actions involved in making a choice does represent a rational type of choice behavior, namely economizing. Furthermore, it illustrates the fact that economizing actions represent a calculating and deliberative process. When an adolescent engages in this kind of decision-making behavior he or she, like economic man, is a highly rational creature.

The economical decision on the part of the adolescent may be more extensive in its effects than those limited to a pleasant surprise for the friend. This decision means that money has been exchanged for the gift, and therefore the shopkeeper has also been satisfied. From the moment the adolescent entered the store, the behavior of the shopkeeper and the customer became regulated by the fact that both of these persons could profit (in different ways) from a possible exchange. The regularized forms of behavior which were organized around these exchanges have been captured in the classical doctrine of "the harmony of interests." Irrespective of the fact that different interests were involved, the adolescent and the shopkeeper integrated their behavior in relation to each other around the possibility of a profitable exchange. Their exchange of money for a gift was an expression of the harmonious relation between their individual self-interests. Their behavior, finally, could have been regarded as "price-making" if they had "higgled" or "bargained" over prices. Their behavior can still be regarded in this fashion if it represented an instance of innumerable, voluntary decisions to buy and sell commodities at prices that fluctuate according to "supply and demand."

In the illustration above only the behavior of the shopkeeper and the young person has been described. It must be remembered, however, that Spencer and many other liberals generalized these relations far beyond the preconditions for their existence. Free exchange based on trade was regarded as being integrative for nations and relations between nations. It was held to be integrative for economic life throughout history. This transhistorical generalization is called "the economistic fallacy" because it assumes that throughout history, personal exchanges and human rationality have been patterned after the nineteenth-century market and its economic "man."

50

NOTES

1. For an interesting discussion of the apologetic and overgeneralized use of integrative exchange notions based on competitive (price-making) markets, see Hopkins (1957).
2. For discussions of economic relations which lie behind these economic experiences, see Marx (1959:35–559).

CHAPTER 7

The Laissez-Faire Liberal Timetable

Spencer Reverses Critical Thrust of Environmentalism

In Spencer's writings, economic ideas are hidden in the most unlikely places. The previous chapter, for instance, has suggested that economic scarcity, competition, and fixed fund notions, in particular, provided the underlying rationale for Spencer's biopsychologistic mechanism of natural selection. Because of this, it is not sufficient to assume that his mechanism was originally derived from biological models which existed at that time, simply because the mechanism was formulated in terms of biological categories.

When examined in this light, Spencer was historically continuous with Malthus in more than one sense. First, Spencer organized his theory around the concept of the "struggle for survival" because of Malthus' influence. Second, Spencer emulated his eminent precursor by drawing heavily from the analytic wellspring of economic liberalism. Thirdly, Spencer agreed wholeheartedly with Malthus that neither radical nor reformist methods of changing human institutions would bring about the perfectibility of humankind. But Spencer also rejected Mathus' dismal prophecy about the limiting effects of population growth and declared, instead, that it was quite possible to achieve a state of perfection within the framework of an intensely competitive, industrial society. Finally, Spencer believed that even though the road upward toward a state of human perfection would be extremely gradual, it would only be traversed by the biologically *superior* individuals and races of humankind.

Spencer certainly was not the first scholar to regard some members of the human species as being biologically fitter than others. (Feudal scholars had already predicated individual worth and privilege on biological lineage.) However, in comparison with the straightforward feudal theories, Spencer's

51

claim that some men were biologically superior showed the influence of environmentalism. He did *not* feel that biological characteristics were immutable. In his opinion, certain men were superior to others because their parents represented superior *adaptations* to highly competitive environmental conditions. These men were also superior because they had inherited the adaptive biological characteristics of their parents.

Thus, Spencer accepted the growing belief that environmental factors determined the individual's development. This belief had its roots in the writings of the eighteenth-century environmentalists. The environmentalists proposed that the moral character of individuals was a direct product of environmental experiences. Taking issue with feudal justifications of class privilege on the basis of lineage, they proposed that irrespective of hereditary influence, radical changes in the nature of human institutions would greatly improve individual character. For instance, the eighteenth-century liberal philosopher, Claude A. Helvetius (1715–71), declared that political institutions were at the center of society and were brought into being by the existing system of laws rather than by supernatural or natural forces beyond human control. For Helvetius (1810), changes in social institutions would change the nature of individual men and women. Furthermore, in his view, radical social changes were possible merely by changing the existing system of laws.

Through Spencer's writings, however, the *radical* liberal perspective of environmentalism was converted into a *conservative* one. Spencer maintained that it was far more likely that radical changes in human institutions would result in social chaos than in the perfection of man and society. In his opinion, radical social changes would have degenerative effects on the human race as a whole.

In order to argue this point effectively Spencer conceded that legislation may effect long-term changes in the biological characteristics of the human species but, by asserting that the human race was forced to compete with other species for survival, Spencer invoked the "adaptive" or competitive ability of the species as a standard for evaluating the potential effects of the legislation. Any reformist or radical legislation (which was allegedly aimed at lowering a human's capacity to compete successfully) augured the possibility of disaster to the human race as a whole. By this logic Spencer *reversed the critical thrust* of the eighteenth-century environmentalists, who had used their doctrines to justify radical changes in existing systems of laws.

Spencer's Political Arguments
Based on *Biological Lag* Theory of Social Change

Spencer's clever logic enabled him to justify conservative doctrines by limiting the rate of optimum *social* change to an alleged rate of optimum *biological* change. He suggested that social change at any given time could not exceed the limits established by the predominant biological characteristics of the species without generating great disruption. Consequently, the evolution of social institutions had to be *synchronized* with the average changes in the evolution of human nature in order to achieve some modicum of social stability and harmony.

Human nature and social institutions, in this Spencerian argument, were analogous to a harnessed team of racing horses. The fastest member of this team was forced to run at the pace of the slowest member in order to achieve a fairly stable, maximum rate of speed for the team as a whole. Furthermore, if one member ran faster than the others, chaos might ensue and the average rate of speed would drop. Other species who were in the race might catch up to the team and pass it by.

Restated, Spencer's political writings proposed that if institutions had to adopt to the predominant biological characteristics of the human species (in order to enable the species to survive), then the progressive evolution of humankind could only take place within the *limits* of the highest possible rate of biological change. The rate of biological change was considered the limiting factor because the biological characteristics of the species changed at a much *slower* pace than the institutional relations among species members. Although social institutions themselves could actually change through legislative fiat at an even faster rate, these changes would not be beneficial because they would exceed the rate at which biological characteristics could be changed.

Spencer's argument was therefore, based on what might be properly called a "biological lag" theory of social change. This way of thinking incorporates a "differential rate of change" notion and was eventually reflected in a number of conservative sociological writings during the twentieth century. William F. Ogburn (1922) notably proposed the existence of various differentials in the rates of change between technological, social, cultural, and biopsychological relationships. In his theory of social change, Ogburn claimed that changes in *cultural* relationships were much more synchronized with the biopsychological relationships than with the social or technological ones. As one would expect, the biöpsychological relationships, and therefore the *cultural* relationships also, changed at a much slower rate than either the social or the technological relationships. Because of this, Ogburn's theory was called a "cultural lag" theory by sociologists. However, one could just as easily— and perhaps more precisely—call his theory a "psychobiological lag" theory. In the context of the twenties, his liberal theory was just as conservative as Spencer's in 1884.

The twentieth-century theorists who subscribed to this differential rate of change notion based their concepts of human nature on Freudian conceptions. Thus, Ogburn and others constructed their influential social myths by claiming that human nature was gradually evolving but primitive instincts of aggression set conservative limits on social change. The personalities of modern men were still too close to those of "stone age" men, to make the ending of poverty, war, and social inequality a short-range possibility.

Criteria for Distinguishing Reductionist Sociological Theory

Because of the consistently conservative manner in which the differential rate of change notion has been applied, it may be informative to further examine the *analytic structure* of the theory which underlies this way of thinking. In addition, the results of this examination might be applicable to a large number of liberal theories, irrespective of whether or not they are explicitly concerned with the analysis of political relationships.

In Spencer's political arguments, the most striking analytic feature resides in the *limiting function* of biological characteristics. In large measure, the credibility of Spencer's arguments were dependent upon the degree to which the rates of change in important social and political institutions could be reduced in tempo to a rate of biological change. This reduction was a logical possibility because Spencer utilized biological categories when formulating his single most important mechanism for social change, namely, the law of natural selection. In this context, the analytic and the political significance of the mechanism for change suggests *possible* analytic criteria for developing a *politically* relevant definition of *reductionist* sociological theories.

On what basis can it be analytically claimed that Spencer's theory is reductionist? One approach is to distinguish the level of analysis (e.g., sociological, psychological, biological) on which his more important *categories* reside. Certain categories in a theory may play more important roles than others, and one of the most crucial categories in Spencer's theory was "the individual." Furthermore the most important characteristics of this category were organized around such terms as "nervous system" and "fertility cells." [1] In Spencer's mechanism, in particular, the individual was essentially defined in biological terms.

Another analytic criterion for judging a reductionist scientific theory can be the level of analysis on which the more important *propositions* are made. Are the more important propositions on a sociological, psychological, or biological level? Propositions in a theoretical system have different "degrees of priority," and this priority can be indicated by a "scientist's reluctance to abandon or even modify the law in an ongoing inquiry" (Kaplan 1964:103). However, in the absence of an empirical inquiry, the centrality of a proposition can be gauged by its specific role in the network of propositions constituting a theory. In this regard, the propositions underlying the theoretical *mechanism* are central to a theoretical system as a whole. From this perspective, it is clear that to understand Spencer's theory of social evolution one requires knowledge of the propositions underlying his biological mechanism.

Are the biological or sociological categories and propositions central to the *mechanism* of Spencer's theory? In Spencer's writings one can find many statements suggesting that institutions have independent effects on the evolution of individuals. At times, in fact, we can find general statements to the effect that there is a two-way interaction between society and individuals. At first glance, therefore, Spencer's theory appears to have avoided problems of reductionism because he discussed the mutual interaction between social institutions and biological characteristics of individuals. But Spencer's biological propositions are absolutely central. (A clue to their centrality is suggested by the title of his 1852 work on natural selection: "A Theory of Population, Deduced from the General Law of *Animal Fertility*" [our emphasis].) Biological statements about animal fertility contributed to the basic mechanism of his evolutionary theory of man and society. From Spencer's point of view, the long-term changes in the biological characteristics of individuals *fundamentally* regulated the course of human civilization.

If a *sociological* theory is defined as reductionist when its mechanism is based on covariation between *biological* elements and / or *psychological* elements, then there can be no question about the reductionist character of Spencer's theory despite his general comments about the independent influence of social institutions or "superorganisms" on human life. The terms "biologism," "biopsychologism," and "psychologism" can be used to represent those strategies of investigating sociological relations which refer to theories utilizing mechanisms with covarying entities appropriate to these classes of reductionism. A nonreductionist sociological theory, on the other hand, contains a mechanism based on the covariation among entities, *each* of which is constituted by ordered *relations* between social types of individuals or social units, such as institutions.

Timetable for Rate of Social Change

Sociologists continuously probe for the speed at which society is changing. Will a better society arrive in the near future or at some far-distant time? Will change be gradual or rapid? Even the most superficial examination of Malthus' or Spencer's theories will reveal that there are no more ideologically significant ideas than those based on rates of social change. We will attempt to capture a sociologist's conception of such change in a notion called the *timetable*.

In Spencer's theory, there is a reductionist timetable linked to his biological mechanism. This mechanism was used to explain the individual changes in species' characteristics over the long range. In this view, the natural forces of competition inevitably kill off inferior human beings and encourage superior persons to survive. This, Spencer maintained, influenced changes in the entire species. By shifting to a level of analysis involving the covariation between the general characteristics of species and the characteristics of social institutions (or societies), Spencer implicitly argued that macroscopic social changes were also dependent upon the rate of change in biological characteristics of the species. From this perspective (and withholding our concern for the moment with the precise ways in which macroscopic changes in institutions or societies can be indicated), we can see that individual changes in the charac-

55

teristics of the species involve variation in the *proportion* of biologically *superior persons* in the society as a whole; progressive or retrogressive sociological changes are completely dependent upon long-term changes in this proportion.

The political dimensions of this reductionist timetable can be illustrated by Spencer's remarks in the chapter entitled "The Coming Slavery" in *The Man versus the State*. Objecting to proposals for social reform, Spencer (1940:50–52) bemoaned the fact that "there seems no getting people to accept the truth . . . that the welfare of society and the justice of its arrangements are at bottom dependent on the characters of its members." There exists, he stated, the "belief, not only of the socialists but also of those so-called Liberals who are diligently preparing the way for them . . . that by due skill an ill-working humanity may be framed into well-working institutions." This belief, he declared emphatically, is "a delusion," because "the defective natures of citizens will show themselves in the bad acting of whatever social structure they are arranged into. There is no political alchemy by which you can get golden conduct out of leaden instincts." The implications of these statements are quite clear: Generally, *social institutions* cannot be changed without first waiting on evolutionary changes in *human nature*. In view of Spencer's mechanism of natural selection, however, these changes involve a long and gradual process and require that the natural evolution of society be left alone. Otherwise, the progress of humanity may not only be slowed, it may even be reversed!

A timetable can now be more generally described. Typically it begins in the present and terminates when society becomes organized around new and qualitatively improved human relationships. It is calibrated by indicating the time intervals during which the fastest socially desirable variation can take place within any given period. This ethically evaluated rate of change will be called an optimum rate. Since the swiftest rate indicates the shortest amount of time during which desired changes can take place, the intervals of the timetable are the minimum intervals; social change can proceed no faster without threatening the end in question.

We must keep in mind that a timetable refers to a historical possibility, namely, the fastest rate of optimum change under a given set of conditions. These conditions, in Spencer's opinion, would be approximated only by laissez-faire capitalism. A timetable also represents an ethicopolitical attitude. It points to the social and political relations that must be maintained or altered in order to effect the fastest desired change in types of social institutions or in society as a whole.

Can the rate of social change in Spencer's theory be described on the basis of the concept of the timetable? In discussing the process of natural selection, Spencer suggested that change in intellectual capacity can be transmitted from one generation to the next. Since *progressive* social changes are totally dependent upon these biological changes, the minimum intervals of Spencer's timetable are based on the length of time necessary for the development of a new generation. However, while it may be assumed that such generational changes can take place in no less than the time necessary to reach puberty (roughly fourteen years) under optimum (laissez-faire) conditions, Spencer still does not specify the *kinds of changes* that might be expected during this time. He merely gives the impression that these changes will be very small because increments in average intelligence for the population as a whole are obviously small.[2] Consequently, the development of human civilization will be very gradual: his perfect society may not come into existence for thousands of years. Calibrated in terms of fourteen-year intervals, therefore, Spencer's timetable extends into the very far and distant future.

NOTES

1. According to Spencer (1852:406), the growth of intelligence is signified by the "capacity of the crania." In a table based on the sizes of crania among various types of human beings, Spencer indicated that on the average, the smallest sizes have been found among Australian aborigines, while the largest were characteristic of Englishmen. Since African and Asian types of persons were also represented in this comparison, it is to be presumed that the English inhabitants of the most industrialized imperialist nation in Europe at the time were superior to most people on earth.

2. In the introduction to *A Plea for Liberty* (McKay 1891:24), for example, Spencer stated: "Nothing but the *slow modification* of human nature by the discipline of social life can produce permanently advantageous changes. A fundamental error pervading the thinking of nearly all parties, political and social is that evils admit of immediate and radical remedies."

PART THREE

Enlightened Despotism: The French and German Reformers

CHAPTER 8

Rationalism and Romanticism

Review and Preview

It has been repeatedly asserted that liberal analytic conceptions, no matter how formal their expression, have structured social reality in a very special way. Although ostensibly without ideological bias, liberal sociological categories, such as structure, function, equilibrium, and natural selection, were used by Spencer to reaffirm the mythical function of the unequal distribution of wealth in industrial capitalist societies. In his opinion, distribution based on competitive striving ensured the slow but nevertheless increasing proportion of biologically superior races and individuals.

The chapters on Spencer's theory have also illustrated the degree to which laissez-faire sociological writings were dependent upon liberalism. Consequently, Spencerism in part represented an extension of liberal economic theories and doctrines into sociological thought. The adoption of Spencerism, to be sure, justified the brutal competition of the American free enterprise system on the basis of *biological* law. But the congenial relationship between Spencerian biology and American free enterprise was possible only because Spencer's biological notions had been modeled, in the first place, after well-established and highly acceptable *economic* liberal ideas.

Soon after it was developed, Spencerism came under sharp attack from many scholars, including most of the major founders of American sociology. By the turn of the twentieth century, capitalist social inequalities were no longer easily justified in terms of a political economy of cellular relationships or the relatively fixed, biological characteristics of individuals. Yet, despite their antipathy, the Americans continued to accept many of the fundamental Spencerian premises with certain qualifications. These qualifications resulted in a modification of the earlier antireform, social Darwinist approach to social inequities.

At the same time, the more basic, liberal premises, such as the belief that competition is the most equitable means for distributing wealth, were explicitly maintained in the newer sociological formulations. They were maintained in spite of the important changes in liberal perspectives that were brought about first by the rapidly growing monopolies and monopoly trusts, and second by the increasing realization that the very same competitive industrial order which Spencer had considered a harbinger of peace and prosperity, had become the staging area for violent, industrial conflicts and imperialist wars.

The newer sociological formulations, however, did not embody the traditional liberal premises in the way they had been used by their classical and laissez-faire predecessors. The Americans also began to selectively adopt eighteenth- and nineteenth-century ideas about the nature of social and political authority and, in the process, they gradually integrated the concepts associated with competition with those related to *social control.*

The following chapters describe additional social and political ideas which were eventually taken up by the American scholars. It will be noted, for example, that French and German writings on "social authority," "the organic society," and "the welfare state," were used along with the classical liberal and laissez-faire liberal notions as solutions to the problem of integration. In this process, liberal-functionalism in the United States became very complex.

Let us now turn to eighteenth- and nineteenth-century developments of both politically *conservative* and politically *radical* systems of thought in order to provide a historical background for the coming chapters. These shades of divergent political thinking were both represented within each of two important intellectual traditions, namely, the tradition of rationalism and the tradition of romanticism. We will also note the limitations inherent in the categories of rationalism and romanticism for understanding the development of sociological thought in the United States.

Rationalist Tradition and *Disagreements* about the Use of Reason

The tradition of rationalism developed during the Enlightenment. Its main tenet was the belief that reason and knowledge would provide the keys to the perfection of man and society. Some of the seventeenth- and eighteenth-century thinkers who contributed to the development of this tradition advocated the use of logical and empirical standards for the achievement of knowledge. Generally, however, the works by men of the Enlightenment clearly indicate that political standards were used for evaluating knowledge: what facts to seek, how and by whom they should be used.

In addition to doctrines predicated on the socially and politically interested search for knowledge, the tradition of rationalism is also noted for its stress on individualism. Individualism was inherited from the classical humanists who, however, generally reconciled their view of man with the authority of feudal institutions. (Other variants of the tradition of individualism continued to maintain the accommodation between prevailing forms of social authority and the individual as a matter of abstract principle, but these variants were not unanimous in favoring the specific authority of either the church or the monarchy.)

During the Enlightenment, scholars also began to emphasize social progress and the management of social affairs as primary standards for evaluating the "positive functions" of scientific knowledge. However, the awareness that scientific knowledge has great power in these respects raised two questions: What *goals* would guide the "enlightened" application of scientific knowledge to social affairs? *Who* in particular should obtain and employ this power?

A brief historical overview of the rationalist tradition suggests that questions like these have not been answered from a libertarian point of view. The scholars of the Renaissance during the fifteenth and sixteenth century, for example, had believed in the power of knowledge but they reconciled these beliefs with ends geared to the maintenance of the social authority of feudal institutions.[1] Later, during the period of the Enlightenment, most scholars also used their "enlightened" but nevertheless elitist conceptions of man and society to buttress legally constituted aristocratic authority. In addition, the creation and application of knowledge was considered the unique province of privileged intellectuals, aristocratic ruling households, and elite groups of civil servants.

At the end of the eighteenth century, scholars advocated the doctrines of "enlightened despotism" because they believed that an informed elite, including ruling households and civil servants, could change and manage *environmental* conditions in order to achieve social progress (Brinton 1963:303). These men simultaneously questioned the conservative authority of religious traditions. Nevertheless, as Crane Brinton (*ibid.:*305) points out, "In most matters the believers in enlightened despotism took an authoritarian position; for them the old authority, the Christian authority, was bad, not the principle of authority; authority in the hands of men *trained* to use enlightened reason was all right—was, in fact, necessary" (our emphasis).

Additional conceptions of man and society were produced by the rationalist writers of the Enlightenment. Some of those who believed in the power of reason even created ideas that became central to philosophical anarchism.

Therefore, in addition to sharing the opinion that human rationality will facilitate the attainment of the dignity and perfection of man in society, they also stressed the inherent goodness of man, as well as the belief in the abolition of all governments because they were essentially evil (*ibid.*:303, 306–307).

In sum, the rationalists agreed with each other in the belief that human beings were capable of discovering the fundamental properties of social and natural phenomena through the exercise of reason. They also felt that knowledge of reality would be used for human betterment. However, in spite of their epistemological agreements—and irrespective of their essentially common attitudes toward the beneficial uses of knowledge—there were very basic disagreements among rationalists about the political application of reason and knowledge. There was even great disagreement about the nature of men and society. Such disagreements become positively critical for differentiating nineteenth-century developments of sociological thought. Also, because of these diverse outlooks, seventeenth- and eighteenth-century rationalism, as a distinct category, becomes insignificant for understanding these later developments.

Some rationalists espoused a radical timetable for social change. They argued that the application of reason to human affairs would radically transform man and his institutions within a generation or two. Some (but by no means all) rationalists also openly opposed the church and depicted humanity as groping in the darkness created by religious superstition and dogma. Their fierce arguments spread widely in France and shattered the hegemony of feudal doctrines. Finally, the French Revolution put an end to the political institutions which sanctioned this hegemony.

Romantic Protest against Rationalism

Around the turn of the nineteenth century, a romantic movement emerged as a reaction to capitalist developments in western Europe. Members of this movement generally agreed that adequate knowledge and insights might be derived from traditional, mystical, or instinctual sources. But very different political and religious persuasions dominated the thinking of the men who shared romantic points of view. Because of their differences, the historical forces which gave expression to the romantic protest against rationalism cannot be forced into a simple explanatory model. For some intellectuals, romanticism reflected their revulsion against the violent course of the French Revolution as well as against the rationalism of its leading members. Still others espoused romantic doctrines simply because they were interested in stabilizing the hegemony of the new rulers of bourgeois societies. Though timeworn, feudal natural-law conceptions of man and feudal doctrines about unquestioning faith in religion and tradition were resurrected because they were found useful for buttressing the newly established authorities. Furthermore, feudal monarchies were still very much alive throughout Europe, and many intellectuals, serving the state and the church, energetically modified old doctrines to meet the new challenges symbolized by the events of the French Revolution or its aftermath. In their view, rationalist doctrines were anathema because rationalism was accountable for the demise of feudal institutions in France.

The complexities of the romantic movement against rationalism are heightened even more by the realization that with the establishment of liberalism as a dominant ideology in countries like England, some intellectuals equated rationalism with economic liberalism and Malthusian doctrines. The operative interpretations of reason, under these conditions, meant the application of a laissez-faire *liberal* metaphysics of normality [2] and *liberal* moral principles in social policy. However, the most widely established liberal theories at the time only provided intellectuals with pseudoscientific apologetics for poverty and starvation. Because of these conditions, many intellectuals were either not familiar with, or could not easily justify socially critical, scientific explanations of the causes of starvation and unemployment. Although some of them deplored the evil consequences of industrialism (e.g., poverty and starvation), they had no plausible "rationalistic" and "scientific" strategy available for a critical analysis of these evils.

With regard to these intellectuals and these conditions, it appears that "romantic" categories filled the breach created by the apologetic character of economic liberalism which was no longer a *critical* ideology. Radical and reformist critics of industrialism turned to faith in traditions which had heretofore sustained the moral economy of feudal communities. Some also turned to utopianism and mysticism, and others to absolute moral principles or emotional revulsion in order to justify their criticism. As long as the liberals had the corner on the market for "scientific" explanations, there seemed to be no plausible *rationalist* grounds for criticism of the existing scheme of things.

Something of this order is implied by Crane Brinton's explanation of the division between the "partisans of the head" and the "partisans of the heart." Brinton states that after 1798, the utilitarians (the "heads") took up Malthus' theory of population changes. Many scholars consequently considered it reasonable to allow poverty-stricken people to starve if they could not earn a living. Brinton (*ibid.*:311) further notes:

We need not debate whether the reasoning of the economists in this matter actually is in accord with what "reason" should mean in [modern economic] tradition. The point is that they claimed they were following reason—and their opponents [i.e., the romanticists] *accepted* their claim. Their opponents said something like this: "We can't see what's wrong with your chain of reasoning. Perhaps the race would be better off if the incompetent were weeded out. But we can't take your argument. We're *sorry* for the poor man. We know you're wrong because we *feel* you're wrong." [our emphasis]

Brinton also indicates that opponents of Malthusian doctrines relied heavily on "sentiments of the heart" such as sympathy, pity, and love. Identifying

Malthus' opponents with the tradition of romanticism, Brinton concludes that "The partisans of the head tended in the later Enlightenment to bolster the side of enlightened despotism, planning and authority; the partisans of the heart tended to bolster the side of democracy, or at least self-government by a numerous middle class, natural spontaneity, and individual liberty" (*ibid.*).

Generally, the romantics rejected the necessity for demonstrating knowledge by means of rational proof as opposed to faith or intuition. The movement degraded the role of reason in human affairs and elevated *faith* and *emotion* as primary guides to moral conduct. The romanticists in the arts, music, and letters were truly represented, as Brinton indicates, by men who shared a deep belief in individual liberty. But romanticists in the field of philosophy, history, law, and political economy also became part of various conservative if not outright reactionary movements. Thus, the romanticists included scholars like Edmund Burke in Britain, who modified liberal ideas to make them more useful for establishing middle-class hegemony. They also included liberal German idealists like Hegel who, although favoring a constitutional monarchy, nevertheless mystified the state. In France, romantic thought was represented by such Catholic reactionaries as Bonald and Maistre.

At the same time, however, other schools of thought appeared, and they were represented, for example, by Saint-Simon and the Saint-Simonians, who reflected the influence of *both* the rationalist and romantic traditions. The Saint-Simonians, who will be discussed in the next chapter, were rationalists because they believed in "scientific" (i.e., economic) planning. But they were also romanticists because they held that the intuition of artists and priests was more reliable for making ultimate decisions about social goals.

Toward the end of the first quarter of the nineteenth century, scholars who wrote in the spirit of rationalism, romanticism, or both, began to create analytic conceptions that profoundly altered the preexisting conceptions of man and society. Elements of these writings, by men like Fourier, Saint-Simon, Hegel and Ricardo, strongly influenced Marx and Engels in later years. During the third decade,[3] romanticism, which had been one of a number of traditions converging in Marxian thought (via Hegel or Fourier), no longer contributed significantly to the development of this ideology.

In the third quarter of the nineteenth century, romanticism still continued as a powerful influence on the works of artists, musicians, and men of letters. But it was rapidly declining in importance as a meaningful determinant of changes in the major styles of reflection leading to the development of modern sociological thought. With the rising tide of science, romanticism lingered among those scholars who were still powerfully influenced by religious conceptions of man and society. Romanticism as a viable social movement had run its course, however, by the middle of the century. Like rationalism, the tradition of romanticism was no longer significant for understanding the analytic developments that led to late nineteenth-century sociological thought.[4]

NOTES

1. This was not only the case with Renaissance scholars like Niccolo Machiavelli (1469–1527). It was also true for the classical humanists during the fifteenth and sixteenth centuries. Crane Brinton (1963:213) points out that these "humanists were not libertarians and democrats in the modern sense. They were a privileged group of learned men . . ." The following chapters of this volume, it should be noted, will repeatedly use the word "humanistic," but this word is not to be interpreted in its classical sense. It is used in a modern sense and connotes libertarian and democratic (antielitist) values.

2. This metaphysics depended heavily on the laissez-faire notion of the self-equilibrating functions of the natural forces of competition.

3. *The German Ideology* (Marx 1845–1846) and *The Poverty of Philosophy* (Marx 1846–1847) are works that represent the turning point from which Marxism emerged as a science.

4. We are aware that there are a number of sociological analyses of the development of modern social thought which contradict this conclusion (notably, Bendix 1970). However, these analyses are formulated on the basis of vague (idealistic) references to "romanticism" and "rationalism," rather than a rigorous investigation of modern social movements (e.g., student movements) and modern social institutions (e.g., the academy).

CHAPTER 9

Enlightened Despots and Industrial Authority

Laissez-Faire Liberals and French Positivists

The general theorists who founded the discipline of sociology in the United States looked primarily to European, not American, predecessors for model interpretations of social relationships. Furthermore, these men were highly selective in choosing among the existing European writings and traditions. This selection, as we will see, was structured by their interest in formulating a technocratically oriented strategy for analyzing social relationships. Scientific knowledge, in their eyes, was a prime instrument of social control and was therefore useful to politicians and social engineers who managed society.

In this chapter we will consider the French positivists whose ideas were used by the North Americans for developing their modern technocratic strategy of analyzing social relationships. These French scholars generally felt that society should be managed by elite groups of individuals and that scientific knowledge would be useful in achieving social stability and progress. It is fitting therefore to view these writers as continuous with the spirit of the early rationalist tradition known as "enlightened despotism," which regarded scientific knowledge as an instrument of enlightened control by ruling elites. At the same time, however, it is also important to keep in mind that most of the authors to be discussed oriented themselves to their own time and did not justify their points of view chiefly in terms of feudal or precapitalist values and authority. They indicated instead that expert knowledge would help achieve "social harmony" and "social efficiency" in the interests of "society." The society in this context was an emerging *industrial* capitalist society.

The French positivists were interested in the direct, theocratic, or political management of economic relationships. Most of the positivists had been liberals at one time or another, but they broke with liberalism as *reconstituted* by the laissez-faire liberals during the nineteenth century. As one would expect, in this process they produced ideas that sharply contrasted with the main trend in liberal thought: laissez-faire liberalism.

On the other hand, a cautionary note should be sounded before leaping to the opposite conclusion; that is, identifying the positivistic writings of Auguste Comte, in particular, as being thoroughly antiliberal on the basis of either his political doctrines or his analytic assumptions. This "antiliberalism" interpretation has been central to the historical writings of most modern liberal sociologists of knowledge.[1] Because of this, it is important to recount the mythical versions of the *liberal state* (against which the "antiliberals" like Comte have been posed) and the mythical categories of "individualism" and "collectivism" which have been used to buttress the notion that nineteenth-century liberalism and positivism were unalterably opposed.

Oversimplification of Liberalism

In the analysis of the relations between positivism and liberalism, one should consider that there is a tendency among scholars to treat nineteenth-century liberalism as being synonymous with laissez-faire liberalism. But this interpretation is categorically wrong and it has been due, in large measure, to the influence of the historical writings by laissez-faire liberals themselves (e.g., Dicey 1905). Laissez-faire historians have regarded their nineteenth-century counterparts as the standard-bearers of "the true liberalism," which, in their view, represented the culmination of a relatively unchanged body of thought originating in the writings of Adam Smith [2] and terminating in laissez-faire theories and doctrines.

In oversimplifying the development of liberalism, historians have uncritically accepted the terms in which nineteenth-century laissez-faire liberals generally posed the ideological issues of their time. These terms have made it appear as if the significant dialogue during the nineteenth century took place between the proponents of "individualism" and the champions of "collectivism." The advocates of "individualism," in this view, supported the laissez-faire liberal state and defined individual liberty in terms of property rights as well as other rights. On the other hand, their political antagonists, including liberals and nonliberals, were regarded as being advocates of a "collectivist state" because they felt, in particular, that the state should actively intervene in economic affairs. This simplistic dichotomy describes nineteenth-century politics inaccurately. "Collectivism" was also used as a catchall term to signify reformism, socialism, positivism, feudalism, and a host of other alternatives as well.

It is possible that the terms in which the nineteenth-century dialogue among bourgeois intellectuals were formulated contributed to this general way of perceiving the political conflicts at that time. But it is just as important to note that the so-called liberal state which defended the interests of "individualists" was a *social myth*. The liberal states in Britain and the United States never adopted a policy of actual noninterference in economic affairs. Instead, the intellectual spokesmen for the British merchant-capitalists and industrialists, for example, employed this mythical conception to justify the curtailment of the property rights of the great landowners. This goal was partly achieved in the third decade of the nineteenth century when British merchants and industrialists began to dominate the Parliament. At that time, in the name of a hands-off policy, they enacted a flood of legislation which ensured that their "liberal state" would *actively intervene* in economic affairs primarily but not exclusively on their own behalf.

Simultaneously, the social myth of the liberal state was turned against the British working classes in order to forestall the enactment of political policies which would enhance their position in the economy. However, the merchants and industrialists never succeeded in completely preventing policies that favored their class antagonists at their own expense because of the coalitions against them, forged between landowners and working-class interests.

Thus, in this welter of conflicting interests, the laissez-faire liberals defended their class interests by creating a mythical opposition based on "individualism" versus "collectivism." In their view liberalism was the fount of "individualism" even though the political standpoints of liberals like John Locke and Jeremy Bentham would, if they were writing at the time, have been regarded by the laissez-faire liberals, as "collectivist" in the extreme.[3] Furthermore, as the century moved along, the growing clashes between the urban working classes and the ruling classes in France, Britain, and elsewhere exposed with great clarity the contradictions between the libertarian and the antilibertarian dimensions of laissez-faire liberal thought. In this process, even laissez-faire liberals like John Stuart Mill (who was forever attempting to forge an eclectic reconciliation between contradictory liberal doctrines) began to vacillate markedly between the notions being associated with the liberal myths of "individualism" and "collectivism."

All of these aforementioned events suggest, first, that "collectivist" views were by no means held by a monopoly of intellectuals who were against liberalism in general. Indeed, for the most part, "collectivist" views countered *laissez-faire* liberalism in particular. Other liberal views continued to have "collectivist" adherents. Second, historians have glossed over the strongly "collectivist" trends in liberal thought which are exemplified by the writings of Locke, Bentham, and Burke, in order to minimize the overlap which did exist between such opposing points of view as liberalism and positivism. Third, the single most important point that was lost or totally ignored in this process is that many of the "collectivist" intellectuals who sharply disagreed with laissez-faire liberals, were *no less committed* than Mill or Spencer to the preservation and development of industrial capitalism. This interest set these "collectivists" apart from the feudalists, the Jacobins, the early communists, and other kinds of "collectivist" points of view. Because of their commitment to some form of *industrial capitalism* (even though they called their versions of capitalism either "socialism," "the Scientific State," or "the Positive State"), the French positivists were much more fundamentally aligned with the liberal than the antiliberal forces.

Oversimplification of Positivism

The French positivists, as we have indicated, were distinguished by the belief that scientific knowledge could be useful for governing society. Our previous remarks also indicated that the positivists preferred industrial capitalism. Positivism, therefore, should not be reduced to a handful of doctrines about the social utilization of scientific knowledge. The positivists, furthermore, should not be regarded as the first scholars to make suggestions about the social utility of scientific knowledge. The science of political economy itself was founded by men who were interested in the politically useful application of knowledge. They were extremely concerned with promoting the welfare of their countries through the scientific management of wealth and other natural resources.

We have seen that virtually every classical liberal scholar shared this view. The same was true of Malthus. After commenting on the retrogressive and progressive oscillations in human societies, Malthus observed, in the famous essay on population, for example, that one principal reason why the inexorable relations had remained unnoticed by previous scholars was that the history of the working classes was insufficiently known. He added:

. . . the histories of mankind which we possess are, in general, histories only of the higher classes. We have not many accounts that can be depended upon of the manners and customs of that part of mankind where these retrograde and progressive movements chiefly take place. A satisfactory history of this kind . . . would require *the constant and minute attention of many observing minds* in local and general remarks on the state of the lower classes of society, and the causes that influence it. [Malthus 1914:10 our emphasis]

Malthus believed that "a branch of statistical knowledge" which generally became identified with developments in economics and sociology would eventually make up the deficiency in the study of working-class relationships. This knowledge could be used to enlighten the men who managed society.

67

Laissez-faire liberals like Herbert Spencer shared similar beliefs, even though they perceived the proper management of society in terms of leaving well-enough alone, when it came to *certain* economic relationships.

Thus, it will be noted that the French positivists were interested in the direct management of economic life. This substantive focus will not be minimized when contrasting their works with statements based on laissez-faire theories and doctrines. But even though some of their accomplishments were very important to the development of early nineteenth-century utopian socialist thought, the French positivists were eager to use scientific knowledge for the preservation of private property. They also shared with liberals a common interest in the use of scientific knowledge for achieving the further development of industrial capitalism. In light of the foregoing discussion, it is believed that they should be regarded as a secondary trend in *bourgeois thought*. Malthus and Spencer, it should be recalled, were representative of the first alternate trend in bourgeois thought.

Saint-Simon: The Visionary Integration of Social Sciences and Industrial Planning

Through the centuries, scholars who espoused one or another form of enlightened despotism justified their elitist doctrines by reference to the authority of God, the prince, the aristocracy, or the commonwealth. During the nineteenth century, however, elitist intellectuals began to speak about a new eminence, the economic and political imperatives of the *industrial* society. Furthermore, knowledge—and social scientific knowledge in particular—was perceived as having considerable utility for organizing and rationalizing human relations under *industrial* conditions.

A French aristocrat, Claude Henri de Rouvroy de Saint-Simon (1760–1825), figured significantly in the development of this new way of thinking about scientific knowledge. During the first quarter of the nineteenth century, Saint-Simon (1964) introduced the philosophy of positivism, a class interpretation of the causes of the French Revolution, and a utopian scheme for integrating society. This scheme was so radical for its time that Marx dubbed it a forerunner of socialist thought. Saint-Simon's writings also stimulated the development of a variant school of thought, organized by a group of his disciples, including Bazard, Laurent, and Enfantin, who were later called the Saint-Simonians. Further, his work exerted a powerful influence on Auguste Comte, who was employed as his secretary for a few years. Some of the ideas flowing from the writings of Comte and the Saint-Simonians were embraced by Emile Durkheim, one of the most eminent of the early corporate-liberal sociologists in Europe. This melange, whose roots were deeply implanted in the work of Saint-Simon, also expressed ideas which appeared in works by early American sociologists. First, then, the writings of Saint-Simon will be spelled out in greater detail.

Saint-Simon was an heir to the spirit of optimistic and universal historical inquiry epitomized by Condorcet and Turgot. In his explanation of social evolution he announced that civilization would not progress appreciably without the further development of an empirical social science. The speculative philosophical method, in his view, was being replaced by the empirical, scientific method aimed at the discovery of the lawlike character of the social universe. A science of "social physiology" was coming into being and would ultimately become the means for guiding the development of a "positive" society. Although his disciples, the Saint-Simonians, also used the term "social physics," while Comte preferred the word "sociology" as the name of this new science, the assumption that a new social science was necessary for social progress belongs to Saint-Simon.[4]

Saint-Simon felt that the golden age of man lay in the future, not the past. He suggested that "parasitic" aristocracies and militaristic feudal "regimes" were being replaced by more productive societies based on "peaceful industry." In the coming "industrial regime," "parasitic" consumers would totally disappear and, as a result, members of society would be limited to the "industrial class." This class would not be limited to the wage earners of industry but would also include manufacturers and merchants. The institution of private property would therefore be maintained and the *business* elite would be given the responsibility of running the government (because they could accomplish this task more efficiently than any other group of "producers"). In time, Saint-Simon speculated, government over men would be replaced with the efficient administration of things by an elite scientific body incorporated within the political state. This group of scientists would organize administrative functions on the basis of "scientific" social planning; and a salient standard for evaluating these governmental activities, in Saint-Simon's view, would consist of meeting the general obligation to maintain a satisfactory standard of living among "the poorest and most numerous class."

In his early works, Saint-Simon explained the development of France, from the sixteenth century to the Revolution, on the basis of class conflict over the ownership and control of private property. This development culminated in the transfer of the ownership of property from the clerical and noble classes to the industrial classes. The Reign of Terror, which had followed the Revolution, was considered a manifestation of the power of the propertyless classes. Generally, on the other hand, Saint-Simon's conception of the *ultimate* causes of social evolution was an idealistic one: ideas ultimately determined history; and scientific knowledge, morality, and religion had independent and important functions in this regard. In his later writings, Saint-Simon elevated morality and religion to a more important position than scientific knowledge in constituting the moving forces of history. This change in emphasis was particularly evident in his last work: *The New Christianity* (1825).[5]

The Saint-Simonians: Social Stability and Theocratic, Technocratic, and Financial Policies

Saint-Simon's followers, the Saint-Simonians, carried many of his ideas to an extreme and eventually degenerated into a religious sect. From approximately 1824 to 1840, however, they enjoyed considerable popularity in France, England, and, to a lesser extent, Germany (Iggers 1958:xxiii–xxv). Like their mentor, Saint-Simon, they argued that the primary problem facing Western civilization was the attainment of social, economic, and political stability. That this had not been achieved was evident in the collapse of the feudal monarchy and the "succession of the transient political regimes; the constitutional monarchy, Jacobinism, the Directory, the Consulate and the Empire, and the Restoration" (*ibid.:*x).

Predating Durkheim's (1933:18–22) highly syndicalist regard for the role of the ancient guild system in maintaining social integration, the Saint-Simonians felt that the economic problems of their time were related to the effects of uncontrolled capitalism on medieval corporate structures. This judgment was reinforced by the depressions of 1816 and 1824, which were also seen as further evidence of the disorganizing effects of uncontrolled capitalism. Instead of urging a return to these feudal corporate structures, however, the Saint-Simonians developed various credit and banking schemes which would, in their view, stabilize and regulate economic relationships. These men, therefore, were among the pioneering advocates of financial policies geared toward stabilizing capitalist economies. They also played an important role in the creation of the first great French trust, the Crédit Mobilier, and figured importantly in the organization of the financial group responsible for the development of the Suez Canal.

Saint-Simon was not the only scholar who influenced the Saint-Simonians. The solutions to the problems of social instability (e.g., respect for traditions and authority) formulated by Bonald and Maistre [6] were also utilized. The Saint-Simonians adopted the conservative insistence on a strongly hierarchal social order. They regarded the French Revolution as the product of socially disorganizing forces set into motion by the Protestant Reformation and the subsequent, skeptical spirit of eighteenth-century philosophical thought. Free rational inquiry, in their view, had ushered in a "critical" period in the development of human civilization which would ultimately be replaced by a new "organic" organization of society. Also, consistent with Saint-Simon's idealist view of history, it was claimed that the critical period would reveal fundamental moral and religious ideas which would be applied by scientists, artists, and industrialists to all phases of life. The systematic application of these ideas would stimulate the development of a new organic stage of history.

Many of the Saint-Simonian formulations had been explicit or implicit in Saint-Simon's works. His disciples, for example, held fast to the notions that society should be led by elite members, that wealth should be distributed unequally, and that each individual should be classified according to his ability and remunerated according to his work performance. But many of their conceptions also represented departures from the writings of Saint-Simon. The Saint-Simonians, for example, went beyond their mentor in proposing that inherited wealth should be completely abolished. They also carried Saint-Simon's later emphasis on religion to an extreme by insisting that in future society the *scientific* and *economic* elites should be totally subordinated to a *religious* elite. In their "social system" the high priests were given the task of commanding the political organization of society.

In effect, the Saint-Simonian vision is similar to Durkheim's mechanical society. The inhabitants of this visionary social system were to be persons who shared the same religion. They would all be members of the same church. As in medieval and Calvinist conceptions of the role of the church, the Saint-Simonian church would be concerned with the management of social and economic life. In their essentially *theocratic* society, science would be relegated to merely descriptive functions and the integration of scientific observations could only be achieved by an individual genius who possessed superior insight into the nature of "fundamental" religious ideas. Saint-Simon had considered science one of the prime movers of human history. This concept of science was greatly modified by the Saint-Simonians. Their attitude toward industrial organization, on the other hand, was consistent with his faith in the positive consequences of technological developments.

Social Authority Based on Imperatives
of Industrial Economy

The Saint-Simonians definitely justified the *private* ownership of property. However, they made *production* a greater test of social usefulness and thereby undermined the forms of industrial and financial authority which were legitimated solely by the private ownership of property (*ibid.*:45). The use of production for evaluating the optimum functioning of an *industrial system* had various critical implications: profit, for example, could be justified as a reward for individual performance in achieving higher production, but the transfer of wealth to young men and women who had *not* been involved in productive enterprises could not be sustained on this basis. Related to this latter view, the Saint-Simonians criticized family *inheritance* because it functioned to maintain "parasitic" classes.[7] This point of view conflicted with traditional bourgeois doctrines which sustained the long-term stability of a ruling class based on the inheritance of wealth and property from one generation to the next.

In light of their strong concern for productive efficiency it is not surprising to find that a number of the Saint-Simonians were engineering students, and were therefore aspiring to join an occupational group that would play a central role in the everyday management of an industrial economy. The Saint-Simonian proposals for economic expansion and production also reflected the increasing awareness of the material abundance made possible by an industrial division of labor and technology. They argued that the industrial economy had its own logic of development for achieving important social goals: with the right mixture of economic planning, fiscal policies, and private competition, national economies would expand. The world could be transformed and a high standard of living ensured for all humankind.

Modern Technologies Instituted Ideologically

Even though Saint-Simon and his disciples eventually elevated religious values and principles as the *ultimate* guides to conduct, they nevertheless influenced modern secular perspectives regarding the social use of knowledge. One of these perspectives, for example, regards scientific knowledge to be useful because it enables men who manage economic institutions to discover the logical principles by which maximum economic expansion and highly efficient production can be achieved within the shortest period of time. In fact, because of the persistent association between scientific knowledge and technological growth, the term "scientific rationality," instead of the older notion of "economic rationality," has come into frequent use by modern liberals to explain the rapid emergence of large scale and highly integrated market institutions.

The new "positivistic" way of thinking about industrial societies during the early nineteenth century has also influenced modern functionalist modes of thought which emphasize the imperatives of social systems rather than individuals. *Individual* needs (imperatives), for example, figured significantly in classical liberal doctrines. However, such standards as economic expansion and productive efficiency replaced this with references to *social* rather than individual imperatives. As standards, these social imperatives, it is true, have been justified by reference to the effects of greater material abundance (engendered by an expanding and productive economy) on the well-being of *individuals*. However, economic growth and efficiency can only be used as standards for evaluating the optimum functioning of a *social system*. These standards do not directly inform us of the effects of that system on the well-being of individuals. This information is not directly available because economic expansion and productive efficiency may produce both positive and negative consequences for individuals. Some men, for example, may become rich because of an increase in productive efficiency; others may become unemployed.

Historical experience clearly shows that in capitalist nations, economic expansion has been a dynamic force behind imperialism; greater productive efficiency has been associated with increased exploitation; and higher production has generated crises of overproduction. With regard to some socialist economies, it has become obvious that highly integrated (centralized) industrial planning and rapid economic growth which have been insensitive to the needs of people have also been harmful. These factors have contributed, in part, toward the development of technocratic socialist elites. They have maintained inequalities in social relationships and undermined attempts to achieve genuine democratic societies. They have consequently negated the significant advantages for improving the well-being of individuals.

Sociologists who have followed in the footsteps of the early positivists have come to believe that science automatically maintains such allegedly "impersonal" social imperatives as economic expansion, productive efficiency, and the emergence of large economic and political institutions. But this belief is fallacious: the automatic identification between modern science and "impersonal" technological policies first of all ignores the fact that in capitalist democracies, scientific resources are monopolized by a plutocratic social class that has little concern for humanistic values. Secondly, although technological developments may appear to be out of control in these nations, they actually do have a "logic of development" which is not independent of ideologically governed purposes. All modern technology is, in fact, instituted ideologically, and "scientific" rationalities which influence technological developments are regulated ideologically.

To be sure, there are some ideologically unforeseen and, therefore, inadvertent consequences of technological developments. But at this stage in the evolution of humankind there are no "runaway" sciences or "scientific" technologies. The sciences or technologies which have appeared "out of control" actually have been subservient to ruling classes or political oligarchies. If they had been organized by humanistic values to begin with, there would be no temptation or justification today to regard them as monstrous instrumentalities which have run amok.

Leaders of modern nations often argue that rapid economic expansion and high productive efficiency will create material abundance. This abundance, in turn, will make men free. But it should be kept in mind that material abundance is not tantamount to freedom. Today, there are alternative possibilities for the development of economic relationships in market economies even if the basic prerequisites for food, shelter, and clothing have not been *fully* secured. Some of these possibilities are conducive to greater freedom while others are not.

The development of market institutions is regulated by various ruling class and nationalist aims in the United States. Private profit is, of course, the most important aim; but other considerations, such as the achievement of military superiority, the accumulation of investment capital, and a favorable position in international trade, also enter into the picture as short- or long-term goals. Without minimizing the economic and political conditions which sustain these aims, however, it should be kept in mind that the development of market institutions can be organized around other ideals. To stand this ideological focus on its head, economic relationships can be made directly conducive to social equality, democratic participation, the prolongation of life, human solidarity, individual dignity, the enrichment of leisure, the optimization of health, the love of knowledge, and the flowering of individual creativity. Although the technocratically organized education of social scientists has rarely examined economic relations in light of these latter aims, there is no doubt that there is no immutable natural law ensuring economic growth and productive efficiency at the expense of all forms of social equality, human solidarity, and individual freedom.

A similar evaluation can be made of the uses of the physical and social sciences. Science need not be used for antihuman and technocratic ends unless the activities of scientists and technicians are regulated by antihuman and technocratic ideologies. With regard to economic relationships, for example, science has power because it is a force of production and is instituted within the context of the prevailing modes of production.[8] Furthermore, just as there are different ideological policies for instituting technologies, there are different "scientific" rationalities for carrying out these ideological policies. There is no "scientific" or "economic" rationality that is *not* associated with some humanistic or antihumanistic ideology.

NOTES

1. The ideal-type opposition between individualism and collectivism has been taken for granted in one way or another by virtually all modern liberal sociologists who have analyzed early nineteenth-century developments. As a result, some of these scholars have erred by regarding the writings of such liberals as Edmund Burke—who argued strongly for the moral and political regulation of social life—as being an anomalous development in liberal thought at that time. There is, however, ample precedent for Burke's way of thinking in classical liberal writings. Similar precedents also exist for Comte's point of view.

2. Adam Smith has usually been taken as a starting point because he felt, among other things, that monopolies prevented prices from seeking their "natural level." His arguments against monopolistic restraints on trade, however, should be analyzed within the context of precapitalist political and social class developments. At that time, for example, monopolies were regarded as functioning in the interests of national policy and were governed by royal patents and decrees. These monopolies, furthermore, were mercantile rather than industrial institutions.

3. For a fascinating discussion of the myth of the liberal state, see Brebner (1947). Brebner also points out that Bentham had maintained that his utilitarian principles should be used to identify the common interests which would bring "the greatest happiness to the greatest number." These principles were to be used by "enlightened" rulers and, because of their abstract form, were easily adjusted to defend the class interests of the landowners. As a result, in the first half of the nineteenth century, parliamentary spokesmen for the landed interests employed Bentham's conception of the common good in order to criticize the negative effects of industrialism on the great mass of people. This conception (as well as Bentham's principle of "local inspectability") was also utilized by royal commissions for justifying state intervention on the behalf of landowners and laborers alike.

4. As Gouldner (1958) has pointed out, Saint-Simon developed the outlines of the positivistic philosophy generally attributed to Comte. (See also Zeitlin 1968:61.)

5. The utopian aspects of his vision are not germane to this discussion.

6. These authors will be discussed briefly in the next chapter on Auguste Comte.

7. This critical point of view was radical in the context of the early nineteenth century. Toward the end of the century, however, it was no longer indicative of a radical perspective. The attitudes toward curbing or eliminating inheritance which were ex-

pressed by Durkheim, Ward, and Small, for example, were expressive of a fully developed corporate-liberal and *technocratic* point of view.

8. The forces of production include not only tools and machines but also the accumulation of experience and knowledge which is necessary to institute a technology at any given stage of economic development.

CHAPTER 10

Counterrevolution and the Philosophy of Auguste Comte

Review

We have seen that profound changes in economic and political relationships in England, initiated by the great industrial revolution, marked the end of the precapitalist period for that nation. Simultaneously, the momentous French Revolution heralded political changes that eventually destroyed the feudal state throughout most of the European continent. Under these new conditions, politically conservative intellectuals reassessed the liberal doctrines of natural rights and found them deficient in their usefulness for the maintenance of ideological hegemony. The Jacobin phase of the French Revolution, in particular, gave rise to frenzied alarm among aristocratic and bourgeois intellectuals. Their concern was directed toward containment and repression of the radical movements unleashed by the emergence of capitalist relationships and the destruction of feudalism.

The French utopians, Saint Simon and the Saint Simonians responded to recent history with optimism and technocratic solutions. Another direction, equally supportive of the expansion of state power but more traditional in its thrust was taken by Comte. His programs for achieving social stability did not emphasize the self-equilibrating economic relationships which were at the heart of Malthus' theory. Instead, Comte's rationales for social order relied more heavily on the stabilizing force of cultural constraints and the integrative functions of oligarchic forms of authority.

Comte's interpretation of social relations with its main emphasis on social control struck a chord of sympathy with some of the early sociologists. The first half of this chapter will discuss Comte's writings which represented one type of French reaction to radicalism as well as to social inequities and instabilities. The remainder of the chapter traces the programs of reform put forth by Comte, the Catholic traditionalists and the Saint Simonians.

Feudal, Technocratic, and Utopian-Socialist Categories Adopted by Theorists of Bourgeois Hegemony

Comte's categories were derived from different traditions in social thought. Some of these traditions were recent in origin and encompassed the rudimentary technocratic conceptions that were rapidly appearing during the early part of the nineteenth century. Others were older because they were rooted in traditionalist ideas that heretofore had been developed most extensively by theological and aristocratic rather than bourgeois scholars.

Many of the traditionalist ideas which were adapted by Comte shared certain common features because they reflected the preeminent fact of class domination. These diverse ideas, therefore, were a product of class-structured societies *in general,* rather than any single class defined by its relation to a specific mode of production. The strategies for resolving the problem of integration on the basis of the binding forces of tradition, religion, or patriarchal authority, for example, predate feudalism and were woven into natural law conceptions in antiquity. During the late eighteenth and early nineteenth centuries, however, bourgeois scholars like Comte modified these notions in order to stabilize *capitalist* rather than other forms of class domination.

The rudimentary technocratic ideas which were used by some of these bourgeois scholars were also reflections of the preeminent fact of class domination because they were squarely based on elitist principles. These principles assumed that ruling class domination has been maintained through other means than overtly repressive policies involving military or police power. Among these other means has been the use of ideology to convince the masses that their proper "station" or proper "function" in life is a subordinate one and that established institutions are natural and inevitable and morally justified. In the nineteenth century, the visionary bourgeois scholars who created ideas of this sort assumed that a stable and progressive social order would become a reality only if effective political power were to reside in oligarchic groups of financiers, industrialists, artists, engineers, priests, or scientists.

The scholars who expressed these ideas can be considered "theorists of bourgeois hegemony." Their analyses of the problem of social integration relied heavily on the objectification of hegemonic forms of social, cultural and political organization as opposed to the competitive "self-equilibrating" forces of nature or the market. In England, for example, Edmund Burke urged that social inequalities in capitalist societies be maintained and that they be justified on the basis of strong traditions. (Nairn 1970:9–10). His writings stimulated a revival of the rhetoric which referred to the solidary forces of ancient traditions and the repression of individualism for the good of society. The necessity for voluntary compliance with the norms of bourgeois institutions (e.g., the constitutional monarchy) was repeatedly justified, for example, on the basis of analogies between the political monarchy and the patriarchal family. It can be seen that in this process early nineteenth-century bourgeois scholars began to deflect the liberating intellectual habits that had been set into motion by the forces of the Enlightenment.[1]

In France, theorists of bourgeois hegemony like Auguste Comte, and (to a lesser extent) the Saint-Simonians, also derived their conceptions of social authority partly from the works of Catholic aristocratic scholars who still defended the feudal monarchy after the French Revolution. A number of French aristocratic and Catholic intellectuals around the turn of the century had urged the abandonment of democratic forms of government. Joseph de Maistre and Louis de Bonald, in particular, attacked the "individualistic" philosophy of the Enlightenment which, in their eyes, ushered in the disintegration of the "organic unity" of social life. Relying, however, on a personified image of society, and an atomistic, dehumanized view of man, they claimed that Society, not the Individual, is the source of the creative development of language, custom, morality, and social institutions. They declared that the basis for social solidarity lies in the individual's respect for tradition rather than self-interest. Secular and spiritual forms of authority such as the "public executioner" and "the Pope of Rome" represented, in their eyes, the "real bond of society" (Maus 1966:10).

The thoughtful reader will reflect that there is great variation in the ways in which the relations of authority are instituted in capitalist societies. The aristocratic Catholic intellectuals, however, abstracted and reified authority relations as an immutable property of the *associated* life of men. Society was considered to be transcendent. It was an entity *sui generis;* greater than and different from the sum of its parts. But the relations which were essential to social integration were the *authority* relations: without authority, society would disintegrate. Because of this, the Catholic aristocratic conceptions adopted by Comte referred to a society that was transcendent and repressive in comparison to the conception of society developed by his liberal contemporaries, the utilitarians.

Technocratic Dimensions of Comtean Thought

Comte also organized his visionary writings about social authority around rudimentary technocratic relationships. In the fourth volume of his *System of Positive Polity,* for example, Comte (1877:641)[2] expressed his agreement with Malthus' theory; however, Malthus' opinion about the necessary and inexorable role played by "natural" checks on population growth was implicitly qualified. Comte stated that "since the appearance of Mr. Malthus' works, it is generally admitted that [the control over population growth] demands a certain degree of *permanent repression* as regards the most energetic of human impulses" (our emphasis). The "energetic impulses" referred to in this statement were the *sexual* desires, and, in Comte's opinion, the repression of these desires could only be carried out effectively by "a moral authority." In Comte's utopian society moral authority and "spiritual power" would be placed in the hands of Scientific Men who alone were competent to understand and judge human behavior. Their scientific explanations would be used as a guide to practical affairs by industrialists and financiers because it was felt that a profound division existed between *theoretical* deliberations (which produced the social plans and principles which are necessary for coordinating social relationships) and the *practical* deliberations which determined the distribution of authority and the combination of administrative institutions on a day-to-day "temporal" basis. Comte insisted vehemently that neither "theory" nor "practice" should be subject to democratic control because, in his view, "the 'sovereignty' of the people tends to dismember the body politic by placing power in the least capable hands . . ." (*ibid.*:532). Instead, he said, as we have seen, "in the system to be constituted [according to his positivistic principles] the spiritual power will be confided to the hands of savants, while the *temporal power* will belong to *the heads of industrial works*" (*ibid.*:544 our emphasis).

The technocratic dimensions of Comte's thought suggest that Comte was both continuous as well as antagonistic with Saint-Simon and the Saint-Simonians. He had contributed to the early development of the Saint-Simonian tradition, even though he had previously disassociated himself from Saint-Simon because of the latter's increasing reliance on religion as a means for achieving social stability. On the other hand, his adherence to the nonreligious aspects of Saint-Simon's positivistic perspective should not obscure the fact that Comte's own "positive" social system was a secularized counterpart to the Saint-Simonian theocracy. Comte's society was to be actually ruled by the *industrialists* rather than the priests.[3] In both his and the Saint-Simonian visions, however, the scientists would function in the roles assigned by modern sociologists to "administrative consultants."

Comte's Attitude toward Private Property, Society, and the Family

Comte's articles on his positivistic philosophy appeared in the *Producteur,* the first periodical published by Saint-Simon's disciples (Iggers 1958:xxii). Toward the end of the 1820s, however, the development of utopian socialist ideas among the disciples of Saint-Simon led to a split between the liberal and the so-called radical members of this group (Lichtheim 1969:46) and, as a consequence, Comte became an antagonist of the group that was formed around that publication. The Saint-Simonians were critical of the bourgeois right of inheritance [4] but, as far as Comte was concerned, bourgeois property relations were inviolate. His positivistic society, moreover, was to be ruled by the industrial entrepreneurs.

The reader of Comte's works will also find the repressive, conservative image of society that had been employed by aristocratic critics of "anarchic" (laissez-faire) "individualism." In his depiction, society was devoid of any substantive economic and political relationships which actually underlie the macroscopic modes of social integration. In place of these institutional relationships Comte formulated and substituted abstract conceptions of self-equilibrating structures; he equipped society with a transcendent drive for order and stability and, on this basis, developed assumptions which became a nucleus for the cardinal methodological strategies developed by corporate liberals such as Emile Durkheim.

Comte therefore concurred with both the conservative Catholic Reconstructionists and the Saint-Simonians that individualistic solutions based on the natural harmony of interests were not sufficient for integrating society. Integration and harmony were more importantly related to the elementary parts of society which consisted of normative structures as well as groups and communities of which "the most basic . . . is the family" (Nisbet 1966:59). In fact, the family was considered to be so crucial to society that Comte denounced "all those, from Luther to the *philosophes,* who had given approval to divorce." He forebodingly declared that divorce was "one of the major manifestations of the 'anarchical spirit' that pervades modern society" (*ibid.:*60). This conclusion was related to his insistence that society transcended the individual. In this, as well as in the notion regarding the self-equilibrating functions of society, he helped prepare the way for twentieth-century sociological perspectives.

Comte's conception of the relation between social order and the family as an institution illustrates the way in which his standpoint gave social scientists a free pass to overlook the causal effects of *economic* and *political* institutions in generating the great social problems of our time. He suggested that the family should be studied in terms of the moral tenor of society. This study would focus on familial contributions to the socialization of individuals and the consequent development of emotional ties that bind men together: individuals, according to Comte, develop their feelings of sympathy, sense of solidarity, and general respect for superior authority within the family.

Comte also proposed that the family could be viewed in terms of its political effects. The inequalities inherent in the patriarchal family were considered to be the prototype for social inequality in the society at large. In Comte's opinion, social inequality is necessary for social integration and, as Robert Nisbet (*ibid.:*61) points out, Comte sharply criticized advocates of egalitarianism as well as utopian socialists who wish, he says, "to carry in the very bosom of the family their anarchic doctrines of levelling." But all of these critical remarks of Comte's were based on the questionable assumption that the main structures of both authority and inequality in capitalist societies were derived from the family rather than economic and political institutions.

Comte: A Bourgeois Counterrevolutionary Scholar

Because of his crass emphasis on authority and order, Comte's works are considered to be medieval or aristocratic in certain aspects.[5] In spite of this, however, Comte is, in fact, a conservative bourgeois philosopher [6] who, in part, revived traditional ways of thinking in order to preserve a new order. His positivistic philosophy is best understood by placing it in the context of the counterrevolutionary reactions, among both bourgeois and aristocratic intellectuals, to what was considered the logical culmination of revolutionary developments in France. (This culmination was represented, above all, by two events—distant from each other in time but similar in portent—the Jacobin phase of the French Revolution just before the turn of the century and the insurrection of the Parisian masses in 1848.) These developments were considered significant, not merely in terms of the actual revolutionary overthrow of feudalism, but also because of the concern for the potential destruction of capitalism, the seeds of which seemed to be contained in the Paris insurrection.

We have become familiar with some of the effects of the Jacobin ideas in previous chapters. Let us obtain an even broader understanding of the political character of Comte's point of view by briefly considering his attitude toward the Paris insurrection which occurred in 1848. But first, the insurrection itself.

The Paris Insurrection

Marx penned the *18th Brumaire of Louis Bonaparte* toward the end of the Paris insurrection and the counterrevolutionary events which shook France from 1848 to 1851.[7] In June of 1848 the Parisian masses held power for three days, after which, in the wake of the defeat of their short-lived insurrection, there followed a period marked by the butchery of more than three thousand of their number. Thousands more were transported (i.e. shipped off in prison hulks) without trial. During the tumultuous period that followed, Marx (1963:64) observed, even the peasantry, goaded by depressed grain prices and increases in taxes and mortgages, "began to bestir themselves in the Departments." The government's answer to peasant unrest came in "a drive against the schoolmasters, who were made subject to the clergy, by a drive against the mayors, who were made subject to the prefects, and by a system of espionage, to which all were made subject." At that time, all the powerful, ultraconservative members of aristocratic and bourgeois parties based on landowning, financial, and industrial capital formed a coalition in order to repress the mass discontent which threatened their existence.

Marx (*ibid.*:65) also noted that following the insurrection there was a resurgent demand for political rights on the part of the workingmen, petty businessmen, and professionals of Paris. However, the "Party of Order," as the ultraconservative coalition was called, opposed every parliamentary maneuver whether it involved "the right of petition or the tax on wine, freedom of the press or free trade . . . protection of personal liberty or regulation of the state budget." These maneuvers were considered harbingers of socialism. Marx reported that taken from this point of view even "bourgeois liberalism [was] declared socialistic, bourgeois enlightenment socialistic, bourgeois financial reform socialistic. It was socialistic to build a railway, where a canal already existed, and it was socialistic to defend oneself with a cane when one was attacked with a rapier." Eventually, the Party of Order was able to muster enough support to revoke the right to universal suffrage in order to ultimately achieve political domination. The political events ushered in by this conservative coalition eventually culminated in the coup d'etat of Louis Bonaparte.

Comte, as the historical sociologist Bernard Stern has noted, opposed parliamentarianism and hailed the coup d'etat of the dictator Louis Bonaparte. "From its futile parliamentary commencement, fit only for the English transition," Comte happily declared, "our republic passes by its own impetus to the *dictatorial stage,* the only one really suited to France, though equally suitable to other Catholic populations, as may be seen in Spanish America" (Stern 1959a:197). "The delusions of constitutionalism being finally set aside," he wrote, "the impossibility of terminating the revolution otherwise than by an effective alliance of Order and Progress is brought into full prominence" (*ibid.*).

The revolutionary events during the nineteenth century, therefore, provide insight into the reasons why Comte and other bourgeois scholars took up the cry of the Catholic Reconstructionists and Legitimists who claimed that the Enlightenment had initiated a socially disorganizing chain of events. Both aristocrats and bourgeois scholars felt that this development was finally detrimental to the whole of Western civilization.

In a letter to Tsar Nicholas, Comte (*ibid.:*196) wrote, "The collective revolt of modern thinkers against all authorities of former times has gradually produced in each individual an habitual insurrection of the mind against the heart, tending to destroy all human discipline. The whole West is thus drifting toward a savage communism in which true liberty would be crushed under degrading Equality."

Comte was not only antagonistic to socialist and communist doctrines, he also objected to the simple and elementary right of workingmen to organize in unions and political associations which aimed at securing social justice. Comte insisted that the "spiritual reconstruction" of the working class was necessary *before* any reconstruction of society could be discussed (Stern 1959a:194–195). His emphasis on the role of education as the prime means for social reform was so great that the American sociologist Lester Ward was considered a Comtean partly because of agreement on this issue.

Utopian Reforms of Traditionalists, Saint-Simonians, and Comte

The early American sociologists proposed various kinds of "constructive" solutions for ameliorating social and economic conditions. Some of these proposals, however, had also been expressed by the Catholic traditionalists, the Saint-Simonians, and Comte. What were these proposals? Why were they advanced by these French utopians in the first half of the nineteenth century?

The proposals advanced by the Catholic traditionalists assumed that feudal relationships could not be reinstituted in precisely the same form as they had existed in the past. For example, parliamentary politics and the rise and fall of French regimes made it apparent that coalition governments would be characteristic of the new bourgeois society. No single political party could hold power for long without the aid of the others. Furthermore, it was obvious that the massive reconstruction of bourgeois society was impossible without the support of either the peasantry or the urban masses. In the eyes of aristocratic Catholic traditionalists, such practical political exigencies dovetailed with idealized conceptions of feudal obligations to maintain the well-being of the rural and urban masses. As a result, these ultraconservative writers developed visionary schemes which proposed to put an end, for all time, to the massive forms of poverty created by capitalism. Their schemes, however, did not advocate a revolutionary change in the existing forms of property relationships. Instead, poverty was to be eliminated by a more equitable distribution of wealth rather than the social ownership of the means of production. Some aspects of these schemes, especially their emphasis on the systematic organization of social life, the control and regulation of marketplace relationships, the emphasis on elitist, hierarchical social structures and principles of equity, influenced the visionary schemes advanced by other intellectual groups such as the Saint-Simonians.

The Saint-Simonian doctrine represented the merging of conservative solutions to the problem of integration with what at that time were conceived to be socialist programs for achieving equality of opportunity and centralized economic planning.[8] Additionally, in spite of the fact that the Saint-Simonians urged the creation of financial trusts and technocratic, industrial, and scientific elites, their utopian schemes can be considered neither fully developed socialist, corporate-liberal, nor technocratic perspectives. They insisted on integrating these economic relationships on the basis of a *theocratic* state and shared the Catholic traditionalist belief that a religious reformation based on a single *church* would provide the basic principle for controlling the further development of capitalism (Iggers 1958:xl).

We have indicated that in addition to the use of financial schemes for integrating the economy, the Saint-Simonians elevated the concept of productive efficiency to a major standard for evaluating the optimum functioning of social institutions or society as a whole. Although this standard of efficiency was coupled with their religious standards as an axiom in their general approach to solving the problem of integration, it is important to see it as an independent feature of their social thought.[9] Furthermore, it is important to note that this feature was often invoked in their attack on laissez-faire capitalism.

The Saint-Simonian emphasis on education assumed that reason had a special role to play in the progressive development of mankind. But as in the other visionary schemes, human rationality was considered meaningful primarily because it was a means for justification and attainment of divine insight and/or social harmony and integration. Comte, for example, was interested in the use of reason for predicting and eventually controlling social developments. The Saint-Simonians were not far apart from Comte in this regard. They represented the intellectual tradition which truly regarded reason, "not as a tool open to every rational individual for attainment of truth, but rather an instrument of total and systematic planning" (*ibid.*:xlii).

There were additional similarities between the writings of Comte, the Catholic traditionalists, and the Saint-Simonians. They all made the individual subservient to a transcendental society or its basic institutions such as the political state and the family. And, although Comte would have preferred to remove the word "religion" from the counterrevolutionary slogan: "Property, Family, Religion and Order!",[10] his view of social relationships was in certain basic respects similar to those advanced by the other writers. His visionary schemes merely substituted a high priest of science for that of religion, and the transcendental and repressive images of the family and the sect for that of the church.

Comte advocated the establishment of a dictatorship and repression of radical movements. But he also insisted that education should be the chief means for reforming society. The Saint-Simonians shared his attitude toward nonviolent, educative persuasion as a means for instituting progressive change. They indicated their disinterest in the "overthrow" of society and stated that the word "overthrow" carried with it "the idea of blind and brutal force which aims at and results in destruction." They took pains to point out that their doctrine "neither advocates nor recognizes for the guidance of men any force other than persuasion and conviction." This doctrine, the Saint-Simonians (*ibid.*:110–111) concluded, "always takes its stand with order, harmony, and positive construction . . . it brings the world a new education, a definitive regeneration."

Comte (Stern 1959a:193) declared, "The essential aim of practical politics is . . . to avoid the violent revolutions which spring from obstacles opposed to the progress of civilization; and to reduce these to a simple *moral movement,* as regularly as, though more intense than, that which gently urges society in ordinary periods." Comte was outspoken about the political direction underlying his conception of the "positive" role of the social scientist (who would function as a sort of societal divining rod). In order to avoid violent revolutions, he insisted that "it is manifestly indispensable that we should know as precisely as possible, the actual tendency of civilization so as to bring our political conduct in harmony with it." Advocating moral and educative instead of political solutions to social problems, he expressed his hopes of inculcating popular acceptance of his positivistic philosophy and thereby preventing "collision with the governing classes" and danger to the institution of private property.[11]

In Book II it will become obvious that to a large degree it was Comte's conservative integration of ideas emerging from works by Catholic traditionalists and Saint-Simon, that appeared in the leading early American sociological writings. However, Comte's works represented by no means the only source of ideas used by the Americans. Classical and laissez-faire liberal as well as contemporaneous works by German, Belgian, and Austro-Hungarian scholars played a significant part in the early development of American sociology. The late nineteenth-century American ethos, which centered on the myth of the self-made man and the value of productive efficiency, was also important in this regard. Nevertheless, some of the ideas advanced by the American sociologists were similar to those advanced by the French utopians even though they were expressed in a different language and social context. A change in status for the working class, for example, was considered only in terms of a more equitable distribution of wealth. Moral and educational regeneration of individuals was given priority. Reason and science were reduced to instruments for social planning and integration. Productive efficiency was made a cardinal standard for evaluating social systems. And society, the political state, and the family were conceived as transcendental and repressive objects.

NOTES

1. This reactionary development was vehemently opposed by such revolutionary liberals as Thomas Paine. This was exemplified in Paine's (1942) famous work on human rights, *The Rights of Man, being an Answer to Mr. Burke's Attack on the French Revolution.* Paine's treatise was systematically organized around a criticism of Edmund Burke's reactionary *liberal* point of view. (Burke was not a feudalist even though he rejected the notion of natural rights and utilized feudal ideas to justify his reactionary standpoint. He accepted the notion of social contract, for example, but gave it the hegemonic quality of a divine sanction.) In his work, Paine criticized Burke's (1910) *Reflections on the French Revolution.*

2. The work referred to in this sentence was originally published in 1854. But Comte's comments on Malthus (as well as the comments which will follow) were also published earlier in 1822.

3. This fact is either underplayed or ignored in modern sociological writings. Also ignored is the degree to which Comte's division between *theory* and *practice* actually placed the most important day-to-day political decisions in the hands of industrialists rather than priests, in spite of the assignment of "spiritual power" to these latter types.

4. Although there were some inconsistencies in their argument, the Saint-Simonians generally rejected criteria favoring social and economic stratification which were merely predicated on the vicissitudes of birth (Iggers 1958:xxxviii–xxxix). However, they also believed that an equal distribution of property would be extremely harmful because inequality was considered an indispensable precondition for social integration. Exploitation, therefore, "was not to be replaced by equal distribution, nor private ownership of the means of production by workers' control. The aim of Saint-Simonian social policy was,

rather, the destruction of arbitrary social and economic stratification based on birth, and the replacement of the aristocracy of wealth by a natural aristocracy of talents" (*ibid.*). Thus, the Saint-Simonians linked the individual's right to own property with the following distributive principle: "From each according to his ability; to each ability according to its works."

Even though the Saint-Simonians coined the word "socialism," Saint-Simonianism was not a socialist movement in the prevailing modern sense of this word. They advocated neither the social ownership of property nor socialism as a transition to communism. Their movement represented one of the "utopian" or "incipient" socialist alternatives which were repeatedly formulated by representatives of middle class movements throughout the first half of the nineteenth century. The rise of the Marxian concept of socialism during the second half of the nineteenth century (and the development of modern socialist movements) placed these "incipient" socialist alternatives in a different context. By the end of the nineteenth century, noted *corporate-liberal* scholars began to advocate utopian schemes which critically attacked the right of inheritance but preserved other bourgeois property relationships. It will be demonstrated in Part Nine that these utopian conceptions, which were formulated by such scholars as Ward, Durkheim, or Small, cannot, by any stretch of the imagination, be justifiably regarded as a convergence with modern (post-Marx) socialist doctrines. (For an argument which supports this "convergence" hypothesis, see Gouldner's [1958:xxiii ff.] introduction to Emile Durkheim's *Socialism and Saint-Simon.*)

5. For example, Nisbet (1966:60) states, "Comte's medieval caste of mind shows in his advocacy of a restoration of the full patriarchical authority within the family that the Revolution had taken away."

6. Bernhard J. Stern (1959a:192) has noted, "Comte was among the many publicists of the post-revolutionary period interested in restoring equilibrium." He also indicated that this equilibrium was not conceived in terms of feudalism.

7. Marx's work was originally published in 1852. The references cited here are to a 1963 edition of the *18th Brumaire.*

8. This peculiar integration foreshadowed the later developments of corporate-liberal as well as fascist ideologies, both of which were often called "socialistic" but which were actually organized around the concept of state capitalism. The Saint-Simonians as Iggers (1958:xxxviii–xxxix) points out, rejected "the class struggle as a means to power . . . [they] considered the masses, as such, politically incompetent. The social revolution must come from above through the leadership of superior men." It is interesting to also note the similarities with Spencer's elitism: The Saint-Simonians believed that "the new social structure in which the masses would be divided into a hierarchy of classes and ruled from above . . . did not imply exploitation, since the *naturally superior man* could better understand the needs of the masses than the masses themselves. *Equality of opportunity* would exist, as the positions in the hierarchy were open to talent" (Iggers 1958:xxxix; our emphasis). (It should be remembered, on the other hand, that the Saint-Simonian program cannot be directly equated with later developments such as fascism or social Darwinism because its advocates conceived their solutions to integration within the framework of a theocratic doctrine.)

9. As Iggers has indicated, "the Saint-Simonians were strongly imbued with the myth of efficiency. To achieve maximum production, the economy must be organized for that purpose: the means of production must pass from the hands of the idle owners [entrusted with them through the accident of birth] to those men most able to administer them effectively" (Iggers 1958:xxvi).

10. After pointing to the correspondence between Comte's rhetoric and the slogans of the Party of Order, Stern (1959a:198) cites Marx's observations:

> During the June days, all other classes and parties united against the proletariat, styling themselves the *Party of Order.* The proletarians were stigmatized as the party of anarchy, socialism and communism. The Party of Order had "saved" society from the "enemies of society." It adopted the watchwords of the old society: Property, the Family, Religion, Order: and made these the passwords of its army. Under this sign you will conquer! said the Party to its counter revolutionary crusaders.

Stern concludes that "Comte opposed the end product, the hereditary Empire. But as one who had rationalized the *coup d'etat* in the name of order, he helped prepare its path to victory over the Republic." In spite of his objections to religion, Comte was simply another counterrevolutionary in the ranks of the men who uttered the passwords: Property, the Family, Religion, and Order!

11. Comte (Stern 1959a:194) was convinced that, "When it is seen why wealth must chiefly abound among the industrial leaders, the positive philosophy will show that it is of small importance to popular interests in what hands capital is deposited, if its employment is duly useful to society at large; and that conditions depend much more on moral than on political methods. . . . The new philosophical action would either obviate or repress all the dangers which attend the institution of property, and correct popular tendencies by a wise analysis of social difficulties, and a salutary conversion of questions of right into questions of duty."

CHAPTER 11

"The Socialists of the Chair"

Usages of the Word "Socialism"

Saint-Simonian doctrines played an active role in state and economic affairs in France and they also achieved some degree of popularity in England and Germany. Partly because of their eclectic combination of theological, technocratic, mercantile, and socialist ideas, the use of the word "socialism," which was coined by the Saint-Simonians, was adopted in self-definitions by middle-class reformists, religious intellectuals, aristocratic reconstructionists, and members of revolutionary movements. The enormous variation in the social usage of the word "socialism" was noted as early as 1847, when Marx and Engels wrote the *Communist Manifesto*. They devoted the entire third and concluding part of their manifesto to a critical review of "feudal socialism," "clerical socialism," "critical-utopian socialism," "bourgeois" and "petty-bourgeois socialism." [1]

During the second half of the nineteenth century, the indeterminacy in the usage of the word "socialism" was increased still further by the fact that reformers were frequently labeled socialists by laissez-faire liberals and other conservative intellectuals. Many conservatives furthermore denounced liberal reformers, aristocratic and religious reconstructionists, and revolutionary socialists alike, as socialists. For example the political economists who formed the Union for Social Politics in 1872 in Germany [2] antagonized laissez-faire liberals and other conservatives, because they advocated building and sanitary codes, the legal limitation of the workday, protectionist legislation for women and children in industry, and the state management of railroads and post offices. These measures would hardly be used as a standard for identifying the differences between liberals and socialists in Europe after the First World War. However, when the German political economists advocated these measures in 1872, a sarcastic newspaper writer labeled them "socialists of the chair" and "sweetwater socialists" (Ely 1883:237). These names stuck even though most of these economists were corporate liberals rather than socialists.[3]

Nineteenth-Century German "Socialists of the Chair"

The Union of Social Politics was established by the "socialists of the chair" during the decade just prior to the onset of the formative years of American sociology. Following this, in the 1880s, some of the leading North American sociologists, including Albion Small and Edward A. Ross, went to German universities for at least part of their graduate education in economics. These scholars were therefore provided with the conceptual guides to contemporary problems that had been developed by a well-established corporate-liberal school of German political economy.

Although members of this school were called "professorial socialists" and "socialists of the chair" (*Kathedersozialisten*), their writings were far closer to the spirit of Comte's conservative doctrines than to the revolutionary socialism of Marx. These German academics also bore a kinship to the Saint-Simonians, who were utopian reformists and wanted to rationalize and stabilize the market economy. Here the similarities cease, however, because in the German situation the political economy in question was to be unequivocally predicated on the advanced formation of a monopoly-state capitalism or simply a state-capitalism, rather than earlier capitalist relationships.

Thus, different social conditions influenced the writings of these German political economists and those of the early French utopians. These differences were not due solely to the economic conditions and national traditions that separated German scholarship in the 1870s and 1880s from the French writers of the 1820s and 1830s. They also stemmed from differences in political relationships. In Germany, republicanism was weaker and aristocratic neo-mercantile traditions stronger. In addition, a socialist working-class movement began to emerge with the rapid industrialization of the German economy. This movement withstood an intensive period of political repression by the German government at the end of the 1870s. It emerged from this repression even stronger than before and became a still more important center of socialist activity than France. Perhaps for the first time on the continent, the rulers of a newly industrialized nation faced a socialist movement that could not be controlled by political repression alone.

An American Economist on Socialist Movements in Germany and France

The relationship between the "socialists of the chair" and the development of working-class socialism in Germany is discussed below. In part this discussion relies on a description of German developments that was published in 1883, the same year in which Lester Ward's *Dynamic Sociology* appeared. This description was published in *French and German Socialism in Modern Times* by Richard T. Ely, a leading North American economist who had studied in Germany during the 1870s. (Ely also advanced his observations of the German developments to his students at Johns Hopkins University. Among his graduate students in later years was Edward A. Ross, who wrote the famous sociological work *Social Control*. Ely, we shall see, figured significantly in both Ross' and Ward's careers.

In the prefatory note to his book, Ely wrote, "The purpose of this work is to provide a perfectly fair, impartial representation of modern communism and socialism in their two strongholds, France and Germany." This intention was engendered by the desire to render "a service to the friends of *law and order*" (our emphasis). Ely's discussion is therefore informative and pertinent here because it symbolized the thinking of North American academics who were beginning to realize the dangers of falsifying or rejecting socialist ideas out of hand.[4] Thus, in spite of his claims to "objective" scholarship, Ely regarded his account of socialist developments to be far more akin to an intellectual reconnaissance of enemy territory than an impartial examination of socialist doctrines.

Ely's discussion of socialist developments is also informational because it provides candid observations of the national circumstances surrounding the rising importance of the "professorial socialists." For example, around the beginning of the 1880s, Bismarck began to repudiate his laissez-faire advisers, attempting to substitute instead the policies recommended by Adolph Wagner and other prominent "socialists of the chair." This change, as Ely points out, came upon the heels of Bismarck's failure at this time to effectively employ outright political repression in order to stem the growing power of socialist movements in Germany.

Universal suffrage had been instituted by the German Empire in 1871. At that time, socialist candidates for the Reichstag received 123,975 votes. By 1877, however, the socialist vote had quadrupled to 493,288. The importance of this increase was underscored by the fact that only 5,401,021 votes were cast at the time. These votes, furthermore, were largely distributed over the nine or ten parties which had achieved representation in the Reichstag.

The extraordinary increase in the relative strength of the socialist movement alarmed the coalition that controlled the German government, and which was composed of aristocratic landowners and members of the newly emergent financial and industrial class. This coalition was even more shocked by the growing strength within the German socialist movement of such individual radical socialists as Karl Liebknecht and August Bebel.[5] Upon advocating passage of antisocialist legislation in 1878, for example, Bismarck referred to the threat symbolized by Bebel's famous 1871 Reichstag speech, which defended the Paris Commune.[6]

In 1878 two unsuccessful attempts had been made upon the life of the German kaiser. Although no official connection between the assailants and the Social Democratic Workingmen's party was established, Bismarck insisted on repressive legislation. The majority of the Reichstag, however, refused to conform to his will. Bismarck thereupon obtained an imperial decree dissolving the Reichstag and, in the hysterical climate whipped up by conservatives, forced a new election, which provided him with sufficient support. After the consequent enactment of antisocialist laws, the German government banned socialist meetings, seized socialist printing presses, suppressed the sale of socialist books and pamphlets, and drove socialist organizations underground. Even hotelkeepers who rented rooms for socialist meetings were liable to imprisonment.

How did Ely respond to these political events? On evaluating the effects of this repression, Ely (*ibid.:*215) stated that "the German government was undoubtedly placed in a trying position but they appear to have made a mistake . . . Every social democratic laborer experienced, to a certain extent, the elevating feelings of martyrdom. They all became secret missionaries, distributing tracts and exhorting individually their fellow laborers to join the struggle for the emancipation of labor." From 1878 to 1882, the German socialists became even more unified in spite of the repression. They established printing presses in Switzerland and smuggled enormous quantities of literature over the border. Even the rural population was beginning to be affected by the movement. In light of these developments, Ely flatly contended that the "severity of the government," after the granting of despotic powers by the Reichstag, had actually "done more harm than good" (*ibid.:*214).

Ely noted further that Bismarck had more comprehensive plans than the repressive acts had demonstrated. The prime minister had acknowledged that the mass discontent on which socialists were building strength was partly justified. He noted that the grounds for the discontent were largely economic in nature and involved low wages, high taxes, unemployment, and anxiety among members of the working class. However, although Bismarck had publicly expressed his acknowledgement and had promised alleviation of these economic conditions, years passed before he offered any concrete plans in this regard. "People," Ely (*ibid.:*217) declared, "began to think that the promises of relief to the poor had been thrown out simply as a bait to catch votes for the bill which became the [anti-] socialistic law. *That they were intended to serve this purpose is undoubted"* (our emphasis).

How did Ely justify this blatant opportunism? While Ely did not doubt Bismarck's political expediency, he also took pains to inform the reader that

Bismarck's memory was good, his will was strong, and his motives pure. Ely added,

More than once Germany has thought that he had forgotten some threat or re-solve because he allowed years to slip by without making any public move to-wards the execution of his plans, but in such cases she has reckoned without her host. It now looks as if Bismarck might have meant all he said when he promised to use the power of the state to relieve the poor classes. He had not for a moment forgotten his promise, but was only working out his plans and waiting for an op-portune moment to execute them.

According to Ely, the German kaiser had also encouraged Bismarck to ame-liorate the conditions confronting German workers. "The old Kaiser," Ely (*ibid.*) noted, "who seems in his way, to have a warm, fatherly affection for his people—professed his distress at the sufferings of the unfortunate, and maintained his sincere desire to relieve them."

In 1882, the Reichstag, at Bismarck's urging, passed two pioneering so-cial-insurance bills which provided accident and sickness insurance for work-ers. In subsequent years, the Reichstag enacted legislation providing for old age insurance (commonly known in the United States as "social security"), industrial sanitation and safety, progressive taxation, protection for women and children, and nationalization of the communication and transportation in-dustries. All of these measures had been championed by a number of socialist movements for some time and by the Social Democratic Workingmen's party after 1875. But the specific form and rationale [7] for these enactments were not derived directly from the Social Democratic party; they were borrowed instead from writings by the "socialists of the chair."

Economic Administrative-Consultants to the Welfare-Warfare State

In 1883 Ely candidly stated in his work on socialism that "Bismarck pro-poses . . . to conquer social democracy by recognizing and adopting into his own platform what there is of good in its demands." Ely also astutely ob-served:

It is curious to notice that friends of Bismarck have even gone so far as to adopt some of the social democratic phrases. They have spoken of the laborers as the "disinherited" classes of society. Yet this originated with the social democrats; and a few years ago the government gave as one reason for prohibiting the sale of a certain book in Germany the fact that it called the laborers the "disinherited" [*die Enterbten*]. Thus far has Bismarck gone in the way of making concessions [Ely 1883:219].

Like many other unscrupulous statesmen at the time, however, Bismarck and his "friends" did not limit their tactics to preempting radical rhetoric, or to compromising when absolutely necessary on any issue, as long as the insti-tution of private property was substantially maintained. He also relied on the "professorial socialists" who in turn were heirs to the traditions developed by a long line of economists who had served German ruling houses in one capacity or another.[8] These economists included the sixteenth-century cameralists, the eighteenth-century "welfare state" (*Wohlfahrsstaat*) economists, and such early "socialist" economists as Rodbertus.

From the sixteenth century onwards, German economists were viewed as having an important role as advisers to governmental bodies. Among the first economists of this kind were the cameralists, who concerned themselves with formulating a viable mercantilist approach to governmental management of economic and social affairs, in the interests of the medieval rulers of the state. (Because of this, Schumpeter [1954:159] refers to the cameralists as "consultant-administrators.") The cameralists, in time, developed a civic theory which viewed the welfare of the state as the source of all other welfare. In this theory, the interests of the individual were subordinated to the interests of the state and the welfare of the state became the basic standard for judging social policy.

The key to the welfare of the state from the cameralists' point of view was securing adequate revenue to supply its needs. Therefore, their social theory was organized around the task of furnishing the state with revenue from public sources. This goal, however, was not perceived in isolation from the needs of the social classes in society.[9] The cameralists assumed that once the maintenance of the established standard of life was assured for any given class, it would be impertinent and presumptuous for members of that class to long for satisfactions in excess of the norms for their social level. On that basis, they argued that if "the conduct of different strata of society could be made to result in an increasing margin of material return, above the aggregate demands of the different class standards, *the state might appropriate that surplus without injustice or hardship to the individual*" (Small 1909:590 our emphasis). The operation of the fiscal policies of the state were presumed, therefore, to be based on *class standards* of distributive justice and normative behavior.

From the sixteenth to eighteenth centuries, the cameralists (who functioned essentially as tough-minded bureaucratic advisers to ruling houses) developed their pragmatic economic principles in order to appropriate the largest possible surplus from the population at large. Some of this surplus was used to promote the general welfare, but the *greater part financed the never-ending wars between feudal principalities*.

In the eighteenth century a number of German economists produced transitional works on the topic of "the welfare state." These economists gave greater weight to advocating governmental responsibility for the general economic welfare. They focused on employment, fire insurance, education, sanitation, and other issues. They also justified the judicious use of price-fixing and tariffs by governmental agencies (Schumpeter 1954:170–173).

Around 1840 Johann Karl Rodbertus-Jagetzow, a monarchist who later became a Prussian minister of education, developed an economic theory that was considered socialist chiefly because it argued that poverty and commercial crises could be solved by state regulation of market relationships. Rodbertus, according to Lichtheim (1969:174), was:

the ancestor of a certain kind of theorizing which proceeds from a critical analysis of the market economy to the indictment of *laissez-faire*. Left to itself (so the argument runs) the free play of economic forces will always depress wages to a subsistence level and at the same time promote cyclical crises. This vicious cycle can only be broken by the state—ideally by a socially enlightened monarchy . . . the state is a living organism and politics the noblest of all arts. Indeed the soul of the state is divine . . .

Rodbertus' theory was an early form of underconsumptionism because he regarded crises as products of the lack of purchasing power brought about by an inequitable distribution of wealth (*ibid.*:175).[10] Because of his blend of "purely meliorist socialism" and conservatism, Rodbertus was also an important precursor "of the Prussian *Kathedersozialisten* of the Bismarck era: men like Adolph Wagner (1835–1917) and Gustav Schmoller (1838–1917) who stood high in the estimation of the ruling elements in German society" (*ibid.*:172).

Programmatic Goals and Socialists of the Chair

At the founding of their Union for Social Politics in 1872, the German "socialists of the chair" conducted a vigorous criticism of laissez-faire political economists (the Manchester school of political economy in particular). According to Ely (1883:240), these academics accused the free-traders of lacking appreciation for "the higher duties of the state." The German academics also said that the laissez-faire liberals had no compassion for the "lower classes" and that they totally ignored the role of ethics in economic relations.

Simultaneously with their attacks on the Manchester school, these German political economists attempted to "reconcile the laborers and the social democrats to society by recognizing and favoring what might be called their just demands" (*ibid.*). These "just demands" included better working conditions, greater economic security, and equity in the distribution of wealth. The "socialists of the chair" also drew selectively upon the religious criticism of early nineteenth-century Catholic writers such as Lammenais, who sought to reconcile the oppressed masses and a revitalized Church into a harmonious alliance against the tyranny of capitalists and kings. At the same time, however, criticism of the German kaiser was studiously avoided. These German scholars also repeatedly urged the reconciliation of capital and labor, and the improvement of social welfare with the aid of the beneficent state.

The "socialists of the chair" insisted upon merging economic and Christian doctrines. Economics was regarded as an ethical science and the state was personified as a moral individual. These "professorial socialists" were also called "state socialists" because of their extremely reverent attitude toward the state. In fact, Ely indicated that it was absolutely impossible to comprehend the teaching of these socialists without first understanding their reverence of the state. He stated (*ibid.*:241): "They regard the state as something sacred and divine, holding that it arises out of the essential characteristics of the human nature given us by God." "In this spirit," Ely concluded, "Professor Schmoller defines the state as the grandest moral institution for the education and development of the human race."

In addition, the "professorial socialists" were gradualists who sharply rejected violent change and "some of them," according to Ely, "did not expect that their ideal will be realized for a thousand years to come." Wagner, the most prominent of these scholars, indicated that eventually the state would own all private enterprises in society. However, unlike Marx's expectations, Wagner argued that this "socialist" state would maintain the same differences in rank as existed in Germany among the governmental employees: The kaiser would preside at the top and the workers at the bottom (*ibid.*:243).

German "Welfare State" Also a "Warfare Society"

The "socialists of the chair" were members of one of the very first corporate-liberal schools of thought in the nineteenth century and they became unequivocally identified with the direct formulation of national policy. Many factors undoubtedly accounted for their acceptance into this inner sanctum, including the strong influence of feudal and mercantile traditions which made German rulers more receptive to extensive and flexible use of state power in all areas of social life.

The "socialists of the chair" pioneered in the construction of the modern welfare state. Eventually all the industrialized Western nations enacted legislation which was similar to that adopted in Germany. At the same time, however, it is important to note that the "professorial socialists" joined with other German academics in expressing their chauvinistic support of German imperial policies. These policies led to the Franco-Prussian War in 1870 and the passage of the naval armament bills around the turn of the twentieth century.[11]

When evaluating the "socialists of the chair," therefore, it should be kept in mind that their goal of "a harmonious social organism" was never achieved even temporarily on the basis of welfare state measures alone. It was attained by their reverent support of the *warfare* state and the brutal destruction of millions of men, women, and children. In order to justify this support, however, these German political economists bypassed the view of the state which had been developed by the republican leaders of the French Revolution. They breathed new life into the Hegelian dichotomy of state and society. (The state remained the embodiment of higher moral principles but society became the repository of all the conflicts and passions inherent in laissez-faire capitalism.) Their creation signified a welfare state and a warfare society. In the process, they generated some of the most important notions that were to appear in the writings of the early North American "sociologists of the chair."

NOTES

1. In later years, Engels (1890:197) wrote that adherents of the various utopian socialist (Owenite, Fourierist, and Saint-Simonian) schemes in France and England had degenerated into sects by the time the *Communist Manifesto* was written. At the same time, "manifold types of social quacks" had emerged and, although professing to be socialists, these writers "wanted to eliminate social abuses through their various universal panaceas and all kinds of patch-work, without hurting capital and profit in the least." For these reasons, Engels explained that "when [the *Communist Manifesto*] appeared we could not have called it a *socialist* manifesto."

2. For further information on the Union of Social Politics, see Oberschall (1965).

3. Some of them were "state socialists" but this kind of socialism placed the control over the means of production in the hands of an aristocratic ruling class and/or a state bourgeoisie.

4. Ely candidly indicated that there were many interpretations of socialist ideas which had backfired because they were patently false. Scholars would be more effective in dealing with the threat of socialism, he suggested, if they approached socialist developments "free of all prejudice and ill-will." ("It is *only* thus that we shall be able to meet and overcome the social dangers which threaten even our own country in a not very distant future" [Ely 1883:25].) In order to underscore his suggestions, he also noted that "We have not had a *permanent* laboring class, but with the increase of population, one is rapidly developing. If it is *now* becoming extremely difficult for the laborer to rise, what will the condition of things be when we number two hundred millions?" (*ibid.*:25–26). Ely concluded his call for truthful scholarship with illustrations of unemployed workingmen responding sympathetically to anarchist speakers (or watching the construction of Vanderbilt's new house in New York) and bitterly muttering about a coming revolution.

5. From the 1860s onwards, German socialists had been greatly influenced by such reformers as Ferdinand Lassalle. In 1877, however, the "left" socialists Karl Leibknecht and August Bebel had achieved considerable prominence as leaders of the newly emergent Social Democratic Workingmen's party. These men had become clearly identified as leftists by their opposition to the Franco-Prussian War in 1870.

6. Bebel (1928:12) declared in that speech to the Reichstag on May 25, 1871: "Gentlemen, even though Paris may now have been put down, I must remind you that the struggle in Paris is only a small outpost skirmish, that the main affair in Europe is still ahead of us, and that before a few decades have passed, the battle cry of the Paris proletariat: 'War on the palaces, peace to the cottages, death to poverty and idleness!' will become the battle cry of the entire European proletariat."

7. Ely pointed out that "bills introduced by government are always accompanied with so-called 'motives' explaining and defending them." The rationale accompanying the accident insurance bill included: "A sound policy should nourish in the indigent classes of the population . . . the view that the state is a beneficial, as well as a necessary, arrangement" (quoted in Ely 1883:219).

8. Bismarck also repudiated the National Liberals in the Reichstag and announced that they were "representatives of a party in which political economy advocates the right of the stronger and deserts the weak in the struggle against the might of capital, and which refers him to free competition, to private insurance, and I do not know what else—in short, refusing him all the help of the state" (quoted in Ely 1883:237). The "political economy" referred to here by Bismarck was composed of the political and economic doctrines of laissez-faire liberalism.

9. Assuming that the medieval principality in which they functioned was composed of various classes, and that a certain standard of life was appropriate to each class, the cameralists used the ruling norms regarding the distribution of wealth and resources as a standard of equity.

10. A criticism of Rodbertus' theory is contained in the preface which was written

by Frederick Engels to the first German edition of Karl Marx's *Poverty of Philosophy*. It is noteworthy that Engels referred to Rodbertus as "the idol of the place hunters of today" (Engels 1847:7). The term "place-hunter" was a term commonly used by Marxists to refer to bureaucratic and academic careerists.

11. Writing from a prison where she had been incarcerated by the German government because of her opposition to the First World War, an *authentic* socialist, Rosa Luxemburg, mentioned the changes in German foreign policy toward the end of the nineteenth century. All of Europe was scrambling about in a deadly race for imperialist possessions: "England seized control of Egypt and created for itself, in South Africa, a powerful colonial empire. France took possession of Tunis in North Africa and Tonkin in East Asia; Italy gained a foothold in Abyssinia; Russia accomplished its conquests in Central Asia and pushed forward into Manchuria; Germany won its first colonies in Africa and in the South Seas, and the United States joined the circle when it procured the Philippines with 'interests' in Eastern Asia. This period of feverish conquests has brought on, beginning with the Chinese-Japanese War in 1895, a practically uninterrupted chain of bloody wars, reaching its height in the Great Chinese invasion and closing with the Russo-Japanese War of 1904" (Luxemburg 1970:281).

PART FOUR

Material Foundations
of Reform Darwinism
and Liberal-Syndicalism

CHAPTER 12

Transitional Social Thought

Preview

The contemporary inspiration for the social theories written by the founders of North American sociology came mainly from two collections of ideas. The first collection was partly developed around Spencer's evolutionary or social Darwinist notions, and in its newly synthesized statement is called *reform Darwinism*. The second focused on contemporary industrial conflicts and is called *liberal-syndicalism*. The contents of these collections are described in this part of Book I. This part also discusses the material foundations for these ideas. Generally, the foundations of reform Darwinism are dealt with first; the material base of liberal-syndicalism is analyzed toward the middle and end of this part of the book.

The reader will discover, in this part of the book, that the ideas developed by the historical precursors of Ward, Ross, Small, and others can be traced like intellectual trajectories which intersect in the varied works of these pioneering sociologists. One can justifiably regard the *dynamics* bringing about this intersection as effects of the interaction between changes in material conditions and in ideological consciousness which existed *at that time*.

Chapter 14 will note that in adopting some of Spencer's liberal ideas, American sociologists realized that Spencerian laissez-faire liberalism did not provide viable solutions to contemporary social conflicts. Because of this, the Americans modified his ideas and produced their own reformist versions of social Darwinism.

Chapter 14 deals mainly with the historical changes that gave meaning to the political ramifications of reform Darwinism. In the previous chapters greater space was devoted to the clarification of the ideological conceptions themselves. This priority is inverted in Chapter 14, and the material foundations of the ideological conceptions are emphasized. Continuing this priority we move through some of the numerous economic and political developments of the nineteenth century; but Chapter 15 and 16 describe the material conditions which influenced the transitional perspective of liberal-syndicalism. The analytic contents of liberal-syndicalism itself are discussed in detail in Chapter 17.

Transitional Periods in Social Thought

Before we begin to discuss the foundations of these sets of ideas, it is important to note that both were *transitional* forms of social thought. During the changing and turbulent period in which monopoly capitalism emerged, these ideas simultaneously represented laissez-faire liberal and corporate-liberal modes of thought. Eventually these ideas were replaced by social theories that were formulated in the corporate-liberal mode of thought alone. This replacement occurred gradually as monopoly capitalism was being stabilized.

These changes in social thought reflect the fact that all ideologies undergo continuous change. Their rates of change are synchronized with changes in political and economic institutions and vary considerably over time. During transitional periods, ideologies first emerge or are substantially revised. During periods of consolidation, ideological conceptions are refined and elaborated.

Under rapidly changing material conditions, intellectuals frequently search the past for suggestive ideas to solutions of new problems. Old categories and phrases are used in a new way. And new ideas become expressed in transitional forms which symbolize both new and old ways of thinking. In time, however, the intellectual traditions being born in this process increasingly manifest more tenuous relations with the past. They are, so to speak, increasingly "rationalized" by intellectuals during periods when economic and political changes are being consolidated. As a result, they eventually lose their transitional characteristics.

During the transitional periods, there is greater opportunity for intellectuals to selectively utilize ideas developed by men of the past in order to reconstitute customary, contemporary styles of thought. Because intellectuals are extremely active agents in the construction of their own history, the organizing and integrating principles used in the search for historical precursors are reconstituted whenever there are significant changes, not only with respect to the emergence of new ideologies, but also in the course of the development of the same ideology.

In the chapters to come we will indicate that the early sociologists created their history in a double sense. First, by formulating new conceptions of social evolution, they made their own history in the literal sense of reconstructing the way in which the past was perceived. They also made history by contributing, as sociologists, to the development of a new liberal ideology. This ideology, in the very process of its emergence, interacted with economic and political events and influenced the changing shape of capitalism in our time.

We will discuss the relationships between the writings of the American sociologists and their historical precursors. This discussion will demonstrate that, compared to their later works, the *first* writings of the American sociologists were influenced much more by their historical predecessors. Almost four decades transpired before highly abstract and formal corporate-liberal conceptions of man, woman, and society fully emerged in the United States. This transition should indicate that a corporate-liberal sociology did not spring fully grown from the minds of these American intellectual pioneers.

From these transitional relationships, it will become apparent why it has been found necessary to first examine a number of classical conceptions that were fully developed roughly between 1776 and 1848. Indeed, at that time, not only utilitarianism, but also a whole family of ethical, epistemological, and theoretical models of man, woman, and society, was integrated and provided by a liberal philosophy of life.[1] These models offered a scheme of ultimate values, a theory of knowledge, a conception of the human mind, a psychological approach to individual behavior, and an explanation of the origins of social institutions. The coherence and plausibility of all these ideas as valid, universal guides to social life could never have been achieved without the growing organization of society along capitalist lines.

Also one should be reminded that the medieval scholars had previously used utilitarian conceptions to characterize human relations mainly in such limited, mundane, and often lowly areas as the shop and the market. The major difference between the feudal view and eighteenth century or classical utilitarianism, however, was that the latter eventually reduced virtually the whole world of human values to the same scheme. But it was precisely because classical liberals had assumed that all aspects of human life were universally structured by the same limited, and relatively invariant individual relations and characteristics, that they were able to produce an enormous variety of behavioral models. Natural-law assumptions were at the heart of these relations and characteristics. They were used to integrate and justify the models of ethical, individual, and social behavior emerging at that time.

Many examples of natural-law and natural-social-law conceptions will be found in Book II when we discuss the writings of such men as Ward, Ross, and Small in great detail. They will be perceived in Ward's conception of genetic evolutionary processes, in Ross' assertion that inequality is functionally necessary for the survival of society, and in Small's conception of interest-group relationships. Ward, Ross, and Small also utilized ideas expressed by the French reformers and the German "socialists of the chair." Nevertheless, in spite of these continuities, neither liberal nor nonliberal individual precursors can account for the particular integration of preexisting and new ideas that was generally achieved by the Americans at that time.

If, as we contend, intellectual traditions are identifiable above all by their most abstract *integrative* ideas, then it can be claimed in a very precise sense that modern sociology in the United States and Europe did not actually originate in the early decades of the nineteenth century, but rather during the formative years, beginning in 1883 and ending in 1922.

Sociology, of course, was not created in isolation from events which transformed every other social science discipline. Between 1880 and 1910, in particular, diverse scholars representing numerous fields throughout the Western world generated a new liberal philosophy of life that eventually led to the construction of a new family of ethical, epistemological, and theoretical models of man, woman, and society. By the twenties of this century, this new liberal family replaced the old.

NOTE

1. The discussion of classical liberal epistemology and laissez-faire concepts of woman will be found in Book III.

CHAPTER 13

The Foundations of Reform Darwinism

Racist theories contained generalizations borrowed from Darwin's works toward the end of the nineteenth century. Because of this, they have been called social *Darwinian* theories, although it was Spencer's laissez-faire liberal works on the evolution of man and society which actually provided the most significant framework for the universal racist categories in use at that time. The degree to which Spencer's theory was permeated with racist ideas cannot be overemphasized. He claimed that "savage" and "semicivilized" people represented a lower stage of biological evolution. These people were regarded as mental and moral inferiors and their sense of justice, according to Spencer, was less evolved than that of the "civilized" races. He maintained further that the intermixture of different racial stocks would lead to racial degeneracy, and pointed to Eurasians in India and "half-breeds" in America as examples. He advised against intermarriage between Europeans and Japanese on similar grounds. He applied this way of thinking to an analysis of conflicts between nations, indicating that France's defeat in the Franco-Prussian War might have been due to racial degeneration (Gossett 1965:151). Conversely, he stated that the United States would produce "a civilization greater than any the world has ever known" because the intermixing was between "the allied varieties of the Aryan race" which were developing in America (Youmans 1883:19–20).

Liberalism, Social Darwinism, and the Justification of Racism and Imperialism

Social Darwinism was a racist product of laissez-faire liberalism. Regarding the relation between racism and liberal thinkers, Gossett (1965:174) states, "If there is one conviction which unites modern liberals, it is a resistance to the idea of explaining innate character and capacity on the basis of race. We need to understand that *liberalism only recently acquired this convention.* The liberals of the latter part of the nineteenth century and the first part of the twentieth were frequently not, it is painfully clear, even liberal on the subject of race" (our emphasis).

American and European social scientists reduced the extraordinary differences among the peoples of many nations to very simple racial schemes of gradation. The upper positions in these graded schemes were occupied by the allegedly more highly "evolved" Anglo-Saxon and Germanic "races." Their "inferiors" in the racial hierarchy were the Slavic and Latin "races" from the Mediterranean and Eastern European countries. But "most inferior" of all were the "savage" races including Indians, Mexicans, Africans, and Asians. A paternalistic view at this time indicated that these "savage" races were being gradually civilized by the white races of Europe and America.

The founders of American sociology adopted social Darwinian ideas in order to buttress their own racist and imperialist doctrines. One example of Ward's racism was expressed in his claim that the Bureau of Indian Affairs had treated the Indians equitably (Ward 1883:I, 477). Moreover, Ward believed that a "Negro" who rapes a white woman is not only driven by lust; he is also motivated by a desire "to raise his race to a little higher level" (quoted in Gossett 1965:166). Ross' racist statements slandered populations in China, India, Africa, and elsewhere. He believed that Jews constituted a distinct race and indicated that the Jews of Eastern Europe, in particular, are "moral cripples, their souls warped and dwarfed" (Ross 1914:150–154). Giddings (1900) attacked the anti-imperialists who opposed the Spanish-American War. He said that if the "racial energies" of Anglo-Saxon Americans were not allowed to express themselves in imperialistic expansion, then they might discharge themselves in anarchistic, socialistic and other "destructive modes" of life. Cooley (1902:268) wrote of the feelings of self which not only distinguished the individual from others, but also the Anglo-Saxon race from its inferiors. He observed that "controlled by intellect and purpose, this passion for differentiation becomes self-reliance, self-discipline, and immutable persistence in private aim: qualities which more than any others make the greater power of superior persons and races." Comparing Northern Europeans to Southern Europeans, Cooley (*ibid.*:288) further wrote that the former, "less given to blind enthusiasm for popular idols have more constructive power in building ideals from various personal sources . . . [they] are more sober and independent in their judgment of particular persons . . . their idealism is all the more potent . . ." etc.

The racist doctrines used by American sociologists were already well grounded in the exploitative relations, which differentiated metropolitan from "underdeveloped" countries in Asia, Africa, and South America. They were also based on the imperialist oppression of racial and national groups within the United States. These *imperialist* relationships, rather than racial, *biological* relationships, represent the proper context for evaluating the theories developed by the sociologists of the chair. The following subsections will consider these imperialist developments because they provide the historical background against which an evaluation of the works of these sociologists must be seen.

The Uneven Development of Nations

Imperialism has existed for centuries, but the dynamics of imperialistic relationships are dependent upon the historical variations in political economies. During the sixteenth, seventeenth, and eighteenth centuries, for example, imperialist policies were generally organized around precapitalist mercantile relationships. Ruling houses in many countries granted royal monopolies and patents to aristocratic conquerors and merchant adventurers. Joint stock companies were formed and these national monopolies reaped huge profits through acts of piracy, brigandage,[1] slavery and genocide. For example,

The frightful barbarism of the Spanish *conquistadores* in the Americas was notorious. In a period of fifty years they exterminated 15 million Indians, if we are to believe Bartholomé de las Casas, or 12 million according to more 'conservative' critics. Densely populated regions like Haiti, Cuba, Nicaragua, the coast of Venezuela, were completely depopulated . . . the Dutch merchants, whose profits depended on their monopoly of spices obtained through conquests in the Indonesian Archipelago, went over to mass destruction of cinnamon trees in the small islands of the Moluccas as soon as prices began to fall in Europe. The 'Hongai voyages' to destroy those trees and massacre the population which for centuries had drawn their livelihood from growing them, set a sinister mark on the history of Dutch colonization, which had, indeed, begun in the same style, Admiral J. P. Coen not shrinking from the extermination of all the male inhabitants of the Banda Islands (Mandel 1970:108).

101

By the eighteenth century, imperialistic monopolies became increasingly dependent on profits realized from the slave trade,[2] and some of the most illustrious men in England, including John Locke, were beneficiaries of slavery.[3] English adventurers and colonists ransacked the world and deposited their plunder in London banks. The interaction of this primitive accumulation of wealth with other political, economic, and technological factors during the eighteenth century, stimulated the beginnings of the industrial revolution in that country.

The number of semicolonial and colonial countries expanded during the precapitalist period. During the nineteenth century European imperialists used outright coercion or bribery to prevent Asian, African, and South American governments from protecting their domestic industries from foreign competition. As a consequence, the indigenous bourgeoisie were ruined in every economic sector which was competitive with imperialist nations. Smallholders were forced off the land and land consolidation was rapidly spurred by the varieties of monoculture ("single crop" agriculture) imposed by the imperialist's market economy. The increasing stagnation of precapitalist economic development in the oppressed countries created enormous numbers of landless and destitute laborers. The continued transformation of variegated economies to monoculture economies systematically exposed the colonial and semicolonial populations to starvation and misery.

On the other hand, the bourgeoisie in the imperialist, metropolitan nations accumulated superprofits [4] from the exploitation of the colonial and semicolonial countries. Some of these superprofits were used as investment capital for the expansion of industry in the metropolitan country itself. As a consequence, a vast superiority in growth and productivity of the metropolitan economy was achieved, in large measure from the intensive exploitation of the colonial and semicolonial nations. One type of political economy grew at the expense of the other. By the middle of the nineteenth century, these uneven economic developments sharply differentiated the "underdeveloped" colonial and semicolonial countries from metropolitan nations.

Changing Modes of Domestic Imperialism

The aforementioned uneven development of nations involved differences *between* metropolitan and semicolonial and colonial nations. This form of imperialist development, however, was paralleled by the uneven development of racial and nationality groups *within* each of these types of nations. The uneven development of racial and nationality groups in the United States involved national policies which led to the settlement of European populations in North America. These populations became the dominant racial and nationality groups on this continent. But their domination was secured by the savage repression of the American Indians, who were the original inhabitants of the "new world."

While the Indians were being overcome, the thirteen English colonies achieved their political independence. But this independence certainly did not lead to the elimination of the policies which maintained the settler's domination over the American Indians. It led instead to the development of a new imperialist nation which expanded rapidly by acquiring the territories located within the continental boundaries of what is now the United States.

The native inhabitants of the North American continent were devastated by the expansionist policies of the United States government. These inhabitants were colonialized even though they lived within the expanding boundaries of an imperialist nation itself. Moreover, as these boundaries widened, the imperialist relations which preserved the dominant status of white settlers were transformed into *domestic* policies. These policies, which were largely based upon apartheid and genocide, can be considered as instrumentalities of a domestic rather than a foreign mode of imperialism.

Apartheid and Genocide: Imperialism's Alternatives for the American Indian

The devastating policies used against the American Indians were implemented by various methods. But two of these, the establishment of reservations and punitive measures against entire tribes, stand out because they clearly symbolize the degree to which policies adopted by the citizens of the new nation were no different from those used by other imperialists during the mercantile period. After the United States was founded, territorial lands possessed by Indians became increasingly valuable to the settlers, who expropriated these lands by violence and deceit. Many Indians were continuously driven further west, where they finally resettled on reservations which exist today. Those who refused to leave their lands and who had not already died from the white man's contagious diseases were massacred. Although there may have been other policies used to deal with "the Indian problem," the most ignominious were apartheid and genocide.

These policies of apartheid and genocide were implemented by legal and extralegal modes of oppression. The founding fathers of America did not approach the Indians as citizens but as members of sovereign political bodies. Economic relations with Indians were therefore legally constituted by treaty arrangements between the government and tribal groups.[5] Guided by imperialist principles, however, men like John Quincy Adams offered an expedient interpretation of what constituted Indian territorial rights, insisting that Indians had no valid claim to land unless it had been settled and cultivated by Indian people (Gossett 1965:230). This interpretation was obviously calculated to take advantage of the fact that many Indian tribes were nomadic or made their livelihood by hunting and fishing rather than by farming.

The state conception of Indian territorial rights was as hypocritical as it was expedient. The democratic institutions among the Iroquois had influenced

PRECURSORS AND MATERIAL FOUNDATIONS

the founding fathers. The Cherokees, on the other hand, not only farmed their land but also modeled their political institutions after the American government. Thomas F. Gossett (1965:232) has indicated, however, that this did not protect these Indians from losing their land through the combined ruthless actions of settlers, the state of Georgia, and the federal government.[6] Similar developments took place in relation to the Creeks and Choctaws in Alabama and Mississippi.

Up to 1825, the Indians had been confined to reservations where it was expected they would take up farming. Once the settlers had set their sights on these lands, however, the United States government initiated policies to force the Indians to relocate themselves on new reservations west of the Mississippi (*ibid.:*231). Attempts to carry out this new policy led to the Black Hawk War of 1832, which terminated only after the massacre of 850 of the thousand men, women, and children who were led by the tribal chieftain Black Hawk. By 1837 nearly two million acres had been taken from Indians who migrated west in order to avoid extermination (*ibid.:*231–232).

The resettlement of the Indians west of the Mississippi was not by any means a permanent solution to "the Indian problem." Indian landholdings in the West were also expropriated by theft and violence. In 1851, California Indians ceded "more than half the state and in exchange were offered perpetual ownership of 7,500,000 acres" (*ibid.:*234). The Bureau of Indian Affairs, however, even deprived them of that acreage,[7] which was sold, instead, to land speculators, farmers, and business interests. Later years witnessed further racist oppression, including the movement against the Colorado Ute Indians after gold and silver had been discovered on their lands.

In 1890 the United States government finally crowned a century of deceit, theft, and murder by reacting violently to the nonviolent and pathetic "ghost dances" which had spread among the oppressed and destitute Sioux Indians of South Dakota who believed that a messiah would free them of the white man. "Mistaking" these mystical dances for a prelude to an Indian uprising, the United States Army, at the Battle of Wounded Knee, murdered almost three hundred Sioux, ninety-eight of whom were disarmed warriors; the remainder were women and children (*ibid.:*236).

The American Indians were crushed and impoverished by the close of the nineteenth century. They had nothing left that could be stolen. But the racism spawned by American imperialism had stamped its indelible mark for the century to come. The candid comments of one of the most important corporate liberals of the early twentieth century, President Theodore Roosevelt, can be taken as an illustration of the criminal arrogance which was still maintained toward the "Indian problem" at that time: "I suppose I should be ashamed to say that I take the Western view of the Indian. I don't go so far as to say that the only good Indians are dead Indians, but I believe that *nine out of every ten are,* and I shouldn't inquire too closely into *the case of the tenth"* (our emphasis).[8]

Enslavement of Africans
and Superexploitation of Their Descendants

The policies directed at African slaves within the United States also represented a form of domestic imperialism although in this case the members of the oppressed population were "conquered" elsewhere and forcibly resettled as slaves within an imperialist country. This process was as brutal as it was profitable. Millions of slaves died chained side-by-side as they were transported to the United States from Africa. Black women went insane and gave birth while chained to corpses during the dreaded "middle passage" (Flexner 1970:19). Merchants, planters, and industrialists amassed great fortunes by tearing black families apart, by using men as beasts of burden and women as breeding stock, by murdering black children who were too weak to work.

The enslavement of African people was rooted in imperialist policies which also generated superprofits for the industrial sectors of such foreign countries as England,[9] as well as the United States. The relation with English textile mills indicated the degree to which, in most cases, the development of racial oppression domestically was interlocked with the development of market relationships on an international scale.

Monoproduction of cotton characterized agricultural developments in the Southern states. The whole economy was effected as international markets made "king cotton" the primary raw material produced by this region. In 1860, the leading manufacturing industry in the United States was cotton manufacturing. Furthermore, after the Emancipation Proclamation, black people in the South continued to provide the army of cheap labor that produced a profitable cash crop for the textile industries at home and abroad. Throughout the post-Civil War period, the majority of blacks continued to labor primarily as domestic workers and in the cotton fields. As late as 1910, in fact, the number of blacks in industries other than cotton production was less than 5 percent.[10] Therefore, the American descendants of African slaves were also, for the most part, highly exploited producers of raw materials. After the Emancipation and Reconstruction, their economic status was not different from the status of the oppressed workers in colonial and semicolonial nations throughout the world.

Black Americans were ostensibly granted freedom and citizenship but events after the Reconstruction proved otherwise; virtually all the legal and extralegal forms of violence that could be employed to maintain the oppressed economic and political position of blacks were used toward this end. These forms of violence included extralegal armed forces such as the Ku Klux Klan, police harassment and brutality, racist courts, and lynch mobs.

105

Colonizing the Mexican Population

American imperialists did not overlook the profitable possibilities involved in the expropriation of Mexican land and the exploitation of Mexican labor. Some of the attitudes expressed toward the Mexican people were similar to those toward the Indian. Sam Houston, for example, insisted that Mexicans could be justifiably cheated out of their land because they were no better than the Indians (Gossett 1965:233).

In the Mexican-American War, Mexico was made to cede the region encompassing New Mexico and areas contiguous to it. In New Mexico proper, an intact colonialized society was simply incorporated within the territory of the United States (Moore 1970:466). Eventually, however, the massive expropriation of land by Anglo interests in this region of the country undermined the village culture and stimulated large scale migration to urban areas.

Following the revolution by North American settlers against the Mexican government, Mexican- and Anglo-Americans in Texas clashed for generations. The power of the leading Mexican families was destroyed by conquest, while such forces as the Texas Rangers suppressed Mexican-American political systems on the village levels. The plight of the Mexican in California, on the other hand, was conditioned by the preexistence of great Spanish landholdings which employed a fund of landless agricultural workers.[11] Later, as Anglos took over these holdings, this fund was periodically increased by the continuous migration from other areas of the Southwest as well as from Mexico itself. This migration was spurred by economic drives and personal necessities similar to those which moved large masses of Europeans to the United States. These Mexicans were met by special legal and extralegal forms of oppression; maintaining highly depressed wage levels among Mexican workers.

Domestic oppression in California forced most Mexicans, and descendants of Mexicans, to become part of the large permanent pool of highly exploited labor which was concentrated in agriculture. The same held true for the Mexicans and Mexican-Americans in other regions of the country. By the turn of the century, Mexican barrios north and south of the Rio Grande provided an unending supply of cheap labor for the great landholdings throughout the Southwest.

Early Sociologists Adopt Spencer's Rather Than Marx's Strategy for Analyzing Historical Relations

The preceding discussion has emphasized the degree to which foreign and domestic imperialism had transformed the United States into a brutally exploitative racist society. It might be concluded on this basis that although the pioneering sociologists were racists, they were also "men of their time" and, therefore, indistinguishable in this respect from most of the white population. This conclusion, however, minimizes their special contribution to the ongoing development of racist ideologies in the United States. It also ignores the fact that Marx had developed a materialist strategy for analyzing historical relations *before* the rise of American sociology (e.g., Marx 1959, Marx and Engels 1972a, 1972b). Marx's writings certainly cannot be regarded as the last word on the topic of nineteenth-century exploitation, colonialism, and imperialism. But they certainly were superior to Spencer's point of view. If applied creatively and systematically to American conditions, a Marxian analysis would have linked racial and national oppression to the historical development of imperialism under changing capitalist conditions. It certainly would not have interpreted these forms of oppression, as did the founding sociologists, in the context of a universal struggle for existence among biologically superior and inferior races. A Marxian analysis would *not* have justified imperialist oppression in the United States.

Consequently, the founders of American sociology should not be considered "waxen tablets" who merely reflected the racism of their times. Their writings were based on the *active selection* of compatible ideological ideas. Their writings, furthermore, reinforced the general system of ideas which had influenced liberals and nonliberals alike.[12] When socialist leaders such as Eugene Debs and William Haywood began to denounce the "race prejudice" which had been expressed for example by such socialists as Victor Berger, they were engaging in an ideological struggle against the effects of liberalism. During the formative years, Spencerism, social Darwinism, and neo-Malthusian ideas, rather than Marxian socialism, structured the racist writings and policies of many socialists.

Spencerism Influences Clergymen, Businessmen, and Journalists

American socialists and sociologists were not the only persons influenced by Spencer's writings. Between 1870 and 1890, Spencerism swept the United States. It became a byword of North American bigotry and capitalist enterprise. Ironmasters, publishers, finance-capitalists, railroad executives, and meatpackers acted as one in their praise of the noted philosopher. Clergymen, journalists, and academics informed the American people that their economic system was regulated by the laws of the cosmos. Outstanding entrepreneurs quoted Spencer at the drop of a hat: "The American Beauty rose," Rockefeller announced in a Sunday School address, "can be produced in the splendor and fragrance which brings cheer to its beholder only by sacrificing the early buds which grow up around it. This is not an evil tendency in business. It is merely the working-out of a law of nature and a law of God" (quoted in Ghent 1902:29). The processes of natural selection which allegedly governed the successful growth of the Standard Oil Trust, according to this logic, were similar to those producing the American Beauty rose. Furthermore, these processes of natural selection were manifested in countless other ways, for example, the superiority of the white Anglo-Saxon and Teutonic races, when compared with the Slavs, Latins, and nonwhite races. The cosmic law epitomized by natural selection was termed "the survival of the fittest."

Spencer's *The Study of Sociology* was first published in the United States in 1872. This work clearly identified social Darwinism with the new social science. As his popularity increased among American businessmen, university governing boards encouraged the employment of sociology professors (Gossett 1965:153). Some of these Spencerian scholars agreed with the ideas of William Graham Sumner, who informed the American people that millionaires were the superior products of natural selection. Sumner also opposed suffrage for black Americans and assured his readers that poverty would be abolished in a few generations, if every man was sober, industrious, prudent, and wise.

Charles H. Cooley (1920:129) once stated: "I imagine that all of us who took up sociology between 1870, say, and 1890 did so at the instigation of Spencer." As late as 1898, Ward (1898:192) also noted that American sociologists were "virtually disciples of Spencer." As the century drew to a close, however, Spencer's thought was being slowly chipped away.

Many sociologists discarded certain parts of Spencer's multifaceted system of ideas, depending upon whether these parts agreed with their estimates of the times. At first glance, the modifications in Spencerian thought which were generated in this process may appear small compared to the main body of social Darwinism. But they were highly significant because they symbolized a developing political cleavage between liberal scholars. Taken as a whole, the revised system of social Darwinist ideas, therefore, is important enough to warrant a special name: *reform Darwinism*.[13]

Emergence of Reform Darwinism: "No-Holds-Barred" Imperialism and Racism

One significant area of revision concerned Spencer's penchant for "peaceful" modes of imperialist penetration. His faith in free trade and his animosity toward the conquest of weaker nations by military force were rapidly rejected by the North Americans. By the turn of the century, for example, Spain had been defeated by the United States' armed forces. Americans colonized the Philippines and Puerto Rico, and Cuba's economy came under American domination.[14] Most of the sociologists in the United States agreed with the famous Columbia University sociologist, Franklin H. Giddings, who publicly proclaimed his support of the imperialist war with Spain. After the war he continued to defend the expansion of the American empire by conquest. In Giddings' view, this expansion was a form of *evolutionary* progress. Among noted sociologists throughout this period, only Sumner spoke against the immorality of American foreign diplomacy.

On the other hand, it is important to note Giddings' justifications for American imperialism. They were organized around such racist notions as the "superiority of the Anglo-Saxon race" and the "decadence of the Latin race." He chastized the anti-imperialists who had opposed the Spanish American War for ignoring "cosmic laws," even though these "laws" were first popularized by the great champion of laissez-faire liberalism, Spencer himself. Giddings, therefore, revised Spencerism to suit his own political stance. He obviously rejected Spencer's laissez-faire opposition to gunboat colonial policies but he kept the faith with Spencer's racism. The same was true of other outstanding founders of American sociology such as Ward, Ross, and Cooley.

Reform Darwinism: Enlightened Intervention into Natural Forces of Competition

Ward, Giddings, Ross, and Cooley rejected some aspects of Spencerian thought because they favored extensive social reforms. These sociologists believed that social reformers, public administrators, and responsible legislators were capable of achieving enlightened *control* of evolutionary social processes. Their opinions about expanding the role of social reform and the political state were used as the conceptual clubs which smashed social Darwinism.[15]

On the other hand, this destructive process took several decades before it was completed. Reform Darwinism emerged because it was possible to modify Spencer's racism, environmentalism, and evolutionary "laws" so that they justified guided social change. After all, Spencer also believed that reformers were quite capable of introducing social changes, even though he felt that these changes could prove biologically disastrous. It was apparent, therefore, that social reformers could adopt a number of Spencer's social Darwinist assumptions to justify their belief in the real possibility of quickening evolutionary developments, in what they considered an *enlightened* manner.

For these and other reasons, many of Spencer's "scientific laws" were adopted by the early sociologists. They ripped these "laws" from their laissez-faire contexts and used them to justify a new set of reformist liberal doctrines. Simultaneously they revised Spencer's "structural" and "functional" analytic strategy for these same ends. The phrase "reform Darwinism," as we have already noted, is used to capture the ideas that emerged in this process.

NOTES

1. For example, "Scott notes that about 1550 there was a marked shortage of capital in England. Within a few years, the pirate expeditions against the Spanish fleet, all of which were organized in the form of joint stock companies, changed the situation.

Drake's first private undertaking, in the years 1577–1580, was launched with a capital of £5,000, to which Queen Elizabeth contributed. It brought in about £6,000,000 profit, half of which went to the Queen. Beard estimates that the pirates introduced some £12 million into England during the reign of Elizabeth" (Mandel 1970:107–108).

2. For example: "Between 1636 and 1645, the Dutch West India Company sold 23,000 Negroes for 6.7 million florins in all. . . . Between 1728 and 1760 ships sailing from Le Havre transported to the Antilles 203,000 slaves bought in Senegal, on the Gold Coast. . . . The sale of these slaves brought in 203 million *livres*. From 1783 to 1793 the slavers of Liverpool sold 300,000 slaves for £15 million, a substantial slice of which went into the foundations of industrial enterprises" (Mandel 1970:109–110).

3. "The New Royal African Company which was engaged down to 1698 in the slave traffic, had partners so distinguished as the Duke of York and the Earl of Shaftesbury, as well as the latter's illustrious friend, the philosopher John Locke" (Mandel 1970:110).

4. The concept of superprofits is operationalized differently, depending on the productive relations being discussed. With regard to monopoly capitalism, superprofits, for example, are higher than the average rate of profit in an industry or industrial sector. For further examples, see (Mandel 1970:419–423).

5. According to the American Constitution, "Congress shall have the power to regulate commerce with foreign nations, and among the several states, and with the Indian tribes."

6. "In Georgia, the Cherokees—a tribe of about *seventeen thousand*—met the requirement that they live upon and farm their land. They maintained schools and had a written constitution based upon the American model with an executive, a legislative, and a judicial branch. Sequoyah, one of their chiefs, had invented an alphabet for the Cherokee language with eighty-five characters and had published parts of the Bible and edited a newspaper, the *Cherokee Phoenix*. *None of this prevented them from losing their land*. Both the federal government and the state of Georgia were determined that they should be removed . . . Then the state legislature of Georgia declared all Cherokee laws to be void, denied the Indians the right to be a party in a legal suit or to testify in court against any white man, and denied them also the right to prospect for gold on their own lands, though white men could do so. In 1830, Congress passed a Removal Bill which authorized the President to resettle any eastern tribe—by force, if necessary, and without regard to any treaties which the government had previously signed. The land of *the Cherokees was ruthlessly taken over by white settlers, debts owing to them were declared canceled, and government agents attempted to induce factions of them to rebel against their leaders*" (Gossett 1965:232, our emphasis).

7. "*By a ruse, the Indian Bureau deprived the Indians of this land.* Because of pressure from *white* politicians in California, the Senate in Washington *did not confirm* these treaties but merely kept them in its *files*. The Indians were not told that the treaties were invalid and at the time had no means of discovering the intricacies of American law. The treaties remained in the files of the Senate until 1905, still unratified; the 7,500,000 acres were sold to white settlers and speculators" (Gossett 1965:234 our emphasis).

8. These remarks are quoted in Gossett (1965:238). The original source is in Roosevelt (*The Winning of the West*, New York: 1889–96, I, 334–335).

9. Englishmen, Frenchmen, and Arabs as well as Americans were involved in the slave trade. England purchased raw cotton produced by slave labor on Southern plantations.

10. Twenty years later, in 1930, almost 70 percent of employed blacks still remained in agriculture or domestic service (Boggs 1970:7).

11. Moore (1970:468–469) states for example: "The New Mexico pattern of social organization on a village level had almost no counterpart in California. Here the Mexican settlements and the economy were built around very large landholdings rather than around villages."

12. This particularly applies to Edward A. Ross, who was a popular writer and who expressed his racist, neo-Malthusian ideas in speeches sponsored by labor and socialist organizations.

13. The term "reform Darwinism" is borrowed from Goldman (1952). Goldman has used this term to indicate the body of scientific and political generalizations which were developed in opposition to Spencer's social Darwinism. It should be noted, however,

110

that our usage of the term "reform Darwinism" is not as loose as Goldman's because he includes under this term anti-Spencerian and anti-racist points of view. (Goldman's usage classifies, among others, Boas' writings as reform Darwinism [*ibid.*:125–128]. In our opinion, however, the theoretical foundations of the Boas school of thought represented too great a departure from the evolutionary or "Darwinian" (neo-Malthusian-Spencerian) nineteenth-century point of view to be given this classification.

The departures from strict, Spencerian, racist points of view have also been captured by Gossett (1965) with the use of the phrases "Darwinian collectivism" and "corporate Darwinism." He contrasted these ideas with what he called "social Darwinist individualism." Gossett's usages of these phrases indicate his sensitivity to different kinds of analytic strategies for justifying racism at that time. Gossett (*ibid.*:160) states that, "the men who challenged the conclusions of Social Darwinist individualism . . . were if anything, more given to race theorizing than were their opponents. They substituted for Social Darwinist individualism a kind of Darwinian collectivism which involved them in certain conclusions about the inherent character of races." He insightfully adds, "men whom we generally think of as liberals and who did the most to loosen the grip of social and economic 'laws' propounded by Spencer and Sumner accomplished part of their task by appeals to race theory."

We have indicated that our usage of the phrase "reform Darwinism" is narrower than Goldman's. On the other hand, it is more general than Gossett's phrases "Darwinian collectivism" or "corporate Darwinism," because they refer to racial and nonracial theories which were directly derived from Spencer's evolutionary ideas.

It should also be noted that, in the process of using Spencerian "laws" to justify the new reformist liberal doctrines, sociologists made significant modifications in the existent stockpile of theoretical categories and generalizations. In addition to the new political doctrines, therefore, our usage of the phrase "Reform Darwinism" also refers to the theoretical categories and generalizations developed by the sociological reformers. Finally, in this volume, the development of reform Darwinism is unequivocally seen as an aspect of the development of corporate liberalism, including its emphasis on the most violent and aggressive forms of imperialism. In this view, Gossett's "Darwinian individualism" emerged within laissez-faire liberalism while his "corporate Darwinism" or "Darwinian collectivism" was an early manifestation of corporate liberalism.

14. The impact of American monopolies on Cuba represents a classic example of the factors involved in the unequal development of semicolonial (or colonial) countries. Fernando Ortiz (1947:53–54) has noted that after the Spanish American War, when Cuba ostensibly achieved her "independence," American capitalism transformed the island into a vast plantation. Simultaneously the small Cuban landowner gradually disappeared into the growing mass of landless labor. Cuban agriculture was restricted to monoculture, primarily based on the production of sugar for export.

15. Social Darwinism was eventually discredited within the field of sociology. But this form of liberal thought was sustained in other fields. Also, a number of social Darwinist works, authored by zoologists, psychologists, etc., were published during the latter sixties.

CHAPTER 14

The Rise of Monopoly Capitalism

Review

Historical materialist analyses of racial and national forms of oppression were actually available to sociology's founding fathers in the nineteenth century, as indicated. But these founders preferred to adopt or modify social Darwinism, when analyzing the conflicts between racial and national groups. They followed in Spencer's footsteps, obfuscating the material foundations of imperialism, and converting racial doctrines into "scientific" theories of racial and national conflict.

Consequently in regard to imperialism there are many similarities between the laissez-faire liberalism of Spencer (or Sumner) and the corporate liberalism of Ward, Giddings, and Ross. Spencer and Sumner opposed specific acts of imperialism: the conquest of colonial markets through gunboat diplomacy (Spencer 1896:236–240) and the Spanish-American War (Starr 1925:275). Still they cannot be considered anti-imperialist unless the meaning of imperialism is limited to the use of armed force in the establishment of imperial domination. In both Great Britain and the United States, imperialist policies have often taken apparently contradictory and disguised forms such as "free trade" or "open door" economic policies. These policies involved attempts to dominate the economies of foreign countries and as such, were merely variant expressions of imperialist relations which characterized the development of capitalism from the very beginning (Stedman-Jones 1970).

Competing Economies and Reevaluation of Free Trade

After the industrial revolution had taken place in Britain, free trade doctrines were used to justify the expansion of imperialist relations. These doctrines had emerged during the precapitalist period when agricultural goods, precious metals, slaves, and luxury items were beginning to assume increasing importance in international trade. In spite of common origins in eighteenth-century mercantile conditions, however, free-trade doctrines were espoused by different groups who viewed them variously as instruments of agrarian, mercantile, or industrial policies. Precapitalist English merchants were inter-

112

ested in free trade because they wanted an opportunity to compete with royal monopolies for profitable domestic and foreign markets; nineteenth-century industrialists espoused free trade because they were opposed to protectionist barriers which would hamper their domination of "underdeveloped" countries throughout the world.

Powerful industrialists and merchants continued to support Spencer's laissez-faire doctrines during the third quarter of the nineteenth century. Further economic developments had indicated that free trade was leading to profitable consequences because industrial growth in Great Britain had been virtually uncontested by other imperialist powers during the first half of the century. All of Europe lagged behind British industrial growth and, as long as superiority in productivity prevailed, British goods were more competitive than those of other nations. The advantages of competitive prices, therefore, enabled the rapid penetration of numerous countries with British rather than other European goods. Moreover, while these conditions prevailed, the continued maintenance of colonial systems seemed overly expensive and there also appeared to be little necessity for investing in further military and political expansion of the empire. The laissez-faire liberal was quick to point out that colonial policies shifted funds which could be used for industrial investments and, therefore, apparently undermined the rate of industrial growth which made British industries superior to those of other countries. From their point of view, gunboat diplomacy and public expenditures for military forces and forceable seisure of political regimes would limit, not encourage, the expansion of British trade.

By the last quarter of the nineteenth century, however, the economic functions of laissez-faire liberalism in Great Britain were rapidly shattered as the gap between the British economy and other European and North American economies increasingly narrowed. The growth of industry and monopoly in the United States, Germany, France, and Belgium, for example, meant the establishment of industrial economies which constituted a threat to British markets. The rise of these economies forced the extensive reevaluation and criticism of free trade and other laissez-faire doctrines which were at the center of Spencerian thought. As competition for world markets increased, British industrialists and bankers reassessed the benefits of the old policies based on colonial conquest and rule. Support for these colonial policies was revived because they provided greater assurance that British industries alone would exploit the underdeveloped countries firmly within its political sphere of influence.

Growth of Industrial Monopolies
in the United States

The rise of North American and European competition with respect to British industrial goods was synchronized with the staggered international development of monopoly capitalism after the middle of the nineteenth century. In the United States, for example, monopolies began to emerge as a significant factor during the post–Civil War era.

At that time, industrial growth completed the development of the foundations for the modern North American industrial economy. This vital phase in American industrial growth, moreover, benefited from the half-century of advances in British technology; North American industry adopted advanced technologies developed elsewhere, and quickly achieved a level of productivity which made American goods highly competitive with those of other nations. Because of the advanced technological developments, the economy of the United States began, early in its post–Civil War expansion, to manifest the trend toward the concentration and centralization of wealth which has accompanied economies of scale in capitalist societies everywhere.

Industrial monopolies during the post–Civil War period were not a totally new feature in American life. Monopoly trusts, or "syndicates" as they were sometimes called at the end of the nineteenth century, had also appeared sporadically prior to the Civil War.[1] In 1874, however, the formation of the first great monopoly trust of the modern period—the Standard Oil Trust— represented the beginnings of a continuing effort on the part of bankers and industrialists to offset falling rates of profit through the formation of trusts or other arrangements among monopolies.[2] These arrangements enabled capitalists to sidestep the effects of national competition, and were usually aimed at controlling prices in order to ensure high rates of profit. These high rates are called superprofits because, in this context, they are higher than the average rate of profit in an industrial sector, or an industry as a whole.

The late nineteenth-century trends toward industrial mergers and monopoly trusts represented aspects of the increasing concentration and centralization of industrial capital in the United States. The concentration of banking capital paralleled this development and eventually played a decisive role in reinforcing these industrial trends. The heads of banking firms began to operate as "finance-capitalists" and promoted waves of mergers from 1890 onwards. By the first two decades of the twentieth century, the American economy became characterized by both oligopolistic and the older competitive sectors. The oligopolistic sectors established the foundations for a stable financial and industrial oligarchy. This oligarchy rapidly became an extremely important—if not the most important—base of the American ruling class.

American Industrialists and Free Trade

Internationally, the rapid development of industrial economies in North America and Europe resulted in sharply increased competition with Britain for foreign markets toward the end of the nineteenth century. Although the laissez-faire doctrine of free trade for Britain was thrown into serious question because of changes in material conditions at the time, the situation in the United States was different. Market relations in Asia as well as Central and

114

South America had become much more favorable to American industrialists and bankers. In spite of the short war with Spain and the outright colonialization which followed it, free-trade doctrines and semicolonial policies as a rule held the upper hand in the determination of American foreign policy. North American imperialists generally penetrated the markets outside of the continental boundaries of the United States by ostensibly "peaceful" means.[3]

By the beginning of the twentieth century, most of the world was divided up among the great imperialist powers. Competitive relations between metropolitan countries eventually generated great conflicts over the control of markets and colonies. Side by side with these competitive relationships, however, finance and industrial capitalists also established working alliances in the form of international cartel arrangements between national monopolies. These arrangements, for example, attempted to minimize competition by tacit agreements about national "spheres of influence" within the world market. Various forms of cooperation between metropolitan nations were also forged in order to further the penetration of vast countries such as China in the name of free trade. American corporations and international cartels encouraged the repression of national movements for self-determination. They assumed virtual sovereignty over an increasing number of countries in South and Central America and the Pacific. Most of these developments occurred during the formative years of sociology in North America.

NOTES

1. "In 1851 the *Cincinnati Gazette* reported: 'About four years ago, the salt manufacturers of the Kanawha River, finding that their capacity to manufacture salt was larger than the demand for consumption . . . and it having consequently went down to a ruinous price, formed themselves into an association, for the purpose of protecting their interest, by fixing the price of the article, and limiting the amount manufactured to the actual wants of the west.' . . . the United States saw the appearance in 1853, of the American Brass Association, 'to meet ruinous competition'; in 1854 the Hampton Country Cotton Spinners' Association, 'to control price policies'; and in 1855 the American Iron Association with the same purpose" (Mandel 1970:400).

2. For a discussion of the relation between business cycles or the fall in price levels and the attempts to maintain profits by formation of monopoly trusts, see Mandel (1970:401–440).

3. These means are denoted *ostensibly* "peaceful" because they were actually preceded and reinforced in many cases by such American armed forces as the United States Marines, as well as by the systematic bribery and corruption of indigenous governments. These governments in South America, for example, used their own military forces to repress nationalist movements which were opposed to the penetration of national economies by North American corporations.

CHAPTER 15

The Growth
of Industrial Violence

Preview

A series of violent clashes between monopoly capital and organized labor in the United States occurred throughout the formative years of American sociology. The great Pullman strike was the largest of these clashes prior to the turn of the century. This strike, moreover, was centered in the Chicago area during the very year in which the University of Chicago established the foundations of the first department of sociology in the world. That department was led by Albion Small.

Small rejected the Marxian concept of class contradictions. He attempted to construct his own social theory around the problem of integration posed by the conflict between capital and labor. This attempt, however, was partly dependent upon the emergence of a general, corporate liberal perspective that examined economic relations within the context of society as a whole, and solved the problem of integration by emphasizing such factors as class harmony, class collaboration, and the "functional interdependence" of economic groups. This perspective, called "liberal-syndicalism," will be discussed in the next chapter.

Thus, reform Darwinism was only one of the politically meaningful, general perspectives developed by the outstanding members of the newly developing sociological discipline. This chapter will provide the historical background for appreciating the issues at stake in the development of another perspective, liberal-syndicalism. It will begin with early nineteenth-century working-class struggles for economic and political rights. It will end with the growth of industrial violence.

British Working-Class Struggles

Workers everywhere were affected by the methods, relations, and results of industrialization. The experiences of the British working class, emanating directly from the early industrialization of Great Britain, were very different from those of the middle class. There were also significant differences in the effects of industrialization on various sections of the working class, such as the skilled and unskilled workers, or between the working classes in a metropolitan country like England or a colonialized country like Ireland.

On a long-term basis, because of the productive technology at home, the new industrial proletarians in the metropolitan countries enjoyed higher standards of living than those in colonialized countries. They also benefited because of the accumulation of wealth accruing from the superexploitative imperialist relations with colonial countries.

From a short-term view, on the other hand, even the workers in metropolitan countries like England were not spared the deprivations accompanying the development of the new capitalist modes of production. During the decades surrounding the turn of the nineteenth century, for example, capitalist modes of production swept like a hurricane through all the traditional institutions that stood in their way. The effects on the smallholders and laboring classes were extraordinary. Properties were foreclosed; the flow of labor from the rural areas to the cities was accelerated; and skilled tradesmen in urban areas felt the devastating effects of the new technology and the capitalist division of labor.

As early as 1811, British workers in Nottingham called the Luddites reacted by forming masked bands to smash the machines in the textile mills. Later, Chartists, utopian socialists such as the Owenites, and early workingmen's associations emerged. The history of these early movements was a continuous reoccurrence of political failure, collapsing utopias, and savage governmental repression. The Chartists, for example, responded to the New Poor Law of 1832 and the economic crisis of 1837 by gathering over a million and a quarter signatures petitioning basic economic and political rights from Parliament. This petition went unheeded, and the leaders of the movement were imprisoned and then hanged in the conflict that followed. By the second half of the century, however, the continual growth of workingmen's and socialist movements began to have greater success in achieving stable organizations and legislative reform.

American Working-Class Responses to Monopoly Capitalism

Similar developments in class-consciousness and workers' protective organizations occurred in America prior to the Civil War (Lens 1969:84–85). During the post-Civil War period the tremendous surge in industrialization provided greater stimulation for the development of labor organizations and working-class consciousness. In addition, the postwar economy was repeatedly seized by wild oscillations: as the century grew older, typical fluctuations in prices were more frequently accompanied by periodic collapse of the market as a whole. Periods of recession and depression lasted longer and were nationwide in scope. From the viewpoint of many workers the whole capitalist system seemed to be coming apart at the seams.

In the twenty-five-year span from 1875 to 1900, for example, the nation witnessed only nine prosperous years (Mitchell 1927:424–434). The first depression in the fourth quarter of the nineteenth century lasted six terrible years; and the last one ran for five. Recessions and depressions were no longer uncommon events; they became the norm.

The responses to these conditions varied greatly depending upon the ideology of working-class movements. But American workers did not have to be socialists to recognize the increasing concentration of wealth which accompanied the frequent prostration of the economy. Early in the last quarter of the century there was extensive evidence of this increase in the extreme contrasts between poverty-stricken workers and fabulously wealthy entrepreneurs.[1] Repeated references to "opportunity for all" and "the self-made man" by conservative journalists, clergymen, and educators could not obscure the numbers of persistently unemployed and underemployed men. In fact, the ideologists' protests bore an inverse relation to the actual living conditions of the unemployed masses.

During the post-Civil War period the response of American workers to the changing economic conditions was to broaden their organizational forms. American labor began to organize and federate on a *national* basis as the national markets for various commodities became significant in determining local wage levels and conditions of work. From 1864 to the panic of 1873, about twenty-six national trade unions were organized with a combined membership of 300,000.

In 1866 the National Labor Union was formed, and for a few years it attempted to achieve a wider representation of labor and a broader approach to the solution of working-class problems. Agitating for an eight-hour day, this organization also focused on legislative and lobbying activities. The National Labor Union pledged its help to Negro labor and also corresponded with the International Workingmen's Association (which had been formed in London in 1861).[2] It admitted women delegates to its conventions and asked for an eight-hour day for women and equal pay for equal work. Toward the end of its short-lived existence, however, the leadership felt that unions could not solve the problem of exploitation in capitalist societies except by making wage laborers into independent small producers through the formation of producers' cooperatives. This utopian solution never occurred.

The Panic of 1873, and the long depression that followed, encompassed events that dealt harshly with the labor movement in the United States. Numerous strikes were occurring on a larger scale than before, but most of them failed to save the workers from the general deterioration in wages and working conditions.[3] The use of terrorism as a weapon by both employers and workers increased considerably, and by 1878 the total membership of all unions had fallen to about 50,000 because of the combined effects of the depression and repression.

From 1880 to 1896, the labor movement grew rapidly once again. The Knights of Labor, an organization favoring industrial rather than craft unions, was formed earlier in 1869. It expanded phenomenally in the eighties and in 1886, at the peak of its strength, totaled 700,000 members. After 1887 the Knights of Labor rapidly declined. Concurrently, the center of nationally federated unions shifted toward the railroad brotherhoods and the American Federation of Labor, which was organized in 1886. During the years following 1886, the number of employers' associations also expanded, and by 1891 they began to engage in industry-wide collective bargaining with the trade unions.

Monopoly Capitalist's Response to American Workers

During the 1870s, corporate leaders had been able to contain militant responses by organized labor through the use of armed scabs, police terror, and other forms of repression. However, the scope of industrial violence began to increase steadily as the turn of the century drew near.

For example, the same year that marked the peak in membership of the Knights of Labor also witnessed the massacre in Chicago's Haymarket Square. On May 3, 1886, members of a Knights of Labor local demonstrated against the scabs hired by the McCormick Harvester Works to replace the striking workers, who advocated higher wages, better working conditions, and an eight-hour day. That day police fired into the striking workers, killing four and wounding many another. After dark of the next day, thousands gathered in Haymarket Square to protest the murder of the McCormick workers. After listening to the final speech the crowd was given an order to disperse by a force of 180 police which suddenly appeared on the scene.[4] A bomb was thrown at the police and six police were killed while many others were wounded. The police fired on the assembly, "chasing, clubbing and shooting down workers. Several were killed (how many is unknown) and at least 200 were wounded" (Foner 1955:106).

The Homestead strike is another illustration of the increase in industrial violence. In 1892, the Amalgamated Association of Iron and Steel workers refused to accept a wage cut demanded by Henry C. Frick, who was the manager of Carnegie Steel. Frick finally locked-out the workers at the Homestead plant in order to break the union. Barges of mercenaries hired by the Pinkerton detective agency were brought in. As the barges landed, shots were exchanged between the Pinkertons and the workers, who had previously urged them to turn back. A thirteen hour armed battle ended in the surrender of the Pinkertons. Even though law, order, and peaceful relations were restored after the battle, the governor dispatched 8,000 troops, to Homestead [5] under the command of General Snowden, who declared: "Philadelphia can hardly appreciate the actual communism of these people. They believe the works are their's quite as much as Carnegie's." After the militia arrived, scabs were brought in to break the strike and the strike leaders were framed on riot and conspiracy charges (*ibid.*:212–215).

A final illustration involves the employees of the Pullman Company which was centered in the Chicago area. These employees struck in 1894 because of a 30–40 percent wage cut and a 30 percent decrease in the labor force (Adamic 1968:115ff). Eugene V. Debs, the president of American Railway Union, which represented these workers, urged the strikers to be nonviolent during the strike. But the crowds of workers crippled engines, overturned freight cars, and sabotaged tracks and switches. Overriding strong objections by Illinois Governor Altgeld, President Cleveland dispatched 10,000 infantry, cavalry, and artillery troops to Chicago to suppress the strike. Estimates of property and business losses eventually produced by the strikers ranged between fifty and one hundred *million* dollars (*ibid.*:121).

The Pullman strike was finally broken and Louis Adamic (*ibid.*:123) has noted that "A few months later the regular army was raised to 50,000 men and more armories were being started in Chicago, New York, and elsewhere, to keep down any possible labor uprising in the future. Military journals printed articles on riot-duty tactics."

During the 1890s, industrial cities and towns were divided into armed camps inhabited on one hand by striking workers and on the other by the armed forces of the corporations and the state. The insatiable demand for capital accumulation had driven the industrial elite to rely increasingly upon savage police reprisals to deal with "its" labor trouble. The strike was the chief weapon used to do battle with the wage cut, the lockout, hazardous working conditions, chronic underemployment, and cyclical depression. The budding socialist movements of the late 1870s found a ready ally within the militant ranks of industrial labor.[6] Although these movements were concentrated among foreign workers, the execution of a Texas anarchist named Albert Parsons, who participated in the Haymarket Riot, indicated that they were also being supported by native-born descendants of old immigrants.

NOTES

1. For instance, when Cornelius Vanderbilt died in 1877, *The Irish World* commented that he had amassed his wealth through swindles, bribery, and corruption. It added, "society itself is to blame. There are fifty thousand men in New York now chained in enforced idleness—rotting away right under the blighting shadow of Vanderbilt's golden pyramid" (quoted in Diamond 1955:58).
2. This international organization is also called the First International and was partly founded by Karl Marx.
3. Regarding a notable strike among miners in the Pennsylvania coal fields at the time, Lens (1969:142) notes "the strike was defeated by hunger. 'Since I last saw you,' a striker wrote in a letter, 'I have buried my youngest child, and on the day before its death there was not one bit of victuals in the house with six children.' The union was smashed. The miners went back to work at wages 20 percent below what they had before."
4. Foner (1955:106) points out that the police were commanded by Captain John Bonfield, "hated throughout the city for his extreme brutality."
5. Upon evaluating the company's destructive tactics toward the union, the amount

of money at stake should be considered. It has been reported (Austin 1949:134) that "during the seventeen years that preceded the strike [Carnegie Steel's] profits amounted to $27,000,000. In the nine years following Homestead it amassed $106,000,000. The historian, Bridges, comments: 'It is believed by the Carnegie officials, and with some show of reason, that this magnificent record was to a great extent made possible by the company's victory at Homestead.' " It should also be noted that five of these nine years had been *depression* years.

6. The Socialist Labor Party was formed in 1877; but the development of socialist movements was, in fact, in the making from the early 1850s (Lens 1969:142).

CHAPTER 16

Liberal-Syndicalism

Cries of anarchism and the development of anarcho-syndicalism as a world view emerged out of this period of industrial violence. Following the violent events in Haymarket Square, newspapers equated "anarchist" bomb-throwing terrorists with the demands for the eight-hour day. However, Foner (1955:107) indicates that "Three years later in an interview, the Chicago chief of police, Captain Frederick Ebersold, admitted that the police . . . deliberately set about organizing anarchist societies and planted bombs and ammunition at these organizations." The identity of the person who threw the bomb at the police was never determined. In spite of this, the leaders of the eight-hour movement were tried for their socialist and anarchist beliefs and sentenced to death.[1]

Early Anarcho-Syndicalism
in France and the United States

Toward the end of the nineteenth century, anarchists abroad developed a utopian philosophy called "anarcho-syndicalism." In the United States, the word "syndicalism" has been traditionally identified with labor unions, or with the "criminal syndicalist" laws enacted toward the end of the last century to prevent the growth of militant labor, anarcho-syndicalist, and other socialist movements. The word itself, however, is derived largely from labor developments in France around the turn of the century. French intellectuals and trade union members had developed a crude syndicalist and class-conscious approach to social change based on the eclectic combination of early socialist, Marxist, anarchist, and trade union ideas. Unlike the socialists, who were

121

led by V. I. Lenin in Russia and Karl Liebknecht in Germany, the French syndicalists regarded labor unions rather than political parties as the most critical change agents in capitalist societies. It was the contention of the French syndicalists that militant union policies which culminated in great "general strikes" would spontaneously bring socialism into being. In their view, the labor union would be the key social unit of socialist societies.

The labor union (as well as other economic organizations or blocs) [2] was called a syndicate in France and syndicalism generally referred to the theory and movement in which national federations of labor (united, perhaps, in "one big union") would ultimately control the economy and society. Existing society was perceived by the French syndicalists in terms of *irreconcilable* economic blocs composed substantially of wage earners and the owners of capital. The wage earners were regarded as members of interdependent and exploited industrial groups bound together in a single social class. Furthermore, the syndicalists envisaged a utopian socialist society predicated chiefly on decentralized trade unions and devoid of privately owned banking and industrial syndicates. Parasitic ruling classes based on the ownership of private property would be replaced forever. In their view, the capitalist state would also disappear. It would be replaced by the trade union state representing "the producers" rather than "the parasites."

The French syndicalists, therefore, did not view the capitalist state as a neutral mediator in industrial conflicts; they regarded the state as an instrument of the ruling class. Unlike the Marxists, however, they felt that parliamentary struggles compromised the class struggle. They rejected both political and parliamentary strategies for social change and restricted their policies for the attainment of socialism to such trade union actions as industrial slowdowns and strikes (Foner 1965:20–21).[3]

Similar developments occurred in the United States at the beginning of this century. William Z. Foster (who was influenced by syndicalism for a time) has indicated that the Socialist Labor party and dissident left-wing members of the Socialist party [4] founded the International Workers of the World, a militant anarcho-syndicalist labor organization. Foster (1947:50) was aware of similar developments in France but minimized their importance in the development of anarcho-syndicalism in the United States. He has suggested that "the syndicalist tendency" in the United States had its roots in "basic American conditions" which restricted the revolutionary consciousness of American workers to the economic field.[5] As a consequence of these conditions, American anarcho-syndicalists were repelled by the "notoriously corrupt American politics" and perceived their immediate grievances chiefly in terms of economic issues involving wages and conditions of work (*ibid.*:52).

The general determinants of American anarcho-syndicalism are arguable.[6] But it is certain that the activities of the anarcho-syndicalists heightened the general awareness of the class contradictions in the United States. The strike actions initiated by these socialists sharply illuminated the degree to which the men who controlled the great corporations had also asserted control over the state and the economy. In addition, these actions deepened the hegemonic crises that had first appeared with the development of industrial unionism in the last quarter of the nineteenth century.

Well before the turn of the century, liberal scholars had begun to search energetically for new ideas which would secure the increasingly unstable popular base for capitalist institutions in the United States. The processes that led to the stabilization of these new ideas, as we will see, were international in scope. These processes were related dialectically to the counterhegemonic ideas that were rapidly emerging among the most militant proletarian movements in the Western nations.

American Syndicalism

In the United States, the corporate liberals, at the opposite end of the political spectrum from the anarcho-syndicalists, began to formulate a body of ideas which William Appleman Williams (1961:358–60) called *American syndicalism*. Williams states:

Americans came increasingly to see their society as one composed of groups— farmers, workers, and businessmen—rather than of individuals and sections. Almost unconsciously at first, but with accelerating awareness, they viewed themselves as members of a bloc that was defined by the political economy of the large corporation. Perhaps nothing characterized the new *Weltanshauung* more revealingly. For given such an attitude, the inherent as well as the conscious drift of thought was to a kind of syndicalism based on organizing, balancing, and co-ordinating different functional groups. [*ibid.:358*]

American syndicalists believed that capitalists were absolutely indispensable to the maintenance of a stable industrial society. Rather than regarding capital and labor as opposing and irreconcilable social classes, they considered them to be interdependent economic blocs or interest groups. The conflicts of interest between these groups, in their view, were quite reconcilable.

Williams (*ibid.:356–357*) has also suggested that the conservative version of American syndicalism, in its earliest form, may have been developed by the desire and efforts on the part of the "interest conscious" (i.e., laissez-faire) capitalists to rationalize and control the marketplace. The view of the market as their *system,* Williams adds "was soon generalized as a result of the observations and reflections on broader issues." These issues were generated by the growing instability of the economy and the rising demands of agrarian and urban groups which challenged the power of the great corporations. Later, aware of these broader "system" problems, "class conscious" (i.e., corporate-liberal) capitalists and their spokesmen began to clothe their proposals for political reform in the same rhetoric of "American syndicalism." They used this rhetoric to emphasize above all the need for equity and co-operation between capital and labor.

Williams also points out another contribution to the development of American syndicalism. Prior to the turn of the century, the cry for equity and co-operation between capital and labor was loudly expressed by a Protestant movement known as the Social Gospel. Members of this movement perceived the church and state as a prime means for ensuring industrial peace and proposed that a harmonious industrial system could only be achieved on the basis of class collaboration. In addition, some of the members eventually developed the conception of Christian capitalism which was shared by such eminent academics as Woodrow Wilson and Richard T. Ely as well as such leading sociologists as Edward A. Ross and Albion Small.

Finally, Williams suggests that another important concept and ideal of American syndicalism at that time was *efficiency*. As early as the 1880's, industrialists, economists, and political scientists began to phrase their policy recommendations in terms of the new liberal ideology which identified the rational management of market institutions with the bureaucratic routine exemplified by the great corporations.[7] Although the notion of corporate efficiency is one of the great myths of our time, it was fast becoming established not only as a perceived "fact of life," but also as a secular ideal, during the very decade in which Ward's *Dynamic Sociology* was first published.

Liberal-Syndicalism

American syndicalism, based on the concept of interest groups, functional interdependence, and efficiency, was not limited to captains of industry. It was also expressed in the very earliest sociological writings. In fact it is likely that the professional writings made a creative contribution to the emergence of this developing liberal perspective. One has only to note Ward's repeated use of the metaphor "efficiency" when describing the "progressive" influence of the state, to realize the degree to which his outlook was shaped by this ideal.[8] Ward, for example, regarded the efficient rationalization of human relations as unattainable without an equitable and harmonious adjustment between capital and labor. Ward was not alone in expressing this point of view.

Book II will describe Edward A. Ross' repeated references to "the perpetual clash and conflict of groups" which characterized modern industrial societies. Ross, too, argued for the development of more equitable relations between capital and labor within the framework of capitalism. Other sociologists with similar conceptions included Albion Small, who insisted that individual rights were conditional upon the performance of a *useful function* as well as upon natural right. While socialists in Britain and elsewhere had declared that the control of economic relations should be transferred away from parasitic, "functionless" owners of capital to those workers who performed a *useful service* to society, sociologists like Small insisted that merchants and industrialists fulfilled a very useful function and because of this, their profits were "well earned wages."

American syndicalist ideas, as we have seen, were formulated by entrepreneurs, clergymen, economists, political scientists, and sociologists. Even a "labor variant" of these syndicalist ideas was expressed by conservative labor leaders.[9] And observations by C. Wright Mills in 1954 suggest that an inchoate "procapitalist syndicalism from the top" still exists among labor leaders in the modern period.[10]

The scope of the national and institutional variations in this body of ideas suggests that Williams' American syndicalism was part of a broader intellectual perspective, developing among liberals from many walks of life within the Western nations. Syndicalist notions were developing simultaneously in Germany, France, and Belgium. For instance, the French sociologist, Emile Durkheim, envisioned a society based on functionally interdependent occupational groups organized on the basis of national industries. In his utopian syndicalist scheme, industrial councils reconciled the conflicts (e.g., between employers and employees) within industries, while the state mediated conflicts between industrial or occupational groups (Durkheim 1933:1–31).

Some of the syndicalist schemes which were developed by scholars abroad were also considered socialist even though they maintained that socialism would be achieved on the basis of reformist policies and class collaboration. These syndicalist schemes, however, can be regarded as being similar in spirit to the corporate-liberal conceptions developed by the German "socialists of the chair" during the last quarter of the nineteenth century. These "professorial socialists" created eclectic combinations of ideas derived from German political economy (e.g., cameralism, German welfare-state economists), Protestantism, utopian socialism, and mercantilism, in order to provide alternative policies which would effectively compete with the radical doctrines being espoused by left socialists like Karl Liebknecht. Similar developments also took place in France and Belgium because of the growth of militant anarcho-syndicalist and Marxian movements.

In Belgium, syndicalist ideas were advanced by Guillaume de Greef, whose influence on the earliest works by the founding sociologists was significant.[11] Greef devised an eclectic combination of syndicalist conceptions and Spencerian evolutionary notions to suggest that forms of human associations had undergone evolutionary changes. Greef utilized the "differential rate of change" notion and indicated that the social structure had become more heterogeneous and its various parts more autonomous. The heterogeneous parts of the social structure exhibited different rates of growth and some of them lagged behind the others. Since all parts were highly dependent upon the economy, he suggested that the state should not encourage some of them to advance too far ahead of the overall economic organization. Instead, legislative reform should concentrate on safeguarding the autonomy of various spheres and developing the means whereby the conflicts between opposing syndicalist forces could be equitably balanced in "a courtroom of interests" (Douglass 1948).

Because of its international scope and ideological character, it may be more appropriate to use the term "liberal-syndicalism" rather than "American syndicalism" to classify the group of important transitional perspectives toward industrial conflict produced by corporate liberals during the formative years. The term *liberal*-syndicalism may be more appropriate for an additional reason: like *anarcho*-syndicalism, it explicitly denotes the major ideology from which it was derived. Unlike anarcho-syndicalism, however, it is concerned not only with liberal explanations of the causes of industrial conflict, but also with identifying the relationships which would reconcile this conflict *within* the framework of capitalism.

Liberal-Syndicalism: The "Schizophrenic" State and the Reconciliation of Industrial Conflict

Liberal-syndicalists in the Western nations borrowed images of society from the feudal and mercantile periods as well as the early nineteenth century. These images, however, were peppered with new social units of analysis. These units, inextricably tied to the emergence of monopoly capitalism, included the liberal perception of society as an interrelated system of industrially based, self-interested social units, such as big businessmen, small businessmen, industrial laborers, skilled "aristocrats" of labor, "syndicates of labor," "combinations of capital," and other "vested interests." Furthermore, as the syndicalist perspective became generalized among liberals, even non-economic groups and the state became defined as interest groups in this scheme of things. Simultaneously with its definition as an interest group, the state was seen as an instrument for arbitrating or integrating the "conflicts of interest" between all opposing blocs in the "interest of society" or the "public" as a whole.

While anarcho-syndicalists abhorred the state for being the guarantor of oppression, liberal-syndicalists revered the state as a neutral adjuster, a benevolent welfare agent, a reconciler of conflicts. While liberal-syndicalists like Ward, Ross, and Small may have agreed with Huxley that laissez-faire capitalism was little more than anarchy with a *policeman,* they assiduously forgot all their critical reservations about the state when they wrote about its integrative role in an "industrial democracy." Their image of the political state was totally schizophrenic. In their *criticisms* of laissez-faire capitalism, they described a liberal state corrupted by men of wealth and power. In their *programmatic* statements about social reforms, they described a beneficent state that dispensed justice in the interests of the population as a whole.

Ward, for example, pointed out that the state in a monarchy was controlled by a ruling class. He also noted that the liberal state was often used as an instrument of "vested interests" to ensure continued exploitation of working people. However, in his programmatic writings he maintained, paradoxically, that the state would increase personal freedom and improve the welfare of the working class. He completely ignored the issue of *who* controlled the state when discussing the effects of state-controlled education. In spite of his criticism of political corruption, he contemplated compulsory universal education within the context of airtight, institutional compartments; he simply assumed that civil bureaucrats and educators would carry out their responsibilities without regard to class realities in industrial societies. This, in essence, typified the liberal-syndicalists' schizophrenic outlook on the history and the role of the state.

Liberal-Syndicalism: Abstract Categories and Integrative Mechanisms

Liberal-syndicalists were fond of talking about the organization of the political economy on the basis of the rational principles of efficient managerial functioning. In actuality, their references to the notions of "efficiency" and "functional interdependence" were largely metaphorical and rhetorical. These references were structured more around corporate-liberal principles of equity than canons of efficient production. These principles of equity were particularly evident in writings about conflict resolution.

Discussion of the processes leading to conflict resolution were at the heart of liberal-syndicalist analyses. This kind of "scientific" discourse was strongly regulated by two types of corporate-liberal doctrines based on the positive effects of *moral regeneration* and *economism* on industrial conflict. Moral regeneration was considered a long-term solution to the amelioration of class and industrial antagonisms. Mechanisms based on the "socialization" of individuals and groups (and even many of the modern usages of the word "socialization" itself) were formulated as liberal-syndicalists concentrated on *long-term* solutions to the problem of industrial integration. Economistic doctrines were utilized for *short-range* solutions to industrial conflicts. "Economism" in this frame of reference generally referred to the resolution of conflict by peaceful means (e.g., collective bargaining). It also denoted doctrines which sharply restricted the conflicts between capital and labor to immediate economic issues involving wages and working conditions. Governmental commissions and public censure of labor unions and corporations were also considered useful for resolving industrial conflicts. But political agitation which threatened the foundations of monopoly and monopoly trusts were rejected as an institutional means by which greater equity for workers could be achieved. In addition, from an analytic point of view, economistic mechanisms were usually formulated on the basis of *market analogies*.

Greef's conception of the process of conflict resolution in modern industrial societies can be taken as an example of a liberal-syndicalist mechanism based on a market analogy. Dorothy W. Douglass (1948:546) points out that Greef's process of reconciliation, involving "the free give and take of interest groups," has been called "contractualism" because it essentially consisted of "a higgling . . . a balancing and weighing of opposite forces in a sort of social market-place." The mechanisms used by North American sociologists to explain "interest-group" reconciliation were also direct or jargonized derivatives from bargaining (i.e., "higgling") relationships between buyers and sellers in price-making market economies. Instead of buyers and sellers, however, the most significant "opposing forces" in early liberal-syndicalist explanations were capital and labor.

There were many secular, religious, and national variations in the development of liberal-syndicalist ideas. We have seen, however, that on an abstract level this brand of syndicalism argued that the modern division of labor was responsible for the creation of functionally interdependent groups. In this view the integration of society as a whole was vitally dependent on class collaboration and the efficient organization of economic relationships. However, as we shall see, the liberal-syndicalists also contended that order and progress were not likely if laissez-faire or socialist doctrines became the predominating influence in industrial relationships. These doctrines would add fuel to class conflicts. Furthermore, laissez-faire and socialist ideas would not enable humankind to achieve order and progress because they either rejected the need for *social control* or were contrary to the *egoistic* nature of man.

Decades after the liberal-syndicalists had passed away, modern American "conflict theorists" and "pluralists" such as Lewis Coser and Robert Dahl mistakenly attributed the developments of the universal conceptions of *conflict* and *accommodation* to early essays by Georg Simmel and James Madison about conflict involving small groups or political parties. Actually, it was the liberal-syndicalist doctrines about the nature of *class conflict* and *class collaboration* which gave rise to these universal liberal-functionalist conceptions. Liberal-syndicalism, as we shall see, provided the fertile intellectual ground from which the modern theories called "conflict theory" and "pluralism" sprang into being.

NOTES

1. In summing up his case against these men before a stacked jury and a prejudicial judge, the state attorney declared "Law is on trial. Anarchy is on trial. These men have been selected, picked out by the grand jury and indicted because they were leaders. They are *no more guilty* than the thousands who follow them. Gentlemen of the jury; convict these men, make *examples* of them, hang them and you save our institutions, our society." (For a description of the trial, the jury, and Judge Gary's attitude toward labor, see Foner [1955:108–109].)

2. The term "syndicate" was also used more generically by persons of different persuasions to refer to many types of economic associations involving bankers, industrialists, or monopolists (e.g., banking syndicates). At times, in the writings of some early American sociologists, for example, the term "syndicated capital" denoted monopoly trusts or employers associations, while "syndicated labor" meant federations of trade unions.

3. The syndicalists also advocated the use of industrial "sabotage" but interpreted this word broadly. It did not necessarily mean the destruction of property; it also referred to nonviolent strategies for interfering with the production process.

4. These dissident members were antagonistic to the reformist policies which prevailed in the Socialist party.

5. For a lengthy list of these economic, political, and ideological conditions, see Foster (1947:51–52).

6. For an alternate view, see Paul Buhle (1970).

7. Williams (1961:357–358) points out that the "idea that efficiency was crucially important to prosperity and the socially tolerable functioning of the system soon gained wide acceptance. Though some businessmen had stressed the axiom earlier, the general discussion was launched by engineering and scientific journals in the 1880's."

8. The metaphor "efficiency" was used to legitimate all sorts of technocratic doctrines. For a description of the varied uses of "efficiency," see Vesey (1965:116–118).

9. Williams points out that the Social Gospel movement included labor leaders who preferred to improve labor's position without attacking the institution of private property. Conservative labor leaders who took similar stands at the time were becoming entrenched in the American Federation of Labor. Foner (1947:524) observes that these leaders sharply rejected the policy of political action which had been raised by earlier associations such as the Knights of Labor. He points out that "the Knights had demanded government ownership of the systems of transportation and communication, but the new Federation did not." The new labor leaders advocated establishment of business unionism modeled upon the "efficient" principles of the large corporation. They restricted union policies to economic issues which involved immediate economic gains for workers. Their narrow policies, however, could only be justified by emphasizing the practical achievement of these goals within the framework of capitalism. Consequently they espoused trade union doctrines which were also organized around the need for equity and cooperation between capital and labor.

10. C. Wright Mills (1963:108–109) wrote that insofar as American labor leaders talk seriously of programs, "they will invariably conceive of them as realizable alongside the present corporations and within the present state framework." As a consequence, unions, in Mills' view, had become "less levers for change of that general framework than they are instruments for more advantageous integration within it. The drift of their actions implement, in terms of the largest projections, a kind of 'procapitalist syndicalism' from the top!" Labor leaders now work for "greater integration at the upper levels of the corporate economy rather than greater power at the lower levels of the work hierarchy, for, in brief, it is the unexpressed desire of American labor leaders to join with owners and managers in running the corporate enterprise system and influencing decisively the political economy as a whole."

11. Burnham (1956:5) has observed that in 1894 "a general bibliography of sociology included only Spencer, Greef, Schaeffle, and Ward." The fact that this bibliography was prepared by Albion Small indicates Greef's significance to the development of the transitional "interest group" and "conflict theory" perspective we have named "liberal syndicalism." Albion Small was perhaps the most important North American liberal syndicalist during the founding period. (Small's bibliography is contained in W. H. Tolman and W. I. Hull, eds., *Handbook of Sociological Information with Especial Reference to New York City*, 1894:5–6.)

PART FIVE
Divisive Trends and Technocratic Intellectuals

CHAPTER 17

Divisive Trends and Popular Movements

Preview

Laissez-faire liberalism was sustained by a variety of doctrines about free trade, free labor, the gold standard, and the (laissez-faire) liberal state. However the growth of imperialism, organized labor, and populist movements undermined these doctrines and encouraged the emergence of alternative points of view. From the 1880's onwards, some of these alternative ideas were buttressed by social theories based on reform-Darwinist and liberal-syndicalist perspectives. These perspectives were compatible with the racial, economic, and political beliefs which had encouraged divisive trends within the working class and collaborative trends between capital and labor.

This chapter describes these divisive trends within the working class. It also acquaints the reader with the degree to which the populist and the progressive movements posed the question of which economic blocs among the white population were to control the American economy. The next chapter will discuss the divisive trends that appeared among capitalist groups. After this is done, we will consider the social class and institutional relationships which mobilized liberal intellectuals toward the goal of a peaceful resolution of economic and political conflict within the framework of capitalism.

Divisive Trends in American Labor Movement

Because of economic instability and repressive violence during the nineteenth century, laissez-faire doctrines about the role of labor and the state, for example, were being indignantly rejected by industrial workers. Both foreign and native-born workers were becoming attracted to radical explanations of industrial relationships. This radical influence, however, was consciously and effectively negated by many labor leaders. Labor organizations were often led by liberals who restricted union activity to economic issues and avoided political solutions to labor problems. As a rule, these organizations had divisive membership policies and excluded unskilled workers, young workers, and women workers as well as members of racial minorities. This exclusiveness further counteracted radical tendencies and, in many regions of the country, for example, organized labor leaders attacked the racial and ethnic minorities as well as the monopoly trusts. On the Pacific Coast, in particular, they frequently resorted to anti-Chinese solutions to labor problems during periods of economic insecurity. Originally Chinese immigration had been encouraged by promoters interested in enlarging the pool of cheap labor for domestic services and, in later years, for railroad building and mining. From the early 1880s onwards, however, members of organized labor groups among white workers led repeated and successful campaigns to restrict Asian immigration in general, and Chinese immigration in particular. Working-class spokesmen such as Dennis Kearny, who helped found the Workingmen's Party of California in 1877, instigated vicious anti-Chinese demonstrations. Workingmen rioted against Chinese laborers; and after these laborers were brought east by employers to break strikes, the Pacific Coast labor movement was able to successfully arouse national support for stopping "coolie" immigration in 1882. The major working-class movements in the United States at the time rejected calls for unity between white workers and Asian, Afro-American, and Mexican-American labor.[1] The combined effects of racism, nativism, and the narrow crafts-union approach to the organization of labor, intensified the fratricidal divisions within the American working class. The white skilled worker eventually obtained some degree of protection through such racist organizations as the American Federation of Labor. But racist, economistic,[2] and chauvinistic doctrines mediated the responses of these workingmen toward the political economy of monopoly capitalism. Because of their influence, these doctrines helped fractionate members of working-class movements irrespective of the widespread agreement among workers about the common dangers presented by the growth of monopolies and monopoly trusts.

The divisions within the American working class as a whole were further intensified after 1882. During the last decades of the century, the commercialization and consolidation of land, the division of labor between town and country, and the expansion of capitalist modes of production in Europe spurred vast immigration to the United States. Almost twenty million immigrants entered the United States during this period, twelve million of whom were from the Mediterranean and Eastern European nations. These "new" immigrants, who first settled in American coastal cities, differed from the "old" settlers who had previously immigrated from England, Wales, Scotland, Ireland, Germany, the Netherlands, and the Scandinavian countries. Represented among these latter arrivals were people from Italy, Russia, Hungary, Poland, Greece, Turkey, and the Balkans. The surge in immigration was accompanied by an unprecedented rise of anti-immigration doctrines among members of white labor organizations.

Control or Regulation of Economic Competition

Generally, the white workingman's labor organizations attempted to maintain income levels by curbing competition between individual workers, just as monopoly trusts attempted to maintain a high profit by restricting competition between individual producers. The demands for curbs on Asian and European immigration should also be seen as expressions of a general trend on the part of large and small economic blocs to control or regulate competition to their advantage. Organized labor's exclusionist policies, for example, were no less consistent with the complex patterns of liberal thought than the advocacy of colonial policies or protectionist legislation (e.g., the tariff) by entrepreneurs who felt the sharp pinch of foreign competition. These exclusionist policies represented but another instance in which economic groups have attempted to control the competitive forces that influenced the price of commodities (including the price of labor) within the framework of capitalism.

Black leaders also advocated exclusionist practices in order to curb foreign competition with black labor. The outstanding liberal spokesman of black Americans, Booker T. Washington, spoke against European immigration at the Atlanta Exposition in 1900, and urged white employers not to "look to the incoming of those of foreign birth and strange tongue and habits for the prosperity of the South." He suggested instead that whites should rely upon the black people "who have, without strikes and labor wars," always provided workers for the economy of the Southern states (Gossett 1965:307).

Because of the influence of white racism and a policy of black gradualism, black liberals were not able to ameliorate the powerless position of black workers. The same held for the emerging "black bourgeoisie" in their attempts to establish a controlling position in the competitive market for goods and services among blacks.

At the turn of the century, white entrepreneurs such as Andrew Carnegie, John D. Rockefeller, and Andrew Mellon supported the black capitalist movement which developed around Booker T. Washington, in order to sidetrack a rising black militancy.[3] Booker T. Washington argued for a gradualist accommodation to the oppressive white political institutions. He also espoused economic separatist policies based on black capitalism, or "the new nationalism" as it was called at the time.[4] In spite of support from finance-capitalists, however, black capitalism failed dismally to achieve progress toward the welfare of blacks in general. It also failed, in any significant degree, to achieve its immediate aim, namely the attainment of profitable monopolies in markets restricted to blacks.[5] Groups of "elite" black professionals and businessmen attempted to establish economic enterprises on their own (Du Bois

132

1968:50–96). But in all of these attempts, the black bourgeoisie were unable to improve the welfare of the black masses.[6]

The Populist and Progressive Movements

During the last quarter of the nineteenth century, the populist movement crystallized the widespread agrarian discontent among American farmers. The National Grange and other farm associations participating in this movement denounced the growth of industrial monopolies and trusts. Because of the need for low-cost loans for feed, seed, building materials, and agricultural machinery, bank monopolies and high interest rates also came under their fire. Railroad monopolies established a differential railroad rebate system which was favorable to industrialists like Rockefeller but highly unfavorable to farmers. The concentration of banking capital also began to affect farmers adversely; and economic crises further compounded their plight by depressing agriculture as well as industry. Small farmers, in particular, began to mobilize in order to regain the political power they had enjoyed before the rise of the great industries and banks.

Turning to federal and state legislation as a way out of their difficult situation, the populists went so far as to propose that the railroads be nationalized. In addition, the 1890 platform of the populist People's Party, which was adopted in Omaha, Nebraska, proposed the direct election of senators, a graduated income tax, postal savings banks, and a bimetallic standard [7] based upon the abandonment of a single monetary gold standard. This platform was widely denounced by conservatives as socialistic and anarchistic.

The populist movement made important strides in state elections, particularly in the West. Moreover, just before the turn of the century, the radical wing of the Democratic party succeeded in inserting the populist stand on the "silver issue" into the Democratic platform. Republican party leaders, however, received heavy financial support from Eastern industrialists and bankers; they were able to win over the working-class voters in the Eastern cities. The standard-bearer of the Democratic party, William Jennings Bryan, lost to Robert McKinley in the national elections and the populist movement subsequently went into sharp decline.

Around this same time, other significant social and political movements began to develop in the American cities. Among the urban middle classes, for example, small businessmen also became concerned about their position in the face of economic instabilities and growing monopolies. By the beginning of the twentieth century, professional, small business and labor organizations formed loose coalitions among themselves as well as with farm groups. These aimed at the control and regulation of large-scale corporations through federal legislation and bureaus. At different stages of their development, these coalitions also included secular and religious urban reformers and "enlightened" corporate capitalists. These shifting coalitions, which were therefore very diverse, were considered to be aspects of a "progressive movement" or "progressive period" by later historians.

A shortcoming of the so-called progressive movement, however, was its significant failure to confront the issue of racism. Not only were blacks impoverished but more than a thousand black individuals were lynched during this period. Instead, racist doctrines were espoused by leading "progressive" Americans (Gossett 1965:106). "Progressive" American politicians did not hesitate to use armed force to repress militant labor organizations; but such force was not utilized to quell outbreaks of lynching and other forms of racist violence (Zinn 1970:173). On the other hand, although the loosely organized and shifting coalitions within the "progressive" movement generally defined their goals within the limits of racist double standards and the private ownership of property—the developments involving the "progressive" movement as well as the labor movement sharply posed the questions of which economic blocs, among the *white* population, were to control and direct the economy.

NOTES

1. Even the National Labor Union, which was distinguished by its broad approach to labor problems, pledged its aid to black labor but did not establish an integrated organization. (Instead, in 1869 blacks organized separately into the Colored National Labor Union.)

2. The tradition of economism sharply restricts the solutions of working-class problems to organizational demands for economic improvements within the framework of capitalism. Economism is generally identified with a pluralist approach to the reconciliation of the conflicts between interest groups, such as corporations and labor unions. It bases organizational policies of trade unions, for example, on what Americans call "immediate bread and butter issues" rather than the eventual elimination of the fundamental causes of economic exploitation and insecurity in capitalist societies.

3. Earl Ofari's work contains two very revealing quotations from Andrew Carnegie and William Dean Howells which, in Ofari's (1970:35) opinion, provide "a good estimate of just how prominently Washington's ideas figured in the plans of white corporate businessmen of that day." For example, Carnegie stated: "Booker Washington's influence is powerfully exerted *to keep the negroes* (sic) from placing *suffrage* in the front. He contends that good moral character and industrial efficiency, resulting in the ownership of property, are the pressing needs and the sure and speedy path to recognition and enfranchisement. A few able negroes (sic) are disposed to press for the free and unrestricted vote *immediately*. We cannot but hope that the wiser policy will prevail . . ." (From a speech delivered before the Philosophical Institute of Edinburgh, 1907, quoted in Ofari (*ibid.* our emphasis).

4. For a discussion of these developments, see the excellent work on black capitalism written by Ofari (1970:30–47).

5. Franklin Frazier pointed to this relation in *The Black Bourgeoisie*. Frazier (1962:139) stated: "The myth of Negro business is tied up with the belief in the possibility of a separate Negro economy . . . Of course, behind the idea of a separate Negro economy is the hope of the black bourgeosie that they will have the monopoly of the Negro market." Ofari (1970:9) notes this relation between black capitalism and a black monopoly and concludes that black capitalists can never hope to achieve a monopoly in a market which is already monopolized to a large extent by great corporations which are owned and controlled by whites. For examples, see Ofari (*ibid.*:66–85).

6. By the end of the formative period of American sociology no industrial or commercial segment of "the third world" in the United States had significantly penetrated even the competitive sectors of the industrial economy, much less the oligarchic sectors which were controlled by the great corporate capitalists. Instead, along with exploited

workers from other undeveloped nations such as China, as we have seen, the vast majority of Indians, Mexican-Americans, and blacks either found their lands expropriated or were pressed into the vast reservoir of superexploited labor.

7. The farmers believed that the adoption of silver as well as gold would bring the price of gold down, and make available inexpensive loans for easier payment of debts. They also perceived this as a means for undercutting the monopolies in bank capital. The provision for postal savings banks was regarded as serving the same purpose. These would also be a superior means for protecting savings in the face of the recurrent bank panics and failures.

CHAPTER 18

Divisive Trends among Capitalist Groups

The growth of the *white* industrial oligarchy, in contrast with the developmental problems of the black bourgeoisie,[1] encountered few barriers from other groups in society.[2] But even though most of the other economic blocs in the United States were less powerful, it did not mean that this industrial oligarchy could completely ignore the potential danger represented by the clamorous outcries against the great corporations which were being expressed by large sections of the population.

American Capitalists Reevaluate Industrial Relations

The passage of the Sherman Act in 1890 was one small indicator of the vast popular anger that was emerging against the monopolies and monopoly-trusts. This anger, which was also expressed in relation to individual monopolists, was maintained throughout the formative years of American sociology. In 1913, for example, there was widespread agreement, upon J. P. Morgan's death, that economic and political power had become dangerously concentrated in the hands of wealthy industrialists and bankers (Diamond 1955:86–87). Morgan was described as "the creation of his environment, the creature of the era of trusts and business consolidations" (*ibid.*:89). It was said that in all of his "great operations" Morgan worked "in partnership with the government" and enabled Wall Street to exploit the country "like a conquered province" (*ibid.*:88).

At the turn of the century, however, men like Morgan and Carnegie began to realize that industrial problems were no longer resolvable by legislation

135

which continued to give up the country's economy to the free play of the market. These industrialists were also alarmed at the impact of the agrarian movements, as shown by the growing interest in political regulation of monopolistic practices. They understood that the recurrent crises created powder-keg conditions among the industrial working classes which would not be securely controlled by military power alone. Even the internecine rivalry among capitalists themselves and the pressures from the more competitive sectors of the economy were undermining the dominating financial position attained by the largest corporate leaders (Kolko 1967:25–26).

During the first few decades of the twentieth century, leading corporate capitalists also became aware that the pillars of laissez-faire capitalism—free labor, the gold standard, and the automatic mechanisms of the market which these implied—would eventually be sharply restricted by the political policies and bureaus which were being created to cope with economic instability and outstanding social problems.

"Progressive" Capitalists and Their Institutional Processes to Clarify Issues and Policies

A number of radical historians,[3] influenced by the highly creative works of William Appleman Williams (1961), have shown that the growth of labor organizations, the exploitative practices of the monopolies, and the changes in thinking of American capitalists around the turn of the century had many consequences. Owners of industrial, banking, and landed capital, for example, began to disagree among themselves about the effectiveness of laissez-faire doctrines as guides to corporate and state policy. In the face of the enormous outcry against the economy and the monopolies, some of these entrepreneurs (the "progressives") began to consider the possibilities inherent in accommodations with "responsible" liberals in the labor movement in order to forestall growing labor militancy. They also began to concern themselves with other political and economic ways to control economic instabilities, repress the development of socialism and anarcho-syndicalism, and preserve the dominating position of the oligopolistic sectors of the economy.

The radical historians have also indicated that during the "progressive" era, these "enlightened" capitalists supported the formation of such organizations as the National Civic Federation. In part, the federation's aim was to bring "representatives" of business, labor, and the public together with "experts" on industrial and other problems in order to help clarify the issues of the day and achieve "constructive" agreement on social policy (Weinstein 1968). Because of the efforts of such organizations, liberals finally came to identify conservatism with those entrepreneurs who publicly advocated laissez-faire policies. These entrepreneurs appeared to construe their own welfare on the basis of the political and economic status quo irrespective of the degree of class conflict engendered by existing policies. On the other hand,

136

the entrepreneurs who publicly advocated reforms, particularly in the relations between the state and the economy, came to be regarded, by most liberals, as "moderates" or "progressives."

The "progressive" capitalists at that time initiated formal and informal discussions which were significant because of their long-term consequences. These deliberative processes helped clarify certain issues and policies even though many of the broader ideological changes wrought by these processes were not translated immediately into practice. Many capitalists, therefore, were called "progressives" in spite of the great chasm between their public statements and the operating policies of their corporations.[4] There was a decided ideological split between "progressive" and "conservative" capitalists; but the most significant changes in practice which were influenced by this split were just beginning to take place. For the most part, these changes were *first* exemplified in the development of those political relationships which safeguarded the *immediate* interests of the great monopolies and monopoly trusts from attacks by radical movements and militant labor unions.[5]

Corporate-Liberal Capitalists and Laissez-Faire Capitalists

The works by radical historians have further indicated that these "progressive capitalists" gradually became conscious of the basic interrelationships and expansionist tendencies which were establishing monopoly capitalism as a viable social system. The progressives' attitudes toward social policy were mixtures of traditional notions (e.g., based on their obligations as "stewards" to society as a whole) and a shrewd, self-interested assessment of the values to be gained from the new forms of political integration and economic growth.

Utilizing theoretical categories for differentiating between the so-called conservative and progressive entrepreneurs, radical historians have employed such terms as "interest-conscious" capitalist and "class-conscious" capitalist (Williams 1961, Weinstein 1968). These categories, however, may lead individuals who are unfamiliar with the historical works from which they are derived, to mistakenly conclude that "interest-conscious" capitalists were not class conscious, or that "class-conscious" capitalists were not concerned with their own selfish interests. In order to achieve analytic precision and avoid confusion, the terms *laissez-faire* capitalist, for the more "interest conscious," and *corporate-liberal* capitalist, for the more "class conscious," are used here to indicate the growing ideological division that emerged between powerful capitalists.

Therefore, the terms "laissez-faire" and "corporate liberal" refer, among other things, to differences in orientation toward preferred modes of political and economic integration. As indicated, laissez-fairism was used during the nineteenth century to advance the penetration of foreign markets abroad and ensure a plentiful supply of cheap industrial labor at home. It justified the use of state power to uphold the expansion of industrial capitalism. Laissez-faire, therefore, represents a particular approach to the overall integration of the political economy.

It should be noted, finally, that this distinction between laissez-faire and corporate-liberal perspectives is in accord with the intentions of the radical historical analyses from which it is derived because it does not represent a division between conservative and radical perspectives. It represents differences among men all of whom were committed to the *preservation* of their class position and the *conservation* of capitalism in the face of economic changes and political conflicts. On certain issues, for example, the "laissez-faire capitalists" had always deferred to the basic priorities of their social class. These priorities included maintenance of the armed forces, selective use of protectionist economic legislation, and the repression of militant labor and radical movements. In this sense, laissez-faire capitalists were *always* class-conscious. Toward the end of the nineteenth century, however, certain political policies which had been justified by laissez-faire doctrines began to fall into disrepute with some entrepreneurs. It was considered necessary to utilize state power to intervene in those marketplace relationships which intensified *politically significant* economic instabilities. Much more comprehensive modes of integration and government involvement were required to preserve the hegemony of the capitalist class and the stability of the capitalist system as a whole. The term "corporate-liberal capitalist" broadly encompasses those members of the upper class who slowly began to realize the importance of reforming the political economy in order to construct these modes of integration.

Whose Interests Served by New Forms of Federal Intervention in Economy?

From 1890 to 1920, new forms of integration between governmental and privately owned corporations were being established in order to cope with the growing economic problems. J. P. Morgan and other powerful American businessmen, for example, became sharply aware that their economic enterprises could no longer weather periodic economic crises supported by their own financial resources. The panic of 1907 indicated clearly that the private banking resources of the nation could not survive a major crisis without massive infusions of credit by the federal government. As Gabriel Kolko (1967:144) points out, "the nation had grown too large, banking had become too complex." During the crisis, "Wall Street, humbled and almost alone, turned from its own resources to the national government."

Some precedents for the private utilization of the resources of the national government had been set within the confines of the nineteenth-century liberal state. The conquerors of the American frontier did not hesitate to use the military power of the state in divesting the native inhabitants of their lands. Federal armed forces and protective legislation served the purposes of expanding American interests in South America, the Caribbean, or the Philippines. The imperialist wars against Mexico and Spain, the military interventions in South America, and the rape of the American Indian were all federally sponsored and rationalized in the name of the civilizing influence of American democracy. Experienced in imperialist policies which dated back to the founding of the nation, American businessmen turned to the federal government to stabilize the economy through support of overseas economic expansion by all means possible, including war and protective legislation at home (Stedman-Jones 1970).

Through various means, a number of corporate capitalists were also able to stimulate and direct the construction of a federal bureaucracy which operated as a shield against the unpredictable actions of state and local governments. Through formal detentes with the executive office, and vague federal laws, some of the leaders of major corporations achieved a stable and politically legitimated existence in the eyes of representatives of the American government as well as many members of the population at large. The antimonopoly reform movements were aborted and in spite of a few antitrust forays by governmental commissions and bureaus into the provinces of private corporate ownership, the federal government vigorously supported the enormous corporate structures which had emerged during this period (Kolko 1967).

Federal Intervention Needed to Secure Market for Powerful Corporate Capitalists

Kolko has criticized the validity of Weberian assumptions about the increasing efficiency of the large-scale corporate enterprise, and the Marxian belief in the inexorable centralization of capital on the basis of market forces alone, for the study of American economic development. He points out, for example, that some early finance-capitalists, primarily interested in maximum, short-range profit-taking through mergers, had watered their stock and replaced competent corporation administrators. Others were insensitive to the new innovations and opportunities developing within the economy. Because of their inefficient practices, their corporations became highly vulnerable to new, aggressive competitors. Powerful industrialists now needed help. They turned to the federal government to establish governmental policies which would secure their dominating position in the economy as a whole and to make it increasingly difficult for parvenu millionaires to enter into parts of the economy controlled by the established upper class (*ibid.*: 25–56, 57–68).[6] Kolko's work suggests, therefore, that without the cooperation of the state, the relations between the competitive and the oligopolistic sectors of the economy would not have been stabilized on a long-term basis.

By the end of the last century, the basic industries, including steel, meat packing, transportation, and power, had become firmly established. By that time, the broad contemporary outlines of American upper-class relations had emerged, and during the present century these relations have not been substantially altered. Having merged with the older landed and business leaders, the new manufacturing and financial elites became the most powerful single assemblage of men representing the new upper class—the men who determined the general policy of the federal government. During the years 1890–1940 the leaders of the largest business and financial institutions directed the development of new federal regulating agencies. In this process, the integrative functions of the automatic price-making market mechanism were seriously restricted by administrative bodies of private corporations. While free competitive relations still influenced certain aspects of the market, the corporate and federal regulating agencies strongly curtailed these influences in other parts of the economy.

Recapping these early years, it has been shown that the heads of large corporations separated themselves into opposing camps of "conservative," laissez-faire liberals and "progressive," corporate liberals. The corporate-liberal capitalists eventually underwrote the new doctrines and legitimations which had emerged among a rising generation of liberal intellectuals. These intellectuals, as we shall see, had begun to diverge markedly from the established schools of laissez-faire liberal thought in advance of the emergence of the opposing camps within the national ruling class.

NOTES

1. For an example of the abortive character of the black capitalism movement see Ofari's (1970) discussion of the Garvey movement.

2. Neither the populists nor the progressives ever succeeded in effectively curbing the growth of monopolies and monopoly trusts in the United States, in spite of the Sherman (antitrust) Act.

3. These historians, in addition to Williams, include among others Kolko (1967), Weinstein (1968), and Sklar (1960).

4. Their corporations, for example, continued to enforce the vicious antiunion "open door" policies which had been long justified by the laissez-faire doctrine of free labor: these so-called progressives did not actually practice accommodation with labor unions until these unions became powerful enough to force an accommodation. (Foner 1964:78–110)

5. Foner (1964:110) states, for example, that the NCF "united A.F. of L. officialdom and powerful financial interests against all aggressive labor leadership in the United States. The A.F. of L. became a 'Morgan Partner' in attacking radicalism wherever it appeared." Weinstein (1968) describes the repressive role of the NCF in regard to the mass media and educational institutions.

6. For a modern parallel see Sweezy and Magdoff, "The Merger Movement: A Study in Power" (1969).

CHAPTER 19

The Intelligentsia and the Intellectuals

Intellectuals, Ideological Categories, and Programmatic Ideas

Liberalism is neither monolithic nor immutable: there are no suprahuman mandates which require that all liberal doctrines have to be eternally fixed and consistent with each other. During highly critical periods in the ongoing development of ideological thought, new doctrines conflict with the old ones, and complex patterns of internal dissension divide persons who are committed to the same general goals. The formative years were such a complicated and critical period in the development of liberalism. At that time, clearly divergent trends in liberal thought became manifest in all walks of life and corporate liberalism emerged as a modal trend even among members of the American ruling class.

Such corporate liberal or "progressive" capitalists as Andrew Carnegie did not actually formulate the new liberal proposals for solving national problems. Instead, these men enabled corporate-liberal *intellectuals* to present their solutions to economic problems before audiences of liberal businessmen and liberal labor leaders. Neither did the "progressive" capitalists create the abstract ruling ideas (e.g., reform Darwinism) during the formative years. These ideas were originally formulated by highly trained corporate-liberal *intellectuals* who worked, for the most part, in American universities. In some cases, these intellectuals conceived their axiomatic conceptions of man and society decades before these ideas were adopted as common sense corporate-liberal guides to reality in the United States.

For example, John R. Commons, a noted political economist who was active in the National Civic Federation, theorized about the ways in which class consciousness among the American working class could be reduced. In a paper before the American Sociological Society in 1907, he indicated that the closing of the frontier meant the disappearance of opportunities for individual mobility and the consequent rise of class consciousness among workers. In his opinion, it was fortunate that the formation of the great corporations was providing new opportunities for individual mobility.[1] These new opportunities—together with the divisive effects of the national rivalries among the new immigrants—would counter the rising development of class consciousness among the American workers.

Commons' remarks about the relation between mobility and class consciousness did more than illustrate ways of thinking that foreshadowed later perspectives among liberals. He also espoused, among other things, a national labor board which would reconcile industrial conflicts by instituting collective bargaining under government auspices. Although his recommendations were not immediately enacted, they affected later practices. Graham Adams (1966:225–227) describes Commons' ideas and writes, "Eighteen years after [Commons'] original proposal . . . labor unions under the NRA found themselves compelled to formulate codes for collective bargaining under government administration."

Other proposals by the early corporate-liberal intellectuals also were not translated into practice immediately. Nevertheless, these corporate-liberal ideas clarified the political options which were open to the most powerful decision-makers in American society, and thereby enabled the American ruling class to come to terms advantageously with the increasingly popular demands for the political regulation of American life. In Commons' case, the options involved the political methods by which militant working-class expressions of class contradictions in industry could be resolved without threatening capitalism itself.

The next chapter discusses the institutional conditions which influenced the emergence of corporate-liberal intellectuals like John R. Commons. These conditions include the rise of the modern American university as well as philanthropic foundations and civic organizations. This chapter, however, will first lay the groundwork for distinguishing the differences between these conservative liberal intellectuals and other intellectuals such as the American "free-lance" novelist Jack London (who also lived during the formative years).

In this work, the word "intelligentsia" will be used to classify the aggregate of persons who devote their activities to the formulation of ideas, or to the creation of artistic representations of ideas, or to the application of ideas (e.g., the application of technical knowledge to human affairs).[2] The word "intellectual," on the other hand, refers to those members of the intelligentsia who actively create new conceptions of reality or impart to these conceptions a coherence they would otherwise not possess.[3] In order to discuss further dimensions in the complex meanings of these terms—and to distinguish corporate-liberal intellectuals from other types of intellectuals—it will be necessary to acquaint the reader with the wide variation in these types of persons. When this is done, we will return to the formative years of American sociology.

Varied Members of Intelligentsia

Previous chapters have noted that working-class Jacobins as well as aristocratic monarchists combined their intellectual and political activities during the Enlightenment. The colonists who led the American Revolution were also political-intellectuals. More than half of the men at the Constitutional Convention in 1787, for example, were educated in colleges and universities, and because of this, Merle Curti (1960:29) observes, this convention has been called "the first American brain trust." Some of the founders, like Benjamin Franklin and James Madison, were scientists or historians. Others were schoolmasters, college presidents, or professors. Both the Federalist and the Republican parties were led by men who were as highly accomplished in scholarship as in politics.

In the nineteenth century, however, we find the rapid development of such inclusive words as "intelligentsia." The word "intelligentsia" in its original Russian form referred to the Russian circles of "intelligent or intellectual ones" which were composed of journalists, novelists, philosophers, and artists.[4] The members of these circles, according to Martin Malia (1960) were alienated from political and social institutions and, as a consequence, shared a sense of common identity, a "moral passion," and various points of view which were sharply opposed to traditional Russian perspectives.

The historical roots of these circles reach back to the social ferment following the December Revolt. The Decembrists, who made their unsuccessful bid for power in 1825, were preintellectuals who placed their social ideals above feudal privilege. But the formulation of ideas was not their major concern although they were composed primarily of young educated gentry who were trained in military schools. From the 1830s onwards, the Russian university system was transformed in order to provide educated civil servants for the new Russian state. Malia reports that this system inadvertently converted the "gentry intellectuals" into "intellectuals from the gentry" and refashioned "dilettante ideologues" into "professional writers, critics and professors." These intellectuals opposed military service and were profoundly influenced by the new ideas about man and society being developed by Western European scholars.

Malia further points out that the Russian university introduced the educated gentry to such liberating currents of thought as German philosophical idealism. The university thereby contributed to the formation of a "rootless" younger gentry with no home but their "ideal vision." Simultaneously, university experiences provided the conditions under which noblemen merged with the *raznochintsy* (people of "diverse rank" or "no estate in particular"), which included sons of civil servants, professionals, and clergymen who made their way into the universities by "tutoring, translations and petty journalism." After the new university system came into existence, this heterogeneous population formed social circles, discussion groups, student communes, and cooperative living groups. They developed a collective, intellectual self-identity, and a highly critical attitude toward established institutions and traditions. The objects of intellectual criticism came to include not only superstition and provincialism, but also the aristocracy, the petty bourgeois family, patriarchal tyranny, the church, and the state.

The French intelligentsia, like the Russian, included artists, writers, scholars, and engineers, all of whom were influenced by market relationships as well as by universities and polytechnical schools. Some of them, for example, secured their unstable and marginal existence by free-lance work in the growing market for paintings, sculpture, literary publications, and journals organized around political and economic topics. The anarchic, individualistic attitudes toward social traditions earned for some of these members of the intelligentsia the title of *bohemian:* a variant of the French word for gypsy.

With regard to the "bohemian" artists, César Graña (1964) indicates that "while the Saint-Simonians and the Fourierists attacked the bourgeoisie at the political and economic level, the artistic faction had as its weapons only the 'brush, the lyre, and the chisel.' " With these artistic tools, however, the bohemians repudiated and mocked what was felt to be the narrow materialistic interests of this new and powerful class. In contrast to those men of letters who became wealthy by selling heroic tales of "brave" entrepreneurs whose fortunes were made by enslaving the savage African and taming the wilderness, the bohemian proclaimed that the constant grubbing for money, status, and power had no redeeming features whatsoever. For bohemians, the organization of life according to bourgeois values was neither imaginative, heroic, nor culturally ennobling.

Democratic Individualists in United States Critical of Class Privilege

Both class and market forces converged in the creation of what Schumpeter (1942:145–152) calls "the collective patron" of the free-lance artist and writer; another name for this patron is the *bourgeois public.* This public provided an important precondition for the development of the intelligentsia throughout Europe. But national and regional peculiarities were also factors influencing the emergence of both bohemians and scholars. These latter factors were particularly important in the determination of intellectual climates. National aristocratic traditions, for example, greatly intensified the elitist quality of life which normally permeated the relationships and works of most European intellectual circles during the nineteenth century.

In the United States, however, aristocratic traditions were weakened considerably in regional areas which were dominated by an agrarian, small-production economy. Although tinged, at times, by a distinctive patrician perspective, Americans in these areas developed a tradition called *democratic individualism.* This tradition first emerged in the struggle among American colonists for what was essentially a white democratic polity. Identified finally with Jeffersonian and Jacksonian principles, the tradition was also given literary expression in the works of Emerson, Thoreau, Whitman, and Mark Twain (all of whom were against slavery). After the rise of the abolitionist movement, the tacit racist limits of this tradition were transcended by some of its advocates who truly believed in the direct popular control of the government, and who severely evaluated political institutions in terms of their service to the common man.

Around the turn of the century, American writers influenced by this older democratic tradition—as well as the new populist tradition—published their work in numerous and inexpensive newspapers, pamphlets, journals, and periodicals. The direction these free-lance intellectuals began to take was in sympathetic response to the current critical situation. These intellectuals, therefore, added their voices to the rising urban discontent. Indignantly labeled "muckrakers" (by Theodore Roosevelt), journalists such as Lincoln Steffens, Ida M. Tarbell, David G. Philips, and others began to publish systematic exposures of corrupt political machines, land frauds, and harmful practices in the food and drug industries. They also centered their fire on fraudulent stock-market manipulations by finance capitalists. They excoriated the "public be damned" attitude of the industrial robber barons and raked the monopolies and monopoly trusts with their scathing criticism.

Jack London's Indictment of "Managing Class"

Simultaneous with the muckrakers, such writers as Theodore Dreiser and Jack London began to publish compelling descriptions of the lives of working people in capitalist nations. A notable work of this kind was Jack London's *People of the Abyss.* Dressing himself in the clothing befitting an unemployed "down-and-out" workingman in Liverpool, England, London lived among the subproletarians who desperately searched for work but could not find steady employment. From his sensitive observations of interpersonal relations and by recording personal conversations, London illustrated the degree to which "the people of the abyss" aided each other in spite of the extraordinary deprivation confronting their everyday existence. His ethnographic observations revealed the compassionate and human qualities of the persons he met, as well as the degree to which their spirit was perpetually menaced by the oppressive poverty which haunted their daily lives.

London wrote other works that were flawed by the racist attitudes so prevalent among West Coast writers and workers (as well as certain sociologists). *The People of the Abyss,* however, was a powerful indictment of "the managing class" which oppressed the working people of England. In order to make this indictment, London (1903:311–317) contrasted this managing class with the primitive Innuit tribe living along the banks of the Yukon River. The Innuit were regarded as an example of "savage folk" [5] who shared their food, shelter, and clothing with each other no matter how little they possessed. London argued that the social organization among these primitive people was *superior* to modern civilization. He *(ibid.*:312) stated, for example, that the Innuit had "their times of plenty and times of famine. In good times they feast; in bad times they die of starvation. But starvation as a chronic condition, present with a large number of them all the time, is a thing unknown." On the other hand, he pointed out, in England the food eaten by "the managing class" as well as "the wine it drinks, the shows it makes, and the fine clothes it wears, are challenged by eight million mouths which have never enough to feed them, and by twice the eight million bodies which have never been sufficiently clothed and housed" *(ibid:*317).

London used participant-observation methods in order to arrive at an understanding of human relations in Liverpool and, in our opinion, he succeeded in producing an outstanding ethnographic work.[6] But *The People of the Abyss* never received any credit in professional histories of urban ethnography in the United States. Perhaps some of the reasons for this are related to the fact that London was a nonprofessional who became a socialist around 1905. Perhaps it was also related to London's *(ibid.*:306–307) belief that social reformers and intellectual "savants" who descended upon slum areas with their "college settlements, missions, charities and what not," were *unequivocal* failures. He believed that in spite of their sincerity, "They do not understand the simple sociology of Christ, yet they come to the miserable and the despised with the pomp of social redeemers." He pointed out that in spite of their perseverance, they have accomplished absolutely nothing "beyond relieving an infinitesimal fraction of the misery and collecting a certain amount of data which might otherwise have been more scientifically and less expensively collected. . . ." "As someone has said," London caustically concluded, "they do everything for the poor except get off their backs."

NOTES

1. Commons (1907:142) stated, for example, "It need not be repeated that a potent reason for the persistent class conflict of the past twenty years is the closing up of the great outlet for agitators, the frontier. But the division of labor [in the great corporations] offers a substitute outlet in the form of promotion." Commons' ideas were derived, in part, from the works of the historian, Frederick Jackson Turner.

2. Members of the intelligentsia therefore would include novelists, artists, journalists, poets, librarians, and scientists. Others representing this category would be corporation managers, city planners, and the various employees who work with ideas in planning and directing human activity in political and economic institutions.

3. The differences among the intelligentsia do not have to be mutually exclusive. For example, some artists are intellectuals and some intellectuals are technicians.

4. Martin Malia (1960) indicates that the word *"intelligentsia"* was introduced in the 1860s by a minor novelist named Boborykin.

5. Sociologists like Weatherly and Ogburn, as we see in later chapters, referred to the "savage" nature of primitive men and alleged that human nature among modern men was not far removed from a bestial state.

6. In fact, even though London's work was written as early as 1903 by a journalist-novelist rather than a social scientist, it surpasses by far every one of the professional works produced by the famous school of urban ethnography at the University of Chicago during the twenties and thirties.

CHAPTER 20

The Hegemonic Intellectuals

Conservative German University Savants

Jack London's sarcasm was directed at social reformers and university "savants" who were quite different from the alienated Russian intelligentsia, the romantic French bohemians, and the democratic American individualist or populist intellectuals. These reformers and savants, on the other hand, shared many similarities with the reformist "socialists of the chair" in the German universities and it may be informative, because of this, to briefly mention an essay by Golo Mann (1960) about the German intelligentsia.

Mann (*ibid.:*459) writes that in the early nineteenth century Germany scarcely tolerated its intelligentsia. Although there were some bohemians like Heinrich Heine, "a free lance publicist could hardly exist [in Germany] until late in the 19th century." In the first half of the century, idealist and materialist German philosophies (embodied in writings by such men as Hegel and Feuerbach) did play a dynamic role in prompting intellectuals to ask critical questions about the nature of their society. But, as Mann observes, "the reactionary state would not hire Feuerbach and the public would not read him." Intellectuals like Karl Marx emigrated to find economic support and surcease from the government censor. The German intelligentsia were often dependent on princely patronage, the university, or the office of "librarian, preacher, tutor, theatre-manager and the like." The university was quite reactionary both before and after the unsuccessful Revolution of 1848 (which has been called "the Revolution of the Intellectuals" [*ibid.:*461]). By the second half of the century, Bismarck had completely "triumphed" over Hegel.

In this reactionary climate, the university scholar generally felt that only experts could deal adequately with economic or political crises. He did not feel that social problems could be solved by serving mass movements which were interested in the establishment of democratic social institutions. The university scholar, moreover, became little more than a bureaucratic agent of the state and, if he had to deal with politics, "it was the natural thing to do so in the interests of the state, to back up with historical arguments, say, the German mission of Prussia if he were teaching at a Prussian university" (*ibid.:*460). In France and England, academic scholars competed with the independent intellectuals and, in fact, "the great novelist, the successful man of letters far outshone the scholar." In Germany, however, "the university enjoyed something like a monopoly" of respectable intellectuals.

147

Mann's observations deal with Germany while London's sarcastic remarks pertain to England. Mann's statements above, furthermore, are concerned with academics while London's also pointed to representatives of religious and philanthropic institutions. Both of these writers, however, appear to be sharply aware of the politically conservative roles played by university scholars.

This chapter and the next describe some of the material relationships which influenced the development of these conservative members of the American intelligentsia. These chapters, moreover, indicate some of the differences between the academic and the free-lance writer; in the process, we will focus on additional factors which gave rise to the American sociologists of the chair. In order to discuss these factors, however, it will be helpful to first introduce the reader to Antonio Gramsci's analytic concepts of "the organic intellectual" and "social hegemony." Let us begin with his notion of "the organic intellectual."

The Organic Intellectual

Antonio Gramsci was an Italian Marxist whose insights into the sociology of the intellectual were scattered throughout his political essays and "prison notebooks." [1] In these essays and notes, he indicated that in every country the behavior of intellectuals had been radically altered by the development of capitalism. Industrial capitalism, in particular, had generated a new type of intellectual, "the technical organizer and specialist of applied science" (Gramsci 1957:42–43). Gramsci, like Marx, regarded the means and relations of capitalist production to be the material bases for the development of the occupational characteristics of these new intellectuals. These intellectuals were considered an expression of the general division of labor between mental and manual labor, as well as the "local forms" (e.g., occupational specialties) which characterized this division in industrial societies. [2] In comparison to other types of intellectuals, therefore, organic intellectuals were directly integrated into the corporate structures of capitalist societies. [3]

The archetype of the organic intellectual, in Gramsci's view, is the intelligent capitalist who structures the perspectives and the activities of workers, buyers, and sellers according to his own entrepreneurial interests. Furthermore, "if not all capitalists, at least an elite of them must have the capacity for organizing society in general, in all its complex organisms of duties up to the State organism, because of the need to create the most favorable conditions for the expansion of their own class . . ." (ibid.:118). This capacity also included the ability to choose "specialized employees" who could be entrusted with "this activity of organizing the general relations outside of their [capitalistic] enterprises." Gramsci called these employees "officers of the ruling class."

What social functions were fulfilled by these "officers of the ruling class?"

Generally, they were "the subordinate functions" of "social hegemony" and "political government." Social hegemony, in this context, refers generally to the process of securing the "spontaneous," that is, *voluntary,* consent "given by the great masses of the population to the direction imprinted on social life by the . . . ruling class." [4] Political government, on the other hand, involves the coercive apparatus of the state. This apparatus, based on bourgeois legality, ensures the discipline of those groups which "do not 'consent' either actively or passively" to the rule of the bourgeoisie. In Gramsci's view, this coercive apparatus was particularly "constituted for the whole of society in anticipation of moments of crises in command and direction when spontaneous consent diminishes" *(ibid.:*124).

The Concept of Social Hegemony

In developing the concept of hegemony, Gramsci went beyond the perception of the organic intellectual as a person who simply organizes, verbalizes, or generalizes the immediate social relations of capitalist production. He also considered organic intellectuals to be necessary for the ascendency of a new ruling class because they included persons who provided this class with its sense of homogeneity and a consciousness of its function, not only in economic fields but also in the social and political fields. In class societies, for example, these intellectuals encouraged rulers to move beyond their own crude economic interests. They conceptualized the relationships between the struggle for ideological domination and the struggle for economic and political power. They also clarified the degree to which political coalitions were required for the maintenance of a stable social order. [5] The ideas which emerge as a result of all of these activities contribute to the establishment of social hegemony.

A number of scholars have provided interpretations of Gramsci's concept of hegemony which illustrate different facts of this complex idea and each interpretation gives it successive clarity. Gwyn Williams (1960:587) writes that hegemony is

an order in which a certain way of life and thought is dominant, in which one concept of reality is diffused throughout society in all its institutional and private manifestations, informing with its spirit all taste, morality, customs, religious and political principles, and all social relations, particularly in their intellectual and moral connotations. [6]

John M. Cammett has also interpreted the concept of hegemony. To lay the groundwork for his interpretation, he reviews various assumptions which appear to underlie Gramsci's view of hegemonic processes. First, Gramsci felt that a ruling class cannot achieve control of the institutions of the state without initially asserting its claims within the realm of ideas. "The founding of a ruling class," Gramsci wrote in this regard, "is equivalent to the founding of a *Weltanshauung.*" Second, Gramsci maintained that these ruling-class ideas conditioned members of the subordinate classes to voluntarily support the political and economic institutions which ensure ruling-class domination. Third, Gramsci used a Hegelian distinction between civil society and political society (civil society is "the totality of private institutions" while political society is "made up of public institutions and organs of coercion"). He suggested that the voluntary relations which supported a ruling class were most evident in civil society. As a result, he noted, "a robust structure of civil society" supports the institutions of the state, particularly in Western nations.[7]

Cammett then interprets the concept of hegemony on the basis of these Gramscian assumptions about the hegemonic functions of ruling ideas and the politically significant impact of certain voluntary relations in civil society. Cammett (1967:204) states that hegemony logically refers to "the preponderance, obtained by consent rather than force, of one class or group over other classes. Hegemony is therefore achieved by the institutions of civil society."

In addition, H. Wolpe has clarified the concept of hegemony in light of other ideas put forward by Gramsci. These ideas refer to the lack of congruence between the *theoretical awareness* of actions and the *actual consequences* of actions. In Wolpe's analysis, the phrase, "theoretical awareness" apparently refers to hegemonically determined awareness which mystifies the consequences of the profound social contradictions inherent in class societies. "Gramsci argues," according to Wolpe [1970:270], "that the hegemonic theoretical consciousness contradicts the real consequences and means of action; it, therefore, disguises a reality which if its 'true' significance were present to the consciousness, would result in its rejection." Wolpe *(ibid.:*271) then states:

For Gramsci "hegemony" refers to the set of ideas which are dominant as a consequence of a particular structure of power. More precisely, as Williams has pointed out, "hegemony" implies a control which corresponds to power conceived of in terms of a ruling class. There is clearly an implication here of "hegemony" as a legitimating mask over the real structure of power.

If Gramsci's concept of hegemony is used to clarify the role of liberalism during the formative years of American sociology, then it can be said that hegemony symbolizes the social process which enabled the employment of liberal ideas for the purpose of ensuring stable forms of bourgeois domination. These liberal ideas masked the real structure of power in society and prevented the masses of people from realizing that the profound social contradictions in capitalist society made it impossible to utilize liberal solutions in order to eliminate such outstanding social problems as imperialist wars, economic exploitation, racial inequality, and sexual inequality.

Further, during the formative years, various institutional relationships, represented by the mass media, the schools, and other economic and political institutions, inculcated a hegemonic liberal consciousness in the population at large. These institutions, concentrating on the relationships within civil so-

150

ciety, reinforced ruling-class domination on the basis of the "spontaneous" consent of the masses.

Hegemonic Intellectuals

The organic intellectual plays an important role in organizing the institutional relationships which *maintain* social hegemony. Before we discuss this further, however, it should be noted that among the many myths in modern social science, there is one which contradicts this assumption by asserting that learned intellectuals are generally critical of established institutions at any given time. This imputation (of a socially critical standpoint) is so ubiquitous that it is even used as a defining criterion for the term intellectual itself.[8] This chapter has indicated, however, that such an unqualified imputation is highly misleading. In fact, social scientists like the British Marxist, Ralph Miliband (1969:259–260), have rightfully pointed out, for example, that *most* intellectuals during any given period are conservators of political and economic systems; their prime function is not to undermine established institutions but to maintain their existence. Among these intellectuals, some are reformers who criticize specific institutional relationships in order to preserve the general scheme of things; but even these reformers are in the minority. (By and large, intellectuals function actively [with little desire for radical change] in the service of those who control their livelihood.)

Many intellectuals, therefore, are involved in occupational activities which support ideological hegemony. Their functions in this regard are fulfilled in a very complex manner and involve the systematic indoctrination of the population as a whole through churches and schools; the reinforcement of these ideas and doctrines via the mass media; and the continuous modification of ruling ideas in institutions of higher learning.[9]

Gramsci's writings clarify some of the economic and political relationships which have generated these intellectuals. We will employ his concept of hegemony and classify the intellectuals who actively formulate or systematize ruling ideas as "hegemonic intellectuals." The phrase "hegemonic intellectuals" will also be used to signify the intellectuals who use scientific and literary methods to provide empirical and moral justifications for hegemonic ideas.[10] This phrase, therefore, classifies those intellectual members of the intelligentsia who have a very direct political and economic significance for the development and the maintenance of political economies.[11]

NOTES

1. Gramsci was imprisoned by Mussolini during the 1920s and 1930s, and died soon after his release. The reader is directed to John Cammett's biographical work: *Antonio Gramsci and the Origins of Italian Communism* (1967) for factual material on the life of Gramsci as well as an overview of his writings. For English translations of Gramsci's works see, for example: Antonio Gramsci, *The Modern Prince and Other Writings* (1957) and *The Open Marxism of Antonio Gramsci,* translated and annotated by Carl

Marzani (1957) and, finally, Antonio Gramsci (1971) *Selections from the Prison Notebooks.*

2. Cammett (1967:202) points out that in Gramsci's view, "new categories of [organic intellectuals] are, in fact, created by 'every social group that originates in the fulfillment of an essential task of economic production!' "

3. John M. Cammett (1967:271) notes, for example, "For Gramsci, organic intellectuals are those specialists attached to particular productive groups in society, for purposes of technical-administrative direction."

4. This consent, according to Gramsci, "comes into existence 'historically' from the 'prestige' (and hence from the trust) accruing to the ruling class from its position and function in the world of production. . . ."

5. See Gramsci (1957:118, 122, 204) for illustrations of his views on these organic intellectuals.

6. The phrase "one concept of reality" in this statement refers either to reality as it is defined by the ruling class ideology or to aspects of this ideology, such as the "ruling ideas" which legitimate ruling class relationships.

7. Because of the degree to which the state was supported by voluntary associations, Gramsci claimed that the working classes could not achieve political power without first achieving victory in civil society. "Hence," Gramsci concluded, "the struggle for hegemony, for cultural and moral predominance, is the main task for Marxists in the advanced countries of the West" (Cammett 1967:206).

8. Carl Becker (1936:93) states, for example, "During the last three hundred years . . . there has emerged a new class of learned men, successors to the priests and scribes, whose function is to increase rather than to preserve knowledge, to *undermine* rather than to stabilize custom and social authority" (our emphasis).

9. Miliband (1969:219–261) presents a clear and penetrating discussion of the role of the mass media, churches, and schools (including institutions of higher learning) in the achievement of hegemony.

10. In this work, the phrase "hegemonic intellectuals" is consequently defined as the intellectuals who formulate, systematize, and justify hegemonic ideas. Hegemonic ideas are interpreted broadly. They include, for example, analytic strategies such as liberal-functionalist strategies, which are necessary for the formulation of hegemonic metatheories and theories.

11. Thus, hegemonic intellectuals are but one part of the broader populations of the intellectuals and the intelligentsia. Furthermore, hegemonic ideas represent only a portion of the total culture within any given society. In capitalist societies, as John Fraser (1971) indicates, culture is not a private monopoly of the bourgeoisie. There are nonhegemonic as well as counterhegemonic members of the intelligentsia. Finally, a single intellectual may produce hegemonic and nonhegemonic ideas during the course of his lifetime. In some cases the same literary or scientific work may contain examples of both types of ideas.

CHAPTER 21

The Technocratic Liberal Intellectuals

Technocratic Intellectuals

In Gramsci's analysis of the "organic intellectuals," the word "organic" appears to signify, minimally, the authoritative, deliberative, and integrative functions of intellectual workers. These intellectuals have an impact on the ways in which capitalist institutions are generated or maintained and they are, therefore, *politically significant* members of the intelligentsia.

There are various types of modern workers who are closely akin to the meaning of Gramsci's general category of intellectuals. One type might be the expert who applies technical-scientific knowledge to human affairs—an expert who is known more simply as a *technocrat*. The technocrat is more than a highly trained technician because he has the effective power to exert a direct or indirect influence on political policy.

The word *technocracy,* therefore, also suggests the element of political power. It has been defined, for example, as "the political situation in which effective power belongs to technologists termed technocrats." [1] This word was popularized by a utopian movement of the same name during the thirties. [2] The leaders of the technocratic movement proposed that society should be ruled by engineers and other "experts" who, by virtue of their specialized competence, would effectively supplant the traditional politician.

Jean Meynaud (1969:12) points out that widespread and popular use of such terms as "technocrat" and "technocracy" has been favored by "the rapid decline of the parliamentary system, allied with the myth of an omnipotent bureaucracy." He further observes that "the desire to exchange politics for technology, and to 'depoliticize' the larger problems of national life are both ideas which enjoy quite a large amount of support today" (*ibid.:*14). But Meynaud objects to the undemocratic implications of these popular ideas and portrays technocracy "as the rise to power of those who possess technical knowledge or ability, to the detriment of the traditional politician." The substitution of the technologist for the politician, in his opinion, ultimately tends to erode "the power of suffrage and the trust of the people" (*ibid.:*29).

Meynaud's observations are timely. However, he seems to take for granted that "traditional politicians" actually represent the masses of people in bourgeois democracies. This assumption, in our opinion, overlooks the degree to which both the politician and the technocrat have functioned within undemocratic institutions in these societies.

Historically, politicians have not generally served as genuine representatives of the common people. Even in bourgeois democracies, these particular persons have functioned largely as representatives of white-middle- and upper-class groups. Some of them, to be sure, have mediated between labor and capital. Others have been sensitive to the needs of working-class groups. But these politicians have generally remained well within the limits established by corporate and private capital. It is not surprising, therefore, to note that the inordinate and decisive control exerted by capital over political officials, as well as technocratic functionaries, has been repeatedly demonstrated by studies of the domestic and foreign policies of the American government.

For example, in spite of the growth of technocratic elites within capitalist economies, the decisive power to determine long-term corporate policies still lies in the hands of the owners of capital. [3] These owners, furthermore, also play a decisive role in determining the long-term trends in both the legislative and administrative branches of government. Their influence has provided the limiting factors which prevent politicians and technocrats from adequately serving the great mass of humanity in American society. Because of this corporate influence, politicians and technocrats attempted to systematically abort the mass movements for participatory democracy which developed during the 1960s.[4] These systematic attempts were made because the movements began to conflict directly with entrenched military and industrial corporate interests.

The diverse functional differences between the traditional politician (e.g., the legislator) and the modern technocrat (e.g., the city manager) are extremely significant because they reflect the extraordinary impact of the evolution of the capitalist division of labor on modern industrial societies, as well as the influence of the great corporations and the modern "corporate state." But an examination of the traditional politician and the modern technocrat admits certain similarities when they are placed within the larger relationships which have characterized the epoch of capitalism from its very beginning. These historical relationships involve the profound contradiction between the socially organized relations of production and the private control of the means of production. This contradiction is expressed in the class struggle. This struggle is at the root of the equally profound political division in capitalist societies between the rulers and the ruled, irrespective of whether the rulers to whom we refer include the owners of capital, or their political and technocratic officers. Consequently both technocrats and traditional politicians are instruments of class domination.

From a Marxian view, there is no more distinguishing characteristic which can be used to define the political functions of the technocratic role than those elitist and antidemocratic activities which attempt to contain the class struggle in all its manifestations. The technocrat, therefore, is not simply an administrator who applies expert knowledge to human affairs. Nor is he merely a technologist who usurps the power of the traditional politician. In capitalist societies, the technocrat is crucially identified by the fact that he institutes administrative and scientific technologies so as to maintain the basic institutional and class structures which make modern capitalism what it is. In socialist societies, the technocrat, where he exists, performs an analogous role by either stimulating new social-class differentiations or maintaining the old, under the control of a political oligarchy.

Hegemonic and Technocratic
Corporate-Liberal Intellectuals

Technocratic intellectuals have earned their livelihoods in a variety of social, economic, and political institutions. Technocratic administrators, for example, have functioned in economic corporations and governmental bureaus. Administrative-consultants, on the other hand, have been employed by universities, research institutions, and private foundations. Furthermore, the administrative-consultants themselves have been supplied with ideological and technical concepts which were formulated by general theorists and researchers employed by these same institutions.

However, neither the technocratic social traditions produced by these new "organic intellectuals"—nor the institutions which provided these intellectuals with a material base—have emerged "full grown" at any given period in the history of Western nations. The state, the university, and the philanthropic foundations have evolved from prior institutional relations. In Europe these relations were historically aligned with the church, the landed gentry, and the aristocracy. In the United States, prior to the formative years, these institutions were supported by various religious denominations, independent farmers, and small as well as large businessmen. The religious, aristocratic, liberal, and even populist traditions which characterized these institutional relations in the United States have had an important impact on the ways in which technocratic intellectual employees initially perceived their relationships with the broader society around them.

Historical traditions created largely by free-lance artists and independent writers have also influenced the ways in which the technocratic intellectuals have perceived their relations with the broader society. In some cases, these historical relations were antagonistic to business and commercial interests. During the formative years this antagonism was heightened by the turbulent populist, "progressive," and socialist movements.

The complex relations between this variety of historical factors and the development of technocratic traditions in the United States defies any simple attempt to equate technocratic writings with corporate liberalism alone. Socialists, for example, also produced technocratic writings. The work of Thorstein Veblen, who became a non-Marxist socialist, illustrates this fact because he proposed that a soviet of production engineers and consulting economists would eventually take over the reins of the economy from the absentee owners (i.e., the finance capitalists). Socialists like Veblen believed that the key to a socialist society merely resided in industrial canons of efficient production which were free of "vested" pecuniary interests.

On the other hand, it is still possible, in spite of the variation in technocratic thought, to separate out and identify the emergence of an integrated body of analytic ideas that were based on technocratic and hegemonic *corporate-liberal* conceptions of man and society. However, the ways in which this integrated body of analytic ideas were first expressed have been complicated by the added historical influence of counterhegemonic and countertechnocratic traditions. In some cases, for example, early corporate-liberal scholars surrounded their hegemonic and technocratic ideas with an individualistic or populist rhetoric which masked the true, analytic dimensions of their writings. For instance, some of the founders of American sociology, like Lester Ward and Edward A. Ross, utilized the populist libertarian rhetoric to justify their reformist and analytic points of view. But Parts Six and Seven show that these scholars merely preempted the libertarian rhetoric for justificatory purposes: this rhetoric did not shape either their *programmatic* or their *analytic* categories. Ward and Ross, as we shall see, were respectively influenced by the populist stands on (1) the nationalization of the railroads and (2) the "silver issue." But the main ideological thrust of their writings, as we will show, was determined less by populism than by the corporate-liberal technocratic ethos that was beginning to emerge among American intellectuals toward the end of the last century.

The difference in attitude toward the *civil bureaucracy* was a prime indicator of the deep chasm which separated the democratic individualists who wrote in the populist spirit, from those intellectuals who reflected the new technocratic ethos whether or not they utilized populist rhetoric. On the one hand, the technocratic reformers, who profoundly influenced the development of American social services and social science disciplines, had high hopes for such schemes as the city management plan and civil service reform. The populists, in contrast, "took over the liberal demand for honest, efficient political leaders, but the reformed government was to be no reflection of upper-income, better-educated America." The notable populist platform created in Omaha, Nebraska, for example, did not emphasize civil service reform because "it smacked too much of establishing a permanent ruling group and contradicted the Jacksonian faith that any well-intentioned American was good enough to carry on government for his fellows" (Goldman 1952:48–49).[5] The populists, therefore, were not interested in creating a new technocratic elite which would strongly mediate the relations between common people and the daily operation of the government. They were already dissatisfied with the degree to which economic and political power had become centralized in the United States. Consequently, they were not about to advocate the creation of a new center of power which would generally serve the "vested interests" rather than the common people.

In sum, the coming chapters will point out that the main ideological thrust of the writings by most of the outstanding early sociologists was corporate liberal and technocratic. As indicated, the institutional foundations for the development of the technocratic ethos were grounded in the operations of such agencies as the modern university, public commissions, philanthropic foundations, research and planning institutes, and governmental bureaus. These institutions began to employ professional analysts and researchers who were neither "men of leisure," "free-lance professionals," nor political functionaries. Nor did they necessarily write for popular consumption. They were, instead, part of a growing, disciplined, bureaucratic army of professionals who were employed to directly manage or aid in the management of social institutions.

Thus, the subsequent chapters will focus on one of the technocratic groups of hegemonic intellectuals which emerged during the formative years. This group was composed entirely of those elite members of the sociological profession who contributed to the dominant theories emerging at that time. These members, at first glance, may not appear to be a technocratic elite because they were generally not involved in the direct management of institu-

156

tions (much less economic institutions). However, the analysis of their writings in the coming chapters will show that these men were committed, above all, to the attainment of stable, rationalized, and harmonious national economic relationships.

The attitudes of members of this group toward the significant growth of militant labor, socialist, and other movements, and their violent repression by armed forces employed by private corporations and the government, is a case in point. The use of armed force was particularly noticeable in such sectors of the economy as the copper, coal, steel, and railroad industries which were being rapidly developed by gigantic corporations (Adamic 1968). The following chapters will show that the men who founded American sociology were very much aware that even the use of armed repression could not fully guarantee the stability of the capitalist system (to which they were totally committed) under the prevailing economic conditions. They also recognized that an uncompromising attitude toward the labor movement might drive labor completely into the hands of the socialists and anarchists. Therefore, within the framework of liberal-syndicalist theories of society, an industrial democracy based on "equity" between capital and labor became increasingly construed as consistent with the basic interests of capital under the new conditions. However, this particular solution to the problem of industrial integration could no longer legitimate a philosophy of free labor. Instead, these sociologists justified the organization of labor and the determination of the price of labor through collective bargaining.

The thoroughgoing technocratic quality of the early works by outstanding sociologists will also be discussed in the chapters to come. But in light of the foregoing discussion of hegemony, it should be kept in mind, while reviewing the social and political contents of the early writings, that the management of economic relationships could no longer be restricted to the rationalization of human relations at the *point of production* alone,—social and political interrelations had to be considered. An example of this extended view lies in the usages of the concept of efficiency. These usages began to be expanded and generalized far beyond their original references to relations in production. The sociologists who referred to the "efficient" and productive adjustment of great masses of people, thought in terms of an adjustment to the political economy as a whole. They envisioned new forms of integration between political and economic institutions which precluded a managerial perspective that was concerned solely with *economic* integration, to the exclusion of *social* or *political* forms of integration. The new forms of integration, therefore, encouraged approaches which encompassed all of society. These approaches received their most abstract expression in the writings of the sociologists who specialized in social problems. The focus on these problems was generally geared to justifying policies aimed at the comprehensive moral management of human beings. And the intellectuals who proposed these policies fulfilled, to the best of their abilities, the authoritative, deliberative, and integrative functions described by Gramsci.

157

NOTES

1. This definition, by the *Dictionnaire de la langue philosophique,* is quoted in Jean Meynaud's (1969:29) *Technocracy.*

2. For an analysis of the "technocratic" movement, see Eisner (1967).

3. Paul A. Baran and Paul M. Sweezy (1966) discuss this issue in great detail. Their work also contains a refutation of the "managerial thesis" which claims that corporate managers, rather than the owners of capital, determine long-term corporate policies.

4. For insights into the role of politicians and technocrats during this period, see Marvin E. Gettleman and David Mermelstein (1967).

5. Goldman has noted that the populists only wanted the civil service to operate as a watchdog over the government ownership of the railroads. He also added (1952:48–49) that "generally, the [populist] platforms had ignored the merit system, and one [populist] document flatly opposed it with the Jacksonian query: 'If this is not the people's government, whose government is it?' "

BOOK II

THE
TRANSITIONAL
FIGURES

INTRODUCTION TO

BOOK II

C. Wright Mills' Analysis of Early Developments in Sociological Thought

As one of the few sociologists to consistently point out the negative effects of liberalism on the development of sociology in the United States, C. Wright Mills stated (1959:85) that in the United States, "liberalism has been the political common denominator of virtually all social study as well as the source of virtually all public rhetoric and ideology." Mills further noted (*ibid.*:84) that in the late nineteenth century, liberal reformers organized the American Social Science Association in order to apply "science" to social problems without resorting to explicitly political tactics. The social science movement which this organization epitomized had run its course by the early decades of the twentieth century. At that time its larger concerns to improve the welfare of lower-class people were transformed into the scattered and limited concerns of social work, associated charities, child welfare, and prison reform.

Mills (*ibid.*:90) claimed that during the first few decades of the twentieth century, sociologists developed a "practical sociology of milieu" which aspired to a "democratic opportunism." Instead of conducting a critical analysis of the political framework of American capitalism, sociologists identified themselves with law or administration and perceived the everyday troubles of men and women from a bureaucratic point of view. Like judges, social workers, mental hygienists, teachers, and local reformers, sociologists thought in terms of individual "situations," and limited their social outlook to existing standards. "Their professional work," Mills stated, "tends to train for an occupational incapacity to rise above a series of 'cases.' " The kinds of opposing notions that reflected their narrow perspective were "adjustment" and "maladjustment." These considerations, Mills added, were "in effect a propaganda for conformity to those norms and traits ideally associated with the small-town middle class."

Mills (*ibid.*:4) also indicated that biological metaphors such as "adaptation" and its entourage "of such socially bare terms as 'existence' and 'survival' . . . often makes evident the acceptance of the ends and the means of the smaller community milieu." Armed with this complement of words, sociologists suggested ameliorative measures without considering "whether or not certain groups or individuals, caught in underprivileged situations, can possibly achieve these goals without modification of the institutional framework as a whole." Mills also asserted that "the ideal man of the earlier generation of sociologists, and of liberal practicality in general, is 'socialized.' Often this means that he is the ethical opposite of 'selfish.' " A "socialized" individual is somewhat extroverted, a member of community organizations; he conforms to conventional morality, comes from an unbroken home, is modestly ambitious, and does not scramble after the big money. The virtues of this adjusted man ". . . correspond with the expected norms of the smaller, independent middle class verbally living out Protestant ideals in the small towns of America" (ibid.:91, also Mills 1943).

During the thirties, forties, and fifties of this century a new perspective emerged alongside of the "older practicality." Using the research in industrial sociology as a prime example, Mills stated: "Liberalism has become less of a reform movement than the administration of social services in a welfare state; sociology has lost its reforming push; its tendencies toward fragmentary problems and scattered causation have been conservatively turned to the use of corporation, army and state." As large bureaucracies have become more dominant in the various parts of society, "the meaning of 'practical' has shifted; that which is thought to serve the purpose of these great institutions is held to be 'practical' " (ibid.:92).

Mills was one of the most trenchant critics of North American sociology and during his lifetime very few members of the profession could match his powerful humanistic grasp of contemporary social problems. On the other hand, although his conception of the relation between liberalism and sociology is correct in its main outlines (and there is no question but that the major founders of the profession came from small midwestern towns and were the sons of clergymen, or clergymen themselves), small-town, Protestant, middleclass ideals may not be the most general factors influencing the shape of early sociology. Examination of the relationship between early sociological ideas and such intellectual developments as the growing defence of the role of the state, American expansionism, and antagonism toward laissez-faire and socialist doctrines, suggests that there were far more general and influential conditions shaping the early development of the field. These conditions involved the increasing class conflict, the economic instability, the further development of domestic and foreign forms of imperialism, the interpenetration of corporate and state forms of monopoly capitalism, and the rise of socialist movements. These conditions sustained the new sociological notions of "race conflict," "social control," "interest group," and "assimilation" as well as the older Spencerian interpretations of "survival" and "adaptation." They also structured the direction of the new developments in sociological thought toward the end of the last century.

In 1965, for example, Dusky Lee Smith noted that major founders of American sociology, such as William Graham Sumner, Lester Ward, Franklin Henry Giddings, Edward Alsworth Ross, and Ulysses Grant Weatherly, did not subscribe to radical intellectual traditions that were well established in the Western world, such as socialism, Marxism, and anarchism. Furthermore, with the exception of Sumner, the "famous paladin of Social Darwinism," these men were in favor of many of the social, economic, and political patterns now associated with "corporate capitalism." While they differed as to "how much of the old and new orders to retain and reject," Smith (1965:402–403) observes, "they were in accord as to the general direction in which change should occur."

After examining and cataloguing various works by these scholars, Smith (*ibid.*:404) points out that Ward not only recommended that the state should be coordinator of the new political economy but he (Ward, 1903:278) also considered money "the root of all good there is in material civilization." Giddings (1900:7) asserted that imperialism helped "the spirit of liberty to grow." Small (1925:441) argued "that no devices are in sight to which we can pin our faith as feasible and comprehensive substitutes for capitalism." Ross (1901:55; 1907:88) recommended the development of a collective capitalism which would "emphasize efficiency and function as well as private property and competition." Weatherly (1926:569) advocated a Christian capitalism based on equitable relations between functional groups in society. In consideration of these and other statements, Smith (1965:401) declares that all of these men "were ideal protagonists for corporate capitalism."

Smith (*ibid.*:410) also points out that Small's identification with capitalism led him to ask the kind of question which has become basic to modern sociology: "How can we insure a better personal building material for our institutions?" (Small 1925:416). Questions like these were raised at a time when "sociology . . . prepared the sketchy and tough blueprint for the total transformation of man into an extension of the system." This was achieved theoretically by identifying the individual's needs with those of society and also depicting society as "the carrier of altruism, democracy, the general welfare, and cooperativeness" (Smith 1965:416). Bound by this image of the good society, sociologists lost their ability to transcend the historical and structural limitations of capitalism. Their criticism finally became institutionalized and in the main sociology "now criticizes only in non-transcendental [1] terms, in perfecting the social structure" (*ibid.*:417).

Lester Ward: Corporate-Liberal Ideologist

In the coming chapters the ideological grounds for the development of early American sociological ideas will be examined. Just as Smith indicates that the founders of American sociology merely differed about what aspects of the old (laissez-faire) and new (monopoly) capitalism were preferable, we will indicate that early theoretical conceptions were formulated from both old (biologically determined) and new (psychologically determined) images of human nature. It will also be pointed out that although the greatest amount of explicit criticism was directed at Spencer and not at Karl Marx, the founders of American sociology were, in fact, direct inheritors of Spencerian liberalism. Despite their criticism, they never went beyond certain basic assumptions defining the liberal heritage. Because of this, it can be shown that neither the frequency nor the targets of criticism are reliable indicators of a truly radical departure from previous frames of reference.

In our discussion of these issues we will concentrate initially on the work of Lester Ward, the first president of the American Sociological Society.[2] There are many reasons for this priority, but above all, in contrast to other founders, Ward was most acrimonious in his criticism of Spencer and it is his unequivocal rejection of some of Spencer's doctrines that has been elevated by historians as a distinguishing feature of his work. It will be maintained, however, that there are very significant parts of Ward's theory that are continuous with Spencer's. In spite of the irreconcilable antagonism which characterized their attitudes toward the state, it will be pointed out that Ward made important additions to the liberal-functionalist approach which was objectified by Spencer. And although Ward's assumptions about the importance of psychic forces in the development of mankind render his explanation more complex than Spencer's, his theoretical ideas involved liberal-functionalist standards and concepts which were similar to those used by Spencer in explaining the evolution of mankind. Both Spencer and Ward were concerned with the problems of social integration and social change. However the resolution of these problems was seen by Spencer to lie in the natural forces of competition while Ward believed their solution resided in the socially enlightened activities of individuals and the institutions of social control. It can therefore be observed that Ward's theory not only departs from Spencer's, but it is also, in certain respects, continuous with his laissez-faire and reductionist approach to man and society.

In examining Ward's theory of the evolution of man and society, his use of terms like "adjustment," "maladjustment," "adaptation," "existence," "survival," and "socialization" will be noted. Mills believed these terms merely indicated that early sociologists subscribed to the norms and values of small-town life. We will inquire into the larger social relationships to which these concepts refer and ask whether or not these relationships were actually constituted by the turbulent and emerging shape of corporate, imperialist America. Another area of interest will be the degree to which Ward's utopian conception of society, called "sociocracy,"[3] approximates a *technocratic* model of optimum human relationships. If considerable correspondence is found, then it can be argued that there is a very significant continuity between the ideas expressed during the founding period of American sociology (which profoundly disturbed C. Wright Mills during the last decades of his life) and the modern technocratic sociology.

Ward's Significance and Hofstadter's Explanation
of Ward's Standpoint

In 1883, Ward (1883:vi) complained that sociology had become "polite amusement" because it had lost sight of the fact that science has but one purpose, the benefit of mankind. Although social scientists had come to realize that natural processes are uncontrolled by man, they erroneously concluded that "nature's way should be man's ways." This attack on the laissez-faire approach toward human relationships was particularly addressed to Spencer, who, according to Ward (*ibid.:*216), had failed to recognize that "if any moral progress is ever to be made other than that which would naturally be brought about by secular influence of cosmical laws, it must be the result of the intelligent direction of the forces of human nature."

In the next chapter it will be seen that the forces of human nature in these remarks were psychic forces, and that it was Ward, not Freud, who anchored modern sociology in psychologism long before Freud's work was disseminated in the United States among members of the profession. It was Ward, not Freud, who represented in his work the most influential point at which American sociologists shifted from nineteenth-century biologism to twentieth-century psychologism. Ward's later reputation apparently contradicts this opinion of his contribution to the development of the field.[4] It is contended, however, that no sociologist outshone Ward in illuminating the great change in liberal thought which eventually produced the discipline of American sociology. His subsequent eclipse, therefore, cannot be explained on the basis of an objective historical evaluation of his work. One must look elsewhere to find the reasons for his obscurity.

Our evaluation of the origins of Ward's ideas will also contradict established interpretations of these sources by scholars who have been sympathetic to Ward. Richard Hofstadter, a noted social historian, has suggested (1959:82), for example, that Ward was in favor of the federal management of economic relations because of his "lower class bias." [5] Sympathy for the lower class, however, seems neither necessary nor sufficient to explain Ward's preferences for state capitalism when his brother C. Osborne Ward (who also had a "lower-class bias") recommended that the federal government be replaced by a socialist state. Lester Ward, on his part, denounced socialism as a solution to national problems because he felt that it created too many "artificial equalities" among the population at large. In light of the fact that proposals for social change may vary considerably despite similar class sympathies, it might be informative to inquire into other fundamental matters, such as Ward's attitude toward the institution of private property and human inequality, in order to understand his view of the state.[6]

Hofstadter (*ibid.:*82) also indicates that Ward's championship of the "underdog" can be explained by his feeling of "a certain alienation from the dominant characters and opinions of American life." Instead of alienation, however, Ward's later works contained numerous references to the number of countries which had adopted social policies recommended by him for many years (e.g., compulsory education, government ownership of the railroads, federal regulation of utilities, etc.).

Intellectual conflict is not an adequate indicator of alienation. By this token, all intellectuals are alienated because there is no intellectual worth his/her salt who is not in conflict with some set of ideas. Ward espoused ideas that were in sharp conflict with major American traditions, but he was one of the pioneers in an intellectual current that swept all antagonists before it.

Ward's career does not suggest an alienated individual. He was denied neither success in the institutions in which he worked, nor recognition by members of the newly emerging discipline of sociology. Ward had served with distinction in the American Civil War. He had earned praise as an original researcher in botany and geology, before his emergence as a sociologist. He was an illustrious figure in national scientific organizations, including the Smithsonian Institute and the Biological Society of Washington (Chugerman 1965:30–31). He was also made librarian of the Bureau of Immigration and chief of the Division of Navigation and Immigration. The National Museum in Washington conferred upon him the title of Honorary Curator of Botany and Paleobotany. During his forty years in the United States civil service, he was appointed geologist in the United States Geological Survey in 1881 and two years later, chief paleontologist (*ibid.*:30–31). He was elected president of l'Institut international de sociologie from 1903 to 1905 and became the first president of the American Sociological Society in 1906 (*ibid.*:64).

The degree to which Ward was accepted rather than alienated in administrative circles in the United States government is further illustrated by a gathering that took place on the very first day of the twentieth century. Ward (1903:vii) stated that on this day, he invited members of the "elite of the National Capital" to a small gathering in order to obtain their "valued counsel" about his most recent scheme for a "system of sociology." He reported that "after free discussion and mature deliberation it was decided that the system would consist of two volumes, as far as possible independent of each other, the first to be entitled *Pure Sociology* and the second, *Applied Sociology,* and the title pages of these volumes were drawn up." The men attending this private gathering included the United States Commissioner of Education, an Assistant Secretary of State, the director of the United States Geological Survey and of the Bureau of American Ethnology, the United States Commissioner of Labor, the superintendent of the National Zoological Park, and others, including a "manufacturer and banker," and a person who later became "the treasurer of Puerto Rico." This "elite" was, for the most part, a federal bureaucratic elite! Events like this are inconsistent with the mere suggestion that Ward was alienated from the dominant character and opinions of American life in his time. They are consistent, on the other hand, with the fact that

Ward was an integral part of a new type of intellectual circle being rapidly generated within an emerging stratum of highly educated technical, professional, and managerial workers. These workers were employed primarily by public and private corporate institutions simultaneously emerging during the latter half of the last century.

Hofstadter's consideration of Ward's lower-class bias and alienation from dominant thoughtways is inadequate for understanding Ward's very significant departures from established modes of thought during a period of great social change. A more fruitful explanation of his theoretical and ameliorative ideas may be obtained by viewing them in relation to the gradual ascendency of new modes of political and economic integration which were an accompaniment to the rise of monopoly capitalism in Europe and North America.

NOTES

1. Smith refers here to the concept of "transcendence" advanced by Herbert Marcuse in *One Dimensional Man* (1964). Marcuse (1964:xi) states, "The terms 'transcend' and 'transcendence' are used throughout in the empirical critical sense: they designate tendencies in theory and practice, which, in a given society, 'overshoot' the established universe of discourse and action toward its historical alternatives (real possibilities)." They refer, therefore, to the factors stimulating individuals to work outside the rhetoric currently in use, while seeking alternative solutions.

2. The society was renamed the American Sociological *Association* in later years.

3. Ward borrowed the term "sociocracy" from Comte.

4. It is on the basis of Ward's later reputation (as well as the absence of references to Ward's works at the *end* of the formative years), that Burnham (1956) has decided that Ward's contribution to the field was insignificant.

5. Hofstadter (1959:82) also writes: "His [Ward's] opposition to the biological argument for individualism stemmed from his democratic faith; his rejection of Sumner and Spencer was partly motivated by his sense of their aristocratic preferences." But Spencer's elitist "preferences" were those of a liberal, not an aristocrat.

6. The fact that Ward defended his own viewpoint on the basis of libertarian principles would indicate that there exist various different interpretations of democracy. Ward's concept of democracy, as we shall see, included the notion that the state could function as an impartial arbiter between conflicting but functionally interrelated groups such as labor and capital. From this point of view, an "industrial democracy" was dependent upon the establishment of *equity* between labor and capital without radically altering the *existing social structure*. At issue was labor's right to obtain its share "of the pie" rather than consideration of fundamental changes in its relationship to capital. Ward's democratic faith, therefore, cannot be described as resting on an absolute belief in human *equality* but was actually closely related to changing conceptions of democracy which were emerging among liberals during his lifetime.

PART SIX

Lester F. Ward:
A Transitional Figure

CHAPTER 22

Social Forces and the Struggle for Existence

The outstanding early sociologists were long-lived and wrote voluminously during their lifetimes. Because of this it is impossible to present all of their ideas. Ward's sociological writings, for example, were embodied in at least twelve volumes and numerous articles, but only a few of them will be considered here. His cosmological principles, for example, will hardly be mentioned, but some of their implicit assumptions will be discussed.

Some standards must operate in selecting certain ideas for presentation and excluding others. One important standard in this work is whether an idea is indicative of a long-term trend in social thought. Another is whether an idea strongly influenced the specific manner in which liberalism was reconstituted by early American sociologists. Ward's hegemonic theory of *social forces,* for example, was among his most important contributions to American sociology. The theory helped to ground American sociology in psychology at the very beginning of the formative years. It also provided a way of looking at social evolution which justified the existence of monopolistic and imperialistic societies.

Social Forces and Psychologism

Ward emphasized the importance of psychological relationships to the study of sociology. He proposed (1903:125) that shortly after the evolution of "the chemical origins of life," the "biological origins of the mind" appeared and

168

the use of the mind itself gave rise to "the feelings, the emotions, the passions, the will." These qualities were particularly vital because they prevented mankind from being "too rigid" in the face of changing environmental conditions. Noting his debt to Spencer and Darwin, both of whom insisted on the importance of biological adaptation, Ward postulated "a law of the survival of the plastic." He asserted that human adaptability is achieved through the operation of feeling, which is "the only conceivable means by which plastic organisms could be preserved from destruction and enabled to perpetuate themselves and develop." Therefore, the "survival of the plastic," enables the survival of the fittest; but plastic people become fittest because they are endowed with *feeling*.

Although a scientific study of individual feelings was considered to be critically important to sociology, Ward (*ibid.:*256–257) noted that this kind of study had not occurred because "the world has always avoided as far as possible the expression of feeling. It is too personal, too near the person or the body. It exposes too plainly the bodily and mental states which are naturally concealed." In spite of the traditional reluctance to discuss feelings, Ward suggested that sociology could not avoid entering into this discussion because "it is upon this *affective* part of mind that sociology rests and not upon its intellectual part." If sociology is to be a science, Ward declared, it must deal with those "psychic forces" which are called "social forces." In his theory, "the social forces [1] are human motives and all motives, in the correct sense of this term, have feeling as their end" (*ibid.:* 108–109). In Ward's classification scheme, the nutritional and reproductive [sexual] forces were the very basic social forces. The reproductive forces were particularly important in solving the problem of integration in his earliest formulations.

Ward's insistence on viewing the social forces as psychic forces, many of which have their proximate origins in biological relations, provides some understanding of why Freudianism was so readily assimilated into American sociology during the twenties and thirties. By that time sociologists had been enculturated into a well-established tradition which already centered on psychic factors as the foundations for sociological relationships. Freud, for example, stated that "pleasure and pain drew up life's program." Ward also considered psychological hedonism to be the ethical principle regulating the social forces; mankind was impelled by the social forces in order to achieve more pleasure than pain. Since these forces were the wellspring of all social relationships, the "general law" regulating their operation was also basic for understanding social integration and change: "All social progress, in the proper sense of the word," Ward (*ibid.:*105) stated, "is a movement from a pain economy toward a pleasure economy, or at least a movement in the direction of the satisfaction of a greater and greater proportion of the desires of men."

Since the social forces are not only inner psychic forces, but also "the dynamic agent in society," and "the motor of the social world," Ward (*ibid.:*101–103) declared that "sociology must have a psychological basis." He also indicated that most of the social forces are themselves highly dependent on biological relationships which he calls "the vital forces." The "vital forces" can be clearly distinguished from the psychic forces, just as biological requirements for food can be differentiated from the psychic desire for particular food delicacies.[2] In contrast to the great variety of behavioral theories based on biological instincts during his lifetime, Ward divided biological and psychological relationships. He placed the dynamic stress on the functions of psychic forces. Because of this Ward became a significant forerunner of customary sociological thought during the twentieth century.

Justification of Class Inequality and Private Property as Expressions of Human Nature

In *Pure Sociology,* Ward *(ibid.:*245) discussed inequality in wealth or resources in an oblique manner by referring to an unequal distribution of "social energies." He indicated, for example, that one sees "vast numbers in whom the social energy is below the level of healthy activity and small groups in whom it is far above the possibility of ever consuming it." What does Ward mean by this statement? When an analytic crowbar is applied to his writings and it becomes understood that "social energies" can be embodied in wealth, property, or consumable commodities, then Ward is simply indicating that there are great inequities between the rich and the poor. The poor do not have enough to sustain healthy life and the rich have more than they can consume.

Ward's observations about social-class inequities, however, should be seen in a larger context; they have to be juxtaposed with his justifications of class inequality in wealth and property. For example, in *Pure Sociology,* Thorstein Veblen's (1899) theory of the leisure class, which emphasized the conspicuous and wasteful modes of leisure-class consumption, was criticized as being a theory which "intentionally" represented a one-sided and therefore biased point of view. Ward *(ibid.)* said in this regard that actually all of nature's processes are wasteful; therefore, by implication, the wasteful use of "energy" by leisure-class members is natural, that is, justified, when compared to less-favored classes. In addition, he flatly remarked that "all social innovation emanates from favored groups and, therefore, one should keep in mind that the 'surplus energy' employed by the upper classes has played an important role in the advancement of human civilization." Ward's observations about the inequitable distribution of "energy" suggest, therefore, that he may have been critical of class inequalities but it should not be inferred that he favored a classless society.

Indeed, Ward proclaimed that it was in the very nature of man to be competitive and avaricious with regard to private property.[3] In one passage he said that "the strongest craving of man's nature is, in one way or another, to be set over one's fellows." Because wealth "provides superiority" and "commands respect and envy," it yields "tremendous power." In light of this,

Ward argued, "the futility of certain reformers to eradicate the passion for property acquisition becomes apparent." He further asserted that this passion would not only continue to be "the ruling element of the industrial state" for an indefinite period, but that it "has done and is still doing incalculable service to society." In another passage, Ward affirmed that "even the amassing of colossal fortunes is not an evil in itself, since the very activity which it requires stimulates industry and benefits a large number." His sole concern regarding these fortunes was their possible transmittal to "inactive and unproductive heirs" with the consequent creation of a "non-industrial class in perpetuity." But he noted that "this could be remedied, without any hardship to any worthy person, by a wise limitation of inheritance."

While on the one hand Veblen's works were concerned with economic crises, growing domination of industry by financiers, and the wasteful and parasitical modes of consumption by upper-class families, Ward *(ibid.:229)* was convinced that "the modern discussion of the problem of social decadence is to no purpose or based on vain imaginings." "The *real problem*," he added, "is how to secure *social stability*" (our emphasis). To show that the problem of stability could not be solved by the establishment of a state of human equality, Ward invoked the operation of a "general law." This "law," discovered originally by Spencer, proposed that action, once begun in a certain direction, "tends more and more to go in that direction until all homogeneity is destroyed." On the basis of this "law," Ward (1903:244) stated that "extremes breed extremes, and a state of equality, if it could be conceived to exist, would be ephemeral. *A state of inequality would quickly replace it*" (our emphasis). Therefore, because of the ephemeral nature of equality, stability must be achieved on other grounds. There is no doubt that Spencer would have heartily concurred in this point of view.

Ward's Concepts of Evolution and Neo-Hobbesian Problem

Ward's opinions about the natural inevitability of inequality and the value of private property were integrated into his concept of social evolution at the beginning of his career as a sociological theorist. In *Dynamic Sociology* he claimed that the unequal distribution of private property has been and would continue to be an essential precondition for social progress in the foreseeable future.

The acquisition of possessions and enjoyment of private property (which is called "the possession of permanent property") became an all-important stimulus for social evolution. Accordingly, the first "rudimentary elements of government" appeared during Ward's third stage of evolution in order to protect property rights. In the spirit of economic liberalism, Ward stated that "the distinguishing feature of this new stage was the recognition of the idea of permanent ownership or possession, and hence it may be styled the proprietary stage of civilization." Possession was linked directly to the essential need for self-preservation, but in the course of human evolution each individual developed "an incentive to industry beyond the mere present demands of his nature" when he recognized that he could retain his property permanently. Private property according to Ward (1883:I,492–493) substituted "a future for present enjoyment and spontaneously begat exchange." [4] The *political state* is important because it prevents savage interaction among men and thereby permits *equitable exchanges* to take place. It is the exchange of privately owned property which integrates society; therefore, the state becomes a precondition for this mode of integration. The state, furthermore, arises because of the necessity to evolve laws regulating sexual relationships (particularly those based on competition between males over the "private possession" of the female), as well as the necessity to regulate other types "of rude property interests" which began to emerge. Ward (1883:I,463) agreed with Hobbes that "man is the worst enemy of man: *homo hominus lupis.*" And this *natural* Hobbesian competition between men established the growing necessity for the creation of institutions such as the state which initiate the third stage of social evolution.

Further contributing to the inevitability of inequality, Ward asserted, exchange relations introduced "a permanent standard" or "measure of value" called money. Money in this scheme of social evolution became the "natural" symbol of all desire because all objects of value acquire monetary values and are thus reduced to private property. "Wealth means safety, ease, the fulfillment of desire. It means happiness." Because "a thing is worth more to anyone in proportion as he is the more absolute owner of it," Ward speculated, "everybody wants to own as many objects as possible, or what becomes equivalent to this, as much money as possible." Two consequences have emerged from this pursuit: first, individuals have become engaged in a struggle to obtain money, and second, "avarice, a wholly derivative sentiment, has come, and naturally too, to be one of the ruling passions" *(ibid.:494)*.

The avaricious pursuit of wealth can be described, according to Ward *(ibid.:516)*, by a general law: the law of acquisition. Behavior regulated by this law has been stimulated by the desire to acquire private property *regardless of the means* employed in this acquisition. If we may use a more modern term and refer to this conduct as socially expedient behavior, then Ward was asserting that such expedience is governed by *natural law* rather than the socially instituted organization of economic activities.

Ward pointed out that the *entire social fabric* rests on soulless competition for economic advantage: "the universal competition . . . which Darwin so tersely described as the 'struggle for existence' has its true counterpart in society in the industrial struggles of men." Under these "natural conditions" of struggle, man is ruled by "the principle of natural justice" and the "morals of nature." This morality regards as justified any act which preserves the individual and advances his own happiness irrespective of its consequences for society *(ibid.:503)*. It is not surprising to find Ward referring to this savage and essentially Hobbesian state of affairs as the "theoretical condition" which again poses the problem of integration in the history of the evolution of civilization.[5]

Ward and Imperialism

In 1883, Ward posed the problem of integration in terms of the Darwinian "struggle for existence" and "the industrial struggles of men." At that time social Darwinism had been strongly influenced by Spencer's early evolutionary laissez-faire writings. Ward's adaptation of Spencer's notions therefore emphasized the competitive relations between atomistic individuals, who were fashioned after the concept of economic man.

In later years, however, social Darwinism had been modified in order to justify the expansion of state power, the imperialist conflicts between metropolitan nations, and the imperialist oppression of races and nations throughout the world. This modification resulted in "race-conflict" theories which placed greater emphasis on racial rather than economic analogues to the Darwinian struggle for existence. Ward was influenced by this development in social thought and by 1903, he expressed his belief in the "race-conflict" perspective which was emerging all over Europe.

Thus, during the period between the publication of *Dynamic Sociology* (1883) and *Pure Sociology* (1903), Ward adopted the theoretical ideas being proposed by such men as Ferguson, Bagehot, Gumplowicz, and Ratzenhofer. These scholars were called "race-conflict" theorists because they classified both racial and nationality groups with the single superordinate term "race" and maintained, in addition, that a universal conflict between "races" stimulated the progressive evolution of human society. Race conflict theorists further claimed that the state had its origins in various social processes which were associated with "race conflict," including the processes of "conflict," "amalgamation," and "assimilation" among racial and national groups. The "race-conflict" theories, taken as a whole, were little more than an apology for imperialism. Ward, however, stated that "any work on the nature of the state that does not recognize and start from this ("race-conflict") standpoint . . . is superficial and worthless" (Ward 1902:762).

Let us look at Ward's justification of *war* as a vital precondition for social progress, for an example of his use of race-conflict theory. (It will also illustrate some of the prevalent ideas about race and group conflict in his time.) In *Pure Sociology,* Ward stated (1903:238) that civilized men are well aware of the horrors of war, and that if sociology had "utilitarian purposes," then one of them would include limiting war. "But pure sociology," he cautions, "is simply an inquiry into the social facts and conditions, and has nothing to do with utilitarian purposes." In making an "objective inquiry" into the social functions of war, he found that "war has been the chief and leading condition of human progress." Ward declared that "this is perfectly obvious to anyone who understands the meaning of the struggle of races. When races stop struggling progress ceases." Asserting further that peace leads to social stagnation, Ward concluded that "we may enlarge to our soul's content on the blessings of peace, but the facts remain as stated, and cannot be successfully disproved."

Turning to "the more civilized races," and their involvement in interracial struggles, Ward *(ibid.:*238–239) pointed out that European populations ("call them Aryan, Indo-Germanic, or anything you please") have been the "repository of the highest culture, they have the largest amount of social efficiency, they have achieved the most and they represent the longest uninterrupted inheritance and transmission of human achievement." But in spite of the fact that they have led the civilization of the world "ever since there were any records," these races have not hesitated to use force in order to achieve their needs. They did not shrink from war. "Indeed," remarked Ward, "the whole movement by which the master race of the planet has extended its dominion over inferior races" does not differ from the processes whereby primitive tribes have extended their dominion over each other. "The effects are different only because of the great disparity in the races engaged, due in turn to the superior social efficiency of the dominant race." The effects have been due to the fact that the differences between the Aryan or Indo-Germanic races and the other races of the earth have been exceedingly great.

In light of his cosmological principle of race conflict and conquest, and in view of the extraordinary differences between the master race and the other races, Ward *(ibid.:*238–239) stated "it seems a waste of breath to urge peace, justice, humanity" when speaking about race conflict. He observed that moral forces are gaining strength and "slowly mitigating the severity of the law of nature." But he hastened to add that "mitigation is all that can be hoped for. The movement must go on, and there seems no place for it to stop until, just as man has gained dominion over the animal world, so the highest type of man shall gain dominion over all the lower types of man."

In concluding his remarks on the inevitability of race conquest and war as a means resulting in technocratic benefits to mankind, Ward *(ibid.:*238–239) stated that most "peace agitation is characterized by total blindness to all the broader cosmic factors and principles and this explains its complete impotence." Identifying individuals who agitate for peace as "effete minds," [6] he noted that "it is the mark of the effete mind to exaggerate small things while ignoring great things," and in spite of his previous statements about the superiority of man's moral attitudes and intellect as guides to social change, he concluded that "the crude instincts of the general public" are far safer guides to the evaluation of war than maudlin sentimentality and . . . certain minds which, from culture or disadvantage, gain the credit of constituting the cream of the most advanced intelligence."

Race-Conflict Theories
and Ward's Sociological Perspective

Hofstadter (1959:78) notes that Ward considered Gumplowicz and Ratzenhofer's ideas to be "the most important contribution thus far made to the science of sociology." But Hofstadter maintains that the conflict school's notions occupy only "a small and transient place in Ward's work," and that there were "grave difficulties in reconciling the conflict theory with his own collectivism." It can be demonstrated, however, that these ideas are not inconsistent with his earlier work, nor with his "collectivism," which, after all, amounts to nothing more than an embracing of monopoly-state capitalism. Even though the conflict school's "race struggle" thesis was adopted by Ward in his last major synthesis of sociological theory (1903), it was part of an emerging justification for war which became widespread in Europe. This justification also identified imperialism with the progressive development of civilization. "Progressive civilization," in this context, also amounted to nothing more than monopoly-state capitalism.

Can it be said that Ward's adoption of the conflict theory represents a drastic departure from his earlier work? It cannot, because even though Ward substituted a conflict theory in *Pure Sociology* for the simple modification of Spencerism expressed in *Dynamic Sociology,* the earlier work contained many passages which were highly consistent with his later viewpoint. For example, the first work stated: "The development of the lower races is being checked by the higher ones. The latter find the former in their way as much as are the wild beasts. Whether they know it or not, whether they intend it or not, the superior races all over the globe are gradually but surely crowding the inferior races out of existence."

In a footnote on the same page as the above statement, Ward indicated that it is possible that the number of Indians in North America may be "nearly or quite as great as it was at the time of the occupancy of the whites." He added that even if this were true, it would not contradict his observation about the disappearance of the inferior races. The reason why the American Indians have not vanished, he stated,

should surprise no one, considering the comparatively gentle treatment which these Indians have received at the hands of the whites, and the earnest efforts made by the United States Government to protect, supply and civilize them. For, notwithstanding some bad faith on the part of agents under great temptations, this national effort has not only been sincere, but on the whole successful, and it is doubtful whether these Indians could have held their own better than they have, had not the whites molested them. [1883:I,477]

Statements of which this is but one example suggest to us that Ward did not have to wait upon Gumplowicz or Ratzenhofer to invent apologies for either domestic or foreign imperialism.[7]

NOTES

1. Ward repeatedly asserted that one of the essential qualities of human feelings is that of seeking an end. Feeling was also called "appetitive," and "appetition" in turn was considered a motive because it "impels to action." Feeling was also called a "force . . . the primary meaning is that which causes or impels." In his discussion, Ward treated words like "psychic motive," "feeling," "appetition," and "desires of whatever kind," as synonyms denoting the presence of a "true natural force" in individual beings. And the *social* forces, from this point of view, were simply "the collective desires of associated man." They were "wants seeking satisfaction through efforts." They were also social motives inspiring activities which either create social structures through social synergy, or modify the social structures already created by various means (1903:261).

2. Since Ward felt that all social institutions were merely manifestations of psychic forces, the classification of these forces was basic to the development of sociological theory. As early as 1880, in a paper entitled "Feeling and Function as Factors in Human Development," he proposed that "the foundations of sociology as a true science must be a logical classification of the social forces."

3. This proposition was an important feature of Ward's theory of social forces, published as early as 1883 in his first major work, *Dynamic Sociology*. See, for example, Ward (1883:I, 488–501).

4. Ward added that with the emergence of exchange all manner of human desires were simply gratified by exchanging surplus production for any chosen commodity. As a result, the stimulation for production on the part of each individual became unlimited and an individual "could not be too industrious" in order to achieve the end of greater and greater happiness. In a manner reminiscent of Bentham's image of man, naturally indolent human beings were propelled into action by the attraction of property and all the "pleasures" it implies.

5. Ward referred to the problem of social integration as "the problem of social mechanics." He stated (1883:I,504), "With the human race . . . the naked law of acquisition . . . and the principle of natural justice would make . . . the wealth of the world . . . the subject of a process of forcible seizure and appropriation, irrespective of proprietorship or of injury to the loser. This is the *theoretical* condition of the problem of social mechanics." (Our emphasis).

6. We don't know who wrote Vice President Spiro Agnew's speech regarding the "effete" intellectuals who engage in agitation against the Vietnamese war, but he may have read Ward beforehand.

7. For the use of Gumplowicz's ideas as justification for war and fascism, see Barnes (1948:203).

CHAPTER 23

Telic (Technocratic) Governance

The previous chapter emphasized the social Darwinist ideas which underlie Ward's theory of social evolution. This chapter discusses the reformist dimensions which indelibly stamp his theory as a product of *reform* Darwinism. These dimensions were expressed as early as 1883, in *Dynamic Sociology*.

176

"Telesis": Ward's Euphemism
for Technocratic Analyses and Intervention

In developing his reformist perspective, Ward departed from Spencer by indicating that social evolution involved very different kinds of processes which could be broadly dichotomized by the terms *telesis* and *genesis*. Genesis was identified with the unconscious control of human relationships by natural forces, while telesis represented the conscious direction of these forces by the human mind. From Ward's standpoint, Spencer was concerned with genesis rather than telesis. Telesis was considered to be superior to the unconscious control of nature because nature is inefficient and only improves the state of mankind very slowly through the process of natural selection. By viewing the relation between the human intellect and social processes in the same terms that a buyer or manager views the means at his disposal, Ward indicated that the intellect tends to economize through foresight and to evaluate means in terms of ends. Since the technological control of means-ends relationships was central to Ward's conception of telesis, social policy developed by technically competent government officials was regarded as the most efficient means for attaining societal goals. Genesis is inefficient and reflective of laissez-faire relationships.

On the face of it, Ward's telesis was highly seductive; everyone likes an efficient government. But efficiency can also be dehumanizing and based on cold bureaucratic norms of efficiency, even though bureaucratic standards are not explicitly contained in Ward's vague formulations. In order to understand the kinds of efficient social policy Ward had in mind, we must turn to his descriptions of legitimate governmental functions. Some of them are familiar to us and include protective services such as police and fire departments. Others were only vaguely indicated and suggested, for example, that the government could represent members of its population and act as an agent "to transact business" in far-removed or restricted localities. Further functions involved the acquisition of personnel who could develop "the skill and dexterity in subjects with which everyone cannot afford time to acquaint himself; and to perform duties by means of organization which individuals, acting independently, would not possess the strength to perform" (Ward 1883:II, 241–242). These functions are performed, however, by many types of government and while a sociocratic government may perform them more efficiently, they do not seem to provide ample justification for either a new society or a new government.

Even though Ward's naivete prevented him from considering the basic issue of how a government frees itself of ruling-class domination, these simple government functions did not offer sufficient justification for the transformation of politicians into social scientists or social scientists into politicians; they did not call for the creation of a stratum of "new mandarins" [1] whose

177

values could regulate the intervention in and control of social processes. This reorganization would merely replace existing forms of class control with control by a new stratum of elites.

There was one set of social and economic functions proposed by Ward which did play a unique and important role in justifying the new mandarins. This set also appeared to be significant in light of the period in which *Pure Sociology* was written. Ward suggested that one of the primary functions of the state was to reconcile conflicting social and economic interests. We have indicated that prior to 1900 the United States was beset by periodic crises and the emergence of militant labor and political organizations. These economic and political developments gave Ward's suggestion special meaning.[2]

In 1895 Ward had already expressed his awareness of the "signal inability of capital and private enterprise to take care of themselves unaided by the state." He pointed out that while entrepreneurs incessantly denounced "paternalism" on the part of the government in opposing governmental aid to the "defenseless laborers and artisans, they are all the while besieging legislators for relief from their own incompetency." (In another statement, Ward noted that if no government existed, capital would commit heinous crimes against labor.) Statements like these revealed Ward's awareness of the lengths to which capitalists would go in order to accumulate wealth. They also revealed Ward's conception of the governmental functions that would defend the interests of functional blocs in society on the basis of "equity." In his opinion, the *accommodative* and the *managerial* functions of the state were the only means for rectifying this chaotic and dangerous development. The accommodative function involved the achievement of accommodative relationships between opposing economic blocs in the interests of equity. The managerial function included both direct management of corporate institutions and indirect management through regulatory bureaus. Both of these functions were being integrated by 1903, into a rudimentary, liberal-syndicalist conception of the state and society.

Monopoly-State Capitalism as Final Solution to Modern Problem of Integration

One cannot exaggerate the extent of Ward's movement toward a statist point of view from 1883 to 1903. *Dynamic Sociology* (1883) dealt primarily with the natural forces of the cosmos, including the evolution of societal relationships based on social forces. While his favorite attitude toward the state was clearly represented in this early work, *Pure Sociology,* published twenty years later (1903), placed a still greater emphasis on the role of the state. Indeed, there is merit to the claim that the later work was almost entirely oriented toward justifying the view of the beneficent political state which was presented in its final chapter.

For Ward, the national government represented the mutually advantageous regulation of unruly, self-interested individuals. Although he admitted that the slow growth of sympathy and other moral sentiments also mitigated human rapaciousness, he indicated that the influence of these sentiments was "less than is commonly supposed." Because of this ineffectuality, "society would have been impossible" without "the beneficent power of the state" (Ward 1903:556). Unlike Spencer, Ward (*ibid.*:564–565) bolstered this claim with a comparison of the functions of the brain and the state in modern industrial society.

Comparing the conscious direction of organic life with the growth of cerebral functioning, Ward proposed that the progressive development of organic life had consisted of "the gradual transfer of unconscious functions to the list of conscious ones, until in all higher animals the cerebral hegemony is complete." This process had its parallel in the social evolution of the state. Since the state was the embodiment of social consciousness and racial intelligence, it was regarded as a vital precondition for the forward-moving development of society. The state was depicted as the homologue of the brain, and the universal growth of Ward's "collectivism" was equated with the growth of intelligence among mankind as a whole. Consequently, "collectivism" was regarded as the outcome of "the natural and normal integration of functions with the development of the social structure" (*ibid.*:567).

Taking issue with Spencer's remarks about the disastrous consequences of state interference in economic affairs, Ward asserted that "the growing collectivism" *has strengthened rather than weakened private enterprise.* Citing a number of articles, including one written in 1899 by the Agent General of South Australia, he pointed out that the government in Australia had brought hope into the life of the farmer by regulating the economy with his interest in mind. Consequently, it had made him "sure of his reward." His profits had not been taken away from him. He had been made more efficient and "instead of sapping private enterprise," the guidance given by the state had assisted this kind of enterprise (*ibid.*:561–564). Thus, in Ward's opinion government regulation and even nationalization of the railroad, power, and communication industries would not destroy competition among the greater number of private entrepreneurs. Indeed, in his view the prevention of unjust forms of economic competition would promote healthy competition by limiting the adverse effects of monopoly and thereby enabling each individual in society to reap a just reward on the basis of his abilities. Ward noted, therefore, that although many nations were moving toward extensive public ownership and regulation of certain kinds of large corporate enterprises, this did not represent a socialist development. In spite of Spencer's claims that the public ownership of utilities, transportation, power, and communications industries was evidence of coming social slavery, Ward construed these changes to be inevitable reactions, on the part of an enlightened public, to the evil effects of the unrestricted forces of competition. These reactions were indicators of the eventual development of a new social order which was to be integrated by both the *exchange* of private property and the political *state*. He called this

179

social order "sociocracy." Today it would be called *monopoly-state capitalism.*

Achieved Status in a Technocratic Utopia

If Ward's antipathies toward socialists and laissez-faire capitalists are kept in mind, then it is obvious that sociocracy would not be represented by either laissez-faire capitalism or socialism. Interestingly, however, in contrasting his sociocracy with these social orders, Ward avoided comparing them on the basis of their forms of integration. Instead, equalitarian or inequalitarian relations between individuals appeared to be the sufficient criterion used to distinguish between them. In his opinion, laissez-faire capitalism and socialism were characterized, respectively, by too many "artificial inequalities" and "artificial equalities." [3] However, we have also seen that he did not believe that an equalitarian society was a practical possibility. Ward had some sort of "natural" inequality in mind as the preferable alternative to these "artificial" relations between individuals. What precisely was the kind of inequality that characterized a sociocratic society? The content of a disagreement between Ward and Spencer provides an answer to this question.

Spencer had asserted that upper-class persons are superior because they are more intelligent than the rest of the population. Ward took issue with Spencer on this question of class superiority. Furthermore, he denied that intellectual attributes are acquired by the offspring of the wealthy on the basis of heredity. Although there are passages in Ward's writings which do suggest that some upper-class persons have acquired their wealth and power because of great intelligence or that upper-class persons have contributed more to social progress than other classes, he claimed that the variation in the human capacity for intelligence *within* classes is greater than the variation *between* classes. Therefore, upper-class individuals are potentially neither more nor less intelligent than members of the lower classes. He further claimed that the differences between the classes are a function of favorable or unfavorable environmental conditions, and a considerable amount of his social criticism was directed toward justifying this repudiation of upper-class superiority on the basis of capacity for intelligence. He insisted that great wealth had often been acquired by antisocial chicanery and accidental advantage rather than by dint of superior intelligence. Persons who acquired upper-class status merely by the accident of being born into an upper-class family were given as an example of individuals who achieved unearned upper-class status. Ward's criticism of Spencer's apologetics for class inequality implied, therefore, that sociocracy would *not* be structured by an inequality based on lineage, forcible appropriation of property, or "deceit."

Ward considered the provision for *universal* public education one of the vitally important means for ensuring equality of opportunity for individuals. Every member of society should be provided with an equal opportunity to realize his intellectual potentiality irrespective of class background. (Spencer, of course, viewed mass education as harmful for the human race.) But it should be noted that Ward's conflict with Spencer in this regard was partly based on a disagreement about *means,* not ends.

Ward differed from Spencer in that he was convinced that a laissez-faire society could not provide equality of opportunity for men of all social classes. Ward suggested that the state should intervene in genetic social processes because of the necessity to restrict the use of naked force or deceitful practices by individuals who are not capable of securing wealth on the basis of their intellectual faculties alone. But this argument with Spencer over the role of the state, including its support of public education, should not obscure their agreement regarding the justice of distributing social rewards on the basis of some form of competition. Nor should it overshadow their mutual belief that individual *merit* should be evaluated on the basis of intelligence. In both their views, the variation in human *intelligence* functioned as the ethical criterion for the right of individuals to a superior standard of living.

The overriding inequality in Ward's utopian society was based on individual intelligence. Spencer also believed that society would continue to be strongly characterized by the same form of human inequality until the day that all dumb human beings would be killed off. Even though Ward was convinced that poverty should be eliminated, and persons with inferior intelligence ought to be treated humanely, it is important to see the very basic common ground on which these two scholars stood.

The crucial importance of their decision to use intelligence as the criterion for judging individual merit is heightened when one considers that the reward for meritorious performance is income, wealth, or property. In all market economies today, monetary rewards are necessary conditions for the fulfillment of a large number of human values which, particularly in capitalist nations, have become associated with adequate medical care, satisfying leisure, advanced education, ample supply of good food, shelter, clothing, and many others. In this light, their intelligence criterion has even greater implicit meaning. (In its Spencerian extreme, it warranted inhuman treatment of mental defectives.) Even more basically it is also the standard used in the ethical justification of the *unequal* distribution of the means for realization of a great number of human rights.

Intelligence: A Self-Serving Criterion for Achieved Status

The socially critical implications of Spencer's and Ward's meritarian proposals are highly questionable because neither of these scholars provided any realistic guides for dealing with the realities of class inequalities based on the private ownership of wealth and property.[4] Indeed, when we place their meritarian proposals in the context of their gradualist evolutionary explanations of social change, these proposals constitute little more than a justification for *conservatizing* the institutions of property ownership which maintain class inequalities in capitalist societies.

At first glance, Spencer's and Ward's criterion of intelligence appears to be a more egalitarian departure from the use of wealth or property as a standard by which to evaluate individual worth. This implication is primarily established by the connection between their meritarian criterion and the liberal doctrine of *equality* of opportunity. But it must be kept in mind that the liberal's concept of equality of opportunity has little to do with egalitarianism. It refers to a rule of equity based on the meritarian premise that *inequalities* in individual talent (e.g., intelligence) or performance should be evaluated *unequally*. This rule usually justifies a set of conditions (e.g., "free competition") under which the unequal distribution of wealth and property is fair. It is a justification for social inequality, not an egalitarian principle.

The meritarian proposals advanced by Spencer and Ward appeared egalitarian because they contrasted sharply with the nonmeritarian *realities* which underlie the great concentrations of wealth and property in capitalist societies. However it should be kept in mind that the upper classes in capitalist societies have not been established on the basis of superiority in individual talents or performances. If these upper classes were based on merit alone, there would be a *massive turnover* in membership within each one of these classes in every generation.

In formulating their conceptions of the liberal myth of the sel-made man, many writers who work for business journals have made much of the idea that outstanding businessmen are superior individuals because they are able to outwit their competitors in business.[5] (In this case "business sagacity" has been taken as the mark of the superior man.) Philosophers and social scientists like Comte, J. S. Mill, and Ward, however, placed greater weight on intellectual abilities in general. In their works, an individual's *general* intelligence was taken as the benchmark for individual superiority.

Why should general intelligence be taken by Spencer, Ward, or anyone else as the criterion for ascertaining whether a man has a right to the goods of this earth? Why not consider manual skills? How about a sense of humor? Isn't there sufficient justification for regarding a man's good deeds, no matter how personally unprofitable, as the standard for providing him and his family with longer life, ample leisure, and the greater happinesses that can be provided by a higher standard of living? It is obvious, when one examines the relation between the criterion of general intelligence and the idealized prerequisites for occupational success among intellectuals, that the liberal scholar's attempt at structuring the inequalities which actually exist—or ought to exist—is no less *self*-serving for intellectuals than the standard of "business sagacity" would be for businessmen, even though it is stated in more abstract terms.

Technocratic Governance

We have demonstrated that Ward and Spencer advocated meritarian doctrines which were based on the criterion of individual intelligence. But Ward must be differentiated from Spencer by placing his doctrine in a broader political framework. Ward suggested that society should be administered by highly intelligent experts and their scientific administrative-consultants. The *political* significance of his meritarian standards, therefore, is explicable only when they are placed within the context of his technocratic perspective.

Various types of technocratic doctrines emerged during the formative years. One of the major trends characterizing this variation was created by technocratic corporate-liberal scholars, of whom Ward was one. These scholars reconciled their technocratic doctrines with the maintenance of the dominant (corporate) forms of private property. This reconciliation eventually generated the fiction that highly trained public servants and enlightened corporation managers, rather than men of great wealth and property, come increasingly into control of the political economy.[6] Another significant corporate-liberal reconciliation is the extraordinary scope of the socially integrative roles they assigned to politically constituted bodies of experts.

Being able to trace the present liberal vogue of technocratic interpretations of society directly back to the rudimentary technocratic conceptions developed almost nine decades ago, (when monopoly capitalism first appeared) comes as no surprise. At that time, however, the corporate-liberal visions of technocratic relationships were completely utopian. They referred to a world that would come into existence, given certain legislative and other "normal" changes in the relations between the state and the economy. These changes seemed to be required by the political necessity of controlling the further development of the great monopolies and monopoly trusts. We must become familiar with some of the rudimentary properties of this earlier perspective by examining Ward's concept of sociocracy.

Additional Technocratic Conceptions
in Ward's Writings

Among his various categories for forms of government, Ward catalogued three "democratic" types: "physiocracy," "plutocracy," and "sociocracy." His definition of the term "physiocracy" was very different from its traditional meaning and expression. Consistent with his reliance on classical liberal myths, Ward reserved this term to describe "laissez-faire governments led by honest men." Plutocracy, on the other hand, was considered a "perversion" of this type of government. According to Ward, plutocracy emerged during the early nineteenth century when the state was manipulated by men of wealth to maintain and advance their own class interests. *Sociocracy,* on the other hand, was seen as a coming stage in the development of the state and represented the administration of government in the public interest rather than in the interest of any particular party or group. In the sociocratic stage, society would inquire in a business way without fear, favor, or bias into everything that concerned its own welfare. "In a word, society would do under the same circumstances just what an intelligent individual would do. It would further in all possible ways its own interests" (Ward 1893:327). However, since governments are run by human beings it is reasonable to inquire into the basis for such publicly interested conduct on the part of government officials. Why would the legislators or executives of Ward's sociocratic state run society with an even, altruistic hand?

The technocratic answer provided by Ward was very simple: government officials would either be social scientists or be trained by social scientists. They would be trained, above all, in the knowledge of the genetic process of human evolution, particularly in those processes bearing on the social forces. They would perform their work like the scientific elites of the Saint-Simonians, the secular priests of Comte's positivist regime, or the mandarins of China who were selected by competitive examination, theoretically from all classes, and recruited into the civil service. The men at the helm of the sociocratic state, therefore, were either "experts" or the spokesmen for "experts."

Ward also envisioned a National Academy of Social Sciences in Washington, managed by a group of social scientists and their research assistants. Not unlike the Committee on Social Trends which was set up by Herbert Hoover or the "Brain Trust" established by Franklin D. Roosevelt, this academy would research every conceivable social problem, indicate social tendencies, and propose desirable economic and political policies to guide government in the interest of the people. Because of their belief in the legitimacy of the academy, legislators would look to the expert members for advice and aid in drafting intelligent and scientific legislation.

The officials in the new quasi-public and public agencies would make considerable use of statistics in determining new legislation. Cooperating with each other,[7] legislative and administrative "experts" would gain knowledge of the nature and means of controlling social forces. Under these conditions sociology would truly realize its potential as a science, because from Ward's point of view a science is primarily concerned with prediction in order to *control* natural phenomena. Applied to the United States, this meant that sociology should be ultimately concerned with the management of the "genetic" and therefore *uncontrolled* aspects of capitalism.

Timetable of Social Control through Equal Education and Opportunity

Although Ward was convinced that genetic forces propelled humanity along the evolutionary path and that war was a precondition to social progress, he also felt that human intelligence, as formalized in sociology, would enable humanity to consciously manage these other forces, so that evolution could take place at a faster rate. In addition he believed that the various branches of government, staffed by social scientists, would develop social policies that would control the unruly social forces in the interests of society as a whole. In this effort, legislative bodies could not suppress the social forces because this would lead to the destruction of the race. Instead, progress could be best promoted by a "telic method" consisting of the invention of "attractive legislation" which would induce men to act in a manner most advantageous to society. The intelligent direction of the forces of human nature, not their repression, is called for; and social policy is aimed at the sublimation of the driving emotional forces of collective behavior into constructive channels. The telic method, or what may be considered "positive" social control, is employed when individuals voluntarily decide that they *want* the kinds of things that are good for society as a whole.

Ward (1883:26) also indicated that society had to do more than invert "attractive legislation." Intelligent control of the social forces required the universal diffusion of knowledge about the animate and inanimate forces of nature through a public education system. The telic method therefore also consisted of a state-supported and state-managed education system which would provide a "scientific and popular" education for all members of society. Mass education would represent an efficient, "businesslike solution to the problems of society" and therefore, the government should spare no effort or expense "to impart to every citizen an equal and adequate amount of useful intelligence." Noting such statements as these, Bernhard J. Stern (1959b:206) has observed that even though socialists were proposing that the ills of society could be healed by the equal distribution of wealth, Lester Ward (1883:II, 597) suggested, instead, an equal distribution of information.

As we have already seen, Ward regarded the educational system as an important instrument for achieving equality of opportunity. And in spite of a liberal attitude toward private property and competition, his unequivocal support of universal education during the last quarter of the nineteenth century brought him into sharp conflict with reactionary scholars (Stern 1959b:203). His new brand of liberalism, however, should not obscure the fact that educational, not political, institutions were viewed as the single most important means for eliminating the individual claim to superior rewards on the basis of upper-class privileges, inheritance, or "antisocial" economic acts. Nor should it obscure the fact that public education was his most important means for achieving the enlightened reconstruction of society. Ward was convinced that social classes would ultimately disappear because of the effects of a mass education system on the population as a whole. A "scientific or popular" education would substitute a "natural" sociocratic form of inequality for class or "artificial inequality."

How well have Ward's education predictions been borne out? Six decades after Ward, another liberal, W. Lloyd Warner, also advocated equality of opportunity through public schooling and directed empirical studies in this area (Warner 1949; Hollingshead 1949). However, even though he and his colleagues, including August Hollingshead, felt that the school would provide lower-class youth with the opportunities denied them in the factory, he was alarmed at the effects of social class on the school system. In his studies, schools were dominated by middle-class values and personnel. There were class barriers to advancement in the school as well as in *all other institutions in the community.* What is particularly ironic, however, is that now, almost nine decades after Ward began to advocate universal education, we find American sociologists and educators still criticizing the influence of class inequality in the very same public education system that Ward offered as a solution to the problem of "artificial inequality." Today, almost *ninety years* after Ward's first major work, similar criticism of public education is being raised by racial and ethnic groups.

Of course, since nine decades are analogous to a blink of the eye in Ward's chronology of cosmological evolution, it may be unfair to be critical of his faith in universal education. Therefore, a judgment of this solution may be premature. Perhaps the mass education system will ultimately reconstruct society. But how long will it take? What, precisely, is Ward's timetable for social change?

While there is no difficulty in finding Ward's conception of an optimum social state (i.e., sociocracy) or the means for attaining this state, it is virtually impossible to locate a specific prediction as to when this state might be reached. Further, it is impossible to find information which may enable us to calibrate the minimal intervals of Ward's reductionist timetable. On the other hand, there are numerous general references which indicate that sociocracy will not take place in the near future. There are, in addition, a number of indications that the rate of change will be extremely gradual. At one point, Ward (1883:I, 521) stated that "the time has not yet fairly come when the finer and nobler qualities shall be those best fitted to preserve, strengthen and perpetuate themselves. We are still in that part of the great circuit of psychological development where the coarse and ruder qualities are those best adapted to achieve success." Instead of reaching the stage of social development wherein "reason shall prevail over passion," Ward noted that "the passion of avarice" will continue to rule men's minds for some time.

James Quayle Dealy, a sociologist who was close to Ward, provides us with some estimates from which we might generally gauge the kind of timetable Ward had in mind. Dealy (1927:86) states Ward's feeling that human achievement, given time, would integrate the human race through "the slow process of assimilation and amalgamation." Dealy adds, "In the long run he [Ward] foresaw the ultimate integration of mankind, the 'long run' being not a few generations but those several *millions* of years during which the earth will remain suited to an advanced civilization." Whether this earth will remain suited in the face of the ever-present threats of germ and chemical warfare, atomic weapons, and the widespread pollution of land, sea, air, and rivers, remains to be seen. But if the human race does survive over the next "several millions of years" it should live to see a peaceful, bright, and unpolluted day, according to Ward's *liberal* estimate.

NOTES

1. The phrase "new mandarins" is borrowed from Chomsky (1967).
2. An example of Ward's sensitivity to monetary crises and inflation is contained in "The Ward-Ross Correspondence, 1891–96" (Stern 1938:399).
3. For example, Ward, like Durkheim, used the term "individualism" to characterize laissez-faire capitalism, and indicated that sociocracy has sometimes been confounded with socialism. "In order to distinguish Sociocracy from socialism and the prevailing competitive regime, or individualism," he stated: "Individualism has created artificial inequalities" and "confers benefits on those only who have the ability to obtain them, by superior power, cunning, intelligence, or accident of position." "Socialism, on the other hand, seeks to create artificial equalities . . . confers the same benefits on all alike, and aims to secure equality of fruition." "Sociocracy," Ward added, "recognized *natural inequalities* and aims to abolish artificial inequalities . . . [and] confer benefits in strict proportion to merit, but insists on *equality of opportunity* as the only means of determining the degree of merit" (1913:292–293. We have emphasized the term *"natural inequalities."* Ward emphasized *"equality of opportunity."*).
4. Ward's proposal for "a wise limitation of inheritance" is obviously inadequate for this purpose. Spencer, of course, had no proposals whatsoever in this regard because he felt that superior intelligence was inherited biologically. This intergenerational transfer of property and wealth therefore was paralleled by the biological transfer of intellectual superiority.
5. After the rise of a wealthy ruling class in the United States, spokesmen for business interests also considered the fact that outstanding businessmen such as J. P. Morgan came from families with substantial property. They incorporated references to "superior" family backgrounds, as well as superior achievement in noneconomic institutions, as justifications for the overall "superiority" of the powerful entrepreneur. For a profound study of the complex development of the reputation of the outstanding American entrepreneur, see Sigmund Diamond (1955).
6. This thesis has been generally identified with "managerialism" (e.g., James Burnham [1941] and Berle [1954]). There are also technocratic, socially critical liberal interpretations of modern trends which should be distinguished from the more blatantly apologetic interpretations. For example, Galbraith's *The New Industrial State* is subject to the technocratic myth. He feels that corporation managers are replacing men of property in controlling the political economy. On the other hand, this work is socially critical because it rightfully reveals the degree to which the great corporations control the political state in their own selfish interest.

Parsons' (1957) corporate-liberal perspective contrasts with Galbraith's point of view. Parsons has asserted that the control of corporations is shifting away from men of property toward professional managers. In addition, however, Parsons argues that the political state has become independent of the economy and also more effective in controlling the economy in the public interest.

The writings by the Marxian economists Baran and Sweezy (1966) contrast sharply with the technocratic writings above. They agree that the managers of large corporations have become less subject to stockholders' control. But they insist that this fact does not place these managers beyond the control of ownership in general. "Quite the contrary," Baran and Sweezy (*ibid.:*34–35) exclaim, "managers are among the biggest owners; and because of the strategic positions they occupy, they function as the protectors and spokesmen for all large scale property. Far from being a separate class, they constitute in reality the leading echelon of the property-owning class."

7. Because all aspects of the state would be guided by scientific principles oriented toward the general welfare, Ward indicated it would *not* be necessary to maintain the check and balance system which diverted the executive and legislative branches of the government. Members of both parts of the government would participate on the same committees.

CHAPTER 24

The Natural-Social-Law Tradition

Preview

This chapter points out that the rudiments of a modern technocratic perspective toward "deviant behavior" were expressed in Ward's writings. Ward used the phrase "wayward behavior" instead of the modern phrase "deviant behavior." Both of these phrases, however, appear to play a similar analytic role in liberal, natural-law theories of moral behavior and social change.

This chapter also discusses some of the historical changes in the natural-law perspective which eventually produced the modern, natural-social-law tradition. This discussion will return us once again to the classical liberal concept of man, but it will terminate in modern structural functional conceptions of deviant relationships.

Ward and the Social Control of "Wayward Tendencies"

According to Ward's evolutionary scheme, man's predatory actions posed the problem of social integration from the very beginning of civilization. In spite of millions of years of human evolution, however, human nature still remains egotistical and, therefore, even highly evolved social arrangements cannot be maintained without coming to terms with this fact. Once formed, all human groups must exert continuing *controls* over individual desires in order to survive.

In discussing the development of social forms of life as they affected the social order, Ward (1883:249) stated that "wayward tendencies" began to emerge among individuals from the very beginnings of their existence as members of groups and that some persons attained their happiness at the expense of the common good. Ward declared that because "wayward tendencies" characterized individual conduct, it became necessary that "everything in society be mobilized for the conservation of the group and the race." As a result, "the *wayward* tendencies of mankind have been subject to the natural and spontaneous *restraints* in the interests of the *social order.*" "This *social* adaptation," Ward added, "is well nigh as complete as *organic* adaptation and it [the uncontrollable wayward tendency] would be impossible for any considerable time without disrupting society altogether. If such has ever been the case such societies have perished and are unknown" (our emphasis).

188

Here *social control* (as an expression of "the interest of the social order") is obviously being explained in the same way the biological instincts or psychic forces are explained, i.e., by the mechanisms of spontaneous restraint and organic adaptation. *Biological* instincts are functional prerequisites for organic adaptation and survival; *psychic* forces are functional prerequisites for the adaptation and survival of individuals; and *social* control mechanisms are functional prerequisites for the adaptation and survival of each group or society. In this approach to human relationships, the dynamic principles developed for the analysis of biological relationships are used to model the psychological relationships. Finally, these principles are applied over again to the sociological level of analysis.

Ideological Conception of Deviancy, Adjustment, and Social Control

Ward's expression "wayward tendencies" is analogous in certain respects to modern liberal-functionalist uses of the term "deviancy." In some contexts, Ward clearly regarded a wayward tendency as deviant in a strictly moral and individual sense; waywardness meant the attainment of egoistic pleasures at the expense of the common good. In other contexts Ward preferred to use the term in reference to the distribution of "tendencies" which might exhibit wide variations from the norm; the extremes were generally classified as "wayward." At first glance, the norm, which tacitly regulated the difference between wayward and nonwayward tendencies, appears to be a statistical one. But further examination can show that Ward was thinking in terms of the departure from a "normal" (i.e., normatively distinguished) case. For example, his references to "anti-social acts" (which were seen as the consequences of wayward tendencies), were tacitly regarded as acts committed by an undefined but apparently small proportion of "extreme" members of society. But this impressionistic use of numbers of wayward individuals has significance only because Ward suggested that if the proportion of individuals became too large, and could not be contained by social controls, then society would become unstable and the forces of synergy would recreate new, equilibrated, social relationships between individuals. The proportion of wayward individuals, therefore, did not have significance in light of a deviation from a statistical norm referring to the actual distribution of conforming or deviant persons in a society. This proportion had theoretical significance only by reference to a tacit liberal-functionalist conception of a "normal," "adjusted," and "stable" social order.

Ward's term *adjustment* is also significant in light of modern sociological solutions to the problems of individual and social integration. Individual adjustment implied more than the satisfaction of *individual* imperatives. In Ward's theory, it meant that "normal" persons must first behave in ways that satisfied the functional imperatives of an established *social* order. Ward (1903:249–250 our emphasis) claimed, for example, that in societies which survive, "human desires are . . . more or less completely adjusted to *individual* and *social* needs, and it is safe to assume that the satisfaction of any *normal* desire also contributes in some degree to the preservation of the life of the *individual* . . . or the maintenance of *society,* or *both.*" It is to this double (individual and social) function that Ward and modern structural-functionalists anchor their conception of a highly stable social system. In this view, therefore, a stable system becomes unstable unless most of its members strive for personal goals which are harmoniously integrated with the functional requirements of the system. The ethical ramifications of this perspective are quite clear: society is stable when people desire the kinds of things that are good for the *maintenance* of established institutions. Personal adjustment, therefore, refers above all to acquisition of those individual desires which maintain a social order.

Around the turn of the century, liberal-functionalists like Ward began to utilize transcendent and repressive concepts in broadening the notion of social control. Vague functionalist references to "society's interests" and "society's reactions" to behavioral departures from the normal case were also at the heart of this intellectual development. These references were used to ground the emerging sociology of social control in allegedly universal (i.e., ahistorical) relationships. As we have seen, Ward believed, for example, that once "wayward tendencies" came into being, "everything in society began to work for the conservation of the group and the race." Because of this, these alleged tendencies must become subject to "natural restraints" that are applied in "the interests of society."

Ward's statements are reminiscent of the classical liberal contradiction between the individual and society. But Ward's resolution of this contradiction admits important differences with the classical liberals. In order to explore the political implications of these differences, we must turn back the clock and consider the natural-law conceptions of "immoral" behavior, which were grounded in universal characteristics of mankind.

Liberal Conceptions of Universal Selfishness

What kind of human relationships contribute to immoral behavior? The classical liberal's answer to this question was simple and direct: Immorality is caused by egotism. Egotism, in turn, was described as a natural, immutable, and universal characteristic of human beings. It was in man's nature to be *selfish.* Are these indisputable assumptions? Are men naturally selfish?

There is little doubt in our minds that every man's desires are his own. In striving to satisfy these desires he may be said to display self-interest. But as the philosopher Barrows Dunham (1947:41) points out, self-interest cannot be equated with selfishness: "Self-interest is the satisfaction of one's desires; selfishness is the satisfaction of one's desires at the expense of someone else." Hence, Dunham reasons that the universal existence of selfishness cannot be inferred from the fact that human beings identify their interest with themselves; it can only be inferred by making the assumption that the satisfaction of individual desires is, by the nature of the event, always at a cost to someone else.

Medieval scholars had their own versions of natural law which ultimately referred to a cosmic design created by God. Classical liberals, as we have seen, anchored their interpretations of natural law in subjective impressions of the empirical world. They admitted that crime, poverty, war, and inequality in wealth have bad consequences, but reasoned that given the universally selfish nature of man, these evils were unavoidable. Of course a few men, like Anthony Shaftesbury (1714), felt uneasy with the arbitrary character of this explanation and suggested that it is just as consistent with human nature to engage in behavior which benefits others; consequently, it cannot be assumed that selfishness is present in all human motives and actions.

The tendency to universally equate self-interest with selfish interest [1] was influenced by the growing organization of life along capitalist lines: more specifically, the proposition of human selfishness became a fundamental axiom of classical liberalism because of the importance of the competitive marketplace to society as a whole. The early liberals abstracted the quality of selfishness, which characterized the competitive relations instituted by the marketplace, and generalized this quality to all humanity. Their fictitious reification of the nature of man posed a spurious problem of integration, which was solved by recourse to further fictions.

If the liberals of the seventeenth, eighteenth, and nineteenth centuries had consciously located human desires in such institutional contexts as the marketplace, spelled them out, and examined their limits, certain parts of their ethical philosophy could have become more accurate. Because it locates human behavior in a specific and historically relative context, an institutional analysis would have greatly restricted the *theoretically* significant domain of socially destructive forms of selfishness to such categories of individuals as merchants and manufacturers, who were at the very center of the competitive relations in the marketplace. Situating individual desires in this manner would have augmented their characterizations of man and led to the realization that precapitalism and capitalism were also generating new forms of human cooperation in the organization of economic life; e.g., there are many individuals who do not compete with each other while earning their livelihood—the products of their labor are produced cooperatively. However, this kind of analysis would also have invited a fresh perception of the problem of selfishness (egotism) and man's inhumanity to man (i.e., the Hobbesian problem). It might have uncovered the fact that if the current social organization of human life brought new modes of selfishness into existence, then a socialist reorganization of human institutions would contain the possibility of removing them altogether.

However, as the early liberals did not situate egotistic desires in their concrete institutional contexts, they attempted instead to establish the credibility of their argument by anchoring universal egotism in those necessities which are truly fundamental to all of human life, such as the need for food, shelter, clothing, companionship, and sexual love. These liberals realized that certain aspects of the ancient functionalist assumptions about the nature of man were valid; the human species cannot truly survive if social institutions demand forms of behavior which frustrate the satisfaction of these fundamental needs. They realized further that this functionalist argument had a powerful justificatory potential and used it to their own advantage by redefining egotism as the desire for private property. They also viewed it as an empirically necessary and morally imperative precondition for the well-being of *all* mankind.

What ideological consequences accompanied the consideration of the selfish desire for property as the essential precondition for human survival? Before this question can be answered, it must be noted that human motives such as selfishness referred to morally evaluated acts and actors rather than merely statements of intended actions. One not only took note of what men did when ascertaining their motives; one also judged the moral value of their actions. In perceiving selfishness as an abstract universal quality, and private property as an essential precondition for human welfare, the classical liberals developed an ethical philosophy that completely obscured the responsibility of the new class of merchants and manufacturers for the prevailing forms of human injustice brought into being by capitalism.

Medieval morality, with all its visions of heaven and hell, had justified its moral conceptions of man on the basis of authoritarian principles transcending the individual and the real world. By grounding moral principles in subjective dispositions of individuals and basic human nature, however, liberalism was ultimately able to reconstitute the evaluation of moral behavior in accordance with the interests of the new men of power. Immoral behavior was eventually seen as referring to private actions which were dysfunctional to the orderly processes of the marketplace. The central target of ethical concern was that body of individual actions and attitudes defined as mendicancy, vagrancy, indolence, alcoholism, and lack of proper manners or aspirations, in addition to the more traditional forms of immorality such as theft, vandalism, and homicide. In this evaluation, moralists of the nineteenth century focused their condemnation on the "moral depravity" of "improvident" working-class individuals instead of on the exploitative and immoral actions of powerful entrepreneurs, even though the latter were far more significant to the welfare of most persons in society.

Early in the nineteenth century, "normal" (laissez-faire) marketplace relationships achieved political legitimation, and selfishness was firmly reinterpreted as working-class immorality or the deviation from the new rules of exchange between buyers and sellers, or factory-owners and laborers. These definitions of "legitimate" exchange were basic to the capitalist principles of equity and the forms of distributive justice. They provided the standards for appropriate forms of accommodation of all members of society to the system of political and economic power established by the middle class.

Towards the end of the nineteenth century, however, new sociological conceptions of human relationships emerged. The economics of the marketplace, in particular, could no longer be regarded as a mere sum of atomistic exchangists. The growing awareness of large corporate institutions transformed the shape of commonsense phenomenological maps of society. But this transformation in subjective awareness by liberal scholars as well as others did not fundamentally alter the liberal approach to ethical relationships. Moral behavior was still analyzed atomistically, although, significantly, this behavior was incorporated into *social* units of analysis that referred to collectivities rather than individuals, and to corporate-liberal rather than laissez-faire rules of equity. These collectivities were constructed around new corporate-liberal types of normal cases.

Technocratic Sociology of Deviancy

As sociology gradually divested itself of the older conceptions of natural law, the apparent character of deviancy was now converted into individual departures from the norms maintaining conventional institutions, or institutional orders, such as the economy. These institutions and their orders were eventually called "social systems," and since the normative properties of these systems were usually taken for granted as being in the interests of the common good, individual departures from these norms were defined as immoral, abnormal, maladjusted, or deviant. This uncritical acceptance of the norms of an established social system as the criteria for defining deviancy became one of the hallmarks of modern technocratic theories of deviant behavior.[2]

This normative approach to deviancy developed slowly along with the emergence of the corporate political economy. During this period of change, however, laissez-faire doctrines still maintained a powerful influence on the prevailing standards for evaluating immoral economic behavior. In addition to using these standards as ideological justification for the subjugation of the working class, laissez-faire liberal economists and sociologists used these notions of morality as causal explanations for the growing concentration and incorporation of wealth. Oligopolistic relations developed, in their view, because of the selfish behavior of those powerful entrepreneurs who were reputed to have little regard for the common good. This explanation assumed that individual selfishness alone was the cause of major institutional changes, such as the growth of monopolies. It also assumed that laissez-faire marketplace relationships were the natural and normal state of economic affairs— and therefore in the interests of the common good. In time, however, laissez-faire standards and descriptions gave way to the newer *corporate*-capitalist principles of equity and the *corporate*-liberal conceptions of a natural and normal (i.e. optimum) case.[3]

New as well as old units of analysis were included in the development of this new normative sociology. The shifts in customary thinking relied heavily on such categories as "societal unit," "social body," and "social forces." Some favored categories, for example, "superorganism," were also carried over from laissez-faire theorists and incorporated into the new analytic framework. The liberal scholars who used these categories originally addressed themselves to microscopic, personal, and interpersonal relationships which were reified and projected onto the level of sociological reality. Furthermore, analytic categories such as "society" and "group" were invested with social "interests," "a group reason," or "a group mind" of their own. In this way, the dynamic properties attributed to these social units were actually based on psychological or social psychological properties of individuals or groups of two or three persons. Relations between major institutions were patterned after the microscopic, interpersonal activities of buyers and sellers in a marketplace as portrayed by classical economists. *Institutions* were perceived as atomistic, egoistic entities and their interrelationships were regulated by the same principles used for interpersonal relationships.

Thus, according to these changed modes of explaining institutional relationships, sociologists emphasized *sociological* rather than *psychological* elements (e.g., theorists referred to *groups* rather than *individuals*). But their dynamic properties were actually reduced to little more than well-established psychological and social psychological mechanisms. For convenience, the term *psychologism* will be used to refer to *both* these types of mechanisms when they appear in a sociological theory.

Liberal Natural-Law Sociologists Produce American Natural-Social-Law Tradition

In light of these changes in liberal-functionalism, it is not surprising to find the Americans increasingly justifying capitalist institutions and relationships by recourse to the "universal" functional "imperatives" or "needs" of *social systems* as well as individuals. The early sociologists were able to utilize the ethical strategy embodied in the natural-law tradition for this justificatory purpose. They regarded sociological relationships in the same functionalist fashion in which they analyzed biological or psychological relationships; and it was the latter which constituted the analytic core of liberal natural-law scholarship.

Certain aspects of the new natural-law view of sociological relationships had appeared previously in earlier nineteenth-century justifications of society as a repressive and transcendent "organism." Awareness of this view undoubtedly expedited the process leading to the development of the new natural-law conceptions of social relationships. But it is also important to note that this trend was fairly gradual. Transitional liberals like Ward still relied more heavily on utilitarian images of man rather than "natural-law" images of social institutions and society, when explaining or justifying the nature of capitalist institutions.

The earlier sociologists' natural-law justifications rationalized social inequality by recourse to the inherent nature of *man* rather than the nature of *society*. However, the development of new liberal-functionalist conceptions of social organization and social control ushered in a period in which academics increasingly used both man's nature and society's nature to justify inequality. Eventually the two natural-law strategies (often embodied in the same theoretical works) became *equally* representative of liberal scholarship during these years and onwards.

The Counterrevolutionary Thrust of Natural-Social-Law Writings

Because of its increasing importance, we will use the phrase "natural-social-law" to underscore this change in customary liberal perspectives. Traditional natural law assumed, among other things, that natural laws exist that are independent of human will. In contrast, natural-social-law assumed the existence of immutable or relatively immutable properties of social organizations involving, for example, pervasive social inequalities and instituted standards based on the rationality of exchange or powerful authoritative norms. These "fundamental" social properties were also regarded as being independent of the social consciousness of individual members of these social organizations. (They were independent in the sense that no revolutionary ideology could be effectively used to transcend these properties.) Consequently, while they were formulating their natural-social-law explanations of class inequality in capitalist societies, liberal sociologists alleged that it would be impossible for socialists to permanently eliminate social classes. The exigencies of social life in modern industrial societies would necessitate the replacement of these classes by *essentially similar* relationships of inequality if modern socialist societies were to survive at all.[4] Like the property of "natural" human selfishness, liberals also regarded certain "fundamental" social properties (expressed by social class or other social inequalities) as being inherently present and inherently necessary.

The early functionalist explanations of social integration and social change eventually made it possible for sociologists today to argue that even if revolutionary programs were not found to be contrary to human nature on psychological grounds, they would certainly be found deficient from an "anthropological" or "sociological" point of view. From this essentially *liberal,* hegemonic point of view, revolutionary demands for equality in the factory, or the educational institution, or the family, or the society as a whole, have been regarded as "unreasonable" and "irrational" and "inconsistent" with the "limits of freedom" inherent in the very nature of socially organized human relationships everywhere.[5]

The natural-social-law tradition epitomizes "ideology" in its most pejorative, hegemonic sense because it illustrates the degree to which *fallacious* ideological views of social reality maintain outstanding social inequalities at any given time. There have been truthful propositions generated by some modern liberal scholars (particularly for the analysis of microscopic social relationships). Often, however, these propositions can be found embedded in general natural-social-law theories of social stability and social change which are scientifically invalid as well as conservative from an ideological point of view. The modern natural-social-law tradition illustrates the degree to which liberal scholars unwittingly view the world on the basis of "a false consciousness" which is organized around ethical, empirical and programmatic myths.

From a Marxist point of view, natural-social-law conceptions, such as "the social imperative for order," are not "prime imperatives for social life." Nor are they *scientific* categories. They are completely fallacious ruling ideas which have been created for ideological purposes. They originated, as this volume will show, when corporate liberals attempted to reconstitute liberal hegemony in the face of a radical challenge, by formulating ideas associated with the notion of social control during the formative years. Furthermore, modern natural-social-law usages clearly demonstrate that the "fundamental" properties attributed to *social* phenomena often serve the very same conservative purposes which were served by natural-law scholars who defined nineteenth-century laissez-faire liberal conceptions of man.

NOTES

1. The term "selfish-interest" in this context connotes the entire gamut of selfish motives which liberals have alleged to be universal qualities of men, including Freud's "aggression," Ward's "avarice," and Warner's "prestige."

2. The adoption of the norms of an established system did not necessarily mean that sociologists were not critical of the normal functioning of established systems. It is quite possible, for example, to conduct a critical analysis of local "institutions of justice" on the basis of implicit or explicit standards which are derived from federal bureaus of the government, or from a conception of the "normal" (i.e., optimum) functioning of capitalist institutions.

3. An example of a call for new principles of equity which departed from what were perceived as "natural" and "spontaneous" (nineteenth-century laissez-faire) relationships, is this statement by Ward (1883:I,517): "Under the natural, or spontaneous, system of society, the accumulation of wealth proceeds in a manner exactly the reverse of that best suited to the true advancement of social and individual welfare. Instead of its equitable distribution in proportion to the amount each contributes to its production, it tends to concentrate in the hands of those who produce least."

4. Modern representatives of natural-social-law interpretations which regard social inequalities as relatively immutable properties of social systems include Davis (1945), Warner (1949), and Moore (1963). Moore (1963:14,196) states, for example, "social inequality is a *necessary* feature of any social system . . ." (Our emphasis).

The American natural-social-law tradition is also exemplified by sociological writings on the family, industrial bureaucracies, social deviancy, and other subjects. In addition to the above mentioned writers, natural-social-law theorists include Talcott Parsons, Peter Berger, Kai Erikson, and many others. European natural social-law scholars such as Emile Durkheim and Max Weber also contributed to the development of this tradition.

5. An example of this logic is contained in Peter Berger's (1971) article about the "blindness of youth." In this "defense of reason," Berger (1971:3) equates the sociologist's "hangups on order" with the "exercise of reason." He misleadingly implies that the notion of "cultural revolution" literally signifies "a *permanent* revolution" and then claims that revolutionary youth do not recognize that "behind [the "hangup on order"]

is the conviction that sociology leads to the understanding that order is *the primary imperative of social* life." Berger adds, "Beginning with language, *every* social institution, no matter how 'nonrepressive' or 'consensual' is an imposition of order. . . . The left, by and large, understands that order is precarious. It generally fails to understand that just because of this precariousness societies will react with almost instinctive violence to any fundamental or long-lasting threat to their order. The idea of 'a permanent revolution' is an *anthropological* fantasy" (our emphasis).

There are many sociologists today who will accept Berger's statement above at face value. But it should be noted that there exists a voluminous radical literature which has been developing over the last century and a half which would reject this statement as totally fallacious. This literature on the historical development of ruling classes and ruling institutions (e.g., the state in particular) would eschew such formal categories and psychologistic metaphors which suggest that "societies" react with almost "instinctive violence" when they face a threat to their order. Members of this radical tradition who are Marxists, for the most part, also recognize that liberal-functionalists like Berger regard the "imperative for order" as a fixed and immutable property of all social systems. Like the natural-law scholars who invested their concepts of man with immutable desires for individual survival, private property, and aggression, these liberals have created a social "imperative" which is transhistorical as well as universal. It is, in liberal-functionalist terms, a "fundamental property of social systems."

PART SEVEN

The Resurrection
of Thomas Hobbes and
the Technocratic Concept
of Social Control

CHAPTER 25

The Resurrection of Thomas Hobbes

The contribution of the early European and American sociologists to corporate liberalism in the United States represents a tangled skein. One of the speckled threads in this development, however, is a rash of historical schemes that appeared around the turn of the century. These schemes often divided the evolution of civilization into two contrasting periods which were classified by such terms as *community* versus *society* (Tönnies 1963). Other early societal pairs which were used for this purpose include *mechanical* versus *organic* (Durkheim 1933), *nondifferentiated* versus *differentiated* (Ross 1901), and *primary* versus *secondary* (Cooley, 1909). Later in the century, adjectives such as *familistic* versus *contractual* (Sorokin 1947), *folk* versus *urban* (Redfield 1947), and *sacred* versus *secular* (Becker, 1950) were also used to distinguish these polarized ideal-type [1] social relationships and historical epochs.

These ideal-type schemes were influenced by a noted historian on the development of law, Henry S. Maine. He suggested that the transition to "modern societies" (i.e., to capitalist societies) be considered a transition from status to contract. Maine (1861) had proposed that individual status was fixed by kinship relations in primitive societies. The individual, Maine added,

198

had replaced the family as the basic unit of social organization in modern societies. In these societies, status relations based on kinship had given way to individual relations based on freely contracted relationships.

Ferdinand Tönnies and the Psychological Determinants of Historical Epochs

Maine's theory reflected his legal interests. His discussion of capitalist relations emphasized the legal (e.g., the contractually governed) expressions of the vast, social, economic and political transformations brought about by capitalism. But Tönnies, a political economist who adopted Maine's categories, focused primarily on economistic rather than legal principles, to explain the transition to capitalism.

In Tönnies' theory, all human history was divided by two ideal-type conceptions called Community (Gemeinschaft) and Society (Gesellschaft). In Communities, men and women were bound together by personal obligations, sacred values and patriarchal authority. Their behavior was an epiphenomenal expression of decision-making principles incorporated under the term "natural will" (Wesenwille). "Natural will" encouraged individual persons to regard social relations in general, and kinship relations in particular, as ends in themselves.

In Societies, however, men and women were bound together by relations of utility. Their behavior was an expression of a "rational will" (Kurwille). "Rational will" encouraged people to regard social relations in general and economic or political relations in particular, as a means for the satisfaction of private, individualistic ends. According to Tönnies, persons "willed" their social institutions into existence. Consequently, the pervasive development of "rational will" ushered in capitalist Societies on a worldwide scale, by encouraging individuals to maximize their own private satisfactions at the expense of traditional values.

Tönnies' analysis was similar to those made by earlier liberals in at least two respects. First, the psychologistic view of social institutions or entire societies, as productions of voluntaristic, self-interested striving, was a hallmark of classical and laissez-faire liberal scholarship. Second, his peculiar use of "rational will" linked his theory with conceptions of economic rationality being developed among "neoclassical" (i.e., laissez-faire) liberal economists. These economists had been developing formalized descriptions of the economistic, decision-making actions of "economic man," and his integrative "exchange relations" in capitalist markets. In Tönnies' theory, the rational principles underlying these formal descriptions were first overgeneralized, second, reified as a "rational will," and third, converted into an explanation of the transition to capitalism.

Tönnies and the Political State
as a Solution to Integration

Tönnies, like other corporate-liberal scholars, was primarily concerned with avoiding violent revolutionary solutions to present problems.[2] But the descriptions of modern societies in his writings indicate that he was quite aware of the violent, exploitative, and chaotic character of capitalism. He highlighted these characteristics by comparing them with the allegedly peaceful and harmonious relations existing during the Community stage of historical development. Although he preferred to use such obscurantist terms as "Community" and "Society," he actually located Community primarily in *feudal* relationships. And considering the fact that there were no other types of industrialized societies during his lifetime, Society obviously referred to *capitalism*. According to Loomis and McKinney (*ibid.*:2), he observed, for example, that in the Middle Ages there was "unity," "solicitous paternalism," "relative peace," "sympathetic relationships," "home production," "barter," and "permanency of abode." In Society, on the other hand, there is "atomization" of human relationships, "exploitation," "wholesale slaughter," "mobility," "world-wide trade," and "capitalist production."

However, Tönnies was optimistic about the future of humankind. He believed that the political *state* would come to be viewed by the common people as "a means and a tool" which would be useful in bettering their condition. Furthermore, a more stable society, with greater equity in the distribution of objects of consumption, could be organized by the state at some future time. As a result of state policies, for example, "the laborer would be allowed a share in production according to his reasonable needs and the leaders in production their share of certain goods which are to be divided for consumption . . ." (Tönnies 1963:259). The state was therefore perceived as a means for eventually controlling laissez-faire capitalism and establishing new principles of equity between capital and labor.

Just as the French utopians developed idealized conceptions of feudal relationships in order to criticize the anarchic characteristics of capitalism, so Tönnies also used feudal relationships as an idealized counterpoint to a critical view of capitalism. However, this similarity does not mean that Tönnies accepted the political doctrines of these utopians. It merely indicates that he used a similar *critical strategy* for his own ends.[3] The significant similarities between Tönnies and the French utopians are more dependent upon their common opposition to laissez-faire capitalism than they are upon their idealizations of feudal periods of social development.

200

Durkheim: Another Example
of This Socially Critical Ideal-Type Strategy

Durkheim did not feel that the differences between individual interests and the coercive influences of culture were sufficiently distinguished in Tönnies' *Community and Society*. In spite of this, Durkheim's concepts of mechanical and organic societies, presented in *The Division of Labor in Society* in 1893, also emphasized the almost total integration, homogeneity, and peaceful nature of traditional or *mechanical* communities. In these communities, men were bound together by common values and obligations. Their lives were regulated by a collective conscience and by repressive law which prevented them from morally refuting and deviating from the cake of custom in which they were embedded. In contrast, *organic* societies, brought about by the continuous development of the division of labor, were still in the process of great change. While they were capable of gradually developing more highly evolved forms of integration on the basis of the political state and occupational morality, life in organic societies was generally characterized by commercialization of values, selfish individualism, and anarchy, as well as the disintegration of the customs, traditions, and institutions of preexisting mechanical communities. Individuals became rootless in organic societies. They acquired socially expedient points of view. Anomie, a condition of normlessness, prevailed in "organic," that is, *capitalist* societies.

Tönnies and Durkheim were not the only scholars who used the same critical strategy to interpret the span of history or social structures at any given time. But these scholars helped set the style of viewing feudal and agrarian economies as the contrasting backdrop to the grave social problems emerging within monopoly capitalist societies. They did not use this sharp contrast, as did the aristocratic French intellectuals before them, to argue for the reinstatement of aristocratic privilege and feudal institutions. To the contrary: their theories were advanced in the hope that capitalism might be reorganized and further developed. Consequently, their contrasting visions of feudalism functioned as ideological justifications. These visions gave greater emphasis to the need for instituting a powerful modern political state and the kinds of social controls which would usher gradual and progressive changes into capitalist nations.

The Hobbesian Problem with a Corporate-Liberal Twist

Tönnies and Durkheim obviously turned the tables on Spencer. They reformulated the liberal perception of social development by making industrial *capitalism,* not militaristic feudalism, the basic condition which posed *the* problem of integration. And consistent with the spirit of corporate liberalism, the feature of capitalism that was chosen to justify this claim was "individualism," that is, *uncontrolled egoism.* Capitalism was considered a progressive form, which, like fire, needed control to prevent its possible destructive efforts. The institutions of social control that had existed in Communities had disintegrated under the effects of individualism. Since no effective controls had replaced these older restrictions, individual self-interest reigned supreme and men were at each other's throats. Clearly, therefore, Tönnies and Durkheim restated the Hobbesian problem but in a very different social, historical, and (monopolistic) economic context.

The *new* liberal social scientists reached out in their criticism beyond capitalism and its relations of production (which they had come to know and partially repudiate). The target of their descriptions went beyond a Society that destroyed Community and left individual egoism uncontrolled. Their hegemonic criticism was also directed at the ideological doctrines which had been used by *liberal* scholars over two centuries as the solution to the problem of integration. For if capitalism was disorganized, then exchange relations in the competitive marketplace were not sufficient for integrating Society.

In order to differentiate the new, *corporate*-liberal conceptions from the type of problem that has become identified with Hobbes, these new concepts will be referred to as the *neo-Hobbesian problem.* It must, however, be kept in mind that for Hobbes, individual egoism posed questions which could only be answered by the creation of an absolute monarchy. For the pioneering corporate liberals, however, the neo-Hobbesian problem could be partly resolved by a modern capitalist state. Since these intellectuals felt that uncontrolled "egoism" was extensively manifested throughout society, they also believed this regulation required new and varied instruments of *social control.*

NOTES

1. The concept of ideal-type was introduced by Weber (1949:90). The definitions of this concept by Weber and others have been highly ambiguous (Martindale 1959:57). (Weber stated, for example, that "an ideal type is formed by the one-sided *accentuation* of one or more points of view and by the synthesis of a great many diffuse, discrete, more or less present and occasionally absent concrete individual phenomena, which are arranged according to those one-sidedly emphasized viewpoints into a unified *analytical* construct.") Generally, however, an ideal-type image of man or society is formulated by abstracting properties which are diachronically or synchronically related to the phenomena being explained. Once this abstract notion is formulated, it appears to be used either as an analytic strategy for developing a theoretical model, or as a theoretical model itself. Tönnies used his ideal-type concepts to explain changes in historical epochs. The next chapter indicates that Ross used ideal-type concepts to explain the historical changes in the methods of social control.

2. Loomis and McKinney (1963:9) point out, for example, that for Tönnies, "the end and meaning of any social order was peaceful relations among men. . . . Maladjustments could best be righted peacefully without resort to revolutions and recasting of the institutions and norms of society."

3. The strategy of counterposing a contemporary state of affairs with an idealized past has been used by both conservative and radical scholars for thousands of years: Plato idealized patrician society and Rousseau did the same with "the natural state of

man" in order to criticize evil in the civilized world. The fact that these writers used a similar critical strategy, however, should not be taken to mean (as Sorokin [1963:vii] implies) that they were addressing themselves to the same *substantive* relationships which were connoted by Tönnies' use of the words "Community" and "Society." Tönnies' society is not Athens. Nor is his Community the agrarian (slave) economy ruled by Greek patricians.

CHAPTER 26

Broadening the Connotations of Social Control

During the eighteenth century, a whole family of ethical, epistemological, and theoretical models of man and society were provided by the liberal ideologists. These conceptual models underwent considerable refinement, modification, and elaboration during the nineteenth century. Toward the end of that century, however, the founders of modern North American sociology began to actively contribute to the second major reconstruction of the liberal world view. Like the first stage in the development of liberalism, this reconstruction generated its own family of theoretical models. Some of their underlying principles were perceived in Ward's evolutionary theory of man and society.

The category of social control became the pivotal concept in the second reconstruction of liberalism. The concept of social control served this central hegemonic function after being applied in one context after another until it was eventually taken for granted that weak or strong social controls were manifest in nearly every single phase of social life.[1] Liberal intellectuals also gradually formulated an analytic strategy for using the concept of social control in further study of human relationships.[2] A theoretical approach to the origins of social control was also fully developed.[3]

Edward Alsworth Ross and Social Controls for Man's Egoistic Nature

The scholar who pioneered most in generating the ideas that became associated with the corporate-liberal concept of social control was Ward's nephew-in-law, Edward A. Ross. Ross began to publish his essays on social control as early as 1895 in the *American Journal of Sociology*. These essays were integrated and published as a volume entitled *Social Control* in 1901.

In order to justify the usefulness of the concept of social control, Ross asserted that social controls have played an integrating role since the very beginning of civilization. "We ought to take for granted," Ross (1901:4–5) indicated, "that men living in propinquity will continually run afoul of one another" because every man has "a *natural* unwillingness to be checked in the hot pursuit of his ends" (our emphasis). Considering that if civilization were "remanded to the zero point of social development," it would be more appropriate to assume a state of disorder than order. Ross asked: "By what means is the human struggle narrowed and limited?" "How has the once brawling torrent of conflicting personal desires been induced to flow smoothly in the channels of legitimate rivalry?" Once again these questions pose the Hobbesian problem of integration.

Ross' Natural Nondifferentiated Man and Society

In *Social Control,* Ross depended heavily on two analytic models of society, the first of which was called the natural, or nondifferentiated society. In describing the natural society, Ross claimed that as civilization evolved, members of small communities became organized on the basis of a common agreement about social values. However, the reciprocal constraints based on this spontaneous consensus about values were not enough to maintain the society after it emerged. Because of the nature of human passions, which include egotistic as well as altruistic elements, individuals had to be restrained, in part by external forces which rely on fear, trust, and admiration of dominating men such as priests, warriors, and political leaders.

Ross' ideal-type model of a natural society contains a number of highly ambiguous psychological assumptions about the nondifferentiated, natural man. Without spelling these out in detail, however, he generally claimed that in a natural society, individuals have *a less evolved* sense of the worthiness of self. However, because the self is not highly developed, natural man is not capable of reflexive social behavior. (Nondifferentiated man was described as being instinctively sympathetic and compassionate, but unable to achieve self-discipline on the basis of abstract moral principles.) As a consequence of their inferiority, the maintenance of social discipline among natural men requires the ever-present fear of external sanctions. The use of undisguised force by "able leaders," in Ross' opinion, is absolutely necessary for the achievement of a stable and orderly nondifferentiated natural society.

Ross' Composite, Differentiated Man and Society

According to Ross, the natural society evolved into the composite or differentiated society. In this evolutionary process, change was inevitably brought about by the emergence of private property and free enterprise, the rapid

204

growth of impersonal and transient urban relationships, a high degree of occupational mobility, deterioration of marriage, kinship, and religious traditions, and technological changes. These enlarged composite societies were also rent by economic conflicts; individual inhabitants deepened their innate concern with selfish interests alone and resorted to socially expedient means no matter what the costs to the public at large. In addition, although it was necessary for the development of civilization, these societies were disrupted by what Ross called "racial conflict" (which actually referred to conflicts between different ethnic, religious, and national groups as well as races). Since increasing differentiation by economic and "racial" factors threatened the foundations of a stable social order, new and highly differentiated social controls were created by "society" in order to achieve stability. As a result, "It is in the composite [differentiated] society . . . where the need of control is most imperative and unremitting, that the various instruments of regulation receive their highest form and finish. Here has been perfected the technique of almost every kind of control" (*ibid.*:57).

It is obvious that Ross' differentiated society included capitalist societies. In capitalism, the forms of social control became most highly refined because of the increasing "social differentiation" brought about by "economic" and "social" factors.

The problem of order presented in Ross' conception of *uncontrolled capitalist societies* is a neo-Hobbesian problem of order. This conception is accompanied by the formulation of a rudimentary concept of neo-Hobbesian man which will be called a *differentiated* man. By contrast, the member of a nondifferentiated society will be called a *nondifferentiated* or *natural* man.

Ross' concept of natural man was influenced by his racial, national, and religious bigotry. The same was true of his concept of the differentiated man. Pointing out that anthropologists distinguish between the "Aryan" or "Germanic people," who are "tall, long-skulled blonds," and the "Celto-Slavs" or "Latin people," who are "shorter, broad-skulled brunets," it was Ross' contention that the former "are more enterprising and variative." These Aryans "conquer," "swarm to the cities," and are "colonists, roamers and pathfinders." They are said to "prize personal liberty, and will not stand policing and surveillance." Because of their "temperament," they are "best controlled through their self-assertion and pride." "With them Protestantism and moral philosophy have real power because they corroborate certain *inner* experiences." In contrast, Ross noted, "the broad-skulled brunets of southern Europe are less individualistic, and more gregarious and dependent." They prefer the farm village, are "tenacious," "bow to authorities," are "emotional" and "artistic in temperament." They feel "the prestige of the past" and are "readily impressed by ceremonies." Since they are "habit loving, they are easily controlled in their ideas of right by means of early religious [Catholic] education" (*ibid.*:439–440).

Internal and External Controls
Required for Superior Races

To a great extent, *Social Control* was written with the United States in mind. Ross perceived a nation filled with different racial, ethnic, religious, and economic groups. The nation as a whole was disrupted by conflicts within and between these groups. In addition, Ross was particularly interested in the forms of integration found among white Anglo-Saxon Protestants (to use current terminology). In his view, this group represented the most ideal model for social control. He stated, for example, "it is the purpose of this inquiry to ascertain how men of the West-European breed are brought to live closely together, and to associate their efforts with that degree of harmony we see about us." [4] As far as he was concerned, the control of the Slav or the Latin primarily revolves around the control of his *unconscious* egotistical feelings, but the social control of the American Aryan is a more complex matter. Because these Aryan and Latin "races" represent different temperamental qualities and since the two are components of the population of the United States, both *internal* and *external* forms of social control are required if these races are to be controlled in "the interests of society." Internal controls, like enlightenment or social ideals, appeal to individual *reason* and *understanding* (and, therefore, involve reflexive thinking.) [5] External controls, like punishment, appeal directly to the will and passions.

Consequently Ross also emphasized the effects of moral persuasion as well as forcible coercion. For example, in an argument about social control with nineteenth-century theorists like Carlyle, he disagreed that the strengthening of custom and religion alone will counter the disruptions of the laissez-faire marketplace. According to Ross, these theorists have overlooked the potentials of capitalism in effectuating the *"moral* method of democracy" which changes individual personalities and permits "the guidance of men by *ideals."* This consequence, it is argued, is particularly noticeable in America "where it is the lineal descendent of Protestantism." Here, "the steadiness of a social control through self-masterhood, lessens both the mood and the need of hero-worship" (*ibid.:*285). And, therefore, instead of relying on strong men, America increasingly turns to the influence of "controlling ideals" to maintain the "interests of society."

Social Types as Instruments of Control

In two chapters devoted to the achievement of conformity by use of "personal ideals" and "personal types," Ross presented the problem of integration anew and suggested a solution to it. He noted that although individuals strenuously pursue their private ends, their interpersonal relationships achieve an equilibrium because "whatever his place in this system, a person must assume certain definite relations to other persons and to other parts of the system." However, since the requirements of social roles are different, one from the other, Ross (1901:218–219) asked, "What prompts each to adjust himself to the demands the social order makes upon him?" He concluded that it is the sentiments of obligation and duty which enable this equilibrium to take place, and that the development of these feelings of duty is achieved by means of "patterns or types which society induces its members to adopt as their guiding ideals." These controlling patterns or types are called "social types" and are known to members of society by such names as "mother," "priest," 'soldier," "diplomat," "chief," and "man of science." Although they are alleged to emerge on the basis of such relationships as "division of labor" within a group or society, they are also regarded as instruments of social control. These types supply individuals with personal ideals. Individuals in society are "induced to admire and aspire to a social type" because social types, as in the case of the soldier, are glorified by literature, canonized by religion, and applauded by the multitudes (*ibid.*:222–223).

Ross' interest in social types was stimulated by his desire to have others use this information to instill moral attitudes in individuals. He stated that by "analyzing social characters into their ultimate elements, we can make a few virtues do the work of many concrete [social] types; but these virtues must be combined in varying degrees and proportions, in order to give the variety of guidance needed in the social system." Excited by the prospect involved, he added (*ibid.*:227), "Vast, indeed, is the gain from this moral alphabet." By bringing people up to "love and imitate" general social qualities, members of society can use knowledge of the socializing influences of social types for the advancement of social progress. Furthermore, social types, as ideals, can be used to inculcate a sense of self-respect or honor on the one hand, and shame on the other; "these taken together constituting a veritable self-acting system of rewards and punishments."

Further Differences in Human Nature
and in Social Control

Ross (*ibid.*:235–236) argued that "there is no good leverage for control unless self be used as a fulcrum." Therefore, it is not possible to control individuals through the inculcation of personal ideals unless they have "a developed self-sense." What groups have this developed sense of self? Generally Ross identified two groups in answering this question: the *Aryans* and the *upper classes*. He declared (*ibid.*:236): "Because it cannot dispense with a vivid consciousness of personal worth, control through ideals flourishes in the higher classes while yet the inferior orders are under the curb of custom and authority." The upper classes, he noted, "are filled with a sense of pride," and the personal ideal appeals, above all, to pride. The "inferior orders," on the other hand, cannot be effectively controlled in this manner because they are still highly influenced by "superstition" and "supernaturalism"—and "supernaturalism makes for humility."

Finally, Ross integrated social class references with nineteenth-century racism by noting that there are also some races that cannot live up to the kinds of exacting ideals exemplified by social types. He noted (*ibid.*:235) that the use of social types as an instrument of control depends upon whether an individual can "appreciate noble aims," and therefore we cannot "expect it of an indolent, unstrenuous race." "On the other hand," he added, "provided it has will and self-control, a race that is *harsh, greedy* and *masterful* in temper may develop into something *noble,* once its allegiance is fixed upon high personal ideals" (our emphasis). He observed that "both the Romans and the English, in spite of their cold and unsociable dispositions, have been able to produce for justice and administration men that cannot be surpassed in integrity."

The Collective Mind
as Benevolent Despot and Arbiter

Ross discussed the ways in which relationships between interest groups could also be controlled. He noted (*ibid.*:302) that the larger the body of people who acted together, the more their action was guided by "group" self-interest. "Consequently, when society seeks to control the conduct of one of its sections or classes, or when one group, sect or community seeks to modify the action of another group, sect or community, it is the language of interest that is used." He suggested that interest groups could be controlled by appealing to their self-interest. When interest groups threaten the "interests of society," however, they can be controlled by the force of "public opinion."

Among corporate liberals, the state functioned as the main arbitrating force or institutional arena within which leaders of groups could reconcile their conflicts of interests. In *Social Control,* on the other hand, Ross also refers to other kinds of relationships such as tradition and public opinion which prevented selfish interest groups from dominating differentiated societies. These relationships were generally classified by the term *collective mind.* This "collective mind" operated, according to Ross, in "the interest of society" or "in the public interest." Whose interests and traditions did the collective mind represent?

Ross (*ibid.*:293) stated: "The thesis of this book is that from the interactions of individuals and generations there emerges a kind of collective mind evincing itself in living ideals, conventions, dogmas, institutions, and religious sentiments which are more or less happily adapted to the task of safeguarding the collective welfare from the ravages of egoism." He then described and differentiated the "collective minds" of natural and differentiated societies. In the former the collective mind was identified with the interest of "a ruling caste," "priestly oligarchies," and "sacred aristocracies." In these societies

Ross generally referred to *ruling classes* or leaders of ruling institutions. However, with regard to modern, differentiated, and obviously democratic capitalist societies, Ross substituted the word "society" for "collective mind" and stated that "the 'society' that 'controls' is today too closely identified with the mass to feel any great aloofness from the individuals it deals with. Originating in the community of many consciousnesses it does not place itself over against the individual in order to bully, browbeat, and exploit him if it can." Ross (*ibid.*:293) conceded that to some extent "this public . . . is, if you will, a despot, but still a paternal, benevolent despot. Hence, it is concerned not only with what harms the community, but with what harms the man himself." This justification of social control is by way of a *democratic rationale* and it will be frequently encountered in works by other American sociologists.

The significance of Ross' avoidance of any reference to a ruling class or oligarchy in modern differentiated societies cannot be overestimated.[6] In his work, the dynamic functions of a ruling class in capitalist societies were replaced by vague references to a mystical collective mind and public consciousness.

Democratic Structure of Differentiated (Capitalist) Societies

Ross perceived American society in ideal-type terms as a "classless" or "democratic" form.[7] As far as Ross was concerned, a society could become dominated by a class if members of the subordinate classes were not provided with "democratic" or "equal" opportunities. Ross did feel that the United States was in danger of being dominated by capitalist blocs, but he was also convinced that countervailing influences such as "public opinion," as well as enlightened capitalists and politicians (e.g.,Theodore Roosevelt) would limit the arbitrary power of the "robber barons."

From this point of view, a society that is not dominated by a ruling class provides the individual with the freedom to *compete* with others in the marketplace. Because of this, it is informative to note the degree to which Ross organized his discussion of American society around such terms as "competitive society" or "democratic society." (He used these terms interchangeably.) For example, in *Social Control,* Ross cautioned the reader not to confuse the different forms of control required in democratic and nondemocratic societies. He pointed out (*ibid.*:393) "it is necessary to distinguish between a parasitic society and a competitive society." Substituting the term "competitive society" for "democratic society," Ross added that in respect to "the economic friction and contrasts of worldly condition, a competitive society may present the same aspect as a society composed of exploiters and exploited." But there is one great difference between these societies; "a difference which has everything to do with the volume and kind of control that will be needed to preserve social order." In a *really* competitive society, the hopelessly poor and wretched are, to a large extent, the weak and incompetent who have accumulated at the lower end of the social scale because they or their parents have failed to meet the tests of the competitive system. (In other words, they deserve their plight.) In an aristocratic society, however, the poor exist because they are oppressed by a parasitic class, "not because they are less capable and energetic than the classes that prey upon them."

With this societal difference in mind, Ross argued that a competitive society will "still require no such elaborate apparatus of control as a parasitic society," no matter how sharply differentiated it is or how "rude the clash of conflicting interests." The controls in a competitive society will "not exhibit the traits of class control, but will show the sincerity, and elasticity that makes the control that is really social" (*ibid.:*393–394). In a chapter on class control, for example, Ross described how "parasitic classes" in natural societies maintain their control over admiring and compliant populations and "inferior orders" through violence, fraud, superstition, ostentatious ceremony, and pomp. These forms of control disappear in a democratic era where "the need of solemn ostentation passes away, and the wealthy employ their riches in keeping up a manner of life very different from that of the great in the aristocratic era." However, in a competitive society, Ross (*ibid.:*391) declared, "government is conducted with less of state, and the ceremony that is still retained for public occassions is religious and ethical rather than spectacular."

As indicated, Ross felt that social control in a democratic society did not exhibit "the traits of class control." Nevertheless he recognized that the social control which replaced class control would have to deal with the discontent generated by economic inequality. "A differentiated society," Ross (*ibid.:*12–13) said, "produces and consecrates stupendous inequalities in condition." Because of this, Ross warned that society cannot depend on the expression of "spontaneous feelings apart from law and morality" as a major instrument of social control. Spontaneous expressions of sympathy cannot hold people together because members of a differentiated society are too envious of each other. Therefore, Ross placed an emphasis on finding ways in which conforming behavior could be produced by public opinion, social myth, laws, custom, religion, and models of social types. In Ross' opinion, "it is *obedience* that articulates the solid, bony framework of the social order; sympathy is but the connective tissue. As well build a skeleton out of soft fibre as construct social òrder out of sympathies. Not friendly aid, but *reliable conduct,* is the cornerstone of great organization" (our emphasis).

NOTES

1. This process of generalization was complex and included, in addition to reification, the continuous scrutiny of instances in which social controls might be made manifest. This scrutiny generated, in time, a very comprehensive field of connotations which were discussed in works on social control by, e.g., Ross (1901) and Lumley (1925) and

were symbolically captured in their chapter headings. These headings included such categories as "law," "public opinion," "art," "personal ideals," "flattery," "laughter," "gossip," "advertising," "slogans," "propaganda," etc., etc.

2. This strategy was developed by men like Ward. The analytic division between genesis and telesis, and other reform Darwinist conceptions (e.g., the spontaneous emergence of social controls as functional prerequisites of social institutions), played important roles in developing a liberal-functionalist strategy in this regard.

3. Ward, for example, pointed out that deviancy occurred when feeling (i.e., individual imperatives) became "opposed" to function (i.e., social imperatives). Unlike Hobbes' political state Leviathan, which came into existence in order to enable individuals to survive, Ward also felt that social controls spontaneously emerged in order to enable groups, institutions, or societies to survive.

4. He does not deny that there exists social disharmony among the American "Aryans" or that the maintenance of a stable social order, "even among the passive, unambitious Hindoos [*sic*], presents a problem for solution." But the American Aryan provides a particularly interesting challenge to Ross because the "restless, striving, doing Aryan, with his personal ambition, his lust for power, fame . . . fortune . . . is under no easy discipline." In Ross' opinion, "the same selective migrations that made the Teuton more self-assertive than the docile Slav or the quiescent Hindoo [*sic*], have made the American more strong-willed and unmanageable than even the West Europeans" (Ross 1901:3).

5. While Ross was developing the category of social control, George H. Mead and Charles H. Cooley were formulating complementary hegemonic metatheoretical perspectives which eventually became the foundations of modern theories of social roles.

6. The relations between Ross' notion of "controlling ideals" and the modern structural-functionalist usage of such phrases as "paramount values" or "value consensus" may appear to be tenuous. But there is certainly a very direct line that connects Ross' social-control view of the "collective mind" and the modern structural-functionalist notion of "social consensus."

7. Usages of the word "class" can be found in Ross' works. But it is important to note that in regard to democratic capitalist societies, Ross actually regarded classes as "interest groups" (e.g., see Ross 1901:401).

CHAPTER 27

Technocratic Consciousness of the Capitalist System

The Technical Expert on the Control of Men and Women

Ross followed up his hardheaded observations with all sorts of crude, "practical" suggestions about achieving "reliable conduct." He concluded his commentary on social types, for instance, with suggestions for utilizing types to achieve conformity. He noted that educators should not "pitch" the ideals embodied in these types "very far above the natural inclination," and he wrote that "a standard nearer to the average will have a more generally useful effect; while one even lower may yet be more useful."

In providing further advice to public administrators of social morality Ross asked, "How can society tell the weapons in its armory from those that are worn out or obsolete or unserviceable?" He then suggested criteria for winnowing the moral wheat from the chaff. One was called "economy"; an economical instrument of moral control should mold individual character rather than particular kinds of conduct because character regulates many kinds of conduct. Another criterion suggested that instruments which inculcate values and voluntary actions are better than those dependent upon external means, such as punishment. In this respect, Ross noted that control of a person's will by precept was preferable to control by sanctions. "Still better tactics than an attack on will is a flank movement aimed at feelings or judgement." In fact, "the best guarantee of a stable control from within is something that reaches at once feeling, reason and will." Simplicity was still another criterion. Those controls which appealed to man's selfish nature or "the immutable conditions of associations" were simplest. Ideology and dogma, on the other hand, were changeable and complex and "must be regarded askance."

Ross (1901:420–425) also suggested that certain limitations should be placed on social control. He advised the moral rulers of society that "Social interference should not lightly excite against itself the passion for liberty." But he also felt that "Social interference should respect the sentiments that are the support of natural order."

Turning to moral deviants, Ross (ibid.:425) resurrected Malthus and Spencer with: "Social interference should not be so paternal as to check self-extinction of the morally ill-constituted," and "Social interference should not limit the struggle for existence as to nullify the selective process." The scope of these principles can be best conceived when the reader considers that Ross (ibid.:422) viewed those who overindulged, such as alcoholics, to be congenital moral defectives: "Those born with the liquor appetite live out their days and plague our descendants with their ill-constituted offspring." The serious consequences of social paternalism entail danger to the human race when it favors these defectives. "The Christian cult of charity as a means of grace," he protested (ibid.:424), "has formed a shelter under which idiots and cretins have crept and bred. The state gathers the deaf mutes into its sheltering arm, and a race of deaf mutes is in process of formation." In fact, his philosophy regarding race improvement through social control was "tastefully" and parsimoniously summed up when he entreated (ibid.) that "we want no purée of human beings."

The tenor of Ross' practical suggestions for race improvement is also revealed in his references to black Americans. "The uplifting of the American negro [sic] is another field for the method of control by social valuations." He considered that "the growth of new and higher wants, coupled with the

212

training to new skill, is the best lever for raising the idle, quarreling, sensual Afro-American," and further pointed out that "the infecting of the backward portion of the race with a high estimate of cleanliness, neatness, family privacy, domestic comfort, and literacy is quite as truly a moralizing agency as dread of future punishments or love for an ethical God" (*ibid.*:336).

In discussing the methods of presenting new ideals to black Americans, or immigrant groups like "the Cossacks and Magyars," who have lost their indigenous traditions in America, Ross pointed out that a discrepancy may arise between what "we commend to our neighbors and what we adopt for ourselves." He therefore counseled those administrators of moral behavior who are concerned with the problem of basing credibility upon honesty to accept the fact that one *cannot be honest* and pursue the use of the new, "inobvious" forms of social control. "For sincerity and frankness," he argued, "let one betake himself to Kabyles or Bedouins," whose conduct is regulated by very obvious external forms of control. "Genuineness," on the other hand, "is not for a society that prefers to maintain its social order by sweet seduction rather than by rude force" (*ibid.*:337).

Ross (*ibid.*:244) extended his remarks about the legitimacy of "sweet seduction" further by stating that "the guidance of men by ideals is just the reverse of guidance by authority." Ideals generate voluntary behavior by "binding" individuals "from within" rather than by external controls. "But when we bind [an individual] from within we must leave him *the illusion of self-direction* even at the very moment he martyrizes himself for the ideal we have sedulously impressed upon him" (our emphasis).

At the conclusion of his work, Ross cautioned the reader not to provide individuals who are being urged "into the straight and narrow way" with too much knowledge about the foundations of the moral order, because this would forearm the individual "in his struggle with society." Ross confessed that "no light responsibility is laid upon the investigator who explores the mysterious processes that take place in the soul of a people, and dissects in public the ideals and affirmations elaborated in the social mind." But he added that "the fact of control is, in good sooth, no gospel to be preached abroad with allegory and parable, with bold type and scare headlines. The secret of order is not to be bawled from every housetop." Because of this, a "wise sociologist will show religion a consideration it has rarely met with from the naturalist. He will venerate a moral system too much to uncover its nakedness. He will not tell . . . the street Arab, or the Elmira [prison] inmate how he is managed. *He will address himself to those who administer the moral capital of society*—to teachers, clergymen, editors, law-makers, and judges, who wield the instruments of control; to poets, artists, thinkers and educators, who guide the human caravan across the waste." In all this, Ross declared, the sociologist "will make himself an accomplice of all good men for the undoing of all bad men" (*ibid.*:441, our emphasis).

These remarks indicate the extent to which Ross' work is more than a theoretical statement. It is also appropriate to regard it as an administrative handbook written by an "expert" on the subject and addressed to persons interested in the efficient control of people. Ross (*ibid.*:436, n.1) regarded *Social Control* in this light: "It is investigation of the kind I have attempted in this book that will enable society to go about the business of control in a *scientific* way" (our emphasis). These remarks were addressed primarily to conventional administrators of moral behavior and not to the population at large. Toward the latter population, Ross suggested that the sociologist should adopt a policy of guile and deception. Because of this it is quite appropriate, in our opinion, to nominate Ross as the American Machiavelli of social control.

Ross' Interpretation of the Enlightenment

Men of the Enlightenment such as Bentham and Helvetius felt, to some extent, that man was innately virtuous or capable of reasoned and prudent self-control. Therefore, given his free and enlightened attentiveness to the desires of other people, each individual would express himself in socially constructive ways. The steady development of an unequivocally selfish conception of man, however, generated the issue of the contradiction between individual and social imperatives during the nineteenth century. Lester Ward's theory of social forces has been described in this work as an attempt to reconcile this contradiction within the framework of a corporate-liberal conception of man and society.

Like Ward, Ross perceived the individual as unalterably opposed to society. At one point in *Social Control,* Ross discussed the ways in which instruments of control can influence judgmental processes apart from feelings. This discussion provides evidence of the peculiar way in which the tradition of the Enlightenment was seen by "social control" theorists like Ross. Echoing the conservative French scholars, Ross regarded the Enlightenment more as the encouragement of "a dissolution of social control" rather than a new morality. This initial interpretation of the Enlightenment is not surprising considering his philosophy of man and society. From his standpoint, *greater individual rationality* stands for *greater ability to circumvent the imperatives of society* when they interfere with the private pursuit of pleasure.

Ross noted that "after we have paraded all the sanctions, there are still many cases in which the virtue or duty that society demands of the individual is hopelessly at variance with his personal welfare." Because the Enlightenment failed to "reach the deep springs of human conduct" it had frequently created a "stereotyped and hollow morality." He had no doubt (*ibid.*:300–301) that "the more intelligent the common people, the safer it is to drop all those distinctions between actions which are founded on religion, convention, or authority, and to influence men in respect to conduct by a frank *expose* of its consequences, personal and social." But Ross (*ibid.*:302) hastened to add that "the *method* of enlightenment is more effective" for modifying the conduct of groups, classes, or parties than the conduct of individuals (our emphasis). "Save in the case of the mob, the rule holds that the larger the body of persons who act together, the more their action is guided by interest and the less it is directed by sentiment." These remarks indicate that Ross perceived the Enlightenment primarily as an era within which a particular *method of social control* was created.

The selective character of Ross' references to the Enlightenment cannot be overstated. Ross, and all the founders who shared his notion of social control, viewed the Enlightenment as the source of the tradition which elevated the importance of human rationality to the detriment of social control. This was not consistent with their *reputed* humanism but rather with an overriding interest in the rational or "efficient" control of large populations of people. What is significantly missing from their view is the recognition of the degree to which the humanism of the Enlightenment elevated human potentiality, not social stability, as the measure of all things. Ross can never be considered an heir to the Enlightenment. On the contrary, Ross *(ibid.:299–300)* clearly stated that rationalism had "clipped the wings of imagination; it cramped the emotions; it misinterpreted the social impulses; it robbed religion of all wonder; it neglected the ebullient side of human nature." Above all, "its cardinal sin was failure to furnish a good cohesive principle for society."

Ross' Consciousness of the Capitalist System

Ross' discussion of enlightened self-interest further detailed an important property of his tacit, natural, and normal conception of society. In this society, the relations between individuals in part, and between groups in general, were to be organized around the principle of a nonmoral prudentialism. One may well view the terms "nonmoral" and "prudential" as somewhat redundant,[1] but they are used here in combination for emphasis because Ross appeared to have converted prudentialism (or "enlightened self-interest") into a "moral" gospel. Prudentialism was so treasured because it was regarded as an instrument of social control leading to stable self-interested *accommodations* between syndicalist elements in society.[2]

Ross' prudentialism is emphasized here because historical sociologists may feel that Protestant traditions are more important for understanding Ross' view of capitalism than his liberal, technocratic beliefs. But Ross' attitude toward social control was based on a profoundly amoral rather than a moral religious view. Ross was certainly influenced by the Social Gospel movement and a utopian perspective based on Christian capitalism. But it is the technocratic and liberal-syndicalist contents of these influences that are critical for understanding his point of view.

Ross regarded his "gospel" as a means for developing a particular consciousness of society as a *total system of relations*. Ross (1901:302) stated, for example, that "the attempt to manage men by enlightenment hurries so-

ciety toward consciousness of itself." Through a recognition of social consequences "the group becomes aware of the processes on which its life depends,
and utilitarianism prepares the way for social science." Once formed, the rational awareness of broader social consciousness can lead, in Ross' opinion,
to an enlightened accommodation on the part of selfish interest groups to the
"interests of society" as a whole.

In a brief review of Ross' work *Sin and Society* it is suggested below that
these "interests of society" are actually carried forward by the most "enlightened" and powerful economic groups in society. In this light, his amoral gospel can be regarded as an attempt to develop a *class-conscious* approach to
the serious disorders and socialist movements existing at the turn of the century.

Saving Corporate Capitalism
by Leashing the "Syndicated" Sinners

It has been suggested that Ross' *Social Control* was essentially a handbook
concerned with operative criteria and principles for moral administration of
diverse national and racial groups in America. His *Sin and Society,* on the
other hand, was aimed at bigger game, as mentioned above: he sought to elu-
cidate principles of equity by which to construct a natural and normal definition of monopoly capitalism.[3]

In the opening pages of *Sin and Society,* Ross (1907:4) explained that new
varieties of sin were appearing as a result of emerging industrial societies.
These varieties were denoted in the first half of the book as immoral social
types and institutions, among which were included the forger, the embezzler,
and the factory system which "makes it possible to work children to death."
In addition to these new sinners, there were also "the blackguard editor,"
"the political blackmailer," "the labor leader," "the policy kings," and "the
saloon-keepers" who buy votes and get "out to the polls the last vote of the
vicious and criminal classes" *(ibid.:*13). The crimes perpetrated by these men
were accepted by many members of society and were therefore lacking "the
tokens of guilt" which were associated with the more traditional forms of
crime. These crimes were impersonal because many obedient henchmen in-
tercede between the powerful new sinners and their victims. Some of the
crimes were doubly impersonal because there was no victim at all. Instead,
the objects of victimization were such customary democratic practices as "the
institution of the ballot," which was assailed by perpetration of election
fraud. Ross accused corrupt political bosses of "murdering representative
government." He particularly centered his fire on the laissez-faire robber barons.

What formula did Ross have for curbing this widespread corruption? He
suggested that public opinion be roused in order to cleanse society of its antisocial elements. He called for a moral awakening of individuals within the

framework of capitalism. While criticizing the idealists who "are dipping their brushes into the sunset for colors bright enough to paint the Utopias that might be if society were quite made over," Ross *(ibid.:*19) begged pardon for himself "for dreaming of what would be possible, even on the plane of *existing institutions,* if only . . . every one was required to act in good faith" (our emphasis).

Who would be entrusted with the task of generating this moral awakening? Ross *(ibid.:*40–43) approached this in a roundabout manner with the suggestion that the impersonality of modern crimes required a high degree of intellectual effort on the part of its opponents. "Our social organization has developed to a stage where the old righteousness is not enough. We need an annual supplement to the Decalogue." This supplement would scrutinize the growth of credit institutions, the spread of fiduciary relations, the enmeshing of industry in law, the interlacing of government and business. "What gateways they open to greed!" Intelligence was the only arsenal of defense because the new reality which encouraged crime was "not to be *seen* and *touched;* it must be *thought* . . . Social defense is coming to be a matter for the *expert.* The rearing of dikes against faithlessness and fraud calls for intelligent *social engineering . . .* there is nothing for it but to turn over the defense of society to *professionals."* [4] (In short, it was the technocrat alone who was capable of analyzing and defending society against these new, impersonal forms of antisocial behavior.)

In *Sin and Society,* Ross dealt primarily with individual types of sinners and advocated public moral censure as the means of control. During the final chapters, however, he turned his attention to "sinning by syndicate" and suggested that public opinion must be augmented by direct government regulation. Ross impugned many syndicalist units in society, including labor, professional, and other groups. There is no question, moreover, that he paid special attention to large corporations in his critique because he was extremely disturbed about the effects of laissez-faire capitalists and managers on the development of socialist movements. As we shall see, Ross justified his economic reforms primarily in terms of a defense of the capitalist system against the revolutionary socialist. The argument for governmental "fixing of responsibility" revolved around the signal importance of the large corporation for society as a whole. However, unless the new corporate institutions were brought into line, Ross feared, the working classes would rise and radically transform the entire society in order to relieve themselves of the inequities brought into being by "antisocial" corporations.

Ross also justified state regulation by asserting *(ibid.:*108–109) that corporations *not* owned by one man have many good as well as bad points. Unlike enterprises owned by the individual businessman, the conduct of the corporation with multiple ownership "is never shaped by political ambitions or social aspirations or the personal feuds with [the owner's] wife." It does not exact personal subservience or "hold back from negotiation with its employees" because of "aristocratic haughtiness." "If it ruins anyone, it does so not from malice, but simply because he stands in the way." "The genuine corporation responds to but one motive. Toward gain it gravitates with the ruthlessness of a lava stream." Although it escapes the vagaries of personal ownership, however, its negative feature is that it does not feel "the restraints that conscience and public sentiment lay on the businessman." Because of this, "you cannot Christianize it." It is beyond public opinion.

On the other hand, Ross (*ibid.*:114–115) found that every year witnessed an increase in the numbers of savings banks, trust companies, and insurance companies coming between the corporate management and those millions of stockholders who furnish the money, "thereby making it harder for their conscience to reach and humanise that management." As a result, a new managerial group was emerging. These men did not possess the "amiable traits" of their stockholders, who are influenced by their community ties and responsibilities. The conduct of these new managerial groups, however, was being perceived by workers who were employed by the corporations as typical of the capitalist class in general. "What, then, is more natural than that those in contact with these agents should take them as representative, should estimate the owners by them, and should accordingly foresee an irrepressible conflict between a lawless, anti-social capitalist class and the masses?"

Therefore, because of the antisocial actions of individual managers, there would spring up "delusion of progress by class war, and the mischievous policy of appealing solely to the class interests of workers instead of chiefly to that *sense of right and justice* which is found at every level and in every quarter of society, and which is *the only power that can settle things so that they stay settled*" (*ibid.*:115 our emphasis). In Ross' (*ibid.*:115–116) opinion, "you cannot sharpen class consciousness without whetting class hatred and loosening social bonds. The only hatred that is wholesome and social and propulsive is the hatred of the righteous for the willfully unrighteous." Consequently, "aggressive corporation men put in a wrong light not only capitalists, but their opponents as well."

How would monopoly capitalism be affected by this aspect of its evolution in which the corporation had become impersonal and nonmoral, unable to mend itself? What resolution could be made when the corporation "has become a machine and Mammon is its master"? Reform could only come by restraints in the combined form of "public opinion and by statute." If this reform was successful, it would create a new and better type of corporation manager and remove "one cause of the needless alienation of classes" (*ibid.*:116–117).

Was Ross interested in dissolving the managerially controlled corporation through legislation? Not at all! He argued instead for strict accountability by managers for their actions, not dissolution of their corporations. In cases where corporations were controlled by financiers through interlocking directorships, he suggested that the managerial forces of these corporations be reconstituted by "enlisting more men with an interest in the technical side of business, or in the community it serves." Other suggestions included provision of greater protection for workers by employing "labor commissioners" or "welfare managers" who would be responsible to a committee of corporation directors. These bureaucratic changes, it was felt, would mitigate the conflict between the classes (*ibid.*:127–131).

Class Conflict and the Rules of the Game

Ross (*ibid.*:135) noted that there had been a time when farmers sustained themselves through their own labor, and questions of the social distribution of wealth or the common welfare were hardly pertinent to their lives. But at the time when he was writing, Ross observed, "every man pours his product into some market, it enters in a way into social wealth and passes out of his control." In order to claim his share of the social wealth, he was obliged to enter into a game and how much he received depended upon his skill in playing the game. The size of his share also depended upon how the rules of the game were constituted and enforced by members of society. (The name of the game was equitable distribution.) In Ross' years, however, the administration of justice had become so feeble that it did not enforce the rules which prevented persons from victimizing one another. In part this had occurred because the owners of saloon dives, gambling dens, betting rings, and poolrooms were able to bribe the police and thereby weaken *all* law. The fact that "only one slayer out of seventy has been brought to the gallows" was also given as evidence of the general weakening of law. The harvest of all this laxity, according to Ross (*ibid.*:138), was "bloodshed, lynching mobs and race friction."

Ross (*ibid.*:138) also pointed out that in addition to crime in its individual forms there was another form of lawlessness which "loosens the masonry of the state itself . . . This is failure to enforce the laws governing the conduct of groups or classes in their economic struggle." This was also considered "failure to uphold the rules of the game." If the government enacted or enforced laws in the interest of one class, "the cheated class fiercely resolves to capture the state and to govern ruthlessly in its own interest." But in this case, the state became "the engine rather than *the arbiter* of conflicting interests" (*ibid.*:139 our emphasis). Because of this, Ross declared, allowing "the big player to violate the rules of the game is doubly dangerous at the present stage." Where this has happened, such occurrences "have narrowed the circle of opportunity for workingmen to achieve independence, and therefore tend powerfully to consolidate wage-earners into a conscious class." It was possible, Ross pointed out, that such developments would destroy the "government by public opinion which has contributed to the good temper and stability of American society." *In view of the modern changes in society, one should accept the fact that there will be a perpetual clash of interests between groups.* However, although the "clash of interests arises as we leave behind the simple, homogeneous society of the early days . . . it is not written that every such conflict shall invade politics and make the state its football" (*ibid.*:142). In light of this danger to society, Ross argued that it was vital that "government as compromise" be reaffirmed so that it might "successfully guard the primary social interests" (*ibid.*:140).

Ross' normal and natural conception of the state was described when he asserted that the state typically inspired reverence on the part of its citizens because "it is felt to express our best selves." As long as government represented a "square deal," people would be content because the fear of having the cards stacked against them would prevail over the desire to stack them against the others. (The rules for fair play and the impartial role of the state are therefore required by the selfish nature of man and his institutions.) If government should turn weak or biased, then "into the law is injected now the greed of this class, now the vengefulness of that," and "this path leads to class war, and beyond that 'the man on horseback' " (*ibid.*:143–45).

The rules of the game could be changed, Ross (*ibid.*:146) argued, only if all individuals and groups were involved in making the changes, and the changes themselves would make the game fairer to all. If there were consensus, these changes would be "righteous" and "those who are hit by them cannot pose as victims of 'class legislation.' " But it must not be "a part of the game founded on private property and free enterprise to grant exclusive perpetual franchises, to exempt surplus values from taxation . . . to legitimate the holding company, to enjoin strikers from the exercise of fundamental rights." Should the existent lawlessness continue, Ross predicted, "there is sure to form a body of tangent opinion denying everything that capitalism affirms and affirming everything that capitalism denies! The Nemesis of treating private property, freedom of enterprise and corporate undertaking as instruments of *private* gain rather than of *public* welfare." The radical "who urges us to escape the Unendurable by taking refuge in the Impossible" would surely gain a toehold if such unfairness continued unabated (*ibid.*:147–148).

Ross indignantly complained that the radical socialist blamed most of the ills in society on the competitive system. According to Ross, however, these ills accrued from monopoly. The radical blamed individualism for the commercialization and corruption of politics, but Ross claimed that these political distortions were due to big business. The radical also argued that the "abysmal inequalities in wealth" were a natural outgrowth of the private ownership of the means of production, but Ross (*ibid.*:148–149) insisted that these inequalities were the "outgrowth of privilege." Ross declared that "in swollen fortunes" the radical saw "the vestibule not to plutocracy but to social revolution." "For a testable working régime," the radical offered "a vague, ill-considered scheme built largely out of antitheses to the actual and sharply at variance with *human nature* on its present plane" (our emphasis).

Ross (*ibid.*:151–152) cautioned that those who put their faith in a moral transfiguration of individualism "should make haste to clean the hull of the old ship for the coming great battle with the opponents of private capital and individual initiative." But if they would "put up a good fight for the ship, it behooves them to rid it of the buccaneers, wreckers, and shanghaiers that now impudently claim the shelter of its flag, and by their sinister presence compromise the efforts of legitimate defenders." It is quite clear that Ross considered social reform to be vital to *the defense of capitalism* at the turn of the century. And his sociological muckraking gave evidence of his energetic efforts in this cause.

These and other remarks by Ross also have suggested several important features of his conception of the modern, differentiated society: namely, the role of the state as an impartial arbiter, the syndicalist organization of society, the perpetual clash of self-interested groups, and the solution to the problem of integration on the basis of accommodation between those groups willing to work within the framework of capitalism. This accommodation would come about only if some attempt were made to force selfish interests to conform to "the rules of the game." If this were not done, Ross argued, there would be no game at all.

NOTES

1. As William K. Frankena (1963:18) notes, "prudentialism or living by the principle of enlightened self-love just is not a kind of *morality* . . . This is not to say that it is immoral, though it may be that too, but that it is nonmoral."

2. Ross (1901:303) noted, for example, that "the prudential method," which he equated with his interpretation of the "method of enlightenment," "flourishes in periods when tradition breaks down." It thrives in "an industrial epoch" and grows apace "in democratic times." The appeal to self-interest insinuates itself into religion, philosophy, and literature. It also "works quietly and unobserved in a humbler sphere, shaping the character of youth through homely proverbs and copy book maxims . . . in any case, we cannot do without it. It never gets in the way of science . . . it is the best custodian of whole fields of conduct."

3. In reviewing *Sin and Society,* Richard Hofstadter (1959:160–161) praises Ross because he "criticized the prevailing code of morals for failing to pierce the veil of impersonal corporate relations of modern society and to fix the blame for social ills on absentee malefactors." Hofstadter adds that Ross had helped loose "the spirit of reform" within the discipline of sociology. It will be suggested here, however, that Ross' *Sin and Society* should be examined in a much larger framework than simply an expression of a particular kind of middle-class reformism. Ross is seen as a contributor to modern sociology who represented a technocratic view of monopoly capitalism which was being developed within the framework of corporate liberalism.

4. The words "seen," "touched," and "thought" were given emphasis by Ross. The rest is our emphasis.

PART EIGHT

The Social Engineers and the Ideological Definitions of Sociology

CHAPTER 28

The Age of Combination

Theodore Roosevelt's Letter to Ross

In a letter to Edward A. Ross, Theodore Roosevelt (Ross 1907:ix) wrote: "It was to Justice Holmes that I owed the pleasure and profit of reading your book on *Social Control*. The Justice spoke of it to me as one of the strongest and most striking presentations of the subject he had ever seen." Roosevelt added that he had also read some parts of *Sin and Society* that had been published as essays in the *American Journal of Sociology*. Roosevelt also expressed his pleasure with these essays and affirmed his "full and hearty sympathy" with Ross' major points. Roosevelt was concerned that "modern society" might be destroyed because politics had become "the mere struggle of class against class." Complimenting Ross on his rejection of "that most mischievous of socialism theses, viz.: that progress is to be secured by the strife of classes," Roosevelt (*ibid.*:xi) joined Ross in a thumping chorus that "all healthy-minded patriots should insist, that public opinion, if only sufficiently enlightened and aroused, is equal to the necessary regenerative tasks and can yet dominate the future."

In his letter, Roosevelt stated that *"the perspective of conduct* must change from age to age, so that our moral judgment may be recast in order more effectively to hold to account *the really dangerous foes* of our present civili-

222

zation" (our emphasis). Politicians and social scientists at the time agreed that these foes were comprised of many others in addition to the revolutionary socialists. As far back as 1883 in Ward's *Dynamic Sociology,* we have seen that these foes also included the "anarchistic" capitalists who were concerned with their own narrow interests. By 1907, Ross clearly identified these laissez-faire capitalists as the cause of political corruption, economic exploitation, and the growth of revolutionary movements.

Although Ross has also been considered a populist because of his muckraking attacks on "irresponsible" monopoly capitalists, his criticism operated well within the limits of the corporate-liberal perspective toward robber barons, which he shared with such liberals as Theodore Roosevelt. These perspectives emerged out of the struggle for economic and political power over several decades. The fundamentals of this new liberal outlook are revealed in the following examination of the various points of view which were expressed in arguments about the proper legal interpretation of the Sherman "Anti-Trust" Act; particularly around the turn of the century.

Conflicting Interpretations of the Sherman (Anti-Trust) Act

The attempts to regulate the large corporation before the turn of the century mainly took the form of antimonopoly legislation. The Sherman Act was passed in 1890, but ironically, the most rapid period of economic (corporate) consolidation actually appeared after its passage. In the eight years from 1897 to 1904, corporate mergers involved assets totaling six billion dollars. Only one-sixth of this amount of money was involved in mergers during the entire twenty-year period prior to 1897 (Weinstein 1968:63). The ambiguities of the Sherman Act and the wave of mergers created an uproar about how this act should be interpreted and applied. During this period, political groups perceived this act in at least two ways. The first, which will be called the antitrust viewpoint, suggested that consolidation of corporations into giant business enterprises or "monopolies" was *illegal.* In this view, "monopoly" was defined popularly as including large holding companies, cartels, and economic pools, as well as very large corporations. The second viewpoint, calling for regulation rather than trust-busting, defined the giant business corporations and agglomerates as *normal* and *inevitable* consequences of capitalism. Consolidation of the market was justified because of its promise of an increasingly productive and wealthy economy.

In the antitrust interpretation, the very size of a corporation made it suspect because big business was seen as inimical to the free market economy. It was felt that a supremely powerful business concern would automatically suppress competition in its own favor; therefore, if honesty were defined as conformity to the mandates of the free competitive market, a big businessman could not be honest. In the second or regulatory interpretation, on the other

223

hand, it was assumed that there were "immoral" business enterprises which "unreasonably" restrained trade, but that their practices could only be distinguished by legal recourse to English and American common law precedents. As James Weinstein (*ibid.*:64) points out, these precedents referred "to the nature of trust and cartel agreements, rather than to the size of a particular enterprise." Also, according to common law, business agreements to control supply, limit output, fix prices, pool profits, or divide markets are legal as long as they are not held to have "unreasonably restrained competition in such a way as to be detrimental to the public interest." The Sherman Act reversed common law procedure by making restraints of trade a criminal as well as a civil offense.

It became obvious that big businessmen in the early part of this century preferred a regulatory interpretation of the Sherman Act since they could not revoke the law altogether. On the other hand, many owners of small and middle-sized businesses, as well as agrarian groups, preferred the narrower, antitrust interpretation. Ultimately, the *regulatory* interpretation was held to be operative by the courts, but not until considerable big business manipulation of government officials and public opinion had taken place.

Political Collusion and Corporate-Liberal Limits of Progressive Movement

Theodore Roosevelt was called the "trustbuster" although his term of office was conspicuous for its reluctance to enforce the Sherman Act. Outside of a few prosecutions (which appear to have been due to his personal peeves with "the Harrimans and the Rockefellers"), he preferred to work out private agreements with entrepreneurs like J. P. Morgan. These agreements favored consolidation, even in the midst of a nationwide (1907) financial panic (Kolko 1967:113–119). As a scion of an upper-class family with roots in the consolidation of land during the early history of the American nation, Roosevelt considered himself a progressive who accepted both the inevitability of consolidation and the use of the large corporation as a means for controlling the economy (*ibid.*:160).

Roosevelt consistently supported the large corporation and a regulatory interpretation of the Sherman Act. As early as 1901, he pointed out the signal importance of the large corporation as representative of the United States in foreign markets. He stated that "business concerns which have the largest means at their disposal . . . take the lead in the strife for commercial supremacy among the nations of the world." He emphasized that "America has only just begun to assume the commanding position in the international business world which we believe will more and more be hers." Because of this, the growth of large corporations should not be jeopardized (Williams 1961:371). Four years later, in his Annual Message to Congress for 1905, Roosevelt invoked the common law or regulatory interpretation of the Sherman Act by stating that *"This is the age of combination"* (our emphasis). Business does not need a "sweeping prohibition of every arrangement good or bad . . . but such adequate supervision and regulation as will prevent any restriction of competition from being to the detriment of the public" (Weinstein 1968:71). Still later, in 1911, Roosevelt insisted that "business cannot be successfully conducted in accordance with the practices and theories of sixty years ago" unless all the modern conditions of modern civilization are abolished. The prohibition of combinations, he asserted, was "bound to fail and ought to fail." He called for business "regulation," not "strangulation" (*ibid.:*149; Roosevelt 1911). In that same year, Senator Robert M. La Follette, referring to Roosevelt's antitrust record, declared that the Sherman Act forbade "that sort of business that Roosevelt characterized as the business which 'honest men' must do under modern business conditions." If Roosevelt had vigorously enforced the law in 1901, La Follette added, he "would have crushed and destroyed the comparatively few trusts which were then in existence" (*ibid.:*66–67; La Follette 1960:91, 92, 296). Thus, Roosevelt's verbal attacks on businessmen had little to do with his concrete political practice. Furthermore, according to Kolko (*ibid.:*279–280), "at no point" during the progressive era "did any major political tendency dealing with the problem of big business in modern society ever try to go beyond the level of high generalization and translate theory into concrete economic programs that would conflict in a fundamental way with business supremacy over the control of wealth."

Moral Censure and Empty Rhetoric

We shall see that the vague generalizations about plutocratic power and the moral propensities of businessmen by early American sociologists such as Ward, Ross, and Small were less than earthshaking. Their writings represented a naive understanding of the major forms of integration in our society. They were also indicative of a critical style which aimed its barbs at corporate owners and managers, but refused to advocate any practical limitation on the increasing development of monopoly capital. Indeed, as far as essentials are concerned, these sociologists justified monopoly capital by defining it as a natural and normal phenomenon.

Ross' remarks about "sinning by syndicate" focused on the fixing of responsibility and the reconstitution of responsible managerial groups. But it is important to note that his recommendations for reform, when taken in their entirety, amounted to little more than moral censure of men like J. P. Morgan, proposals for minor bureaucratic adjustments, and the enactment of federal antitrust laws. History clearly indicates that these proposals did not militate against either the development of gigantic monopolies or the great inequities in the distribution of wealth and power. The muckraking articles, and the federal bureaus and legislative reform, merely provided the illusion that something was being done about these relationships.

Nor can Ross' call for the use of public opinion as a means of controlling the giant corporations be taken seriously. Even Ross' mentor, Lester Ward, believed that "back of the politician and demagogue lie the 'vested interests' and these it is that are 'making public opinion' " (Ward 1903:486–487). During the twentieth century, business manipulation of the press had become all too obvious. In 1912, for example, La Follette remarked that "one would think that in a democracy like ours, people seeking the truth" would be aided by the press. This help, however, is not forthcoming because "the money power" has a firm grasp with each of its tentacles on industry, government, and also the press. In La Follette's view, newspaper columnist opinions had been salaried (Weinstein 1968:159).

While Ross' faith in public opinion was naive, his excoriating attack on interest-conscious corporation owners and managers in 1907 had prophetic overtones. During the first two decades of this century, the increasingly violent conflicts between capital and labor appeared momentarily to herald a revolutionary transformation of American institutions. During that time, there were many persons who agreed with sociological experts like Ross that "sinning by syndicates" had to be taken in hand.

The Ludlow Massacre

One part of the public that registered justifiable disapproval of the antisocial practices of the corporations was organized labor. A miners' strike during the early years of the twentieth century serves as an illustration of this disapproval. It also demonstrates the explosive potential that was still being generated by the development of monopolies in the United States.

In 1913, Colorado mine workers downed their tools in a strike for an eight-hour day, wage increases, union recognition, effective enforcement of state laws which allegedly guaranteed safe conditions in the mines, the removal of armed company guards, abolition of company scrip in company stores, election of checkweighmen, and the miners' right to live in other than company houses if he desired (Adams 1966:151–152). These houses were appropriately called "hovels, shacks and dugouts that are unfit . . . for human beings" by a company social worker at the time (Weinstein 1968:192).[1]

At the beginning of this strike, ten thousand miners and their families left their company shacks in sleet and snow at the onset of a harsh fall and winter season (*ibid.*:193–194). They set up their tent colonies in the Colorado canyons and prepared for a long drawn-out struggle. Violent conflict between strikers, strikebreakers, company police, deputies, and sheriffs promptly erupted; company police armed with machine guns were confronted by striking miners wielding small arms. Strikers and police became engaged in pitched battles and the strike rapidly escalated into guerrilla warfare. Finally the state governor called upon the militia to restore peace to the minefields.

His original instructions to the militia ordered them not to provide armed protection for the strikebreakers, but subsequent pressure from corporation officials and financiers caused him to rescind these instructions. The strikers therefore clashed directly with the militia and according to union reports, the militia turned to protecting scabs, and robbing and looting the miners and their colonies. The criminal actions of the militia became particularly flagrant in areas like Ludlow, which was controlled by the Colorado Fuel and Iron Company, a Rockefeller corporation. The struggle between the miners and militia in Ludlow reached its climax when, after a fierce battle, the militia routed the workers and burned their tent colony to the ground. Two women and eleven children were burned alive under the flaming tents.

The miners in the state of Colorado were enraged by the Ludlow massacre. State Federation of Labor officials sounded a call to arms and thousands of miners responded. The workers

. . . seized possession of Ludlow and Trinidad. Then they pounced upon mine after mine in rampaging assaults which ranged 250 miles from their base. One battalion stormed and captured Empire mine, killed three guards, and left the property in ashes. A few days later some 300 beseiged the Walsen and McNally mines. After a fifty-hour gun battle, wrathful laborers dynamited the property. At Forbes, hundreds swarmed into the hills and discharged terrific fusillades into the canyon below. They killed nine strikebreakers and policemen. Afterward these marauders set company buildings afire and laid waste to CFI holdings 30 miles around. Similar armed bands burned, pillaged, and desolated company resources at Delagua, Aguilar, Hastings, and Black Hills. . . . for ten days a workers' army which controlled vast areas of territory clashed with state and company forces. [Adams 1966:160]

On April 28, 1914, President Wilson dispatched federal troops to the scene to secure the mine owners' property rights.[2]

In 1915, a federally established Industrial Relations Commission conducted hearings into the causes of the Ludlow Massacre in Denver, Colorado. At the hearings, Judge Ben B. Lindsey and others exposed Rockefeller's control of the judiciary and the state government in Colorado. The Colorado Fuel and Iron Company was accused of owning "judges on the bench as they have owned their office boys." The company was also accused of controlling attorneys and governors. Lindsey stated that the company fashioned the law to suit its own wishes, and prevented the enforcement of laws protecting miners' rights, such as the eight-hour day.[3] "This is violence," and a "condition of terror," Judge Lindsey declared. Echoing sentiments similar to those expressed by Ross (regarding laissez-faire capitalists) at the beginning of the century, Lindsey noted that the "power of capital had become 'superior to that of the President of the United States' " and that if nothing was going to be done about this, "the republican form of government would not be possible." [4]

NOTES

1. The conditions in the company towns are reported in detail by Adams (1966:48–49). He notes, for example, "Within these settlements unsanitary conditions easily spread disease. In 1912–13 alone, 151 persons contracted typhoid. Seepage water 'with a distinctively dead-rat-essence,' reported a physician . . . was supplied to three camps 'because it was cheaper than to tap the main pipeline' . . . for more than a year a cesspool a few feet from a company store overflowed into the main street. . . . If a workman protested these conditions too vigorously, he risked the simultaneous loss of his job, his dwelling, and his right to remain in the community."

2. Zinn (1970:95–97) reports that President Wilson's response was delayed because he was busily involved in organizing an armed imperialist attack on Mexico. In his message to Congress, asking for the right to use armed forces in order to kill Mexicans, Wilson indicated that these forces were necessary to maintain dignity, preserve liberty, and benefit mankind (*ibid.*).

3. The Colorado Fuel and Iron Company also exercised strong control over the miners' education, religion, and intellectual freedom. For example, Adams (1966:149) states that "mine superintendent and company officers dictated the selection of school teachers and dismissed those to whom they objected. No one could erect a church building without CFI permission. J. F. Wellborn, president of the company, considered it management's prerogative to fire ministers who opposed the firm or who exhibited 'socialistic tendencies.' A Commission inspector discovered that the firm censored movies, books, and magazines. It proscribed not only anti-capitalist literature but such works as Darwin's *Origin of the Species.*"

4. Judge Lindsey's remarks are quoted in Weinstein (1968:195).

======

CHAPTER 29

The Social Engineers

Preview

This chapter focuses on the arguments generated by the activities of John R. Commons and Charles V. McCarthy, within the same Industrial Relations Commission that conducted hearings on the Ludlow Massacre. These arguments, which centered on social engineering, will lay the groundwork for the analysis of Albion Small's writings. It will also enable us to reveal the broader social ramifications of Small's commitment to the principles of social engineering which had been developed by German political economists during the Bismarck era.

Ideological Conflict between
Walsh and Social Engineers

The Industrial Relations Commission's hearings on the Ludlow Massacre grew out of insistent demands by various groups for industrial reforms. These demands included proposals for a thorough investigation of the conditions leading to the increasing violence in American industrial life. The Commission was charged with the responsibility for conducting this investigation and began its work under the chairmanship of Frank P. Walsh, a Kansas City attorney and social worker. Walsh's populist leanings and his high regard for public exposure as a step toward achieving reform resulted in sharp disagreement with John R. Commons, another Commission member, and Charles V. McCarthy, the Commission's research director. Commons and McCarthy were also members of a circle of "social engineers" at the University of Wisconsin (Weinstein 1968:185).

The disagreements between Walsh and the other men arose from his ideological objections to the concept of social engineering when it was applied to the concrete problems directly facing the Commission. These disagreements became particularly acute during the Denver, Colorado, hearings into the violence culminating in the Ludlow massacre and the subsequent guerrilla warfare.

At the Denver hearings, Rockefeller denied that he had any knowledge of the Colorado Fuel and Iron Company's outrageous policy toward the miner's union. Walsh, however, produced company communications collected by his staff which proved that Rockefeller not only had full knowledge of the events leading to the strike, but had also endorsed the company's adamant refusal to deal with the union. Furthermore, Walsh produced evidence directly implicating Rockefeller in the pressure placed on Colorado's Governor Ammons to rescind his original order to the state militia. (This act enabled the militia to support the strikebreakers and precipitated the most violent phase of the strike.) Testimony from Judge Lipset and others further revealed the degree to which the Rockefeller interests controlled public officials in the state (*ibid.:*196–198).

Walsh (*ibid.:*198) was outraged by this outright manipulation of public officials. He felt that industrial conflicts should be resolved in public, often with the aid of impartial government officials. In Colorado, however, the government was actually at the beck and call of business interests. By manipulating public officials, Rockefeller and his corporation managers had subverted democratic principles.

In light of this, it is not surprising that Walsh became increasingly disturbed by the opposition from Commons and McCarthy over the way the Commission was functioning. "Commons and McCarthy," Weinstein (*ibid.:*189) observes, "sought reform through the removal of issues from politics and their solution by private conferences or through representative bodies

229

of experts." As Commons put it, when dissenting from Walsh's final report, their differences turned on "whether the labor movement should be directed toward politics or toward collective bargaining" (*ibid.*:202). Commons' opinion of proper direction favored private agreements between conflicting parties. It also resulted in opposition to Walsh's plans to give greater priority to open public hearings rather than to closed hearings on the Ludlow Massacre.

The Commission was also charged with the drafting of model legislation for the prevention of industrial violence. However, Commons' interpretation (*ibid.*:198–199) of the best way to fulfill this responsibility was to conduct informal conferences with union and company officials in order to reach agreements on legislative reforms in those areas where there was the least amount of conflict. The drafting of model bills was to be based on a policy of consensus rather than on critical inquiry into the causes of industrial violence. Walsh, on the other hand, favored the public airing of the undemocratic use of power by men like Rockefeller. Although he recognized that this would undoubtedly lead to greater "class politics" or "agitation" of "class feelings," Walsh believed that these consequences would be in the interests of social justice in the long run. Commons and McCarthy, guided by principles of social engineering, opposed Walsh; they felt that Walsh's methods would not achieve consensus. Indeed, in their opinion, Walsh's "frontal attacks on men of great wealth, even those admittedly as irresponsible as Rockefeller, would make cooperation and compromise with others difficult, if not impossible" (*ibid.*). In spite of Commons and McCarthy's opposition to Walsh, the open hearings were held and the role of Rockefeller was exposed in public.

The "Wisconsin Idea": Corporate Interests Manipulate Experts

It is important to underscore the degree to which Commons' and McCarthy's policies were integrated with a *professional* ideal that had become identified with the state of Wisconsin and its leading academic institution. This ideal was called "the Wisconsin idea" and McCarthy had played the most important role in pioneering it. In 1901 he had arrived in Wisconsin's state capital and established a Legislative Reference Library. The aim of the library was to circumvent legislation by "interest groups" by providing individual legislators and other politicians with up-to-date social analyses, statistics, and general information on current political issues. Furthermore, as Graham Adams (1966:205) notes, "Staff librarians then drew up tentative drafts of proposals based on this information. McCarthy also dispatched copies of these prospective statutes to hundreds of experts, commissions, and attorneys for criticism and modification." Some referred to McCarthy's bureau as "Wisconsin's bill factory." But he claimed that his bureau epitomized the application of *disinterested* scientific methods to social affairs.

Walsh was also very skeptical about the disinterested "scientific" nature of the "Wisconsin idea." From Walsh's standpoint (Weinstein 1968:205–206), McCarthy as well as Commons were committed to an approach which favored "interminable bill-drafting" by "countless employees, experts and the like, of 'scientific training,'—the very thought of which should throw the legal profession into spasms of delight and the proletariat into hopeless despair" (*ibid.*).

Walsh further remarked that the new "scientific" methods and opinions were not necessarily impartial merely because they had been espoused by experts. He asserted (*ibid.*) that Commons and McCarthy were supported by "the philanthropic trust [1] in New York." As far as he was concerned, this "trust," which he opposed, was making "strenuous efforts to apply the methods of scientific philanthropy to the work of this Commission." The foundations or "trusts," Walsh declared, would make "the whole profession of scientists, social workers and economists" subservient to wealthy men. He noted (*ibid.*) that "these professions [were] receiving subsidies, either directly or indirectly, from the Rockefeller estate." If professionals wanted to "take any step toward effective economic, social and industrial reform" they would come into conflict with "the interests of their benefactor." It was, therefore, impossible to believe that "research workers, publicists and teachers [could] be subsidized with money obtained from the exploitation of workers without being profoundly influenced in their points of view and in the energy and enthusiasm with which they might otherwise attack economic abuses." Walsh's criticism touched on the blatant manipulation of scholars by Rockefeller during the early decades of this century. No analysis of the development of the social sciences can ignore the degree to which powerful social institutions can buy outright the intellectual products of scholars. But there were more subtle hegemonic factors which played an even greater role in determing the conduct of academic social scientists.

German Reformism and Technocratic Management of Human Beings

More important than the simple view of technocratic intellectuals as persons who are "bought off" by the system, was the formation of a committed corps of social scientists, research personnel, and social engineers. This corps of technical experts was fashioned by ideological as well as material conditions. The commitments of the corps members to reformist doctrines, such as those developed by the "German socialists of the chair," encouraged and guided the energetic development of a "rational," "scientific," approach to the management of the population. There is no better illustration of the relation between German reformism and the technocratic nature of social engineering than Charles V. McCarthy's direct testimony to the 1915 Industrial Relations Commission prior to his employment as its research director.

In this testimony McCarthy gave frank expression to his admiration for Bismarck's solutions to the dangers represented by the rise of socialist movements in Germany. McCarthy also expressed admiration for the methods used by the German government in managing and stabilizing the economy. He stated that Germany was a "wonderful example to the rest of the world as showing what a country can do" (Weinstein 1968:201). In regard to social planning, he observed that "Bismarck did a great deal of that planning, and the men around him, Wagner, and other university men were brought in by him." England was also considered to be "imitating Germany," and McCarthy added, "Lloyd George told me himself that he had constantly gone to Germany" to study "the methods of the German government." He informed the Commission that "the great industrial commission act" which had been passed in Wisconsin, was "after all based upon the suggestion of the German act."

McCarthy's testimony revealed one significant aspect of the German reformist doctrines. This was the technocratic interest in shaping the physical well-being and attitudes of individuals so that they could be of "service" to their country. This "service" was usually interpreted by American corporate-liberal scholars to mean voluntary adjustment by individuals to the standards of the institutions which were most significant to the maintenance of corporate capitalism. Because of this, social engineers were concerned, above all, with each individual's qualities as a member of the work force, and they gave greatest priority to biological and characterological requisites for industrial tasks. When asked what he considered the backbone of society, for example, McCarthy replied (*ibid.*:202) to the commission members that "the backbone, here, is that the state must invest in human beings in the same way you invest in *cattle* on a farm. . . . You have got to have *better human beings*" (our emphasis). One of the commission members asked McCarthy whether his idea "is to build people up physically?" McCarthy answered affirmatively, but added that he was "using the word 'physical' in a big sense; physically, mentally and all those things. A man will produce more, and the employer will get more for his money, and the state will get more out of the man, and my idea is that the state ought to invest in the health, strength, intelligence and ability of the people who make up the state."

In spite of Ross' spirited celebration of the Aryan segment of the population in *Social Control,* McCarthy's conception of working people as domesticated animals was not inconsistent with the views of man revealed in Ross' work. Nor, as we shall see in a moment, was it far removed from Small's orientation toward the social management of human beings.

Albion Small's Study of German Cameralists

Albion Small, one of the major founders of American sociology and a champion of Ward's *Dynamic Sociology* [2] during the early 1890s, was also strongly influenced by German reformist doctrines. This influence was illustrated in his 1909 publication, *The Cameralists,* which examined the important philosophical and political perspectives toward governmental policies developed in the German principalities from the middle of the sixteenth to the end of the eighteenth century.[3] The cameralists were scholars who concerned themselves with formulating a viable mercantilist approach to governmental management of economic and social affairs in the interests of the medieval rulers of the state.[4] According to Small (1909:588), the policies founded on their perspective were based on maxims of prudence compared to the "individualism in America" which had "degenerated into the license of some to invade the rights of others." Small felt that exponents of laissez-faire doctrines in America had been ruthless in their management of national affairs.

Small urged that his study should not be used "to glorify German bureaucracy at the expense of American republicanism." He insisted that the knowledge of German institutions for Americans should not consist in imitating them, but rather in "adapting whatever may be learned from their workings to the improvement of our own [American] institutions." Pointing out that the Hegelians would say that "it is a typical manifestation of the nature of things that the German and American politics would tend to complete each other," Small conjectured that the American assumes the individual is important while the German views the state in this light. In his opinion (*ibid.*:xvi), "experience has shown that neither assumption is the whole truth, and that the social problem rests hard upon the need of a reconstruction which shall organize these two phases of truth into a convincing basis for present social action." Although it is to be understood that Small was not calling for an imitative or mechanical adaptation to German institutions, the message of his study was clear. The reader was urged to consider some modification of laissez-faire policies in the direction of the cameralist philosophy of state management, such as the development of government bureaus, in order to solve the social problems of the day.

It is important to note that Small did not use the works of the cameralists in order to develop a broader theoretical understanding of the *social* foundations which underlie cameralist class conceptions of equity in the distribution of wealth and resources. Nor did he view the cameralists as philosophical scholars who developed important justifications for the exploitation of the population in the interests of a ruling class. Instead, the state was merely perceived as an instrumentality of a ruling house (not a class) and the cameralists themselves were defined as practical, hardheaded bureaucratic advisers. Cameralism was viewed by Small (*ibid.*:590–591) solely as an "administrative technology" oriented to the "practical" solution of the problems of the day. This view of "administrative technology" which blithely ignores the consequences of class-dominated policies for professional conduct is, as we shall see, another indicator of a technocratic sociological mentality.

Small, McCarthy, and the New Cameralistic Science

McCarthy's testimony to the Industrial Relations Commission prior to his acceptance as its research director, suggested the kinds of elitist and instrumental definitions of common people which were being generated by the operative interpretation of such notions as "efficiency," "scientific planning," and "social engineering." That these notions were not only current in Wisconsin University is clear from the many similarities between McCarthy's and Small's orientations. The differences between McCarthy and Small were merely exaggerated by the fact that Small, whose activities were heavily centered in the university, was not called upon to translate his moral rhetoric into practice. Because of this, he was able to assume a "statesmanlike" position and construct vague justifications for the kind of social engineering McCarthy had in mind. It is important to note that Small shared McCarthy's definitions of social engineering. However, in order to realize that each of these men represented an elaboration of the same ideological tradition in American social science, it is necessary to cut through Small's vague allusions to social responsibility, human perfection, and the ethical goals of science, and to note the kinds of examples he constructed and the specific schools of thought to which he referred his major ideas.

A most affirmative indicator of the similarities between McCarthy and Small was their common admiration for Germany's reformist doctrines. We have seen evidence of this admiration in McCarthy's testimony before the Commission prior to his position as research director. Small's view is merely suggested in his study of the German cameralists; but it is particularly evident in his final major work, *Origins of Sociology* (1967:235), in which, for example, he referred to Adolph Wagner as the John the Baptist of the ethical school developing in German economics. As McCarthy pointed out, Wagner provided assistance to Bismarck in formulating a "social engineering" approach to social policy. From Wagner's point of view, this policy involved the watchful and calculated intervention of the state in industrial relations. Both Small and McCarthy favored the development of a new "cameralistic science," which was to be created by modern administrative-consultants in the service of the state.

Both McCarthy and Small were also committed to a program of physical and moral "engineering" or "eugenics." Although Small did not explicitly compare human beings to cattle, his view of the common man was no less instrumental than McCarthy's. Small (1925:456) asserted that the change from laissez-faire capitalism to a better society would necessitate consideration of the "problem of *physical, mental* and *moral* eugenics" (our emphasis). This problem consisted of *"breeding* a population whose individual and collective wishes will aggregate a collective demand for something different from [laissez-faire] capitalism" (our emphasis).[5] In fact, any solution which did not "insure better personal building material for our institutions," Small declared, "is nothing more than a 'superficial and deceptive renovation of our institutions.' "

Moral Eugenics and Sociology of Socialization

Even though Small felt that moral eugenics involved "in its technique and details . . . a problem for all the arts of physical, mental and moral influences, or of educators in the widest sense," it was also "in its totality, a *sociological* problem" (*ibid.*:456). In Small's view, eugenics pointed to one of the substantive areas that defined a field, and in this case, the problem under study came to be called "socialization" of individuals or groups.

The term "socialization" attained broader and alternative meanings in later years, but men like Small regarded it in a narrower sense during the early development of the field. (For example, since the individual was naturally greedy, socialization meant the individual acquisition of "cooperative" values. Small believed that human beings always wanted "something for nothing" under laissez-faire capitalism and that socialization was an antidote to *egoism*.) Socialization at that time meant, in particular, learning to conform *efficiently* to conventional (social) imperatives or "functions." Socialization therefore referred to the acquisition of those attitudes and dispositions which enabled individuals to adjust to a naturally normal social system, whether these systems referred to small groups, major institutions, or society as a whole. With regard to these systems, socialization also referred to the cooperative, interpersonal, or intergroup processes culminating in the reconciliation of conflict; it therefore catalogued the determinants of harmoniously integrated social relationships. In time, this view of socialization provided a major analytic tool for the sociology of deviancy. The lack of socialization, or "inadequate socialization," meant that individuals, alone or in groups, were arrested in their natural state of selfishness and were not "functionally" adjusted to established institutions.

NOTES

1. One "trust" Walsh had in mind was the Rockefeller Foundation, which had established an industrial relations division and conducted a "scholarly" investigation into the United Mine Workers' strike. Walsh felt that the testimony of the scholar who directed this investigation was outrageously biased. He declared that this "scholar of highest reputation apparently drew no line, in lending his cooperation, between the Rockefeller philanthropies and the Rockefeller exploiting industries." In regard to the Rockefeller Foundation, Walsh stated that "even in the power to do good, no one man, or group of men, should hold a monopoly" (Weinstein 1968:206).

2. A contemporary said that in 1890, upon reading *Dynamic Sociology,* Albion Small "fearlessly proclaimed it to be the most vital diagnosis in the last two centuries of cosmic and social problems."

3. The cameralists were feudal counterparts to the economic advisors to the modern state. Because of this, Schumpeter (1954:159) calls the cameralists "consultant-administrators."

4. Small (1909:16) stressed that *"the salient fact about the cameralistic civic theory*

was its fundamental assumption of the paramount value of the collective interests, or in other words, the subordination of the interests of the individual to the interests of the community."

5. We have inserted the term "laissez-faire" in this statement because of our interpretation of Small's usage of the term "capitalism" in a number of his works. In a later chapter on the transitional nature of early sociological rhetoric, it will be noted that generally, when Small used the term "capitalism," he specifically meant *laissez-faire* capitalism; that is, in his terms: a society which placed no restraints on "greedy" businessmen.

CHAPTER 30

Ideological Parameters of the Field

Early Attempt to Define Sociology

What kind of sociology did Small favor? Small, together with one of his students, Vincent, defined the kinds of ideas appropriate to the domain of a "systematic sociology" in the first textbook published in the field (1894). This sociology was identified with the use of empirical research methods or the advocacy of their use. As an example of "systematic sociology" the authors pointed to Pierre Le Play's concrete research on family household budgets.[1] Also, because of his high regard for scientific methods, Lester Ward was considered to have made "the most important American contribution to systematic sociology" (Small and Vincent 1894:50).

Small and Vincent (*ibid.*:48) also identified a "constructive sociology" and provided examples of "German scientific thought" indicating that social science could be used "for construction of *an ideal* toward which social endeavor should aim" (our emphasis). The economist, Paul von Lilienfeld was cited here; and another example was the economist and sociologist August Shäffle. Shäffle had reputedly discovered the foundations of a constructive sociology when he pointed out that "the functional adaptation of social parts disclosed . . . the beginnings of ultimate Social Ethics." It can be seen, therefore, that constructive sociology had an *ethical* basis. Small and Vincent (*ibid.*:50) reiterated this in their classification of Schäffle as a "constructive" sociologist because he "dissects society in order to discover the *immanent* needs and *possibilities* of society, which knowledge shall in turn become the foundation for intelligent social endeavor" (our emphasis). According to Small and Vincent, Schäffle's goal was "synthetic" because he was concerned with the complete adaptation of social action to the functional imperatives of social groups or society as a whole.

Small and Vincent's constructive sociology was not identical to Ward's notion of applied sociology, although it would undoubtedly hasten and rationalize the development of applied knowledge. Small and Vincent were concerned with identifying the ways of thinking that would eventually lead to the *discovery* of functional prerequisites of normal (optimum) social relationships and, consequently, to the identification of conditions necessary to meet the "immanent needs" of society. They were also interested in a sociology that would delineate historical possibilities inherent in contemporary developments. These future "possibilities of society"—as they were called—could provide guidelines for applied scientists, but they did not necessarily represent knowledge that would actually have immediate utility for controlling social relationships.

From Small and Vincent's limited references to a constructive sociology, one can infer that they were somewhat aware of the interrelations between prescriptive and descriptive propositions in liberal-functionalist thought. The notion of constructive sociology attempted to make a few of these interrelations explicit. During the first two decades of the twentieth century, however, the attempt to delineate an ethical or "constructive" sociology was discarded. In this gradual movement toward a contemporary positivist stance, American sociologists conspicuously obscured the fact that their theories were tacitly regulated by ethical presuppositions. By the twenties, academic sociologists preferred to think of themselves as scholars who were engaged in the disinterested search for knowledge. However, their descriptions of the world as it existed were profoundly influenced by their liberal political preferences for the possible ways in which the world *ought* to develop. This was the case irrespective of whether these scholars were aware of it or not.

Criteria for a Constructive Sociology

Ward might also have been considered a constructive sociologist because of his stress on the functional imperatives of society. He had advanced, in addition, a visionary conception called sociocracy which represented one of the historical possibilities which could be achieved by the "intelligent" application of science to social problems. However, from Small and Vincent's point of view, these properties were apparently insufficient to qualify Ward as a constructive sociologist. Additional defining criteria must have been used by these authors for classifying sociologists as "constructive." What were these criteria? Why did Small and Vincent exclude Ward's writings from the classification of "constructive sociology"?

Ward's *positivism* may provide us with a clue to why he was not accorded "constructive" sociologist status. For example, he made a sharp distinction between "pure" and "applied" sociology, both of which had legitimate functions. His positivistic pure sociology had to be value-free; it, therefore, need only be concerned with "objective" social reality. Small, on the other hand, while sharing Ward's belief that applied sociology should be made relevant to the problems of their time, insisted that even sociological theorizing should be explicitly governed by an ethical point of view; otherwise it tended to be "descriptive" rather than "synthetic."

At first glance the differences between Small and Ward in this respect appear trivial and contradictory since Small (*ibid.:*51) had lauded the fact that Ward was "teleological" (i.e., Ward was interested in the intelligent application of scientific knowledge to social affairs). But it is quite clear that Small was insisting that a branch of sociological theory be *explicitly* and *simultaneously* judged on the basis of prescriptive as well as analytic (logical and research) standards. A constructive sociology had to be both *ethically relevant* and *empirically correct* because it was the combination of both ethical and descriptive propositions that enabled man to adapt "scientifically" to the functional imperatives of social groups or society as a whole.

The Sectarian Schism between Small and Ward

The differences between Ward and Small appear to have stemmed, but only in part, from their respective attitudes toward the significance of *religion* for progressive social change.[2] Ward considered religion a hindrance to the development of science. Ward's attitude is illustrated by his response to a proposal for constructing the foundations of sociology from theology, during an informal gathering at the American Economic Association. When this proposal was made, Small observed (1967:344) that "Ward threw himself back in a chair with a gasp that was almost a groan, and a legible look of disgust and despair."

Small, on the other hand, was originally trained for the ministry and never fully abandoned his beliefs about the compatibility of science and religion. Because of this he was not completely at ease with the antireligious aspects of Ward's reform Darwinism. In a letter written to Ward in 1895, for example, Small (Stern 1933:171) expressed his belief that competent Christian sociologists would make important contributions to the field specifically because of their religious beliefs. However, Ward's attitude toward a "Christian sociology" was expressed with wit and pointed sarcasm. He consistently refused to take Small's advice on not antagonizing members of the clergy [3] and stated (*ibid.:*171–172) publicly: "I am in the habit of considering sociology as a science, not a religion, cult or programme of action, and therefore, 'Christian Sociology' sounds to me about as would 'Christian Mathematics,' 'Mohammedan Biology,' or 'Buddhist Chemistry.' "

Although the relationship between these two men became very strained toward the end, Small, for the most part, appeared to take Ward's contentious remarks in stride.[4] He attempted to find part-time teaching positions for

238

Ward. He also advised him about the advantages accruing from public lectures and, for example, in one communication during 1897, Small (Stern 1936:179) wrote, "Among your hearers will be a Miss Crozier, who has already written to you quite freely I judge. She seems to be quite a Queen Bee among the Southern Women's Clubs, and I hope you will cultivate her for the sake of possible results through these organs."

Small's acceptance of Ward was conditioned by the fact that he did not have a dogmatic attitude toward "secular" theorists and because of his respect for Ward's methodological approach. His regard for Ward was, therefore, not merely based on the fact that he first established his early reputation as a sociological thinker by actively espousing Ward's theory of social forces.[5] Small felt that empirical research had much to contribute to a "constructive sociology." He even went so far in the other direction as to criticize professionals and laymen in the camp of Christian sociology for their lack of scientific rigor and claimed that they had much to gain by being attentive to works by secular scholars.[6]

Sharp Boundaries
of Ideologically Acceptable Sociology

Small's attitude toward Ward symbolized the degree to which Christian capitalist sociologists had reconciled the contradictions between science and Protestantism which had become so critical following the spread of nineteenth-century Darwinism. This modern reconciliation frankly admitted the existence of certain *tolerable* and even mutually advantageous differences between positivist and Christian capitalist sociologists in the United States.

But the tolerable clash of religious and positivistic traditions among sophisticated liberal scholars during the formative years should not obscure the fact that there were certain scholarly inclinations which were not tolerated by men like Small. Positivism was acceptable because positivistic social scientists adhered to corporate-liberal standards. But the laissez-faire liberalism of Spencer and the socialism of Marx were not considered acceptable.

Small and Vincent's pioneering textbook in sociology discussed works by Spencer and Marx. This discussion contained certain reservations about what should be called scientific sociological theory. Upon examination, for example, we find that Small and Vincent evaluated Spencer's and Marx's theories as neither systematic nor constructive sociology. (Indeed, there is some question whether they considered them sociological theories at all.) It is clear that these theories were regarded as historical contributions, but with regard to Spencer, Small and Vincent stated that *"Spencer's sociology ends precisely where Sociology proper should begin"* (our emphasis). Forever concerned with justifying sociology in terms of both a scientific methodology and its social usefulness in advancing "progress," Small and Vincent (*ibid.:*46) insisted that while Spencer's sociology was descriptive, it was *merely* descriptive.

Spencer's sociology, therefore, "can have no [more] direct influence upon human progress than a census of the waves of the ocean could have upon the speed of a ship." The authors added that "De Greef, a Belgian sociologist, has very justly asserted that Mr. Spencer not only fails to show that there is a place for Sociology but his own reasoning proves more than anything else that there is no social science superior to Biology."

Small and Vincent did not dismiss the works of socialists as lightly as they did Spencer's. They placed sociological theories by socialists into a body of knowledge they called "Systematic *Socialism*" (rather than systematic sociology). In their view, "Systematic Socialism has both directly and indirectly promoted the development of Sociology." However, these authors hastened to add that "doctrinal tendencies represented by Saint Simon, Rodbertus, Proudhon, Bakunin, Marx and their interpreters and imitators," stood for "deliberate indictments of society." [7] Represented as a criticism of society, these tendencies were also considered to be "mainly negative" and had "not been equally positive in proposal of remedies." In these remarks it appeared that Small and Vincent had decided that the adequacy of social theories was dependent upon whether or not they had proposed "positive" remedies for social problems.

When Small and Vincent (*ibid.*:41) turned to "Socialism's contribution to nineteenth century thought," they argued that "Sociology appears to have come into existence less from choice than from necessity. In the Hegelian idiom, conventionality is the thesis, Socialism is the antithesis, Sociology is the synthesis." If this example is too murky for clarifying how these authors regarded theoretical works by socialists, then perhaps the following statement will make it clearer: "Sociology must be distinguished from Socialism . . . at present Socialism is related to Sociology much as Astrology was to the early history of Astronomy, or Alchemy to the beginnings of Chemistry" (*ibid.*:76).

This dialectical example may be helpful in summarizing their definition of the domain of sociological theorizing, if certain relevant hypothetical substitutions are made: if we (1) insert *laissez-faire* theories (in place of conventionality) as the thesis, (2) *socialist* theories remain the antithesis, and (3) *corporate-liberal* theories become the synthesis. In this substitute dialectic, corporate-liberal sociology would be considered the highest form of sociological theorizing. But even if these substitutions were not made, it would still be clear that whatever Small and Vincent's sociology consisted of, from their point of view it transcended the "limited" theoretical perspectives developed by others such as Spencer and Marx. Furthermore, by restricting the domain of sociology to two types of sociological enterprises; namely, empirical research and reformist corporate-liberal theorizing, the men who operated outside of this domain were dismissed as socialists, "negative" critics of society, and laissez-faire dogmatists. It is, therefore, consummately obvious that the latter were not considered social *scientists*.

240

Spencerian Attack on Small
and Vincent's Definition of Sociology

Small and Vincent were not alone in calling for a socially relevant social science. Similar developments were occurring in other academic disciplines and professions. In addition, their vague description of a constructive sociology expressed some of the corporate-liberal assumptions which were tacitly governing the development of sociological theorizing. Thus, even though their religious bias structured their operating interpretations, they made explicit in formal terms the ethical presuppositions that were implicitly shaping the functionalist ideas being generated by such earlier "systematic" sociologists as Lester Ward.

Small and Vincent's attempt to define a normatively governed realm of sociological discourse did not escape the attention of laissez-faire liberal scholars in other disciplines who were outraged by the emergence of an entire discipline led by men who openly advocated social reforms. In 1909, for example, a political scientist from Princeton, Henry Jones Ford, declared that sociology was some sort of intellectual hoax. Advocating a "Darwinian" approach to the study of social relationships, Ford declared that sociology consisted of a heap of vague empirical observations and flimsy generalizations which had no claim to scientific validity; sociology, furthermore, was a hotbed of radicalism!

In pursuing his attack on American sociology, Ford centered his fire on Ward's explanation of the origin of the political state and his *visionary* conception of equality of the sexes. He not only considered Ward's scholarly contributions worthless, but generalized this evaluation to all American sociologists. Those sociological concepts having any value, according to Ford, had been derived from other fields such as history, psychology, economics, and anthropology. "So far as sociology differs from established sciences," Ford (1909a:102) exclaimed, "it is an asylum for their castaways." Some of these castaways, his remarks implied, favored free love and the disintegration of the family.[8]

Ford's criticism of sociology is also of interest because it stressed the fact that by 1909 sociologists were using a number of definitions of the field. In order to emphasize the discrepancies between these definitions, Ford remarked that Small and Vincent's textbook regarded Comte's writings as offering little of value to students in sociology even though he had introduced the word "sociology."[9] Ford (*ibid.:*98) also pointed out that the 1895 textbook claimed that "Spencer's sociology ends precisely where sociology proper should begin," even though Spencer's writings had helped establish the discipline itself. To make the problem of definition appear even more ludicrous, Ford added that Ward's *Pure Sociology* contains a reference to at least twelve definitions of sociology which were being used in 1903. Furthermore, Ward offered another definition of his own. Ford (*ibid.*) exclaimed, therefore,

"What claim has any body of knowledge to rank as a science whose students have yet to arrive at some agreement as to what it is or as to how it is to be defined?"

With regard to the problem of definition, Ford (*ibid.:*99) finally remarked sarcastically that "the latest official bulletin is probably that issued by Professor Small." In that 1908 "bulletin," Small stated: "Whether or not there is, or ever shall be, a science of sociology, there is and will hardly cease to be something which, for lack of a better name, we may call the *sociological movement.*" Ford indignantly asked "What . . . is the sociological movement?" There was nothing in Small's vague description of the essence of this movement, Ford added, to suggest that it had any right to call itself a science.[10]

Toward the end of this critique, Ford (*ibid.:*103) returned to Small's remarks about sociology being a social movement and insightfully indicated that these remarks disguised the fact that American sociologists were involved in a *political* enterprise. He argued that "there is, indeed, a world-wide movement for social reform involving extensive readjustments of public order and of governmental function. Civilization is apparently engaged in the dangerous but periodically unavoidable process of exuviation, when old forms are cast and new forms are shaped. But in Europe this is a *political* movement, and if in the United States it is regarded as a distinctly *sociological* movement, American scholarship is at fault" (our emphasis). Ford fingered Small in particular because Small "defined sociology, not only as a science, but also as a social movement which is concerned about instituting social reforms." Since Ford felt that sociology lacked "scientific validity," he concluded that "it cannot give safe guidance to any movement and its invasion of the political arena is an added peril." As far as he (*ibid.*) was concerned, "Instead of inspiring caution, [sociology] encourages haste, levity and sensationalism in dealing with social problems. . . . We shall be lucky if we get through the present era of Jacobinism in ethics and politics without serious disaster."

Defense of American Sociology in Name of Order and Progress

Although Ford's criticism did reveal that sociologists disagreed about the definition of their field, the ideological differences expressed in these disagreements were all confined to *liberal* points of view. Charles A. Ellwood's (1909b) reply to Ford's attack provides insight into the limited ideological scope and emphasis of this aspect of sociological discussion at the time.

Ellwood, who later became a president of the American Sociological Society, was an eminent American sociologist. He was noted for his interest in grounding sociology in psychology, particularly in instinct theory.[11] In addition to proselytizing racist notions,[12] he formulated a corporate-liberal "social control" theory of revolutions, which were in his view "distinctly pathological" phenomena of change.[13] In responding to Ford, Ellwood's defense of the field was by way of pointing out that the latter had not distinguished sufficiently between sociologists and social radicals or revolutionaries. Therefore, Ellwood (*ibid.:*105) made up this "deficiency" as follows:

There is scarcely one in the whole list of "established sciences" which has not in some stage of its development been exploited by quacks and visionaries. This is notably true of political science or philosophy, which produced a whole new crop of dangerous radicals from Hobbes to Rousseau . . . As a matter of fact, very few sociologists of reputed standing endorse the revolutionary ideas which he [Ford] credits all with possessing . . . A few socialists and revolutionaries have put forward these ideas in the name of sociology but not sociologists in the sense of *scientific* students of society. [our emphasis]

Ellwood also pointed out that neither Ward nor Spencer was representative of sociological theorizing at the beginning of the second decade of the twentieth century because their basic works had been formulated at least a quarter century earlier. In his discussion, he presented his own views of what constituted appropriate problems for sociological study. He stated (*ibid.:*106) that human society is the object of study by all the social sciences, but that "none of these study it from the same point of view, or with the same problems in mind." On the other hand, he judged that "sociological literature from Comte down to the present shows that *all sociologists worthy of the name have had practically the same problems in mind.* These problems were set by *Comte* himself, viz., problems of the organization or *order* of society on the one hand, and problems of the *progress* or evolution of society on the other" (our emphasis).

In concluding his reply to Ford, Ellwood (*ibid.:*109−110) declared:

Sociology has, on one hand, stood for applying the methods of positive science to the problems of the social life; on the other, for obtaining an all-sided, comprehensive view of the social life as opposed to fractional or one-sided views. The scientific importance of this endeavor, it seems to me, cannot be overestimated. If the right development of the humanistic sciences depends upon getting rid of one-sided views of collective human life; if sociology is simply the name for the larger, completer view of the social life; if, finally, the social sciences can furnish man with the means of mastering his social environment . . . then it would seem not unreasonable to say that he who opposes sociology as such is unconsciously *an enemy of mankind.* [our emphasis]

Ostensibly, Ellwood's reply to Ford was concerned with defending the worthiness of a scientific discipline. This defense, however, was by no means divested of political content. To the contrary, Ford's criticism was countered by an eminently political defense which insisted that the men most worthy of being identified as sociologists had the same problems of "order" and "progress" in mind. No one who is familiar with the writings of that ultraconservative paladin of a totalitarian bourgeois state, Auguste Comte, can deny that Ellwood was referring to the preservation of capitalism when he refurbished the counterrevolutionary French slogans of Order and Progress in order to symbolize the directions for the new "humanistic" social science.

Disappearance of Christian Capitalist
Definitions of Sociology

There were additional implications in Ellwood's use of Comte's secular writings for purposes of justifying the existence of sociology as a scientific discipline. At the end of the first decade of this century, ideological definitions of the discipline which were influenced by American Protestantism and German reformism were being implicitly, if not explicitly, called into question. Scholars increasingly rejected Small and Vincent's distinction between a *constructive* and a *systematic sociology* in favor of nonethical defining criteria inherent in the single, secular, positivistic category: *scientific sociology*. The orientation toward science which had been expressed by men like Lilienfeld and Schäffle was relegated to the dustbin of history.

In 1918 almost every eminent American sociologist expressed his patriotic desire to "make the world safe for democracy" and supported the entrance of the United States into the imperialist war between the Allies and the Central Powers in Europe. In the mad dash to condemn the "barbarism" of the nation they had once admired greatly, these sociologists conveniently forgot about the attractiveness of German corporate-liberal ideas and ideals. German political economy had provided the leading hegemonic intellectuals in American sociology with ethicopolitical guidelines during the formative years. With the passage of time, however, the awareness of the nature of this unique, historical linkage between German and American scholarship has virtually disappeared.

NOTES

1. Le Play's lifetime spanned 1806–82.

2. Other differences between Ward and Small are reflected in Ward's vision of sociocracy. Although this vision was little more than an imaginative description of state capitalism, Ward's attitude toward public ownership of property went far beyond Small's concept of social reform. As far as Small was concerned, existent industrial, familial, and governmental structures should be preserved; social reforms should not alter these structures in any significant manner. Small's written material would indicate that he was more conservative than Ward.

3. In a letter dated October 3, 1890, Small (Stern 1933:165–166) wrote: "I fear that I have not made myself perfectly clear as to my opinion about your religious utterances. I mean that simply from the strategic or rhetorical point of view I regret that you could not have refrained from certain details, which, whatever their importance in the argument, necessarily shock people who would otherwise follow you very much further and would accept very much more of your instruction, than they will consent to take when they see in what direction it tends. There are thousands of men who hold to the substance of the traditional evangelical doctrines who are yet theoretically unwilling to be convinced that any one of them is yet untenable . . . It is better in dealing with such men, it seems to me, to adopt Beecher's advice 'Don't let too many cats out of the bag at once.' "

4. In 1895, for example, Small (Stern 1933:171) wrote Ward about the Institute of Christian Sociology, which was founded by Richard T. Ely (an economist who figures significantly in coming chapters). Small advised Ward that the majority of the members of the institute "want to build a Scientific Sociology." Small added, "I hope you

[Ward] will consent to cooperate with them with the understanding that there is neither pre-scription nor pro-scription in the matter of free thought and speech."

In this same letter, however, Small gives evidence about the limits of his tolerance by complaining about the "Herron faction" which "practically wrecked the Institute." He added that there was a "general revolt against allowing Herron to speak for members of that society." In an additional footnote to the letter, Stern (*ibid.*:n.3) indicated that "Professor George D. Herron, who had occupied the chair of Applied Sociology at Iowa College, incurred the wrathful protests of the clergy against his criticisms of capitalism, although these criticisms were merely based on an evaluation of capitalism in terms of 'Christian ethics' without reference to a political program."

5. Personal correspondence between Small and Ward suggests, for example, that as early as 1890, Small forestalled Ward's abandonment of sociology (in favor of his other scientific interests) by becoming champion of the theory of social forces. Furthermore, while president of Colby College, Small began to build his sociological curriculum around Ward's theory. In 1895, when Small received his appointment to the University of Chicago, the *Popular Science Monthly* announced: "The University of Chicago recognizes the claims of [social science] studies by putting Professor Small, whose teaching has been based in good degree on the views set forth in Ward's *Dynamic Sociology*, in charge of a well-equipped department of social sciences" (Stern 1933:171). By supporting Ward's theory, Small contributed to the rapid formation of a corporate-liberal sociology and the eventual demise of Spencer's laissez-faire liberal hold on American sociologists.

6. Small wrote Ward (Stern 1933:171), "My personal belief is that Christ's life was the most effective object lesson in history as to the *quality* of rational human life, but that it showed comparatively little about the *processes*. Hence, no matter how extensive our resemblance to Christ in disposition, we are as little equipped thereby for social service as a raw recruit with loyalty alone for war. Other things being equal, honest Christians ought to be the best social functionaries. Therefore I am glad to help get *social knowledge in circulation among them*, even if I do not hope *to get much help from them in enlarging knowledge*" (our emphasis).

7. It should be noted that Small indiscriminately lumped together all sorts of scholars in this list, as long as they were called anarchists or socialists, including the Prussian monarchist Rodbertus.

8. This criticism appears to have been addressed specifically to Ward, who advocated the sexes being allowed to compete "equally" in occupational life. Ward also felt that in the distant future there would be a cyclical return to the forms of sexual equality that existed in prehistoric relationships.

9. Ford (1909a:97) indicated that Small and Vincent had warned students not to regard Comte as an authority in sociology: they stated "all that is of permanent value in the six volumes entitled *Positive Philosophy*, and in the four later volumes entitled *System of Positive Polity* might be reported in a few paragraphs."

10. Ford (1909a:99) clarified this by stating: "We are told that the movement is fundamentally 'a declaration of faith that the closest approach to ultimate organization of knowledge which finite intelligence can ever reach must be a formulation of the relations of all alleged knowledge to the central process of human experience.' But has not that been the object of philosophy ever since it originated in ancient Greece? At any rate, it is clear that this movement, this faith, on its own showing, has no right to rank as a science or to set up any kind of authority."

11. Typically, Ellwood's psychological view of man was rooted in natural law. In opposition to the growing number of scholars who were insisting that instinct theory was inadequate, Ellwood (1909a:618) claimed that objections to the theory of instincts were tantamount to rejection of "modern psychology." Furthermore, in his view the inability to explain social "processes in psychological terms" meant an inability to formulate an adequate sociological explanation.

12. In attacking the concept of "imitation," Ellwood stated (1900:735): "If the process of growth by imitation were not limited and modified by innate tendencies, we should expect children of different races, when reared in the same cultural environment, to develop the same general mental and moral characteristics. But the negro [sic] child, even when reared in a white family under the most favorable conditions, fails to take on the mental and moral characteristics of the Caucasian race."

13. "My theory of revolutions," Ellwood (1909a:609) stated, is ". . . that they are disturbances in the social order due to the breakdown of social habits under conditions which make difficult the reconstruction of these habits, that is, of a new social order. Such social disturbances as revolutions, with their confusion, anarchy, and conflicts between classes, are distinctly pathological."

PART NINE

Liberal-Syndicalism as a Solution to the Neo-Hobbesian Problem

CHAPTER 31

Small's Syndicalist Vision

Alternative Syndicalist Utopias

Among the persons invited to the Industrial Relations hearings on industrial violence in 1915, was William ("Big Bill") Haywood, a leader of the International Workers of the World. The "Wobblies," as the members of the I.W.W. were called, were led by socialists who had suffered from the savage industrial conditions maintained by corporation owners and managers. Haywood himself had been an early victim of industrial conditions, losing an eye at the age of nine as a child laborer in the mines. Familiar with the brutal suppression of unions, he had declared that the Industrial Workers would not follow in the footsteps of other labor organizations by submitting passively to violent repression by the state militia.

Although there was little disagreement between the members of the Industrial Relations Commission about the need to reconcile the conflict between capital and labor, they received no support from Haywood in this regard. Haywood believed that the elimination of capitalism, rather than the reconciliation of industrial conflict, would solve the "labor problem." In response to questions by the Commission members, Haywood (Lynd 1966:237) testified that his labor organization advocated an industrial society wherein each person would become a citizen of industry; "moving from place to place, belonging to his union, wherever he went he would step in the union hall, show his card, register, and he at once has a voice in the conduct of affairs pertaining to his welfare." This citizen's rights, according to Haywood, would not be derived from a state or nation because such social units played no functional role in his *anarcho-syndicalist* society. There would be no state or nation; society, instead, would consist of loosely but functionally interrelated industrial syndicalist units. There would be no capitalists either, because Haywood's utopia was reserved for workingmen only. As far as Big Bill was concerned, capitalists were "parasites," and he plainly stated that "you never saw [a capitalist] on the stormy end of a No. 2 shovel" or "with his hand on the throttle" (*ibid.*:299).

About a thousand miles east of the Colorado Fuel and Iron Company, a very different kind of syndicalism was being developed in another institution heavily indebted to John D. Rockefeller. This institution, the University of Chicago, originally a Baptist school, had been revived and reorganized following its receipt of a fifteen-million-dollar Rockefeller grant (Odum 1927:156–157). When the new faculty of the university was being recruited, Albion Small was asked to chair the department that was to be known, throughout the early decades of the field, as the foremost department of sociology in the country (Lundberg 1929:50). After assuming this position, Small devoted some of his energies to the task of elaborating a syndicalist conception of society. This liberal endeavor, aiming at a moral renaissance and industrial peace, represented the antithesis of Haywood's labor syndicalism because it defined the capitalist's profit as a well-earned wage, the state as a functionally necessary social unit, and the conflict between capital and labor as reconcilable.

As early as 1905, for example, Small described "the great problem" facing scientists and the public. He noted that high production, machine technology, and "the syndicated control of capital and the syndicated organization of labor" have introduced many social problems. These problems included "the collision of interests in distribution," "the widening chasm between luxury and poverty," "the domination of politics by pecuniary interests," "the growth of capitalist world-politics," and "the futility or fractionality of most ameliorative programs." Small (1905:653) argued that "all these are making men wonder how long we can go on in a fashion that no one quite understands and that everyone feels at liberty to condemn."

In order to explain the underlying causes of these relationships, Small claimed (*ibid.*:302–303) that the incorporation of capital has awarded it legal personification; "Capital thus becomes a titanic superman, incomparably superior to the natural persons who find their interest challenged by this artificial being." The struggle between capital and labor was a struggle between a "Leviathan" and all "natural persons" for dominance as a "social force."

The dynamic agent in this struggle was reputed, in Small's very early works, to be the *universal conflict of interests* between groups which are organized around such values as health, sociability, beauty, knowledge, rightness, and *wealth.* Thus, while previous liberal (natural-law) scholars had regarded the striving for private property as a basic part of *individual* human nature, Small also considered the interest in private property (wealth) a natural and universal property of social groups. Assumptions of this kind can be regarded as another expression of the natural-social-law tradition.

Small and the Concept of Social Efficiency

Small held Ward's theory in such high regard that he organized his very early courses around such concepts as evolution of society, social forces, and genesis and telesis. He said that he would rather have written Ward's *Dynamic Sociology* than any other book. In eulogizing Lester Ward, Small (and Vincent 1894:50) commented that "it is a patriotic as well as a scientific duty" to mention Ward's works as "the most important American contribution to Systematic Sociology."

In 1894, as we have seen, Small coauthored the first textbook published in the field. In it he stated: "In this preliminary survey of social relations, the aim is to familiarize students with the more general conceptions which the sociological method employs and to induce the habit of regarding all social phenomena as *normal* or *abnormal,* progressive or retrogressive . . . in the realization of immanent social economy" (our emphasis).

Did Small provide any insights into the hegemonic, sociological view of "normal" social relations? What kind of natural and normal society did he finally propose as a standard for identifying "abnormal" social phenomena? In 1914, the year of the Ludlow Massacre, Small published "A Vision of Social Efficiency," which he had previously delivered as a presidential address before the meeting of the American Sociological Association. With the typical technocrat's penchant for such terms as "rationality" and "efficiency," he proceeded to project a vision of "a relatively rational society" (1914:434–436). In this utopian vision, society was portrayed as an "enormous enterprise," with a "common interest" always having priority over "minor aims." He declared that in this progressive dream world, social and natural resources "will always be regarded as a trust to be administered by the community as an endowment for the human process in which the enterprise finds its ultimate expression." Small's hegemonic generalizations did not provide a concrete description of the specific nature of these human processes, but these processes were not based on the spontaneous expression of *individual* interests. They required a "system of control" which discouraged abnormal (retrogressive) characteristics while it evoked "in each individual . . . the highest degree of every excellence which can be harmonized with the efficiency of the whole process of human development."

In Small's essay, human perfectibility was represented by a close personal adjustment to a vaguely defined common good or general interest. However, who was to be the definer of this common good? How would behavior that was in the general interest be secured? Who would control the "system of control"? Although Small did not address himself to the problem of the locus of power in this essay, it will presently be seen that he tackled the problem elsewhere.

In his vision, Small (*ibid.*:437) foresaw that from "decade to decade the enterprise will show an increasing surplus" and that "experience will develop a *code of equity* to govern the administration of this . . . wealth" (our emphasis).[1] Small had standards for his concept of equity. Equity appeared to refer to any set of principles which encouraged or coerced individuals to become "worthy," "socially fit," "socially useful," or "socially efficient." But what precisely did all these synonyms for social efficiency signify? In Small's visionary society, they simply signified behavior which was necessary to achieve the common good and they were applied to institutions or "interest groups" as well as individuals. A socially efficient institution, for example, was one that harmonized with the "interests" of society as a whole. In light of this, the terms "good adjustment" or "functional adjustment" merely indicated that individuals were efficiently servicing the goals of institutions, and that these institutions, in turn, were efficiently servicing the goals of society as a whole. Small's utopia, therefore, was simply overflowing with good, adjusted, and efficient individuals and institutions!

More than half a century has passed since Small described his efficient society. At present, Small's usage of words such as "efficiency," "adjustment," and "social interests" appear vague and old fashioned. But while it cannot be determined whether Small preferred conspicuously vague expressions because of opportunistic bureaucratic motives, it does seem clear that his terminological usages in this regard were related to the fetish of efficiency which accompanied the emergence of the large corporation. This development was accompanied by the elevation of the term "efficiency" into a "master symbol of legitimation" (Gerth and Mills 1954:276), and Small appears to have cleverly adapted it for his own sociological usage.

In this adaptation of prevailing symbols, sociological and business justifications appear indistinguishable; for example, Small's objections to exploitation of the labor force were not tied into the fundamental moral issues involved in industrial exploitation. Rather, Small looked upon exploitation as a *waste* of human resources within an industrial or mercantile perspective. If persons were encouraged to produce industrial products voluntarily, they would produce more and waste less; and they would therefore be *efficient*. Concepts like efficiency and adjustment were clearly associated with economizing activity rather than the fulfillment of human potentials and human values.

Small expressed his vision of an efficient society in order to help identify the abnormal society as well as the normal one. He noted (1914:440) in this regard that "the social problem of the twentieth century is whether the civilized nations can restore themselves to sanity after the nineteenth century aberrations of individualism and capitalism." He pointed out that American capital had, for example, been personified by members of society and allocated an inequitable amount of power. Capital has not only exploited labor, it has taken advantage of the public. In this process, the public has subordinated its interest to capital even though capital has not fulfilled its obligations to the public. According to Small (*ibid.*:442), therefore, "The illusion that the way to live is to subordinate life to the lifeless thing capital is the most astounding of the paganisms." He declared that there was "something radically mistaken in the capitalistic system itself," and although the last three presidents (Roosevelt, Taft, and Wilson) had grappled with the problem of clarifying and ameliorating social conditions, they had had difficulty in accomplishing these aims. Small was not in favor of abolishing capitalism, but rather sought adequate means of controlling it. He insisted that sociologists could be doing more toward reconciling or clarifying divergent social aims and "the confused modern consciousness." Even though "no scholars in the world have a fairer field . . . for durable social service," American sociologists were not doing their share in developing constructive visions of the good society.

With an astute eye on the present, Small noted that "reorganization of social relations is going on, with us or in spite of us." Sociologists faced a choice: "We may consent to be mere bookkeepers of other men's deeds, or we may be 'instead of eyes' to men with more force than insight for rational progress" (*ibid.*:445). This suggestion for providing "eyes" to users of force rather than insight, was undoubtedly addressed to such individuals as John D. Rockefeller and "Big Bill" Haywood. Presumably, were these men to be equipped with farseeing sociological vision, their energies would be put to use urging capital and labor to conform with the general interests of society. They would renounce force in favor of a peaceful and just reconciliation of their differences. They would become part of a good, not a bad, syndicalist society.

Liberal-Syndicalism: The Small Variety

Small's liberal-syndicalist theory was based on a conception of intergroup conflict followed by a conciliation of conflict. The state is seen as an impartial arbiter or referee, and reconciles conflicting interests through compromise. The state, therefore, is above all, "a union of disunions, a conciliation of conflicts, a harmony of discords" (Small 1905:252–253).

Many of Small's conflict theory notions were derived from Ratzenhofer, Shäffle, and Gumplowicz. However he also incorporated ideas developed by Ward and Ross into a unilinear evolutionary theory of his own. Accommodative relations between groups were seen to generate "general interests" or "common values." The state and other forms of "civilization" emerge from the conflict between interest groups, and, in turn, regulate or integrate these interests in light of the common values. This synthesizing activity, which he called *sociali-*

251

zation, involved intelligent (telic) control of social conflicts, in the interest of "more and better life by more and better people." One of the consequences of socialization, according to Small, was a redistribution of the nation's wealth, with each person sharing more equitably in the spiritual and material goods of life (*ibid.:*522–523).

This equitable state, resulting from "socialization" or "synthesizing" or "cooperative" process (they all mean the same thing), was regarded as an inevitable and progressive evolutionary development. At the same time, however, Small appeared to have little faith in the mutability of human nature. In the "Sociology of Profits," he illustrates this with a Hobbesian view of the nature of humanity. It is not surprising that socialization processes were needed when "not capitalists alone are greedy, but . . . we belong to *a human race that is greedy*" (our emphasis). Small viewed capitalism as "both a program of greed" and a "program for restricting greed." Without *capitalistic* restraints on human greed, the world would be "full of wholly unrestrained greedy people."

Equitable, Unequal Distribution of Wealth and Property

At first glance, Small's utopian vision appears to suggest that capitalism should be discarded in favor of another type of society. But Small was merely trading-in the already outdated utopian model for a more timely one. If men (and their interest groups) were considered basically greedy, how would Small's principles of equity have resolved conflicts between fellow men? He suggested the resolution of these conflicts by an impartial political state and an unassailable criterion for distributive justice. Small (*ibid.:*441) described it as a *functional* criterion. It would be thoroughly moral because it rewards individuals unequally but equitably on the basis of their different "functions" or services. By this means, it would constitute a society "based on function" rather than property and "private profit." Upon examination, however, Small's society "based on function" was a meritarian, capitalist society which still utilized individual competition for wealth. Function, in this case, merely referred to the criterion for estimating the particular values to be paid for the performance of each occupational type. Equity simply meant that wealth should be distributed *less* unequally, *not* that it should be distributed equally.

Who is a "functioner" and what types of incomes were envisioned? Small (*ibid.:*443) suggested that a profit could be considered a businessman's wage because "genetically, and in their elementary forms, profits are merely wages in disguise. It is accordingly an embarrassing blunder for socialism . . . to risk its fortunes upon representations to the contrary." Small did not specify who would determine the value of each function (e.g., how much an occupational type should be paid). But he did suggest that morally enlightened members of society should get together and make this decision *peaceably*. He also claimed that these peaceful means could be augmented by enlightened corporation policies, for example, he viewed Henry Ford's profit-sharing scheme as "a desirable kind of cooperative economic trend" (Page 1940:139). He insisted (Small 1925:446–447) that force and violence cannot be a proper method for adjusting "conflicting claims about justice" because granting "one of the contending parties more *arbitrary power* than the other to settle the dispute between them is so obviously a confusing of the relations between co-operators" (our emphasis). Such a state of affairs, he claimed, "will not be permanently tolerated in human society." Unfortunately, the meaning of the term "arbitrary power" in the above statement is unspecified. Small was also vague about meanings of the terms "force" and "violence," but in some of his writings, he (1905:315) placed "peaceful picketing" in this category when he remonstrated against it as "a manifestation of 'terrorism' " (Page 1940:140).

Generally, Small appeared to suggest that in a functionally integrated society, syndicalist groups must exist in a roughly equal position of parity, and that collective bargaining and arbitration by an impartial party were justifiable ways to resolve conflicting interests. Given these forms of cooperation between economic interest groups, capital and labor would eventually settle outstanding issues peacefully. Society would gradually but inevitably develop an unequal but nevertheless equitable distribution of wealth. And in this harmonious and tranquil setting each and every "functioner" would perform his or her tasks very efficiently.

NOTE

1. He added further that this wealth would be judiciously allocated to "all persons and processes . . . worthy of exceptional support . . . [and] every interest in the community . . . that give[s] assurance of contributing ultimately to the good of the whole." Persons who were unfit through no fault of their own would "be enlisted for the most useful employments of which they are capable, and . . . the deficit between their services and a reasonable appraisal of their needs will be a charge upon the insurance reserve." Persons who are culpably unfit for the community, on the other hand, would "be held to . . . disciplinary restraints" until they acquired some "social fitness" and preferred "a tolerable measure of usefulness in the general undertaking. . . ."

CHAPTER 32

The Parallels between Durkheim and the Americans

Some of the ideas in Small's presidential address to the American Sociological Society, "The Vision of Social Efficiency," appeared in his earliest writings.[1] On the other hand, this address was published in 1914, and by that time Small's writings (as well as works by other American sociologists) began to provide greater evidence that Durkheim was having a broad influence on American theorists. Small did not cite Durkheim in his presidential address. However, his objections to inheritance laws (1914:440–441), and his repetitive use of such terms as "efficiency," "cooperators," and "functioners," are reminiscent not only of the French utopians Comte and the Saint-Simonians, but also of Durkheim's (1933) syndicalist preface to the second edition of *The Division of Labor*.

It is important to point out, as a matter of historical record, that Durkheim's works apparently did not have a strong influence on the early writings of American sociologists. (Prior to the second decade of the twentieth century, one can hardly find theoretically significant references to his works by Ward, Small, Giddings, Cooley, Thomas, or the others.) Durkheim's writings did take a critical view of Spencer, contained a functionalist analysis of deviancy, showed a high regard for efficiency, proposed an abstract syndicalist conception of social developments, and stated a very broad interpretation of the concept of social control. Ward, however, had also attacked Spencer and stressed the notion of efficiency an entire decade before the publication of Durkheim's *The Division of Labor*. In the 1890s, syndicalist notions were emerging rapidly, not only in Europe, but in the United States as well. Prior to the turn of the century, the functions of deviancy and social control had been analytically and substantively discussed in essays by Small and Ross. Indeed, parallel intellectual developments of this type were occurring in every advanced capitalist nation at the time.

This chapter will briefly review Durkheim's *The Division of Labor* in order to provide a striking illustration of the parallel developments in social thought. This review will not be concerned with the work as a whole, but rather with those features deemed to be also representative of the early evolution of social thought among the leading American sociologists. This review will, in

254

addition, enable us to contrast Durkheim's and Small's syndicalist ideas in a later chapter.

Durkheim: An Influential Bourgeois Propagandist

Our review of Durkheim's writings should be set against his relations with the professional French sociology journal and the French government. Durkheim was the dominating figure of the single most important sociological journal (*Anée Sociologique*) in France from 1898 to World War I. He also became a very highly placed academic administrator in state-controlled academic institutions, and his position enabled him to influence the choice of scholars appointed to institutions of higher learning.[2] Durkheim's influence also extended far beyond the academy, and by 1914 "Durkheimian doctrine had become the standard fare of courses in civic morality in primary schools" (Coser 1971:168). Because of this, the French Marxian, Paul Nizan, sarcastically suggested that "the founder of French sociology had written *The Division of Labor* in order to allow obscure administrators to put together a course of instruction for primary teachers." He added that "the introduction of sociology into normal schools consecrates the administrative victory of official morality . . . In the name of science, primary teachers teach children to respect *la patrie française,* to justify class collaboration, to accept everything, to commune in the cult of the flag and bourgeois democracy" (quoted in *ibid.:*169). To Nizan, Durkheim's success appeared to be chiefly derived from his usefulness as a *moral* propagandist.

Durkheim's scholarly works had been greeted with contempt by outstanding Marxist scholars long before the incorporation of his moral doctrines into elementary school education. In 1900, for example, Paul Lafargue[3] criticized French schools in a speech before a group of students in Paris. He used *The Division of Labor* as an example of the "hopeless nearsightedness" of French academics (Lafargue 1967:38). In his address, Lafargue also pointed out that recent technological developments had created the conditions for the emergence of French "factories" (i.e., schools) for turning out intellectuals.[4] Lafargue wrote that the Marquis of Foucault had declared, in 1790, a laborer did not need to know how to read or write. Modern industries, however, "compel the capitalist of today to speak in language altogether different; and his economic interests and not his love of humanity and of science force him to encourage and to develop both elementary and higher education" (*ibid.:*16).

Lafargue further indicated that intellectual capacities had become merely merchandise in highly industrialized capitalist societies. Scientists and technicians were being transformed into wage slaves whose salaries fluctuated with supply and demand. A crisis of overproduction of chemists existed in France at the time and their wage levels were being depressed to those of laborers. Science, he exclaimed, was being used as a tool of exploitation and academics had become apologists who rationalized the crimes of capitalism. A veritable "intellectual priesthood of capitalism" had emerged and some of the "job hunters" who were members of this priesthood had even "invaded the French socialist movement." According to Lafargue, these "socialists" were "perverting" the socialist movement with their doctrines of class collaboration (*ibid.:*17–36).

Although a number of his colleagues were "professorial socialists" who were criticized by Lafargue, Durkheim himself did not become a socialist. Instead, he unofficially skirted the edges of a movement called *solidarism* which had been started by "radical socialists" (i.e., "republicans of the left who were neither particularly radical nor particularly socialist" [Coser 1971:171]). Solidarism closely epitomized the technocratic, statist, and corporate-liberal spirit of Durkheim's writings. According to Coser (*ibid.*), "Solidarism was a kind of *welfare-state* philosophy in French garb, a vague and elastic doctrine that stressed the need for solidarity among all the citizens of the republic; it had a social welfare approach rather similar to that practiced at the time by the Lloyd George Liberals in England and taught by the 'socialists of the chair' in Germany" (our emphasis).

Durkheim's Mechanical *Community* and Organic *Society*

Durkheim presented his theory of the evolution of human civilization in *The Division of Labor*. Conforming to the new fashion in liberal analysis, he split the development of civilization into two ideal-typical configurations: mechanical and organic. *Mechanical* relations were dominated by tradition. They were characterized by consensus, common ownership of property, and conformity of individuals to a "collective conscience." Each person was enmeshed in a cake of custom structured by kinship obligations and religious beliefs. Primitive societies were organized around mechanical relationships.

Durkheim's second ideal-type, the *organic* society, was considered to have come into existence with the development of technology and the liberation of individuals from traditional constraints. These changes had ushered in voluntarism, individualism, and contractually governed exchange relations.

Organic societies were represented by modern industrial nations where "great concentrations of forces and capital" have led to "the extreme division of labor." This division of labor was characteristic of both economic and noneconomic relations. In economic relations, the division of labor was expressed by the "functional interdependence" of occupational roles and groups. This interdependence was based on exchange relations, competition, and the pursuit of private interests.

Durkheim's Critique of Spencer:
Integration and Social Control

Durkheim felt that the "harmony of interests" which is spontaneously generated by exchange relations, competition, and the pursuit of private interests, was not sufficient for integrating organic societies. His criticism of Spencer's writings, therefore, minimized the integrative functions of individual interests.

Spencer's theory implied to Durkheim (1933:200–203) that "social solidarity would then be nothing else than the spontaneous accord of individual interests." It further suggested that the typical social relationship would be sheerly economic, "stripped of all regulation and resulting from the free initiative of [contracting] parties." These implications were considered absurd because they took for granted that social relationships can exist without social control. Assuming the opposite, that human relationships are *social* only if they are socially *controlled,* Durkheim declared that the natural harmony of interests is devoid of "any action *properly* social coming to regulate this exchange" (our emphasis). Therefore, by definition, complementary or shared interests cannot solve the problem of *social* integration.

Certain factors, in Durkheim's opinion, prevented exchange relations from being integrated by the natural harmony of interests alone. In the first place, this harmony could not provide for enduring exchange relationships because it was based on temporary expedience; consequently, when interests brought men together, it was never for more than a few moments. But even more important in this regard was the fact that Durkheim felt that the "harmony of *interests* conceals a *latent* or *deferred conflict"* which threatens to destroy exchange: "For where interest is the only ruling force *each individual* finds himself *in a state of war with every other* since nothing comes to mollify the *egos,* and any truce in this *eternal antagonism* would not be of long duration" (*ibid.:*204 our emphasis). Since conflict was latent in exchange, Durkheim concluded that there *must* exist some form of social control to repress or regulate this conflict. Otherwise, no social relationship could endure.

Two important assumptions underlie these critical statements: first, exchange is social only if it is regulated by society. Second, if exchange relationships are not socially controlled, men will destroy each other. Since Durkheim implicitly was discussing the nature of exchange between members of *capitalist* societies, his assault on Spencer was but another convoluted echo in the general attack by proponents of corporate capitalism against laissez-faire capitalism. Durkheim's critique was based on the familiar neo-Hobbesian corporate-liberal problem of order, and his solution to this problem, as we shall continue to see, was firmly anchored by the broad concept of social control. This solution, furthermore, was considered to be part of a "normal" evolutionary state of affairs. One cannot ask for more striking parallels among Durkheim and other corporate-liberal sociologists!

Changes in Evolutionary Development
of Social Controls

Like Ward and Ross, Durkheim (*ibid*.:204–205) also emphasized historical developments in the scope and complexity of social controls both in the past and the future. In his polemic against Spencer, Durkheim indicated that Spencer did not conduct a rigorous *historical* analysis of changes in the relationships between the individual and society. Spencer had ignored the degree to which societal constraints had changed over time. He had only cited facts "taken at random," instead of examining historically "the way in which social action [5] has essentially manifested itself." Had Spencer been more competent, he would have found that "far from diminishing, social action grows greater and greater and becomes more and more complex" in industrial societies.

In what way had social control become more complex and broad in scope? Firstly, Durkheim claimed that restitutive law,[6] which had not existed in primitive societies, came into being alongside traditional forms of repressive law. Secondly, domestic laws involving "the different species of juridical relations to which family life gives rise [became] much more numerous than heretofore." The obligations which resulted from this also gave rise to a highly influential noncontractual system of rights and duties. According to Durkheim (*ibid*.:206–210), ideational systems of this sort controlled the evolutionary changes in the kinship ties in modern societies.

Durkheim also stated that the legal regulation of contractual relationships were no less normal in organic societies than the legal and extralegal control of domestic relationships. In order to buttress this point, Durkheim proposed that the division of labor was necessary for social solidarity. He then added (*ibid*.:214) that contractual law was the decisive factor in maintaining the harmony of interests between exchangists: it "expresses the *normal* conditions of equilibrium." Consistent with his systematic blindness to the historical development of market relationships, Durkheim also regarded the functional necessity of contractual law in terms of a final cause, namely the necessity for establishing nonconflicting, equilibrated relationships.[7]

Although Durkheim, like Spencer, had indicated that "division of labor makes interests solidary," he departed from Spencer by noting that the mere fact of interdependence does not guarantee continued order because "each of the contractants while needing the other seeks to obtain what he needs at the least expense." [8] Therefore, he concluded, it had been necessary to establish persistent order on other grounds than interests. These grounds were constituted by a system of rules which regulated contractual relationships. Moreover, these rules were not merely concerned with regulating individuals in typical or predictable situations; they were also developed in order to regulate situations which might arise even though they were not taken into account by the interested parties (*ibid*.:213). As a result of the accumulation of past experiences, Durkheim asserted, "what we cannot foresee individually" is provided for by society. What "we cannot regulate is therefore regulated, and this regulation imposes itself upon us, although it may not be our handiwork, but that of society and tradition." "From this point of view," Durkheim (*ibid.*:214) exclaimed, "the law of contract appears in an entirely new light." "It is no longer simply a useful complement of individual conventions; it is their *fundamental norm. Imposing itself upon us with the authority of traditional experience,* it constitutes the foundation of our contractual relations" (our emphasis).

Although he considered it most decisive, the legal code was not the only normative system which sustained contractual relations: there was also custom. Custom included rules which, although not sanctioned "either directly or indirectly by any legal code, are none the less imperative." These rules were represented by professional obligations which could be very strict even though they were "purely moral." Moreover, these rules, according to Durkheim (*ibid.*:215), were also multiplying in modern societies. Thus, modern industrial societies were not only integrated by complex systems of contractual rules at any one time—they were being increasingly integrated by custom as they developed progressively over time.

Durkheim's denunciation of Spencer should not obscure the fundamentally liberal grounds on which this criticism was formulated. His argument did not *deny* the significance of microscopic exchange relations as a solution to the problem of integration. It merely *modified* the concept of exchange in the manner of the times to include the notion of social control.

Expansion of Political State Defined as *Normal* Phenomenon

A much more significant departure from Spencer's laissez-faire liberal ideology was represented by Durkheim's attitude toward the role of the political state. Since Durkheim felt that the basic function of the state was its social control function, it should be no surprise that he found Spencer an antagonist in this area, too. In *The Division of Labor,* Durkheim (*ibid.*:218–219) attacked Spencer on grounds similar to those stated later by Lester Ward: he accused Spencer of not providing a proper analogue between the role of the state in a "social organism" and the role of the brain in a biological organism. Durkheim (*ibid.*:219) then made his own analogy between the brain and the state, proposing that administrative law consists of the "totality of rules" which determine the functions of the "central organ" and the "organs" which are "immediately subordinate to it." He added that "if we may again borrow biological terminology . . . we may say that these rules determine the way in which the cerebro-spinal system of the social organism functions. This system, in current parlance, is designated by the name, State."

After drastically reducing the essential aspects of the state to a *system of rules,* Durkheim declared that Spencer's reasons for the withering away of the state in industrial society were "remarkably poor." The functions of the state were not only *not* disappearing, but instead "these functions are becoming more and more numerous and varied." Furthermore, these functions were absolutely necessary in order to integrate a society which was becoming progressively differentiated because of the evolution of the division of labor. Pointing to the increasing expansion of state functions in industrialized societies, Durkheim (*ibid.*:219–222) added that "it is thus contrary to . . . regard the present [i.e., expanding] dimensions of the governmental organ as a symptom of social illness . . . Everything forces us to see in it a normal phenomenon."

Durkheim also justified the expansion of the state by referring to the effects of the concentration of capital on economic stability. He suggested (*ibid.*:224–225) that because of industrial development, large-scale industry was being substituted for small. As the small businesses were eliminated, "the number of different enterprises" grew less. Consequently, "each has more relative importance," and finally "the failure of a great industrial company results . . . in public distress." Since "distress of some general scope cannot be produced without affecting the higher centers," these "centers," such as the political state and its "subsidiary organs," were increasingly "forced to intervene" out of self-preservation to ameliorate this distress.

Durkheim justified the political control of corporations on the basis of this simplistic explanation of the causes of state intervention into economic relations within monopoly capitalism. In regard to individual control, however, Durkheim stressed functional obligations and political dependency; "because we fill some domestic or social function," he stated (*ibid.*:227),:

we are involved in a complex of obligations from which we have *no right to free ourselves*. There is, above all, an organ upon which we are tending to depend more and more; this is the state. The points at which we are in contact with it multiply as do the occasions when it is entrusted with the duty of reminding us of the sentiment of common solidarity. [our emphasis]

Durkheim justified his stance in the name of social stability and solidarity. But one cannot ask for a more blatant call for the general subservience of the individual to the authority of the state.

NOTES

1. As early as 1894, for example, there are emphasized references to the notion that *"in a normal state of society, there is no wage without function"* (Small and Vincent 1894:239).

2. For further discussion on this topic see Clark (1968).

3. In 1911, Daniel De Leon said of Lafargue: "Paul Lafargue, a Cuban by birth, was of French-Jewish and Cuban Mulatto extraction. When asked at Lille, France, by the writer . . . whether he [Lafargue] had any predilection for any of the races through whose loins he was strained, he promptly answered, 'Yes,' and added 'I am proudest of my Negro extraction.' The statement gives a cue to the understanding of Lafargue's characteristics and career" (quoted in Lafargue 1967:41).

4. Lafargue (1967:15–16) indicated that "Dollfus, Scherer-Kestner Alsace, the most intelligent, most philanthropic and consequently the heaviest exploiters in France be-

fore the [Franco-Prussian] war, had founded with their spare pennies at Mulhouse, schools of design, of chemistry and physics, where the brightest children of their workingmen are instructed gratis, in order that they might always have at hand and at a reasonable figure the intellectual capacities required for carrying on their industries."

5. Durkheim used the term "social action" to refer to the regulating influence of law, custom, tradition, and social obligations.

6. Restitutive law, stimulated by the development of the division of labor, and representing *originally a liberal syndicalist conception of law*, regulates, according to Durkheim, "the special relations between different *functions.*"

7. Spencer, according to Durkheim (*ibid.*:217), had not realized that contract is exchange *governed* by law; therefore, it is *social control* which gives exchange its *normal* form.

8. It should be noted in passing that this observation by Durkheim implicitly rests on the assumption that economistic activity and therefore "scarcity" poses a problem of integration in organic societies.

CHAPTER 33

Durkheim's Syndicalist Vision

Durkheim claimed that governmental institutions and occupational groups would eventually evolve into the basic units of social organization in "organic" societies. In pursuing this line of thought, Durkheim developed a utopian vision which unequivocally stamps him as a liberal-syndicalist theorist.

Liberal-Syndicalism and Durkheim's Vision of Society

In the preface to the second edition of *The Division of Labor,* Durkheim reflected on the direction in which modern "organic" societies were moving. He began the preface (1933:1) by noting his concern with "the question of the role that occupational groups are destined to play in the contemporary social order." [1] His scholarly works had focused on the fact that "in the economic order, occupational ethics exist only in the most rudimentary state." Consequently, he felt, society is lawless. Although professional ethics exist in some occupations, the economy is generally characterized by "juridical and moral anomy." "The most blameworthy acts," he sadly remarked, "are so often absolved by success that the boundary between what is permitted and what is prohibited, what is just and what is unjust, has nothing fixed about it, but seems susceptible to almost arbitrary change by individuals" (*ibid.*:1–2).

Durkheim (*ibid.*:2) flatly declared that "this juridical and moral anomy" is the cause "of the incessantly recurrent conflicts, and the multifarious disorders of which the economic world exhibits so sad a spectacle." What is more, he emphasized, "truces arrived at after violence, are never anything but provisional, and satisfy no one. Human passions stop only before a moral power they respect. If all authority of this kind is waning, the law of the strongest prevails, and latent or active, the state of war is necessarily chronic." Characterizing this "anomic" (i.e., laissez-faire capitalist) state of affairs as "anarchy," he added that it "is an unhealthy phenomenon . . . since it runs counter to the aim of society, which is to suppress, or at least to moderate, war among men, subordinating the law of the strongest to a higher law."

How could social order replace the anarchic conditions in capitalist societies at the turn of the century? The only answer, in Durkheim's opinion, was the formation of *national-corporate* organizations based on similar occupations or industries. These national corporations would replace or subsume the "only groups which have a certain permanence today"; namely, "those called syndicates composed of either employers or workmen." In Durkheim's view, these syndicates represented "a beginning of occupational organization, but still are quite formless and rudimentary." Therefore, they have not evolved into the higher national-corporate organization he had in mind. The syndicates in existence were still private associations "without legal authority and deprived, consequently, of all regulatory power." Furthermore, the number of existing syndicates was "theoretically limitless, even in the interior of the same industrial category; and as each of them is independent of the others, if they do not federate or unify there is nothing intrinsic in them expressing the unity of the occupation in its entirety." Finally, *"the syndicates of employers* and *the syndicates of employees* are distinct from each other, which is *legitimate and necessary,* but with no regular contact between them" (*ibid.:*6 our emphasis). Durkheim's proposed national corporations would be certified by the state; limited to an industry or occupational group, they would include both *workers and capitalists* in one big happy family.

The allusion to a "happy family" is suggested by Durkheim himself in his claim that the "corporation" is a modern evolvement of the family. He stated (*ibid.:*17), "indeed, the corporation has been, in a sense, *the heir of the family.* As long as industry is exclusively agriculture, it has, in the family and in the village, which is itself only a sort of great family, its immediate organ, and it needs no other." But the growth of exchange forces people to move outside of the family: "For to live by a trade, customers are necessary, as is having relations with competitors . . . in addition, trades demand cities, and cities have always been formed and recruited principally from the ranks of immigrants, individuals who have left their native homes. A new form of activity was thus constituted which burst from the old familiar form." Guided by this fantastic logic, Durkheim (*ibid.:*17–18) concluded that "this is the origin of the *corporation;* it was substituted for the *family* in the exercise of a function which had first been domestic, but which could no longer keep this character" (our emphasis).[2]

Returning full circle to the state, Durkheim considered the election of members to its executive and legislative bodies. First, as mentioned previously, he indicated (*ibid.*:27) that "society, instead of remaining what it is today, an aggregate of juxtaposed territorial districts, would become *a vast system* of national corporations. From various quarters it is asked that elective assemblies be formed by *occupations,* and not by territorial divisions." In this way, "political assemblies . . . would be a more faithful picture of *social life in its entirety*" (our emphasis).

Durkheim also integrated the familiar class divisions in capitalist societies into his corporate liberal vision of social evolution. He indicated that each national corporation would have its own elected assemblies comprised of representatives of employees and representatives of employers. Workers and capitalists had to be separately represented because "they form distinct and independent groups" at the "base of the corporation." In addition, Durkheim observed in passing, in order to be able "to go about their ways freely, they (i.e., the workers and the capitalists) must go about their ways separately" (*ibid.*:25n.1).

Durkheim's Mechanism: Political Economy of Syndicalist Relationships

When sociologists describe the mechanism in Durkheim's theory of the division of labor, they usually offer a summary approximation in the form of the following generalization: The division of labor increases as the population size and density increases. This growth in "divided" labor poses a problem which is *literally* conceived as "the task of integrating" or "coordinating" different or competing specialties of labor. The reader has seen, however, that liberal theorists generally based their conceptions of man and the integration of society on mechanisms involving notions of *competition* and *scarcity*. Not one liberal theorist (and Durkheim is no exception) since Malthus has posed the problem of integration for society as a whole on the basis of demographic characteristics (e.g., population size, "volume," or density) *alone*. In one way or another, these theorists have explicitly emphasized or implicitly asserted that the problem of integration is *universally* posed by the voluntaristic, internecine, warlike activity for scarce goods which characterizes life in capitalist societies. In the later nineteenth century, this contention was buttressed by recourse to Darwin's observations on intraspecies competition. Durkheim justified his theory in this same manner.

For example, Durkheim (*ibid.*:262) did state that if the division of labor "progresses in a continuous manner in the course of social development, it is because societies become regularly denser and generally more voluminous." He *added* (*ibid.*:266), however, that "if work becomes divided more as societies become more voluminous and denser, it is not because external circumstances are more varied, but because *struggle for existence is more acute*" (our emphasis). Citing Darwin's observations in intraspecies competition,

Durkheim claimed that members of different species are able to "co-exist" because they "do not feed in the same manner and do not lead the same kind of life . . . What is advantageous to one is without value to the others." On the other hand, members of the same species have "the same needs" and pursue "the same objects" and are "in rivalry everywhere."

In Malthus' theory, population growth initiated a specified series of significant social changes when it outstripped the food supply. While Durkheim never took the trouble to inform the reader about the detailed nature of the general condition of scarcity, the increase in population density was clearly being related to a decrease in the availability of valued goods. He stated (*ibid.*:266) that as long as members of a population "have more resources than they need, they can still live side by side, but if their number increases to such a proportion that all appetites can no longer be sufficiently satisfied, war breaks out, and it is as violent as this insufficiency is more marked; that is to say, as the number in the struggle increase." In these statements, Durkheim was obviously assuming that the supply of goods was limited in some absolute sense, or that it could not keep up with the rate of population growth. It is important to keep in mind that this fallacious assumption was made by Durkheim at the end of the nineteenth century, when the vast power of an industrial technology was already clearly observable to any scholar interested in understanding the real nature of human relationships. It had been patently clear for some time that even natural calamities were no longer sufficient for explaining the condition of scarcity in advanced capitalist nations.

It is also important to note that Durkheim could have examined the ways in which scarcity is *instituted* through the economy. His work refers time and again to human relationships as relationships among "cooperators." Why did he not deem it possible for human beings to cooperate by sharing the goods of life without external constraint? What caused individuals to war against each other rather than engage in a planned production and distribution of goods according to need? These questions do not enter into his analysis. The fact of the competitive struggle for scarce values is merely assumed as a *fundamental fact of nature*. Human beings are considered to be like all other species. People, as we shall see, are held to obey fallacious social Darwinist "laws" governing intraspecies competition. These "laws" structure the mechanisms in Durkheim's theory.[3]

Durkheimian Mechanisms and the Sociobiological Leap

Durkheim detailed the nature of his theoretical mechanism by constantly shifting between human relationships and biological or plant analogies. His warrant for the mechanism, therefore, is heavily dependent upon analogy. In order to construct this analogy, Durkheim first claimed that intraspecies relations are dominated by competition while interspecies relations are characterized by peaceful coexistence.[4] After making this patently ridiculous claim, Durkheim declared: "Men submit to the same law. In the same city, different occupations can co-exist without being obliged mutually to destroy one another, for they pursue different objects." On the other hand, although "the judge is never in competition with the businessman" because their occupations are different, "the brewer and the winegrower, the clothier and the manufacturer of silks, the poet and the musician, often try to supplant each other." Thus, the greater the similarities in "function," the greater the competition between occupations.

The consequences of this competition between functionally similar occupations, according to Durkheim, depend upon the conditions under which the competition takes place. If the "occupations" communicate with each other frequently, the competition is more intense. If "they" are both strong, "they" will limit each other and their "mutual relationships" are generally unchanged. However, the creation of new occupational specializations and therefore an increase in the division of labor result from *one* condition regardless of all other conditions. If some of the contending "occupations" are *inferior* to the others, these "occupations" will have to "yield ground." According to Durkheim (*ibid.:*269), "they no longer have any alternative but to disappear or transform and this *transformation must necessarily end in a new specialization*" (our emphasis).

Durkheim's general discussion of his mechanism occupies almost a hundred pages. Many of the nuances described seem to be implicitly organized around Durkheim's belief in the importance of detailing the conditions under which occupational failures in competitive struggles choose alternative courses of action in an effort to escape their painful situation.[5] For example, it is noted that members of unsuccessfully competing occupations do not have to create new occupations in order to maintain their economic identity within a nation. They can emigrate and become the colonizers of other lands. They can become resigned to their defeat and live out their lives in despair. They can even turn to suicide! Of course, these individuals can also choose to become members of an existing occupational group, but, as Durkheim (*ibid.:* 285–286) noted, this merely transfers the competitive struggle to another arena.

It would be pointless to make a summary of all the nuances of Durkheim's interminable discussion of the multitude of conditions, or modes of *adaptation* to personal failure. It can be easily demonstrated, however, that most of this discussion amounts to little more than the wholesale projection of atomistic and economistic decision-making processes onto the domain of occupational relationships. New occupational groups are reputed to come into existence because individuals have not been able to compete successfully with others in maintaining their occupational identity. New "specializations," in this context, merely represent the substitution of an alternative course of individual action in the face of unsuccessful competition. The complex development of occupations such as those represented by biologists, doctors, electricians, plumbers, or policemen, for that matter, are thus reduced to consequences of economistic choice-behavior and voluntaristic competitive striving.[6]

Durkheim's theory of occupational development is pure fiction. But even more fallacious was his contention that this theory could be generalized to "all social functions." Thus Durkheim was not merely talking about occupations but about all forms of "divided" labor, including, for example, the relationships based on the division of labor within the family. Durkheim's theory is but another example of the way in which early sociologists applied trivial psychological and social psychological paradigms to one likely aspect of social life, and then generalized their analysis to all aspects of social life.

NOTES

1. This concern, Durkheim added, was reflected in *The Division of Labor*, his famous study *Suicide*, and various other works.

2. How did Durkheim perceive the relations between his national corporations and the state? According to Durkheim (1933:24–25), the state should be concerned with regulation of the interrelationships between the national corporations. The corporation, on its part, is concerned with the relationships between its members, including the overseeing of meritarian and competitive distribution of wealth between its individual members.

3. Durkheim's theory is dependent on the notion that social disorganization can be ameliorated by the development of new functional relationships and their social controls. Therefore, it can be regarded as an illustration of reform Darwinism. However, his mechanism, taken by itself, is *directly* derived from a social Darwinist approach to a sociology of occupations.

4. In regard to this latter claim, Durkheim provided an example taken from Darwin, in which "twenty" species of plants, belonging to eighteen genera and eight classes; "can live side by side one another on a three by four foot turf." "This," Durkheim (1933:266) happily declared, "clearly proves how differentiated they are."

5. In discussing these alternative possibilities, Durkheim (1933:285) indicated that it is unlikely that the occupational failures in "less developed" societies will choose an occupation which is forbidden by prevailing norms because social controls are very strong in these societies. He pointed out that it is also unlikely that they will choose occupations which "are held in *low esteem* by public opinion." The pressure, therefore, is to move individuals into activity which represents new "specialized functions" where this is at all possible. This is more satisfying to persons who are searching for a new, acceptable identity. It is also, in our opinion, very rational and very economistic.

6. Thus, on the basis of Durkheim's theory, it would be logical to claim that the occupation of sociology came into existence when it did (after the other sciences) because the founders of sociology were inferior persons who could not make the grade in competition with the other occupations.

CHAPTER 34

Moral Integration of the Capitalist Division of Labor

How did the concept of social control enter into Durkheim's theory of the evolution of "organic" society? He indicated (1933:287–302) that as society grew and its population became more dense, small communities disintegrated, great cities emerged, and, as a consequence, the individual was less enveloped by "mechanical" relationships. The individual thereby became free of collective bonds and lost his or her habits of unquestioned obedience to communal forms of authority and the collective conscience. One result was an increased access to means which departed from those sanctioned by tradition. The disintegration of traditional controls, therefore, enabled the individual to specialize in other ways than those determined and sanctioned by the preferences of previous generations. Social control entered into Durkheim's theory, therefore, as *one* of the factors influencing the conditions of *individual choice behavior* (*ibid.*:290–291, 330–331, 333).

Social control was also used to indicate the ways in which the *occupational specialities* of "organic" society were maintained after they had emerged. "In so far as labor is divided," Durkheim (*ibid.*:302) stated, "there arises a multitude of occupational moralities and laws." (The form of this social control therefore consisted of "moralities and laws.") These "moralities" replaced the older, "collective conscience," and regulated competitive and other forms of behavior within and between occupational groups. This kind of regulation, however, was much less binding than that of mechanical societies. It was free enough so that the organic society maintained the flexibility to adapt to constantly changing circumstances. The occupational moralities of organic societies, for example, admitted sufficient anomie so that orderly changes could take place indefinitely (*ibid.*:302–304). At least this was the case with what Durkheim called "normal" organic societies. There were also "pathological" organic societies such as laissez-faire capitalist societies, which were ridden with uncontrolled conflicts and greater anomie.

In further detailing his mechanism, Durkheim (*ibid.*:272) asserted that a new occupational specialization, once in existence, cannot be maintained unless it also meets some "need of society," and that new needs are stimulated by larger individual brains. In support of this contrived functionalist assertion, Durkheim indicated that the same competition which generated the

267

growth of new occupations also stimulated the growth of the nervous system. (According to Durkheim, it is the nervous system which supports the varied "burdens" of competitive life and devises "ingenious methods to keep up the struggle" between individuals.) Arguing that "cerebral life develops . . . at the same time that competition becomes keener," Durkheim (*ibid.:*272–273) stated that "a more voluminous and more delicate brain makes greater demands than a less refined one." As a result of these "great demands," "intellectual" and other "social" needs developed and thus provided the functional preconditions for maintaining the increasing division of labor.[1]

In sum, the universal existence of intraspecies competition creates both an increasing division of labor and an increasing "social" need to maintain this division of labor. In the course of time, occupations emerge which are sufficiently different from the existing occupations to enable peaceful coexistence. Although there does exist some rivalry within and between occupations, this is regulated by occupational "moralities." As a result, in "normal societies" competition does not generate class struggle, poverty, crime, or imperialism. Instead, the competition for "scarce" resources in capitalism produces harmony, goodwill, peace, equilibrium, cooperation, a mutually beneficial interdependence between specialized "functioners," and a higher morality.

Futhermore, in this grand process each man's inferiority becomes a positive attribute. Individuals with strong bodies but poor brains can specialize in occupations which require great muscles but little thought. Others with weak bodies but powerful brains can specialize in occupations which require little muscular exertion but considerable intellect. Individual inferiority is thus transcended by the growth of occupational specializations and each person is allocated to a "rightful" place in the natural scheme of things. Indeed, the blessings of the increasing division of labor are so great, Durkheim declared, that a comparison would illustrate their good work: "Among primitive tribes, the vanquished enemy is put to death," but "where industrial functions are separated from military functions he lives as a *slave* beside the conqueror" (our emphasis).

In the eighteenth century, Adam Smith suggested that frequent commerce promotes trust. In the nineteenth century, Herbert Spencer regarded the exchange of private property to be the stimulus for peaceful world order. Emile Durkheim, at the dawn of the twentieth century, felt that the growth of functionally interdependent groups, organized on the basis of the division of labor, would usher in a stable and harmonious capitalist society. It may be contended that Durkheim should not be criticized for overestimating the positive effects of the industrial organization on monopoly capitalism (at the turn of the century there were few liberals who could have predicted the full magnitude of the horrors yet to be produced by this form of capitalism). It is possible, however, in light of the fact that Marx had taken similar uses to task in the 1840s, to hold Durkheim responsible for the incompetent use of the concept of the division of labor.

Marx's View of Division of Labor

During the 1840s, a half-century before Durkheim's work, M. Proudhon published his *Philosophy of Poverty,* which also relied heavily on the concept of the division of labor. In 1847, Marx's scathing criticism, satirically entitled *The Poverty of Philosophy,* carefully dissected Proudhon's work. Some of Marx's remarks are also pertinent to an understanding of both the empirical inadequacies and the ideological functions of Durkheim's *Division of Labor.* Most of Marx's remarks were focused on the division of labor in the workshop. But in spite of this focus, these remarks will provide some indication why it is virtually impossible, in terms of Durkheim's simple liberal formulas, to intelligently analyze the development of the division of labor in a single economic institution, much less in all of society.

In criticizing Proudhon's theory, Marx (1847:109) indicated that economists and philosophers generally prefer to see the development of society in terms of eternal, immutable, and fixed categories. But intellectual ideas and categories, he noted, "are as little eternal as the relations they express. They are historical and transitory products." From this point of view the division of labor should be examined in respect to its concrete historical context. This examination would show that the development of the division of labor is *not* continuous. During any given epoch the division of labor was dependent upon the mode of production and the latter had undergone qualitatively different historical changes. The division of labor which was characteristic of the separation between urban and rural areas in modern nations, for example, took centuries to develop and was related to the formation of a national market economy. As a result, Marx stated (*ibid.*:134), "the separation of the different parts of labor, leaving to each one the opportunity of devoting himself to the specialty best suited to him—a separation which M. Proudhon dates from the beginning of the world—exists only in *modern* industry under the rule of competition" (our emphasis).

Marx felt that the notion of "divided" labor had capitalized heavily upon a commonsense awareness of the modern industrial specialization of labor. When fully analyzed, however, it became apparent that it was frequently not occupational specialization, but historically specific modes of production and distribution that were actually referred to when scholars used the concept of division of labor. In Proudhon's case, the model for the division of labor, mistakenly generalized to all societies throughout history, was actually based on the industrial workshop. As Marx pointed out, however, the division of labor in the workshop was not highly developed in previous historical epochs. Furthermore, he noted that even in modern societies, the complex system of social, political, and economic authority could not be equated with the simple authoritarian system of the workshop.

Marx further indicated that Proudhon's concept of the "continuous" development of the division of labor in the workshop was also in error. In certain respects this criticism can be extrapolated to Durkheim's (1933:39) belief that modern industry "advances steadily towards . . . great concentrations of forces and capital, and consequently to the extreme division of labor." With regard to the concentration of capital in the nineteenth century, Marx would *not* have disagreed. (In fact, his work, *Capital,* represented an important economic theory which attempted to explain this concentration before it had fully developed.) However, his dissent was with the consequent "extreme division of labor" resulting from this development. His criticism of Proudhon's concept of the division of labor in the industrial workshop pointed out that machine technology not only destroyed previous occupational specialties such as those characterized by the feudal artisan, but this technology often rendered useless occupations created by a previous development *in the very same* (machine) technology. This was particularly true in what Marx called the "automatic workshop" in which workers were transformed into mere "onlookers" who tended machines. New machines brought into being new specialties. These same machines also frequently replaced a larger number of others. Thus, Marx contended, the development of the workshop did not necessarily represent the development of more numerous specialties. It often represented the *opposite.* In 1847, at the time Marx's work was written, "machine tenders" were often women and children who were trained for this labor within a few hours. Their "functions," according to Marx, did not represent an *occupational specialty* in the sense that we normally use this term. These persons could not even be termed "semiskilled" workers although their particular function may have had a distinctive name. In fact, not only were these persons "mere appendages to the machine," but their functions were often taken over by the machine itself in the further development of technology.[2]

Durkheim expressed the belief that the division of labor increased because of frustrated competitive striving on the part of occupational failures. This striving was stimulated by the growth in population density and the intensity of competition. Marx, on the other hand, insisted that population changes were inextricably tied to changes in the mode of production. He pointed out that the division of labor in the workshop was only made possible by the agrarian revolution and the formation of the modern industrial class system. He noted that a massive transformation of agricultural populations had been underway for centuries before the emergence of the industrial workshop. In this process, a merchant and manufacturing class had come into being and a new class of *wage earners* became *concentrated* in urban communities. The first workshops had often retained a traditional division of labor, but they had concentrated artisans under a single merchant-manufacturer. The development of machine technology toward the end of the eighteenth century was rapidly integrated into the workshop system because of these previous developments. Thus, it was not the mere density of the population *in general* but the transformation in class structure and the concentration of forces of production (e.g., workers) which made possible the workshop and its consequent division of labor.[3]

Marx also noted that further development of the division of labor in the workshop required a constant feedback between the development of machine technology and the previous organization of the division of labor. The previous organization of labor stimulated the invention of new machines and vice versa. When placed within the context of the general growth in market relationships, this interaction was also part of other political and economic processes which encompassed workers in different nations. Not only did there arise a division of labor between town and country, but also between nations. The English worker, for example, spun cotton and processed tea that was grown and gathered by farm laborers in America and Ceylon. This development was accompanied by profound political and economic changes throughout the world. The development of capitalist forms of the division of labor in the nineteenth century, therefore, could not, in Marx's view, be described without also discussing the development of imperialism. In light of the merits of this analysis, an explanation of the division of labor which bases its development on a continuous tendency toward high population density, specialization, and "organic" integration is very misleading.

Part of Marx's critique is devoted to Proudhon's belief that competition is an invariable feature of societal development. Proudhon anchored his assumption in human nature. Marx (1847:147) insisted, however, that *"all history is nothing but a continuous transformation of human nature"* (our emphasis). Further, competition, as a prime mover of individual striving, was relegated to the epoch of capitalism and rooted in capitalist modes of production. Competition, therefore, was not considered a "necessity of the human soul."

Although Durkheim vaguely indicated that the division of labor was maintained by the development of new "social" needs, competition was actually viewed as the cause of both the division of labor as well as these "social" needs: competitive striving was taken as an immutable force within individuals which was set free with the disintegration of traditional controls. The organic society was perceived as the result of egoistic striving and was the product of each man's highly rational (economistic) attempt to choose a means for expressing his peculiar talents without being destroyed by other competitors. In sharp contrast with this viewpoint, Marx explicitly maintained that the *division of labor* created the *inequality* in human talents. Men were conditioned to inequality in performance by their work life. Furthermore, more often than not, this conditioning *limited human potentiality* and produced what Marx called the specialized "craft idiocy" that is typical in modern industrial societies.

Occupational Morality: Panacea for Social Conflict

Where today, Durkheim inquired, are the moral forces capable of establishing and maintaining the necessary discipline for integrating social life? They can be found in the moral attitudes and authority generated by professional groupings in industrial societies. If these groups were granted the power necessary to resolve conflicts among their members and "apply the general laws of society" according to their specific variety of labor, they would eventually acquire the "moral authority" to *restrain* their members. What is more, without this restraint, Durkheim (1933:203–204) declared, "there could be no *economic* stability." This was a technocratic solution different only in its locus from those developed elsewhere.[4]

Almost a century before the publication of Durkheim's work, Charles Fourier had excoriated the kind of occupational attitudes that had become prevalent in capitalist societies. He indicated that members of such specializations as window-glazing and medicine had become so dominated by materialistic standards that they welcomed hail-storms and epidemics as opportunities to make money. Undoubtedly Fourier's observations and criticisms appeared crudely perverse to Durkheim, because the latter felt that occupational ethics would, in time, transcend the special interests of individuals or even of the occupational group as a whole. After all, if economic stability is merely dependent upon moral restraint, forward-looking occupational groups should become very concerned about checking their greedy interests in favor of "society."

It is now seven decades since Durkheim's moral solution and more than a century and a half since Fourier's cynical comments about occupational morality. Americans are concerned with the extent of consumer fraud, the rate at which both industrial and craft unions are being riddled with racketeers or undemocratic leadership, and the scandalous extent to which corporation managers and owners are implicated in milking the public.

When city planners attempt to formulate plans for the general welfare, they are confronted by the myriad conflicting interests of real estate agents, merchants, manufacturers, civil servants, electricians, plumbers, and carpenters (Jacobs 1969). Has either the general welfare or the ethical quality of occupational life increased in any significant way because each specialty has become organized?

Durkheim's universal tendency toward equilibrium and solidarity does not characterize the development of occupational relations. Instead, Fourier seems to have been much closer to the mark, for it is the old-fashioned laws of capitalist competition that have not only generated organized associations within each specialty but also *maintained* the socially expedient morality of these associations. The only transformation in this development has involved the emergence of attitudes and practices that aim at the restraint of competition within and between specialties. And this transformation aims at the maximization of profits and earnings, not solidarity.

Durkheim's view of the generally positive consequences of the development of occupational moralities seem even less defensible than his view of the capitalist division of labor. His moral solution not only ignores the most obvious regularities which were pointed out by Fourier, but it is also blind to the fact that capitalism influences occupational morality by instituting pecuniary remuneration as an overriding value. There are, in addition, more general ideological influences that determine how a member of an occupational group will evaluate the conditions under which he will service others. The American Medical Association, for example, fought, and still is fighting, "socialized medicine" in the United States. This antagonistic stand was taken even though the lives of poor people were clearly being foreshortened by the lack of adequate care.[5] What can be said of a professional morality that cannot override its member professionals who are morally culpable for the premature deaths of literally millions of Americans? If the medical profession generally refused to adhere to its own professed obligations to serve humanity unless this service was rendered in the name of free enterprise, what can be said about other occupations in this regard?

NOTES

1. It should be noted that aside from these vague references to biological changes, Durkheim gives us few, if any, clues to the specific nature of these "social" needs, outside of a hypostasized need for social integration.

2. Applying Marx's argument to the second half of the twentieth century, the further development of the automatic workshop and of self-regulating machines in other types of institutions, now heralds a major reorganization of labor. The cybernetic revolution, as it is called, will undoubtedly defy any simpleminded attempt to describe the organization of occupations in terms of the continuous growth in *specialization*. The opposite may well be the case.

3. Durkheim, therefore, was basing his model on a demographic change, but Marx referred instead to *sociological* phenomena involving the relations between human beings, not their mere numbers or density.

4. Durkheim (1958) also pointed out in a work on Saint-Simon that his own "moral solution" would be superior to those offered by other philosophers. The professional group's authority, Durkheim explained, "no longer stirs questions of classes; it no longer opposes rich to poor, employers to workers—as if the only possible solution consisted of diminishing the portion of one in order to augment the other." Instead, according to Durkheim, the moral solution "declares, in the interests of both, the necessity of a curb from above which checks appetites and so sets a limit on the stages of disarrangement, excitement, and frenzied agitation, which do not spring from social activity and which even make it suffer." "Put differently," Durkheim (*ibid.*:203–204) concluded, "the social question, posed in this way, is not a question of money or force; it is a question of moral agents. What dominates it is not the state of our *economy*, but much more, the state of our *morality* . . ."

5. The consequences of the lack of medical care are compounded when racism is combined with poverty. Nathan Hare (1970:6), for example, notes that blacks are more than twice as likely to die of pneumonia and influenza. Their "life expectancy is almost ten years less than that of whites, black infant mortality rates are at the level which whites exhibited twenty years ago. Black women are more than four times as likely to die of childbirth, and black children are about three times as likely to succumb to post-natal mortality."

CHAPTER 35

From Syndicalism to Pluralism

The syndicalism of Ross and Durkheim was soon to be superceded in a closely related yet more abstract conceptualization—pluralism. The social-political mechanisms described by Small were also largely transitional and therefore important to understanding the new development. Small believed that capitalism was gradually evolving toward a full democracy based on co-operation between such conflicting interests as capital and labor. This utopian development was preferable when contrasted with solutions offered by "traditional individualism" and "modern socialism." The former, Small declared, would maintain a semianarchistic (laissez-faire) society while the latter meant totalitarianism. Small's own alternative was a "middle course" produced by the "cooperative" processes which he called "socialization." Small suggested further that the "direct line of truth" was a position between Adam Smith's and Karl Marx's conceptions of society (Page 1940:138).

Small was aware that capitalism was undergoing significant changes during his lifetime. He also knew that these changes heralded the broad political outlines of a new "middle of the road" society. Like the classical liberals, Small considered "politics at bottom . . . largely a maneuvering to control the means of controlling wealth" (*ibid.*:125). But instead of regarding politics as an arena wherein atomistic egoists strove to maximize their personal power, Small felt that the significant unit of analysis for political behavior was the *group* rather than the *individual,* and also argued, for example, that capitalists were beginning to realize that the individual ballot was useless unless it was an instrument of group policy. The ballot had become a means for changing the balance of political power between competing syndicalist units, rather than simply a means for expressing majority opinion.

Furthermore, Small recognized that the power of "syndicated" capital far exceeded organized labor's political power. In the interest of achieving distributive justice, he suggested that unjustified privilege and power monopolized by "large capital" should be allocated to other groups. If the general intent and theoretical significance of his political remarks [1] were summarized and translated into modern terms, then Small was proposing that a balance of power (synchronized with the development of a social control system managed by the state) be established between economic units. Driven by group *competition* and *interests,* the relationships between these units would undergo a continuously equilibrated series of adjustments over time. The process organized around this series of adjustments would be self-acting because of the perpetual clash of interests. It would also be self-regulating; firstly, the state forever seeks to maintain a homeostatic "balance of power" between the units within the framework of capitalism. Secondly, the syndicalist units themselves would ideologically be committed to accommodating themselves within this framework. An important indicator of this commitment would be their *tolerance,* rather than uncompromising rejection, of competing syndicalist units. (Tolerance manifests itself in their grudging willingness to operate within the framework of capitalism; or as Ross and Small would agree to putting it, a willingness "to compete according to the rules of the game.")

Pluralism in Historical Perspective

Toward the end of the formative years, this general conception of political relationships gradually became associated with the term *pluralism,* partly because of the absence of a single locus of power. Political power was to be allocated among a plurality of two or more economic or noneconomic "interest groups." Furthermore, since a highly skewed distribution of power was contrary to the assumptions underlying the model (e.g., its self-regulating adjustments cannot occur if only one unit has all the power), a degree of parity had to exist between the interest groups. The groups did not have to be equal in power, but the weakest group required sufficient power to strike a bargain in its own interest. Because the *rationality of exchange* and the dynamics of the *competitive market* still remained at the heart of this updated, liberal model of political relationships between groups, political "power" within this paradigm was merely an analogue of money (the marketplace unit of exchange) [2] and the weakest unit needed to have enough "power" to "force" an exchange in its interest with stronger groups. (Or, at a minimum, members of the weakest group had to *believe* that it possessed the power to make this exchange.) Diffusion of power among interest groups and having an attitude of tolerance were regarded as necessary preconditions for behavior in the political arena. Since these preconditions had certain "democratic" (ethical) connotations, the model was sometimes called a *democratic* pluralist model.

It should be noted that this political model contained two interrelated but analytically distinguishable sets of propositions, one of which was empirical and the other ethical. The empirical propositions referred to such relationships as interest groups, group perspectives, and power to strike a bargain. The second set referred to ethical propositions associated with such terms as "good" and "greed" as well as "vested [selfish] interests," "tolerance," and "pluralism." Previous chapters have indicated the importance of distinguishing sociological theories containing moral imperatives even when they presuppose certain kinds of empirical relationships. In this work, the term *syndicalism* is primarily used to refer to such a theoretical model when it explains the "behavior" of functionally interdependent *economic* groups. Further, although the term "pluralism" is used by modern sociologists for this purpose, it will be indicated in later chapters that today the term also denotes interest-group relationships among *noneconomic* groups, as well as relationships among economic groups which are not functionally dependent upon one another. As such, the concept of pluralism represents a higher level of formal abstraction than syndicalism.

Although both Spencer and Marx (whose works bear on this model) assumed that power was highly concentrated in society, Spencer sharply disagreed with Marx with regard to the basis of power, claiming that this concentration was a function of the natural inequality of human ability. The syndicalist model developed by American corporate-liberal sociologists like Ross and Small was an alternative to both laissez-faire and Marxian theories. In this model, the locus of social, economic, and political power resided in competing groups whose selfish interests mitigated against the achievement of permanent accommodations. By depicting the state as either an impartial arbiter or a politically instituted nexus of accommodation, liberal-syndicalism sustained the democratic aura surrounding the legally institutionalized expressions of power. At the same time, this view of the state appeared to dissolve into innumerable interest groups, the reality of the social-class basis on which power rests in the United States. As a consequence, liberal-syndicalism not only provided an empirical warrant for the corporate-liberal state, it also enabled American sociologists to formulate a democratic rationale for the real social inequalities in capitalist societies.

During the early decades of this century, both the ethical connotations (e.g., democracy, tolerance, and equity) and the empirical contents (e.g., interest groups and group conflict) of liberal-syndicalism continued to be viewed mainly as emergent properties of American capitalism. In the views of both Ross and Small, syndicalism referred to a coming, utopian state of affairs. In concluding his textbook *Principles of Sociology,* for example, Ross (1930:585) stated:

In the piloting of society no valuable element should have too little influence or too much influence . . . Thus we arrive at the principle of balance which may be formulated as follows: In the guidance of society *each social element should share according to the intelligence and public spirit of its members* AND NONE SHOULD DOMINATE.

(The quotation above is an exact reproduction of Ross' original ending, including emphasis and capitalization.) Ross shouted these imperatives at the very end of his book because he felt that the United States had not yet arrived at this ideal democratic condition. (By the fifth decade of this century, however, many sociologists had come to believe that the ethical model of pluralism was, in fact, an accurate empirical description of American industrial democracy.)

Liberal-Syndicalism and Pluralist Doctrines and Categories

Liberal-syndicalism therefore represented a transitional stage in the development of pluralism. Taking shape prior to and during the "progressive" era, liberal-syndicalism explicitly reflected the concern of reformist liberals with the violent class conflicts that were emerging before their eyes.

The pluralist formulations generated by the liberal-syndicalists during the 1920s and onwards, underwent important changes. In spite of these changes, the ideological function of this orientation, taken in its entirety, has remained highly consistent throughout this century. During the thirties for example, many corporate-liberal sociologists could no longer ignore the overriding importance of *class*. It was one of the most important new considerations, but in typical liberal fashion the class structure was seen as resulting from the necessity to vary social rewards with inequalities in *individual* performance. As a consequence, these corporate liberals established their identities as modern exponents of the same individualistic, liberal tradition represented by Spencer and Malthus.

Modern liberal sociologists, on the other hand, were not wholly in this tradition. They departed from the classical and laissez-faire tradition by incorporating a pluralist viewpoint within the framework of their conception of class. This was not difficult to do because their classes were either conceived as styles of life based on inequality in individual attitudes and rewards, or as unanalyzed aggregations of different types of interest groups (i.e., each class was generally defined as containing its own collection of interest groups).[3]

Liberal-syndicalism was particularly important because it also provided the major categories from which pluralism was derived. In the process of derivation, however, the ideological emphasis on the more equitable distribution of wealth [4] (rather than control over the means of production) that had been highly *explicit* in liberal-syndicalism became *implicit* in pluralism. In addition, the ideational shift away from such structural units of analysis as capital and labor (which were characteristic of liberal-syndicalist theories) was very marked in pluralist formulations. Pluralism eventually envisioned highly fluid and adjustable functional relationships between an infinite variety of interest groups and, as a result, was highly effective in obfuscating the social-class dynamics that actually determined long-term changes in capitalist societies.

NOTES

1. Remarks of this kind were not by any means restricted to Small. Other American political economists like Ross and Commons had expressed similar ideas.
2. During the formative years, this relation was repeatedly made apparent by the use of the analogy between interest-group relationships and the "higgling" or bargaining relationships between individuals in the market.
3. For example, see Arnold M. Rose's (1967) pluralist work, *The Power Structure*. Note also G. William Domhoff's (1969) critical review of Rose's work. Domhoff points

out that Rose's references to professional, "voluntary," and other kinds of middle-class interest groups totally obscure the role and identity of the economic elite in the United States.

4. In later years questions of the distribution of wealth and other forms of distributive justice were systematically encompassed under a sociological concept called the "problem of allocation."

CHAPTER 36

Corporate Liberalism and Economic Classes

It has been noted that some of the hegemonic intellectuals in sociology began to regard the phenomenon of interest groups as being somewhat universal—related to the fundamental principles of social organization allegedly existing in all industrial societies. Nevertheless, examination of their writings revealed that these sociologists and their ideas were firmly located within transitory historical conditions.

It has been further observed that these intellectuals defined the problem of social integration primarily in terms of highly conflicting economic blocs that were regarded as "natural" products of any industrial "division of labor." In actuality, these blocs were in no way natural: they were generated by the rise of monopoly capitalism, and represented products of its modal technological and institutional changes. Monopoly capitalism had created the historically situated contradictions which, in turn, had posed the most significant aspects of the problem of social integration. The monopoly trusts, which were the most general organizations of capital, and the militant associations of labor unions, which were the most class-conscious organizations of proletarians, were at the very heart of the corporate-liberal problem of social integration.

The preceding chapters have also clarified the grounds for the selection of the term "syndicalism" to classify a body of highly varied transitional liberal writings about industrial harmony. This term has been found helpful for highlighting the degree to which modern pluralism was *historically grounded* in a definable body of liberal writings dealing with the *reconciliation of class contradictions* during the formative years.

Liberal-Syndicalist Dialogue with Marxians

The formative years in America appeared on the heels of Marx's death in Europe. In 1883, Marxism had just begun to take hold among the most class-conscious sectors of the working classes in the Western nations. Before the turn of the century, Marxists like Karl Liebknecht and August Bebel rose to leadership in the powerful German Social Democratic Labor party. By the end of the first two decades of the twentieth century, V. I. Lenin held the reins of the Russian Social Democratic Labor party. Across the rest of Europe and America, however, non-Marxian as well as Marxian socialists dominated both the political and the labor organizations that had developed among middle-class groups and class-conscious proletarians.

Liberal-syndicalism developed in reaction to ideological as well as material conditions. But these ideological conditions were generally represented by non-Marxian as well as Marxian socialist perspectives. As a consequence, the national peculiarities of liberal-syndicalist writings also depended greatly upon the differences in socialist movements [1] as well as the relative differences in the strength of laissez-faire capitalists and traditions in the various Western nations.

The founders of American sociology were aware of Marxian and non-Marxian socialist ideas. The Ross-Ward letters also contain references to Ross' pleasure in reading the economic writings of Eugen Von Böhm-Bawerk who, in 1894, wrote one of the most famous liberal criticisms of Marx's labor theory of value. In addition, Ward made reference to Marxism in a comment at the Second Annual Meeting of the American Sociological Society in 1907. Ostensibly speaking for himself and his colleagues in the society, Ward (1907:30) stated:

Most of us appreciate the vastness of the economic struggle, but the more I look at the general doctrine of historical materialism . . . the more it narrows down relatively to the other motives and factors of history. . . . The more we look at it, the more the economic side contracts and the more the reproductive, the aesthetic, moral, and all the sociogenetic motives loom upon the horizon of our sociological discussion.

Ward's comment is particularly informative because it reveals the degree to which the outstanding American sociologists regarded their own psychologistic conceptions as an alternative to such "economic" approaches to social change as the materialist conception of history. On the other hand, there is very little by way of references to Marxism in the early liberal writings to suggest that these sociologists had seriously *come to terms* with Marxism, or even comprehended accurately what Marxism was all about.

Albion Small: Sociological Expert on Marxism

Among the early liberals, Small was reputed to be knowledgeable in Marxism. However, he turned his knowledge to undermining Marx's influence on colleagues and students. Small, of course, did not perform solo in being responsible for the subsequent failure of American sociology to consider Marxism as a body of scientific explanations or analytic perspectives. (Giddings and Ross were also noted for their crude and derogatory references to socialist ideas.) However, according to Charles H. Page (1940:38), Small was reputed to be an outstanding sociological *expert* on Marx's works (even though the level of his scholarly approach to Marx was exemplified by some grotesque notions: for example, that Marx's "doctrine of profits" was a proposal that "no capitalist deserves profits"). Small did conduct a "famous" course on the "Conflict of Classes" (Barnes 1948:775) and probably was one of the only leaders in the field to focus on Karl Marx in both courses and publications (*ibid.:*791).[2]

Small's antagonistic attitude toward Marx was easy to distinguish. Although Louis Wirth has indicated that Small was a "critical and sympathetic student of Marx," Small himself has stated that "Marx's ideal of economic society has never appealed to me as plausible, desirable or possible." Further, he somewhat crudely added that those "who were attempting to abolish classes were often interested in avoiding labor!" (Page 1940:140). Like Ross, Small argued that socialists "err in attributing the blame for our 'pathologies' to the institution of private property" (*ibid.:*133). "Socialistic and anarchistic dogma," Small declared, "mistakenly assigns a 'radical vice' to the social system itself. Furthermore they are *foreign* importations having little application to the American scene" (*ibid.:*140 our emphasis). Small (whose notions, in part, were no less a "foreign" importation) felt that "a perpetual conflict for moral control of the terms of cooperation" existed between groups, rather than a Marxian conflict between classes (*ibid.:*134).[3] Thus, although Small conceded that "Marx was one of the really great thinkers in the history of the social sciences," Page (*ibid.*) has wisely pointed out that "such appraisals are in *no sense* an indication of Small's adherence to Marxism" (our emphasis).

Small's Interest-Group Theory of Classes

Small also made many statements which evoked the belief that his theories were "semi-socialistic" or derived, in part, from Marxism, but a closer examination of his syndicalist perspective suggests that this resemblance should be taken with a very large pinch of salt. To a great extent, the superficial similarities resulted from Small's penchant for borrowing words (as well as ideas) from many different sources. These sources apparently included socialist publications.

In part this eclectic combination of words was forced by the absence of a fairly stable and widely standardized corpus of corporate-liberal sociological categories. (These categories did not become stabilized in American sociological usage until the twenties.) During Small's lifetime a corporate-liberal vocabulary was coming into being. But because the field itself was new, it was constructed by men who were not originally trained in sociology. From 1880 to 1920, the backgrounds of these men included paleontology, biology, history, theology, philosophy, journalism, and, above all, political economy. It is therefore not surprising to see in Small's works the influence of Ward's positivistic, secular, and biological categories. Nor is it surprising to see philosophical and moral categories originally used by German scholars or American Protestant clergymen. Economic terms were also studded throughout the writings of the founding sociologists. To complicate matters further, psychiatric, psychological, and social psychological categories were being rapidly developed in France and Germany around the beginning of the century, and they too were being adapted by American sociologists. (Terms like "abnormal," "social pathology," and "social disease," for example, are to be found throughout Small and Vincent's [1894] textbook.)

This complicated terminological situation provides some understanding of the apparent inconsistency in Small's writings about capitalism. On the one hand, Small was highly critical of "capitalism," but on the other, he defended the meritarian and property relations which are so central to capitalism. The inconsistence reflected by this approach, however, was more apparent than real, for it must be remembered that there was no available socially standardized category for monopoly-state capitalism. (This was the form of capitalism that Small and others were proposing as an ideal.) While it is true that he used such euphemisms as "an efficient society" to describe his conception of what this form of monopoly capitalism should be like, it is also true that there existed no standardized term for the new political economy within the profession as a whole. In light of the terminological chaos during the formative years, it is understandable, therefore, that later sociologists would be confused by Small's attitude toward capitalism.

Small's apparently inconsistent attitude toward capitalism can be easily reconciled when it is noted that his referent for both the term "capitalism" and his criticism of it was *laissez-faire* capitalism. On the other hand, the terms "efficient society," "democracy," and "industrial democracy" were often used to refer to his moral vision of *an optimum* capitalist society. His apparently inconsistent attitude toward the state can also be conciliated by observing his general association of business corruption and political domination with *laissez-faire* capitalism. Because of this association Small's theory appeared at first glance to be a class theory of the state. But when the rhetorical phrases are pushed aside, it is found that Small actually viewed social class as merely one among many "interest groups" which were attempting to control the state in order to advance their own "selfish interests." The dynamics which regulated his conception of the state were fully derived from liberal-syndicalism—not at all from Marxism. And liberal-syndicalism essentially maintained that the United States was a classless society. Thus, while Small developed the ability to pepper his papers with "progressive" phrases, these phrases were always incorporated into conservative, although reformist, social doctrines.

Before the eventual development of an extensive body of sociological categories, men like Small had to "make do" with categories like "class" or "class struggle." But it is now obvious that Small's use of these terms was very different from their use by radical contemporaries. Although he maintained that "class struggle" was an "axiom" of social science (e.g., "No one gets through a primer on social science today without learning that class conflict is to the social process what friction is to mechanics" [*ibid.:*126]), Small's notion of class struggle was a liberal-syndicalist one; and classes were merely functionally interrelated interest groups. His definition of class was as vague as the use of the term "vested interests" in the commonsense discourse of his time. The only stable defining criteria that Small invoked were *psychological*. A class was defined according to its "interests" and its selfish or tolerant attitudes toward engaging in conflict or conciliation with other classes.

The liberal-syndicalism being developed by Ward, Ross, Small, Giddings, and others was also of little value for conducting a profound analysis of class conflict in the United States. When analyzing labor unrest, for example, these men thought in terms of a competitive struggle for scarce values among individuals or interest groups. They reduced the dynamics of this conflict, in this context, to the mere presence or absence of opportunities for individual mobility [4] or the reestablishment of equity between interest groups. Because of this, Small felt that "the reorganization of our institutions would in no way guarantee the removal of our social problems." Equal opportunities plus equitable distribution were more likely candidates for fruitful change.

Page (*ibid.:*251) has indicated that "the close of the [first] World War signaled a period in the history of American sociology quite different from the years of the [Founding] Fathers." In the twenties, in contrast with the earlier years when class was regularly discussed, "the problems of class were largely neglected." Instead of perceiving the twenties as a marked departure from the formative years, however, it is suggested here that the twenties represented a logical outcome of the pseudoclass theories advanced by men like Small. In Small's analysis of capitalism, class conflict was only perceived as a significant factor when its locus was placed within laissez-faire relationships. Small's theory was never a *class theory* of capitalism; it was an *interest-group theory* of classes. When the terminological confusion of the early period is swept aside, then it becomes clear that monopoly-state capitalism was perceived as a classless society in the sense that (the Marxian notion of) the class struggle was not a fundamental mechanism by which qualitative *long-term* change could be explained. The only possible forms of evolutionary change that could be stabilized were "ordered changes" based on accommodations rather than conflicts between syndicalist units.

This assumption did not mean that men like Albion Small ignored the existence of the class struggle. But the conflicts between the two fundamental economic groups referred to by the subjectively defined term "class" (or by "capital" and "labor") were being sharply confined, in their theoretical formulations to laissez-faire capitalism. Because of this operative restriction, it is not surprising to find later sociologists viewing the United States as a "classless" society when they became convinced that an "ordered" (capitalist) society was finally coming into existence!

This conviction, as we shall see, crystallized toward the end of the formative years, when thousands of radicals, like Eugene Debs, Victor Berger, Scott Nearing, Nicola Sacco, and Bartolomeo Vanzetti, were being imprisoned, fired from their jobs, deported en masse, or murdered for their political beliefs.

NOTES

1. These movements did not have to appear within the United States in order to affect the writings of Americans. Albion Small's "Sociology of Profits," for example, represents a critical attack on Guild Socialism in Great Britain. This attack occurred in 1925, toward the end of Small's career. It should be noted however, that G. D. H. Cole (1918:6) has pointed out that Guild Socialism was derived, in part, from the "American Industrial Unionist Movement" (e.g., the IWW) and "French [anarcho] Syndicalism."

2. David Horowitz (1971:7–9) discusses the misleading liberal interpretations of Marxian concepts which have been put forward by *modern* liberal scholars like Robert Nisbet. It should be noted, in addition, that liberal scholars often believe that they have been influenced by Marxian concepts when, in actuality, the concepts being referred to are liberal conceptions that have been mistakenly attributed to Marx. Weber's concept of economic class is one example of a liberal conception which is frequently attributed to Marxian influence. Richard Hofstadter's comment about the influence of Marxism on his own thinking also reveals a conception of class which is essentially liberal rather than Marxian in character. Hofstadter (1970:9) states, for example; "My own assertion of consensus history in 1948 had its sources in the Marxism of the 1930's. Political struggles, as manifested in the major parties, I argued, had 'always been bounded by the horizons of property and enterprise . . . American traditions . . . show a strong bias in favor of equalitarian democracy, but it has been a democracy in cupidity rather than a democracy of fraternity' " (*The American Political Tradition,* vii.). This comment by Hofstadter could just as easily have been written by Albion Small, who not only favored American democracy but also wrote, "I meant by the term 'capitalism' . . . old fashioned 'cupidity' getting in its work all along the line. . . ." (Stern 1936:182). Hofstadter's writings actually were based on the liberal interest-group theory of class rather than the concept of class epitomized by "the Marxism of the 1930's."

3. Page (1940:134) has also noted that Small condemned "Russian nihilism, German socialism, French and Italian anarchism, and English and American trade unionism." Small regarded these movements as "senseless extremes."

4. Page (*ibid.:*140) has noted, for example, that Small "questioned whether an *unemployed* class was a sign of *institutional* weakness of our social order, though he pointed out that if proof could be obtained of an actual decrease of economic opportunity such would indicate 'institutional disarrangement' " (our emphasis). On the other hand, the presence of defective, dependent, and delinquent classes "neither proves nor fairly tends to prove, that the evil points to *structural* defects in the social order" (our emphasis).

BOOK III

CONSOLIDATION
AND
OPPRESSION

INTRODUCTION TO

BOOK III

THE preceding books have discussed the historical precursors and the material relationships that influenced the founding fathers of American sociology. These books have maintained that the leading members of the field were hegemonic intellectuals who helped reconstitute liberal thought. Their transitional writings played an active conceptive role in the generation of corporate liberalism in the United States.

The formative years of North American sociology spanned the four decades between 1883 and 1922. During this entire period, leading American sociologists never completely divorced themselves from the analytic perspectives of such laissez-faire writers as Herbert Spencer. The primary transition from a laissez-faire to a corporate-liberal perspective was completed during the first decade of the twentieth century. Simultaneously, the leading American sociologists began to consolidate the development of their new conceptions of social reality.

During the period of consolidation, the hegemonic intellectuals in the field of sociology systematized, elaborated, and refined the basic ideas which had been, or were actually being established at the time. These refinements served many purposes: they enabled scholars, for example, to construct "plausible" explanations of the revolutionary movements which had become very significant during the "progressive" era. The reductionist mechanisms generally assumed that revolutionary conduct was based on irrational, egoistic behavior and thereby encouraged the adoption of a social-control perspective toward this behavior.

This final book will also demonstrate that the reduction of the dynamics of radical relationships (to irrational and selfish motives of individuals) has had at least three ideological consequences. First, it has justified a never-ending production of scholarly treatises which, in the name of science, have viciously slandered the profoundly humanistic hopes and dreams shared by members of radical movements. Second, it has enabled liberal scholars to utilize the entire conceptual armament associated with the category of social control for the "scientific" analysis of radical movements. Third, it has provided a major ideological linkage between the activities of professionals who have analyzed "social unrest" and those of professionals who have been energetically developing so-called reforms aimed, in part, at aborting revolutionary movements in the United States.

Technocratic Tradition in Academic Sociology

The coming chapters will also demonstrate that the linkage between the *professional* social analyst and the *professional* social reformer has undermined every democratic American precept that has heretofore justified the direct control over political institutions by the population at large. This linkage, as we shall see, has provided the justification for removing some of the most significant urban issues from politics. It has redefined these issues as the province of a vast network of private and public bureaucratic structures which are regulated on an everyday basis by technocratic administrators and their equally technocratic administrative-consultants. It has led to the systematic ridicule of radical proposals for genuine grass-roots administration and control over the institutions that affect the daily lives of common people.[1]

This book maintains the spirit of the previous one, demonstrating further that critical intellectual perspectives characterized the development of sociology from the very inception of the field. But it will also continue to show that these perspectives represented, at best, criticism from *within* the ideology of liberalism. In addition, it will be noted that pioneering sociologists formulated technocratic criticisms of institutional functioning. These "critical" perspectives provided ideas which continued to legitimate the oppressive nature of these institutions in the face of alternative, radical ways of thinking and acting. Furthermore, like the modern sociologists who usurp the rhetoric of radicals to make their own ideas more palatable in turbulent times, the sociologists of the chair made reference to "the perfection of man" in order to justify their technocratic points of view. In fact, the editors of the very first edition of the conference papers, to be published by the American Sociological Society, stated a desire to establish a social science which would unify all the social sciences in order to further an understanding of *"the quality of life* as it is capable of becoming . . ." (American Sociological Society 1906: 1–2 our emphasis).

There is no better way to begin this book than by reviewing the early sociological writings on sexual relationships. In writing about the subjection of women, as well as about marriage and the family, the *corporate-liberal* sociologists Lester F. Ward and W. I. Thomas critically declared that the biological doctrines of male superiority which existed in their time were fallacious. Sharp criticisms of these biological doctrines were also made by the noted *laissez-faire* liberal, John Stuart Mill, and the outstanding *Marxist,* Frederick Engels. All of these ideological perspectives, therefore, produced critical statements. However, one of these criticisms was an authentically radical criticism while the other, as we shall see, explicitly or implicitly replaced the older biological doctrines with new sexist interpretations of human relationships.

NOTE

1. A statement by Peter Berger (1971:4–5) provides us with an example of this kind of ridicule: "The currently fashionable left ideal of full participation in the sense that everybody will participate in every decision affecting his life, would, if realized, constitute a nightmare comparable to unending sleeplessness."

We know of no radical work which has advocated, as Berger indicates, that literally *"everybody* will participate in *every* decision affecting his life" (our emphasis). If there exists such a work, we are sure that it is in no way representative of the "currently fashionable left ideal of full participation." On the other hand, we do know of a recent work which is certainly in the spirit of this ideal. It was written by a surgeon, Joshua Horn, who administered a hospital in China. Horn (1971) also had questions about the effects of the systematic meeting between hospital staff and patients. A reader of this work will quickly perceive, however, that Horn became convinced of the great importance of democratic participation in the hospital setting. Horn movingly describes the extraordinary and positive effects that this participation had on the services provided hospital patients. He points to the truly humanistic impact of genuine participation on what, in the United States and elsewhere, is regarded as one of the most properly authoritarian institutions and elitest professions in existence, namely, the hospital and the medical profession. Berger's article is entitled "Sociology and Freedom," but it is Horn's work that provides us with insight into what professionalism and freedom are all about in the United States, even though he is writing about his experiences as a medical professional in China.

PART TEN

The Subjection of Women: Ideological Views and Solutions

CHAPTER 37

The Subjection of Women

Background and Preview

There were many differences among such leading sociologists as Ward, Thomas, Small, Giddings, Chapin, Weatherly, Park, and Burgess. Unlike Sumner,[1] these men were all corporate-liberal and technocratic analysts. Even if Sumner is included, the differences between them can be considered bourgeois "family" differences. This is particularly true of their writings about women: the scholars who played an outstanding role in the founding of sociology were *sexists to a man*.

One of the single most important generalizations that can be made about sexist writings in early North American sociology is that the analytic strategies used for explaining sexual relationships were similar to those employed for explaining all other outstanding forms of social inequality, including those based on racism, imperialism, and class exploitation. At that time, for example, both social Darwinism and reform Darwinism justified sexist doctrines concerning the origins of the family and the subjugation of women as well as comprehensive racist doctrines about the superiority of the Anglo-Saxon and Teutonic races.

The warrant for this conclusion will be presented in the last four chapters of this part of Book III. Before this is done, however, it is important to men-

290

tion other significant features of the sexist writings during the formative years. We will also place these writings in the context of their time.

The writings on women by the pioneers in the field ranged from the paternalistic notions of Lester F. Ward and W. I. Thomas to the rank sexism of Edward A. Ross and Ulysses G. Weatherly. Among the leading men in the new social science, however, Ward and Thomas were the first outstanding North American sociologists who purported to develop a scientific theory of the subjection of women. Ward's explanation appeared in 1883 in his famous *Dynamic Sociology*. Thomas' sexist essays, on the other hand, appeared individually from 1897 onward in professional journals like the *American Journal of Sociology*. They were published together in a single volume entitled *Sex and Society* in 1907. Thomas' essays were also racist. Furthermore, they appeared at the beginning of his career and played an important role in establishing his reputation as an outstanding sociologist.

Ward's and Thomas' works were distinguished by the fact that they contained general theories of the origins of marriage and the family, as well as the subjection of women. Because the first of their theoretical works appeared in 1883, it can be safely argued that sexism was an integral feature of North American sociology from its inception. Our interest in Ward and Thomas, however, is not merely antiquarian. These men, as we shall see, constructed their sexist theories with the avowed purpose of emancipating women from male oppression. If history can provide guidelines to the present and the future, then an account of their efforts may be helpful for evaluating similar approaches today. In order to maximize this possibility, we will mention writings on women by John Stuart Mill, Lewis Henry Morgan, Frederick Engels, Otis Tufton Mason, Auguste Comte, Herbert Spencer, and others. Their works are relevant to the theories under consideration, and a brief but critical review of their ideas will also heighten the appreciation of the corporate-liberal spirit behind Ward's and Thomas' explanations.

This and the following chapters will concentrate, therefore, on *ethical* and *analytic* ideas relevant to theories about marriage, the family, and the subjugation of women. In this chapter we will discuss Mill's ethical standpoint toward the subjection of women. The next two chapters will disclose some aspects of Morgan's and Engels' evolutionary theories of society. These three chapters will provide an understanding of the contemporary intellectual milieu and the alternative ideas Ward and Thomas had at their disposal. This intellectual context is necessary for a critical evaluation of Ward's and Thomas' theoretical works.

A Defense of Women's Rights

The Subjection of Women was published in 1869, under John Stuart Mill's name alone. Mill, however, based this work on an essay, *The Enfranchisement of Women,* which was written by Harriet Taylor in 1851. Taylor, who eventually became Mill's wife, was coauthor of a number of works including those central to his reputation (e.g., *Principles of Political Economy, On Liberty,* and so on). She was not actually given publication credits for these books; ostensibly out of acquiescence to the prejudices of the period.

Taylor had died before Mill expanded some of the ideas in her 1851 essay. Although it was written earlier, Mill published *The Subjection of Women* in 1869 as a "memento for Harriet" (Borchard 1957:129–130). If she had lived, Mill might have analyzed the subject from a broader perspective: in contrast with his publication, Taylor's work, *The Enfranchisement of Women,* mentioned the disenfranchisement of working-class men; the inequities inherent in the favored position of the middle class; the need for child labor laws; and the *disbelief* that "the division of mankind into capitalists and hired labourers, and the regulation of the reward of labourers mainly by demand and supply, will be forever, or even much longer, the rule of the world." *The Enfranchisement of Women,* moreover, was decidedly more militant and more consistent than *The Subjection of Women* on the question of economic independence for women. Nevertheless, the latter work has a number of positive aspects which will be described in this section. Following this, we will deal with the limitations imposed on this work by Mill's laissez-faire perspective.

The Subjection of Women was a passionate plea for feminine legal rights, including women's suffrage, women's equal claim to their own children, the equality of married women before the law, and the right of married women to have exclusive control over their own property. Mill's work was a positive document because of its major stress on the equal capacity and capabilities of women. The work castigated theories and doctrines of female inferiority and emphasized, instead, the effects of culture and environment in determining the differences between the sexes. In addition to legislative change, Mill pleaded for the reversal of the ill effects of the culture on women by availing them of a "better and more complete intellectual education" (Mill 1970:83). Consequently, Mill defended women's rights and criticized male supremacy at a time when the vast majority of liberal intellectuals were undeniably sexists in this regard.

Consistent with their atomistic analysis of the problem, Mill, like many other liberals to come, sharply restricted their very general solutions regarding the subjection of women to the modification of individual intellectual and emotional differences. These modifications were possible, Mill argued, because nearly all the differences between the sexes were environmentally conditioned and therefore educatable. The most important causes of the subjection of women were the customary attitudes of individual men. Therefore, prime *long-term* solutions to sexual inequality, in his view, involved appeals to male compassion and the correction of erroneous male thinking about the nature of women. Prior to any universal moral regeneration brought about by educational and moral suasion, of course, legislative sanctions would be required to cope with those individual men who, by temperament, were inclined to abuse their power over women.

292

Because of this orientation, *The Subjection of Women* focused much of its theoretical attention on the fallaciousness of doctrines about women's inferiority. Mill argued, in the spirit of Helvétius, that human nature was infinitely malleable: virtually all of the personality characteristics that have distinguished the sexes were products of the environment. Consequently, with regard to the nurture-nature controversy, Mill generally rejected arguments favoring women's *natural* inferiority or superiority.

Laissez-Faire Dimensions of Mill's Work

When it is placed, as it should be, in a historical perspective, Mill's work represents the limits of a nineteenth-century laissez-faire middle-class defense of women's rights. These rights involved primarily but not exclusively those of interest to middle-class women. The work did not support divorce laws,[2] nor did it raise economic demands, such as equal pay for equal work, that were being expressed by women's movements, labor organizations, and socialist groups at the time. When compared with the demands raised decades earlier by the revolutionary women of the third estate in France at the turn of the nineteenth century, Mill's defense becomes particularly limited.[3]

Nor can Mill's work be considered innovating when compared solely with the writings of male intellectuals. It is undeniably noteworthy when contrasted with the great mass of sexist trash being written by some of his contemporaries; but its significance as a step forward can only be claimed within the liberal or other conservatizing traditions of the nineteenth century. Throughout the nineteenth century from Charles Fourier onwards, leading socialist writers had repeatedly advocated the liberation of women from their most oppressive institutions—marriage and the bourgeois family. As an intellectual analysis, therefore, Mill's work suffers when compared with socialist writings and, in spite of the encouragement it must have given to the liberal women who led women's rights movements, it provided no *new scientific or political* insights that would have aided the liberation of women. Thus, although it was widely read and acclaimed, much of its content was, as Wendell Robert Carr has noted, already commonplace.[4]

Mill's argument against the subjection of women was analytically grounded in a laissez-faire liberal metaphysics of reality. This was exemplified by the egoistic concept of man underlying his analysis. However, Mill did not utilize that hoary concept of egoistic man which was predicated on the avaricious pursuit of *wealth*. Instead, he constructed his utilitarian conception around the value of *power*. He employed as his analytic cutting-edge what is currently and commonly called the concept of "political man." [5] He predicated his theory on personal desires for power in political, economic, and family relationships. These desires allegedly characterized the universal nature of man. This did not mean, however, that the desire for power was necessarily expressed egotistically. There were many circumstances which prevented the selfish use of power.

Most of the psychological assumptions underlying Mill's analysis were as old as liberalism. The far-reaching effect of male egoism is one example of his time-honored categories. However, in arguing that the unrestricted power of men over women inadvertently hampered the great moral education of succeeding generations, Mill (*ibid.*:43) limited his discussion of this assumption to its effects on the *family* setting. The effect of the socializing influence of male supremacy in the family was considered to be so extraordinary that Mill (*ibid.*:80) declared, *"All* the *selfish propensities, self-worship,* the *unjust self-preference,* which exist among mankind, have their source and root in, and derive their principle nourishment from the present constitution of the relation between men and women"* (our emphasis). The development of a selfish desire for *power* was an important example of the influence of an improper moral education.

According to Mill's analytic logic, therefore, male supremacy encouraged the socialization of megalomania and egotistical desires in individual children and was counterproductive to the common good. The family, consequently, was seen as the prime institutional locus of power relationships which generated, inflamed, and maintained the egotistical nature of man. Nevertheless, although the great classical concept of egoism has time and again been used to reify and reduce these relationships to relatively immutable properties of man, it was the capitalist mode of production based on the institution of private property—not the family—that generalized selfish human relationships. (This can be claimed, independent of the lengthy list of nineteenth-century liberal subscribers to the family as the source of worldly ills, because the family relation *itself* was structured by capitalism.)

With the exception of his stand on education, Mill's programmatic approach to women's emancipation was largely legalistic and moral. He was aware of the almost unlimited power that "present social institutions" in his day gave to husbands over their wives. He advocated piecemeal legislative changes that would prevent male "abuses of power." Because of his laissez-faire liberalism, he did not perceive jural relationships as subservient to broader institutional relations; nor did he regard systems of jural relations as expressions of the political economy as a whole. Neither kinship, political, nor economic systems—nor the functional relationships between these institutional orders—were thrown into question by his myopic analysis of the subjection of women.

Mill's ethical and legal suggestions for limiting the abuse of power by men over women will be discussed shortly. First, however, it is important to ask whether Mill perceived this selfish abuse in relation to other forms of social oppression during the nineteenth century. Did Mill make any connection between the subjection of women, class exploitation, colonialism, or racism? The answer is unequivocally negative. Mill (*ibid.*:21) claimed that the subjection of women stood out as a lone case: "as an *isolated fact* in modern social institutions" (our emphasis). He further declared (*ibid.*) that the subjection of women was not only isolated but, in addition, "in *no instance* except this

. . . are the higher social functions closed against anyone by a fatality of *birth* which no exertions, and no change of circumstances can overcome . . ." (our emphasis).[6] To arrive at this point, Mill had to totally ignore the brutal nineteenth-century capitalist oppression of working classes, colonial populations, and national and racial minorities and majorities throughout the world.

"Complementarity" and Sexist Role Relationships

It is understandable, in light of Mill's laissez-faire liberal philosophy, that the analytic generalizations in *The Subjection of Women* were firmly locked into an egoistic, atomistic, and utilitarian framework. Less understandable, however, are his sexist references to complementary male-female relationships. These references appear to contradict his stated belief in sexual equality. Carr (1970:xxi) has noted that Mill's "entire discussion of the question [of masculine and feminine natures] was torn by an implicit tension between his concept of women as complementary to man and his desire to affirm the basic equality of the sexes." For example, Mill (*ibid.:*59) pointed out that there was much to be gained from intellectual cooperation between the sexes. The male's ability to engage in highly abstract speculation could be complemented by the female's "lively perception and ever-present sense of objective fact." Furthermore, although men of theory might lose sight of the legitimate purpose of speculation altogether,

a woman seldom runs wild after an *abstraction*. The habitual direction of her mind [tends] to dealing with things as *individuals* rather than in *groups* . . . Women's thoughts are thus useful in giving reality to those of thinking men, as men's thoughts in giving width and largeness to those of women. In *depth*, as distinguished from *breadth*, I greatly doubt if even now, women, compared with men, are at any disadvantage. [*ibid*. our emphasis]

Does this not also imply women's *lesser* ability to abstract? Because of these kinds of observations, Carr (*ibid.:*xxii) has concluded that Mill affirmed "two apparently incompatible versions of woman's relations to man. At times, he [Mill] honored women as man's inspiring complement; at others, he insisted on the basic identity of masculine and feminine natures."

It is important to note, however, that Mill was apparently unaware of the sexist implications of the complementary roles he perceived as ideal relations for men and women. For example, he explicitly referred to concrete forms of complementary male and female behavior without labeling their interdependence with the term "complementarity" or with any other special formal name. (The actual formulation of the theoretical category of complementarity and its application for classifying sexist relations is a later liberal development which became manifest by the end of the formative years.[7]

Laissez-Faire Interpretations of Women's Rights

Mill contended that women were slaves of men from "the earliest twilight of society" and, therefore, that long ago women, along with certain men, were born to their place in life. Consequently, he could not agree that women originally had been equal or superior, as Bachofen (1861) had claimed, and were unjustly oppressed at a later time in the early stages of civilization. If he had assumed that women's status had changed for the worse, then he might have sought for the historical causes of this development. But he did not concern himself with historical or anthropological analyses of sexual or other social inequalities. He simply took women's oppressed status as a historical constant and suggested that their continued oppression was predicated on what appeared to be a cultural lag. Custom and tradition, he argued, still kept women in bondage even though industrial developments and liberal rules of equity had swept away the aristocratic doctrine that human beings were justifiably born to their station in life.

Mill therefore argued that women's status should not be based on *ascribed* characteristics that were determined at birth. Women should be given the chance to *achieve* status by their own efforts. At first glance, Mill's attack on status by ascription appears to be egalitarian. In actuality, however, the core of his argument for the liberal emancipation of women was based on a thoroughly elitist liberal doctrine that a woman's status in society should be established on the basis of free competition for the determination of the *fittest* individuals. Far from being egalitarian, this doctrine was merely a meritarian *rule of equity* which stipulated the conditions under which social inequalities of a certain kind could be considered *fair*.

Seventeen years before the publication of Mill's work, Spencer (1851:155) had already captured this meritarian rule with the words: "Equity knows no difference in sex." (This sentence opened a chapter entitled "The Rights of Women.") Mill's ethical discussion of the subjection of women certainly justified the necessity for curbing the unlimited power of males. Beyond this, however, his work represented, in large part, an elaborate, logical, ethical, and empirical warrant for Spencer's declaration. A careful reading of Mill's work will reveal page after page of ethical discourse justifying in every conceivable manner—not the liberation of women in general—but rather the premise that there existed individual women who were already fit enough— or who could be made fit enough by favorable circumstances—to compete *successfully* with men.[8]

On the other hand, it can be justifiably contended that Mill expressed the spirit of egalitarianism when he urged that women be given equal *treatment* with men before the law. This approach to equality ostensibly removed sex criteria from being relevant to the determination of the *differences* between contending legal claims. (In this context, sex, for example, would make no difference in deciding who would take possession of children in cases of divorce. The decision regarding custody would be made on *other* grounds.) However, history has repeatedly shown that this negative and legalistic approach leaves ample room for the accommodation of other antiegalitarian criteria, some of which may be de facto concomitants of the subjection of women. It is also not surprising, in light of this, to find that attempts to establish equality by law are frequently made ineffective because the law itself is not comprehensive enough, or its operational interpretation is highly discriminatory.

It is impossible to evaluate the laissez-faire liberal conception of human rights without underscoring the operational interpretations of these rights. These latter interpretations were important because they determined whether many men could enjoy even their legally established rights. During the second half of the nineteenth century, many legal rights were allegedly established universally as rights of men. These rights, however, were highly contingent, ideally and practically, on whether individual men were also members of the white race, property owners, free of criminal convictions, "literate" members of the population, residents of an area for a specified length of time, above the minimum legal "age of manhood," or possessed of any of the other legal or extralegal qualifications that determined who could actually claim an established right. Some of these qualifications, obviously, were highly discriminatory from a social-class and racial point of view. Even though male blacks were legally given the right to vote in the United States, for example, suffrage was operatively denied them, in the Southern states in particular, until well into the twentieth century. Reflecting on the degree to which the law guaranteed equality, Anatole France cynically remarked: "The law, in its majestic equality, forbids all men to sleep under bridges, to beg in the streets, and to steal bread—*the rich* as well as *the poor*" (our emphasis). From a liberal point of view, the essential warrant for women's rights was based on the extension of those established rights of "men" to women. But the oversimplified equation between *men* in general and established *right* did violence to the facts of nineteenth-century life. Irrespective of this, however, this equation became a central reference point in laissez-faire liberal arguments for women's rights. Thus, for example, concluding a chapter on women's rights in *Social Statics,* Spencer (1851:171) wrote, " . . . it has been shown that the rights of women must stand or fall with those of men; derived as they are from the same authority; involved in the same axiom; demonstrated by the same argument."

Space limitations prevent us from evaluating Mill's place in the historical development of the liberal conceptions of equality, liberty, and right. It can be demonstrated, however, that in the eighteenth century these conceptions were revolutionary and justified far more than the ownership of private property. In the nineteenth century, on the other hand, even the truly liberating qualities of these liberal conceptions (which are often associated with the Bill of Rights in the United States) were emasculated by laissez-faire intellectuals of Imperial Britain. These scholars generated a vast storehouse of ideological rationalizations to buttress the denial of the freedom of the oppressed people of four continents. Indeed, the *eclectic reconciliation* of the most glaring contradictions between the liberal profession of equality, liberty, or right, and the oppression of social classes or entire nations at home and abroad, became one of the hallmarks of laissez-faire liberalism in Great Britain. (We have seen that even the blatant imperialist penetration of the world in the name of free trade was justified by men like Spencer, for example, as a "peaceful" and "anti-imperialist" alternative to colonialism.) Mill himself was employed as an official for the East India Company, the great prototype of the monopolies spawned by British imperialism, and was no exception to this general trend.

When the effects of the liberal notions of equality are evaluated in this century, one can hardly overstate the degree to which (1) the meritarian rules, and (2) the negative concepts of right encompassed by these notions, have repeatedly served to justify all sorts of social, political, and economic *inequalities*. (This general observation is valid even though liberal notions of equality have been properly used, at times, in defense of the achievement of more equitable conditions for outstanding individual members of an oppressed population.) These notions have never been, and will never be used successfully to establish egalitarian relationships on a collective basis, particularly for the most oppressed groups in our society.

The struggle for women's liberation has had to contend with the doctrines of male supremacy, not merely because of the effects of male hegemony on the personal aspirations, attitudes, and emotions of women, but also because the very grounds on which this struggle for liberation has been waged have been largely determined by liberal principles. In the modern period, however, radical scholars are no longer content with definitions of human rights unless they are inextricably linked with a liberating praxis. They are interested in individual needs and sisterhood, not individual merit and competition. They recognize that the reductionist power relationships that Mill regarded as fundamental were *symptoms* rather than causes. In their view, the subjection of women in modern societies has been primarily grounded in the political and economic relationships that John Stuart Mill spent his lifetime defending.

NOTES

1. Sumner, it should be recalled, was a Spencerian laissez-faire liberal.

2. Carr (1970:vii) has noted that Mill felt that women should raise the issue of divorce and indicated that its omission would facilitate a more sympathetic male response to the cause of women's rights. Mill's justification for its omission, however, is much too expedient when compared to the stand on this issue not only by women but also by male socialist contemporaries.

3. Revolutionary women in France about three quarters of a century prior to the publication of Mill's work, had made much more comprehensive social, political, and economic demands for women's rights (Racz 1970). To be sure, some of their revolutionary demands represented only the feminist desire to "secure equality with men in sharing the fruits of the middle class triumph of 1789" (*ibid.*:30), but others transcended contemporary liberal perspectives by advocating divorce laws and guarantees of economic security.

4. Carr (1970:xxv) states, for example, ". . . as late as 1914 Havelock Ellis testified

that in nearly half a century since the appearance of *The Subjection of Women* 'no book on this subject published in any country—with the single exception of Bebel's *Woman*—has been so widely read or influential!' " Carr adds, however: "Though such claims may well be correct, they can be verified only through references to *The Subjection of Women* by persons actually involved in the movement for women's rights. And by this standard, what strikes one is not the abundance but the paucity of documentation." Furthermore, according to Carr (*ibid.*:xxvii), "by the time *The Subjection of Women* was published in 1869, Mill's arguments were already commonplace among those involved in the women's rights movement. To these persons what mattered was not the fact that their arguments had been stated, but that it was the renowned John Stuart Mill who had stated them."

5. The favored egotistical "values" or "propensities" that have been used in the varied general theories of human behavior by liberals include, above all, wealth, power, sex, and status. These "values" are considered useful "scientific fictions" or "hypothetical constructs" today. Actually, they are reifications of human relationships that have very clear institutional and historical boundaries.

6. Mill realized that the subjection of women involved half the human race, but one need only compare his assumptions about the isolated nature of this problem with statements by socialist writers to become aware of the importance of social-class, national, and racial oppression for the subjection of women. Mill's philosophy stemmed from the conviction that individual men achieved their social and economic statuses in *free* competition with each other in capitalist societies. This fallacious notion, however, was and still is one of the greatest hoaxes ever perpetrated by liberal scholars and nonscholars alike, in both the nineteenth and twentieth centuries.

7. Nevertheless, the intellectual preconditions for the use of the notion of complementarity as a *formalized* and ostensibly *noninvidious* statement of inegalitarian relationships were already present in Mill's work. These preconditions actually consisted of the perception of sexist adjustments in the family, the market, and any other instituted relationship, as the product of a "natural" division of labor based on a harmony of interests between the sexes, and sexual differences in abilities or temperament. The concept of integrative exchange became central to complementarity because of its correlative notion of social relationships as the product of free choice; no other liberal mechanism connotes the simultaneous existence of individual freedom and an integrated order more effectively than that of exchange. In modern times, the concept of complementarity has been used very broadly and it is still repeatedly applied to the study of sexist family relationships without bringing into question the basic political and economic institutions which maintained these forms of sexual exploitation.

8. From a laissez-faire perspective, one of the strongest arguments employed by Mill was that the probable existence of fit women, no matter how few, was sufficient for justifying the right of all women to compete "equally" for, let us say, occupational status or political representation. All women must be allowed to compete "equally" with men because the laissez-faire outlook would also contend that the natural forces of competition alone can determine whether there actually existed individual women who were equal or superior to individual men.

299

CHAPTER 38

The State, Private Property, and the Family

Background

During the same decade in which John Stuart Mill's famous work on the subjection of women appeared and ten years before Morgan published *Ancient Society,* a brilliant Swiss mystic, Johann J. Bachofen, published his analysis of classical ancient literature. Entitled *The Mother Right* (1861), this work represented an early history of the family. Bachofen claimed that numerous passages from classical documents and myths indicated an original state of promiscuity between the sexes, and, furthermore, that in antiquity, descent had been determined according to matrilineality (i.e., by "mother-right" rather than "father-right"). According to Bachofen, women were not only respected by their children because they clearly represented parental identity; women also *ruled* the entire primitive community. (Mill apparently discounted or was not aware of the implications of this seminal work.)

Bachofen also suggested that the instituted relations between the sexes were determined by the evolution of religious ideas. Historically, these sexual relations have been transformed from the ancient rule of women based on "mother-right" to the rule of men and "father-right." These changes corresponded to the emergence of monogamous relations in which the women became the exclusive property of one man.

In 1865, J. F. McLennan published his theory of the prehistoric development of marriage and family relationships. McLennan's theory, which was partly based on assumptions provided by economic liberalism, alleged, among other things,[1] that "savages" practiced a custom of killing off their female children. This practice created a *scarcity* of females and generated polyandry (the possession of one wife by a number of men) as well as "marriage by abduction" (the forcible seizure of wives from other tribes). These forms of marriage represented attempts by males to redress the unbalanced sex ratio. McLennan also wrote about polygamous and monogamous forms of marriage; and in 1870, the social scientific literature on early sexual relations was further supplemented by John Lubbock's discussion of "group marriage" in which the men of a primitive group possessed the women of the group in common.

300

In 1871, however, the account of prehistoric relations between men and women was integrated into a very general theory of the evolution of society. This theory, by Lewis Henry Morgan, was an eclectic embodiment of conflicting materialistic and idealistic analytic strategies which, divorced from one another, influenced the divergent theories about the origins of women, marriage, and the family by Frederick Engels and Lester F. Ward, Engels generally adapted the materialist aspects and ignored the idealism. Ward, on the other hand, appears to have selected some of Morgan's idealist notions. (Ward is discussed in another chapter.)

Morgan's Views on Origin of Family, Property, and State

After research and study,[2] Morgan maintained that human communities had evolved through three stages of savagery, barbarism, and civilization.[3] His evolutionary theory suggested that the family was preceded by units exhibited all over the globe and known as the gens, phratry or tribe. The gens lived, worked, and owned the means of production communally. There was no private property under this form of social organization. The gens members depended upon each other for help, defense, and redress of injuries. Democratically governed social organizations consisting of gentes, phratries, or tribes, had preceded the state. The war chief and the peace chief were chosen in a council of all the adult members, male and female, who voted equally.

Morgan felt these forms of social organization had been adversely effected by the development of private property and the state. His explanation of these economic and political changes, however, included both idealistic and materialistic explanations of social evolution. The institution of private property, as well as other "domestic institutions," was considered an epiphenomenal expression of "the growth of certain *ideas* and *passions*" (Morgan 1963:4). (He felt that the idea of property grew in the human mind where it had "commenced in feebleness and ended in becoming its *master passion*" [*ibid.*:512 our emphasis].) Other aspects of Morgan's idealism were expressed in his theory of the origins of the stage of *civilization*. This particular stage of evolutionary development was generated by the emergence of private property, class relationships, social disorganization (caused by the disintegration of the gentile organization), and the political state.

Morgan's idealism appeared, most ironically, in the area which gave greatest sustenance but not its actual content to Engels—the function and meaning of private property and social class. The concept of class is crucial for understanding the evolution of economic relations based on the institution of private property. Morgan's use of the term "social class," however, was very rudimentary.[4] This observation also applies to his conception of the political state. According to Morgan, the organization of social classes and the state began in Greece about 850 B.C. Prior to this time communal-living relations had declined and communal ownership of property ceased to exist: private "property [became] the new element that had been gradually remoulding Grecian institutions to prepare the way for political society, of which it was to be the mainspring as well as the foundation." The old gentes, phratries, and tribes were eventually divested of their influence. The state was developed in Athens in order to cope with the governmental problems and complications accruing from the accumulation of private property, growth of productivity, and extended mercantile relationships.

To further develop his explanation of the origins of the state, Morgan also used a "great man" theory of history; Theseus' rule was regarded, for example, as a turning point in the Grecian attempt to resolve the outstanding problems which had accrued from the changes in modes of production and the disintegration of older forms of social organization. Further political changes occurred during Solon's rule. Both of these leaders attempted to divide the people by political edict into *classes* in order to integrate society under existing conditions. As a consequence, civilization began with class society.

The efforts of Theseus and Solon failed, according to Morgan, and finally, in 509 B.C., Cleisthenes sharply delineated the townships and founded a new plan of social organization based upon territory and property inclusive of all citizens. "As a consequence of the legislation of Cleisthenes," Morgan (*ibid.*:280) noted, "the gentes, phratries and tribes were divested of their influence." Morgan also asserted that Athens was thenceforth a class*less* society.[5]

Morgan's theory of class relations, at bottom, was an idealistic conception based analytically on a sociopolitical problem of social integration. Although he was aware that material developments wrought changes in the evolution of society, he relied heavily on the notions of ruling *passions* and individual *genius* as causes. As indicated previously, he saw the idea of property as a dominant passion above all other passions, and the institution of property as the commencement of civilization. Consistent with this he unwittingly presented a "great man" theory of history; Theseus and Solon were seen as creators, or as figures representing culminating points, in the processes leading to integrated class societies by political edict. Cleisthenes, on the other hand, was viewed as the destroyer of class relationships.

Engels' Adaptation of Morgan's Theory

Morgan's orientation was eclectic, but sections of his work appeared to confirm the materialist conception of history which had been previously developed by Karl Marx and Frederick Engels. His three major stages of savagery, barbarism, and civilization were, more or less, based on the development of forces and modes of production. The successive kinship forms which culminated in the family as we know it today, roughly paralleled these evolutionary stages and their requisite modes of production.

Morgan's attitude toward relations between man and woman was particularly radical in the context of his time. He felt (1963:398) that the relation between men and women became oppressive within the "monogamian" stage of the family which "owes its *origin* to property." (In addition, his outlook toward *future* sexual relations coincided with that of numerous socialists.)

As with all other human social institutions, the monogamian family was seen as constantly in a process of change. Morgan (*ibid.*:399–400) pointed out that "we have a record of the monogamian family, running back nearly three thousand years, during which, it may be claimed, there has been a gradual but continuous improvement in its character. It is destined to progress still further, until the equality of the sexes is acknowledged, and the equities of the marriage relation are completely recognized."

Socialist theorists like Marx and Engels felt a kinship with some of his expressed views.[6] For example, Morgan deplored the inequities of class, the subservient relations of women, and the excesses brought about by private property. He also reacted sharply to the class differences he perceived in his European travels. He wondered, "how long the masses will bear this . . . rather than rise in revolution and resort to force" (White 1937:325). On another occasion he reflected on the Paris Commune, which he felt had been "unjustly condemned" (*ibid.*:343). Morgan had indicated that around 850 B.C. civilization was ushered in, after a million years of social evolution and with the development of social classes and the patriarchal family (which was characterized by the ownership of private property and by despotic relations between the patriarch and his servile and dependent relations, including wives, children, servants, and slaves). He was dismayed at the overall effects of private property. It was hard for him to believe that man was merely destined to fulfill a career aimed at the accumulation of private possessions. Significant parts of Morgan's view were immediately adopted by Marx and Engels. In 1884, only seven years after the publication of *Ancient Society,* Engels, writing partially from the notes left by the late Marx, published *The Origin of the Family, Private Property, and the State.* Engels concluded this work by noting one of Morgan's final statements, in which the force of nineteenth-century laissez-faire liberalism (with its emphasis on competition among owners of private property) was contrasted with the relations of "liberty, equality and fraternity of the ancient gentes," among whom property was *communally* owned.[7]

Engels' discussion of the emergence of class society was less dependent on Morgan's than on his own and Marx's knowledge of the development of slavery in Greece. But he was sufficiently impressed with Morgan's achievement to adopt major portions of Morgan's discussions of savagery and barbarism. These portions, however, were chosen carefully. With a few exceptions, Engels utilized only those insights which were indicative of a materialist analysis and, because of his "skillful editing," Marvin Harris (1968:248), an anthropologist, has claimed that "it is Engels and not Morgan who presents the first clear-cut periodization of prehistory, based on the mode of production." [8]

In contrast with Morgan's writings, Engels asserted that in Theseus' time the owners of substantial property had *already* begun to form groups that acted as a privileged class. The political state merely gave sanction to the already established social-class relationships. Private ownership of land and commodities for exchange was a fact of Athenian life. The most crucial factor of this development was the emergence of class relationships based on the ownership of slaves.

Property relationships, Engels further noted, were maintained by the establishment of usurious interest rates. When debtors could not fulfill their contracts they were forced to sell their children and finally themselves into slavery. (Because this development was accompanied by the development of the family, Engels [1968:110] declared, "The sale of his children by the father—such was the first fruit of father right and monogamy!") Therefore, although the specific "class" systems legislated by Theseus and by Solon were unsuccessful, Athens did, in fact, become a class society based on *slavery*. Somehow, Morgan missed the extraordinary significance of slavery as a stage in the origin of class society.

Engels on the Subjection of Women

Engels' view of women's relation to man and the family was analytically closer to Morgan than to John Stuart Mill. His assumptions and background material were so divergent from Mill's that the most they held in common was the general desire to see woman set free. Engels did not subscribe to Mill's view that prehistoric women were born into slavery. Engels (1968:49) wrote: "That woman was the slave of man at the commencement of society is one of the most absurd notions that have come down to us from the period of Enlightenment of the eighteenth century." According to Engels, woman had a proud and productive heritage. Furthermore, Engels believed that very early sexual relations were organized within the "communistic household" and group marriage,[9] in which "whole groups of men and whole groups of women belong to one another" (*ibid.*:36). In time this early structure evolved into the pairing family. Within this communistic household (enclosing several families), women held a position of supremacy.

Engels also suggested a causal relation between the work performed by primitive women and the respect or high position which they commanded. In fact, coming after woman's earlier exalted position, Engles perceived that "the overthrow of mother right was the world-historic defeat of the female sex. The man seized the reins in the house also, the woman was degraded, enthralled, the slave of the man's lust, a mere instrument for breeding children" (*ibid.*:57).

Engels indicated further that the subjection of women within the patriarchal monogamous family was inextricably linked with the formation of *the state* and *social-class* relations based on *private property*. Following Morgan,

Engels emphasized that the state emerged as the culmination of social and economic processes which had begun long before the time of Cleisthenes. In the Grecian heroic age the gentile system was still viable, but the emergence of father-right and the inheritance of property by children encouraged the accumulation of private wealth by individual families. Wealthy families began to rival the gens as centers of power and their development generated the rudiments of hereditary aristocratic class.

Slave-produced wealth swelled the power of this early class. At first slavery was limited to prisoners of war; but the processes leading to the eventual enslavement of fellow members of the tribe and gens were initiated with the increasing deployment of tribal forces in systematic raids for cattle, slaves, and treasure. Only one thing was missing in order to guarantee the crystallization of these into long-term trends in the form of a stable class society:

. . . an institution that would not only safeguard the newly-acquired property of private individuals against the communistic traditions of the gentile order, would not only sanctify private property, formerly held in such light esteem, and pronounce this sanctification the highest purpose of human society, but would also stamp the gradually developing new forms of acquiring property, and consequently, of constantly accelerating the increase in wealth, with the seal of general public recognition; an institution that would perpetuate, not only the newly-rising class division of society, but also the right of the possessing class to exploit the non-possessing classes and the rule of the former over the latter. [*ibid.*:107]

This "institution" was the political *state*.

Thus, Engels indicated, although the "formal" legally established classes of Solon were abolished in the time of Cleisthenes, the new state perpetuated the existent and growing cleavage into classes of slavers and slaves, exploiters and exploited, within the newly formalized territorial divisions. The state itself was the institutional embodiment of the political rights of the ruling class; it sanctioned the rule of this class. The newly emergent but gradually evolving state also secured for the ruling class the goods of the earth which were being created by the labor of male as well as female slaves.

The state not only destroyed the gentile organization of society, according to Engels, but also the gentile institutions of communal property, equal access to the necessities of life, and mother-right. The family replaced the gens as the social unit of life; and accumulation of wealth within the family gave rise to the inheritance of wealth by the father's children. Riches were generally respected and praised as the highest good.

Engels (*ibid.*:100) remarked that all historians, especially those of the eighteenth century, have assumed that "the monogamous individual family, an institution scarcely older than civilization, is the nucleus around which society and the state gradually crystallized." He noted however, that this type of kinship relation was not a unit of the venerable [10] gentile social organization. The monogamous family developed instead,

. . . in the transition period from the middle to the upper stage of barbarism. . . . It is based on the supremacy of the man; its express aim is the begetting of children of undisputed paternity, this paternity being required in order that these children may in due time inherit their father's wealth as his natural heirs. [*ibid.:*62]

As an example of this development Engels used this Athenian "family" which increasingly became, according to him, a model for many others. In this family he found the origin of monogamy; a system which was then and is now debased with pecuniary values. Indeed, this family

. . . was not in any way the fruit of individual sex love, with which it had absolutely nothing in common, for the marriages remained marriages of convenience, as before. It was the first form of the family based not on natural but on economic condition, namely, on the victory of private property over original, naturally developed, common ownership. [*ibid.:*65]

To underscore this interpretation, Engels observed that the Roman word *familia*—from which the modern term "family" is derived—did not signify a married couple and their children, but only the totality of slaves belonging to one person [*ibid.:*58].

Reductionist Aspects of Engels' Work

Engels departed to some extent from the traditional materialist strategy [11] of historical analysis developed by Marx. He insisted (*ibid.:*5–6) that "the determining factor in history is the production and *reproduction* of immediate life" (our emphasis). He defined the concept of production in Marxist terms, i.e., it referred to "the production of the means of subsistence, of articles of food, clothing, dwellings, and of the tools necessary for that production." His concept of reproduction, however, was Darwinian and referred to "the propagation of the species." Furthermore, as Harris (1968:247) indicates, Engels explained "the origin of the nuclear family, incest taboos, and clan exogamy, only by subscribing to Morgan's Darwinian hypothesis concerning the deleterious effects of inbreeding." [12]

According to Harris (*ibid.*), Engels' explanation of the origin of monogamy, derived from Bachofen and Morgan, was also inconsistent with Marx's analytic strategy. Harris adds that Engels decided that "primitive sexual communism came to an end because in effect the woman enjoyed it less than the men." [13] In some respects, therefore, Engels had not fully departed from the biologistic and psychologistic interpretations of historical change which were prevalent among his liberal contemporaries.

Engels' work, dependent as it was upon Morgan's anthropological observations and generalizations, suffered from the inaccuracies in Morgan's unilinear theory of social evolution. Furthermore, it expressed Morgan's simple equation between matrilineality and sexual equality. Today, after almost a century of professional anthropological research, evolutionary processes are being seen as multilinear. In addition, research on *observable* societies indicates that such relations as matrilineal descent and sexual equality may be highly independent. Generalizing from observable relations, for example,

306

Kathleen Gough (1971:52–53) states: "All known societies have been male dominant to some extent, although the extent varies greatly and it seems to be true that, in general, pre-state societies (bands, tribes, and chiefdoms) offer greater freedom for women than do primitive or archaic states, and matrilineal horticultural tribes the greatest freedom of all."

Engels: Women's Liberation and Marxist Timetable for Change

Engels' writings were apparently not completely free of the reductionism that pervaded contemporary liberal thought. However, the major thrust of his work was materialistic; and because of the identity he had established between Morgan's theory and Marxism, liberal cultural anthropologists quickly reacted by attacking Morgan's theory as well as evolutionary theory in general. Beginning with the last decades of the nineteenth century, the development of anthropology, like that of sociology, was powerfully determined by the liberal reaction to Marxism.

On the other hand, whatever anthropologists have thought about Engels' theory, there is little question but that he was strongly in favor of the liberation of women. Furthermore, he expressed his thoughts as early as 1845 in *The Holy Family* written with Marx, and in the same year in his *The Conditions of the Working Class in England*. Engels, to be sure, also romanticized the sexual relations between individual men and women in the oppressed class, the proletariat, as opposed to those in the ruling class, the bourgeoisie; [14] but he was unequivocal about the importance of creating the social foundations for sexual relations based on mutual affection and voluntary choice. These foundations included, among other things, (1) the transformation of "private housekeeping" into a "social industry," (2) the public care and education of children ("irrespective of whether they are born in wedlock or not"), and (3) the elimination of the family as an *economic unit* of society (1968:76). Engels, therefore, foresaw a time when monogamy would be divested of "all the characteristics stamped on it in consequence of its having arisen out of property relationships." These characteristics included, above all, "the dominance of the man" and "the indissolubility of marriage." As far as divorce was concerned, Engels remarked, "If only marriages that are based on love are moral, then, also, only those are moral in which love continues" (*ibid.*:82).

The previous chapters note that while intellectuals have often painted the future in glowing colors, upon examination their timetables for social change predict the coming of utopia after many millennia. Engels, however, did not project a gradualist timetable; he expected socialism in the near future and spoke about the impending overthrow of the capitalist system. He predicted an end to women's subjection and stated that "since large-scale industry has transferred the woman from the house to the labor market and the factory, and makes her, often enough, the bread-winner of the family, the last remnants of male domination in the proletarian home have lost all foundation—except, perhaps, for some of that brutality towards women which became firmly rooted with the establishment of monogamy" (*ibid.:*72). He also indicated that it was impossible to predict the shape of a socialist society in detail. Regarding relations between men and women he said:

What we can now conjecture about the way in which sexual relations will be ordered after the impending overthrow of capitalist production is mainly of a negative character, limited for the most part to what will disappear. But what will there be new? That will be answered when a new generation has grown up: a generation of men who never in their lives have known what it is to buy a woman's surrender with money or any other social instrument of power; a generation of women who have never known what it is to give themselves to a man from any other considerations than real love, or to refuse to give themselves to their lover from fear of the economic consequences. When these people are in the world, they will care precious little what anybody today thinks they ought to do; they will make their own practice and their corresponding public opinion about the practice of each individual—and that will be the end of it. [*ibid.:*82–83]

NOTES

1. McLennan developed much of his theory around exogamy (marriage out of the group) and endogamy (marriage within the group). Exogamy and polyandry, he thought, always went together and served the same purpose—balance between the sexes.

2. Morgan was a president of the American Association for the Advancement of Science and the founder of its anthropology subsection. Prior to his major work, *Ancient Society,* first published in 1877, he also wrote *Letters on the Iroquois* in 1847 and *The League of the Iroquois* in 1851. In 1881, he published *Houses and House-Life of the North American Aborigines.*

3. Harris (1968:29) indicates that similar schemes had been proposed earlier by Montesquieu and others. In addition, some of Morgan's views have been justifiably criticized as erroneous and racist. As Eleanor Burke Leacock points out, he wrote (1963:382) that "savagery in its lowest forms, cannibalism included, and barbarism in its lowest forms prevail over the greater part of the continent" of Africa. Modern anthropologists have substituted new terminology for Morgan's obviously negative designations. "Savagery" is called the "hunting and gathering" and Paleolithic period; barbarism is denoted variously as the "slash and burn agriculture" and the Neolithic period. "Urban culture" is increasingly being used in place of "civilization."

4. This was exemplified by the fact that Morgan believed the United States was a classless society. He stated (1963:561), for example, "Although several thousand years have passed away without the overthrow of privileged classes, *excepting* in the United States, their burdensome character upon society has been demonstrated (our emphasis). His protest against the evils of class oppression was marred by his lack of understanding of the nature of class society.

5. Morgan stated (1963:281) in this respect that "the classes, both those instituted by Theseus and those afterwards created by Solon, disappeared after the time of Cleisthenes."

6. Marx and Engels did not adopt Morgan's concept of class relationships but nevertheless agreed that class society was ushered in toward the end of barbarism and that the development of the family was dynamically related to the changes in modes of production as well as class relationships.

7. In the passage quoted by Engels, Morgan (1963:561–562) protested: "A mere property career is not the final destiny of mankind, if progress is to be the law of the future as it has been of the past. The time which has passed away since civilization began is but a fragment of the past duration of man's existence; and but a fragment of the ages yet to

come. The dissolution of society bids fair to become the termination of a career of which property is the end and aim; because such a career contains the elements of self-destruction. Democracy in government, brotherhood in society, equality in rights and privileges, and universal education, foreshadow the next higher plane of society to which experience, intelligence and knowledge are steadily tending. It will be a revival, in a higher form, of the liberty, equality and fraternity of the ancient gentes."

8. Harris (1968:248) quotes part of the following statement by Engles (1968:28–29) to illustrate the latter scholar's succinct and coherent grasp of these evolutionary stages: "For the time being we can generalize Morgan's periodization as follows: Savagery— the period in which the appropriation of natural products, ready for use, predominated: the things produced by man were, in the main, instruments that facilitated this appropriation. Barbarism—the period in which knowledge of cattle breeding and land cultivation was acquired, in which methods of increasing the productivity of nature through human activity were learnt. Civilization—the period in which knowledge of the further working up of natural products, of industry proper, and of art was acquired."

9. Today anthropologists do not support the hypothesis that group marriage was the earliest form of family relationship.

10. Morgan and Engels indicated that human social organization began and endured for many millennia during the precivilization stages of society.

11. Ten years after the publication of Engles' work, Otis Tufton Mason explored the division of labor between men and women. He also stressed women's material contributions such as inventions of tools, discoveries of new edible plants and medicines, as well as the development of trades like stone cutting. For a detailed account refer to *Women's Share in Primitive Culture* (1894). In 1927, the knowledge about women's positive contributions to technology and productive relations in early societies was further enlarged in *The Mothers* by Robert Briffault. These works tend to refute Spencerian generalizations about women in enslaved and dependency roles in the past.

12. Harris (1968:247) further indicates that Engels quoted directly from Morgan's *Ancient Society* in regard to this point: "In this ever widening exclusion of blood relatives from marriage," Engels [1968:47] stated "natural selection also continues to have its effect. In Morgan's words, marriage between non-consanguineous gentes 'tended to create a more vigorous stock physically and mentally. When two advancing tribes are blended into one people . . . the new skull and brain would widen and lengthen to the sum of the capabilities of both.' "

13. Engels (1968:53) had stated, for example, that "Bachofen is again absolutely right when he contends throughout that the transition . . . to monogamy was brought about essentially by the women. The more the old traditional sexual relations lost their naive, primitive jungle character, as a result of the development of the economic conditions of life . . . the more degrading and oppressive must they have appeared to women; the more fervently must they have longed for the right to chastity, to temporary or permanent marriage with one man only, as a deliverance. This advance could not have originated from the men, if only for the reason that they have never— not even to the present day—dreamed of renouncing the pleasures of actual group marriage. Only after the transition to pairing marriage had been effected by the women could the men introduce strict monogamy—for the women only, of course."

14. For example, in addition to the quotation above (Engels 1968:72), Engels stated that "the ruling class continues to be dominated by the familiar economic influences and, therefore, only in *exceptional* cases can it show really *voluntary* marriages; whereas, as we have seen, these are *the rule* among the dominated class" (our emphasis). In this statement Engels is underestimating the complexities of middle-class family relationships, and the influence of ideological hegemony and socioeconomic factors other than inheritance on middle-class and working-class marriages.

CHAPTER 39

Ward and Thomas:
The Subjection of Women

Preview

This chapter brings us back to two American sociologists, Ward and Thomas, who wrote extensively on the relations between women and men. We will begin with a very brief consideration of Comte's and Spencer's writings on women because Ward criticized their conservative positions while developing his own. Then we will outline the contrasting positions of Ward and Engels, in order to emphasize the ideological assumptions underlying Ward's view. The remainder of the chapter examines the reasoning and writing of Ward and Thomas on the subjection of women.

Comte and Spencer: Subjection of Women

Prior to Ward and Thomas, the two men most closely identified with the development of liberal *sociology* proper and having something to say about the position and function of women, were Comte and Spencer. Book I has indicated that Comte was an early nineteenth-century precursor of North American sociology. But his views on women are considerably less well known today than his identity as a positivist, as a bourgeois philosopher, and as the man who coined the term "sociology." With regard to women, Comte maintained that women were constitutionally inferior to men because their maturation was arrested at childhood. He insisted that patriarchal authority (as well as a political dictatorship) was absolutely indispensable for "Order and Progress" in France. Accordingly, he proposed that women were justifiably subordinated to men when they married. Divorce should be unequivocally denied them: women should be the pampered slaves of men. To begin with, therefore, Comte touted sociology as a powerful new method for halting the drift of Western nations toward "a savage communism" and "degrading equality." However, after he raised the curtain on the new discipline, it became equally patent that it would be useful for justifying, in the name of science, the oppression of women for the good of society!

Later in the nineteenth century, Spencer became most representative of the developments leading to the emergence of North American sociology. With his earlier writings, in 1851, Spencer championed laissez-faire rights to individual women (e.g., the right to become truly "free labor" in the competitive market). This was consistent with his key belief that all men have the right to compete savagely with each other for *unequal* positions in life. Later, however, he reversed himself and urged that women be denied the right to engage in free competition for occupations with men. He completely abandoned his limited defense of women's rights and contended that educating women to compete for business and political careers, for example, would be positively "mischievous." Speaking about the aspirations of women, Spencer (1894:774) added benevolently that "if women comprehended all that is contained in the domestic sphere they would ask no other."

Liberal-Functional Categories and Marxian-Materialist Categories

Ward wrote at great length about the subjection of women. He was a scholar who read widely and was therefore subject to many influences.[1] In order to heighten Ward's identity as an *active ideologue* it may be useful to counterpose his theory to Engels' work on women which appeared only one year later but which followed other socialist writings about women and the social order. These men faced similar analytic options and, at least in part, the same theoretical problems. Both of them rejected the prevalent notion that women were slaves of men in the earliest prehistoric times. Each of them, moreover, predicted equality for women in the future.

Anthropological interest and theories regarding women, marriage, and the family were developing rapidly during the two decades prior to the publication in 1883 of Ward's first major theoretical work.[2] Although it is true that comparative knowledge was far from systematically developed, Ward and Engels had available the same wide assortment of analytic categories and mechanisms concerning evolutionary changes in social relationships. These included social Darwinist categories based on the notion of natural selection; psychological categories such as instinct, which tapped man's aggressive propensities; technological categories that linked evolutionary developments with the cumulative effects of inventions; socio-economic categories that involved changing modes of production; and an array of political categories that had been found useful for solving the problem of social integration. As the most plausible keys to the subjection of women and the origin of marriage and the family, Ward, oriented toward liberal-functionalism, chose man's *sexual passion,* man's passion for *private property,* woman's *desire* for *security,* and various mechanisms organized around the concepts of *natural selection* and *scarce resources.* Engels, moving in a materialist direction, based the major part of his explanation on changes in the modes of production and the development of the political state. In Engels' view, as we have seen, the Athenian family (which other Greeks and Greek colonies accepted as a model) "was not in *any* way the fruit of individual sex-love, with which it had *nothing whatever to do*" (Engels 1968:62 our emphasis).

The influence of ideology is even illustrated by the differences in the ways both Engels and Ward used the mechanism of natural selection. It will be recalled that according to Harris, Engels departed from the Marxian materialist strategy by subscribing to one of Morgan's Darwinian hypotheses. This hypothesis indicated the positive effects of certain family taboos, for example, in terms of natural selection. Unlike Ward and Thomas, however, Engels did not employ the concept of natural selection in order to create a new pseudo-scientific doctrine of male supremacy. Indeed, he attempted to develop a materialistic explanation for the development of male supremacy without any equivocation about the unjust character of the subjection of any woman, irrespective of her personal (biological or psychological) qualifications. Engels did not use the concept of natural selection to assert that women had become biologically inferior to men. But Ward and Thomas did!

One of the most intriguing features of nineteenth-century liberal works on the subjection of women is the liberal preoccupation with biological or psychological doctrines of male supremacy. Even Mill,[3] who concentrated on refuting these doctrines on environmentalist grounds, was equivocal in this regard. This was not inconsistent because Mill was surrounded by other intellectuals who were representative of the very traditions and ideologies that had regarded women as naturally inferior for centuries. One of these ideologies was liberalism itself.

It is not surprising, in light of this, that Mill had come to terms with himself, in one way or another, with the biological doctrines of male superiority. The same can be said about Ward and Thomas. But the need to develop elaborate justifications or refutations of these doctrines was comparatively absent from works by such socialists as Engels or Bebel. Outstanding nineteenth-century socialists appeared to take for granted that women were equal to men. They also felt that biological or psychological differences between the sexes were absolutely irrelevant to the issue at hand. From their nineteenth-century socialist point of view, the major issue bearing on the subjection of women was the reconstruction of society in order to eliminate the coercive economic and political pressures that sustained sexist relationships. With this very brief background let us consider Ward's polemic regarding the subjection of women.

Ward's and Comte's "Flimsy Fallacies"

Although most of the early sociologists in the United States cut their milk teeth on writings of Comte and Spencer, sharp differences were expressed when it came to Spencer's laissez-faire doctrines; and some, like Ward, also rejected Comte's view of women.[4] Ward expressed his contempt for Comte's pernicious allegation that women were biologically incapable of achieving equality with men. He also rebuked other scholars who brought in animal analogies to further substantiate their claims that the inferior status of women served nature's purposes.[5] These "natural-law" theories and analogies were fallacious, Ward declared, because the mentalities of women had come about generally from their *adaptation* to male desires. Indeed, primitive woman had been man's superior or equal! If woman had changed once from a state of equality or dominance to inequality, she could change again under new conditions; in fact, the redemption of woman's lost equality, Ward (1883:I,657) proclaimed, "will be the regeneration of humanity."

A "Wardian" Dream:
Woman Defeated in Prehistoric Battle of the Sexes

What were the empirical grounds for Ward's ringing declaration? He proposed that at the very dawn of society men and women lived side by side in full equality because women possessed complete self-determination in regard to *sexual intercourse.* Women, Ward (*ibid.*:614) stated, had "supremacy" in deciding "all matters pertaining to sex." This implied that women alone decided whether or not to have children; or whether and when men themselves could obtain sexual gratification from intercourse.[6] Men, on the other hand, were endowed by nature with much stronger *passions* than women. "The sexual desire of man is quite different from that of woman." His passion is "uniform and uninterrupted, while hers is more or less periodical and intermittent" (*ibid.*:I,608).[7] Apparently, however, the emotional conflicts one would expect from this relation between the sexes remained latent for thousands of years, and during that time men had to keep their horny intentions well in hand.

As Ward's theory is further unveiled it becomes painfully obvious that he also found it necessary to rely in part on the kinds of analogical and biological reasoning which he considered so objectionable in the writings of other scholars.[8] Ward claimed, for example, that men were more bold and aggressive than women because of their psychobiological makeup. Women, on the other hand, were constitutionally shy and timid. Over a long period of time in prehistory, it was man's aggressiveness and passion that precipitated a series of circumstances that destroyed male-female equality.

The turnabout from woman's good fortune took place in the following manner: Forever driven by his sexual passion, man desperately needed to succeed in courtship. For this he required greater cunning and intelligence in order to manipulate woman so that she would acquiesce to his sexual demands more frequently. Fortunately, Ward argued, man was "plastic." Through the processes of natural selection, man was biologically adaptable to his changing environment. This biological adaptability enabled him to become more intelligent than woman.

313

What were the specific means by which men superseded women intellectually? The first of these was represented by man's role in relation to food and the need to cope with its scarcity. In the process of laboring to overcome this problem, he becomes more cunning than woman. The second was created by the consequences of his overly passionate nature: "The sexual passion in man," Ward (*ibid.:*649) remarked, "was one cause of a more rapid intellectual development in him than in woman." ("Superior cunning," he added, ". . . may be regarded as a secondary sexual characteristic as much as the tusks of the boar or the spurs of the cock.") The third was produced by man's desire for the private ownership of property: According to Ward (*ibid.:*495), "the idea of permanent possession . . . has not only given [man] life, it has given intelligence." [9]

Therefore, in sum, because of his *emotional* makeup and conditions of scarcity, man became superior intellectually: his mental powers expanded as he successfully pursued his need to overcome a *scarcity* of food as well as a *scarcity* of opportunities to obtain sexual gratification through intercourse with women. Although the kind of man being discussed in his theory actually lived before the dawn of social history, Ward's explanation implied that man was equipped with the "economic rationality" usually associated with the "scarcity postulate" and the "rationality of exchange," formulated and described by classical and neoclassical liberal economists (Polanyi 1957:246).

The "hidden hand" of economic liberalism is completely revealed when we discover Ward's use of the concept of exchange as an *integrative mechanism*. We shall see momentarily that Ward introduced this mechanism to explain the emergence of the voluntary *accommodation* of women to the domination of men.

Sex for Sale!
In the Substructure (Bargain Basement) of Civilization

Ward argued that once man had obtained mental superiority, he became capable of wooing woman with gifts; and that by appealing "to her imagination and reason" (1883:I,633), he won in *exchange* the surrender of her "right of choice" and "right of refusal" in matters pertaining to sexual intercourse. Like buyers and sellers in a competitive market, man bargained with woman about her price of exchange. The scarce values at stake also appeared to include her "right" to dictate the price of her body thereafter. Thus, eventually man was voluntarily accorded the "right" to manage the conditions under which sexual exchanges were to take place: all because woman was *duped* into renouncing her "right to refusal" to engage in sexual intercourse!

As a final biological proof of her complete renunciation of rights, Ward cited the fact that female menstruation, otherwise referred to as the "curse" (not only by Ward), became a monthly occurrence only among the human species. This frequency, he pointed out, could scarcely have been left up to the woman alone. "It is therefore most reasonable," Ward (*ibid.*) continued, "to suppose that the present process [of menstruation] is the result of the surrender of this right of choice, the subjection of her person to the excessive attentions of the male sex." The domination of woman was finally achieved and civilization proper now proceeded to unfold.

W. I. Thomas: Women Are Stationary—Men Are Mobile "Look! Jane, See Dick Run! Look! Dick, See Jane Hide!"

Thomas, like Ward, objected strenuously to the assumption, expressed by many anthropologists at the time, that "woman is an inferior creature." He further protested (1907:50–51), on environmentalist grounds, that these anthropologists "have almost totally neglected to distinguish between the congenital characters of woman and those acquired as a result of a totally different relation to society on the part of women and men. They have also failed to appreciate the fact that differences from man are not necessarily points of inferiority, but *adaptations* to different and specialized modes of functioning" (our emphasis). At first glance, therefore, Thomas also seemed to move beyond the male supremist theories of his time.

In constructing his own theory, however, Thomas relied on biological analogies as well as instinct theory, natural-law concepts, and an ahistorical interpretation of evolutionary change. The use of these analytic concepts and assumptions inevitably led to another particularly inane solution to the problem under study: Thomas claimed, for example, that the female's metabolism, like that of the plants, tends to store and construct nutrition, while the male destroys nutrients through "katabolism" (*sic*) and thereby creates energy. On this basis, Thomas asserted that "woman stands nearer to plant processes than man" and therefore woman is more constructive than man.[10] Women, Thomas concluded, were by nature "stationary,"[11] while men were wont to seek and wander.

It is impossible to overstate the degree to which Thomas' description of the differences between men and women contained a rude mixture of fiction, truth, and triviality. Although called "main propositions" about sexual differences, his descriptions read like an accountant's ledger of assets:

Man consumes energy more rapidly; woman is more conservative of it. The structural variability of man is mainly toward motion; woman's variational tendency is not towards motion, but toward reproduction. Man is fitted for feats of strength and bursts of energy; woman has more stability and endurance. While woman remains nearer to the infantile type, man approaches more to the senile. The extreme variational tendency of man expresses itself in a larger percentage of genius, insanity, and idiocy; woman remains more nearly normal. [*ibid.*:51]

It is important to also keep in mind that as far as Thomas was concerned, these "adaptive traits" represented the complementary characteristics enabling men and women to aid each other's performance as a functionally necessary unit.

Value-Laden Dimensions
of a "Value-Free" Approach to Women

Thomas was one of the new breed of sociologists who eschewed an expressed commitment to ethical goals as a scientist. The social analyses produced by this breed were considered merely "objective," "value-free" commentaries on human behavior. However, the kinds of behavior that Thomas did not necessarily consider "points of inferiority" were, in fact, the very same ones previously used by sexists as an empirical warrant for male supremacy. In Thomas' theory, moreover, these kinds of adaptive behavior were also regarded as "functional prerequisites" for the evolution of "society," "civilization" and the continued survival of the "human species." In the context of this functionalist perspective, the ostensibly unbiased and scientifically objective terms "adaptation" and "specialized modes of functioning," merely restated older sexist doctrines of male supremacy in a new way. Thomas' theory implicitly was very much "value-laden."

Thomas also discussed the differences between "higher and lower races" in his writing about the differences between the sexes. Sexist writers like Thomas interchangeably used the same liberal-functionalist strategies for justifying racial and sexual inequality. He specified that "higher and lower races" differed because they came from very different environments.[12] According to Thomas, sexual differences were due less to environmental variations than to "certain organic conditions" (metabolic rates) and "historical incidents" (functional modes) which have enclosed the woman "in habits which she neither can nor will fracture." These differences, he added, "have also set up in the mind of man an attitude toward her which renders her almost as alien to man's interests and practices as if she were spatially separated from them" (*ibid.:*291).

Thomas' description of the "historical incidents" that led to sexual differences in temperament contained strong hints that his theory of social change was as reductionist as Ward's, and that it was in fact heavily dependent upon the latter scholar's notions of *adaptation* and *adjustment*. Thomas, however, expressed additional comments about history which made more explicit the *psychologism* and philosophical *idealism* that underlie both of their approaches to historical change. Thomas (*ibid.:*277) proclaimed, for example, that "the institutions and practices of a people are a product of the mind." In *his* mind (*ibid.:*287–288), moreover, there was no doubt that:

. . . it is a notorious fact that the course of human history has been largely without prevision or direction. Things have drifted and forces have arisen. Under these conditions an unusual incident—the emergence of a *great mind* or a forcible personality, or the operation of influences as subtle as those which determine fashions in dress—may establish social habits and duties which will give a distinct character to the modes of attention and mental life of the group. [our emphasis]

316

To a great extent, therefore, the disadvantaged position of women today has come about because of fortuitous circumstances and the active nature and mind of man.

The Story of Chicken Little and Thomas' Explanation of Greater Male Intelligence

Thomas constructed a pseudoscientific and foreshortened presentation of the events in the development of women. He argued, in particular, that the capacities of women in prehistory were not inferior; they were merely *complementary* to men. Because women tended toward reproduction rather than "motion," they contributed to the size and the strength of the group. While men were out hunting, women protected themselves and their young by building and maintaining shelters that were a comfort to the family. In supplementing the vicissitudes of the hunt, they also dug roots and cultivated growing things.[13]

Why did women develop activities that were structured almost entirely in terms of their complementary functions? Why didn't women do the same things as men? What made this division of labor—and women's obviously subordinate position in this division of labor—so necessary in the first place? When we ask these questions and Thomas' explanation is pushed back into its fundamental categories and mechanisms, we find the following tale: In the early beginnings of human development women spent a great deal of their time hiding and evading natural predators—man and beast—while men moved about and fought them actively. The differences in the social habits and interests of the sexes originated with the *motion* of one as opposed to the *stability* of the other.

These different modes of existence were generated by the persistence of organic differences between the sexes. Among these "organic differences" were differences in intellectual and sensory capacities. According to Thomas, "the development of *intelligence* and *motion* have gone along side by side in all animal forms. Through motion changes and experiences are multiplied . . . the organs of sense and the intelligence are developed to take note of and manipulate the outside world" (*ibid.*:292 our emphasis). Obviously, if greater motion is correlated with greater intelligence and sensory abilities, then by their active lives, men become *superior* to women in these respects.

We will borrow Thomas' own strategy of analogy to other forms of life to modify his explanation of the differences between the sexes during prehistoric times. This modification assumes, however, that Thomas' speculation about the differences in mobility between the sexes is only partly accurate: our observation of birds, for example, suggests that the relation between motion and intelligence is an *inverse* rather than a direct relation. (Birds exhibit an extraordinary degree of motion. However as a species [as any second grader would know, having heard the story of Chicken Little] birds are conspicuous for

317

their *lack* of intelligence.) Consequently, it is woman, not man, who has become more intelligent and sensitive to the world about her: man is her intellectual inferior precisely because of his active nature!

Thus revised, Thomas' theory can be called the *Chicken Little* theory of the sexes.

NOTES

1. Ward expressed admiration for Mill's outlook on the emancipation of women (Ward 1935:275). He later indicated (1883:I,211) substantial agreement with Spencer's writings on "domestic relations." Moreover, he considered Lubbock, McLennan, and Tylor to be informative about the institutions of marriage, the family, and religion (*ibid.*:I,619;II,262). Ward, in fact, generally derived his explanations of polygamy and polyandry from McLennan's notions about the "scarcity" of females who were desirable or of females in the population as a whole. Ward's central focus on the relations between private property, male supremacy, and the evolution of civilization is also strongly reminiscent of Morgan, who is cited in the bibliography at the end of the second volume of *Dynamic Sociology*. We find no reference to Bachofen in that work, even though Ward was in agreement with his view that woman's position in prehistorical societies was superior to that of men. Both Morgan and Bachofen are cited in Ward's later publication, *Pure Sociology* (1903).

2. It is interesting to note that Ward actually started the draft of *Dynamic Sociology* in 1869, by which time he had already shown an interest, along with his wife, in the rights of women. "Lizzie is stirred to the depths on the subject of suffrage for women" (Ward 1935:282). For further allusion to his early concerns with education, suffrage, and dress reforms for women, see *Young Ward's Diary*, ed. Bernhard J. Stern, 1935.

3. Ward followed the work of Mill and expressed agreement with it. In 1868, he amused himself by writing a letter, which he never sent, to an editor who criticized Mill for his lack of religion. Ward extolled Mill for his work in the "great cause of human enfranchisement . . . of both men and women" (Ward 1935:275).

4. Ward [1883:130–131] attacked Comte's view of the family, which he styled as detestable.

5. Ward (*ibid.*:659) vigorously protested that "arguments of this kind, coming from high scientific sources, have great weight, especially as those to whom they are chiefly addressed are incompetent as a rule, to judge of the adequacy of the premises and accept them as resting upon authority."

6. Ward is still alive and well today, reincarnated as Norman Mailer, who also reduces sexism to questions of equity involving power and exchange relations between individual men and women.

7. Further comments on Ward's sexual theory include: "While the sexuality of a savage is scarcely less localized than that of a brute, that of a cultivated and enlightened man or woman is widely diffused, and blends with all the other emotions and with the intellect itself." Additionally, "All love emanates from the sexual system, of which the mammary glands are a part, particularly in woman, and the higher sentiment of love seems to have its chief seat in the breast of man as well as of woman" (Ward 1883:I,609–610).

8. Women's "natural modesty" is found "among the females of many animals. . . . All this has its counterpart in the human race, where the normal condition universally is, that the males should take the initiative and active, and the females the defensive and passive character in the courtship" (Ward 1883:I,608–609).

9. While all of these energetic male developments were taking place, women, it appears, were passively allowing their "brains" to fall into disuse. Furthermore, according to Ward (1883:II,616), the "brain can only develop by use. It must languish from disuse. The causal faculty of women has no exercise, therefore it has not developed."

10. Men were considered more "disruptive" or "destructive." These and other words (e.g., "fighting instincts") connoted the personality characteristics that are now generally associated with the psychoanalytic metaphor "aggression." It is not surprising in light of

this and other features of Thomas' work that Freud's writings influenced his perspective in later years.

11. At least Thomas did not suggest that it was their nature to be always "prone"; he left this for one of our own contemporaries, Stokely Carmichael (Morgan 1970:35).

12. Sex differences could not be explained on this basis because, as Thomas (1907:291) wrote, "Woman . . . exists in the white man's world of practical and scientific activity, but is excluded from full participation in it."

13. For a factual alternative theory of women's contributions to "primitive" culture, published before Thomas' first essay on women, see Otis Tufton Mason's fine work *Women's Share in Primitive Culture* (1894).

CHAPTER 40

Ward and Thomas: Marriage and the Family

Ward: Family and Marriage Grounded in Male Egoism

In the previous chapter we considered theories of the subjection of women on all general institutional levels—social, economic, and political. The discussion in this chapter centers on the origins of two overlapping yet distinct institutions, the family and marriage which were conceived as natural settings of male domination by Ward and Thomas.

Prior to the publication of Ward's *Dynamic Sociology*, Lewis Henry Morgan had supplied a very significant framework for studying the development of marriage and the family in prehistory. In *Ancient Society*, Morgan carefully traced the linkage of the origin of the family with the institution of private property and the emergence of class society. Ward and Thomas, however, either revised or ignored Morgan's framework. Morgan described "primitive communism" as matriarchal and organized around maternal gentes or clans which *later* developed into the family unit, tending toward the institution as we know it today. Ward, on the other hand, followed established perspectives by reversing this ordering of prehistory. According to Ward's theory, the "reproductive forces" gave rise to "the family, and out of the family have grown gentes, tribes and nations" (Ward 1883:I,604).

In Ward's explanation, as we previously indicated, the emergence of the family was not synchronized with changes in modes of production and political institutions. Instead, he argued that men established families with women in order to guarantee a stable source of sexual gratification for themselves

319

and, in exchange, they provided regular food and protection. Children were a consequence of the reproductive act, and they ultimately provided for their parents. But the direct object of man's pursuits was his interest in his own survival through gratification of his own needs, not love for family members. Egoistic male desire was considered a functional prerequisite for the family and, in Ward's view, this institution emerged largely as an unintended consequence of man's pursuit of his own selfish needs.

To be sure, Ward was concerned with the existence of "sexual-social inequalities in contemporary societies." He was interested in seeking "their causes and establishing if possible a genesis of their existence in society." However, in formulating his explanations, he considered subjective factors to be the fundamental causes. Furthermore, even though these factors were located in both men and women, he primarily emphasized male egoism as the cause of the institutional forms of sexual inequality.

Consequently, Ward (*ibid.*:616) conceived of the following explanation for the genesis of all sexual relationships.

The motive power, the propelling force [of sexual relations] *is in man*, whom . . . we shall find to have shaped all the facts relating to the sexes pretty much after *his own mind*. The activities which have been put forth in this department of life, like all other activities, are but a series of struggles for the *gratification of desire*. Here, as everywhere else, *pleasure* is the object of all action. [our emphasis]

Quite consistently, this Benthamesque explanation was used in his discussion of the institution of *marriage,* to which he also ascribed hedonistic origins. Man's effort activates "all sexual-social phenomena [and] marriage, in whatever form, is but the successful issue of these efforts" (*ibid*). And the subjection of women was to be found, according to Ward, in the microscopic relations emanating solely within *this* institution. (The reader is urged to compare this with the source of woman's subjection discussed by Morgan and Engels.) The causal factors accounting for marriage were, therefore, man's invariable desire for sex, the aggressive acts which were the outcome of the desire, and women's modification of it.

Status of Women as Property Grounded in Male Egoism

Ward noted that he perceived the importance of private property in shaping marriage relations; but again, it was merely as the effect of male egoism and not as an effect of larger social and economic forces. In this process, as we shall see, the institution of marriage was seen as the cause of woman's status as property. Woman's status as property was not determined in the manner by which property had been generally instituted in society as a whole.

Ward's view of private property becomes logical, however, only when placed in the spirit of economic liberalism and the natural-law tradition. For example, he claimed that man was naturally bounded by his individual need for survival. Furthermore, man's life was regulated by a utilitarian desire for pleasure and the avoidance of pain. Wealth was the universal equivalent of the objects which enabled individuals to survive; therefore, "the pursuit of wealth is only the pursuit of happiness" (*ibid.:*494). In Ward's opinion, "the conception of permanent possession [1] is what gave to civilization its initial impulse" (*ibid.:*496). From axioms of this kind, Ward derived the portion of his theory that applied to marriage; it was only natural, Ward argued, for man to seek the sole and permanent possession of woman, who represented the ultimate in pleasure. After woman surrendered to man in the matter of sexual unions, she

at once becomes property, since any thing that affords its possessor gratification is property. Woman was capable of affording man the highest of gratifications, and therefore became property of the highest value. Marriage, under the prevailing form, became the symbol of transfer of ownership in the same manner as the formal seizin [*sic*] of lands. [*ibid.:*649]

Because of the interaction of the innate features of man and woman the transition from woman's high state to one of subjection occurred and:

the passivity of woman, coupled with the ardor of man, soon placed her wholly out of the account, and reduced her to the condition of a mere possession . . . differing little from that of any other class of property. [*ibid.:*617]

Thus we have one phase of the natural history of marriage.

Ward: Marriage as Solution to Hobbesian Problem

Scholars of ancient Greece and Rome had already described the limits of marriage in early class societies. Only the propertied classes possessed the right to marry.[2] Eventually,

Universal marriage, covering all classes, became prevalent in Western civilization along with the rise of bourgeois relations. Even then it took some time to mature as a legal mandate. The poor and propertyless passed through a period of "common law" marriage before they achieved the same kind of legal marriage ties sanctioned by the state, as did the wealthy classes. [Reed 1971:53]

Looking backward, however, Ward conjured up an institution that did not fit the social facts of that day.

The institution of marriage and the institution of the family are not necessarily identical; marriage can be considered a jural expression of family relations between men and women. The form and purpose of marriage are interpreted by the theorist according to the meaning and history he attaches to the family. In Ward's theory, the need for marriage was seen in Hobbesian terms as a problem of integration. According to Ward:

Like the seizure-method of obtaining other kinds of property, it [the seizure form of marriage] involved the race in perpetual combat, and rendered existence precarious and social progress impossible. Just as government was instituted to protect society from such ruthless modes of acquisition, so formal marriage was also instituted for the possession and retention of women. [*ibid.*]

Marriage, like Hobbes' Leviathan, was instituted in order to preserve the social order and prevent males from mutual destruction. It was a means for limiting the internecine struggle for the "scarce goods" (i.e., women) of this earth and therefore a form of social control.

Thomas: "Not Conceivable" that Women Could Control "Society" for Long

Thomas' explanation was structured by an attempted historical view of women, marriage, and the family through the use of such phrases as "in early times," "at a later time," and "in modern times." [3] His work, however, was basically ahistorical. His use of the undifferentiated term "primitivism" under which he incorporated all his observations of precapitalist relationships, was related to his emphasis on biological differences as determinants of male and female behavior. The primitive stages of humankind, moreover, were seen analogously to *childhood* and the maturational stages of childhood itself were perceived in terms of "the recapitulation of the race." [4] Thomas applied the racist *social Darwinist* conceptions of his time to the study of human evolution.

Although he purported to present a historical work, Thomas actually constructed an inchoate natural-law theory about the subjection of woman, a subjection institutionalized in the family. His theory, in recognizing the new "discoveries" of Bachofen and Morgan, alleged that a personified Mother Nature "obviously started out on the plan of having *woman the dominant force,* with man as an aid; but after a certain time there was a reversal of plan and *man became dominant* and woman dropped back into a somewhat unstable and adventitious relation to the social process" (*ibid.:*224 our emphasis). The turning point in woman's evolution and her true downfall came about with the advent of private property followed by the acquisition of larger territories. Woman became the subject of ownership by her husband, and indeed a tool to be used in the collecting, carrying, and producing of increased quantities of private property. The physical confrontation between groups of men who fought to gain more territory resulted in despotism, slavery, and the subjection of women.

Clarifying the egoistic conditions and the "law of might" underlying the downfall of women, Thomas proposed that man was sexually attracted to woman and secondarily interested in the child. However, the woman could not be separated from the child. Therefore, in the beginning the social group or mass "took place unconsciously about the female" (*ibid.:*69).[5] Thomas (*ibid.:*67) partly agreed with Bachofen "that the so-called 'mother-right' has everywhere preceded 'father-right'; and was the fund from which the latter was evolved." Nevertheless, while he found it quite reasonable that the mother's offspring and male admirer should congregate around the woman, "it is *not conceivable* that woman should definitely or long control the activities of society. In view of his superior power of making movements and applying force, the male must *inevitably* assume control of the life direction of the group, no matter what the genesis of the group" (*ibid*. our emphasis). Because "the law of might" has always existed and dominated social relations, Thomas indicated that it was only natural that in *exchange* for woman's much desired sexual favors, the male contributed his superior fighting capacity to protect her body and personal belongings. Thomas' conception of the origins of the family had a number of similarities with Ward's theory from which it was partly derived. It should also be noted in passing that Freud's explanation of the origins of the family in prehistory, which appeared in *Civilization and Its Discontents* almost fifty years after Ward's explanation, is partly based on very similar premises.

Thomas: Women's Education, "Equal Opportunity," and Technocratic Service

In *Sex and Society,* Thomas (1907:312) claimed that the existing differences between the white man and men of the "lower races . . . are no greater than they should be in view of the existing differences in opportunity." Thomas was fond of comparing women with the so-called lower races since lack of equal opportunity was also considered the means which held women down. Thomas proposed that the proper adaptation of women to modern culture could occur only by providing equal opportunities for women to participate "in the world of intellectual life." Orderly changes in the status of women, as well as "the remedy for the irregularity, pettiness, ill-health, and unserviceableness of modern women seems to lie, therefore, along educational lines" (*ibid.:*245). Ward was not alone in seeing education as a panacea for the oppression of women.

Although Thomas recognized women's formal right to equality, its enactment was restricted by existent institutional limits, for example, by marriage. Therefore the substance of women's rights was, in actuality, abandoned when he addressed himself to a consideration of what he euphemistically called "the good of mankind" or "the good of the species." Operationally, he found that "the function of morality is to regulate the activities of associated life so that all may have what we call fair play" (*ibid.:*149). Physical force was seen as one of nature's means to the maintenance of an orderly and stable society. But additional stabilizing forces were also needed and these, he asserted, were *marriage* and the *family*.

Marriage as a stabilizing force was needed because man, by nature, was equipped with the tendency to motion and wandering. In addition, marriage, according to Thomas (*ibid.:*227), "is a union favored by the scheme of nature because it is favorable to *the rearing and training of children,* and the groups practicing marriage . . . have the best chance of survival" (our emphasis). Thomas, to be sure, recognized that when female students married they became engulfed by the marriage and were therefore prevented from continuing their education or participating in the larger world. His remarks about the higher nature of the necessary relations between marriage, family, social stability, and group survival indicated, however, that he was ready to have women make the sacrifice of themselves and their emotional and intellectual development for "the good of mankind."

It might be argued that Thomas was not completely callous to the condition of women in the family setting; for example, he did offer "helpful hints" to men and women for alleviating the stultifying effects of family life on women. Regarding so-called happy marriages, he noted (*ibid.:*246) the existence of a trade-off, with the wife looking after the husband as another of her children, and the husband extending to his wife "that nurture and affection which is in his nature to give to *pets* and all *helpless* (and preferably *dumb*) creatures" (our emphasis).[6] If the woman gives her man motherly care—the man should generously grant her the privilege of seeking an occupation of her own choosing. In Thomas' writings, therefore, greater equity for women could be achieved through what was considered an "enlightened" accommodation between the sexes, regulated by tolerance of women's desires on the part of men, and affectionate regard for men on the part of women.

Gradualist Solutions to Subjection of Women

Ward's and Thomas' works signified a change in liberal theorizing about the subjection of women. Their writings represented the first shift in analytic emphasis among sociologists, from biological to *psychobiological* and *psychosocial* causation. Long before the North Americans became acquainted with Freudian terminology, they used the phrase "the social forces" to signify this new way of thinking about human relationships. Ward can be given much of the credit for popularizing this phrase because his evolutionary theory of society was known as the "theory of the social forces." Reproduction, for example, was classified under "reproductive forces." These were also considered to be a "social force," since reproductive forces were regarded as functional prerequisites for such basic social institutions as the family. They were therefore not regarded as necessary for the survival of the individual alone.

From an ideological point of view, however, there were certain continuities between the new and the traditional ways of thinking about women. We have noted, for example, that Thomas disputed with anthropologists who claimed that women were constitutionally inferior from the beginnings of time. But his writings make it clear that his counter-claim did no more than sidestep the basic issue. He became an accessory to Ward in modernizing sexist doctrines that were falling into disrepute. Their criticism, as we shall see, was typically liberal because it was linked to espousal of gradualist and ameliorative practices that maintained rather than eliminated sexually oppressive institutional relationships.

324

Ward: Education and
"Equal Opportunity" for Women

In regard to women, Ward felt that education was indispensable for hastening the evolutionary tendency toward the "ultimate restoration of the primeval state of nature." Ward declared that "even in our times we are beginning to observe the most unmistakable signs of the eventual resumption by woman of her lost scepter, and of her restoration to that empire over the emotional nature of man which the females of nearly all other animals exercise" (*ibid.*:615). Ward did not indicate what these "signs" of greater equality might actually consist of,[7] but it is possible that he was thinking primarily of the struggle for women's rights which was surging around him.

According to the logic of Ward's argument, however, women's rights could not be achieved on the basis of the proposals advanced by either militant social reformers or conservative laissez-faire liberals. What were the grounds for his middle-of-the-road, corporate-liberal logic? First, in arguing against militant reformers, Ward enunciated his utilitarian view that human progress (in this case represented by an extension of rights to a deserving group) should ultimately be measured in terms of happiness achieved. He indicated, however, that one cannot voluntarily decide to be happy, nor can happiness be achieved directly on the command of others. Because of this, reform by direct legal means could not be used to make people happy. He stated: "Social reform however clearly perceived by the legislator can not be brought about by direct legislation, either positive . . . or negative" [*ibid.*:II, 545]. On the other hand, with regard to laissez-faire solutions, Ward was aware that in the case of those most in need, the laissez-faire liberal approach to happiness would fail. Because he also included women among the neediest, Ward thereby implied that the natural forces of competition would not ameliorate their needy condition. After these casuistic ruminations, Ward finally suggested that the most indirect and comprehensive means for achieving happiness for women was universal, compulsory, state-supported education.

Ward and Thomas were not surrounded merely by scholarly works on the subjection of women. During the period in which they wrote, the United States was conspicuously distinguished by the activities of women's rights movements that were more advanced than those in England. These movements also encompassed struggles for social, economic, and political equality (Flexner 1970:113 ff.). The fact that Wyoming and Utah granted suffrage during the 1870s points to the growing power of the women's movements. In 1878 the Anthony amendment for woman suffrage (which eventually passed in 1920 as the nineteenth amendment to the Constitution) was introduced for the first time. One year before the publication of Ward's *Dynamic Sociology,* both houses of Congress, composed, of course, entirely of men, appointed select committees on woman suffrage. Both of these committees made favorable reports. It is highly likely that the intense feminist activities that began in the first half of the nineteenth century were instrumental in bringing about

Ward's substantial treatment of the subjection of women in the first place. He is known to have attended women's reform meetings in the 1860s.[8]

It should be noted that Ward ignored the persistent criticism of bourgeois family relationships by socialists during the nineteenth century. It should be further noted that although he selected education from among the variety of proposals expressed by the women's rights movements, no mention was made of the struggle for women's participation in government. One wonders why he supported women's suffrage in his private life but refrained from discussing it in his major theoretical works. Perhaps the motivation behind this omission can be discovered in his later work, *Applied Sociology* (1906), in which he specifically warned sociologists about the dangers of organizing applied sociological inquiries around immediate political issues.

Ward's failings are made even more salient by comparing his 1883 "middle-of-the-road" argument against legislative reform with John Stuart Mill's 1869 work on women entitled *The Subjection of Women*.[9] Mill had argued (as did Ward and Thomas) that the rights of women should *not* be determined by the power of might, which was exercised in this case by the absolutely unchecked male desire for power. But Mill was able to nullify the notion that women were by nature inferior and, at the same time, to justify and argue directly for legislation regarding woman suffrage, women's equal claim to their own children, the equality of married women before the law, and the right of married women to have exclusive control over their property. On the other hand, Ward, the sociologist, as we have seen, abandoned even a minimal short-range political solution to the subjection of women. In his major theoretical works he focused entirely on a *gradualist* solution to this problem.[10]

Ward's Gradualism

Ward was fully aware that radical alternatives to his gradualism were being expressed by socialist movements.[11] Consequently, as early as 1883 we find him comparing his own approach with more radical attempts toward greater economic equality:

Others will wonder why so little is said in this work of the great social economic problems: why the distribution of wealth, rather than of education, is not insisted upon, since happiness depends greatly upon the possession of the objects of desire. . . . The answer to all such criticisms must be that the sole object of this treatise is to arrive at the initial means. . . . And it is high time for socialists to perceive that, as a rule, they are working at the roof instead of at the foundation of the structure which they desire to erect. . . . The distribution of knowledge underlies all social reform. [*ibid.*:597–598 our emphasis]

The socialists were outspoken about the repressive effects of poverty on family life. They were also indignant about the exploitation of women who labored in sweatshops and textile mills. They believed that the eradication of the great inequalities in wealth [12] in the United States should be an important goal for those interested in the liberation of most women in the country. Incredible as it may seem, however, Ward felt that an equal distribution of *knowledge* rather than wealth, for example, would do more for the emancipation of women. The demand for the equal distribution of knowledge was also considered much more fundamental for achieving sexual equality than all the socialist schemes in this regard. Even when Ward's objections to Spencer's neo-Malthusian conception of competition are taken into account, it becomes obvious that his approach to sexual equality was circumscribed by an undying commitment to competition in the marketplace. This competition was regarded as the only feasible means to equity in the realizable future— irrespective of whether the values at stake involved loaves of bread or sexual equality.

NOTES

1. The "conception of permanent pleasure" was a euphemism to symbolize a desire for the private ownership of property. This desire was considered a derivative of man's basic needs for reproduction and nutrition, in much the same way that Locke considered the desire for private property to be a derivative of the individual's need to survive.

2. "Patriarchal Roman marriage was instituted by the patricians for their own purposes. . . . The patrician privilege consisted in having a legally recognized heir. The propertied patricians did not recognize the marriage arrangements of the propertyless plebians as being marriage at all. . . . Moreover, they refused to allow them to adopt legal marriage because they would thereby have become patricians, recognized owners of property" (Briffault 1959:231).

3. It was the methodological fashion at the turn of the century to present historical supporting statements, including a detailed analysis of prehistoric social relations. Other notable examples of this fashion were Bebel's *Woman in the Past, Present and Future* and Ward's *Dynamic Sociology*. These were triggered by the contemporary research published by anthropologists such as Bachofen, Morgan, Tylor, and McLennan.

4. Thomas (1907:281–282) stated some disagreement with this theory with regard to the maturational stages of childhood itself. But his disagreement indicated his *agreement* with the *general* conception because in disagreeing he merely stated that some children escape the socialization effects which enabled them to become mature. Consequently they never outgrow their "savage" characteristics.

5. This embryonic group evolved into marriage; for Thomas (*ibid.:*227) agreed with Westermarck that "children are not the result of marriage, but marriage is the result of children."

6. All parts of this quotation, including the parenthetical remark, belong to Thomas. We have only added the emphases.

7. Ward did suggest that differences in dress, fashions, speech, etc., between the sexes would disappear as women obtained greater equality with men. This development, however, was much more in the nature of a prediction than a description of conditions in 1883.

8. Reference to attendance at these meetings with his wife can be found in his diary (see Ward 1935).

9. This comparison is apt because the title "The Subjection of Women," applied to one of the most important sections of Ward's discussion of women, marriage, and the family, which was borrowed from Mill (Ward 1883:I,648).

10. However, although Ward's gradualist solution to sexual inequality may lack credibility, it was certainly not inconsistent with his evolutionary theory of the subjection of women. It should be recalled that his theory provided a pseudoscientific warrant for the doctrine of female inferiority. Men, according to this theory, were indeed intellectually superior to women because of long-standing environmental conditioning. What

could be a more logical solution to women's inequality than education in this sexist frame of reference? If Ward's arguments were stated in the language of modern liberalism, it would be said that given women's intellectual inferiority to men, by all means educate them! Give them "equal opportunities" to overcome their alleged stupidity and to compete with men in "true equality." Break the vicious cycle of female inferiority! (Any relation between these corporate-liberal demands for sexual equality and the "equal opportunity—war on poverty" approaches today will not seem accidental to the thoughtful reader.)

11. It should be noted that socialist works by Marx and Engels had discussed the subjection of women and the bourgeois family as early as the late 1840's.' Bebel's *Die Frau und der Sozialismus* was published in 1879, and English translations appeared in the United States toward the end of the century.

12. In nineteenth-century America, small groups of radical women struck for the ten-hour working day and equal pay for equal work. Emma Goldman and Victoria Woodhull were labeled "free lovers" because of their forthright statements and actions regarding the "outrage" of bourgeois marriage laws. These laws were based on the idea of property and compulsion rather than love and free choice.

European socialists saw an inherent connection between what they called the "women question" and the entire oppressive social system. August Bebel (1897:2–3) expressed this problem and its solution in a way typical of the radicals before the turn of the century. The problem was of such an extreme nature that a *"complete solution of the Women's Question is as unattainable as the solution of the Labor Question under the existing social and political institutions."*

CHAPTER 41

Sexism and Corporate Liberalism

Ward and Thomas conceded that women should be given the formal right to sexual equality and equal educational opportunity. But these rights were merely formal because they were not supported by the advocacy of institutional changes in either the family or the market. These men talked about rights and opportunities for women without considering significant changes in family relationships where, for example, housekeeping and child-raising chores have the huge dimensions and dark depths of an iceberg. In addition to "educational opportunity," like other leading sociologists, Ward and Thomas offered the carrot of the Promised Land of Hearth and Home but neglected to warn the unwary of its voracious appetite which consumes the emotions, physical strength, and mental energy, and leaves little over to be applied to woman's own growth and development. Nor were changes envisaged in the political economy of capitalism, with its emphasis on acquisition and consumption of private property, conformity with political institutions, and the encouragement of competition with one's peers. Surely the possibility of achieving the liberation of women in the forseeable future was furthest from their minds.

What explains the theoretical directions developed by Ward and Thomas? Why did these sociological "experts" on sexual relationships contrive such pseudoscientific nonsense about the subjection of women and its solution? Indeed, a more significant question would ask: Why did none of the leading sociologists during the formative years play a positive role with regard to the liberation of women? This question can be answered if sexist writings during these years are evaluated within a more comprehensive ideological framework.

Same Categories and Strategies for Sexual, Racial, and National Inequality

Book I has shown that during the formative years, classical and laissez-faire liberal assumptions about man and society were being modified by leading scholars. It will be noted in later chapters that this modification was occurring not only in sociology but in every other social science discipline and professional field. A new variant of the liberal ideology, corporate liberalism, came into being. This variant provided a new ethical and analytic liberal vocabulary for explaining and justifying sexist institutions and sexual inequality. This "scientific" vocabulary certainly played no positive role in liberating womankind.

Book I has also indicated the events leading to the generation of corporate-liberal ideas among sociologists. The reconstitution of classical and laissez-faire modes of liberal thought was necessitated by the tumultuous social instabilities accompanying the rise of monopoly capitalism in the United States. Concomitant with the widespread economic and political instability, large-scale industrial violence increasingly characterized the relations between capital and labor. National traditions seemed to be jeopardized by extensive immigration and rapid industrial change. The very foundations of capitalism itself were being attacked by new, militant socialist and anarchist movements.

The responses of elite North American sociologists to the issue of women's equality were inextricably interwoven with their ideological reactions to these other nationwide developments. Because of this, one of the most significant generalizations about the formative years is that the theoretical categories and analytic strategies that were crucial to Ward's and Thomas' analyses of *sexual* inequality, were similar to those being used to explain *racial* and *national* inequality. Indeed, even their proposals for reform of inequitable sexual relationships differed little from the gradualist and ameliorative proposals being advanced for assimilating immigrants or "upgrading" oppressed racial groups. Neither their sexist writings nor their sexual reforms were independent of corporate-liberal attitudes and technocratic solutions to other outstanding issues of the time.

329

Women and Family:
Instruments of Social Control

Turning to long-range solutions to social problems, the leading North American sociologists focused on educative institutions and socialization practices which would lead to the moral regeneration of the population. They favored Americanization programs aimed at the social and political indoctrination of immigrants. They also emphasized the kinds of family relationships which would facilitate "normal" adjustments to established institutions. Operationally interpreted, "normality" and "adjustment" meant the inculcation in men of firm industrial discipline, strong personal ambition, and the harmonious blend of the conforming and aggressive characteristics required for a smoothly functioning industrial labor force.

The family was also perceived in a larger frame. Improvident behavior, extreme selfishness, prejudicial attitudes, and the lack of personal ambition were being defined as the *causes* of social *unrest, crime, racism, war,* and *poverty*. Consequently, the family was considered important precisely because it was eventually regarded as a prime institutional means for achieving social stability and order. The family could be expected to eliminate the causes of outstanding social problems through the proper socialization of individual moral values, self-control, status attitudes, and ethnic or racial tolerance.

In this technocratic and corporate-liberal frame of reference, women were conceived chiefly as *instruments* of social control. Their activities were theoretically organized around the "obligation" to properly socialize the present and future members of the labor force, their husbands and children. (These inadequately socialized individuals were also the likely candidates for criminal and revolutionary behavior.) This obligation, furthermore, was given the force of their psychologized version of natural law: women's nature was defined as "shy," "timid," "passive," "stationary," "stable," "maternal," "accommodating," "nurturant," and "sympathetic." Moreover, "the role of the woman," "the mother role," and "the wifely role" were perceived as "adaptations" to "specialized" or "complementary" modes of functioning. These modes buttressed male temperaments and male activities outside the home, satisfying the social imperatives of major institutions in capitalist societies.

In addition to being instruments of social control, women, as we shall presently see, were also regarded as *objects* of social control. Ward and Thomas, for example, felt that education would improve women's chances for equality with men. But the technocratic belief that women would also become more "serviceable" to society, remained in the foreground of their thoughts. Women were perceived as a factor in "social" production, whose management would increase or decrease social "expenses" and the "efficient" functioning of society.

Technocratic Justifications
for Ameliorative Change

At the beginning of the nineteenth century, class domination, imperialist exploitation, and the subjection of women were not defined by liberals as benefiting ruling classes, metropolitan imperialist nations, or male supremists alone. Most of humanity (including the very persons who were the victims of exploitation, racism, and sexism) were alleged to be the beneficiaries of these forms of oppression. Toward the end of the nineteenth century, many scholars continued to structure their justifications of class, sex, and other oppression on the basis of hedonistic utilitarianism, which was one of the most important ethical perspectives developed by classical liberal-functionalists. With the rise of the modern North American universities, however, corporate-liberal functionalism also began to provide a new general analytic strategy for justifying all outstanding forms of social inequality. This strategy was constituted, in part, by defining inequality as a necessary precondition for the survival of major institutions that were central to capitalist political economies. At first, the new corporate liberals, like those before them, justified their liberal policies on the basis of the "greatest happiness" for the greatest number. In time, however, the hedonistic rhetoric was generally abandoned in favor of a *technocratic* rhetoric.

We have seen, for example, that Ward was a hedonistic utilitarian; however, he was also a transitional figure who helped bridge laissez-faire liberalism and corporate liberalism by modifying Spencer's social Darwinism and creating a *reform* Darwinist approach to social change. As a consequence, Ward justified his social reforms in two ways. He grounded universal education, firstly, in *individual* happiness (and therefore in individual needs). But he also justified education by reference to the alleged *social* imperatives that were necessary (i.e., functional prerequisites) for the survival of groups, institutions, political economies, or the entire human species. Ward's concept of universal education, therefore, generally referred less to individual potentiality than to the *adjustment* by individuals to the norms of established institutions.

During the formative years of North American sociology, the leading scholars also talked in terms of "social efficiency," "social engineering," and the "domestication" or "socialization" of people. Book I noted that Ward preferred to use the term "efficiency." As a corollary, Ward repeatedly referred to the *expense* to "society" of uneducated groups.[1] Of course, from an operational point of view, "society" generally meant *capitalism*. He further argued that society should not be concerned solely with these expensive losses; it should also be interested in maximizing progress. To accomplish this, however, "society" needed an educated work force; therefore, it could ill afford to lose the potential of 51 percent of the population. Indeed, "society" could *profit* greatly from sexual equality. Sexual equality was good because it was beneficial to "society."

Thomas' writings were no exception to this development of technocratic justifications. In the last paragraph of his work *Sex and Society,* for example, Thomas stated that the increasing participation of "women and the lower races" would make a positive contribution to the development of civilization because it would ultimately reconstruct "our habits on more sympathetic and equitable principles." [2] He concluded that this would enable our civilization to remain "the highest" (i.e., the fittest), for "certain it is that no civilization can remain the highest if another civilization adds to the intelligence of its men the intelligence of its women" (*ibid. :*314). Sexual equality is good because it enables "civilization" to survive by becoming even fitter than it was before; all humankind is therefore "benefited" by sexual and racial equality.

Thomas, like Ward, did not use the terms "capitalism" or "imperialism." But it is not difficult to determine the particular kind of society Thomas referred to when writing about "women and the lower races." It can be easily demonstrated that such terms as "social groups," "present civilization," "society as a whole," "the human species," or "the race," usually functioned as euphemisms for capitalist and imperialist institutions, or capitalist political economies as a whole.

Ward's Sexual Theories Ridiculed

Ward protected his theories with careful qualifications. He took pains to note that his writings on sexual equality should not be regarded as a critical statement about men: he wrote, for example, "I have only been seeking to study the condition of society not to criticize the conduct of its members" (1883:II,656).[3] Ward's advocacy of sexual equality was also carefully circumscribed by a gradualist program for social change: sexual equality was considered a definite possibility but it would come about in the far and distant future. The chapters to come will note, however, that despite his mousy apologies and tortoiselike programs, by 1909 scholars like Charles Ellwood and Henry Ford Jones were taking Ward to task for his writings on sexual equality. In particular, his prediction of the distant cyclical revival of prehistoric sexual customs (by which men and women could dissolve their marriages by mutual consent) was stoutly ridiculed.[4] An increasingly conservative trend in social and political thought was occurring among the leading sociologists. Finally, Ward's muted vision of full sexual equality at home and in the market was completely washed away by the initial wave of Freudian thought, with its antiegalitarian concepts of adjustment and instincts as well as its emphasis on the individual, subjective sources of human misery.

Ward's and Thomas' theories about women and the family were very limited. The corporate-liberal, atomistic approach to social problems was a far cry from an integrated, consistent moral statement of effective action. Their analytic approaches were studded with inaccuracies, inconsistencies, and justifications that belied their proclaimed advocacy of women's rights. Ward and Thomas failed to present these rights as a *humanistic* necessity. They perpetuated the myth that women made almost no contribution to the development of civilization.[5] They ignored the relation between class privilege and educational opportunities.[6] And their trust in the liberating force of male tolerance for women's interests was positively ludicrous.

There is a different spirit among many sociologists today. Some of them are becoming aware of the implicit ideological bias that has accompanied the vision of the family as an "equilibrated social system"—others are evaluating the concept of woman as complementary to man. They are able to recognize the antihuman, technocratic obsession with social stability and order that underlie Ward's (1883:I,657) suggestion that "it is high time that all the forces of society were brought into action, and it is especially necessary that those vast complementary forces which woman alone can wield will be given free rein, and the whole machinery of society be set into full and harmonious operation."

These scholars are no longer following the corporate-liberal tradition which men like Ward established in the United States. They are no longer applying conceptual band-aids to a decrepit and alienating capitalist society. They are concerned, instead, with the liberating quality of daily interchanges between men and women, and are questioning the fundamental causes of the subjection of women in both capitalist and socialist societies. Today there is a growing number of scholars who recognize that these causes are embedded in such basic institutions as the patriarchal family and the private ownership of property; that the problems of sexism are not epiphenomenal expressions of individual egoism but expressions of the political economy as a whole.

NOTES

1. Here are two examples from Ward's *Dynamic Sociology:*
   From an economical point of view, an uneducated class is an expensive class. [1883:II,589]

   The total cost of supporting, punishing, and guarding against [ignorant paupers, beggars and criminals] constitutes half the charge of all legitimate government. [*ibid.*:II,594]
2. These changes, Thomas (1907:314) indicated, would temper male egoism (i.e., "man's fighting instincts and techniques"), which was seen by corporate-liberal scholars as the basis for the problem of social *order* in laissez-faire capitalist societies.
3. This statement was made specifically in reference to the implications for men of his writings on sexual equality.
4. Chapter 30 above noted that in 1909, Ford (a self-styled [social] "Darwinian" political scientist) singled out Ward in his critique of sociologists and what to him was their espousal of free love and the destruction of America's most sacrosanct institutions. He wrote (1909a:101): "That is just what Professor Ward holds to be the end of social effort and the blessed consummation of the labors of the sociologists . . . robust sociologists contend that we should all be as free to find our affinities as cats or dogs. Suggestions of trial marriage are made simply as a temporary palliative of an enslaving institution. The trouble with divorce laws is not that they are loose, but that there should be any laws at all. Human beings should be free to mate as they please, and separate as

they please, like other animals enjoying their natural freedom." Charles Ellwood (1909b:105) joined this argument with: "Very few sociologists of reputed standing endorse the revolutionary ideas which he [Ford] credits all with possessing. Free love, trial marriage, divorce by mutual consent . . . and other anarchist ideas . . . have, perhaps, been *more powerfully combated by them* than by any other class of scientific men" (our emphasis).

5. "Civilization and progress," Ward (1883:I,657) wrote, "have hitherto been carried forward by the male half alone."

6. Ward (1883:II,594) claimed, for example, that the application of education as a means of social progress has been left to chance throughout history. He stated that the reason why "civilization," which is due to "knowledge" achieved by education, has not reached the masses is because education has been left to chance. This contention, however, is absurd. Education has been historically controlled by representatives of the ruling classes. In the main, education previously was available to clerical and aristocratic students and later to wealthy or middle-class families which could afford to have sons devoted to academic and intellectual pursuits. Even today, educational opportunities from the end of high school onwards still seem largely a middle-class affair.

PART ELEVEN

The Construction
of the
Freud-Thomas Bridge

CHAPTER 42

*Freudianism
and Corporate Liberalism*

The previous chapters have discussed transitional corporate-liberal writings about marriage, the family, and the subjection of women. Although the coming chapters consider Freud's work, they will relate to other issues, and we will hardly touch on his well-known male chauvinist views. In fact, these chapters will focus on another significant topic; namely, certain developments regarding liberal theories of "deviant behavior," radical movements, and social change. Since these particular developments involved Freudian ideas, this chapter will introduce this topic through a discussion of his social philosophy. Subsequent chapters will point out that although the leading second generation Americans may have generally rejected Freud's concept of the libido, such men as Thomas, Weatherly, Park, Chapin, and Ogburn accepted other psychoanalytic assumptions. In his later writings, Thomas, for instance, coupled Freud's mechanisms of defense with his own notions about individual "definitions" of "critical" situations. He used this combination of ideas to explain various types of personal "adaptations" to "socially disorganized" (e.g., neo-Hobbesian) conditions.

Before our discussion begins, it is important to emphasize its limited scope. The following analysis of Freud's perspective is addressed *only* to his major solutions to the problems of social integration and social change. It is *not*

335

concerned with the clinical aspects of psychoanalysis. These aspects of Freud's work are extremely varied and complex; they also involve standards, norms and operating principles that may depart greatly from Freud's *social* philosophy. In turning our attention to the relation between his personality conceptions and the problems of social integration and social change, we shall concentrate on *Civilization and Its Discontents* (1957). This work represents one of Freud's last attempts to apply psychoanalytic principles to macroscopic sociological relationships. Although it was published after the formative years in the development of sociology, it represents a concise statement of hegemonic ideas that were being adopted by sociologists from his earlier works.

In interpreting Freud's "sociological" explanations in *Civilization and Its Discontents* as expressive of a *corporate-liberal* standpoint, we shall briefly illustrate the thesis that Freud's theory of man and society was accepted precisely because it supplied hegemonic conceptions that were complementary, both ideologically and descriptively, to the sociological conceptions being generated during the rise of monopoly capitalism, not only in the United States but throughout the Western World.

Psychological Reductionism in Sociological Analysis

The discussion of the impact of Sigmund Freud on American sociology must take into account the prevalence of psychological assumptions about the nature of sociological relationships that were in wide currency among American scholars before they became associated with psychoanalysis. American scholars had viewed social structures as expressions of instincts or feelings, and personality categories that were functionally equivalent to the "superego" had also appeared among them by the turn of the century. In formulating theories about the relationships between psychic forces, social control and the economistic allocation of human resources, the pioneering sociologists invariably fell back on psychologistic variables and mechanisms. Individuals were driven by basic needs; instituted behavior was a manifestation of group minds or group interests; the relations between institutions were based on conflicting but reconcilable interests, and social stability was achieved by accommodations between "right-minded" individuals or groups.

Seventeenth- and eighteenth-century scholars had also perceived the importance of psychological factors as prime movers of individual conduct. Nor were these factors overlooked by nineteenth-century scholars. In the early nineteenth century, Comte was to be found stating (Chugerman 1965:276) that "the affections, the inclinations, the passions constitute the principal motor forces of human life." In light of this many-centuried historical development, therefore, Ward's psychic forces were not unique in the annals of social science. However, his socially imperative psychic forces (i.e., the social forces) were particularly significant because they were integrated into a rudimentary corporate-liberal theory of man and society. This theory went beyond Comtean and Spencerian justifications for competition and private property, for it also supported a new stage of economic development, the concentration of privately owned capital, the expansion of imperialism, and the development of the corporate-liberal state.[1]

Even critical discussions between men like Ward, Giddings, and Small neglected to challenge the psychological foundations on which the field was being constructed. In objecting to Ward's view that "feeling" was the motive power for social change, for example, Giddings in actuality extended psychologism by claiming that feeling also accounted for "static" (i.e., stable) social formations. According to the logic of Giddings' argument, Ward did not go far enough in his psychologistic analysis of the social functions of feeling. When everything was said and done, all agreed with Ward (1903:101) that "sociology must have a psychological basis." Giddings (Stern 1938:392, n34) proclaimed, "Sociology is a psychological science." Small unequivocally declared, "Nothing is social which is not psychical." (Hinkle 1957:576–577).

Psychoanalytic Principles and Macrosocial Relationships

Both Freud and Ward considered the individual's need to satisfy hunger and to reproduce as important human motives. For example, Ward regarded *psychic forces* as the proximate cause of social relationships even though some of these forces were believed to be derivatives of biological or "vital forces." He asserted in 1883, for example, that the *nutritional* and *reproductive* desires "constitute the motive, either direct or indirect, to the greater part of all his [man's] acts." To this, Ward (1903:256–257) added the observation that if, as a result of the satisfaction of desires, a feeling is pleasurable, "there is either an ascetic sense of its sinfulness or a sense of shame at its avowal." However, unlike Freud, Ward did not detail the dynamics of guilt or shame. Nor did he utilize personality conceptions that departed greatly from the slightly modified eighteenth-century utilitarian models used by Spencerians.

Freud, on the other hand—and at a later date—placed little emphasis on nutritional needs in explaining social relations, although he (1957:95) wrote: "At the beginning, I took as my starting-point the poet-philosopher Schiller's aphorism, that *hunger* and *love* make the world go around." In Freud's earlier view, "hunger would serve to represent those instincts which aim at preservation of the individual; love seeks for objects; its chief function . . . is preservation of the species." He reflected that this contrast between ego instincts and object instincts was one of the first to arise. It is interesting to note that certain aspects of this contrast appear to be based on the classical dichotomy between individual and social imperatives. Hunger was regarded as functionally necessary for individuals while love was imperative for society. However, Freud generally placed greater emphasis on love, which he *also* regarded as necessary for individuals. The main point, however, is that his counterpart to Ward's psychic forces was constituted, in this case, by love and its derivatives; these "instincts" were both individually *and* socially imperative. Freud, like Ward, employed these "forces" in explaining the origin of family and nonfamily relationships. Freud, thus far, was walking a familiar path.

In *Civilization and Its Discontents* Freud did not approach the development of the modern problem of social integration with a single simple historical scheme. He perceived the evolution of civilization in terms of a loose, if not almost totally disconnected series of system states, the *last* of which posed the modern problem of integration. Let us examine the first of these evolutionary "stages."

Inquiring into the origins of culture,[2] Freud suggested that families originated in a fair exchange between males and females during the period when the desire for "genital satisfaction" was inhibited. The male, according to Freud (*ibid.*:65–66), needed to keep his "sexual objects" near him, while the female needed protection by the stronger male. However, with the birth of children, this fair exchange was considered insufficient for integrating the family arrangement within a "cultural" framework. It was noted that "the one *essential* feature of culture" was lacking: "the will of the father, the head of it [the family] was *unfettered*" (our emphasis). It was also claimed that the sons discovered that "several men united can be stronger than a single man" by overpowering the father. After making this discovery of social control, the sons initiated the "totemic stage of culture," which was apparently integrated in the main by bringing under collective control the uncontrollable authority of a single, powerful man. *Individualism* was regulated by the "will" of the *collective* body; the family as a "cultural entity" was now stabilized. In Freud's opinion, this first stage of social development was "founded upon the *restrictions* that the [members of the] *band* were obliged to impose on one another in order to maintain this new system" (our emphasis).

We have previously encountered "scarcity" or "limited" fund notions in the mechanisms employed by Malthus, Spencer, and Durkheim. Freud introduced a new mechanism in order to explain the development of social ties beyond the family. This mechanism was analogous to an imaginative political economy of biopsychological relationships, which was organized around the economistic allocations of a limited fund of "libidinal energy."

In *Civilization and Its Discontents,* Freud assumed the existence of a limited fund of psychic energy and that the wise allocation of this scarce resource could be used to explain the emergence of social relations outside of the family. The wisdom of this allocation was based on various assumptions, including the assumption that the classical contradiction between the individual and society was embodied within each and every individual. The contradictions expressed by this natural law assumption were particularly salient in Freud's concept of primitive man.

338

Freud's *Primitive* Economistic, Prudent, and Chauvinistic Man

Upon describing the personalities of primitive men, Freud oscillated between his description of these personalities and personality dynamics which allegedly held true for all times and places. Freud (*ibid.*:135–136) stated, for example, that two trends exist in every individual: "one toward personal happiness and the other towards unity with the rest of humanity." These two trends "must contend with each other," but the conflict between personal happiness (the individual good) and the unity of humanity (the social good) was not considered irreconcilable in every instance. When applied to prehistoric man, this conflict was merely considered "a dissension in the camp of the libido itself, comparable to the contest between the *ego* and its *objects* for a *share of the libido* and it does eventually admit of a solution in the individual . . ." (our emphasis). The eternal "contest" between ego and its objects was also comparable to competition between competitors in a marketplace; Freud encouraged this comparison by adding that "happiness is a problem in the *economics* of the libido in each individual . . . just as a cautious *businessman* avoids *investing all his capital in one concern,* so wisdom would probably admonish us not to anticipate all our happiness from one quarter alone" (*ibid.*:41 our emphasis).

The economics of the libido encouraged long-term rather than short-term gratifications. Freud (*ibid.*:28–29) declared that "unbridled gratification of all desires forces itself into the foreground as the most alluring guiding principle, but it entails preferring enjoyment to caution and penalizes itself after short indulgences." Consequently, in regard to primitive man, Freud's economistic analysis of the allocation of scarce libidinal resources was concerned with achievement of long-term, that is, *stable,* gratification. Like a corporation manager who wants to maximize the average rate of profit over a long period of time, Freud argued that "success is never certain" and organized his claims around future contingencies that might decrease individual happiness.

The economics of the libido also called for a diversification of investments. Freud (*ibid.*:69) noted that primitive "man . . . found by experience that sexual [genital] love afforded him his greatest satisfaction." Consequently, genital love became in effect "a prototype of all happiness to him" and he "must have been thereby impelled to seek his happiness further along the path of sexual relations, to make genital eroticism the central point of his life." But because his love was confined to his mate, prehistoric man became "to a very dangerous degree dependent on a part of the outer world, namely, on his chosen love-object, and this exposes him to most painful suffering if he is rejected by it or loses it through death or defection."

According to Freud (*ibid.*:71–72), the "wise men of all ages have warned man against becoming totally dependent for gratification on a single person."

Heeding the warning to avoid this all-or-nothing solution to happiness, man has learned to inhibit his love and create a derivative from the original genital love called "aim-inhibited" love. He has reached out "beyond the family and [created] new bonds with others who before were strangers." Thus, "genital love leads to the forming of new families, aim-inhibited love to 'friendships' which are valuable culturally because they do not entail many of the limitations of genital love—for instance, its exclusiveness." In short, faced with an all-or-nothing possibility, primitive men are alleged to have acted like rational businessmen who are overly anxious about investing all their money in one enterprise. The former learned to diversify their investments. Hence, it was claimed that for ordinary men, prudent behavior would net a greater amount of happiness when the balance of pleasure and pain was shrewdly calculated over the long range. Primitive man was obviously a modern finance-capitalist in disguise.

Freud and the Subjection of Women

Freud's concept of primitive man was also organized around a chauvinistic as well as an economic model of man. Male supremist standards were used to define both the family and nonfamily identifications as *natural* and *normal* states for men. These standards, as we shall see, excluded that which was naturally normal for women.

What were the optimum conditions for maximizing the happiness of women? What relationships were they experiencing while the men were busily protecting themselves against unwise single-person relationships? According to Freud (*ibid.*:72–73) women reacted negatively and created "discord" because of their "conservative" opposition to the "cultural trends" which were determined by men. Women still represented "the interests of the family and sexual life" even though "the work of civilization [became] more and more men's business." This work compelled men "to sublimations of instinct which women [were] not easily able to achieve." Furthermore, "Since man has not an unlimited amount of mental energy at his disposal, he must accomplish his tasks by distributing his libido to the best advantage." As a result, primitive man diversified his libidinal investments and thereby became more attentive to the imperatives of his culture, while women found themselves "forced into the background by the claims of [this] culture and she adopts an inimical attitude towards it."

Freud's *Modern,* Socially Controlled, Economic Man

In *Civilization and Its Discontents,* Freud outlined his normative concept of modern man. The political implications of this normative concept can be clarified by reference to Ward, Ross, Small and Durkheim. It will be recalled that none of these corporate liberals felt that social integration was possible merely on the basis of the functional interdependence of individuals or groups established by marketplace exchanges and the division of labor. In their view, the natural (i.e., the unregulated) forces of competition undermined social solidarity in modern societies. Freud was also a natural-law scholar who questioned the integrative effects of the free marketplace. But Freud used the category of aggression rather than egoism to reify the competitive and possessive relationships that he perceived among his fellow men during his lifetime.

Freud (*ibid.*:102) vaguely noted, for example, that libidinal ties must reinforce the "advantages of common work" in order to maintain a stable and integrated civilization because "the natural instinct of *aggressiveness* in man, the hostility of each one against all and of all against each one, opposes this programme of civilization" (our emphasis). Once his "aggression" is recognized as functioning like the "natural" forces of competition, and his "advantages of common work" are recognized as analogous to exchange and division of labor, then Freud's affinity with contemporary corporate liberal scholars becomes clear. In his opinion (*ibid.*), aggressive instincts constituted "the most powerful obstacle to culture." In fact, "the *fateful question* of the human species," Freud (*ibid.*:143–144) declared, is whether the culture "will succeed in mastering the derangements of communal life caused by the human instinct of aggression and self-destruction" (our emphasis).

According to Freud (*ibid.*:43), aggressiveness was at the seat of the modern problem of integration primarily because of the "inadequacy of our method of *regulating* human relations in the family, the community and the state" (our emphasis). Insofar as this inadequacy was based on human nature, Freud felt it might not be possible to institute ameliorative changes in any but a slow and painful manner. However, if mankind was interested in progressive change, it would have to pay attention to certain "scientific principles" (i.e., technocratic principles) necessary for developing more adequate methods of regulating human aggression. These principles were based, above all, on an explanation of the process whereby guilt was socialized in children.

Freud asserted that during the socialization of the child, the fear of punishment from "external" authority figures gives rise to feelings of shame. In time, these feelings are replaced by a sense of guilt. Once internalized, the mechanism of guilt enables the child to regulate his instinctual desires without the direct, authoritative presence of his parents or other representatives of the moral standpoint of the larger community. In developing a sense of guilt, each individual acquires an ever-present reminder of significant authority figures whose actions typically integrate and control various aspects of the social order (father-family, state-society). Moreover, because it becomes an autonomous self-regulating mechanism, the sense of guilt also becomes a significant mode of integration independent of preexisting agencies of social control. This mechanism enables the precepts of stable forms of social authority to be transmitted from one generation to the next. *Prevailing forms of social control thereby become enduring forms of control.*

Liberal-Syndicalism and Modern Freudian Man

Many parallels exist between Freud's concept of modern man and liberal-syndicalist solutions to the problem of social integration. In liberal-syndicalist writings, for example, socialization originally referred to those processes primarily influencing the moral regeneration of interest groups. Such processes included the authoritative presence of the state. The state was conceived as an integrative mechanism that would keep watch over interest groups and maintain equitable forms of distributive justice. Although some sociologists replaced the state by vague references to society, mores, public opinion, or the judgement of mankind, some *agent of social control* was perceived to be the prime necessity for social stability. Furthermore, whether or not sociologists used the term "accommodation" instead of "socialization," there was still a need for some *organizing principle* to account for progressive changes as well as stability in a "properly" controlled society.

In Freud's writings, personal control is considered an extremely important prerequisite for the progressive development of civilization (*ibid.:*123). In his view (*ibid.:*105), the sense of guilt enables "civilization" to obtain "the mastery over the dangerous love of aggression in individuals by enfeebling and disarming it and setting up an institution within their minds to keep watch over it like a garrison within a conquered city." The function of guilt, therefore, is analogous to the functions of the "state," "society," "mores," "public opinion," and "the judgement of mankind" in liberal-syndicalism.

Of course, Freud's analysis of the necessary conditions for the progressive development of civilization was primarily directed toward psychological relationships and control over the instinct of aggression rather than social relationships and control over interest groups. Despite this psychological emphasis, Freud's theory did have preferable social agents of control and they usually consisted of significant authority figures in the family. These persons represented the individual's "social reality"; and "maturation" was achieved by way of the *accommodation* between the natural qualities of individuals and the "matured" representatives of this social reality. It was claimed that this accommodative process generated a moral awareness in the individual, and this awareness was called a sense of guilt. The implications of guilt for social progress and distributive justice will be clear in a moment.

Freud's concept of social progress was formulated by considering the consequences of these accommodative developments for both individuals and society. Since his concepts of man and society were based on atomistic and psychologistic premises, the development of a sense of guilt in many individuals had aggregative consequences; an unspecified distribution of guilty persons throughout society was necessary for social stability and more equitable forms of distributive justice. Thus, although the individual (natural) impulses were called upon to make the greatest sacrifice in the accommodation to social reality, this accommodation resulted in a normal or "optimum" state of

342

social affairs. The optimum state benefited the many as well as the individual in the long run. Progress occurred even though "the price of progress in civilization is paid in forfeiting happiness through the heightening of the sense of guilt" (*ibid.:*123).

In Freudian theory, aggression poses the problem of integration. Freud, therefore, asked for the solution to this problem when he inquired: "What means does civilization make use of to hold in check the aggressiveness that opposes it, to make it harmless, perhaps to get rid of it?" His answer treated the problem on two levels. In referring to social institutions (e.g., family or "culture"), Freud focused on the problem primarily via mechanisms of *social* control and the presence of *socially* regulated opportunities for the gratification of instincts. In regard to personality, he dealt with the problem in terms of *personal* control mechanisms (guilt) and the *personal* regulation of instinctual desires. This utilization of similar dynamics for the analysis of social and individual relationships appears to be very similar to the analytic strategies utilized by other corporate-liberal scholars during Freud's lifetime.

Like American corporate liberals who advocated regulation instead of elimination of the competitive struggle for property (which they considered natural for society), Freud argued for the regulation (through "socialization") rather than the total elimination of aggression (which he saw as natural to man). This was significant because his use of the concept of aggression appears to be *the psychological analogue* to the competitive relations that were considered genetic features of society. But if *unrestricted* aggression is the analogue to *laissez-faire* competition, then *"socialized* aggression" is an analogue to *socially controlled* competition!

The parallel modes of thought that characterized the ideas being advanced by Freud (primarily on the individual level of analysis) and by the corporate liberal-syndicalists (primarily on a social level of analysis) are most extraordinary. These parallel modes are not merely formal; they permeate the very substance and dynamics of their sociological and psychological ideas. Ignoring historical realities, for example, the liberal-syndicalists inquired into the disintegrative consequences of what was considered to be a universal or *"perpetual* clash" of interest groups. Freud (*ibid.:*86) also searched for ahistorical universals (e.g., aggression) that would explain the anarchic and internecine character of society: he argued that "civilization is *perpetually* menaced with disintegration through this primary hostility of men towards one another" (our emphasis).

The liberal-syndicalists, objecting to the classical doctrine of the harmony of interests, insisted that the mutual aims arising out of functionally interdependent economic (e.g., occupational) groups were not sufficient for integrating society in the face of uncontrolled egoism. After commenting on the divisive effects of aggression, Freud likewise felt that "their [men's] interests in their common work would not hold them together; the passions of instinct are stronger than reasoned interests" (*ibid.*).

The liberal-syndicalists argued further that "society," "the state," or "public opinion" were rational means for checking the unreasonable demands of such interest groups as "syndicated" capital and labor. Although Freud also referred to the society, the state, and especially the parental figure as agents of control, his preferred term "culture" was the most inclusive category used in this regard. Both the liberal-syndicalists and Freud visualized society and culture as being chiefly a social-control agent. And, as we shall see in a moment, Freud did not differ from the Americans in considering revolutionary alternatives to capitalism as unnatural to man.

Rejection of Revolutionary Alternatives

American sociologists believed that "vested interests" should be regulated within the framework of capitalism. This assumed that capitalist forms of competition and private property should be preserved. To this day, this ideological position is justified by recourse to natural-law assumptions and individual differences in ability; according to this received doctrine, no society, however utopian, can transcend the selfish nature of man and the social necessity for competition in the face of human inequality. Freud, on his part, bravely declared that because of man's inhumanity to man, it was necessary to demystify utopian proposals for change and "illusory anticipations with which in our youth we regard our fellow man." In advising youth about the objective nature of social reality, he cautioned, however, that there were many proposals for changing society; that some of these denied the *indispensable* nature of competition and were uncritically opposed to social authority. Mindful of the misuse of criticism, Freud (*ibid.:*87–88) stated: "It would be unfair . . . to reproach culture with trying to eliminate all disputes and *competition* from human concerns. These things are undoubtedly indispensable; but opposition is not necessarily enmity, only it may be misused to make an opening for it."

As if to ensure that *his* criticism of man's inhumanity was not construed as a communistic attack on capitalism, Freud (*ibid.:*87–88) attached the following disclaimer: "The communists believe that they have found a way of delivering us from this evil. Man is wholeheartedly good and friendly to his neighbour, they say, but the system of private property has corrupted his nature . . . If private property were abolished . . . ill-will and enmity would disappear from among men." According to Freud, however, these beliefs are "founded on an untenable illusion. By abolishing private property one deprives the human love of aggression of one of its instruments." Furthermore, "it in no way alters the individual differences in power and influence which are turned by aggressiveness to its own use, nor does it change the nature of the instinct in any way."

Thus, Freud argued that present forms of inequality are consistent with the imperfect nature of man. He opposed "the misconception that civilization is synonymous with becoming perfect." He claimed that distributive justice based on inequalities in human ability was originally instituted by nature rather than society. Consequently, he declared (*ibid.:*88,n.1) that if an attempt is to be made to base the fight against the economic inequality of men "upon an abstract demand for *equality for all* in the name of justice, there is a very obvious objection to be made, namely, that *nature began the injustice* by the highly unequal way in which she endows individuals physically and mentally, *for which there is no help"* (our emphasis). Freud therefore concluded that a truly egalitarian society was contrary to human nature: It was an unattainable dream!

NOTES

1. Henry Steele Commager (1950) called Ward "the Prophet of the New Deal." In a similar spirit, Ross (Chugerman 1965:39) astutely remarked after Ward's death that "few realize that Ward's . . . *Psychic Factors of Civilization* . . . furnishes the philosophy that lies at the base of the recent great extension of functions by contemporary governments."
2. The terms "civilization," "culture," and "society" were used interchangeably by Freud.

CHAPTER 43

Ideological Dimensions of Freudianism

The generally liberal character of Freudianism has been apparent to scholars for some time (e.g., Rieff 1959). Freud's philosophical and theoretical attitudes toward social authority, however, went beyond old-fashioned liberal natural-law justifications for competition, inequality, and private property. His perspective justified the concepts of social authority that had emerged among corporate-liberal intellectuals throughout the Western world.

The corporate-liberal dimensions of Freudianism are sometimes difficult to discern because there are so many qualifications in Freud's expressions of his theoretical ideas. In fact, he proferred an apparently contradictory view of social authority which superficially suggested that it must be socially maintained and individually repulsed. In a chapter titled "Politics and the Individual," Philip Rieff (*ibid.:*248) claims, for example, that Freud envisaged "*accommodation* to social authority . . . not its abolition" (our emphasis). However, Rieff adds, paradoxically, "in yet another sense Freud's familial models militate *against* authority" (our emphasis).[1] Since Freud considered all politics to be corrupt, it has also been said that he fundamentally questioned established criteria for discriminating one political regime from another, "let alone for determining the *best regime*" (our emphasis). Rieff (*ibid.:*247) further claims that Freud's "recognition of the necessity of social coercion—in the psychoanalytic currency, repression—hardly makes him an advocate of this or that *repressive* system" (our emphasis). Is Freud supporting or opposing these authority relationships? Rieff implies that he is doing both. He points out that Freud debunked authority but urged accommodation to it. He considered social coercion necessary but did not champion any repressive system. He regarded social rebellion as an infantile regression but gave it a justifiable "place in the normal course of human affairs" (*ibid.:*247).

Reiff paints Freudianism as an incredibly flexible, ideologically neutral [2] set of ideas. In our opinion, however, Freud's comments about authority, political systems, and revolutions must, at the very minimum, be taken in the context of his larger view of individual and social possibilities. As long as he felt that radical transformations of society were outside of the bounds of human nature at present, then one must conclude that he had *some* standards for defining an optimum system of authority.

The consistent features of these standards can be discovered only when it is observed that Freud generally regarded all types of society from a negative point of view; hence, they were all *more or less repressive.* The analysis of Freud's preferences among social systems, therefore, must take into account that with regard to civilized relationships, his optimum state is always a *lesser of evils.* This fact does not strip his theory of all operating standards for defining optimum conditions. Millions of Americans enter polling booths and utilize similar operating standards ever year when they vote for lesser evils. Obviously, individual disgust, cynicism, or other negative evaluations of "repressive" realities do not prevent one from choosing the "best" candidate even if the list of candidates only contains a choice of evils.

It can be seen, therefore, that Rieff is incorrect when he informs us that Freud equated a "best regime" with an "absolutely good regime." Furthermore, Rieff's ambiguous juggling of Freudian ideas overlooks the ideological implications of Freud's attitudes toward war, private property, competition, human inequality, and the political state.[3] Freud's ideological posture implied the existence of corporate-liberal *standards* for evaluating political systems. In light of his liberal standards, Freud's political debunking can be taken for what it implied with regard to individual behavior; a cynical, knowledgeable accommodation to modern capitalism because it was the best of a sorry list of alternatives.

In all fairness to Rieff, it should be pointed out that Freud personally insisted on his own ideological neutrality. In *Civilization and Its Discontents,* for example, Freud (1957:142–143) declared that "for various reasons, it is very far from my intention to express any opinion concerning the value of human civilization. I have endeavored to guard myself against the enthusiastic partiality which believes our civilization to be the most precious thing that we possess or could acquire and think it must inevitably lead to undreamt of heights of perfection." After insisting on his personal neutrality, however, Freud added, "my impartiality is all the easier to me since I know very little about these things and am sure only of one thing, that the judgements of value made by mankind . . . are attempts to prop up their illusions with arguments." Before taking statements like these at their face value, it should be kept in mind that Americans like Small, Ogburn, Park, and Burgess also professed to be impartial, even though their biases were blantantly obvious to anyone who did not share their world view.

Freud was fond of debunking social myths in the name of his limited expertise. (As we have seen above, he indicated that he knew "very little" about issues that appeared to transcend strictly professional concerns.) His argument for the regulation of private property was advanced in these terms: Freud (*ibid.:* 88) declared that he had "no concern with any economic criticisms of the communistic system; I cannot enquire into whether the abolition of private property is advantageous and expedient." He gratuitously noted in passing, however, his ability "to recognize that *psychologically* it [the *abolition* of private property] is founded on an *untenable* illusion" (our emphasis). Ostensibly, therefore, Freud was speaking only within the limits of his role as an "expert"; however, one must be extremely naive to be taken in by such rhetoric.

Freud, like other corporate liberals, claimed that public issues could be explained and ameliorated by psychological models and methods. Although Freudianism distinguished between public issues and ethical principles, it regarded them both as the outcome of personal affairs. One of the consequences of this was the incorporation of technocratic and corporate-liberal values into the medical vocabulary. Such terms as "social control" were transformed into "therapy," and as a result of Freud's influence, modern sociologists speak, for example, of a "therapeutic" or "mental health" model of deviancy. With these models, political issues and behavior are regarded as problems of individual adjustment. It is plain, however, that the use of these models never allowed sociologists to analyze "deviancy" in a nonpolitical manner. Their models have been no less political because deviancy has been considered to be the product of personal conflict or because their analytic categories have been reputed to be ideologically neutral.

Freud: Technocratic Concepts
of Leadership and Democracy

From Ward onwards, corporate-liberal sociologists became interested in studying the "natural" characteristics of man and society in a social control context. As a result, a well-established theoretical perspective had already developed by the time Freud influenced American sociologists. Freud contributed very few original insights to these topics; his sociological work was heavily dependent on Le Bon's publications. Consequently Freud's sociological work was influenced by elitist, liberal ideas [4] that were already very familiar to the Americans.[5]

As far as the topic of democratic participation was concerned, Freud generally reinforced rather than originated the established elitist viewpoint. As liberals, sociologists believed that working people were hardly capable of governing themselves; a "democratic" society functioned properly if it provided free competitive opportunities for selection of an elite body. This elite, consisting of the most intelligent men available, was necessary in order to occupy positions of greatest authority.

The source of Freud's elitism was not located solely in his belief that coercive institutions were necessary in order to force the indolent masses to work (Rieff 1959:245), nor was it in his conviction that the competitive distribution of rewards was justified by natural inequalities among men. Nor was his theory technocratic merely because of his continual protestations of ideological neutrality. Freud's theory was formulated at a time when new corporate-liberal *alternatives* to populist and revolutionary concepts of individual freedom and democratic participation were being proposed in America and Europe. These alternatives were represented by the liberal-syndicalist justifications of government administered by experts rather than common people. They were contained in a round of theories which reached back into the eighteenth century to justify the definition of the masses or racial and national minorities as a swinish, indolent, and irrational population.[6] They were also manifested by theoreticians who attributed morally suspect intentions to persons who were passionately committed to social change in order to achieve greater individual liberty and democracy. Freudianism fit each of these perspectives as a hand fits a glove.

With slight modifications, Freud's theory of human personality integrated almost every major idea or assumption developed by liberals over the previous centuries into a single explanation of human behavior. These included such classical conceptions as egoism, reason, altruism, quietism, atomism, prudentialism, utilitarianism, hedonism, and the dichotomy between the functional imperatives of individuals and society. Also, utilizing such technocratic notions as social control and individual adjustment, Freud's theory could convey every significant new ethical notion in the liberal lexicon. This theory had unlimited potential for the development of ideological rhetoric.

Freud: Democratic Rationale
for Suppressing Revolutionary Behavior

Like the American sociologists, Freud constructed his critique of revolutionary behavior around the investment of democratic qualities in established forms of social authority. (They mutually interpreted institutionalized authority, therefore, as the embodiment of social justice.) American sociologists organized their concepts of justice around the authority of the "state," "society," "the public," "the will of the people," or "the judgement of mankind," and explicitly or implicitly grounded these corporate entities in a democratic rationale.[7] The "mores," for example, represented the opinions of most persons and, therefore, had to be given greater priority than opinions of single entrepreneurs or syndicated labor, capital, and other "vested interests." Working primarily with categories based on family relations, Freud developed a similar rationale for his notions of justice and authority. In *Civilization and Its Discontents,* an analogy is drawn between the conflict over authority between family members and the conflicts involving single individuals and groups in society. Generalizations from the "findings" about the former were made to the latter. In this process, as we shall see, Freud constructed a democratic rationale for the authority of the larger group against the single individual or smaller groups of individuals.

Freud (*ibid.*:59) stated, for example, that "the first attempt ever made to regulate . . . social relations already contained the essential elements of civilization." This attempt involved the control over the authority of the father by the sons. "Had no such attempt been made, [social] relations would be subject to the wills of individuals; that is to say, the man who was physically strongest would decide things in accordance with *his own interests* and desires." In Freud's view, "human life in communities only becomes possible when a *number of men* unite together in strength superior to *any single individual* and remain united against *all single individuals*" (our emphasis). According to Freud (*ibid.*), "the substitution of the power of a united number for the power of the single man is the decisive step toward civilization." By uniting with each other, "members of the community have restricted their possibilities of gratification, whereas the individual recognizes no such restrictions." Consequently, *"the first requisite of culture . . . is justice*—that is, the assurance that a law once made will not be broken in favor of any *individual* . . . the further course of cultural development seems to tend toward ensuring that the law shall no longer represent the will of *any small body*—caste, tribe, section of the population—which may behave like a *predatory individual* toward other groups perhaps containing larger numbers" (our emphasis). It is clear that in the context of this statement, Freud's notions of primitive justice, and of the imperatives of primitive society, were organized around very *modern* analogues. At the very least, these analogues were based on the notion of interest groups, the concept of democratic right, and the egoistic image of man which had emerged during the epoch of capitalism.

It is important to note, on the other hand, that Freud's analytic categories have not been inseparable from his own ethical referents. The superego, for example, need not refer to norms and values of *established* institutions. Instincts can and have been extended; new, ethically significant derivatives have been added to love and aggression. By this means, a scholar can change the ethical implications of Freud's theory and still employ many of his dynamic principles. Some of these principles can even be extended or discarded in favor of others.

It is because they are couched in such abstract terms that Freud's analytic categories can be reinterpreted and separated from the standards and organizing principles used in his own analytic work. However, as the term "orthodox Freudianism" suggests, there are limitations to the range of these interpretations; theoretical works outside of these limits have been considered outside the domain of psychoanalysis as prescribed by Freud. Scholars like Eric Fromm, Karen Horney, Harry Stack Sullivan, and Herbert Marcuse, who went beyond these limits, have either justifiably been called "revisionists" or considered outside the pale of psychoanalytic theory, no matter how loosely this theory is defined.

Counterrevolutionary Dimensions of Freudianism

American sociologists developed various arguments to reconcile the contradictions between their concepts of individual liberty and social control. They employed a democratic rationale for this purpose. First, regulation of individual freedom was functionally imperative for capitalism. (The regulation of laissez-faire capitalists, for example, was held to favor the interests of "society" [i.e., capitalism] rather than the selfish individual or group of individuals.) Second, it was also claimed that individual liberty had to be content with the choice of less freedom or none at all. Either freedom was restricted or "society" would be destroyed.

In order to reconcile the contradiction between liberty and control, Freud also relied on the democratic rationale and the functional necessity for social controls. His reasons for accommodation to the repression of individual liberty, however, were not confined to democratic authority and social imperatives. Like Park and Burgess, Freud formulated a pathological model for revolutionary behavior that implicitly transformed altruistic striving into irrational acts of individual selfishness. Freud (*ibid.*:60) declared, for example: "The liberty of the individual is not a benefit of culture. It was greatest before any culture . . . . Liberty has undergone restrictions through the evolution of civilization, and justice demands that these restrictions shall apply to all." Recognizing and admitting that the desire for freedom could represent "a revolt against some existing injustice," Freud insisted, however, that "this desire may also have its origins in the primitive roots of the personality, still unfettered by civilizing influences and so become a source of antagonism to culture."

Thus revolutionary behavior was converted into fundamentally selfish individual behavior resulting from inadequate socialization of primal (i.e., "unfettered") desires. Furthermore, revolutionists, in this model, could be classed with common murderers whose violent crimes were also considered expressions of unsocialized aggressive impulses. The usefulness of this model in repudiating activist demands for change is inherent in its broad flexibility and formalized categories. Moreover, given situations in which the family relations of revolutionary individuals were considered to be inconsistent with this causal analysis, other Freudian dynamics could be brought into play to arrive

350

at the same ethical conclusion. Revolutionists, for example, could also be depicted as persons who displaced, toward the state, hostility developed in the family, or who discharged their excessive or irrational feelings of guilt through apparent acts of altruism. These explanations of revolutionary behavior ignored the real social issues posed by revolutionary socialists. They also provide technocratic scholars with new psychological justifications for legitimating political and social deviations from established norms as objects for social control.

Freudian Man: Personality Homologue of Conceptualized Social Relationships

In Social Control, Ross (1901:280) stated that "personal control is all the positive control there is." The Freudian concept of modern man rested on similar assumptions; nevertheless, liberal social control theorists have not utilized this concept on the basis of these ideological assumptions alone. The ideological utility of this concept is sustained by the *mode of analogical reasoning* which underlies the concept itself. This historically complex, cognitive mode has special relevance for liberal social scientists because they are required to justify their reifications on the basis of an immediately apprehendable reality. The contradictions between social myths and social reality must be resolved in order to justify the "reality" of the myths. Analogical thought is used to formulate a "noncontradictory," "theoretical" correspondence between a reified reality and the actual behavior signified by the reification.

The ideological utility of Freud's concept of modern man for liberal sociologists is also sustained by the *homologous relations* between this concept and their own conceptions of social reality. If the theorized structure and/or dynamic relations of a *personality* system correspond to the structure and/or dynamic relations of a *social* system, then the personality system is homologous to the social system. Freud's concept of man is a homologue of corporate-liberal conceptions of the political and economic relationships that had emerged throughout the Western world during the formative years. Because of this we will call the Freudian concept of modern man a *personal homologue* of these conceptualized social relationships. Examples of homologous structural and dynamic relations are: first, a liberal-syndicalist model of government and its homologue of the ego mediating between the id and superego in the individual; and second, economizing behavior on the part of both corporate institutions and the individual in corporate-liberal societies. Other homologous relations would involve the correspondence between the concept of social control and the concept of the superego, etc. Let us pursue this way of thinking by further discussing the way in which Freud supplied a model of personal decision-making mechanisms corresponding to those used in contemporary liberal solutions to the problems of social integration and social change. This discussion will also address itself to Rieff's (1959) characterization of Freudian man as a "psychological man."

351

Psychological Man:
A Socially Controlled Economic Man

Rieff calls the Freudian concept of modern man "the psychological man." Rieff (*ibid.*:356) recognizes that the personality of Freud's psychological man is partly organized around the "nervous habits" and personal ideals of his "father," economic man, who is "anti-heroic, shrewd, carefully counting his satisfactions, and dissatisfactions, studying unprofitable commitments as the sins most to be avoided." Rieff indicates that Freud's "psychological man" has additional characteristics that seem to be organized around the concepts of personal control: "The psychological man," Rieff (*ibid.*:355–356) adds, "lives neither by the ideal of might nor by the ideal of right which confused his ancestors, political man and religious man. Psychological man lives by the ideal of insight . . . leading to the *mastery* of his own personality. The psychological man has withdrawn into a world always at war, where the ego is an armed force capable of achieving *armistices* but not peace" (our emphasis). However unstable, the characteristic of *personal control* appears to be the main reason why Rieff preferred to call Freud's concept, "psychological man," rather than "economic man."

But can Freudian man be uniquely defined on the basis of *personal* mastery of inner conflicts? How different is *personal* mastery from *social* control? It is not possible to define the concept of man independently of time and place. Economic man was squarely related to the development of the competitive market in capitalist societies. What are the social relations behind Freud's concept of man? Why is Freudian man cynical about power but nevertheless accommodative to power he cannot resist? What forces are actually in *control* of Freudian man? We suggest that it is the same monopoly capitalist society that preoccupied the American scholars—and the same social controls they had in mind for stabilizing and optimizing this society.

Corporate liberal conceptions of social control, which were developing in Europe as well as America, are *intrinsic* to the very use of the *basic analytic categories* on which Freud's philosophy and theory stand. Consequently the achievement of individual self-mastery in this context can be considered the epitome of social control rather than of individual freedom. The terms of self realization were sharply limited by such Freudian ideals as private property, prudentialism, an accommodating disposition, sexual determinism, and economistic habits of mind. These personal ideals and behavioral principles excluded self-realization by such alternatives as communal ownership of the means of production, sharing according to need, participation in revolutionary socialist pursuits, equality for women, and service to the people. The limited ideals of principles which underlie Freud's general philosophy (which by no means are exhaustive) have been clearly stated in the description of the counterrevolutionary aspects of Freudianism, and Freud's "professional" justifications of competition, meritocratic relationships, and social authority, as well as his attitudes toward women.

Freud expressed his liberal social-control orientation and demonstrated homologous thinking in his repeated references (*ibid.:*62, 133, 136, 141) to the similarities between personality relationships and social relationships. In comparing "the cultural process in humanity with the socializing process in the individual," he concluded (*ibid.:*133) "without much hesitation that the two are very similar in nature, if not in fact *the same process* applied to a different kind of object" (our emphasis). Arguing that the "whole of humanity" may have "become 'neurotic' under the pressure of the civilizing trends," Freud (*ibid.:*141) stated that "the evolution of civilization has . . . a far reaching similarity with the development of the individual, and . . . *the same methods* are involved in both (our emphasis). In Freud's case, the homologous correspondence is not only predicated on structural similarities, as we have seen, but also on the use of the same dynamic principles for psychological and sociological levels of analysis.

Why has homologous thinking been acceptable to scholars? Certain historical conditions appear to have influenced this embracing of the notion that similar structural and dynamic principles can be used on each level of reality. The most important condition is the ideology of liberalism. One common denominator of liberal thinking has generally been to regard great social inequities and disorders in capitalism as the products of personal morality. In the first decades of this century, the analytic categories and strategies that underlay liberal conceptions of the origins of crime, imperialist war, and economic inequality, for example, were captured by Freud's variation on this theme— i.e., his personal homologue of conceptualized social relationships. In the name of ideological neutrality and psychological expertise—and under the guise of a technocratic gospel of personal mastery of inner conflicts—Freud formulated a homologous model capable of explaining every significant social, political, and economic event imaginable by merely describing the relations directly encompassed within the homologue itself. But how fundamentally different was the function of this homologue in social theory from Malthus' hoary notion of moral impropriety? Malthus, as we have seen, located the origins of poverty and war in the moral depravity of individual working people. In *certain* basic respects Freud did not really go far beyond Malthus' moralistic and reductionist assumptions.

In spite of the parallels between Freud and Malthus however, it is also important to note the developmental differences that become evident when we consider that Freud's concept of man was indicative of a different stage in liberal thought. At this later stage, the theoretical explanations of personal and social relationships became extraordinarily complex; in regard to each level of analysis as well as to the relations between levels.

Since the last part of the nineteenth century, corporate-liberal scholars have been generating the thoroughgoing application (at each level of biological, psychological, and sociological realities) of homologous thinking (similar structural and dynamic relations) to the atomistic conceptions that had been shared by classical liberal scholars and nineteenth-century theorists. By the turn of the century, corporate liberalism had become the dominating influence on sociology in the United States, and eventually, by the twenties, it was such reductionist approaches as the social disorganization tradition, produced and sustained by this ideology, which also made explicit the claim that similar structural and dynamic relations could be fruitful for explaining variations on each qualitative level of human reality. In the second half of this century, liberal sociologists still maintain that similar structural and dynamic relations characterize personality and social systems (e.g., Smelser and Smelser 1963). But neither the classical liberals nor the modern structural functionalists have ever successfully utilized homologous thinking in order to develop an "objective," "value free" conception of human relationships.

Historical works suggest that valid homologous explanations of personality and social systems are *not* likely. The evidence shows that homologous explanations of personality and social systems are little more than insidious ideological formulations that disregard even the most obvious truths. Eighteenth-century philosophers argued that a correspondence between human nature and the marketplace justified the institution of private property. During the nineteenth century it was proposed that the development of the individual recapitulated the development of the race. (This theory was used repeatedly by imperialists to claim that African tribesmen, for example, were racial inferiors because they were in an arrested stage of evolutionary development.) In the twentieth century, as we have seen, scholars have attributed labor and political unrest to pathological personality relationships on the basis of a correspondence between personality and social disorganization. These examples represent but a minute sample of the kind of historical traditions that have generally sustained reductionist explanations based on personal homologues of social relationships.

After more than two hundred years of reductionist thought, liberal scholars are still constructing personality systems whose structures and dynamic principles are similar to social systems. Because these systems are conceived in highly formal terms (Wallace 1969:36–44) in modern sociology, they appear to have no ideological functions at all. This appearance, however, should not blind us to the fact that it is the ideology of liberalism which still maintains the plausibility of personal homologues of social relationships.

If Freud's stated aims are taken at face value, then his homologous concept of man has its origins in his concern for scientific knowledge and the psychotherapeutic application of this knowledge. But the very basic categories used in this enterprise are not explainable by recourse to his stated aims. In *Civilization and Its Discontents,* Freud's personal homologue of syndicalist relationships has little meaning without reference to a concern for the problem of *social* integration; not merely the concern for a scientific description of *individual* behavior. When this work is taken as a whole, it becomes obvious that Freud is engaged in an ideological enterprise and that his personal homologue plays a crucial role in this undertaking because the regulation of the *personal homologue,* from an atomistic viewpoint, is tantamount to the regulation of the *social order.* If regulation is interpreted operatively in terms of personal ideals, then the resolution of personal conflicts and the widespread achievement of *personal* integration by the development of an unheroic, shrewd, calculating, expedient, prudent, and accommodating disposition is also tantamount to the achievement of long-lasting *social* integration.

In light of this, it is not paradoxical to assert that individual self-mastery in Freud's theory is the ultimate in social control. Nor is it illogical to regard homologous thinking as an important ideological means for achieving this control. However, the notion that the application of this homologue can provide a satisfactory solution to the problem of integration on the societal or personal level is not only an improbable fiction, but its acceptance on a broad scale in the United States has been positively disastrous for militant social reformist traditions in one professional field after another.

NOTES

1. Rieff (1959:248) quotes Freud in this regard: "The human individual must devote himself to the great task of *freeing* himself from his parents." Therefore, "in likening citizens to children, and leaders to fathers, he [Freud] tarnishes whatever halo may remain around political authority."

2. Rieff's major point is that Freud was a liberal moralist. He continuously provides evidence for this in his citations. In our opinion, however, it is impossible to overstate the degree to which Rieff's work is in the spirit of "giving with one hand" and "taking away with the other." Rieff suggests that Freudianism is an ideologically committed set of ideas. But his *operative* interpretation of Freudianism completely neutralizes this suggestion: the phrase "ideologically neutral" (in the above text), refers to the operative interpretation made by Rieff.

3. This oversight is implied when Rieff argues that Freud fundamentally questioned established criteria for evaluating political and economic systems when, in fact, these criteria were being clearly *revitalized* by Freud and other corporate-liberal scholars during the formative years.

4. In modern sociological literature on "collective" (e.g., riot) behavior Le Bon's work is usually called aristocratic. However, Le Bon was a liberal and his Spencerian, elitist orientation was consistent with nineteenth-century liberalism.

5. American journals published reviews of Le Bon's works as early as the last decade of the nineteenth century.

6. For an excellent discussion of Freud's attitudes toward the masses, see Rieff (1959:228–238, 245). For example, Rieff states: "In his political psychology Freud was no innovator. The mixed suspicion and sympathy with which he described the masses echoes both the best and the worst political writing of the late nineteenth century. Suspicion bulks larger than sympathy . . . So little did Freud consider his own disdain of the masses to be distinguished from that of his sources that in *Group Psychology* he copied out whole passages from the most profoundly anti-democratic of these polemics raised to the level of social psychology—Le Bon's *The Crowd* (1895)" (*ibid.*:229–230).

7. The phrase, "democratic rationale," in this work, refers to types of justifications which allege, in essence, that a set of relationships serve the interests of the majority of individuals or of society as a whole.

CHAPTER 44

The Freudian Bridge
between Desires and Institutions

Background

Modeling basic human nature after such socioeconomic relationships as private property and competition has been a very familiar practice among American sociologists. Even more ancient is the practice of inventing theories born of the notion that women are naturally oriented to the institution of the familial hearth and home. In 1920, Freud was being associated with these conservative ideas; [1] and because of his personality homologue of liberal conceptions, he was considered a major authority on the nature of humankind. The eminent sociologist Ulysses G. Weatherly (1920:27) acclaimed Freud for opening up "new vistas in the interpretation of individual wishes." He also declared that in examining the relationship between frustrated wishes and popular unrest, it was Freud who pointed out that the "real wish, repressed into the unconscious . . . has ways of asserting itself that are generally pathological." Militant expressions of social unrest during the progressive era were certainly considered to be pathological; they demonstrated, according to Weatherly (*ibid.*), that "latent powers which find no outlet in normal functioning may break out in those abortive, capricious acts of popular will which will bring discredit on the very name of democracy."

What were the factors that determined Freud's influence on American sociology? One previously mentioned factor was the symmetry between Freud's world view and liberal-syndicalism in America. Park, Burgess, Weatherly, Chapin, Ogburn, and every other leading sociologist who advocated Freudian ideas believed that capitalism afforded the optimum conditions for the development of mankind. They asserted the necessity for achieving accommodations that would enable the system to function in an orderly manner. Freud's doctrines were obviously congenial with this ideological point of view. His theory took firm hold when corporate liberalism finally became the dominant world view of American sociology.

On the other hand, although quite necessary, ideological similarities alone cannot help us understand why sociologists began to accept certain parts of Freud's concept of man but not others. The American sociologists, for example, accepted Freud's mechanism but eventually rejected his concept of in-

356

stincts. In order to clarify the historical relationships that regulated the highly selective diffusion of Freud's ideas, it is necessary to examine the usages of his notions being made by sociologists at the time; and to evaluate the purposes to which these uses were put.

This chapter points out that Freud's ideas were considered particularly significant because they helped bridge the relationships between individual desire and social institutions in reductionist solutions to the problem of *social change*. It also points out that the American sociologists had come under fire in the first decade of this century because they were formulating reductionist theories which did not solve the contradiction between individual and social imperatives satisfactorily from a psychological point of view. By the second decade of this century it was clear that there was a critical chasm in customary sociological thinking. This chasm, as we will see, was bridged by the Freudian mechanisms of defense.

Ward's Contradiction
between Individual and Society

Early scholars generally integrated social relationships on the basis of the natural harmony of interests. With the rise of monopoly capitalism, however, it was no longer possible to reconcile the liberal contradiction between the individual and society in so simple a manner. Ward's theory represents a crude attempt to depart from this traditional harmony of interests approach to the contradiction; he reconciled the contradiction by regarding an institution like the family, for example, not as an altruistic relationship but as an inadvertent by-product of egotistic striving. A brief review of his theoretical argument in this regard will enable us to understand the kind of criticism directed at the theory of social forces by psychologists. It will also illustrate the degree to which ideology determined the logical difficulties a liberal functionalist faced when constructing an explanation of social change. Finally, it will reveal the nature of the chasm that was eventually bridged by the Freudian mechanisms of defense.

As we have seen previously, the contradiction between egotism and the social good was a major concern to classical liberals as well as to twentieth-century reductionist theorists. *In fact, this concern exists in every reductionist theory of social development based either partly or wholly on a natural-law conception of egotistic desire.* As long as egotism is held to be a universal characteristic of man, some attention must be paid to the implications of this characteristic for the problems of social integration and change. It does not matter whether or not a scholar uses a dualistic scheme based on egotism and altruism; if his reductionist explanation assumes the dynamic functions of egotism, certain questions are forced into the foreground.

In Ward's theory, for example, the potentially destructive effects of egotism are contained by the influence of human institutions. But how do these institutions come into being? It is obvious from Ward's theory that individuals in society, as a rule, create social institutions in order to meet their own personal needs. But individuals are interested in satisfying themselves, not others. At *first* glance, therefore, individual striving seems to be the least important determinant of social institutions or society in general. In fact, since this striving is considered to be egotistic, it is generally opposed to the forms of cooperation required by society and its institutions. Thus, while the concept of universal selfish desire may appear to have great generalizing power, it is obvious that without some other theoretical propositions, the persistent and integrative features of society are not consequences attributable to egotism alone. In fact, when joined with the concept of natural law, the opposite is implicated; if we leave individuals in their "natural state" they will destroy each other.

What kinds of propositions were used by Ward to causally bridge the contradiction between egotistic desire and the persistence of social institutions? Step by step it will be demonstrated that he felt institutions survive as an unintended consequence of the pursuit of personal desires. First, he identified those forms of egotistic desire which ultimately produce a stable social order and called them social forces. Second, he differentiated between the *direct* and *indirect* consequences of these forces. Third, he asserted that when the resultant changes in institutions are considered, "the salient fact which it behooves us especially to notice is that these results [stable institutions] are the indirect [inadvertent] products of the social forces, and have no relation to the real object sought by the agents who accomplish them." According to Ward, the *real* object of individual attention is simply "the temporary satisfaction of an immediate physical demand, and the advancement of civilization or social well-being is never for a moment contemplated." On this basis, he concluded that "in the pursuit of feeling, men raise families and their children provide for them in their old age." But *personal interest* in survival, not the institution of the family, is the *direct object* of their pursuits. Because the family arises and is maintained in this process, however, the individual's interest in survival becomes more than a personal desire, in that it is converted inadvertently into a functionally necessary condition for the existence and maintenance of the family. Therefore, Ward stated (1903:126), as an *"unintended"* consequence of this pursuit, " [individual] feeling becomes related to [social] function." The family is depicted in this explanation as an accidental by-product of *egotistic striving*.

The Bridge of Hedonism and Inadvertent Consequences

During the two decades following its publication, Ward was not confronted with seriously critical questions regarding the superficial nature of the psychological processes described in his *Dynamic Sociology*. Nor was there much question raised about his notion of inadvertent consequences, even though it was used to explain the origin of a major social institution. He was called a "biologic theorist" by one economist because his "essential" needs (e.g., nutritional and reproductive needs) were derived from "vital" biological forces (Stern 1938:384). Nevertheless, scholars who were very familiar with his work knew that it was grounded primarily in psychological relationships. They also recognized that Ward believed "the biological viewpoint affords everywhere a meagre, insufficient, inadequate view" of human relationships (*ibid.:*386). As far as men like Small or Ross were concerned, Ward was the trailblazer of a radically new approach to sociology: Ross (*ibid.:*365) wrote to Ward in 1892 that "everything I read now suggests to me something concerning the psychology of the social forces." He added that his classes "were wildly enthusiastic" about *Dynamic Sociology.* As the founding sociologists departed from traditional standpoints, they created an exciting intellectual atmosphere. As a result, Ross (*ibid.:*391) was able to state in 1895 that "the other day I found myself compelled to use the phrase 'classical sociology' " in a reference to Spencer. "Soon," Ross happily added, "we shall have the 'old school,' 'the new school' and all the rest."

There was, of course, some early criticism of Ward's theory. But prior to the turn of the century, this criticism did not touch directly on the weakest parts of his theory. In 1892, for example, Ross (*ibid.:*373) offered Ward advice about a new manuscript in which the "transition from psychology to sociology seemed too abrupt and needed some explanation in the title." Ross himself had very little to offer Ward in this respect, aside from the use of a metaphor like "social synthesis" to symbolize the complex processes involved in this transition. Like other sociologists, Ross and Ward did not seem overly concerned about whether their psychological mechanisms established a logically consistent and empirically adequate relationship between individual desires and social institutions. During the founding period, metaphors like "social synthesis" and "synergetic processes" and cursory references to "inadvertent" or "latent consequences" proliferated and appeared sufficient for this purpose.

Shortly after the publication of Ward's *Pure Sociology* in 1903, however, a psychologist, H. Heath Bawden, wrote a devastating review of the psychological assumptions underlying Ward's theory. Bawden (1903:408) began his criticism by asserting that "from a psychological point of view, this book is more instructive in what it attempts but *fails* to do than in what it actually accomplishes." He noted that "the author's avowed aim is to ground sociology in psychology. If he falls short of attaining this end, it is because of the character of the psychological conceptions which he employs." Bawden interspersed his description of Ward's ideas with such comments as "the psychological concepts are not fully developed" and "the psychological doctrines do not form a coherent view taken by themselves." They "notably fail to articulate in any organic way with the biological and sociological parts of the system." Highly contradictory statements made by Ward in discussing psychological processes were also cited repeatedly. One of the significant doubts raised by Bawden concerned Ward's principle of "creative synthesis." This principle amounted to the notion that feeling alone is an efficient cause of new human relationships. Ward also used the term "synergy" to classify the interaction between the physical, psychical, and social forces involved in this "creative" process. Synergy represented the mechanisms by which social structures came into existence. However, since these mechanisms were never adequately described, Bawden (*ibid.:*409) called creative synergy a "magical phrase." He wryly noted that "the logic of modern science has not prepared us" for the meanings associated with this phrase.

Toward the end of his review, Bawden stated, "finally, we come to what is in some respects the most important psychological conception in the book, because of its relation to sociology." This conception described the processes by which the individual achieved *socially* significant relationships. It is observed that Ward claimed individuals strive for egoistic ends but are unconscious of the social consequences of this striving. Bawden insisted, however, that this claim does not represent an adequate description of the processes involved, because "the really social nature of individual consciousness and the important function of the individual in the reconstruction of [social] experience are vaguely assumed throughout the book." As far as Bawden (*ibid.:*414) was concerned, "this is perhaps the most important question at the present time in both psychology and sociology—the relation between the *social* processes . . . and the *psychic* processes which take place in individual consciousness" (our emphasis). While it was granted that suggestive statements were made by Ward in this regard, Bawden concluded that Ward's "inadequate psychology precludes any statement" of a satisfactory solution to this question. As far as Bawden was concerned, Ward's explanation of the psychological processes (which transform egoistic striving into enduring social relationships) was completely unacceptable.

Although sociologists utilized more complex conceptions of man as time went on, none of them was able to detail a psychological mechanism that bridged the concepts of basic *individual desire* and the origin of *social institutions* in a way that made sense to more sophisticated psychologists. In time, members of the psychological profession themselves provided the reductionist mechanisms for sociology.

Unprecedented Discussion:
Relation between Freudianism and Sociology

If we leave the very early period and examine the discipline in which graduate training was taken by each of the nineteen presidents of the American Sociological Society between 1906 and 1929, it will be found that none of these men were trained in psychology. This is striking, considering that they were busily involved in grounding the entire sociological discipline in psychology. In light of this deficiency it is not surprising to find a professional psychologist like Bawden sharply attacking the crude psychological processes being formulated by the early sociologists. The awareness of theoretical gaps and flaws spelled out by this criticism provides a partial understanding of why Freud's mechanisms of defense, in particular, were eagerly grasped by the Americans.

The conservative climate among the second generation of sociologists provides additional insight into their receptivity to Freud's ideas. The conservative atmosphere within which Freudianism was diffused among American sociologists is illustrated in the papers presented at the American Sociological Society's annual meeting during the very first session dealing with the relation between psychoanalytic theory and sociology. This session was held in 1920, after the United States government had blatantly ignored constitutional rights in the attempt to "normalize" industrial relations [2] and destroy socialist parties and the IWW.[3] In the atmosphere engendered by the political repression, "college graduates were calling for the dismissal of professors suspected of radicalism; school teachers were being made to sign oaths of allegiance; business men with unorthodox political or economic ideas were learning to hold their tongues if they wanted to hold their jobs" (Allen 1959:41).

The ideology of corporate liberalism and the atmosphere of economic and political unrest and repression provide keys to the social priorities and the analytic strategies that were very much in evidence at the Sociological Society's 1920 session on "The Sociological Significance of Psychoanalytic Sociology." Although they expressed themselves in very formal professional jargon, most of the participants in the session focused on the problem of controlling "social unrest" (e.g., militant reformist, labor, or radical "agitation"). The remarks by these participants reveal the degree to which psychoanalytic rhetoric was being used to reinforce the same ameliorative and repressive doctrines contained in other liberal-functionalist languages.

Ross set the theme for this session at the turn of the century when he advised administrators not to flaunt the professional secrets of social control. But in 1920, one of the session participants, E. R. Groves (1920:205), warned that "a multitude of people are conscious of the processes of social control and for different desires and in different ways are *in revolt against social discipline*" (our emphasis). It is unfortunate, Groves sadly suggested, that "we have arrived at a time . . . when more people than ever before, out of sympathy with the object of specific repressions, are conscious of the methods of social discipline and therefore are sensitive to what they interpret as unjustified coercion." Indeed *"at a time when we especially need social self-control,"* Groves indignantly declared, "we have been taught the impatience with slow processes and as a society we would rush pell-mell to our objectives." Implying by his Freudian terminology that this uncontrolled rush might be checked by psychoanalytic insights, Groves noted that "there is certainly need of a clear knowledge of the technique of social *sublimation,"* and expressed the hope that "the tremendous mass of restless energy brought forth by modern conditions from our basic instincts may be drained by educational processes into channels that sweep toward *security* [4] and *progress"* (our emphasis).

Another participant, Iva L. Peters (1920:215), recognized that "many impartial students have been unable to agree with all of Freud's conclusions, especially in making sex so all-dominating a factor of the psychic life of past and present." Nevertheless, he felt that psychoanalysis could be useful for making social predictions. He noted that the opportunities afforded by the American frontier had been closed. In addition, existent forms of social control were becoming outmoded because they did not provide for *alternative opportunities* for gratification. Given these conditions, he concluded (*ibid.:*216), "the psychoanalytic hypothesis would lead us to expect (in the absence of rationalization) increasing *conflict* with recrudescence of ancient *racial* and *class* hatreds, and a reinforcement of the collective emotion of crowds, all molded by the pattern conflicts of past generations" (our emphasis).

Still another participant, William A. Whyte, revealed some of the key liberal assumptions and priorities underlying the scholarly papers at the session. He observed (1920:208) that "society is composed of individuals and *the problem of society* is to *integrate their activities* . . . the individual in his cultural progress brings his *instincts* under increasingly better *control; he sublimates* his instinctive activities to higher and progressively more socially valuable ends" (our emphasis). In Whyte's opinion, society socializes the individual by enabling him "to act in *conformity* with the interests of the group" (our emphasis). Taking a cue from Spencer by referring to society as a "superorganism," Whyte suggested that one law distinguished by scholars (who have studied how individual behavior is integrated in superorganisms) is "the law of the *resolution of the conflict"* (our emphasis). He illustrated the importance of this law by noting that "the various groups that make up society . . . are in continuous conflict." These groups, such as "labor and capital" or "conservatives and radicals," "occupy positions with reference to some specific questions that are diametrically opposed to each other." "Now this," Whyte declared, "is precisely the situation in an intrapsychic conflict." The study of conflict shows that "no solution . . . can be reached on the level of the conflict, that the solution can only eventuate when the two diametrically opposed interests are integrated at a higher level and at that higher level both opposing interests are *equally* satisfied" (our emphasis). After this liberal-syndicalist plea for accommodation, integration, and equity, Whyte concluded: "It seems to me that an appreciation of this law [of conflict resolution] taken over *from psychoanalysis to sociology* would be of immense importance to the latter" (our emphasis).

Whyte's "law of the resolution of the conflict" reflects syndicalist ideas which had actually been established *before* psychoanalytic doctrines influenced sociology in the United States. Whyte, however, did not seem to recognize the possibility that the basic principles used by Freud to organize psychological phenomena may have actually been derived from sociological conceptions that had generally emerged in Europe and America. Nor did he note that, as its basic characteristics were gradually being formulated, parts of the homologous Freudian conception of man were being selectively incorporated into the further development of the growing corporate-liberal family of sociological models.

NOTES

1. After criticizing the representative form of government and extolling Freud's psychology, Weatherly (1920:29) claimed, for example, that human nature is not "inherently radical." "Worthy enthusiasm," therefore, should not be wasted on "ephemeral issues that do not spring from elemental passions." Most women are innately conservative and "their entrance into politics ought normally to augment the conservative tendency, for with women even more than men, the primary passions center about the hearth and home." According to Weatherly, "people are, at bottom, fairly conservative in temper . . . their fundamental concerns, those in which they function naturally . . . are matters of *family, property,* and *personal ambitions*" (our emphasis).

2. In 1919, Preston (1963:191–192) points out "a marked increase in unemployment, labor unrest, and radicalism accompanied the readjustment to a peacetime economy . . . Industry's open-shop drive symbolized its resolution not to remove the grievances responsible for much of the agitation. The employers' American Plan foresaw the destruction of, rather than any concession to labor's aims. As a result, the United States witnessed 'an eruption of mass strikes on a scale never before seen in American society.' Over four million workers walked out in protest before 1919 came to an end."

3. Although every branch of the government was involved in the repressive attempts (Preston 1963:180–237), the attorney general's office was most conspicuous. Attorney General Mitchell Palmer conducted a series of nationwide raids which resulted in the deportation of thousands of "subversive aliens." Borenzweig (1970) reports that "the apex of Mr. Palmer's career was his arrest of over six thousand men attending Communist Party meetings in scores of cities all over the United States, on New Year's Day in 1920."

4. It should be noted that with the psychoanalytic equation of personal "security" with social stability, Comte's cry for *order* and progress was transformed into a call for conditions which would ensure *security* and progress. In this context, of course, the notion of (personal) security was interpreted from a psychoanalytic point of view.

CHAPTER 45

Ideological Usages
of Behaviorist
and Psychoanalytic Mechanisms

Background and Preview

The men who dominated the field of sociology firmly anchored the discipline as a whole in reductionist psychological mechanisms. It is not surprising to find, therefore, that by the second decade of this century, liberal sociologists had become utterly dependent on the field of psychology for replenishing their stockpile of theoretical mechanisms with the most sophisticated and up-to-date models. By that time, sociology had become little more than an applied psychology as far as theoretical activity is concerned.

During the formative years, corporate liberals interested in the origins of such social relationships as war, crime, the family, social classes, the political state, and the economy, seriously entertained only two very basic types of mechanisms. The first were learning mechanisms based on the concept of the conditioned reflex and produced by mechanistic behaviorist psychologists. The second consisted of the mechanisms of defense, produced primarily by psychoanalytic psychologists.

This chapter will continue to review the historical factors that regulated the selective diffusion of Freudian ideas. But it will also briefly discuss the "battle of the mechanisms," which became extremely important in the sociology of crime and delinquency after the formative years.[1] Behaviorist "learning mechanisms" were well established in American psychology long before the Freudian mechanisms were introduced. It is therefore important to consider why the Freudian mechanisms were eventually considered more useful for solving the problem of social change.

Behaviorism and the Problem of Social Change

To understand some of the reasons why American sociologists generally rejected the behaviorist in favor of psychoanalytic mechanisms, it is first necessary to make the general point that behaviorism at the turn of the century was deeply rooted in hedonistic utilitarianism and associationist (learning) principles, both of which were succinctly expressed in Thorndike's (1898) "law of effect" ("Pleasure stamps in; pain stamps out"). Utilitarianism and associationism, no matter how expressed, were under attack by corporate liberals in every discipline, even though they had been considerably refined throughout the nineteenth century. (In contrast with the older hedonistic conceptions, for example, the newer notions stemming primarily from the work of John Stuart Mill, and later political economists, emphasized such decision-making processes as those influencing price-making market activities, which enabled men to be selectively attentive and to actively engage characteristic features of their environment. Ward's *Social Dynamics* serves as an illustration of this development among sociologists; his concepts, for example, embodied the more sophisticated utilitarian view of man as a [tropismatic] cluster of interests or "psychic forces" that regulated the individual's attention and engagement with the complex of forces constituting his environment.)

Toward the end of the last century, utilitarian theorists in economics refined the notion of self-regulating processes particularly in their analysis of economizing and bargaining relationships (Veblen 1900). But no matter what the degree of refinement, the psychological relationships in these theories were very often based on associationist principles. By the end of the century these principles were being succinctly represented by such notions as "habit patterns" among sociologists and "conditioned reflexes" among psychologists; thus, for example, while it was felt that the individual's interests regulated his selection and engagement with environmental stimuli, his *habituated* or *conditioned associations,* in great part, determined the manner and direction of his responses.

By the turn of the century "the law of effect" described the relationships usually identified as behaviorist reinforcement theories today (Allport 1954:15). This "law" represented the most sophisticated and general statement of the kind of mechanism developed among psychologists who were hedonistic utilitarians and associationists. But irrespective of whether sociologists specified this law—or used terms such as "learning," "suggestion," "habit," or "imitation" instead—they could not explain a new response except by taking a new stimulus situation for granted; accordingly, individuals habitually behaved in a new, socially interrelated manner, for example, only if they were first stimulated to respond to each other in this way.

In this view, the repetitive occurrence of a new stimulus situation, in part, leads to persistent changes in individual behavior. Because of this, conditioned reflexes or "learning" mechanisms have been used by sociologists for explaining the diffusion of new ideas or the persistence of institutional patterns *after* these ideas and patterns have come into existence. But, as will be noted in a moment, it is precisely the *new* stimulus that could not be taken for granted in solving the problem of social change, and because of this, reductionist behavioristic mechanisms have never been successfully applied in an explanation of the origins of *new* patterns of socially *instituted* behavior.

The increasing disrepute of simple schemes based on clusters of biological instincts or psychological forces created a serious problem for scholars who were particularly interested in explaining institutional *change*. Generally these sociologists had little question about using the concepts of conditioning, imitation, or habit in their explanations of social integration. Sociologists used these notions in order to account for the *persistence* of instituted relationships. But the conceptual problem of social change did not consist of the search for causes of persistent conduct; the sociologists of change were not interested in why people continued to act in a particular way. They wanted to explain why *new* forms of activity came into being. Because of this they could not take the "new social stimuli" for granted. These stimuli were indeed the very object of explanation. In light of this, neither term, "habit" or "imitation"—nor the behaviorist's concept of the conditioned reflex—seemed to make sense for explaining the original occurrence of new forms of socially instituted conduct.[2]

Freudian Mechanisms and "Pathological" Social Change

Social scientists are highly inventive persons and logical limitations have never presented them with insurmountable obstacles. Because of this, the reasons for the general acceptance of Freudian mechanisms and the rejection of most behaviorist mechanisms also have to be sought on other than merely logical grounds. Some of these other grounds involved the existence of *ideological* pressures against the use of learning mechanisms for explaining the origins of nonconforming (i.e., "pathological") behavior. These pressures were particularly acute toward the close of the formative years.

Freudian theory began to affect American sociology toward the end of the second decade of this century (e.g., Park 1967:43). The formative years were drawing to a close: the militant liberal reformist thrust against laissez-faire capitalism, which had spawned, in its earliest years, Ward's visionary dream of a sociocratic society, was fast disappearing. As we shall see in the coming chapters, eminent scholars had generally come to agree on the standards for optimizing "healthy" human relationships as well as the corporate-liberal "industrial democracy" produced by this optimization. These leaders in social thought had agreed for some time that behavior which departed from these standards was pathological. Implicit in this agreement, as we shall see, was the notion that the *institutions* within which individuals could fulfill their basic needs and realize their potentialities, either *existed* already or were *actually coming into being*. These desirable institutions were generally considered to be the outcome of the "division of labor" in (capitalist) industrial societies, and it was believed that these institutional relationships, no matter how rudimentary, were being adversely affected by the anarchic and competitive conditions of laissez-faire capitalism. Their origins, on the other hand, were now no longer problematic for sociologists. It was their persistence, stabilization, and further development which had to be explained.

Generally, liberal sociologists believed that ideologically acceptable social movements or institutions would, in fact, become stabilized because they satisfied "healthy" human needs. Learning theory could be plausibly used to explain the persistence of these movements: obviously, if an institution serves to satisfy needs, a theory that stresses individual conformity on the basis of institutional learning rather than frustration, would more likely be used to explain its continued existence. Ideologically unacceptable (i.e., "pathological") movements and institutions, on the other hand, were judged differently; they did not stabilize because they were considered to be *contrary* to human nature. The notion of frustration in this context, moreover, was not only used to explain their emergence: they also flourished because of the *persistence of the frustrating conditions* that had produced them as a defensive "pathological" response in the first place. Their continued existence was, therefore, not primarily attributed to learning mechanisms, as was the case, for example, with established institutions.

It is suggested, therefore, that the mechanisms of defense were not merely associated with "pathological" social relationships because they were developed by psychologists interested in "abnormal" individual conduct. This association was made because of the expansion of ideological pressures against viewing established institutions as *causes of social pathology* toward the end of the formative years. Ideologically acceptable institutions were generally viewed as permanently satisfying basic human needs. They did not account for the widespread frustration in American society. Instead, this frustration was caused by "rapid social change," "cultural lags," or "socially disorganized" relationships that would soon be corrected by the progressive development and modification of established institutions. Until this correction was fully accomplished, however, individual frustration would be expressed, according to this point of view, by passing fads, fashions, financial panics, revolutionary movements, and other forms of "collective" behavior.

Positive Attitude toward Psychoanalytic Mechanisms

The 1920 discussion on the significance of psychoanalysis for sociology, described above, took place when these ideological developments were being spurred across the finish line by massive political repression of radical movements and intellectuals. In the panel discussion, Iva L. Peters made references to behaviorist and psychoanalytic mechanisms [3] that illustrate the points made previously in this chapter. For example, Peters (1920:215) felt that as far as *conventional* behavior was concerned, "the fear of group disapproval . . . is sufficient explanation of the incessant *reconditioning* which begins at birth, continues through life, and thus from the beginning *conventionalizes* the methods of gratification" (our emphasis). However, he felt that lack of socialization (i.e., lack of guilt-producing sanctions) explained antisocial behavior. He noted that the "environment may exercise a warping effect on native endowment and capacities by means of the early establishment of bad-conditioned reflexes." Even if a child has not been socialized properly, his adjustment to social sanctions later as an adult may be conventional and "it is possible that studies now being made of the drive [in] back of the patterns or motor sets of which we are speaking may show that the tendency of emotions *inhibited* at one outlet to seek other outlets may be too complex to be completely explained by conditioned reflexes. All that can be said at present [and here Peters in a roundabout language may have been suggesting sublimation] is that emotional pressure is drained off through channels made possible by environment and hereditary factors" (our emphasis).

Thus Peters' explanation differed from the behavioristic model (which might consider delinquency and revolutionary behavior, for example, to be the consequences of learned responses) when he suggested that the concept of the conditioned reflex did not provide adequate insight into the psychological origins of what is called "deviant" or "collective" behavior by liberal sociologists. Consequently, he concluded (*ibid.:*214): "The psychoanalytic hypothesis gives a new approach to the field of investigation admittedly *sociological,* that of *the origin of* many of the standardized forms of *collective behavior"* (our emphasis). These and other remarks by participants in the 1920 session (e.g., Blanchard 1920:210) indicate the degree to which psychoanalytic notions were considered complementary to sociological thinking about delinquency, prostitution, labor agitation, revolutionary movements, and other manifestations of "social unrest," "social problems," and "collective behavior."

From 1915 to 1930, many sociologists influenced by Freud simply used the single term "sublimation" to signify the psychological processes involved in a specific theory of social stability and change. In 1926, Freud revived the concept of defense, which had been abandoned early in his writings in favor of the term "repression." He defined defense "as the general name for all the techniques, other than the normal ones, which the ego uses in putting down conflicts" (Hall and Lindzey 1954:162). After the twenties, sociologists increasingly referred to specific mechanisms such as reaction-formation, compensation, projection, repression, and sublimation in their theories.

Subjectivism versus Objectivism

During the second decade of this century there was an open market for the sale of highly general psychological mechanisms, particularly in explanations of social change. The arguments and category distinctions which took place in the face of the increasing attacks on utilitarian and associationist doctrines became very brisk indeed. The controversies over the question of why people associated in short- or long-lived social relationships were peppered with endless distinctions about the meanings of such categories as "imitation," "like-mindedness," and "common purposes." The disputes which dichotomized between "objective" and "subjective" relationships figured very importantly in these controversies.

Associationism, for example, was often perceived as irrevocably opposed to "subjectivism" because behaviorist models made minimal reference, by contrast to others, to the subjective dynamics that mediated between a stimulus situation and an individual response. The individual's subjective state mirrored his objective situation in the narrow sense that the objective (stimulus) situation directly accounted for his feelings and activities in a very simple, direct, utilitarian fashion. In fact, when the utilitarian and associationist mechanisms were finally formalized, it was apparent that the utilitarian propositions about the emotional effects of pleasurable and painful stimuli were so simple that they could largely be taken for granted. As a consequence it was assumed that the ordered relations between stimulus situations and the feelings of pleasure and pain could be directly inferred from *overt* behavioral responses.

These general remarks enable us to evaluate Charles A. Ellwood's criticism of behaviorist theories and rejection of "objectivism" in 1916 when Freud's theory was beginning to take hold among eminent sociologists. Ellwood noted (1916:289–290) that a movement to produce an "objective" science had emerged among behavioristic social scientists. These scientists, according to Ellwood, were in opposition to the use of data based on introspection, and admitted references only to directly observable activity in their explanations. Ellwood defended analytic strategies based on assumptions about the "subjective" nature of man and indignantly pointed out that the movement toward "objectivism" in the social sciences had been a problem for a long time. He complained (*ibid.*:291), moreover, that "it has even been claimed that Comte was the father of the [objective] movement. A careful reading of Comte, however, will show that there is little foundation for this view." Although Comte did not feel that introspection would be used as a valid method in the social sciences,[4] Ellwood pointed out, "no one was ever more insistent than he [Comte] upon the essentially psychic nature of human society—that it was dominated by a developing tradition, or ' social mind,' as we should say. In the *Positive Polity,* indeed, he goes so far as to say that sociology is 'reducible to true mental science.' "

In lining up support for his views, Ellwood examined Durkheim's statements. Durkheim (1938) had claimed that for sociology to become scientific, sociologists must study social facts independently of the conscious subjects in whose minds they existed. Although Ellwood was aware of this, he saw blatant inconsistencies in Durkheim's argument. Sociology, in Durkheim's stated view, did not consider individual consciousness and therefore did not have to be based on psychology. However, as Ellwood (*ibid.*:292) pointed out, Durkheim's concept of "collective representations" was very similar to the concept of the "social mind" being used by American sociologists. In Ellwood's opinion, Durkheim's "objectivism" therefore ended in "a subjectivism of the worst sort." Consequently Ellwood concluded that "Durkheim is no more entitled to be called an objective sociologist than Giddings or Cooley, whom he criticizes for their subjectivity."

Ellwood (*ibid.*:304) acknowledged that behaviorists were correct in insisting that "the scientific student of society . . . must begin his description with activity and end with activity." However, he questioned whether sociologists could explain significant changes in social life "without bringing in those *psychic processes* through which all the *active adaptations* of social life take place" (our emphasis). These psychic processes called "instruments of adaptation" made "the whole adaptive process . . . susceptible of intelligent guidance." They "mediated objective life processes." "They were *bridges* between two types of activity" (our emphasis).

Ellwood's remarks were written in 1916, but similar criticisms by subsequent generations of sociologists have echoed repeatedly in the halls, books, and journals dedicated to sociology. However, it is important to note that when Ellwood referred to psychic mediational processes, he was not speaking about the complex interaction between *ideology* and *socially instituted* forms of human activity. He reduced these mediational processes instead to the narrow framework provided by atomistic liberal concepts of man; he was speaking about a universal conception of an atomistic act, an atomistic consciousness, and an egoistic response to situational exigencies. We shall see in later chapters that even the description of these situational exigencies were organized by W. I. Thomas around atomistic and egoistic assumptions.

Although the "objectivist" scholars grounded their theories in a mechanical materialism, others, like Ellwood, mired their analytic strategies in the morass of subjective idealism. On the whole, however, it was the idealist, not the materialist, who prevailed in this platonic tug of war over the conflicts produced by these alternative liberal points of view. And the very significant gap in the armament of theoretical ideas—representing a need for a universal and systematic explanation of atomistic human responses—on the part of corporate-liberal sociologists interested in social change, was eventually filled by Sigmund Freud and his followers. Freudian "mechanisms of defense" supplanted Ellwood's vague reference to "instruments of [active] adaptation." They finally *bridged* the great reductionist chasm between social causes and social effects which had appeared when classical utilitarianism was swept to the side by new critical developments in psychological thought.

NOTES

1. In later years, the battle of the mechanisms was represented, on the one hand, by behaviorist sociologists like Edwin H. Sutherland, and, on the other, by "means-ends" theorists like Robert K. Merton. (Although Merton asserted that his "theory of anomie" was an alternative to Freudian revisionism, it can be demonstrated that the differences between Merton's theory and psychoanalytic theories are superficial. It is of no mean consequence that the two major theories of delinquency, organized around Merton's meta-theory (Cohen 1955, Cloward and Ohlin 1960) are dependent on Freudian mechanisms of defense.

2. Since the emergence of the social stimuli, not the individual response, was the object of inquiry in a problem of social change, the behaviorist strategies seemed to lead theorists in a closed conceptual circle. This circle was broken later by the development of behaviorist "coping mechanisms" which have theoretical functions very similar to those of psychoanalytic mechanisms of defense.

370

3. Peters believed that "it has been left to the physiological and behavioristic psychologists to *supplement* the work in psychoanalysis by the study of conditioned reflexes" (our emphasis).

4. It should be noted in passing that Comte found his model for the nature of man in the ludicrous phrenological system of Franz Josef Gall (Allport 1954:8).

———

CHAPTER 46

W. I. Thomas and the Entrance to the Freudian Bridge

Background

W. I. Thomas' publications exemplify the developments sketched in previous chapters. In addition, his new conceptual categories helped bridge over the profound chasm existing in sociology at the time. His first major work (1907) was concerned, among other things, with a solution to the Hobbesian problem of order and was organized around blatant male-supremist doctrines. Early in his career, he took (1909:viii) sharp issue with Herbert Spencer; nevertheless, he felt that there was some merit in Darwinism (*ibid.:*vii); and advised (*ibid.:*13–14) students to read "notable" works by Small, Gumplovicz, Durkheim, Greef, and Giddings. The racism underlying his evolutionary theories, furthermore, was no different from that of all the other corporate-liberal scholars we have considered.

Thomas' affinity for corporate liberalism is also evident in his infatuation with the concept of social control. As early as 1909, Thomas (*ibid.:*14–16) stated that "control . . . is the object of all purposive activity." Man, according to Thomas, "extends his control through the use of animals" and other objects. (Thus, "fire is a precious element in control" and mechanical inventions are "forms of control.") But Thomas went much further than merely suggesting that animate and inanimate tools are useful for controlling the environment. He also stated that "the gregariousness of animals and the *associated life of men* are modes of control." "Forms of government are aids to control. Religion assists control. . . . Art aids control. . . . Play is an organic preparation . . . for control. Marriage. . . . Medicine. . . . Liberty is favorable to control. . . . The human mind is pre-eminently the organ of . . . control. Knowledge . . . becomes the great force in control . . . all conflict, exploitation, showing off, boasting, gambling, and violations of the

371

decalogue, are designed to secure control." In Thomas' view, all aspects of life could be regarded from the standpoint of social control.

Although control is the end to be secured, Thomas (*ibid.:*17–18) asserted that individual or group "attention" is the means to that end. While attention, as the application of rational thought process to the solution of a problem was the *subjective* means, control, as the end, was considered the *objective* side of the same process. Through attention, man takes note of the "outside world and manipulates it"; attention is accommodation to crises. Attention is seen to combine with habit and crisis—normally persons act habitually but when habitual patterns are disturbed, "attention is called into play and [it] devises a new mode of behavior which will meet the crisis." Attention, therefore, enables the establishment of new and adequate habits in response to crisis situations. (In Thomas' later works, one of the paramount uses of the term *definition of the situation* was to classify *the field and objects of attention* to which the individual or group responded particularly in *crisis situations.*)

Thomas regarded attention as a means for securing social and personal control; therefore, his analysis of the subjective dimensions of accommodation to crises is tightly regulated by the broad concept of control. Since there is no doubt that the term "crisis" is used to refer to a significant personal moment in the process of all social change, it must also be regarded as a necessary condition for new forms of social or personal integration. When atomistic individuals become attentive to certain aspects of their disorganized environment because of personal crises, they may make decisions that lead to new forms of social or personal integration. As such, the situation becomes defined because it is a possible prelude to *order*. In Thomas' theories, the definitional process is the very first theoretically significant step taken by individuals in *controlling* heretofore *uncontrolled* social changes.

Individualizing Critical Situations in Laissez-Faire Capitalism

Generally, Thomas' analysis of contemporary capitalist society consisted of enumerating a list of factors making for "social disorganization." Like Ross, Thomas suggested that modern societies were characterized by "culture conflict," "social disorganization," "technological changes," "secondary institutions," "commercialization," and "individualism." Individually contracted relationships and "individualization of definitions of the situation" [1] replaced "the cake of custom" of less evolved, "primitive societies."

Under these disorganized neo-Hobbesian conditions Thomas claimed that individual crises became a normal feature of modern societies. In order to better understand social disorganization he (*ibid.:*22) suggested that "the best course that students can follow is to keep *individual* crisis constantly in mind" when making an analysis of change (our emphasis). This generally meant that the student should concern himself with an analytic strategy for studying change based on a combination of the concepts of "the four wishes," which specified the *motive* for choosing, and "the definition of the situation," which specified the *grounds* for choice.

It is our contention that Thomas reinforced the reductionist trends among American sociologists. However, on the basis of Thomas' methodological *advice* to sociological theorists, it is possible to argue that he did not "treat personality as a microcosm of culture, and culture itself, as 'personality writ large' " (Parenti 1967:xiv). It can also be contended that Thomas considered reductionism as an "evasion of the critical problems of socio-cultural analysis." Or that, "for Thomas, the individual is never simply determined by culture, but always by culture in conjunction with physiological, psychological and social forces" (*ibid.*:24). But there are glaring contradictions between Thomas' analytic recommendations and his own empirical studies. Even though Thomas may have explicitly favored a nonreductionist sociology, he did not *actually* construct his theories with this in mind. And although he may have suggested that all levels of analysis be considered, one can look in vain for any significant *dynamically* integrated references on the level of either physiological or macroscopic social relationships when examining his theories of concrete social behavior.

Thus, Thomas would have explicitly disagreed with Jeremy Bentham's opinion that society is the mere sum of its individuals. But Thomas' notion of social disorganization ultimately reduced society to its constituent parts. And these parts consisted of little more than atomistic individuals who were defined in terms of personal desires and individual "definitions" of social relationships. Thomas' analytic reflections, therefore, must be separated from the empirical assertions at the heart of his research. Like other sociologists, he was concerned with justifying his professional status as a *sociologist* on the basis of *non*reductionist principles. However, this concern did not override the effects of his liberal ideology.

In order to avoid becoming involved in interminable wrangling over what is meant by Thomas' concept of "the definition of the situation," let us examine the way in which this concept was *actually* applied. Thomas' theory of the adolescent prostitute can be taken as an excellent illustration of the *operative interpretation* of this notion and of the workings of the four wishes in the creation of normal and deviant social types.

The Prostitute and Social Disorganization

Every person, according to Thomas, possessed the desire for *security,* new *experience, response* and *recognition*. Of these four, the first two are quite fundamental to his analysis of social integration and change. The desire for security referred to fear, individual avoidance of death, conservatism, and "generally made for stability in habits and accumulation of property." The desire for new experience, on the other hand, could be expressed as the preference for personal change, individual curiosity, instability and social irresponsibility (Thomas 1967:14; Hinkle 1951:88).

Thomas referred to the four wishes in the first chapter of *The Unadjusted Girl*. He described the necessary conditions for the natural and normal (optimum) state by assuming that "an individual life cannot be called normal in which all the four types of wishes are not satisfied in some measure or some form" (1967:40). Different types of satisfactions must be acquired in relatively equal doses, because no single wish should "dominate" the others. The unnatural and abnormal condition is dominated or "overdetermined" by a single wish. "The social type known as the 'bohemian' and 'philistine' are determined respectively by the domination of the desire for new experience and the desire for security," while the miser signifies that "the means of security has become an end in itself" (*ibid.:*12). Like Freud's psychological man, Thomas' normal and natural man abhorred extremes and kept to the middle of the road; Thomas' prudent man balanced the imperatives of security with those of new experience; he was also responsive to others but not excessively so.

In the second chapter of his book, Thomas (*ibid.:*43) noted that there is an inevitable contradiction between the individual's imperatives and those of society. Because individuals are interested in personal pleasure and change, "society" must protect itself. "An *organized* society seeks . . . to *regulate* the *conflict and competition* inevitable between its members in the pursuit of their wishes" (our emphasis). An *unregulated* society however is doomed to *disintegration.*[2]

A moral code arises in order to regulate competition and conflict among individuals. This code "is a set of rules or behavior norms, regulating the expression of the wishes, and which is built up by *successive definitions of the situation.*" "Morality is thus the generally accepted definition of the situation," whether expressed in public opinion, religious commandments, or the mores. These "moral" or "social" definitions are thus instruments of social control. Because these definitions are acquired in primary relationships within the community, groups like the family and the neighborhood circle are "defining agencies" and are also instruments of control (our emphasis).

Thomas indicated that "the typical community is vanishing and it would be neither possible nor desirable to restore it in its old form." But, he added, although it does not "correspond to the present direction of social evolution," it will have to be restored in "some form of cooperation" in accordance with human nature in order to "secure a balanced and normal society." Thomas then detailed (*ibid.:*44–69) the necessary preconditions for returning to normality by way of community control of individual behavior. Unanimity and consensus about the definitions of the situation were suggested means to this end. Consensus was reflected in the "winks, shrugs, nudges, laughter, sneers, haughtiness, coldness" and "gossip" directed by most inhabitants toward individuals who deviated from established rules. The best kinds of means for "standardizing" the individual, however, were love and affection. These were means that could be employed by members of the community in cooperation with the family, and the outcome would be the achievement of a thoroughgoing regulation of individual behavior.

Unfortunately, members of typical modern communities are confronted with socially disorganized definitions of individual behavior. These definitions "press in" on the community and take such forms as "woman's rights" (*ibid.:*62). Modern women are encouraged to make their own way in the world. "Young people leave home for larger opportunities." The unadjusted girl is caught up unprepared and without communal support in this situation of rapid change. "Girls leave home to work in factories, stores, offices, and studies." They leave their primary relationships and become enmeshed in casual, secondary relationships. This movement is regarded as part and parcel of an evolutionary process involving technological developments, "the growth of cities, business organization, the capitalistic system, specialized occupations, scientific research, doctrines of freedom, the revolutionary view of life, etc. . . ." (*ibid.:*71). All these processes *weaken* social control and introduce conflicting definitions of the situation that may "demoralize" individual girls.

Thomas points out that traditional girls consider such things as "virginity" and "purity" to have "almost a magical value." These girls learn to value themselves in these terms. By sublimating their wishes according to these definitions, they acquire respect and adoration. However, "this sublimation of life *is an investment*" (*ibid.:*98). "It requires incessant attention and effort . . . and goes on best when life is economically secure." But in contemporary communities *"there are families and whole strata of society where life affords no investments.* There is little to gain and little to lose" (our emphasis). Under these conditions, girls are not rewarded for morally regulated striving and never acquire a moral code. They regard their sexual attributes in a socially expedient manner: *"Their sex* is used as a condition of the realization of other wishes. *It is their capital"* (our emphasis).

In short, Thomas proposed that girls were turning to prostitution because social change destroyed the traditional social controls and exchange relationships that supported the "values" of "virginity" and "purity." Under these uncontrolled and unrewarding conditions, girls created new opportunities for achieving gratification. They exchanged their sexual talents for money or its equivalents. These were used, in turn, to satisfy such fundamental desires as security, new experience, and response. Although their adjustment to frustration might be an abnormal one, it was very economical.

Definitions: Reason Controls Passion

Prostitution has been in existence for thousands of years in class societies. However, instead of conducting a comparative historical analysis of this persistent form of socially instituted behavior, Thomas regarded it as a product of individual choice and social disorganization created by technological and social changes occurring in the wake of capitalism. Prostitution was also considered unlikely among populations controlled by local customs and traditions; but his vague, historical testimonial to a "cake of custom" which tightly controlled the behavior of individuals in primitive tribes, agrarian communities, and small towns has long been discredited by anthropological and sociological research. His fictitious references served primarily as a backdrop for an economistic analysis of decision-making processes. They also provided an empirical warrant for the reformist critique of laissez-faire capitalism that was implicit in his description of technological and social changes. According to his analysis, these changes, introduced by the uncontrolled capitalist market, were responsible for the destruction of traditional primary relationships and for the demoralization (in the sense of *lowering* the morals) of large sections of the population. Prostitution was a product of this demoralization. It was ultimately caused by *crisis* situations emerging under uncontrolled and unrewarding "urban" (i.e., capitalist) conditions.

"Preliminary to any self-determined act of behavior," Thomas (*ibid.:*42) asserted, "there is always *a stage of examination and deliberation* which we can call the definition of the situation" (our emphasis). Confronted with a personal crisis the individual (e.g., the prostitute) is forced to make a decision in order to obtain some measure of gratification. The "definition," therefore, represents the objective relationships that are rationally considered by the individual just before making this decision. Classical liberals would have similarly interpreted the "definition" as the very beginning of an ideational process in which *reason takes control over passion*.

On the other hand, Thomas' "definition of the situation" was a refinement of the liberal concept of reason. It was also a response to several decades of analytic concentration on the socialization of individuals. Liberals have always regarded the policies dictated by reason as learned from life experience. It is therefore not surprising to find Thomas stating that the individual acquires his definitions of the situation "by experience." Corporate-liberal sociologists, concerned with the control of large populations, had begun to construct the concepts of attitudes and values and derived the concept of culture from these subjective components of individual consciousness. They turned their attention to the ways in which social relationships on many levels influenced individual decision-making. Even though they still subscribed to natural conceptions of man, they realized that macroscopic social changes were powerful influences on individual behavior. Thomas' concept of "the definition of the situation" provided a *link between sociological relationships and individual choice behavior*. He tied the knot between the two when he declared (*ibid.:*43): "Not only concrete acts are dependent on the definition of the situation, but gradually a whole life policy and the personality of the individual himself follow from a series of such definitions."

Definitions: Reason and Free Will

In the introduction to the *Unadjusted Girl,* Michael Parenti (1967:xi) has said: "To grasp the situation we need to study the institutional and cultural settings of family, church, gang, school, etc. and the attitudes and values which come into conflict or join forces with one's predilections and 'train of experiences,' in short, all the cues . . . that represent the beliefs and directives of the cultural systems along with the social agents who mediate such cues in any particular area of action." At first glance, this advice suggests that everything must be taken into account in order to describe the individual's definition of the situation. However, irrespective of whether a scholar's analytic definition of the "definition of the situation" includes every seemingly possible social determinant of the subjective qualities of individuals or not, only a very highly selected group of factors can be *theoretically* plausible when applying this concept in a concrete explanation of behavior.

Thomas wrongly suggested that a vast range of social factors enter into the "definition of the situation," especially when it is implied that these encompass "all the cues" to the exclusion of other components. In fact, psychological factors governed its actual application. Liberal sociologists cannot transform psychology into sociology. Scholars who used Thomas' "definition of the situation" or similar ideas about choice-making behavior, tacitly adopt the psychological assumptions at the heart of the families of theoretical models in general use. Thomas' awareness of psychological principles regulated his application of the concept of "the definition of the situation." Consequently, in spite of the fact that he suggested that the entire life history of the prostitute influenced her "definitions" in times of crisis, only very small fragments of her biographical account were actually made relevant to the study. Only those personal and social events that *justified the use of Freudian mechanisms and the rationality of exchange were considered important.* Sex was employed to satisfy her wishes and as her coin of exchange.

Chapter 6 described the major formal assumptions subsumed under the economic "postulate of scarcity," including, in part, (1) that there exists a condition of scarcity, (2) that means have alternative uses, and (3) that ends are graded in order of preference. In addition to voluntary choice-making, Thomas' "definition of the situation" emphasized, in particular, the individual's awareness of the rewards and risks attending to the various uses to which a socially constituted means could be put. This awareness also included an assessment of the nature of the social factors that influenced these rewards and risks.

It can be shown that Thomas' "definition of the situation" was primarily organized around the necessary grounds for choice. Choice, as conceived by Thomas, was a deliberate procedure. The grounds for choice, therefore, required evaluation by the individual. They were evaluated in that part of the sequence of economizing activity which was initiated by a condition of scarcity (of opportunities) and terminated in the rational assessment of the use values (sex as a commodity) as a means. His definition of the situation, therefore, simply detailed the processes of the traditional liberal concept of reason and free will on the basis of a nineteenth-century market analogy.

Although it is not obvious in Thomas' analysis, the prostitute's assessment of her use value was implicitly influenced by consideration of graded ends in terms of possible risks as well as gains. This became apparent with the realization that Thomas introduced his *analytic* definition of "the definition of the situation" in the chapter devoted to the influence of social controls on individual behavior. In that chapter he noted that, in general, powerful negative sanctions are used to exact conforming behavior. In the very next chapter, however, it was noted specifically that the young prostitute did not find herself seriously confronted with these sanctions because she was not embedded in cohesive, primary relationships. Primary relationships are weakened in modern societies and, as a consequence, these young women were confronted with neither definite risks nor definite rewards from family and community members. Furthermore, since Thomas believed that these young women had never acquired a moral code, they were not confronted with guilt either. As a result, the most economical solution to their problem was prostitution. How could it be otherwise? The young women needed to gratify their basic desires; however, all the legitimate uses to which these young women had put themselves involved low-paying factory jobs, unsatisfying school work, or other possibilities of this order. Along with the absence of rewards from family members for conforming behavior, these legitimate uses had low values and, in an indirect manner, established the condition of scarcity which characterized the means actually available for achieving gratification. Since the exchange of their only marketable "capital"—sex—for money, favors, or enjoyable experiences, did not involve significant references to external or internal sanctions, the decision to become a prostitute was the most logical one possible. Solving her problem in the sex market was eminently logical. (It involved the least effort and pain; it netted the greatest amount of satisfaction.) But this logic rested squarely on the postulate of scarcity, the rationality of exchange, and utilitarian assumptions about the nature of (wo)man.

Thus, a two-stage process was gradually differentiated and elaborated in the analysis of choice behavior. Sociologists used the first stage to establish the link between the broader social environment and individual consciousness. The second stage of the decision-making process provided the vitally necessary link between individual consciousness and socially instituted forms of new behavior. The bridge was now complete! Sociologists could finally claim that they had achieved a fully integrated theoretical strategy for solving the problems of social integration and change!

The Demise of Instinct Theory

Preoccupation with the personality processes related to social control had several consequences. It encouraged analysis of the socialization processes on the individual and the small group level. It also led to a focus on individual choice behavior in critical situations. In 1909 for example, W. I. Thomas encouraged students to examine crisis situations because he believed that significant changes in social relations occurred at these times. By the twenties, sociologists concerned with social control had generated an ensemble of analytic categories denoted by the terms "attitude," "value," and "definition of the situation." These terms referred to social-psychological characteristics acquired through experience and these characteristics were considered important determinants of individual choices (particularly under frustrating conditions).

By the middle of the twenties, American sociologists had generally used the notions of attitudes, values, and definition of the situation in an effort to reconceptualize material previously covered by such terms as "reason" and "instinct." It became unfashionable to derive psychological prime movers from the "vital" biological forces. Increasing numbers of sociologists had become convinced that the most important psychological motives influencing social integration and social change were acquired through social experience rather than heredity.

However, it is instructive to stop a moment for consideration of some of the logical characteristics of instinct theories. Even though other parts of the psychoanalytic model were being integrated into major sociological works, the general rejection by sociologists of the concept of instincts sheds light on their disapproval of Freud's instincts of love and aggression. This review will also deepen our appreciation of why Freud's analytic ideas were adopted by the Americans in a very *selective* way.

Illustration: Early Instinct Theory

One study based on instinct theory is doubly informative because of its historical role—it ranked among the earliest empirical inquiries into the origin and nature of adolescent gangs. In 1905, "a graduate student and fellow at Clark University," J. Adam Puffer, reported on his interviews of "sixty-six boys who were members of gangs" (Puffer 1912:iii). His article was later incorporated into a larger work entitled *The Boy and His Gang* (1912). Consistent with prevailing usage, the term "gang" in this work was used broadly to refer to any male adolescent group irrespective of its delinquent status.

How did Puffer explain gangs? He first claimed that the development of the child recapitulated the development of the race: "The young of each species . . . tends to reproduce in the course of its youth, the successive stages

379

in the history of its ancestors." In this sense, "the *normal* boy between ten and sixteen is really living through the historical period which for the race of Northern Europe began somewhere this side of the glacial period and came to an end with . . . the early middle ages" (our emphasis). On the basis of this assumption, Puffer (*ibid.*:78) asserted that a boy joins a gang because of his savage, herding instincts. He is "essentially a savage, with the interests of a savage, the body of a savage, and to no small extent, the soul of one. He thinks and feels like a savage; he has the savage virtues and the savage vices; and the gang is his tribe."

According to Puffer (*ibid.*:6), the gang, which he compared with the family, was "formed like a pack and flock and hive, in respect to *deep-seated but unconscious need* . . . The boy's reaction to his gang is neither more nor less reasonable than the reaction of a mother to her babe, the tribesman to his chief, or the lover to his sweetheart. All these alike belong to the ancient instinctive, ultra-rational parts of our human nature." Puffer also asserted that thievery was an expression of acquisitiveness which was "an entirely natural instinct." The "fighting impulse" was also a basic part of human nature, and "pugnacity," like all other instincts, arose because it was functionally necessary for mankind. The same held for the boy's growing interest in the opposite sex. This interest was stimulated by his "mating instincts," and sexual desire, like all other instincts, was beyond the rational part of human nature.

Puffer's advice to parents and teachers illustrates other facets of his instinctualism. He suggested (*ibid.*:108), for example, that "the problem of the school is to utilize to the full the great moving passions of boyhood." It was also suggested that "too much belligerency needs to be curtailed; too little needs to be increased." On the other hand, adults were urged to let nature generally have its way. Some of his advice sounded like Spencer's belief in the generally positive effects of natural processes: in Puffer's opinion, "the best way to deal with the gang instincts is to gratify them." *Normal* members of play groups have "just the right amount" of pugnaciousness and therefore "need a good deal of letting alone."

One of the gangs described in Puffer's work was *the Dowser Glums.* Its members seemed to take a positive delight in violating the law. In regard to such groups, Puffer suggested that parents and teachers should not attempt to "root out" the instincts that caused "evil" behavior. Instead, some *alternative* and constructive *means* for gratifying these instinctive *ends* should be found. It was indicated (*ibid.*:96), for example, that the adolescent's acquisitive instincts stimulated him to "acquire property of his own," and "we may keep a boy from becoming a thief by making him a collector . . . We help him to satisfy his natural desires for property in one way, and we check his tendency to satisfy it for himself in another."

A Total of 15,789 Concrete and Abstract Instincts

In Puffer's work a boy was thought to convert from a "solitary" into a "social animal" by his herding instinct; he stole because of his acquisitive instinct; fought because of his pugnacious instinct; and became interested in girls because of his mating instinct. These instincts appeared to refer to a limited range of acts or human relationships. Puffer also referred to more *abstract* instincts, such as the instinct for adventure and excitement and the predatory instincts of adolescent boys. Boys hunted, fished, and camped out of doors because of a desire for adventure and excitement; they were cruel to strangers or weaker boys, on the other hand, because of their predatory desires. In Puffer's theory, one instinct appeared to be more abstract than another if it "explained" a greater number of adolescent activities or relationships. Concrete instincts referred to a single type of act. The most abstract instincts "explained" a whole panorama of human acts or relationships. A concrete fighting instinct was expressed in fighting; an abstract instinct for adventure was expressed in hunting, fishing, camping, or traveling to strange places.

Whether a scholar used abstract or concrete instincts appeared arbitrary. If he used an abstract instinct, then a larger range of discrete types of individual behavior was depicted as offering alternative means of gratifying the instinct. By this means, scholars were able to claim that their theories had considerable generality. A few abstract instincts such as love or aggression could be used, for example, to "explain" every possible form of individual behavior; whereas many instincts on a lower level of abstraction would have to be listed in order to encompass these varied forms of conduct.

In the early twenties, sociologists became concerned about the tautological and unclear usage of "instincts" on all levels of abstraction. They were also distressed about the extraordinary number of instincts mentioned in the biological and social science literature. For example, Ellsworth Faris (1921a:181) exclaimed, "At the present time there is the widest diversity of opinion as to what an instinct is; there is the utmost confusion as to how many there are."

In another critical essay, Faris (1926:25) suggested that "a zoologist who describes the migrating salmon or the breeding habits of seals is dealing with a single species whose members exhibit a universality of action." But when this kind of explanation is applied to social customs, Faris added, then "every tribe or race must be assumed to have different instincts, and the basic error of the whole instinct psychology stands revealed. *Then instinct merely becomes another name for custom.*" Illustrating the logical extreme of such a substitution, Faris indicated that the Shakers might be erroneously explained by "assuming a selection of people who had no sex instincts, or very weak ones." "The peaceful tribes" could be considered "lacking in the instincts of pugnacity." It can also be concluded on the basis of instincts that "the French have a different instinct from the English" or that Anglo-Saxons have an "in-

CONSOLIDATION AND OPPRESSION

stinct for representative government which the Italians and Orientals are assumed to lack." Although "traditional instincts" were an important part of the "popular psychology" of the day, Faris reiterated that they were "mere tautologies for ancient customs."

The most telling blow administered to instinct theorists in American sociology was represented by L. L. Bernard's 1924 study of approximately two thousand books in the biological and social disciplines. Bernard found the extraordinary total of 15,789 separate instincts listed; these were classified under 6,131 separate but more abstract instincts. Furthermore, many of these instincts referred to learned behavior. It became obvious that the concept of instincts was being used in arbitrary and contradictory ways. Because of Bernard's study, the use of the crude concept of unconditioned instincts to explain sociological relationships was completely discredited. Although a few modern scholars still espouse biological theories of sociological relationships, the twenties marked the final and well-earned demise of biologism and psychobiologism among American scholars. With a few exceptions, the crude biologism which had been so popular during Spencer's lifetime had been irrevocably put aside by members of the profession. Furthermore, neither Freud's growing popularity nor the greater (psychobiological) complexity of his concept of instincts could save this concept from the widespread disfavor into which instincts in general had fallen.

In time, American sociologists not only abandoned the concept of instincts but also rejected the practice, characteristic among the founding sociologists, of formulating a list of universal desires or interests. Ogburn's eleven desires and Thomas' four wishes represented the tail end of this customary practice.

NOTES

1. The terms "individualization of choice" and "individualization of definitions of the situation," in this context, prepared the groundwork for an atomistic analysis of social change.

2. These propositions were based on natural social-law rather than traditional natural law. They were introduced to justify the use of social control as a solution to the problem of integration.

PART TWELVE

Park and Burgess' Natural Social-Laws and the Stabilization of a New Formalism

CHAPTER 47

The Consolidation of Theoretical Ideas

During the first half of the formative years, Small was a staunch champion of Ward's theoretical writings. However, around the turn of the century Small was influenced by the critical reactions to Ward's theoretical analysis of genetic relationships. Small changed his appraisal of Ward's work and this cut deeply. In a 1903 letter to an admirer, Ward (Stern 1937:318) wrote that Small was only interested in listening to his [Ward's] critics. He added that "a change had come over the spirit of his [Small's] dreams, and I can only account for it on the hypothesis that he is under instructions from the capitalist censorship that controls the U. of C. [University of Chicago]." Ross (*ibid.*:320), on becoming aware of Ward's estrangement from Small, wrote to Ward, "I am much dismayed too at the mistrust growing up in your mind against Small . . . It does not appeal to me as reasonable that the authorities of the University of Chicago would interest themselves in heading off the diffusion of such *general ideas* as sociologists deal in. They can see in them *no concrete menace to property* or to the Standard Oil *monopoly*" (our emphasis).

Ross was undoubtedly correct about the attitudes of University trustees toward *academic* sociological theories written by leading sociologists. But the

383

publication of *Pure Sociology* and *Applied Sociology* did reveal that one of Ward's major ideas was the utopian belief that outright public ownership of major industries such as power and transportation was socially desirable.[1] Ward, of course, took pains to point out that nationalization of highly centralized industries would help perpetuate rather than subvert capitalism. He supported his argument by referring to the operation of nationalized industries in capitalist England, France, Germany, and Australia. In spite of this, however, Ward's notions did not sit well with more conservative scholars. For example, in a review of *Applied Sociology,* Thorndike (1907:291) referred to Ward's views in this work as "intellectual communism." Although Ward's advocacy of a secular sociology and a monopoly-state capitalism was a far cry from communism, this combination became objectionable to religious and politically conservative leaders in the field, among them Ulysses G. Weatherly.

Stabilization of Complementary Sets of Theoretical Ideas

Ward never suggested that his utopian society would come into being in the near future. Nevertheless, by 1920, Ulysses G. Weatherly, who became president of the American Sociological Society [2] only a few years later, stated that Ward's "gospel of sociocracy" was predicated upon a radical change in human nature which "is outside the bounds of reasonable expectation." Furthermore, it was Weatherly's opinion (1920:32) that neither the "wild Russian experiment in group economy" nor any other attempt to realize "the utopian ideal of social solidarity" in the present or near future, would achieve "effective common action for the general welfare."

Weatherly (*ibid.:*23–26) claimed that the primitive nature of man prevented collective activity which would improve the general welfare or achieve "the utopian ideal of social solidarity." He even declared that personal qualities such as love, hate, avarice, and revenge "are almost as largely the content of life as they were in the Stone Age . . . human nature, and particularly youthful human nature, psychologists tell us, has not changed in kind since the earliest recorded time." In other words, since men are basically savages, they cannot build a truly civilized society.

Turning his professional attention to the state, it was Weatherly's belief that "representative government is verging toward bankruptcy, both as a political mechanism and as a mode of group self-expression." This situation had developed not because the idea of democratic representation was morally wrong, but because it was no longer adequate in light of changing social circumstances. Because of these changes, "the unitary [i.e., the laissez-faire liberal] political state in which [individual representation] grew up is itself passing over into the social [i.e., the corporate liberal] state." Political democracy previously concerned itself with such relationships as the rights of individuals, social equality, and police power. "In the social state now evolving the [interest] group is the unit and the adjustment of group relationships is the state's prime function." Weatherly's remarks illustrate the degree to which a highly formal vocabulary, based on liberal-syndicalist and interest group notions, had become standardized among academic sociologists.

A 1919 article, "Democracy and Class Relations," by F. Stuart Chapin—who later became a president of the American Sociological Society—illustrates the use of several Freudian notions in an explanation of "pathological" social change. Chapin (1919:100) stated that "deep in the original nature of all men there is a powerful urge toward self-realization." [3] The repression of this urge will cause "disharmony" and "internal conflict" in individuals. Referring to the defensive mechanisms of displacement, projection, symbolism, compensation, and rationalization, all explained most thoroughly by Freud, Chapin claimed that "states of internal disquietude and turmoil . . . may have strange consequences." Investigation shows that these consequences included "vague industrial unrest" and "inflamed" radicalism involving "direct action and sabotage" (*ibid.*:102).

Explaining the causes of this unrest, Chapin (*ibid.*:104) stated that "the centralization of ownership and directing power" in the economy was an important "cultural more" which repressed the instincts of curiosity, of self-assertion, and of acquisition among the "masses of laboring men." Men's reactions to this repression, he said, "take the form of certain well known psychological defenses, curious adaptations of the organism or of the group to forces in the environment which produce internal conflict." Although Chapin alternated between the individual and societal levels he had specific conflicts in mind and these became clear from his conclusion that "class and industrial conflict are the products of repressed instincts."

After this reductionist interpretation of class and industrial conflicts, Chapin (*ibid.*:108) echoed the liberal-syndicalist sentiments of his day by indicating that "the time element involved in thoroughgoing readjustment and reorganization of class relations is considerable." Because change can only occur very slowly and because survival and order were central desires of man, he proposed that members of society must show patience and should engage in "frank efforts to meet existing conflicts with compromise." "Accommodation" and "compromise" will be seen as two terms sharing a common meaning.

The organizing ideas behind these diverse views can be indicated: Weatherly's discussion of the coming industrial democracy had been organized primarily around syndicalist notions while containing a few references to psychoanalytic conceptions. By contrast, Chapin's comments were organized primarily around psychoanalytic ideas, but they also contained liberal-syndicalist sentiments. By 1921, however, differences in emphasis or jargon could not mask the fact that sociologists had begun to use systematically interrelated sets of ideas developed over the previous forty years. Some of these ideas, notably the theories created by Small, Ross, and Durkheim, thoroughly reflected a corporate-liberal perspective. Liberal-syndicalists grounded their analysis in the relations leading to industrial stability. Freudian mechanisms explained pathological social change. Other theoretical ideas were clustered around reform Darwinist conceptions, the reconciliation of racial and ethnic conflicts, and the assimilation of racial and ethnic groups. However, even though great diversity appeared to characterize the sociological notions developed since the 1880s, and there were disagreements between individual theorists, their ideas fell into related sets when they were theoretically consolidated by sociologists over time.

Park and Burgess' Synthesis of Preexisting Ideas

The existence of systematic interrelationships among established theoretical ideas became clearly evident in 1921. At that time, Park and Burgess published their highly formal "synthesis" of the major ideas in the field of sociology. One of the features of their work was the proposal that all types of sociological relationships could be classified according to four universal and interrelated processes of social interaction called competition, conflict, accommodation, and assimilation. Among other things, *competition* classified the vast, unconscious, and impersonal processes of nature which gave rise to both interdependent and conflicting relations between individuals or groups. *Conflict,* on the other hand, referred to the emergence of human consciousness of competitive processes and the conscious attempts to control these in favor of individual or group interests. *Accommodation* and *assimilation* represented further steps in the development of this process of control; accommodation was the process by which interest groups reconciled their conflicts to the "public interest," while assimilation classified the stable, institutionalized products of long-term reconciliation. These processes included modifications in individual personalities.

Park and Burgess' categories were dependent upon preexisting liberal ideas. Pure competition, for example, differed from the other universal processes in that it resembled Ward's genetic processes. The purest forms of competition referred to "the natural forces of competition." The processes of conflict, accommodation, and assimilation, on the other hand, were produced, like telic processes, by attempts to intelligently comprehend and control competitive forces.

The category of assimilation partly represented reform Darwinist ideas which had gradually evolved from the theoretical generalizations and the educational and moral doctrines produced by national chauvinists and racists, including Park himself. An example of Park's assimilation theory had already appeared in a 1918 article that discussed various aspects of foreign and domestic imperialism. The work of missionaries in this article was unabashedly viewed as "essentially one of colonization" in the sense that they reconcile conflicting cultures or "graft" and "fuse" a "new culture" onto an older one

(Park 1918:40). Park (*ibid.*:40) asked, "How far do racial characteristics and innate biological interests determine the characteristic features of an alien civilization?" Underlying his answers to such questions was the acceptance of the notion of a "racial temperament" which consisted of "a few elementary but distinctive characteristics." An example of racial temperament was contained in the following statement: "The Negro is, by natural disposition, neither an intellectual nor an idealist, like the Jew; nor a brooding introspective, like the East Indian; nor a pioneer and frontiersman, like the Anglo Saxon. He is primarily an artist, loving life for its own sake. His *métier* is expression rather than action." The Jew, Park (*ibid.*:60) added, is a "natural-born idealist, internationalist doctrinaire, and revolutionist, while the Negro . . . has uniformly shown a disposition to loyalty during slavery to his master and during freedom to the South and the country as a whole."

The relations among the processes of conflict, accommodation, and assimilation also referred to well-established liberal-syndicalist solutions to the reconciliation of class conflict. These relations incorporated all the processes generating very stable patterns of social subordination and domination for different races, classes, and ethnic groups.

Still further similarities between Park and Burgess' categories and preexisting ideas will be pointed out in the chapters that follow. It will be shown that their abstract categories encompassed virtually every outstanding corporate-liberal idea developed during the formative years. Moreover, entire theories were symbolized in their concept of "universal processes of social interaction." In fact, it was alleged that their natural-social-law categories could be used in the study of virtually every significant human relationship throughout history.

Because of that total comprehensiveness, we will borrow a term from C. Wright Mills (1959:25–49) and call Park and Burgess' conceptual system "a grand theory."

NOTES

1. In the first chapter of *Applied Sociology,* in spite of his animus toward socialism, Ward (1906:10) went so far as to say that socialist parties might someday achieve control of the state. He stated that: "Statistics show that the socialist vote is increasing in all countries where it is made a political issue, and the time may arrive when the party will come into power somewhat generally." His comment about statistical trends was quite accurate. The size of the socialist vote in a number of major European countries has been increasing fairly steadily from the last quarter of the nineteenth century onwards.

2. This society changed its name in later years to American Sociological Association.

3. Chapin added, "*Moderate* self-expression of the instincts of workmanship, curiosity, ownership or acquisition, self-assertion and pugnacity, is *natural* and *normal*" (our emphasis).

CHAPTER 48

A Natural-Social-Law Conception of Competitive Processes

Overview of Park and Burgess' Chapter on Competition

Park and Burgess' discussion of the universal processes of competition opened with a brief summary of "the popular conceptions of competition." These conceptions by and large viewed competition as a social good. In this summary, the authors (1924:504) claimed that eighteenth-century economists and physiocrats had revealed that competition promoted a harmony of interests. Evolutionary biologists, in their study of "the struggle for existence," had discovered competition "as a universal phenomenon." Scholars also realized that competition, guided by laissez-faire principles, had "created a world economy where previously there were only local markets." Competition, on the other hand, had generated an industrial division of labor and invidious class distinctions. It had even created a demand, in modern industrial societies, for control of "unfair competition" in the interests of "competition itself" (*ibid.*:505–506).

The remainder of Park and Burgess' chapter on competition was devoted to a presentation of their loosely connected propositions about the "universal features of competition." The chapter also contained a sample of reading materials intended to illustrate these "universal" qualities. Migratory, demographic, interracial, economic, and ecological relationships were also provided as concrete illustrations of competitive relationships. By the end of the chapter, the authors had made the point that the diverse effects of competition revealed that "a competitive order" has existed everywhere and always among living things.

Ascending Phylogenetic Order: Laissez-Faire Plant Life to Corporate-Liberal Human Life

To clarify the principles behind Park and Burgess' analysis of competitive processes, it should be recalled that prior to the 1920s, liberal sociologists utilized two conflicting perspectives toward competition as a universal phenomenon: *social* Darwinism and *reform* Darwinism. Both of these perspectives viewed competitive relationships among nonhuman species in terms of the natural forces of competition and the survival of the fittest. But they strongly disagreed about competitive relations among human beings. Whereas the social Darwinians were laissez-faire in their orientation to human competition, reform Darwinists had come to view social control as an inherently necessary aspect of human evolution. Competition, therefore, required some degree of social control.

The reform Darwinist perspective toward competitive relations was reflected in its explanatory mechanisms. If *nonhuman* relationships were under examination, then the analytic propositions were organized around the ecological "exchanges" that created "functionally interdependent" forms of plant, insect, or animal life. On the other hand, if *human* relationships were under consideration, then the analytic propositions were organized around social control as well as exchange mechanisms.

Park and Burgess viewed universal competitive processes from a reform Darwinist vantage point. Accordingly, they classified natural processes that were as elemental as plant life. It was noted that competition created "functionally interdependent" relations among plants and other living things. Moreover, social Darwinian concepts based on "the survival of the fittest" were considered adequate for explaining "competitive processes" among nonhuman members of the animal kingdom. But "the competitive process," according to Park and Burgess (1924:664) "exists only in plant communities . . . in its absolute form." By contrast, competitive human processes involve social control.

Park and Burgess:
Opponents of Laissez-Faire Competition

Because of Park and Burgess' Darwinian (ecological) analogies, it has been maintained that they derived their concept of competition from Herbert Spencer. In fact, their "ecological" analysis of city life has been seen as reflecting a straightforward Spencerian view.[1] We have noted that they were influenced by Spencer. Nevertheless it will be maintained here that Park and Burgess' analysis of competitive human relations was actually a corporate-liberal analysis. This contention implies that they proposed ideas common to both classical and laissez-faire liberals. But it also indicates that these authors departed from traditional liberal ideas, particularly in their use of the concept of social control.

Our interpretation of Park and Burgess' work is confirmed by their evaluation of laissez-faire doctrines. These authors indicated (*ibid.:*505) that "competitive processes" had led to the development of worldwide markets. Agreeing with Spencer, they (*ibid.:*507) noted that competition contributes to the social good in human relations. On a person-to-person level, "competition invariably tends to create an impersonal social order in which each individual, being free to pursue his own profit . . . inevitably contributes . . . to the common welfare." Thus far, Park and Burgess had one foot in traditional liberal doctrines.

But Park and Burgess' other foot was planted one step ahead in newer soil: they indicated that "the growth of large scale production" has made it necessary to control competition. They declared that English legislation, "in spite of Herbert Spencer," has moved "in the direction of a collectivistic social order." The reason for this was simply that "the growth of communication, economic organization and cities . . . have so increased the mutual interdependence of all members of society as to render illusory and unreal the old freedoms and liberties which the system of laissez-faire was supposed to guarantee" (ibid.:558–559).

Once again, referring to Spencer, Park and Burgess (ibid.:512) flatly said that "the absolute free play of competition is neither desirable nor even possible." For justification they added that control over competition is not only synonymous with "individual movement" (i.e., individual freedom), it is also identified with "telesis" (i.e., intelligent social control).

Thus, prior to the publication of Park and Burgess' book, social Darwinism had been reinterpreted and integrated into the new corporate-liberal world view. It had *become* reform Darwinism. By 1921, however, reform Darwinism itself had been so highly attenuated that sociologists like Park and Burgess could no longer admit the assumption of *totally* unrestricted "pure" competition as a preexisting state of human affairs. Pure competition had only existed among plants. Every human society exerts some control over competitive processes: competition among humans operates within "the limits the cultural process creates, and custom, law, and institutions impose" (ibid.:507).

Competition, Distributive Justice, and Individual Freedom

Competition, in Park and Burgess' theory, was used to clarify the notions of individual freedom and distributive justice. Because their concepts are so interrelated, we must describe their concept of individual freedom before we can understand their view of distributive justice. In their discussion about individual freedom, Park and Burgess first suggested that society was "made up of individuals *spacially* separated, *territorially* distributed, and capable of independent *locomotion*" (our emphasis). With regard to "locomotion" by atomistic individuals, they stated that it "is the basis and the symbol of every other form of locomotion . . . *Freedom* is fundamentally freedom to *move* and individuality is inconceivable without the capacity and the *opportunity* to gain an individual experience as a result of independent action" (our emphasis). In these statements, Park and Burgess used analogical phrases like "spacial dis-

390

tribution" and "locomotion" as surrogates for historically substantive and clearly understandable liberal ideas about individual freedom. Freedom was largely defined in terms of geographic mobility and "the opportunity to gain individual experience as a result of independent action." This mobility and independence, however, makes ethical sense only if it implies the ability of individuals to free themselves of ties to the land, to royal decrees, or to national identities, in order to move about in search for a more profitable existence. In regard to "competition," this concept of freedom was plausible because liberals believed that the serf became free because he was free to *compete* for wages in cities; the trader became free because he could freely *compete* in all corners of the earth without hindrance from royal monopolies, patents, and edicts; and the industrial worker was free because he could move about in order to *compete* with all other workers.

Perhaps the clearest example of the usage of the concept of free, competitive relations was Park and Burgess' political and economic determinants of distributive justice and economic inequality. Distributive justice was primarily considered in the context of the orderly "spacial distribution" of the individuals, involving the location of the breadwinner and his family in a wealthy or poor residential area. This kind of distribution was obviously based on the distribution of wealth and resources in society, even though it confused competitive processes with what they perceived as the "ecological" effects of these processes.

It can be demonstrated from examination of their theory as a whole, that Park and Burgess regarded competitive processes as being so "fundamental" that they could be regulated but never fully transcended by planned social intervention. Therefore, the main determinants of distributive justice which underlie the inequalities in the distribution of wealth and resources were, to some extent, beyond human control. Humanity, in this view, was free to move about and engage in competitive relationships, but human nature imposed sharp limits on the freedom to transcend the forces of competition. Consequently, Park and Burgess' notions of "universal competitive processes" represented another statement of the natural-social-law tradition. The ideological function of the concept competition, in the theory as a whole, was to establish the limited terms in which the arguments about distributive justice could be waged. This "empirical" perspective set the ground rules for the solution to integration as an "allocation problem" which is solved by the "universal processes" of *conflict* and *accommodation* among interest groups.

Panconflictism and Enduring Conflict Resolution

Park and Burgess (1924:508) shared the twentieth-century liberal concern with social integration and believed that the functions of social control "inevitably" made control "the central problem of sociology." They felt that all of their various universal processes of social interaction were effected by social controls but not in equal measure. Conflict, accommodation, and assimilation were distinguished from competition because they were "all *intimately* related to control" (our emphasis). Competition among humans was socially controlled. By comparison with other universal processes of social interaction, however, human competition was *relatively* uncontrolled.

Park and Burgess (*ibid.*:509) stated that "in periods of crisis, when men are making new and conscious efforts to control the conditions of their common life . . . the forces with which they are competing get identified with persons, and *competition* is converted into *conflict*" (our emphasis). This conversion of one type of "social interaction" into another, the authors argued, occurred within the political arena because it is in this arena that society consciously deals with its crises. The political process, as we shall see, introduces such "telic" relations as "public opinion" and "the judgement of mankind" into the universal processes of social interaction.

As indicated previously, the shadow of Ward's great division between the unconscious forces of nature or genesis, and the conscious forces of human intelligence or telesis, loomed large over Park and Burgess' theory in general. For example, it was felt that the processes of conflict arose when individuals developed consciousness of their relative "statuses" or "positions" in life, particularly through group conflict. The conscious awareness of competitive processes through conflict transformed the nature of human relationships because consciousness was considered a precondition for the arbitration of issues raised by competition. The consciousness of various kinds of group conflict, including war, therefore, was considered the necessary condition which led to the eventual regulation of competition through "social control."

Park and Burgess' analysis of conflict was based on reform Darwinist and liberal-syndicalist assumptions. For example, they used syndicalist notions about the perpetual clash of interest groups when describing the universal nature of conflict. For a review of basic syndicalist assumptions the reader is referred to Chapter 16. The following discussion will concentrate, instead, on their analysis of war as a prime expression of group conflict.

Conflict: "War the Political Process Par Excellence"

When Park and Burgess turned their attention to the various forms of conflict, they stated (*ibid.*:575–576), "it is interesting . . . that political and judicial forms of procedure are conducted on a conflict pattern. An election is a contest in which we count noses when we do not break heads. A trial by jury is a contest in which the parties are represented by champions, as in the judicial duels of an earlier time." In fact, "in general . . . one may say competition becomes conscious and personal in conflict" and "competitors are transformed into rivals and enemies." In the most abstract, or "higher forms" of conflict, such as "war,"

conflict becomes impersonal—a struggle to establish and maintain rules of justice and a moral order. In this case, the welfare not merely of individual men but of the community is involved . . . [and] the issues are not determined by the force and weight of the contestants *immediately* involved, but to a greater or lesser extent, by the force and weight of public opinion of the community, and eventually, by the judgement of mankind (our emphasis).

In developing this argument they claimed: "War is the political process par excellence. It is in war that the great decisions are made." This does not mean that other political relations are unimportant; "political organizations exist for the purpose of dealing with conflict situations." But it is nevertheless the case that such political relationships as "parties, parliaments and courts, public discussion and voting are to be considered simply as substitutes for war" (*ibid.*).

Furthermore, just as there is broad participation in other political processes, there is great "human interest" in wars. Among the spectators, conflict develops between the noncombatants who take sides and create public opinion. "This has raised war from a mere play of physical forces and given it the tragic significance of a moral struggle, a conflict of good and evil." "The result," according to Park and Burgess, "is that war *tends to assume the character of litigation,* a judicial procedure, in which *custom* determines the method of procedure, and the issue of the struggle is *accepted* as a judgement in the case" (our emphasis).

On the basis of their assumptions, it can be logically argued that World War I, which Park and Burgess had witnessed and supported shortly before the publication of their textbook, was merely a ceremonial affair and that the division of African colonies among imperialist powers, for example, was the outcome of an essentially juridical procedure.

By way of summary, *competition* in Park and Burgess' work involved formalized notions about the economic order, while *conflict* was identified with the political order. Finally, the ideological functions of conflict in their theory were particularly centered on the justification of racial, national, and class inequalities. Competition and conflict initiated the sequential process which maintained or revised the distribution of power and wealth among individuals. Furthermore, although restrained by custom, litigation, and "the judgement of mankind," different degrees of conflict, including war, were responsible for the distribution of wealth and power on a worldwide basis.

Accommodation: Universalizing the Liberal-Syndicalist Class Differentiation

Park and Burgess considered the third concept, accommodation, as being "associated with the social order that is fixed and established in custom and the mores" (*ibid.:*510). Accommodation can be grasped by contrasting it with adaptation. In Darwin's theory, according to Park and Burgess, adaptation referred to species characteristics that had "survival value"; i.e., it was associated with the biological order. By contrast with adaptation, accommodation referred to "all the social heritages, traditions, sentiments, cultures and techniques" which are "socially and not biologically transmitted" (*ibid.*:163).

Park and Burgess (*ibid.*:665) further distinguished accommodation by utilizing images and terms that were prevalent in works by "social engineers" during the formative years. Park and Burgess had stated that in the process of being "domesticated" man modified the inheritable biological traits of plants and animals. When animals were "tamed," however, a species which was "naturally in conflict with man" became accommodated to him. Man could likewise be regarded as "tamed," rather than "domesticated," when he became educated. In fulfilling this end, education, in Park and Burgess' opinion, represented "a program of accommodation."

Park and Burgess perceived society along liberal-syndicalist lines; that is, in terms of functionally interdependent blocs, conflicts of interest, and integrations through accommodations. These categories, however, were stated in *exceedingly* formal terms: "Every society represents an organization of elements more or less antagonistic to each other but united for the moment, at least, by an arrangement which defines the reciprocal relations and respective spheres of action of each." This arrangement or adjustment involved accommodation and referred to "any alteration of function resulting in a better *adjustment* to environment and to the functional changes which are thus effected" (*ibid.*:663).

Although Park and Burgess had apparently *abstracted* and then *formalized* certain basic notions from liberal-syndicalism as it was developed among the American sociologists, they also *generalized* these formal notions into *universal* features of social life: these notions, therefore, applied to all human societies. Panconflictism was a salient feature of their conflict-control theory. Conflicting groups were said to characterize *all* societies—tribal, slave, feudal, and capitalist, although the duration of the accommodations between them varied from society to society. Accommodations might be "relatively permanent" in a caste society or "quite transitory" in "societies made up of open classes" (*ibid.*:665). Like Spencer, these authors also remade *all* human societies in their image of American capitalism; however, at a further state of its development. Instead of using Spencer's "economistic fallacy" for this purpose, Park and Burgess reconceptualized all human societies on the basis of what should properly be called an "interest group fallacy."

Competition, Conflict, and Accommodation
Explain Class Relations

In Park and Burgess' theory, the processes of competition and conflict were used to introduce the inequalities in the distribution of power and wealth within and between societies. Accommodative relations then modified or stabilized established distributive arrangements among small groups, occupational groups, nationality groups, sexual groups, and racial groups. Accommodative processes also influenced distributive relations in all preexisting

394

societies. In addition, class relations and the relations between imperialist and colonial nations were stabilized by accommodative processes.

In their discussion, Park and Burgess (*ibid.*:667) stated that there had been four historical types of societal-wide structures based on accommodation. The structure of primitive society was alleged to be determined by accommodative relations between kinship groupings. It was maintained that the structure of ancient society was essentially an outcome of the accommodative relations between two groups called "masters" and "slaves" ("with some special form of accommodation for the freeman and the stranger who was not a citizen to be sure but was not a slave either"). In medieval societies, groups accommodated themselves in "a system of class approaching castes." Social and economic classes constituted the dominant group formations in modern societies. These classes were first stabilized by accommodative processes; but in time they were regulated by the mores.

According to Park and Burgess, competition could only take place "between members of the same status" in a caste system and therefore individuals were *denied* the opportunities of mobility (*ibid.*). In happy contrast with medieval society, however, modern society contained "economic and social classes with freedom of economic competition and freedom in passage therefore from one class to another." Since all preexisting societies were based on "accommodated groups," irrespective of whether they were called kinship groups, masters, slaves, castes, or classes, by logical extension, the structure of modern society was also predicated upon *accommodation* between classes.

Corporate liberals had previously used the *state,* a political arbiter, as the prime means for reconciling group conflicts. Park and Burgess' formulation had greater generality. It could also be used to analyze nonpolitical relationships. It could be applied to family relations, delinquent group relations, or union relationships. Like competition, individual or group accommodation was *universal;* it could be applied to any "social order."

Although the theory was formulated in abstract and formal terms, Park and Burgess' discussion did pinpoint one issue very clearly. Accommodation did *not* take place on the basis of *force and violence*. Submission or subjugation by force involved conflict rather than accommodation. In spite of these conflicts, the authors claimed (*ibid.*), for example, that "even where accommodation has been imposed, as in the case of slavery, by force, the personal relations of master and slave are invariably supported by appropriate attitudes and sentiments." These attitudes and sentiments included "the self-complacent and reverential loyalty on the part of the slave" because "in order to impose his will on his slaves, it was necessary for the master to retain their respect" (*ibid.*:667–668).

Particular kinds of psychological and social psychological relationships supported accommodative processes. Conflict groups did not have to be "likeminded." They could differ from one another with regard to goals. But they also had to be "diverse-minded" or *tolerant* about their differences (*ibid.*:664). Furthermore, "prestige," "personal influence," and "authority"

395

were the kinds of personal controls that enhanced accommodation. These controls, which were generally referred to as control by "suggestion," subtly influenced conflicting groups or individuals to accommodate to one another (*ibid.*:668).

Assimilation: Long-Term Solution to Integration

In Park and Burgess' theory, accommodation between individuals and groups led to rapid modifications in attitudes and status relations. But these modifications might only remain in effect for a short time. Conflict, latent in the accommodative processes, can break out again with changes in social, economic, or political relationships. In order to endure, accommodative relations must be "assimilated" into the traditions of groups and the personalities of individuals.

Assimilation enabled accommodation to function as a *long-term* solution to the problem of integration because it involved processes which, above all, changed the nature of individual personalities. Since Park and Burgess also felt that these changes could only occur in intimate primary groups such as the family, they suggested (*ibid.*:510) that "assimilation, as distinguished from accommodation, implies a more thoroughgoing transformation of the personality—a transformation which takes place gradually under the influence of social contracts of the most concrete and intimate sort."

As groups or individuals were accommodated, traditions which appeared to be strange and foreign at first became acceptable and deemed worthy of imitation. Since mutually respectful relations of superordination and subordination were involved in accommodative processes, the positive cultural characteristics of groups were suggested as worthy of adoption. In this climate of tolerance, modification of group traditions and individual attitudes was initiated by the mechanisms of imitation and suggestion. "Assimilation," according to Park and Burgess (*ibid.*:735), "is a process of interpenetration and fusion in which persons and groups acquire the memories, sentiments, and attitudes of other persons or groups, and, by sharing their experience and history, are incorporated with them in a *common* cultural life" (our emphasis).

Reassuring their readers once again, Park and Burgess insisted that the process of assimilation did not assume that persons would come to think and act *alike*. Referring to the "Americanization" of the immigrant, they noted that the immigrant contributed "something of his own temperament, culture and philosophy of life to the future American civilization." They added that "this recognition of diversity in the elements entering into the cultural process is not, of course, inconsistent with the expectation of an *ultimate homogeneity* of the product" (our emphasis). Although the authors called attention to the fact that assimilation "is concerned with differences quite as much as with likeness," the ultimate outcome of assimilation was the merging of these differences into a common culture. Enduring stability or integration was

396

achieved by national consensus and cultural homogeneity. On the other hand, the United States was viewed as embodying both pluralistic and homogeneous elements, each of which was characteristic of a stage in the accommodation and assimilation processes.

The concept assimilation was applicable to diverse relations involving, for example, immigrants, racial groups, and nations. Assimilation through primary relations, and the regulation of social relations on the basis of a common culture, was seen to have a universal importance: "Fundamentally," the authors stated (*ibid.*:734), "the problem of maintaining a democratic form of government in a southern village composed of whites and blacks, and the problem of maintaining an international order based on anything but force are the same. The ultimate basis of the existing moral and political order is still kinship and culture." And as we have seen, kinship and cultural groups were the breeding places of assimilated relationships.

Finally, it can be noted that assimilation could only take place gradually and that as a rule individuals were unconscious of their assimilation. Also, assimilation took place through primary rather than secondary contacts because it was based on a "unit of experience and orientation." Since it eventuated in a "community of purpose and action" (i.e., *common* purpose and *common* action), assimilation involved a process of communication for which a common language was indispensable (*ibid.*:736–737). After being assimilated, individuals and groups regulated themselves according to internalized, consensually based norms and values. An enduring process of conflict resolution was the result. And this was essential in a world requiring integration in order to progress.

Other than formalizing their generalization about assimilation, Park and Burgess differed little in their "assimilationist" resolution to the problem of integration, from their predecessors, the French positivist, Auguste Comte, and the English liberal, Edmund Burke. In Park and Burgess' view (*ibid.*:510), "the permanence and solidarity of the group rest finally upon this body of common experience and tradition." The permanence and general structure of each community, as well as of society in general, also rested on this consensual body of experience and tradition. The corollary therefore, was that the stability of communities composed of black sharecroppers and white planters as well as that of societies composed of workers and capitalists did *not*, ultimately, rest on the ideological control and management of public opinion, or on the operation of the police, the judges, and the armies of the state. It rested on a grand and voluntary consensus.

NOTE

1. Scott Greer (1926:8) states, ". . . the assumptions of laissez-faire are built into the ecological image. Competition, conflict, accommodation, and assimilation take place within a framework of rules approximately the same as those advocated by Herbert Spencer—with room for social evolution, enterprise and the survival of those most fit to survive."

CHAPTER 49

The Disappearance of the State

The Mystique of the Public

In 1907 John R. Commons, a political economist and noted labor historian, delivered a paper on class conflict before the second annual gathering of the newly formed American Sociological Society. Commons (1907:146) declared that class conflict might be growing but that its growth certainly would not be inevitable if "the public" were given the opportunity to control the struggle between capital and labor. The democratic public was regarded as constituting at least two-thirds of the population. And, in Common's view, this silent majority was capable of functioning more effectively as a stabilizing force in society than the state because it was "too big and too exposed for the wire-pulling of classes." [1] The "public" was so idealized by Commons that it was neither corruptible nor co-optable. The political party, the political machine, the legislature, and the judge, on the other hand, were regarded as being more easily corrupted and manipulated by class interests.

Commons indicated that state officials had denied the public the right to determine the course of events that eventually led to the violent encounter between capital and labor at Cripple Creek, Colorado. If the public had been given this right, the violence would not have occurred. [2]

Commons explicitly invoked the common myth about "the public's" reified penchant for fair play when he remarked:

Class antagonism will not disappear as long as there is wealth to distribute, but it can be transferred to the jury of the people. Then we can expect social classes to state their case in the open and to wait upon the gradual process of education rather than plunge into battle. [*ibid.:*147]

It was, therefore, clearly evident that although Commons felt that the public *ought to* regulate the ways in which class antagonisms are *ultimately* resolved, this regulation had *not* actually been instituted in American life.

Park and Burgess:
Ultimate Forces Control Institutions of State

The mystique of the bourgeois democratic public also figured large in Park and Burgess' theory. However, they did not speak about a morally preferable state of affairs (based on how the public *should* function in relation to such social problems as class conflict). Park and Burgess assumed, fourteen years later, that the public had *actually* operated as a penultimate, if not the ultimate, controlling agent throughout history. This assumption was particularly salient in their discussion of the relation between the state and the public.

In a chapter devoted specifically to social control, Park and Burgess contrasted the commonsense, and the sociological, concepts of social control. They stated that when common people talked about social control, they ordinarily associated it with its most obvious representations, namely, "the machinery" by which law is made and enforced. But contrary to popular beliefs, Park and Burgess hastily added, such obvious aspects of this "machinery" as the legislature, courts, and police were not quite adequate for the sociological conception of social control. More importantly, they stated (1924:786) that though it was "not quite as obvious," it was their belief that "legislation and the police must, in the long run, have the support of public opinion. A king or a political 'boss' having an army or a political 'machine' at his command can do much . . . but neither the king nor the boss will, if he be wise, challenge the mores and the commonsense of the community." Functionally it is not the legal machinery but the public which has the real power to control. According to this example, social control did not "ultimately" reside in the *political state;* it was lodged penultimately, as we will presently see, in *the mores* and *public opinion.*

In further pursuit of the ultimate locus of social control, Park and Burgess noted that in time the mores and public opinion represented "the response of the community to changing situations." As a consequence of this sensitivity to change, these entities "are themselves subject to change and variation." Moreover, these authors add, "the mores" and "public opinion" develop according to "what we have called fundamental human nature, that is, certain traits which, in some form or another, are reproduced in every form of society." In other words, public opinion and the mores were actually sociological reflections of still more fundamental [natural-law] relationships. Established leaders and institutions by being dependent upon public opinion and the mores were, at bottom, dependent upon the ultimate—the relatively unchanging—i.e., "fundamental human nature." Social control was a democratic manifestation of natural laws.

Upon reflection, Park and Burgess' analytic mode of reasoning appears to shift the locus of social control through a series of categorical entities, each of which was regarded as being more "ultimate" than the other. Furthermore, these "penultimate" and "ultimate" causal entities loomed larger than the state in controlling human relationships.

These insights suggest that Park and Burgess were not merely abstracting the common *empirical* assumptions that had been incorporated in a larger number of theories prior to 1921. They were also abstracting the common properties of ideological rationales for these theories. For example, these authors appeared to have chosen as "ultimate" and "elementary," the very same analytic categories that had functioned previously as justifications for a projected syndicalist state of affairs.[3] It appears, therefore, that Park and Burgess' ideas were also constituted by transforming *ideological rationales* into *theoretical categories*. According to the authors, these categories represented universal properties of human forms of life. In actuality, however, they were merely liberal reifications of historically transient social phenomena.

Analysis: Park and Burgess' Amoral Political Perspective

Most of the eminent early sociologists in the United States felt that the federal and local forms of the state should have been given increased power to institute and implement badly needed social reforms. Compared with Ward and the other founders' preoccupation with the use of the state as an equitable and progressive means of achieving ordered economic changes and social reforms, Park and Burgess' theory contains very few systematic *analytic* references to the independent functions of a modern political state. In fact, although these authors descriptively indicated throughout their textbook that there are such institutional entities as police, courts, legislatures, and "political machines," it is notable that the modern state was nominally defined as having almost no independent institutional identities to which it could be uniquely referred: the state itself was made of little consequence by merely considering it "an organization of groups that have been in conflict, i.e. classes or castes; or of groups that are in conflict, i.e. political parties" (*ibid.*:647−648).

In fact, their depiction of the state is reminiscent of the liberal-syndicalists' *society*. In liberal-syndicalist theory, it should be recalled, society as a whole was often considered little more than a collection of functionally interdependent but conflicting economic groups. The *state,* on the other hand, had been perceived as a special kind of institution (conceived separately from "society") that facilitated the reconciliation of economic conflicts. It is obvious, because of this, that if the modern state was now also defined by Park and Burgess as a collection of interest groups (whose interests are usually related to various "competitive" [e.g., socioeconomic] processes), then there were few differences on the face of it between their conceptions of the state, for example, and the conception of society or the economy as a whole which had been firmly established by liberal-syndicalists during the formative years.[4]

400

On the other hand, there were some differences between these points of view in spite of the analytic similarities between the syndicalist conception of society and Park and Burgess' conception of the state. During the formative years, liberal syndicalists had regarded the state in a highly contradictory manner. But in their schizoid descriptions of the state they had indicated that it would *altruistically* serve the population at large even though it was also recognized that legislative offices had often been controlled by vested interests. Park and Burgess, however, ignored the contradictions inherent in their view of the state. These men merely regarded the state as an expression of a plurality of interest groups. Their theoretical strategy for analyzing political relationships did not even attempt to justify the state as a higher embodiment of moral rules or a facilitation for mediating conflicts.

Of course, Park and Burgess did reflect the spirit of liberal-syndicalism when they argued that conflict permeated "the political order." Interest-group accommodation, furthermore, was regarded as the single most important feature of a democratic polity and higgling between representatives of interest groups was also implicit in their view of the democratic process. However, Park and Burgess stopped short at this point. No matter how *inequitable* the outcome, a democratic process based on higgling between selfish groups justified the kinds of policies eventually implemented by the state. For all intents and purposes, political authority was legitimated on this basis alone.

We shall presently demonstrate Park and Burgess' free substitution of words and phrases like "society" and "the public interest" for "the state," and also their argument that the state was democratic and expressed the will of "society." On this basis, they virtually eliminated the possibility that the state was the representative of any single "vested interest" (e.g., a ruling class). But their argument was made credible only by stripping such terms as "democratic process" and "democratic will" of any significant moral content. Their democratic rationale for the state made sense to corporate liberals because it was squarely based on an essentially *amoral* view of political relationships.

Park and Burgess' theoretical categories made it possible to move beyond a syndicalist perspective into a completely *formal* perspective which ignored the enduring moral and political realities engendered by class relations in the United States. By restricting the process of conflict to the political arena but subsuming the products of conflict under accommodation and assimilation, these authors set into motion a mode of analysis which strongly influenced the kinds of analytic activity that stressed both (1) the diversity of conflicting interests and (2) the democratic rationale, and eventually produced the very abstract and highly axiomatic brand of pluralism (Dahl 1967) which has provided corporate-liberal sociologists with a source of indescribable joy.

Democratic Rationale
for Antidemocratic Administrative-Consultant

It should be recalled that Ward objected to Spencer's refusal to make the same analogy between the brain's relationship to other parts of the organism, and the functions of the political state in relation to other parts of the society. The *state*, Ward suggested, was like the *brain* of an organism insofar as it regulated the parts of a social organism. Small, in agreement on this point, added and stressed that the state ruled in the name of "society."

In light of its ideological significance in the early years, it is an interesting comparison again to find Park and Burgess' continuity with Ward's analogy regarding the integrating functions of the state for society as a whole. In their scheme, however, the word "mind" was substituted for "brain" and, as indicated, *society* replaced the *state*. They stated (*ibid.*:848): "*Society,* insofar as it can be distinguished from the individuals that compose it, performs for these individuals the functions of a *mind*. Like the mind in the individual man, society is a *control* organization" (our emphasis).[5] Park and Burgess utilized this analogy in a chapter entitled "Social Control," and it is clear that they utilized the word "society" to provide a democratic rationale for the administrative consultant's implementation of social control. The term "collective mind" has the same meaning and uses in Ross' work. In a discussion of Ross' use of this term it was suggested that he also scrupulously avoided making any reference to ruling classes or ruling oligarchies in "differentiated" (capitalist) societies. The dynamic functions of the ruling class in capitalism were replaced in his work by vague references to a collective mind and public consciousness.[6] In the differentiated and democratic ("competitive") societies, Ross substituted the word "society" for "collective mind" and indicated that "society" controls the individuals and groups in the interests of the community and its individual members.

In Park and Burgess' theory, however, the aforementioned avoidance of any mention of the political realities engendered by the monopolies and monopoly trusts in societies like the United States, extended their work to the most absurd heights of obscurantist abstraction. But this omission was, nevertheless, consistent with previous tendencies in customary thinking. The political state was increasingly seen as a microcosm of the processes that allegedly existed in society as a whole, and because of this was disappearing from the theoretical horizon. It was being operatively replaced by such vacuous terms as "society," "the mores," "public opinion," and "the will of the people." As indicated, the existence of ruling classes in capitalist societies was not even recognized. Because of the obvious contradictions within the theory as a whole, there was no analytic category in Park and Burgess' system that could be used to objectively pinpoint the extraordinary concentration of power in modern bourgeois democratic societies. Power had been dissipated among all the instruments of social control which had occupied the fertile imagination of the early sociologists.

An unbelievable irrationality and a profound irony is expressed in the fact that Park and Burgess' categories represented the triumphant culmination of the formative years. Their theory represented the end result of four decades of exhausting and prolific intellectual activity. But it also demonstrated that a host of American academics never *actually* discovered the most vital sources of social, political, and economic power, even though they were positively obsessed with an endless search for these sources in the name of social control.

NOTES

1. Commons (1907:146) added, "And [the public] does not consent that one class shall have an advantage over another. It does not favor either radicals or reactionaries. When the public shall have more direct means of expressing its will, through direct nomination, direct elections, initiative, or referendum then we may expect class conflict to subside."

2. Commons (1907:147) stated, for example: "The class war in Colorado broke out because the legislature refused to carry out the will of the people as expressed by a constitutional amendment."

3. These categories had not functioned primarily as descriptive assertions about the actual nature of nineteenth-century capitalism.

4. The differences between their concepts of the state and society became further narrowed when it is noted that such "conflict groups" as "classes" and "castes" in Park and Burgess' definition of the state were usually considered economic interest groups or blocs by liberal syndicalists.

5. Park and Burgess (1924:848) added that "the literature on social control, in the widest extension of that term, embraces *most that has been written and all that is fundamental* to the subject of society" (our emphasis).

6. This omission reflected a false consciousness of what were actually *class*-controlled bourgeois societies.

CHAPTER 50

Technocratic Analysis of Social Change

Park and Burgess, along with the earlier American sociologists, were concerned with regulating social change. Their theoretical perspective anticipated two general kinds of social change, progressive and retrogressive. Progressive change eventuated in very natural and normal outcomes. Examples of this change, which terminated in accommodative and assimilative relationships, have been given. The authors, however, reserved the term "pathological" for

403

the second kind of social change, which started in disorganization and terminated in unnatural and abnormal relationships. It is important in this chapter to know where Park and Burgess were "coming from" and where they were going. Their starting point was a capitalist America but they had a future vision of a modern social system which represented the grand consequence of beneficial social changes.

Park and Burgess' Vision
of Industrial Democracy

It has been shown that in Park and Burgess' vision, progress occurred by small increments in "social efficiency," and although these authors insisted that no one could determine with finality what would happen to the human race, they predicted *progressive* change in the United States. The anticipated progressive changes would take place through changing mores. Although the mores change slowly, "they change in *one direction* and they change *steadily*" (Park and Burgess 1924:831–832 our emphasis). What would be the shape of the society produced by these steady changes? Park and Burgess observed that "there are profound changes going on in our social organization today. *Industrial democracy,* or something corresponding to it, is *coming.* It is coming not entirely because of social agitation. It is coming, perhaps, in spite of agitation" (*ibid.* our emphasis). And, this industrial democracy would undoubtedly be based on a grand consensus as well as tolerant accommodations between industrial, religious, ethnic, and racial groups.

Technocratic Dynamics
of Progressive and Retrogressive Change

Park and Burgess still lived in the savage realities of modern life. In their view, laissez-faire capitalism had brought about a weakening of traditional controls and changes in economic relations that did not automatically lead to new forms of human solidarity. The new economic relations motivated individuals to engage in selfish striving. People now had little concern for obligations to traditional groups or society as a whole. Even the "rules of the game" established by the free competitive marketplace were ignored in the attempt to amass individual wealth and power. Freedom of competition itself had become threatened: the unregulated forces of competition had destroyed the most sacred and sacrosanct norms by which individuals organized their relations with one another. The natural outcome of this stage of development was social unrest marked by social disorganization, increased conflict, the heightening of individual egoism, and a state of normlessness. Social unrest, social disorganization, and social instability posed a neo-Hobbesian problem of integration.

404

Various states of social stability or instability based on degrees of conflict were described in Park and Burgess' theory. One state involved accommodative relations but it also contained "latent conflict." Another state included the relatively "conflict-free" condition of fully assimilated relationships. (In this state the conflict "latent in the organization of individuals or groups is likely to be wholly dissolved.") Park and Burgess (*ibid.:*665) also suggested still another possibility: the state of *unrest*. "With a change in the situation, the adjustment that had hitherto successfully held in control the antagonistic forces, fails. There is confusion and unrest which may issue in open conflict."

The state of unrest was said to emerge from modern conditions of life. These conditions included the expansion of worldwide markets. These markets have made nations interdependent but they have also undermined certain solidary groups. The family has ceased to be an economic unit and therefore "ceases to function as an organ of social control." Furthermore, different nationalities have "interpenetrated one another" and as a result, "the old solidarities, the common loyalties and common hatreds that formerly bound men together in primitive kinship and local groups" have been destroyed. Individualism has become rife and in Europe, Asia, and Africa, "new cultural contacts have undermined and broken down old cultures. The effect has been to loosen all the social bonds and reduce society to its individual atoms . . . Out of this confusion new and strange political movements arise, which represent the groping of men for a new social order" (*ibid.:*867).

In this context, Park and Burgess' (*ibid.:*924–925) definition of collective behavior took on special meaning. Collective behavior, in this almost classical liberal view, was built around a notion of "elementary forms" of human relations which, like atomistic pieces of a puzzle, became scattered in a state of unrest or reformed in a subsequent state of order. Park and Burgess also referred to this state by such terms as "social disorganization." Students of this behavior were referred to the study of "the processes by which societies are *disintegrated* into their constituent elements *and* the processes by which these elements are *brought together to form new societies*" (*ibid.* our emphasis).

Various forms of social unrest were considered socially beneficial. These forms included the medieval crusade, which "at bottom . . . was an inner restlessness, that sought peace in great hardship and inspiring action." Contemporary religious movements such as the Women's Christian Temperance League also were seen to be beneficial because they are radical attempts to correct a recognized evil (*ibid.:*878). With regard to revolutionary movements, they stated that "the most radical and the most successful of them have been religious." Becoming more specific, a prime example of "revolution" in this regard was Christianity itself (*ibid.:*874). Were there no socially beneficial changes initiated under *secular* auspices? To be sure there were. The authors referred to the "restlessness" of the immigrants who swarm like "members of a hive" to the new world and eventually become fully Americanized. This form of "social unrest" could be regarded as socially beneficial at least in the long run.

Moral Rearmament

How did Park and Burgess proceed with the formulation of their solution to this new liberal conception of the problem of integration? Like other corporate liberals who had modified laissez-faire ideas before incorporating them into their theories, Park and Burgess subtly transformed Le Bon's Spencerian ideas in order to make them congenial with their solution to the problem of integration. This was accomplished by abstracting Le Bon's concept of the crowd and Tarde's concept of the public. The crowd and the public were then defined as parts of different *phases* in a process of interaction—i.e., the crowd was described as emerging at a beginning stage of an evolutionary change. At the highest stage of its development, it became a (democratic) public. This public was thereupon defined as an essential characteristic of a corporate-liberal industrial democracy. Citing Le Bon, Park and Burgess first agreed that "the crowd . . . is a slave of its impulses," neither discussing nor reflecting on its actions. "The crowd simply 'mills.' " They then departed from Le Bon and argued (*ibid.*:868–869) that the public "presupposes a *higher* state of social development . . . [wherein] interaction takes the form of discussion. Individuals tend to act upon one another critically; issues are raised and parties form. Opinions clash and thus modify and moderate one another" (our emphasis). In other words, a rational social product came from the interactions of individuals in a rational corporate economy; the public was a refinement of crowd relations whose impulse was governed by a certain amount of reason. At times, we will use the phrase "the democratic public" instead of "the public." This substitution emphasizes the "tolerance," "diversity," and bourgeois "rationality," which is implicit in Park and Burgess' conception of the public, when compared to the "intolerant," "biased," and "unreasoning" crowd.

In Park and Burgess' theory, the democratic public was a corporate-liberal antithesis of the crowd, in the same way that reason was perceived as the antithesis of passion in classical liberalism. The classical dichotomy between reason and passion in individuals was simply elevated to the realm of sociological discourse in order to distinguish the relations between two social units of analysis; the crowd and the public.

By what process does the first stage evolve into the second stage; i.e., how does a crowd become a democratic public? First it must endure over time in order to become that form of a "chronic crowd" called a "sect." "A sect [as a chronic crowd] is at war with the existing mores" and "seeks to cultivate a state of mind and morals different from the world around it." A sect is a movement that attempts to reform the "inner life of the community." Eventually, after the sect accommodates itself to other groups in society, it "becomes tolerated and is tolerant." It "assumes the form of a denomination." In the process of change, that which began as a crowd has been "institutionalized" with the development of "the denomination." Finally, through

406

accommodation and assimilation, the denominational view of life is absorbed into the public (*ibid*.:872–874). In Park and Burgess' theory, the transformation of a crowd into a denomination was taken as the archetype of all non-pathological social changes involving fundamental reorganization of institutional structures.

It was still not surprising in 1921 to find a religious group being used as a paradigm case for social change. However, the Protestant rhetoric should not obscure the fundamentally secular, corporate-liberal system of natural-social-laws being standardized by Park and Burgess. In their theory, the gradual and steady development of the mores was given the crucial role of establishing an industrial democracy. The effects of "chronic crowds" became very crucial in this respect because they were seen as potential agents for changing the mores. Because of this, the "chronic crowd" or "sect" was also regarded "as a movement of social reform and regeneration" that might ultimately become "institutionalized."

Like Ross and Small before them, Park and Burgess had their eyes firmly fixed on the main target: the moral rearmament of the American people. The standards defining this moral rearmament were concocted from transitional rhetoric based on a unique American blend of white, Anglo-Saxon, Protestant, bluenose, corporate-liberal precepts. And these same precepts informed Park and Burgess of the pathological states of unrest. What were the pathological examples differentiated by these standards? They were unrest created by socialists, bolsheviks, anarcho-syndicalists, criminal and delinquent immigrants or sons of immigrants, all of whom had not gratified their fundamental wishes in the new world. Pathological social unrest also included unrest created by militant labor agitators like the organizers of the International Workers of the World. These Wobblies were considered red-blooded Americans who had been made homeless by the impersonal forces of the modern world. Their militant labor movement was regarded to be a result of the pathological substitution of reckless dreams of anarcho-syndicalism and bolshevism for older religions and moralities that were no longer viable in modern societies!

According to Park and Burgess, new social movements arose with the disintegration of traditional social relationships. These movements represented the first stage of a process which might eventuate in either an interminable state of unrest or the stable reorganization of society along new lines. Generally, socially beneficial movements terminated in stable accommodation and therefore reorganization of social relationships. Pathological movements did not! Normal and natural social changes eventually became equilibrated and therefore solved the problem of order posed by the anomic or socially disorganized relationships. Pathological adaptations did not solve this problem. The ultimate criterion for evaluating social change was whether change contributed to integration of the established institutions. Progressive change made this contribution. Regressive changes did not!

Analysis: Elementary Parts
of Reductionist Mechanism for Social Unrest

Park and Burgess' concepts of change and social unrest were based on homologous corporate-liberal conceptions of personal and social relationships. Some of their assumptions had been generated previously by scholars like Freud and Thomas in order to solve the problem of social change. Consequently, it was maintained that "All social changes . . . are preceded by a certain degree of *social* and *individual* disorganization" (our emphasis). Now we will briefly examine the degree to which "elementary parts" of their mechanism for social change had become firmly identified with Freud's and Thomas' works rather than Ward's.

Park and Burgess (*ibid.*:788–789) alleged that certain *elementary forces* were ultimately responsible for such collective forms of behavior as the Napoleonic war against Russia, the Franco-Prussian War of 1812, and the financial panics and depressions which troubled capitalist societies. These elementary forces were expressed in the development of a general state of unrest and a widespread state of alarm. An inexorable outcome of this development was that segments of the population milled about like "restless cattle," only to plunge into an irrational panic or war at the slightest provocation.

In identifying these elementary forces, Park and Burgess first indicated that institutions and organizations should not be used as the *ultimate* candidates [1] for locating the forces. Similarly, "the individual" was not considered the proper locus of the "social forces" because an individual was really "not the same person" at different places and times.[2] Since Park and Burgess believed that all social and individual relationships were ultimately manifestations of the most elementary parts of human nature, they concluded (*ibid.*:473) that of necessity "sociologists invariably sought the *sociological* element, not in the individual, but in his *appetites, desires, wishes*—the human motives that move him to action" (our emphasis). Thus, after a search for the smallest and indivisible unit of sociological analysis (which represented an "elementary part" of the process of integration and change), the concept of "human motives" was considered to embody the "social forces."

Park and Burgess' notion of motives as social forces was obviously identical to the idea advanced by Ward at the very beginning of the formative years. However, they did not credit Ward with the more sophisticated formulations of this notion. In addition, these authors did not use any portion of Ward's famous work on the social forces, *Dynamic Sociology,* as reading material for a chapter specifically entitled "Social Forces." [3] Instead, in that chapter they provided readings by Ely, Dicey, Small, McDougall, Park, and Holt, and most of this material, in Park and Burgess' estimation, expressed the varied formulations of the concept of the social forces. These forces, they noted, had been previously designated "social tendencies," "instincts," "sentiments," "interests," "wishes," "desires," and "attitudes."

408

Although Park and Burgess (*ibid:*497) briefly cited one of Ward's definitions of the social forces,[4] they conspicuously avoided an evaluation of the place of his work in the historical development of the concept in American sociology. They vaguely suggested that this notion had first been introduced by "historians" and had subsequently undergone various changes in meaning. They credited the most adequately developed interpretation of the concept of social forces to psychoanalytic theorists. In addition W. I. Thomas was regarded as having "reintroduced" the psychoanalytic conception of social forces into sociology "under the title of the 'four wishes' " (*ibid.:*438).

By 1921, therefore, the elementary social forces were equated with either the original or the modified versions of the psychoanalytic concepts of "instincts," "desires," and "wishes." A short time later, as we have noted, the concepts of instincts and wishes gave way to complex but logically interrelated models of psychological processes involving the mechanisms of defense and socially acquired values, internalized norms, and definitions of the situation—all of which now represented the elementary social forces. In this process, the final curtain began to drop at the end of the formative years. The habitual association between Ward and the social forces that had signaled the once powerful presence of his utopian work *Dynamic Sociology* was finally extinguished.

NOTES

1. Their description of this matter involved identification of "locus candidates" for the social forces rather than the specific substantively defined forces themselves (e.g., *nutritional* or *reproductive* forces). For a discussion of the concept of locus candidates, see Edel (1959).

2. This obscure remark presumably meant that situational variations in individual behavior did not reveal the "elementary forms" (i.e., "the social forces") that Park and Burgess were looking for.

3. It should be recalled that Park and Burgess included reading material (abstracted from a large selection of theoretical works) in their textbook. The textbook, therefore, was a cross between a traditional text and a modern "reader."

4. Park and Burgess noted that "Ward had stated that 'the social forces are wants seeking satisfaction through efforts, and are thus the social motives or motors inspiring activities which either create *social structures* through social synergy or modify the structures already created through innovation and conation" (our emphasis).

PART THIRTEEN

The Liberal Sins of Reification

CHAPTER 51

The Reciprocity between Formal and Substantive Ideas

Preview

Very abstract liberal categories like social control, and very abstract theories like Park and Burgess' grand theory, exhibit peculiar analytic properties which will be described in the following chapters. Familiarity with these properties will enable the reader to discount on epistemological grounds, the belief among early sociologists in the existence of an empirically "pure sociology." This belief is basic to the modern claim that sociology is a "value-free" social science.

The epistemological issues which are presented by the early sociological theories cannot be confronted directly without emphasizing the degree to which these theories were *formal expressions* of preexisting modes of theorizing. This emphasis, however, requires the description of a complex method of theory construction which is based on the reciprocal relations between formal and substantive liberal ideas. This chapter describes this method by using as examples Ward's mechanism of "synergetic process" and Park and Burgess' grand theory. The description of this method prepares the groundwork for a critical analysis of the notion of "pure sociology" in the next chapter.

Universals: "Process of Equilibrium"
and "Processes of Social Interaction"

Park and Burgess' theory by itself consisted of four master categories and a large set of formal generalizations. Examples of similarities between Park and Burgess' categories and preexisting ideas have been presented in previous chapters. To further clarify the significant connections between their grand theory and preexisting theories, and because it makes their method of theory construction immediately apprehendable, it may be informative to briefly discuss Ward's concept of synergy. By 1903 synergy connoted several crucial ideas that would eventually become associated with Park and Burgess' "universal processes of social interaction."

Synergy, according to Ward (1903:175), was a *universal* "process of *equilibrium*" which encompassed all acts of "social creation." It emerged after various conflicting "forces" were first brought together in a state of "partial equilibration." Synergy, therefore, "begins in collision, *conflict,* antagonism, and opposition, but as no motion can be lost it is transformed, and we have the milder phases of antithesis, *competition* and interaction passing next into a *modus vivendi,* or compromise, and ending in *collaboration* and *cooperation*" (our emphasis).

The concept of synergy was an attempt to formulate a sociological mechanism within the constraints imposed by liberal predilections. But the mechanism itself has multiple facets and appears to consist of a list of superordinate categories such as "conflict," "competition," "collaboration," and "cooperation," each of which tacitly refer to other "genetic," or "telic," relationships such as imperialist conquest and colonization. Ward (1903:203–204) believed that the "struggle between races" also reflected the universal effects of synergetic processes in the social world.[1]

In the mechanism of synergy, the categories of conflict, competition, collaboration, and cooperation were related to each other as part of a larger process called the synergetic "process" or "interaction." As Ward's critic, Heath Bawden, indicated, however, the words "process" and "interaction" covered a lot of highly unexplored and unexplained ground; nevertheless, when Ward's "synergy" is compared with Park and Burgess' grand theory, it appears that the latter theory constituted an enterprise that actually charted this highly unexplored ground. Park and Burgess' theory produced a far more detailed view of the social world than Ward's mechanism, but the differences between their theoretical ideas should not obscure the fact that social reality was being analyzed from similar *methodological* as well as ideological vantage points.

Formal Abstractives Defined

Virtually all of the social meanings which were associated with Ward's concept of synergy or with Park and Burgess' superordinates, were based on the liberal selection and simple classification of common properties and generalizations in preexisting theories. The phrase *formal abstractives* will capture the methodological principles underlying this classification process. The sociologists who use these principles to develop such categories as "synergy," "conflict," "competition," "process," and "interaction," spend many hours— if not years—continuously surveying and abstracting common characteristics from contemporary theories. After this is done, they classify these abstracted notions with a formal name, or reconceptualize them on the basis of formal generalizations.

Put more succinctly and precisely: formal abstractives are formulated by first abstracting and then, by the use of comprehensive terms or generalizations, classifying and reconceptualizing various properties, relations, and mechanisms commonly designated by preexisting theories. In some cases, a formal abstractive may refer to a whole family of theories because they exhibit certain properties in common.

Taken-for-Granted Qualities
of Formal Abstractives

Thus, categories such as "competition," "conflict," and "accommodation," in Park and Burgess' theory, partly represented the end products of a method of theory construction. As formal abstractives, these categories signified properties, relationships, and mechanisms that were originally specified in a preexisting body of theories. Park and Burgess used these abstractives to systematize rather than extend preexisting ideas. Their chapters on competition, conflict, etc., for example, identified and sorted out the kinds of mechanisms which had commonly functioned in various short-term as well as long-term solutions to economic, political, and social problems. Certain mechanisms were considered particularly applicable to theories of *competition* between individual workers. Others were more useful for analyzing *conflict* between political parties. Still others were regarded as particularly pertinent for the study of *accommodation* between capital and labor or the *assimilation* of national ideals among immigrants or conquered populations. After being abstracted from the theories of their origin, these common mechanisms were reformulated in formal, metaphorical, or analogical terms, and incorporated into the stockpile of mechanisms embodied in the theory as a whole.

Park and Burgess' abstractives originally had explanatory utility only because other relevant categories, axioms, or full-fledged members of a family of models (e.g., entire theories) were actually being *taken for granted* when the abstractives were first formulated and used. Ward's "synergy" is an example of this kind of taken-for-granted category. However, once formulated, Park and Burgess' abstractives broadened the perception of the interrelationships among preexisting categories and theories. Categories and theories, which had heretofore been regarded as disparate, now appeared to be related to each other.

Park and Burgess' grand theory had significant analytic gaps due to its eclectic character. But there is no question that it appeared to provide a unified analytic framework for many sociologists at the time. The appearance of unity was primarily created by the use of (1) the notion of "universal process" and by (2) various intuitive associations made on the basis of the superordinate categories, which signified the major stages of a universal social process. Thus, the superordinate categories—competition, conflict, accommodation, and assimilation—appeared to "hang together" because they were considered sequential stages in a process. This sequence, moreover, did not have to move in one direction; accommodation could be disrupted by conflict, just as accommodation could result from conflict. It was taken for granted that an enormous variety of social changes could be explained as lateral or multilateral oscillations between these stages. But it was also taken for granted that the overall integration of all of these major states was epitomized by the development of industrial capitalism. Industrial capitalism, in Park and Burgess' view, was evolving out of the relatively uncontrolled competitive stage of development, through the stages of conflict and accommodation, toward the final "moving equilibrium" of assimilation.

Key-Concept Defined

It may be useful to see each one of Park and Burgess' formal abstractives as a figurative master key to a large bin or stockpile filled with analytic strategies, concepts, generalizations, and entire theories of animate and inanimate forms of life. The category of competition, for example, is the "key" to a stockpile of notions about biological adaptation among birds or men, and classical economic theories about economic activity in competitive, price-making markets. Because of this the term *key-concept method* will be used to designate the analytic process involving the utilization of formal abstractives for the construction of new theories on a lower level of abstraction. The two phrases, "formal abstractive" and "key-concept," therefore, refer to the same categories but relate these categories to *different* analytic usages. The category of assimilation, for example, is a key-concept as well as a formal abstractive. This category structured the formulation of new theories on lower levels of abstraction. Because they were less general than Park and Burgess' theory, the new theories, when formulated, were incorporated into the families of models which had been tacitly established by Park and Burgess' grand theory. In this process, the families of models were expanded and often brought up to date.

Thus, Park and Burgess' formal abstractives encouraged social scientists who were studying specific types of social interaction, to create new theories by analyzing these concrete types of interaction as special instances of competitive, conflicted, accommodative, or assimilative processes. For example, until Frederick M. Thrasher adapted these ideas to his theoretical work on delinquency, Park and Burgess' theory merely constituted a strategy for the analysis of conflict between delinquent groups. The theory may have been suggestive of some theoretical ideas but it did not actually constitute a theory of delinquency. With regard to delinquency, moreover, Park and Burgess' categories were not associated with any new *substantive* insights into this type of social relationship until Thrasher's work was published in 1927.

Park and Burgess' Categories: Indeterminate Fields of Meanings

Each of the formal abstractives has its own formal definition alluding to the characteristics in the theories with which it shares features in common; but when used as a key-concept, the formal abstractive does not function as a "heuristic" concept which sensitizes researchers to the immediate discovery of factual relationships in the real world. The key-concept sensitizes theorists instead to analytic ideas which (1) are presumed to aid the development of new theories, or (2) are actually theoretical explanations in themselves. In short, the key-concept is a word surrogate or an associative cue for *theoretical* ideas.

Because of this, it is impossible to fully grasp "Park and Burgess" by merely quoting their formal definitions of the concepts of competition, conflict, accommodation, and assimilation. Operatively, their key-concepts eventually served as cues to a virtually indeterminate, taken-for-granted body of ideas.

The realization of this fact placed an extraordinary burden on our review of Park and Burgess' theory. A thorough review should have taken into consideration the substantive contents of the theories they referred to. This, however, would have been an impossible task, because the number of these theories literally have *no upper boundary*. Park and Burgess' text itself was over a thousand pages. It included selective writings from works by Thorndike, Davenport, Keller, Espinas, Wheeler, Ellwood, Warming, Hobhouse, Durkheim, Small, Sighele, Hocking, Bacon, Knowlson, Hudson, Galpin, Thomas, Shaler, James, Ripley, Cooley, Richards, Tönnies, Sombart, Simmel, Gumplowicz, Darwin, Dugas, Morgan, Müller, Judd, Adam Smith, Becterew, Ely, Simons, Dicey, Bentley, McDougall, Holt, Watson, Crile, Le Bon, Giddings, Dewey, and others. Furthermore, their theoretical approach did not limit the reader to these selections. There were still other theorists included in the extensive bibliographies following each chapter. And, there were additional theorists who followed during the later twenties and thirties and whose ideas became subsumed under this approach.

414

On the other hand, the indeterminacy in meanings associated with Park and Burgess' categories is more apparent than real. These meanings were abstracted, in the first place, according to well-established ideological principles and precepts. Because of this selectivity, our analysis in the previous chapters described a few of these basic principles and precepts in order to show how closely the grand theory's meanings were confined to the ideology of liberalism. The same kind of ideological analysis is appropriate to all the models of the allegedly "universal" processes of equilibrium which have been produced by liberal sociologists.

NOTE

1. Consequently Ward not only interpreted synergy on the basis of the naturalistic fallacy (e.g., social structures which survived were conceived as the "best" structures; see Ward [1903:184]); he also used synergy systematically in combination with the chauvinistic race-conflict theories.

CHAPTER 52

Liberalism and Canons of Adequate Knowledge

Review and Preview

The previous chapter emphasized the degree to which Park and Burgess' grand theory was an expression of preexisting modes of theorizing. It also described the complex method of theory construction which underlies their theory. Finally, the notions of "formal abstractive" and "key-concept" were introduced in order to clarify the active and reactive relations among different types of liberal theorists.

These analytic ideas were especially introduced in order to clarify the reciprocal relations between *formal* and *substantive* liberal ideas. They were also considered necessary because the activities of theoreticians, who engaged in analyses of many different types, increasingly mediated the politically significant interaction between grand theory and the liberal practices in the family, the corporation, or the state. The activities of "applied" sociologists who directly supply technocratic justifications and technocratic intelligence to the mass media, the social agencies, and the governmental bureaucracies, interact with the activities of leading social scientists who supply them with abstract conceptions of social reality. These scholars "concretize" and extend these abstract conceptions; however, they do not usually generate these conceptions by themselves.

The direct connections which mediate the relations between "abstract" liberal theorists, "applied" liberal theorists, and professional liberal "practitioners" were obfuscated during the formative years by positivistic myths about the sharp separation between "pure sociology" and "applied sociology." It was claimed, in this context, that "pure sociologists" were not concerned with the way society *ought to be*. In modern times, this claim has been used to justify the activities of "value free" sociologists who are ostensibly devoted to "the disinterested pursuit of knowledge," even though, in many cases, this "disinterested pursuit" is funded by governmental agencies and philanthropic foundations because of its practical relevance.

This chapter describes the epistemological tradition of philosophical empiricism, which justified a sharp cleavage between "facts" and "values" among classical liberals. This tradition laid the groundwork for the later development of such notions as "pure sociology" and "value free" sociology. Knowledge of this tradition will enable the reader to appreciate the degree to which the early sociologists were ideologically *engaged* under the cover of a rhetoric of ideological *neutrality*. After this classical tradition is described, the chapter will return to such notions as they were prescribed by Ward, Park, and Burgess.

Philosophical Empiricism and the Factual Domain of Scientific Inquiry

For centuries, liberal-functionalists have justified the existence of a separation between scientific judgments and value judgments. This alleged separation is fundamental to the so-called "value-free" social science. However, sociologists of knowledge generally credit the origination of the modern doctrines of a value-free science to positivistic philosophy; but, in some respects the controversies involving philosophical empiricism and other aspects of the classical liberal approach to knowledge anticipated modern positivism. These controversies among philosophers launched the arguments in favor of sharply restricting the domain of scientific inquiries to what were allegedly the "factual" areas of human conduct. As a result, many liberal social scientists have become convinced that value judgments about economic or political relationships can, and should, be matters of individual preference. Therefore, these judgments are not and ought not to be germane to the formulation of their scientific categories and methodologies.

Philosophical empiricism had its own roots in the medieval schoolmen. But even though the medieval scholastics generally recognized that considerable knowledge emerges from empirical observations, they argued from first causes when theorizing about the general nature of man. Scholars of the sev-

416

enteenth and eighteenth centuries, on the other hand, increasingly departed from this theological tradition and attempted to ground their theories in references to empirical relationships. Hobbes, for instance, not only justified the propriety of grounding theories of man and society in empirical relationships, he also asserted that objective knowledge generally referred to a world existing independently of human consciousness; and consequently, propositions about the existence of supernatural entities who transcended and created the real world were absurd.

While Hobbes placed priority and primacy on the existence of objects and relationships in a world external to human consciousness, Locke (1632–1704) argued afterwards that human understanding is very limited because individuals can only grasp the appearance of things. Reasoning from the basic premises of his philosophical empiricism, he indicated that science cannot provide information about anything other than sense impressions. Since scientific theory cannot penetrate beyond these appearances, a scientific argument can only be valid if it is about things as they affect our senses. The valid object of scientific inquiry, therefore, cannot consist of questioning the ultimate reality of ideas, which appear only in the mind's eye.

Moving beyond Locke but still within the framework of philosophical empiricism which characterized classical liberal epistemology, Hume (1711–1776) acknowledged and distinguished between propositions demonstrated by logical or mathematical reasoning and beliefs about empirical relationships. He then argued that matters of fact cannot be demonstrated merely on the basis of logical relationships. Consistent with his extreme version of philosophical empiricism, he asserted that demonstrable knowledge can only be based on the impressions in existence at the moment the individual is aware of them. Because of this, it is also impossible to demonstrate the existence of either God or the real world because both of these entities are reputed to exist independently of individual awareness. Thus, philosophical issues involving controversies about objective causal relations existing in the real world were fruitless issues for empiricists. Concomitantly, religion was also considered to be outside the realm of demonstrable empirical knowledge, since it had nothing to do with matters of fact. This way of thinking proved to be convenient for individuals interested in reconciling the conflict between religion and science. Hume as well as other agnostics used it to argue that there was no *intrinsic* conflict between these two ways of comprehending the universe; religion and science simply referred to two *mutually exclusive* beliefs, one based on *faith* and the other on *facts*.

Although Hume thought that scientific observations would lead to a greater understanding of human nature, he refused to see man as subject to any determinants outside of this nature. He also took for granted that the driving force of human conduct is individual "passion," and consistent with natural-law tradition, he asserted that "the rules of morality are not conclusions of our reason" (Cornforth 1967:12).

In order to support this argument, Hume pointed out that a human act cannot, by itself, serve as an objective example of vice. It is possible to define an act as vicious only if a person feels disapproval of the act and evaluates it according to some personal standard. Consequently, he stated that "when you pronounce any action to be vicious, you mean nothing but that from the constitution of your nature you have a feeling or sentiment of blame from the contemplation of it." From this he concluded: "Morality therefore is more properly felt than judged of" (*ibid.:* 53). If morality is simply a matter of personal feelings, volitions, motives, or passions in the eye of the beholder, then the criteria for verifying the truth or falsity of good or bad human relationships are *extra*scientific. Furthermore, the moral status of any reality cannot be directly inferred from its empirical existence and, in Hume's opinion, propositions containing the verbs *ought* and *ought not* cannot be deduced from those containing *is* or *is not,* because these propositions refer to relationships which are of a qualitatively different order.

This way of thinking about scientific relationships was adopted by succeeding generations of liberal social scientists.[1] Consequently these tenets of philosophical empiricism were used to restrict the range of valid objectives for "pure" science. While the causes of ethical principles could be investigated by recourse to inquiries into human nature, the verification of these principles for mankind was not considered to be within the domain of science. Goodness was reduced to a matter of individual opinion. This also applied to religion and, above all, to aesthetic values or moral judgments.

The liberal's scientific inquiries into personal choices of religious, aesthetic, ethical, or political values eventually became concerned ostensibly only with the search for the functional relationships between these choices and the egoistic intentions of *individual* men. But when we examine what was generally considered a "factual" interpretation of moral behavior from this perspective, we find once again implicit judgmental characterizations. Religious, ethical, or political choices were described, for example, as being "reasonable" or "unreasonable." And the "unreasonable" choices were invariably made by radical personages who were called pathological fanatics, blind revolutionaries, members of dogmatic sects, and partisans of all sorts of "extreme" causes. These persons were not considered "amiable," "prudent," or "tolerant" individuals. Hume's judgments about people were no exception to this rule (*ibid.:*54).

Basic Axioms as Ideological Conceptions

During the Enlightenment, the growing separation between "matters of fact" and "matters of faith" was accompanied by an increasingly sophisticated awareness of the differences between factual statements and logical statements, i.e., sets of acceptable rules for reasoning, such as the rules of *deduction.* (Deduction is a process of reasoning from general principles to particular instances according to set procedures.) As early as the seventeenth century, for example,

René Descartes (1596–1650) had already asserted that the primary criteria for effectively demonstrating the truth or falsity of knowledge should be based on the logical juxtaposition of "clear and distinct ideas" about the nature or essence of things (*ibid.*:22–23). In the case of deduction, such useful ideas are achieved by means of a connected series of propositions, each of which proceeds logically from the propositions preceding it. The original propositions in this series are denoted as *basic axioms* because they are taken for granted and accepted, a priori, without proof. The final propositions in this series are called *theorems* and are regarded as being deductively derived from the axioms irrespective of their validity from an empirical point of view. On the other hand, it is also generally assumed that if the basic axioms and the other important propositions are, in fact, valid (empirical) statements about reality, then the theorems (derived deductively from these axioms and propositions) will also be truthful in an empirical sense.

Modern scholars have utilized deductive principles for formulating theorems about the real world which are called hypotheses or predictions. These scholars have departed from Descartes by introducing methods for determining the validity of these theorems by empirical test rather than logical consistency. On this basis they claim on empirical grounds to have proven their theories as a whole. They further assume that their theories are therefore worthy on the basis of their heuristic value [i.e., their value for the *discovery* of empirically testable relationships]. But this assumption has obscured the fact that the only ideas in a deductive model which are capable of being directly subjected to empirical test are the theorems. Moreover, as indicated, the theorems are deduced from a set of basic axioms; and, in highly general theories of human relationships, these axioms, we shall argue, are *invariably* structured by ideological considerations.

Liberal-functionalism has been significant ideologically because it has helped shape the very basic axioms of general theories of human behavior. As an analytic strategy, liberal-functionalism did not merely describe types of individuals or societies; it also referred to properties based on natural laws that were beyond the control of human institutions. However, these properties were inextricably bound to such historically relative ideas as the ethical premise that the goods of life should be distributed unequally. Premises like this were fundamental to the egoistic conceptions of man and, during the seventeenth and eighteenth centuries, they began to reflect the moral imperatives of an emerging society based on the competitive struggle for the ownership of wealth and property. In the nineteenth century, these imperatives were modified in order to maintain ruling class institutions which were rapidly establishing bourgeois hegemony throughout the Western world.

Mythology of "Pure Sociology"

The nineteenth-century corporate liberals who founded American sociology challenged many of the axiomatic principles which had sustained laissez-faire liberalism. But most of them held fast to philosophical empiricism. Small even accommodated himself to Hume's distinction between facts and values although he had recommended that sociologists should generate "a constructive sociology," by integrating their facts with Protestant values. Small recognized the existence of "a systematic sociology" and congratulated Ward for being a foremost example of this empirically oriented approach.

Ward believed that sociology should be dichotomized into "pure" and "applied" categories. He suggested that sociologists should develop a pure sociology in order to study the origin and nature of genetic processes, which developed more or less spontaneously among human beings. He (1903) was also convinced that

Pure sociology has no concern with what society *ought* to be, or with any social ideals. It confines itself strictly to the present and the past, allowing the future to take care of itself. It totally ignores the purpose of the science and aims at truth wholly for its own sake. [our emphasis]

Applied sociology, on the other hand, was the application of "intelligence" to human affairs. This application would result in control over genetic processes. But applied sociology was not at all concerned with everyday political decision-making: "The most it claims to do," Ward (1906:10) declared, "is to lay down certain general principles as guides to social and political action." Ward then clarified his remarks with a technocratic admonition:

But in this [applied sociology] must be *exceedingly* cautious. The [general] principles can consist only of the highest generalizations. They can have only the most general bearing on current events and the popular or burning questions of the hour. The sociologist who undertakes to discuss these, especially *to take sides* on them, *abandons* his *science* and becomes a politician. [our emphasis]

Ward's dichotomy between "pure" and "applied" sociology was full of contradictions. His mechanism of synergy was embodied in a "pure" sociological theory; hence, when applied to contemporary relations this mechanism was very concerned with what these relations *ought to be*. Ward's advocacy of universal state-supported education was embodied in his "applied" sociological theory; when addressed to social problems, his technocratic doctrines, which included gradualist educational proposals, were an eminent *political* strategy for resolving social conflicts.

420

Ideological Engagement Under Cover of Ideological Neutrality

Early American sociologists like Ward were concerned with how things ought to be when they formulated their "empirical theories," even when they have persistently denied that this is the case. Furthermore, every last one of the sharp distinctions between prescriptive and descriptive systems of thought vanished in the formation of their grand theories. It was impossible to separate prescriptive from descriptive judgments when formulating natural-law categories and axioms about the nature of man, woman, or society.

Paradoxically, however, the developments in grand theory toward the end of the formative years thoroughly obscured but effectively maintained the technocratic character of the liberal pursuit of scientific knowledge. For decades, the more astute sociologists, such as Ward, Ross, and Small, realized at least that their activity must eventually be justified on the basis of ideological (i.e., political and social) utility or practice. The disinterested search for knowledge, although regarded as appropriate in Ward's case, was not generally considered a sufficient justification for this pursuit. By the end of the formative years, however, it became unfashionable to explicitly declare such ideological commitments. Corporate-liberal scientists merely declared their commitment to a theoretical orientation. This declaration, moreover, appeared increasingly to be confirmed by their own scientific practices.[2] In actuality, however, social science theory and practice in academic institutions had been regulated on a long-term basis by ideological principles.

Because corporate-liberal theory mediated the relationship between ideology and the professional consciousness of scientific practice, scholars became conscious of their theoretical commitment rather than of the liberal ideology behind it. This consequence was directly attributable to the amoral and technocratic character of liberal-functionalism itself. Differing from theory developed, for example, by Marxist scholars, the theory that prevailed among liberal scholars specifically laid claim to ideological neutrality and therefore engendered a false awareness of the relationship between ideology and theory as well as theory and other forms of liberal practice.

There is no better example of a false awareness than the attitude taken by American sociologists toward Park and Burgess' grand theory. This theory was generally considered to be a statement of the universal processes of social interaction. But it was actually a reification and generalization of the concrete relations considered necessary for the emergence of a *stable* and *harmonious* capitalist society. Park and Burgess' theory went far beyond the world as it existed during their lifetime: it directed American sociologists to think in terms of future possibilities. It also influenced their social analyses so that they could make these possibilities come into being.

Park and Burgess' key concepts portrayed a larger picture of the world than the one that was a contemporary social reality. In addition, these concepts served as a map that indicated the operating principles of a world they felt was coming into existence. Although this complex vision of an equitable society was based on conflict and control—on control and exchange—on order and change—on the constant oscillation between competition, conflict, accommodation, and assimilation; it did not represent a simple idealistic quest for a totally controlled utopian community. Park and Burgess' metatheory was visionary but it was also rooted in their practical awareness of the disordered realities of modern capitalism.

Park and Burgess' implicit extrapolation of existing realities was based on certain assumptions about the nature of the present. They began, in regard to these assumptions, with obscurantist natural-social-law generalizations about the savage *competition* and *conflicts* in imperialistic capitalist societies. Their terminating point, however, was at the end of a straight line into the future: it was represented by their vision of an industrial society that *should* exist. The "empirical" principles which would bring this society into being were derived by abstracting, generalizing and classifying (with the key-concepts *accommodation* and *assimilation)* liberal conceptions of certain institutional practices. These practices (e.g., labor arbitration, education of immigrants) had emerged during the formative years in order to reestablish ideological hegemony and social stability under the new political and economic conditions.

Thus, Park and Burgess' emerging world was critically dependent on the continuing and successful application of specific types of institutional practices. These practices, however, had come into being *before* Park and Burgess labeled them and formulated their theory. In addition, they had already been articulated in theoretical (e.g. syndicalist and psychoanalytic) works. The theory therefore merely abstracted and generalized the organizing principles that were considered to have practical utility and had found theoretical statement regarding the social integration of American society.

Although obscured by the technocratic doctrine of ideological neutrality, the use of Park and Burgess' theory also contributed to the achievement of their corporate-liberal vision of the emerging industrial democracy. Their doctrines were influential because they became a powerful means for ensuring *professional* engagement and commitment to established political policies and ameliorative programs. Ideological engagement and commitment to corporate capitalism had produced the theory: this involvement now also determined its practical application! During the twenties, as subsequent chapters will demonstrate, American sociologists developed a complementary relationship with professional social workers, urban planners, and public administrators. These former, the so-called ideologically neutral, "pure" scientists, provided the kinds of social analyses and research that were useful to professional practitioners (e.g., social workers, public administrators) if only as justifications for established institutional practice. The linkage between the professional social analyst and professional ameliorative practice was forged, in particular, with the aid of the ideas associated with the key-concepts of accommodation and assimilation, as well as the all-inclusive category of social control.

Thus, ideological (e.g., meliorative) practices had first generated the ideas that were abstracted and generalized in this theory. The application of the theory, on the other hand, was obviously also aimed at the reinforcement of these ideological practices. Next, the conceptual generalization of established institutional practice enabled American academics to examine further aspects of social life which had not been previously subjected to this kind of "social engineering." Their examination, therefore, represented the extension of these principles into the analysis of such areas as crime, delinquency, the family, the play group, and relations in industry. As a result, an extraordinary variety of human relationships were soon being studied with the application of these ideological principles in mind. And finally, the empirical findings produced by the methodological application of these theoretical ideas provided useful, technocratic intelligence and technocratic rationalizations for psychologists, social workers, community organizers, urban planners, and administrators, in public and private institutions.

NOTES

1. This argument anticipated the concept of the "naturalistic fallacy" which was formulated by philosopher G. E. Moore in an attack on hedonism, a major doctrine of classical liberalism. According to Moore (1903), it is impossible to infer a moral rule directly from a factual assertion.

2. Among sociologists, for example, the meaning of scientific practice subsequently emphasized quantifiable and controlled methods of study, and the relationship between research practice and theory was made more systematic.

CHAPTER 53

The Fragmentation of Professional Consciousness

The standardization of a professional sociological vocabulary at the end of the formative years influenced theory and research for decades to come. The implications of the new theoretical categories, developed by such men as Park and Burgess, were just as important for the analytical methods eventually stressed in sociology. The significance of particular methods for classical as well as corporate liberals will be suggested in the following chapters; thus, it will be seen that in each case, certain analytic methods, including the use of the hypothetico-deductive model of inference for the development of theorems, were considered especially significant only after the theoretical categories of the previous epochs had been sharply attacked, discarded, and replaced with a new and highly formalized body of ideas. To discuss this issue (i.e., the import of analytical methods) in depth, however, it is necessary to dwell in this chapter on the analytic properties of grand theory and to a lesser extent on a more modern variant, "middle range theory," which utilized some of the earlier theoretical assumptions.

Concept of Metatheory Defined

During the formative years, the intellectuals who contributed heavily to theoretical developments, like Lester Ward, were general theorists: their work usually represented abstract attempts to solve the problems of social integration and social change everywhere and always. Their writing stamped them as intellectuals' intellectuals, and the products of their labor provided analytic methods, analytic categories, basic assumptions of man, woman, and nature, and an ensemble of mechanisms which might be fruitful to theorists interested in delimited areas of social behavior.

At times these hegemonic intellectuals did formulate specific theories of social relationships. But the uniqueness of their contribution to the development of sociology lies in their ability, first, to distinguish various trends in social thought; second, to abstract their common categories and generalizations and; third, to reconceptualize and formalize their meanings on a more abstract level. These men were also adept at reflecting on the implicit analytic strategies by which theorists arrived at their explanations and, after distinguishing these strategies, reconceptualizing them so that they were made explicitly available to others.

The notion of "formal abstractive" has been introduced in order to familiarize the reader with some of the methodological principles underlying the formation of grand theories. But this notion is not sufficient for classifying all the complex ideas which were developed by such men as Ward, Ross, Small, Park, and Burgess. The word "metatheory" is now introduced in order to rectify this deficiency.

"Metatheory" is used to classify all the abstract products of the reflexive intellectual labor among grand theorists, including formal abstractives. In this work, metatheory refers partly to an unsystematic ensemble of formal categories, formal generalizations, and basic assumptions about the nature of man and society. Metatheory also includes conceptual *systems* of relatively formal generalizations as, for example, are contained in Lester Ward's "wayward behavior," Albion Small's "interest groups," Park and Burgess' "universal processes of social interaction" or, for that matter, Talcott Parsons' "social action."

Metatheory, in this work, also encompasses the stockpile of certain mechanisms, including, for example, the formal exchange mechanisms, which have been derived from the notion of harmony of interest. It also classifies the analytic strategies which are typically used by scholars in order to formulate theories of social relationships. These strategies are included in metatheory rather than a separate category such as metasociology (e.g., Furfey 1959:510) because they are dynamically related to metatheoretical assumptions about the nature of man, woman, and society. For example, liberal-functionalist strategies, as we have seen, hardly make sense without their psychologistic assumptions about the nature of man, woman, and society. The methods of analyzing social reality presuppose basic assumptions about the nature of that reality.

The concept of metatheory, like that of "formal abstractive," is considered useful because it specifically distinguishes formal theoretical concepts from other theoretical concepts on epistemological grounds. Among liberal sociologists, metatheory arises when scholars reflect on the diverse theories from which they then abstract common properties and relationships. The prefix *meta,* in metatheory, therefore, symbolizes a process of abstracting properties and relationships contained in theories; [1] the element, *theory,* indicates that the objects of study are theories.[2] The object of study which produces metatheory, consequently, is not the real world, but theories of that world.

Metatheory plays an important role in graduate training when students acquire the broad analytic frameworks and the styles of inquiry that eventually legitimate their status as professionals. In graduate schools, young scholars are usually informed by conventional sociologists that analytic ideas and strategies facilitate the discovery of empirical knowledge by deductive inference from a current stockpile of basic categories, axioms, and mechanisms. For the sake of clarity, the formal, or most abstract, nominally defined ideas in this stockpile have been referred to as metatheoretical ideas.

Middle-Range Metatheory

The metatheoretical efforts of the pioneering sociologists were often constructed in the grand style because they were interested in the analysis of great historical epochs, or the historical evolution of human civilization as a whole. Metatheoretical formulations on this level are rare today; metatheoretical "systems" for the analysis of total societies or institutional spheres are more frequent.[3] By the end of the thirties, moreover, metatheories of specific subject matter and "social-problem" areas in sociology began to emerge on a frequent basis and today much of the metatheoretical activity among sociologists consists of similar kinds of activity. In certain respects this activity is not very different from that of the pioneering metatheoreticians. Some of the work today consists mainly of rephrasing or updating (explicating) *fragments* of older metatheoretical systems.

Part of Merton's (1938) study of deviant behavior will be used in order to clarify the meaning of metatheory in the "middle-range." In illustrating his metatheory, Merton indicated that contemporary American culture is characterized by a heavy emphasis on wealth as a basic symbol of success, without a corresponding emphasis on legitimate ways of attaining success. Merton added, moreover, that there are relatively limited opportunities available for realizing success, particularly among the lower classes in America. While persons in the lower classes are conditioned to believe that their place could be at the top, they find themselves deprived of "access to legitimate means" by which they can attain this "paramount goal." Thus, "a considerable part of the same population" believing in the Horatio Alger model of success cannot achieve their greatest ambitions, no matter how hard they strive. Their frustration under these conditions clears the path to "deviant" behavior.[4]

In Merton's metatheory, "deviant" behavior is the outcome of the ways in which individuals evaluate and react to legitimate *means* for obtaining commonly desired *ends*.[5] It is important, therefore, that it is not the substantive quality of the ends which Merton considers metatheoretically relevant, because members of a population may subscribe to new social goals over time.[6] Furthermore, the new goals, like the old ones, may contribute to widespread "deviancy" as long as the population generally values them as *more* important than the prescribed means for their achievement—it is the *relative* value of the abstract ends with respect to the means that is metatheoretically significant, not the relations between the specific *contents* of the ends and the means.[7] Consequently, the "end" in Merton's metatheory can be interpreted to mean *any* end; this word is a purely *formal* term.

Merton's "means-ends" paradigm, as it is often called, did not arise in an intellectual vacuum. Some of the basic principles used to construct this paradigm were ultimately derived, for example, from theoretical ideas developed originally by classical political economists. Other principles were derived from such assumptions as the notion that mobility is integrative in American society[8] (this notion was firmly established even among the pioneering sociologists; for example, Small). Merton's "theory" is therefore considered a metatheory on two counts: it is expressed primarily in terms of formal propositions and it is derived, wittingly or unwittingly, from *numerous* theoretical explanations which, although formulated in concrete terms, have been most representative of analytic thought among liberals for decades, if not centuries.

Conservation of Shared Misconceptions

In comparing metatheories with theories it will be noted that the former are called upon to do the work of the latter. However, because *some* of the important categories in Merton's metatheory, for example, are purely formal, it has been necessary to develop an operative interpretation of their meanings prior to their use in structuring new theoretical explanations about specific types of deviancy in particular societies.[9] This process of creative interpretation substitutes ideas which have substantive or objective references for such formal categories as "means" and "ends." After the substantive interpretations of a metatheory have been made for some time, however, the formal categories may undergo a transformation in meaning and acquire a substantive theoretical status. These categories may then be directly associated with concrete referents and appear to have a substantive "reality" of their own. Because of this, a metatheory can also be regarded as different from theories in *degree* rather than kind. This observation is supported by the fact that no "substantive" theory is devoid of formal categories, and no metatheory is devoid of substantive connotations. In fact, metatheory is plausible primarily because of its substantive connotations, even though these may be taken for granted in conversation between scholars.

The previous discussion on formal abstractives applies to other kinds of metatheoretical categories. Sociologists also construct metatheoretical categories on the basis of formal similarities between established theories (these can be called *source theories* in this context). The general outcome of this activity is a kind of "theory building" which usually consists of the formal classification and restatement of substantive categories and/or the formal interpretation of the mechanisms of source theories. However, in the development of such theory after this classification and interpretation are made, the formal categories and propositions are then applied to a particular area of inquiry; they need only be explicated by a *new* set of substantive referents that have not been used previously in the field of inquiry. By this means, the more abstract formulation helps generate new theories despite the fact that its source may have been in established theories in the *same* field. The abstract formulation, therefore, may *feed back* or stimulate theoretical development by the mere addition of a variant theory to the body of theories from which it has been derived.

The generation of new theories from metatheories can be a fruitful source of new knowledge. In sociology, however, this process most often seems to have proceeded without concern for the systematic confirmation or disconfirmation of the ideas encountered in the source theories. Consequently, this process of theory building drives *unconfirmed and often fallacious ideas to a higher level of abstraction.* On this high level, it becomes far more difficult to convince researchers to generate valid metatheoretical formulations, because the invalid ones can always be explicated in a new way.

It appears to be the case, therefore, that the search for abstract formulations by *the mere contemplation of the run of theory* is guaranteed to result in little more than the preservation of social myths. In light of the historical development of the field of sociology, an actual inadvertent consequence of this process of theory building has been the conservation of shared misconceptions rather than the discovery of new empirical uniformities.

Using Heuristic and Occupational Standards
to Justify Liberal Metatheories

The possibility of generating never-ending sets of fruitful, empirical hypotheses, based on newly specified applications of metatheory, is often a primary justification for retaining the metatheory in current use. Positivists and pragmatists call this justification the heuristic doctrine. In this context, the word "heuristic" suggests that these metatheoretical formulations are "useful fictions" because they have value for the discovery of empirical uniformities. However, when liberal metatheories actually do yield genuinely new information, the ideologically selective nature of these empirical "discoveries" makes the heuristic doctrine highly suspect as an ultimate justification for social science theorizing. Indeed, in this context, the heuristic doctrine generally appears to function primarily as a justification of theoretical activities which facilitate the development of technocratic rationalizations and technocratic intelligence. Because of this, it can be argued that in the social sciences, "scientific revolutions" resulting from significant changes related to metatheory are due more to the active and reactive relations between theoretical consciousness and politically significant practices than to theoretical consciousness and research practices.

The heuristic doctrine is part of a number of doctrines which are usually identified with "the scientific method." During the formative years, the unbounded faith in "scientific methods" encouraged the rise of a variety of corporate liberal scientific circles in American universities. These intellectual circles emerged in social science disciplines and professional schools: the social engineers held forth at Wisconsin; the legal realists at Yale; the industrial psychologists at the Carnegie Institute of Technology, and the reformist urban ethnographers at the University of Chicago. These and other new liberal schools of thought believed that social analyses or social policy could be benefited by "scientific methods." But a critical examination of the works by these scholars demonstrates that their so-called scientific methods were not the actual standards ultimately used to formulate their theories or policies about human relationships and the burning issues of the day.[10]

In much the same way, the fields which influenced the methods of social science, such as philosophy, were affected. The philosophy of science, for example, increasingly emphasized a formal analysis of the linguistic conventions used by scientists to arrive at and to validate knowledge. They also helped develop formal classification systems for types of theoretical formulations and definitional usages. At the same time, however, the great questions about the origins of comprehensive views of social life, which had figured large in classical epistemologies, were either ranked low on the scale of professional priorities or excluded from philosophy altogether. Because of the influence of corporate liberalism, philosophers of scientific knowledge analyzed linguistic conventions among scientists as if these conventions were part of a *closed system* which included scientists but excluded the rest of the world. They narrowed the scope of their professional goals by making involvement in the solutions of *logical* problems the measure of competence.[11] This was during the time when study should have concentrated on competing ideologies that had more to do with theoretical developments in social science than all the competing philosophical reconstructions of scientific practice.

These developments led to the stabilization of *systemic* standards, that is, to standards which appeared to be systematically related *only* to the activity of social scientists rather than to the ideological relationships in the society at large. Supported by such notions as the heuristic doctrine, these standards generally preempted the study of those standards referring to social or political utility. Even the expression of the vague humanistic or technocratic standards which had been previously found in Ward's notion of "social achievement," Small's "efficient society," and Dewey's concepts of "growth" and "progress" eventually became unfashionable.

Because of these developments, the academic social scientist's awareness of the influence of corporate liberalism was thoroughly cloaked in a fallacious technocratic mystique. Conceiving their relations to society at large in terms of this mystique, they saw ideological regulation of their conduct simply as a problem of what "values" governed a limited range of theoretical and methodological choices. Even the phrase *"value-free"* or *"fact-value"* rather than *"ideologically* free" or *"ideologically* neutral" is an expression of how narrow and formalistic this debate has been seen at times.[12]

The peculiarly restricted awareness of the relation between ideology and professional practice in sociology was strongly reinforced by periodic restraint of radical thought, such as the postwar political repression which accompanied the standardization of the corporate-liberal metatheory at the turn of the twenties and the rise of structural-functionalism during the fifties. During these repressive periods, sociologists generally subscribed to the erroneous belief that objective scientific standards had finally replaced "the value-laden" standards that had previously operated in their profession. By the beginning of the sixties, for example, Daniel Bell (1960) confidently declared that contemporary scholars had finally witnessed the "exhaustion" of the great nineteenth-century political ideologies throughout the Western world.[13] This assertion, as it is well known at this point, is one of the outstanding sociological fiascoes of the modern period.

This work has demonstrated that liberal ideology did not end with nineteenth century laissez-faire liberalism. Moreover, many of the fundamental assumptions underlying laissez-faire liberalism have been carried forward by corporate liberals in the twentieth century. Neither has the great Marxist tradition of the nineteenth century vanished from the modern world. Also, fundamental aspects of Marxism have been carried forward into the twentieth century, even though this world view has undergone change. In fact, Marxism is undergoing a substantial revival in Western nations today. The same certainly cannot be said for the ideology of liberalism. Liberal ideologists like

Bell [14] today are merely refining and elaborating the corporate-liberal conceptions which were laid down more than four decades ago.

In Bell's 1960 epilogue, he restricted his ("end of ideology") analysis to "western societies" because he must have felt that changes in ideological modes of thought in the third world were having little effect on social thought in advanced capitalist nations. Although this restriction may have increased the plausibility of his analysis among American liberals, it has become quite clear that significant changes in Marxism in capitalist nations have originated in the Marxist extensions and revisions made by writers who participated in revolutionary movements in Asia, Africa, and South America during the cold war years. Obviously, Marxism, like all other major world views, has no national boundaries. Consequently, when Bell wrote about the exhaustion of older ideologies, he mistakenly reversed the actual trends in social thought. It was liberalism, the patriarch among current ideologies, that was exhausted and impoverished, while Marxism was being creatively developed throughout the world.

NOTES

1. For examples of metatheoretical formulations, see Walter L. Wallace's 1969 text, *Sociological Theory*.
2. The source theories which are used to develop metatheories can include preexisting metatheories.
3. For a famous critical discussion of modern metatheory in the grand style, see C. Wright Mills' chapter on "grand theory" in *The Sociological Imagination* (1959:25–49).
4. The remainder of Merton's theory consists of an explanation of how the various types of deviant behavior result from the possible adaptations of lower-class persons to these frustrating conditions. It is important to note in passing that Merton's criteria for deviancy are never stated. This fact, in the face of the popularity of Merton's theory, testifies to a broad consensus among sociologists about the meanings of this metatheoretical term (i.e., "deviancy"). It might be suggested, on the basis of his concrete illustrations of this term (e.g., overconformist workers, revolutionaries, narcotics addicts, robber barons, all acts which are defined as "crime" [and therefore assigned this definition by the political state], etc.) that while radical and laissez-faire scholars might agree with some of his concrete interpretations of deviancy, a corporate liberal would agree with all of them.
5. Merton regards these relationships on an abstract plane although he applies the metatheory to the United States. This application produces a theory which specifies that Americans commonly share a "paramount desire" for social mobility or pecuniary success.
6. The metatheory in Merton's view can be applied to *any* society. The society, for example, can be a theocratic society and the "paramount goals" might therefore be constituted by religious perspectives.
7. Presumably, therefore, the pursuit of companionship or love will be just as conducive to "deviancy" as the pursuit of money, as long as these ends are generally considered more important than the means for attaining them.
8. Basic to Merton's theory, therefore, is the natural-social-law assumption that all social structures are the product of innumerable multilateral exchanges; society is essentially a vast exchange system wherein each individual exchanges his personal talents for status or wealth. The rate of mobility in this view is actually a rate of exchange. Also, classes in this model are actually reduced to "opportunity structures" which vary in their degree of "openness" (that is, in the degree to which they provide opportunities for exchange). Exchange, furthermore, is the key to social integration and change; without opportunities for exchange, there would be crime and revolution. With *sufficient* opportunities there would be an innovative but stable and ordered social change.

9. The word "specification" or "explication" is sometimes used to refer to this process of creative interpretation.

10. Weinstein (1968) extracts the ideological standards of the social engineers. Baritz (1960) describes the technocratic perspectives of the industrial psychologists. We will briefly comment on the ideological orientation of some of the reformist urban ethnographers such as Thrasher and Zorbaugh in Part Fourteen.

11. There is no better example of the trivialization and reduction of *epistemological* problems to *logical* problems than the dispute among philosophers of science regarding the question, is there a "logic" of discovery? Norwood R. Hanson (1969:73) points out that the approved (although not his) answer to this dispute is that there is no logic of discovery: "Thus," Hanson states, "Popper argues: 'The initial stage, the act of conceiving or inventing a theory, seems to me neither to call for logical analysis nor to be susceptible of it.' Again, 'There is no such thing as a logical method of having new ideas, or a logical reconstruction of this process.' Reichenbach writes that the philosophy of science 'cannot be concerned with [reasons for suggesting hypotheses], but only with [reasons for accepting hypotheses].' Braithwaite elaborates: 'The solution of these historical problems involves the individual psychology of thinking and the sociology of thought. None of these questions are our business here.' " Against this negative chorus, however, Hanson adds in disagreement, "the 'Ayes' have *not* had it. Aristotle (*Prior Analytics II*) and Pierce hinted that in science there may be more problems for the logician than just analyzing the arguments supporting already invented hypotheses."

We agree with Hanson but suggest that the fruitful analysis of logics of discovery will undoubtedly require substantial modification of the approved standards by which logic is defined. It is doubtful, however, that this will be done as long as philosophers relegate problems which have been central to their field for centuries, to psychology and sociology. Although this narrowed scope may free scholarly efforts for solutions to problems which enhance technical services for other disciplines (e.g., clarification of the logic of verification or explanation), it certainly contributes little to the development of a critical epistemology.

12. In spite of the admonitions of men like C. Wright Mills (1943, 1959:85–90), who underscored the significance of liberal ideology in the development of social science in the United States, sociologists generally ignored the implications of ideological hegemony for their daily practice. They avoided the implication that their controversies about the relation between theory and values, no matter how tumultuous, were within a limited universe of ideological discourse.

13. This assertion is sometimes sustained today by the claim that modern forms of Marxist thought, for example, are not identical with Marx's theory. Aside from assuming an erroneous view of post-Marx developments, this claim not only ignores the fact that Marx revised his work during his own lifetime, but that ideology is not the product of any one man. Marxism as well as liberalism underwent changes throughout the nineteenth century. During the twentieth century it has undergone further changes. At present, new and substantial revisions and extensions are also being made.

14. For example, Bell's (1953) theory of organized crime, which is considered a significant work in the sociology of crime and delinquency, is merely an elaborated version of the categories, generalizations, and mechanisms established during the formative years.

CHAPTER 54

Classical Liberal
and Corporate-Liberal Critiques
of Formalism

This chapter will broaden the previous discussions about the changes in analytic methods during the formative years. Before doing so, it returns briefly to the methodological perspectives of the classical and the laissez-faire liberal philosophers of science. Then, it discusses the late nineteenth century revolt against the formalism which had been justified by these earlier methodological perspectives.

Background

As noted previously, a liberal philosophy of science came into being during the seventeenth and eighteenth centuries. Identified with such scholars as Thomas Hobbes, David Hume, Adam Smith, John Locke, Jeremy Bentham, and James Mill, this philosophical approach eschewed the syllogistic logic and political conservatism of precapitalist scholasticism. In its most mature expression, it attempted to revitalize social science by equating a theory of science with a theory of language usage.

As finally stressed in the works of Bentham and James Mill, this approach equated a theory of science with a theory of "signs" or "useful fictions." These scientific "fictions" were ultimately derived, according to the utilitarians, from archetypal individual sensations caused by objective reality. It was also believed that scientific "fictions" were influenced by historically evolved language conventions which mediated the relationship between primal individual sensations and theoretical ideas. The utilitarians claimed that many of these linguistic conventions were not conducive to clear thinking because they were based on "false" or "abusive" uses of language. As a result of the influence of these linguistic errors, scientific ideas distorted the meanings of impressions or sensations of the real world. These false language conventions had to be replaced by proper usages and a logic of science which was more conducive to objective thinking.[1]

The liberal philosophers also considered scientific ideas to be valid if they had practical (i.e., political) utility. James F. Becker (1964) indicates that scholars have overlooked the degree to which the philosophical radicalism of these early liberals (particularly as expressed by such utilitarians as Jeremy Bentham and James Mill) incorporated *political* utility as a criterion of truth. Becker does not deny that the utilitarians were interested in formulating objective criteria for validating competing theories as well as logical principles which could be useful for theory construction. However, Becker also points out that the utilitarians were just as concerned with "a logic of science" which could be useful for the common good (a political category) by revitalizing a decrepit and conservative scholastic tradition. For example, to Bentham, the "principles of action" which were revealed in classical political economy served as the *ultimate* criterion for validating scientific theory. Bentham was interested in creating a science which was relevant to the social problems of their time and regarded their "logic of science" to be eminently practical for scientists and society: the utilitarians believed their philosophy of science was valid, therefore, because it had both *logical* and *political* utility.[2]

Thus, in this classical liberal perspective, scientific ideas were valid ideas if they were found to be syntactically consistent and reducible to primal sense impressions and, in addition, if they had political utility. Rejecting the epistemology of preceding generations of scholars, this philosophical approach to science laid the foundations of the leading liberal philosophies of science today.

The classical doctrines of political economy were structured around other basic liberal axioms which had achieved the status of ruling ideas. In the nineteenth century, these axioms were increasingly expressed in formal terms, and the criterion of political utility, which had previously served to justify the rejection of precapitalist perspectives toward science, was no longer necessary for reconstituting and revitalizing social science. Less concerned with the invention of basic axioms about the nature of man and society, liberal philosophers and political economists began to focus instead on the clarification of logics of deduction and verification. These facilitated the development of empirically testable generalizations of a lower order of abstraction. The contributions of scholars at that time, such as John Stuart Mill, consisted primarily of an elaboration and systematization rather than a major reconstruction of basic liberal premises.

In advancing the liberal philosophy of science, John Stuart Mill clarified the distinction between static and dynamic ideas which had been implicated in Hume's and James Mill's comparisons of types of individual sensations generated by momentary as opposed to repetitive phenomena. As a result of John Stuart Mill's analysis of the relation between types of individual sensations and types of language use among scientists, scholars distinguished between "static" and "dynamic" theories. Static theories included the kinds of theories which were eventually called "equilibrium models" by modern social scientists. These models often assumed the existence of "formal principles" or "tendencies" toward "equilibrated" social relationships.

J. S. Mill also attempted to make a clear distinction between political economy and social life in general by reference to a set of axioms which he felt dominated the study of economic relations. He noted (1844:137–138), for example, that the study of the political economy was concerned solely with individual man "as a being who desires to possess wealth, and who is capable of judging the comparative efficacy of attaining that end." This economic view of man was necessary, he said, in order to predict "only such of the phenomena of the social state as take place in consequence of the pursuit of wealth." This limited and abstract concept of man was commonly referred to as the concept of "economic man" and, as we have seen, it was central to the liberal study of economic relationships.[3]

In further analyzing modes of scientific theorizing, Mill distinguished the deductive or "a priori"[4] mode of reasoning. This mode referred to the logical principles used in deducing empirical generalizations (theorems) from a small set of basic axioms. Mill considered such axioms hypothetical because they were merely abstractions and referred to noninclusive phenomena in the real world. He, therefore, was fully aware that, for example, his references to certain qualities, such as the interest in wealth, were constructed because they might be useful for predicting *economic* behavior. He did not assert that wealth was actually the *sole* motive of man. In fact, as Morton G. White (1947:143) has noted, Mill actually denied (*ibid.:*139) that any "political economist was ever so absurd to suppose that mankind are really thus constituted." Mill simply regarded the basic axioms of classical liberal theories as "useful fictions."

Throughout the nineteenth century, however, such useful fictions as "economic man" provided the central pillars on which scholarly enterprises in American university departments were supported. These "fictions," as we have seen, came under sharp attack by corporate liberals at the turn of the century. Of equal importance, in the process of raising serious questions about the validity and usefulness of these "fictions," corporate-liberal scholars also challenged the epistemological assumptions and logical principles that justified the ways in which these "fictions" were integrated into scientific theories. These particular challenges figured large in what came to be called the "revolt against formalism." But it should be noted that this "revolt" was the *second* "revolt" against formalism to have been launched and consummated by liberal scholarship. The first, the authentic revolution in ideas, was conducted by classical liberals against *precapitalist scholasticism*. The second, the "palace revolt," was directed by corporate liberals against the analytic methods that prevailed among *laissez-faire liberals* during the nineteenth century.

Neoclassical Economics and the Metaphysics of Normality

Morton G. White has indicated that the "revolt against formalism" toward the end of the last century included a number of leading scholars, such as Dewey, Holmes, and Veblen. In his analysis, White (*ibid.*:144) specifically pointed out that Veblen felt that John Stuart Mill's definition of political economy was fallacious because it was based on universal and inclusive characteristics of man.[5] However, White also amends Veblen's statement, indicating that Mill did not regard his descriptions of man as unconditional statements of human behavior.[6] Mill was aware that his assumptions were merely hypothetical.

But the developments in liberal thought throughout the nineteenth century suggest that whether Mill considered his concepts of man to be "hypothetical constructions," "useful fictions," or "conditional assertions" was of little consequence from an operative point of view. Whether he qualified his concept of man in terms of a positivistic or pragmatic view of concept formation did not alter the fact that liberal economists had actually behaved as if no other assumptions than those implicated, for example, by egoism, atomism, scarcity, economizing, and free competition were necessary for the study of economic relationships. Mill may have felt that no political economist "was ever so absurd as to suppose that mankind" was only interested in the pursuit of wealth; but to all intents and purposes, political economists were indeed "absurd" because they proceeded to theorize about economic processes primarily from this point of reference. And a careful examination of Veblen's criticism of classical economics will reveal that it was precisely this obvious regularity in *actual* scholarship which accounted for his challenge to the basic axioms and epistemological assumptions advanced by such classical scholars as John Stuart Mill.

In a sharp criticism of classical schools of economics, Veblen (1900:253–256) declared that economists had developed a "metaphysics of normality" which was directly reflected or deducible from what these scholars called "hypothetical truths" or "very concise assumptions concerning human nature." Because he recognized that ethical criteria identified the optimum relations described by these "hypothetical truths," Veblen considered the science of political economy to be analogous to "a theory of the normal case." [7] He also felt that the hypothetico-deductive mode of reasoning encouraged static analyses organized around theoretical equilibrium models, rather than causal analyses of the dynamic processes which actually took place in industrial societies. Neoclassical theorists, such as Marshall, he contended, were concerned only with "explaining the mutual adjustments and interrelation of elements in a system," rather than dynamic evolutionary institutional processes.[8] Although he also declared at that time that there was the possibility that certain German and English economists, including Keynes, might "provide a fuller account of the genesis and developmental continuity of all features of modern life," Veblen (*ibid.*:263) indicated that this possibility had not yet been realized.

Veblen reacted strongly against the logical principles of the hypothetico-deductive model of influence because, as indicated, they played an important role in static analyses. In his opinion, moreover, this deductive way of thinking had created the false impression that economists were dealing solely with questions of fact rather than questions of value. The classical "metaphysics of normality" or "theoretical reality" was ostensibly "colorless" and concerned only with "matter of fact events." But, Veblen (*ibid.*:256) pointed out, "in the work actually done by these economists this standpoint of rigorous normality is not consistently maintained." Instead, value judgments entered into the basic assumptions used by economists; they were especially manifested in the prevailing belief that *laissez-faire* economic principles *legitimately* as well as objectively characterized the nature of economic life at the turn of the century. The use of deductive principles therefore obscured the fact that economists were heavily involved in an ideological enterprise.

In short, Veblen felt that economics had been reduced to a "taxonomic science" because it was organized around a laissez-faire and utilitarian "metaphysics of normality." The consequences of this metaphysics were considered disastrous for economic theory because they prevented an "evolutionary" (i.e., historical) study of economic processes, as well as the proper institutional study of the "proliferation of economic processes." Furthermore, economic analysis had become constricted to the study of individual choices and bargaining relationships. In his words, the "metaphysics of normality had narrowed the range of discretionary [voluntaristic] teleological action to the human agent alone." [9]

Rejection of Prevailing Analytic Methods

The classical liberal and corporate-liberal rejection of formalism occurred a century apart from each other. A comparison of these "uprisings" suggests that in every major critique of a preexisting ideology, its methods of inquiry generally come under attack along with its most abstract categories and paradigmatic generalizations. Taken as a whole, the categories, generalizations, and methodological canons are critically labeled "formal" and "insubstantive" because they refer to highly abstract or very general properties, relations, and rules which are no longer considered plausible or useful for scientific and social purposes. However, even though the widespread criticism of these relations around the turn of the century has been seen as a "revolt against formalism" (White 1947), what is actually being classified by this phrase is a revolt against established liberal metatheory. This attack encountered the metatheory as a whole, but it also singled out methodological canons and analytic strategies. The differences between these strategies and other aspects of the metatheory are not absolute because it is *impossible* to mount a

436

comprehensive criticism of the former (e.g., methodological canons and analytical strategies) without the latter (e.g., basic concepts of man, woman, and society).

During the last two decades of the nineteenth century, the revolt against formalism in fields other than sociology was led by such outstanding scholars as Holmes,[10] Dewey, Veblen, and Beard. These men condemned legal, philosophical, economic, and historical "scholasticism." In each case, very general notions and logical strategies of inquiry in their respective fields were called "false," "formal" or "lifeless" abstractions. These abstract ideas, as White (*ibid.*:132) points out, were rejected in favor of those centering on human "experience," "processes," "growth," "social contexts," and "evolution." They declared that life was not "static." Ideas were related to their time and every period in history involved complex, interdependent, and changing relationships.[11]

It should surprise no one to find that, as the new formalism was being created, the *deductive* method was coming under attack around the turn of the century. The use of deductive methods for generating theories in certain social science fields has been utterly dependent upon the plausibility of highly abstract and universal ideas that have been firmly established by preceding generations of scholars. These ideas were losing plausibility, however, because they were being challenged at the turn of the century by eminent members of the *new generation* of liberal scholars. Some of these new scholars advocated the use of *historical* methods of inquiry because these methods were considered useful for deriving new insights into the changing nature of man and society. Historical methods were therefore found useful for attacking the metaphysics of normality which had been carefully constructed by classical and laissez-faire scholars. Used critically, these methods also stimulated the growing acceptance of the emerging *corporate*-liberal metaphysics of normality.

Formal Elaborations and the Post-Formative Years

Toward the end of the formative period a corporate-liberal sociological metatheory was finally standardized and, in time, the grand theories developed by the earlier founders of the field also came under attack as "global" and "vacuous" interpretations of the evolutionary developments of human civilization. During the period between the great wars, the insistence on the importance of empirical research came to mean little more than the application of newly established metatheory to the study of specific subject-matter areas. Even historical research was organized around the metatheoretical categories and generalizations that were now dominating the field. The expansion of sociological research, moreover, influenced the levels on which metatheoretical reorganization took place. Toward the end of the period between the two world wars, as indicated in the previous chapter, sociologists, led by Robert K. Merton, became aware of the fact that the repetitive use of certain generalizations by researchers in various subject-matter areas had led to the increasing formalization of theoretical ideas. Following this, during the early post–World War II years, these theoreticians urged a program of "codification" and standardization of "middle-range" (meta)theory or "paradigms" (i.e., axiomatic generalizations) in specific subject matter areas (Merton 1957:12–16).

The extraordinary complexity of metatheoretical activity during the postwar period provided the precondition for the revitalization and the domination of the hypothetico-deductive model of inference among sociologists. Although some sociologists utilized what was mistakenly called an "inductive" method [12] and others espoused historical approaches (Mills 1959:143–64), none of the other methods functioned so effectively as a sign of professional (analytic) competence. This tacit insistence that scientific theorizing must involve the use of the deductive model of inference, however, was, from an operative standpoint, little more than a plea for conformity to a dominant ideology and its metatheoretical generalizations.

NOTES

1. For politically significant insights into the philosophy of science developed by men like Smith, Bentham, and Mill, see James F. Becker (1961, 1964). See also, Halevy's (1955) comprehensive work on the "philosophical radicals."
2. For Adam Smith's interest in the formulation of a theory of political economy for persuasive political discourse, see also Becker (1961).
3. White (1947:143) notes that Mill indicated political economy *is to be* distinguished from "social economy" or "speculative politics" ("the latter treating 'the whole of man's nature as modified by the social state' ") on the basis of the concept of economic man. Actually, Mill pointed out that political economy *had become* defined in these narrow terms. He stated (1844:136–137) that the previous conception of political economy had been in tune with M. Say's definition (which embraced "every part of man's nature") but "the words 'political economy' *have long ceased* to have so large a meaning . . . What is now commonly understood by the term 'Political Economy' . . . is concerned with [man] solely as a being who desires to possess wealth . . ." (our emphasis).
4. Mill (1844:145) stated, "The *à priori* method . . . is . . . the only method by which truth can possibly be attained in any department of the social science." Mill (*ibid.*:143–145) further stated: "By the method *à priori* we mean . . . reasoning from an assumed hypothesis; which is not a practice confined to mathematics, but is of the essence of all science which admits of general reasoning at all. To verify the hypothesis itself *à posteriori* . . . is . . . [an] *application* of science. In the definition . . . of Political Economy, we have characterized it as essentially an *abstract* science, and its method as the method *à priori* . . . Political Economy, therefore, reasons from *assumed* premises—from premises which might be totally without foundation in fact, and which are not pretended to be universally in accordance with it. The conclusions of Political Economy, consequently, like those of geometry, are only true, as the common phrase is, *in the abstract;* that is, they are only true under certain suppositions, in which none but general causes—causes common to the *whole class* of cases under consideration—are taken into account" (our emphasis).
5. Veblen also stated that Mill's assertion represented the acme of "faulty psychology." The theorems which were being deduced from this classical concept of man, in his opinion, were highly suspect.
6. White (1947:143) stated that "the important point in Mill's [*ibid.*] view of the political economy is his use of the subjective conditional mode of assertion in the following passage: 'Political economy considers mankind as occupied solely in acquiring and

consuming wealth; and aims at showing what is the course of action into which mankind, living in a state of society, *would* (my italics) be impelled *if* (my italics) that motive . . . *were* (my italics) absolute ruler of all their actions.' " "I emphasize the subjunctive mood of the statement," White added, "for it is clear that Mill is not saying that in fact the pursuit of wealth *is* the sole motive of man. Indeed, he goes on to say that the economist does *not* put this forth as a description of man's actual behavior.

It is our opinion, however, that Mill's statements have to be evaluated in the general context of his view of political economy. As long as Mill agreed with other liberal economists that political economy was based on the behavior of economic man, then his qualifications about the "hypothetical" status of this conception have to be taken with a grain of sand. In 1844, Mill (1844:136–137) indicated that the field of political economy as a whole had been narrowly redefined with reference to the concept of economic man.

7. He stated (1900:255), for example, that the theory represented "a discussion of the concrete facts of life in respect to their approximation of the normal case." Moreover, he declared that political and economic relationships *not* encompassed or deducible from the basic axioms of this normal case, if entering into theoretical consideration at all, did so by way of qualification rather than causal analyses based on different basic premises. Veblen (*ibid.*:254) stated, "The concrete premises from which proceeds the systematic knowledge of this generation of economists are certain very concise assumptions concerning human nature . . . these postulates afford the standard of normality. Whatever situation or course of events can be shown to express these postulates without mitigation is normal; and wherever a departure from this normal course of things occurs, it is due to disturbing causes,—that is to say, to causes not comprised in the main premises of the science,—and such departures are to be taken account of by way of qualification."

8. Veblen, interestingly, illustrated this point by referring to the significant changes in what he called the analysis of "normal value." Originally, Veblen noted, classical economists such as Smith and Ricardo had emphasized such factors as costs of production (including above all the cost of "personal labor") in arriving at "normal value" of commodities. However, the sophisticated changes in hedonistic utilitarianism made by J. S. Mill and elaborated by later neoclassical economists had resulted in the analysis of "normal value" on the basis of equilibrium models involving, according to Veblen, "the law of reciprocal demand." As a result, Veblen (1900:259–260) indicated, "the factor of cost falls into the background; and the process of bargaining which is in the foreground, being a process of valuation, a balancing of individual demand and supply, it follows that a law of reciprocal demand comes in to supplant the law of cost. In all this the proximate causes at work in the determination of values are plainly taken into account of more adequately than in earlier cost-of-production doctrines; but they are taken account of with a view to explaining the mutual adjustment and interrelation of elements in a system rather than to explaining either a developmental sequence or the working out of a foreordained end." Obviously Veblen is discussing here the shift from macroscopic economic analysis based on the classical interpretations of the labor theory of value, to microscopic analysis of short-term price fluctuations based on supply and demand propositions, etc.

9. Veblen's phrase "the metaphysics of normality" is useful, in our opinion, for classifying, in addition to the classical, the corporate-liberal assumptions about the nature of man and society. This phrase, however, should be modified within the framework of the critical perspective enunciated in prior chapters. In making this modification, for example, it should be kept in mind that Veblen generally implied that basic assumptions about the nature of man and society could somehow be formulated independently of questions of value. Because of this, he implied that the science of political economy would be enhanced if facts and values were separated from one another. It is our opinion, however, that this separation is an impossibility because ideology and metatheory are inseparable. The history of the development of social science throughout the centuries indicates that with regard to the genesis of metatheoretical assumptions, there exists no distinction between what Veblen referred to as "the avowed identification of the normal with the right," and what the sociologist Donald Martindale (1957:341) calls "normative" and "empirical" theories. The various metaphysics of reality have been and still are at once normative and empirical.

10. Holmes is cited because he expressed the need for change very early in this development. When Roscoe Pound formulated his conception of sociological jurisprudence, on the other hand, American sociology had been firmly established. Pound's formulations were heavily dependent on Ross' and Small's concepts of social control and interest groups. His works represent an excellent example of the influence of corporate liberalism on changes in a professional field. (For a discussion of the relation between Pound and the American sociologists, see Geis [1964].)

11. It should be emphasized that *corporate liberals* as well as radical liberal and socialist intellectuals were advancing ideas of this sort. Later developments in American universities have obscured the degree to which American social scientists and philosophers were concerned with the dynamics of changing social relationships.

12. The utilization of an "analytic-induction method" is operatively represented by Lindesmith's (1947), Becker's (1953), and Cressey's (1953) works. There is also the implication that Glaser and Strauss' (1967) method of "the discovery of grounded theory" is inductive. The method used by all of these scholars, however, is not based on induction. It is analogous to the method of retroduction. For a discussion of the concepts of induction, deduction, and retroduction, see Willer (1967:25–29) and Pierce (1932:137).

CHAPTER 55

Formalism and Reification

The attack on "formalism" toward the end of the nineteenth century was distributed among the disciplines and professions in the United States. Leading scholars in each field assaulted metatheoretical categories, formal paradigms, and analytic methods that were closest to their own substantive concerns: logical systems used by philosophers, scientists, and educators loomed large in Dewey's iconoclastic writings; Veblen deprecated the psychological and the deductive methods of neoclassical economists; Beard regarded the formal interpretations of the constitution as fruitless for understanding its historical origins; Holmes declared "The life of law has not been logic: it has been experience," while Pound decried the "legal monks who pass their lives in an atmosphere of pure law." Each academic discipline and professional field dealt with its own body of formal metatheoretical ideas.

The critics of "formalism" encountered the reified realities of associationism and utilitarianism. Farseeing liberals such as John Dewey rejected the quietistic assumptions underlying the classical liberal conception of man.[1] They also indicated that a "wholistic" and "organic" approach to man should be developed.[2] This approach, it was contended, would unify human qualities heretofore segmented by such concepts as natural man, political man, economic man, and religious man. However, when these scholars—as well as succeeding generations of liberals—eventually evolved their own comprehensive versions of a self-regulated man, they retained the

440

classical preferences for prudentialism, competition, scarcity and egoism. They combined their notions of social control and these older concepts into a pluralistic web. Finally, they embedded their concept of man within the social context of ordered conflict: this "whole" man—with all his liberal tensions and nervous afflictions—was considered the key to an equally conflicted but nevertheless equally "organic" society. In this process, a new ensemble of liberal reifications began to shape the academic view of social life.

Widening Critique of Established Metatheories

The developing revolt against established metatheories in one field influenced other fields. Although lagging at first, sociologists, for example, eventually caught up with corporate-liberal developments in the field of psychology. Significant analytic changes in other fields such as law (Geis 1964) drew from developments in sociology. In time, therefore, the uneven developments in each field were adjusted in light of significant changes in other fields. These "adjustments" in sociology, as we have previously seen, were stimulated by controversies arising from papers and reviews published in the *American Journal of Sociology* but written by psychologists, philosophers, and political scientists. Ward's, Small's, and Ross' personal correspondence indicate that the early sociologists read widely. Because of this, theoretical works published by members of other disciplines and professions also influenced their developing orientations.

Universities such as Johns Hopkins, Chicago, and Wisconsin played a very significant role in stimulating the breadth of changes in every social science discipline. A high concentration of corporate-liberal scholars appeared in these institutions prior to the turn of the century and provided the crucial opportunities for direct interaction between men with similar ideological perspectives but from different disciplines. Their interaction reinforced the revolt against the "formalism" of preceding generations of scholars. It also generalized this revolt and, as a consequence, the opposition to hedonistic utilitarianism or associationism, for example, was not restricted to psychology or sociology alone. This opposition became manifest throughout all the social science disciplines.

Formal Principles for Empirical Generalizations: Criticism from the Left

We have seen that Veblen attacked neoclassical economists on methodological as well as substantive grounds. He criticized them for using abstractions such as "perfect competition" and "economic man" instead of organizing their theories around evolutionary economic processes. These abstractions were not only considered to be unrelated to the realities of economic life, they also represented a style of inquiry which overlooked the interdependence between psychological and institutional relationships. The classical abstractions, in Veblen's view, were divorced from larger social contexts. They were attentive neither to historical processes nor to the total pattern of institutional relationships at any given time.

Veblen's critique was not new however; parts of it had been expressed centuries before by such French environmentalists as Helvetius; most of it repeated comments previously made by Marx. However, Marx had also pointed out that classical modes of thought had been influenced by the idealist's penchant for universal formal principles. One of these idealistic principles, for example, rooted capitalistic division of labor in an eternal quest for greater efficiency. Others based the origin of the division of labor in a vague quest for pure reason or higher morality. (It was alleged that these "quests," "generalizations," or "empirical laws" were universal because they were found in all forms of human association.) But Marx also noted that these "eternal tendencies" were merely formal principles substituted for a concrete historical analysis of the changes in the organization of social, political, and economic life. Because of this, he urged the sharp rejection of theories of social evolution based on these "immutable principles." He stated that these principles, and the categories embedded within them, "are as little eternal as the relations they express. They are historical and transitory products."

When applied to the problem of social integration or change it was pointed out that these formal principles were conjoined with equally formal social units of analysis (e.g. groups, institutions, or society). The increasing specialization of occupational groups, for example, was considered by Durkheim (1933:269) to be a "means" whose primary "function" was the reduction of competition and the maintenance of an equilibrated social order. Occupational groups, in Durkheim's work, were compared to "organs" which are "battling and trying to supplant one another." Even society as a whole was perceived as a type of organic Leviathan which mobilized itself against the individuals and groups within it in order to regulate social conflict and maintain social stability. Robert Nisbet (1966:87) indicates that Durkheim's *Rules of Sociological Method* was criticized when it was published because "it must have appeared—in that ultraindividualistic age of social science—as hardly more than a vision of the absolute social mind, a scholastic exercise in reification." Nisbet feels, however, that this impression was inaccurate; it represents a distortion of Durkheim's work. We suggest, in contrast, that this impression was neither inaccurate nor distorted. We will also suggest, toward the end of this chapter, what kinds of social relationships were reified by Durkheim.

Hegemonic Function of New Metaphysics

In our discussion of *The Division of Labor in Society* in Chapter 32, it was noted that Durkheim had no qualms about defining the political state merely as a set of administrative rules. A quarter of a century later, Park and Burgess (1924:33–40) took Durkheim's metaphysical claims at face value; they also asserted that groups, institutions, and societies have "a real corporate existence" independent of the individuals comprising them (*ibid.*:33). For support they noted further that Durkheim, in the *Rules of Sociological Method,* considered definitions of this kind to be valid because the moral rules governing life in social groups were the qualities which gave them their "corporate reality."

Durkheim's moral metaphysics emphasized individual duties rather than rights. It pointed to the functional necessity of moral principles and certain normative relationships as the ultimate keystones of social reality. By the end of the formative years the basic substructure of this new liberal metaphysics of reality was clearly staked out by such categories as "the collective conscience," "a group mind," "systems of rules," "social consensus," and "societal mores."

Why did Durkheim—or the Americans for that matter—ground metaphysical reality in analytic references to moral rules, a general consensus, or social mores? There are many possibilities, but the most significant touch upon the hegemonic functions of these reifications at the turn of the century. The formative period in American and European sociology took place on the heels of the advent of monopoly capitalism; at that time, new instruments of social control were made urgent by the conflicts which accompanied the great changes in the political economy and the widespread disillusionment with laissez-faire liberalism. Under these conditions, the Americans who became preoccupied with the concept of social control generally refrained from analyzing the systematic use of violence for the maintenance and expansion of capitalism. At the same time, these scholars stressed, above all, the role of mutual obligations and social ideals in achieving an optimum industrial democracy. Their repeated references to mutual obligations and value consensus suggest, moreover, that they were fully aware that the police, state militia, and federal troops did not, by themselves, guarantee long-term social stability in the United States.

The leading American sociologists blended their descriptions of society with the ways in which moral obligations and ideals *ought* to function in the new liberal metaphysics of industrial reality. As a consequence, the formal categories created by these men *imperceptibly structured* the scholar's orientation to the study of certain human relations at the very *outset* of an analytic enterprise. These hegemonic categories selectively oriented social scientists toward social relationships that maintained or weakened voluntary compliance to the established "rules of the game." This ideological aim indicated the *real* heuristic functions of the natural-social-law categories developed by the end of the formative years.

What other kinds of formal conceptual creations could one expect from these technocratic students of moral relationships? Considering their points of view, what more effectively pragmatic units of analysis could be formulated for studying and monitoring hegemonic relationships based on the new corporate-liberal morality?

The Moral *Politics* of "The Social Science Movement"

The American concentration on moral relationships is also not surprising in light of the close identification between sociology and certain kinds of institutional structures. These structures, including social work, public welfare, and sectarian or nonsectarian philanthropic agencies, attempted to ameliorate the problems of working-class people chiefly through *moral* means. The American social sciences generally emerged out of an earlier liberal reform "social science movement" [3] which had encouraged the application of social science to social problems. Long after the demise of this specific movement, however, sociology still maintained a very close relation with institutions attempting to manage or reform social problems without recourse to outright political (much less revolutionary) tactics.

The historical development of certain kinds of social theory and social practice provides some understanding of why the early sociologists were men who generally specialized in the development of moral ideas and moral strategies (for maintaining ideological hegemony). However, it is also noteworthy that this specialized function had been fulfilled heretofore chiefly by clerical intellectuals. For centuries, clerical institutions had cornered most of the intellectual market in the moral management of the population at large.[4] In light of this, it is to be expected that a high proportion of leading sociologists during the formative years were sons of clergymen or had actually been trained for ministerial service themselves. Irrespective of the increasingly secular orientations that characterized the field, from what other source would men interested primarily in moral behavior have come at that time?

The Liberal Sins of Reification

In *The Rules of Sociological Method,* Durkheim (1938:3) stated that his concept of "social fact" referred to "ways of acting, thinking and feeling, external to the individual and endowed with a power of coercion by reason of which they control him." His operative interpretation of this formal notion (i.e., "social fact") with regard to *modern* industrial societies suggests that he committed a conceptual "sin of reification." The concept of social fact, at the very least, is a blatant reification of all the hegemonically significant aspects of social life, which are presumed to be governable by restitutive laws," "administrative rules," "occupational moralities," and other bourgeois rules of conduct.

It should be apparent by now that Durkheim's sins of reification were merely instances of a general regularity in intellectual thought. This regularity was expressed in representative works of a legion of scholars in the technologically advanced capitalist nations during the formative years. The early American representatives of this intellectual trend, of course, had their own national reasons which divided the social reality as it was into the *established* world based on the ravages of egoism and the *emergent* one based on social control. As a point of fact, however, liberal scholars in the Western European countries also formulated similar reasons and categories for their analyses of social relationships.

On the other hand, the American sociologists operated in much more favorable institutional circumstances with regard to the formation of their profession. They rode the initial wave of modern university development relatively unencumbered by ancient academic traditions. Their status as members of an independent discipline was rapidly institutionalized within the academy. They established separate sociology departments much earlier than the Europeans and were able to train a much larger core of professional sociologists who applied the new ways of thinking more systematically to greater varieties of social issues. As a consequence, the Americans were far more capable of fulfilling the programmatic implications of such formal natural-social-law categories as social control, which stressed moral relationships but also implicated every conceivable manner by which social and political hegemony had been, was being, and could be maintained.

The Americans, it is true, derived many of their metatheoretical concepts from European scholarship, but these concepts had been developed for the most part by classical and laissez-faire scholars such as Smith, Bentham, Mill, and Spencer. And even though the Americans were strongly influenced by their European contemporaries, the strength of their own national contribution to a great period in the development of analytic liberal thought should not be minimized. The great magnitude of this contribution is symbolized by the fact that there is perhaps only *one* other natural law category which is as significant in its theoretical pervasiveness as the category of social control in this regard. That category is egoism.

The categories of egoism and social control represent two great moments in analytic liberal thought because they symbolized the conditions emerging at two very significant periods of time. Egoism, it should be recalled, reified the individualistic and internecine conditions in precapitalist price-making markets and generalized these relations as being universally necessary for human survival. On the other hand, social control categorized all the regulatory and coercive relationships which maintained human institutions throughout history. But it especially reified the hegemonic conditions necessary for capitalist institutions and justified these conditions as being necessary for the survival of all humankind.

NOTES

1. Mead should also be mentioned in this regard: there is a need for a thoroughgoing study of the liberalism underlying his conception of self and role (e.g., note the reifications of the corporate liberal contradiction between the individual and society in his discussion of the relations between the "I" and the "Me"). For insight into Dewey's liberalism, see C. Wright Mills (1966:356 ff.). Mills, for example, states that many pages in Ward's *Dynamic Sociology,* which criticize laissez-faire notions, could have been written by Dewey (*ibid.:*462,fn.1). The final chapter on Mills' analysis of the history of pragmatism deals with Dewey's social psychology. It is entitled, "Social Psychology: Model for Liberals."

2. White (1947) refers to this approach as "cultural organicism." It represented, in our opinion, a rudimentary "systems" approach to behavioral relations developed by scholars who were taking a broader view of capitalist relations, and who were using "culture" as the idealistic, social control mechanism for solving the problem of social integration.

3. This movement was organized around the American Social Science Association, which was formed in 1965 (Mills 1959:84).

4. From this point of view, it is the relations between certain kinds of liberal theoretical activity and the institutional structures at the time which encouraged a high concentration of scholars with religious backgrounds. Thus, although there was undoubtedly a reinforcing relation between the religious background characteristics of individual sociologists and the general nature of the field, these characteristics did not *initially* determine the general concern with moral forms of integration.

From the turn of the century onwards, the further development of secular institutions of higher learning and the increasing diversity of sociological interests began to provide the conditions for the decrease in the significance of religious background characteristics for the specialized study and control of moral as well as other human relationships.

PART FOURTEEN
The Pragmatic Timetable, the Subversion of Democracy, and Technocratic Professionalism

CHAPTER 56
The Demise of the Utopian Timetable

A number of the utopian conceptions of society were expressed in liberal writings during the formative years. Spencer's utopia was embodied in his concept of the laissez-faire industrial society. Ward enunciated his conception of sociocracy early in his sociological career. Durkheim proposed a national liberal-syndicalist scheme in the preface to the second edition of *The Division of Labor*. And Small presented his utopian vision of the "Efficient Society" in a presidential address before American sociologists. By the end of the formative years, however, utopian thinking was becoming unfashionable and its principal protagonists no longer dominated the professional scene. This chapter will briefly describe the demise of the laissez-faire and Protestant traditions which had sustained the gradualist, utopian timetable.

The Demise of Spencerism

The early sociologists had two types of intellectual opponents: (1) laissez-faire liberals; (2) radicals, such as socialists and anarchists. At the beginning of the formative years, when Ward's *Dynamic Sociology* was written, the laissez-faire liberal, Herbert Spencer, clearly overshadowed all other opponents of the emerging corporate-liberal tradition. Four decades later, however, laissez-faire *slogans* were being retained as part of the folklore of capitalism (Arnold 1937) but laissez-faire liberalism was vanishing as a viable intellectual alternative to corporate liberalism. In 1913, Ross (Small 1913:65) declared upon Ward's death, "Dr. Ward lived to see his philosophy triumph in the minds of leaders of thought and opinion. Today there is *nothing* left of the Spencerian theory of the state which thirty years ago dominated the political thought of intellectuals, with the exception of a handful of socialists . . ." (our emphasis).

Spencerism was also laid to rest outside sociological circles. Howard W. Odum (1927:159) has pointed out that "during the first decades of Professor Small's connection with the University of Chicago," the laissez-faire doctrine "was the summary and conclusion of economic teaching as presented by the majority of its professors in the United States." In 1917, however, "the meeting of the American Economic Association held in Philadelphia . . . including a joint session with the American Sociological Society, celebrated the funeral obsequies of the doctrine of laissez-faire."

Utopia Revised

The founding fathers of American sociology replaced Spencer's "industrial society" with a utopian vision of their own. These corporate liberals advanced this vision in the name of social justice and individual liberty. But in certain respects, their fervent desire for justice and liberty was little more than a transformation of the meritocratic, capitalist society Spencer had in mind. Of course, Spencer's savage principles of equity were replaced by intellectual pleading for a furtherance of "humane" principles based on a more equitable balance of power between such "interest groups" as capital and labor. During the end of the second decade of this century, however, even militant expressions of a desire for justice appeared to give way before the overriding alarm concerning the stability of capitalism.

Some of the founders' visions of an equitable society were integrated by references to voluntary exchanges and to a powerful authoritative state. Others were integrated by normative, functionalist definitions of rights and duties, which efficiently induced each individual into service for the betterment of the corporate economy. At times, as we have seen, these visions were supported by crude laissez-faire justifications, exemplified by Ross' (1930:360) comment that "private property is a social welfare institution because the hope of acquiring property powerfully stimulates the economic activities of the capable." At other times, this utopian vision was buttressed by more sophisticated arguments, such as Small's liberal-syndicalist ethic of cooperation within the framework of corporate capitalism. This cooperation entailed a *tolerant* attitude on the part of all members of groups representing functionally interrelated parts of society. It also required a basic commitment to corporate capitalism exclusive of allegiance to any other political or economic system.

In 1910, Ward sadly defended his telic conception of the sociocratic state when he lamented that "political economy has become a sort of quietism [which] bade people hush and cease to disturb the social order" (Stern, 1937:325). But what precisely did men like Ward, Ross, and Small propose as viable alternatives to this "quietism"? They went no further than vague indications of piecemeal and ameliorative reform, development of mass education, and calls for the mere arousal of public criticism against the robber barons. They also suggested that the federal government sponsor advisory councils of scientists and encourage the moral rejuvenation of individual persons. In addition, all of them believed that significant reforms could be achieved by appealing to disinterested sympathy on the part of upper-class individuals.

When Small insisted that science must provide an ethical philosophy of life, his thoughts did not end with improving the moral conduct of public officials or the population at large. He also stated (1905:728–729) early in the century that "there must be *credible* sociologists in order that there may be farseeing economists and statesmen and moralists, and that each of us may be an *intelligent* specialist at his particular post." And although Small interwove these remarks with vague references to the general welfare and the promise of human reason, he was not at all ambiguous about the kinds of standards that should pervade the field. It was corporate liberalism which informed him of the "intelligent" directions in which the field and its personnel should develop.

Another consequence of the emerging corporate-liberal sociology was the intrusion of technocratic criteria into major substantive areas of sociology. The important topics were not the study of human beings striving to enjoy life to the fullest at work or at play, but rather the study of industrial discipline, occupational aspirations, and personal commitment to the legal codes. The technocratic bias inherent in these writings generally resulted in a search for all types of extra-legal methods of social control and the creation of the illusion that a "stable" family, "American" education, various "regulatory" agencies, and "social" engineering were effective means for reshaping society. Similar technocratic attitudes toward reform were also expressed in the writings of the *second* generation of American sociologists, but they were expressed in an atmosphere of increasing optimism about the achievement of economic and political stability in the United States.

The End of an Era

In 1920, some sociologists were beginning to feel that the era of uncontrolled industrial conflicts between interest groups was coming to an end. In reviewing the events of this period, which was now behind him, Weatherly (1920:34–35) sarcastically observed that the history of reform could be divided into three periods: the "soapbox," "parlor," and "statehouse" eras. In the soapbox era, according to Weatherly, muckrakers vituperatively attacked social problems. During the parlor era, "brittle intellectuals" speculatively developed visionary programs for social reform. However, during the final, "statehouse" era, legislators conservatively developed "the solid mass of statutory measures" out of the "gusty airs of reform sentiments." As a consequence, things would be different now. Society was becoming increasingly integrated and Weatherly (ibid.:35) observed that "a renovated economic system is in the process of formation." Obviously, however, the three reform periods did not progress smoothly or in absence of setbacks. Nor was everyone satisfied with the outcome of these periods, as indicated by Weatherly's observation that "the man of the soapbox era" (who is "rarely of the kind to be satisfied with anything") felt that "his cause has been *betrayed*" by the legislation produced during the "statehouse era" (our emphasis).

Weatherly's remarks alluded to the widespread sense of betrayal experienced by many liberals in all walks of life during and after President Wilson's administration. These liberal reformers were justified in feeling betrayed. Instead of being decreased, the power of great corporations continued increasing during Woodrow Wilson's administration. Utilizing the rhetoric of the Christian capitalist wing of the progressive movement, Wilson gave lip service to achieving a balance between capital and labor. Integrating Taft's and Roosevelt's positions on the giant corporations, he favored regulation, not dissolution of the great corporation "in the public interest" (Sklar 1960:25; Weinstein 1968:162). The legislative tools for this regulation had come into existence during the "progressive" period, and by 1914 Wilson had stated that "the antagonism between business and labor is over." But the depression during that very same year indicated that the economic contradictions of capitalism had never disappeared.

Furthermore, Wilson initiated a program of overseas expansion as the solution to America's economic contradictions. The first phase of this strategy for sustaining the economy linked the United States with the Allied cause in the war. Under the aegis of the preparedness movement, the demand side of the economy was firmed up through large expenditures by the federal government. During World War I itself, federal bureaucracies, staffed by representatives of the business community, achieved a degree of political and economic integration which made apparent to all concerned the relationship between governmental planning, regulation, and unprecedented corporation profits. "What was done in those war years," Bernard Baruch said, "was never to be completely forgotten" (Williams 1961:425).

Another national policy was based on Wilson's recognition of the danger to capitalism inherent in the Russian Revolution. He recommended that the United States government lead in the construction of the "Road Away from Revolution" (ibid.:422). He initiated the vigorous repression of radical movements in the United States. Following World War I, Wilson applied his rhetoric to the justification of the "open-door" policy in Asia. He directed American foreign policy, including the use of armed forces, toward the containment of revolutionary movements in Europe, Asia, and South America. He also "proposed a consortium of advanced industrial nations led by the United States as the first and most powerful among equals that would regulate and reform the development of all the Chinas of the world" (*ibid.*). The defeat of this grand strategy brought home the fact that Wilson could not offer any alternative to stabilization of the economy short of a continuous state of imperialist expansion and war. The vague functionalist proposals for establishing equity between capital and labor, eliminating poverty, and regulating the economy, were not adequate to meet the problems posed by corporate capitalism at home. The collapse of Wilson's policies revealed the failure of the "progressive" movement, and the Christian capitalist wing in particular, to provide a realistic blueprint for a new social order based on lasting peace and an equitable distribution of wealth.

Williams (*ibid.*:424) indicates that the events occurring during and immediately after World War I "produced a shock of disillusionment that converted many reformers into cynics disguised as realists, and turned many Americans against extensive reforms." Although it has been noted (Kolko 1967:286) that this sense of betrayal was not confined to liberals or to the United States,[1] it was particularly acute among many American liberals because of their personal involvement in the election of Wilson on a platform of peace and the new Freedoms. Traces of the rhetoric of Christian capitalism, which had been very much in evidence in writings by Ross and Small, vanished rapidly from sociology after the collapse of the progressive movement. This rhetoric, with its visions of the neomercantile Christian capitalist commonwealth, had provided many eminent sociologists with their utopian standards. With its disappearance, scholars confined their discussions of optimum change to secularized "pluralist" and "assimilationist" conceptions that had been developing slowly during the founding period. These no less visionary conceptions of society were shorn of their explicit utopian references and underwent rapid changes. In this process, the nonutopian timetable of modern corporate liberalism appeared.

NOTE

1. "The fetish of government regulation of the economy as a positive social good," Kolko (1967:286) notes, "was one that [also] sidetracked a substantial portion of European socialism as well, and was not unique to American experience. Such axiomatic and simplistic assumptions of what federal regulation would bring did not take into account problems of democratic control and participation and in effect assumed that the power of government was neutral and socially beneficient."

CHAPTER 57

The Pragmatic Timetable and "Social Problems"

Background

Before the discussion of the nonutopian timetable begins, it should be reiterated that the utopian destiny for mankind proposed by Spencer and Ward was far off in the distant future. Weatherly (1920), on the other hand, justified his claim that it was useless to even speculate about the future because a radical change in human nature was "outside the bounds of reasonable expectation." He equated modern man with Stone Age man and asserted that human equality was no more than a pipe dream. He hastened to suggest that progress was possible, but only within the framework of a new industrial democracy. This democracy, or new social "synthesis," he declared, was emerging from "recent experiences in the evolution of economic adjustment" in the United States. Weatherly believed (like Park and Burgess, who also felt that laissez-faire capitalism was giving birth to the great society) [1] that this social synthesis would not be devoid of interest-group conflict, but that it would be virtually free of the class conflict Karl Marx had in mind.

Since Weatherly refused to speculate about the future, his vision of an emerging industrial democracy did not provide utopian criteria for evaluating the optimum rate of social change. Instead, as we shall see in a subsequent chapter, his necessary criteria for optimum social change included accommodated interest groups, a technocratic elite, and a corporate-liberal state.

Weatherly's timetable will be called a technocratic, nonutopian timetable, because it was devoid of any standards other than those favoring a pragmatic, ameliorative approach to integration. Technocratic timetables, however, were frequently invoked even though the scholar did not explicitly mention the ultimate standards regulating his evaluation of social change. In such cases, these standards were taken for granted by the writer because they were rarely challenged. Sometimes they were "de facto" or "systemic" occupational standards because the scholar was projecting rates of social change ostensibly on the basis of a *method* (such as the scientific method) for bringing about change. An example of a technocratic timetable explicitly organized around a method for social change is contained in George Herbert Mead's approach to social reform, which will be described in the following section. It will be seen

452

that Mead's methodological proposals fitted hand in glove with the piecemeal social control orientation developing concomitantly among American sociologists.

Pragmatic Sophistry and Piecemeal Approach to Social Change

Mead's perspective toward social reform was detailed in two articles published in 1899. The first (Mead 1899a), which was entitled "The Working Hypothesis in Social Reform," justified what *he* called an "opportunistic" approach to social reform. The second (Mead, 1899b) consisted of a sharply critical review of "the Anglo Saxon individualism" inherent in Le Bon's Spencerian work, *The Psychology of Socialism* (1899). In these articles Mead indicated his distaste for socialist and laissez-faire doctrines because they were based on utopian models of society and were therefore automatically unworkable. Secondly, Mead referred to sociologists with utopian conceptions as *programmists*. But those who guided their reformist activities by reference to the "scientific method of reform," were called *opportunists*. Mead was firmly convinced that the programmist (utopian) approach to reform had no scientific usefulness because it was virtually impossible to develop a detailed utopian "vision on the mount" which could be used as an accurate guide to optimum social change. What was the basis for this conclusion?

According to Mead (1899a:369), long-range planning and prediction were fool's play because "it is impossible to so forecast any future condition that depends upon the evolution of society as to be able to govern our conduct by such a forecast." In his opinion, "it is always the unexpected that happens, for we have to recognize, not only the immediate change that is to take place, but also the reaction back upon this of the whole world within which the change takes place, and no human foresight is equal to this." Theories, therefore, must be couched in terms of a working hypothesis which operates according to one ultimate standard, namely that "the hypothesis shall work in the complex of forces in which we introduce it." Because it is impossible to set up a *"detailed statement* of the conditions that are to be realized," scientists only have "a *method and control* in application, not an *ideal* to work toward" (our emphasis).

Mead (*ibid.:*367) stated flatly that "socialist utopias have been recognized as impotent to lead to better conditions, and opportunists have succeeded the programmists." In spite of this, he felt that there were still many people deluding themselves into believing that it would "be possible to effect by constructive legislation radical changes that will lead to greater social equality." This delusion had spread because there had been some successful attempts to expand municipal ownership of public utilities. As far as Mead was concerned, however, the confidence that this success could be generalized and achieved in other kinds of industries was inspired "by the socialistic schemes of an essentially a priori character, rather than by the study of the conditions which these municipal concerns represent." Familiarity with these conditions would show that public ownership of economic institutions could only be managed according to economic rules prevailing in the *private* businesses of a capitalist economy.

In his further discussion of this issue, Mead (*ibid.*:368) revealed a firm, personal commitment to maintaining the priority of capitalist forms of property. He insisted that "there is no reason why the German government . . . should not buy up and manage such a business as the railroad . . ." But the government should undertake only "a very limited number of industrial and commercial concerns, which business evolution has carried to such a point of perfection that they lie safely within its domain." At all times, Mead suggested, it is the business world, not the public, which establishes the ground rules for the public selection and management of industrial enterprises.

Prior to the turn of the century, some but not all socialists were aware of the fact that government control of economic enterprises actually strengthened and stabilized the control by the upper classes over the economy as a whole.[2] Mead's liberal conceptualization of government control, however, bore no resemblance to their view of this matter. Although he cautioned against violation of basic capitalist principles by municipal or federal ownership of the "public utilities" or other services and industries, his concern was not for the long-term effects of such measures on the *political and economic organization* of the nation as a whole. He believed that public ownership could not successfully supplant private property in any case. In his opinion, planning and management of the economy could not conceivably go beyond the "rules of the business world" simply because we cannot foresee *the future*. Therefore, it was hopeless to conceive of reconstructing society on the basis of a utopian vision that transcended "the world as it is."

Underlying Mead's analysis is the epistemology of pragmatism which, at the turn of the century, often based its assumptions on philosophical contemplation by *individuals* in atypical circumstances. For Mead the *experimental act* was the paradigm case (or typical event) from which he constructed his generalizations. Mead used this act and its model of *individual problem-solving* as an analogous guide to the behavior of social and political movements. The logic of this model suggested that the so-called utopian conceptions being produced by laissez-faire liberals, anarcho-syndicalists, neopopulists, corporate liberals, and socialists represented activities of *isolated* individuals such as theoreticians and political leaders, who were concerned with an *isolated* social problem. But the fact is that these politically important "utopian" and scientific conceptions did not arise from this kind of atomistic process. These conceptions were formed in a complex web of reciprocal relationships among contemporaries.

The experimental laboratory situation was not an appropriate, analogous guide to social movements and ideological or scientific conceptions of the future. The complex issues raging at the turn of the century did not involve a single social problem. Because of this, these conceptions cannot be generally compared to a single experimental hypothesis without seriously compromising the epistemological analysis of utopian or scientific thought. The scientific socialist conception, in particular, emerged when it became apparent that an extraordinary variety of problems were so interconnected that no one of them could be solved without a socialist transformation of society. Furthermore, even the utopian corporate liberal conceptions were not merely expressive of a theoretical statement of the world as it existed; they were the products of an *ideological* statement of that world. Utopian statements were produced by the complex social conditions that generated the ideologies themselves.

An Amoral Justification for Piecemeal Reform

Mead also argued that persons *cannot* be made social by legislative enactment. Instead, we can only "allow the essentially social nature of their actions to come to expression under conditions which favor this." But what kinds of social organization will allow man to express his "essential" social nature? Mead indicated that there is no answer to this question, because "what the form of this social organization will be depends on conditions that lie necessarily beyond our ken."

To arrive at this conclusion he asked the question: "What is the function of reflective consciousness in its attempt to direct conduct? The common answer is that we carry in thought the world as it should be, and fashion our conduct to bring this about. As we have already seen, if this implies a 'vision on the mount' [i.e., utopian thinking] which represents in *detail* what is to be, we are utterly incapable of conceiving it" (our emphasis). After indicating the limits of human precognition, Mead (*ibid.*:371) leaped to the conclusion that "every attempt to direct thought by a fixed idea of the world of the future must be, not only a failure, but also pernicious." [3]

Mead was correct in stating that a utopian model cannot map the future in all its *detail*. But if the word "detail" means awareness of all the variation involved, then this limitation of human precognition is *universal;* it therefore also applies to exponents of ameliorative change. Indeed, even the laboratory scientist cannot map the future in all its detail; his hypothesis can only be confirmed on a probabilistic basis. Consequently, Mead's argument was sheer sophistry because his most important empirical criterion for distinguishing between the adequacy of ameliorative and utopian models was applied in an arbitrary fashion. He claimed that socialists could not develop a *detailed* blueprint of the future when, in fact, Engels himself had indicated that it was impossible to develop this kind of blueprint. Furthermore, no adequate history of the ameliorative programs instituted during Mead's lifetime, such as the juvenile court system or the enactment of compulsory universal secondary education laws, can state that these programs fulfilled the expectations of their staunchest advocates. Nor can it be claimed that the opportunistic followers of Mead's approach to social reform have developed anything other than a priori formulations of the nature of social change. What was particularly ironical about Mead's working hypothesis of social reform, therefore, was the amount of error actually characterizing Mead's "opportunistic" method of feasible and predictable reform. Obviously, the "programmists" are not the only persons who have had difficulty in forecasting the consequences of their actions and the accuracy of their dreams.

Mead's discussion represented a very early attempt to justify ameliorative models of social intervention on the basis of a pragmatic phenomenology of a scientific act.[4] His article also provided an example of the kinds of philosophical notions incorporated into social engineering directed toward the planned, technocratic control of social relationships. Social engineers were concerned with "social efficiency," "industrial reconciliation," and the "perfection of the individual's adjustment" to established institutions. The secular philosophy of ethics and science for individuals engaged in this enterprise at the turn of the century was pragmatism.[5] It enabled professional corporate-liberal reformers to imperiously claim that their activity involved the application of scientific methods to social problems. It provided these men with an amoral rhetoric, and justified their methods on the basis of the ultimate standards of "practicality," "workability," and "efficiency."

But pragmatism masked the real imposition of technocratic values which were being instituted by corporate liberals as guides to optimum individual and institutional functioning. Terms like "scientific method," "practicality," and "workability" did *not* explicitly contain the ultimate standards that operatively regulated technocratic evaluations of human conduct. The norms and values of state agencies manned by politicians and civil servants, or those of the large corporations owned by businessmen, provided the working standards for evaluating social conduct. They provided these standards in spite of all the sophistry about the validity of "scientific methods" as ultimate, professional, standards of social reform.

NOTES

1. The term "Great Society" appeared several times in Park and Burgess' textbook. (It did not originate during the Johnson administration.) The term was originally popularized in a corporate-liberal work entitled *The Great Society* by Graham Wallas (1914).

2. In a note to *Socialism: Utopian and Scientific*, Engels (1882:179) indicated, for example, in relation to Germany: "Recently . . . since Bismarck adopted state ownership, a certain spurious socialism has made its appearance—here and there even degenerating into a kind of flunkeyism—which declares that *all* taking over by the state, even the Bismarckian kind, is in itself socialistic. If, however, the taking over of the tobacco trade by the state was socialistic, Napoleon and Metternich would rank among the founders of socialism . . . if Bismarck . . . took over the main railway lines in Prussia, simply in order to be better able to organize and use them for war, to train the railway officials as the government's voting cattle, and especially to secure a new source of revenue independent of parliamentary votes; such actions were in no sense socialist measures, whether direct or indirect, conscious or unconscious. Otherwise, the Royal Maritime Company, the Royal Porcelain Manufacture, and even the regimental tailors

in the army, would be socialist institutions, or even, as was seriously proposed by a sly dog in the reign of Frederick William III, the taking over by the state of the—brothels."

3. What is more, utopian schemes were dangerous because "a conception of a different world comes to us always as a result of some specific problem which involves readjustment of the world as it is . . . and the test of the effort lies in the possibility of *this readjustment fitting into the world as it is* . . ." (Mead 1899a:371 our emphasis).

4. Liberal-functionalists today have still not moved beyond Mead's myopic analytic strategy to any significant degree. Modern sociologists, however, often use various highly formalized and pragmatic (e.g., "symbolic interactionist") phenomenologies of interpersonal or "small-group" relationships as the basis for their liberal epistemologies (e.g., Berger and Luckmann 1966), or as empirical warrants for social reforms (e.g., labeling theories in the sociology of delinquency).

5. The "positivistic" doctrines used to justify sociological inquiry from the twenties onwards were, in actuality, based on an eclectic combination of (older) positivistic and (newer) pragmatic doctrines.

CHAPTER 58

Technocratic Concepts of Progress and Cultural Lag

Mead developed his philosophical justification for the technocratic timetable at the turn of the century, but eminent sociologists in general did not emphatically reject utopian thinking until the end of the formative years. At that later time, the opportunistic or nonutopian timetable was incorporated into the latest natural-law conceptions of man and society being formulated by men like Weatherly, Chapin, Park, and Burgess. Their conceptions became the basis for a much more complex sociological warrant for the timetable. Park and Burgess' metatheoretical reinterpretation of the conception of progress (which had prevailed since the Enlightenment) provides an illustration of this development.

Progress: A Social Myth

According to Park and Burgess (1924:959–962), the idea of progress as a sociological *datum* represented the hopes of the people and, as such, was totally "an act of faith." Concepts of progress, in this context, were likened to a "popular religion," "superstition," or "social myth." Because of this, it was suggested that popular notions of progress could be treated as a category of "social facts" which "cannot be proven to be either true or false." The "popular" conceptions of progress were, therefore, to be seen as matters of individual or group opinion, in much the same way as the eighteenth-century philosopher David Hume conceived of religious or aesthetic preferences. There were no true or false notions of progress; there were only different points of view.

Just as the logic of Bentham had argued that a pushpin was as good as poetry if it contributed the same amount of happiness to an individual, so Park and Burgess contended that substantive differences in popular conceptions of progress were equally useful depending on the point of view. Progress, as a social datum, was sociologically significant merely because, like other social myths of its kind, it was a stimulus to social action among members of the population at large.

It will become clear that Park and Burgess' insistence on the rejection of any "objective" conceptions of progress cleared the way for a technocratic (but no less "objective") definition of its proper use. This definition reduced the concept of progress to a piecemeal and pragmatic approach to change by first suggesting that utopian ideals (usually encompassing extensive changes) were only social myths. Secondly, scientists, according to Park and Burgess (*ibid.*), were supplanting the notion of progress with the concept of social control.[1] This notion of social control, in their opinion, was stimulating individuals to define each social problem, including "poverty, disease, crime, vice, intemperance or war" as a *"separate* enterprise."[2]

In this particular context, the concept of progress was reduced to a methodological tool that was considered useful because it measured the *effectiveness* of control. As a methodological tool, moreover, progress could not refer to a utopian conception of social change: it could only be used for evaluating whether society was changing on *schedule*. This schedule, as we shall see, was to be supplied by the opportunistic (social problems) timetable.

Progress: A Methodological Tool

Park and Burgess indicated that the concept of progress could be shared by sociologists as long as it was regarded as a methodological tool. Progress, as a methodological tool, could be used by social scientists to evaluate the "new" social goal. This "methodological tool" embodied various "social indices" or "factors of progress" in order to "objectively" measure the degree to which communities were functioning at an optimum level.

The index of progress that Park and Burgess had adopted was social efficiency; and the units on which progress was measured were limited to specific problems. They declared (*ibid.*:1001–1002) for example that "progress may be considered as the addition to the sum of accumulated experience, tradition, and technical devices organized for *social efficiency*. This is at once a definition of progress and of civilization in which civilization is the *sum of social efficiencies* and progress consists of the units [additions] of which it is

458

composed" (our emphasis). Furthermore, they claimed (*ibid*.) that "there is just as much, and *no more*, reason for a sociologist to formulate a doctrine of social progress as there is for the physician to do so. Both are concerned with *specific* problems for which they are seeking specific remedies" (our emphasis). Consequently, "it is not impossible to formulate a definition of progress which does *not* assume the perfectibility of mankind, which does *not* regard progress as a necessity, and which does *not* presume to say with finality what has happened or is likely to happen to humanity as a whole" (our emphasis).

In short, progress and civilization were tantamount to social efficiency and, in spite of all the objections to *utopian* or *objective* interpretations of progress, Park and Burgess, by defining progress within the safe and narrow limits of atomistic problems, returned to the same technocratic standards that underlie Small's vision of an "efficient society."

In other words, according to this perspective, sociological *research* regarding the question of progress did not involve a critical, empirical inquiry into the fundamental *values* for measuring progress. These values were accepted as given and their sourcepoints were the established institutions. Consequently, as far as Park and Burgess (*ibid.:*1003) were concerned, "from the point of view of social research, the problem of progress is mainly one of getting *devices* that will measure all the different factors of progress . . . of the community" (our emphasis). This meant that community "score cards," based on indices of progress and retrogression, could be developed to evaluate whether community well-being was increasing or decreasing. The amount of crime, personal income, or health could be measured, and community progress could be indicated by the sum of scores on each of these dimensions at varying points in time.[3] This, then, was the modus operandi for applying the "scientific method" in their evaluation of progress.

Familiarity with this justification leads one to realize that these authors recommended the abandonment of the sociologist's moral responsibility for arriving at his or her own ethical criteria for social progress independently of established institutions. This abandonment was given a democratic rationale even though the "indices of progress" which resulted from Park and Burgess' analysis were actually based on technocratic rather than participatory democratic standards. Their justification for the concept of progress as a methodological tool obviously required selection of some standards by which to measure progressive and retrogressive changes. But their previous argument about the popular conceptions of progress explicitly indicated that there are no objective standards. Park and Burgess (*ibid.:*1000–1001) concluded that the question of the criteria for progress is insoluble. It involves "a problem in philosophy which sociology is not bound to solve before it undertakes to describe society. *It does not even need to discuss it.* Sociology, just as any other natural science, accepts the *current values* of the community" (our emphasis). After stressing this opinion again, these authors not only declared that sociologists should limit themselves to the use of *established norms* as criteria of progress but that they also *should not question this use.*

The technocratic justification of the index of progress was not new to sociology. Park and Burgess, however, integrated the concept of progress into a rounded corporate-liberal system of ideas. Progress was now operatively related to pragmatic and technocratic criteria. It was relativistic. It was also defined in terms of social control and piecemeal reform. On the other hand, Park and Burgess' loose formulation of social change did not provide enough information about whether progress was, in fact, taking place. Social change, according to Park and Burgess, could oscillate retrogressively or progressively. And although they were personally convinced that a new industrial democracy was coming into being, their relativistic approach to progress did not provide a clear sense that capitalism was inexorably moving forward solely on the basis of internal, ameliorative adjustments.

Ogburn's Technocratic Version
of Inverted Spencerian Timetable

In 1922, William F. Ogburn, who claimed a prior interest in socialism,[4] provided a theory suggesting the empirical conditions for progress. Capitalism, which played a clearly defined role in this theory, was unequivocally perceived as an *inherently* progressive system. In developing his theory of social change, Ogburn devised a scheme based on social and individual dichotomies. Culture was divided into material and nonmaterial culture, and human nature into biological and psychological attributes. Working with a flexible paradigm which assumed that each one of these divisions changed at different rates, he suggested that material culture, which included technology in particular, changed faster than other components of man and society. Because Ogburn reflected the optimistic view of technological change which was widespread in America, he identified technological advancement as the relationship which ostensibly determined human progress. In this sense, Ogburn inverted the dynamics of the Spencerian timetable by locating the mechanism which accounted for *progressive* social change in the cultural environment of persons (giving primacy to technological determinants) rather than by their biological natures. Ogburn's mechanism for changes in *material culture,* however, was little more than a loose concoction of culture contact and diffusionist ideas borrowed from Alfred Kroeber and the Boaz school of anthropology.

Ogburn further indicated that although the *rate of change* of material culture had accelerated, human nature was still changing at *a very slow rate.* In fact, if man's biological nature was examined, according to Ogburn (1922:287–288), it would be found that it "may very probably be fundamentally the same now as in the last glacial period." Man's nature is therefore "like that of the cave men," and a great many social problems such as war, crime, insanity, homosexuality, unhappiness, "arise because of the inability or difficulty of the *original nature* of man to adapt itself to modern conditions and cultural standards" (our emphasis). Some disorders, such as nervousness and insanity, originate in the "lack of adjustment between culture and the psychological equipment of man" (*ibid.*:312). These disorders include the functional disorders such as hysteria, morbid compulsions, anxiety-neurosis, paranoia, melancholia, manic-depression, and so on.[5]

Psychological Causality Again Emphasized in Discussion of Society's Ills

Ogburn (*ibid.*:334–335) also indicated that many social problems arise because of the fundamentally egotistical nature of man. In fact, he stated, "perhaps the psychological factor underlying the *largest* number of social problems is *selfishness*" (our emphasis). Thus, for example, "a large number of modern social problems flow from the unequal distribution of property," including "poverty, unemployment, disease, taxation, labor, government, war, and many other problems." And "one reason why wealth is so unequally accumulated is the pursuit of one's *selfish interest* with not enough considerations [*sic*] for the interests of others, and another reason is the scarcity of *social limitations* upon such selfish actions" (our emphasis). According to Ogburn (*ibid.*) "a highly developed accumulation of material culture . . . provides a wonderful opportunity for an apparently ruthless exploitation of selfish interests." Thus, a high accumulation of material culture gives rise to uncontrolled egoism which, in turn, creates a neo-Hobbesian problem of integration.

Ogburn addressed himself to methods for alleviating the maladjustments between human nature and modern culture. He indicated that it might be possible to change the economic order but little could be accomplished by this. He stated (*ibid.*:363), for example, that "there are no doubt many merits in socialism, and surely we can imagine a better economic order which would be accompanied by less injustice; but even assuming a fundamental change in the economic order to have occurred, social problems would not have disappeared; there would still be inequalities in the rate of cultural change, and many problems involving human nature would remain." Instead of proposing a new economic order, therefore, Ogburn suggested that social problems such as *war, crime* or *insanity* could be ameliorated by *games* and other forms of *personal recreation* which permitted the "constructive" expression of repressed instincts. Other proposals of this nature were also made. However, this portion of his work (*ibid.*:353–361) is so superficial that there is no point in reviewing it.

Considering the possibilities for "better adjustments" between man and culture, Ogburn (*ibid.*:347) also indicated that it was not necessary for the forces of change "to have all power or even to make wholesale changes in culture." In fact, "it is conceivable that by making certain changes in culture, *relatively minor* compared to the plan of directing culture *as a whole,* a more harmonious adjustment may be attained" (our emphasis). The attempts to bring about "better adjustment" should focus "chiefly on *particular* fields" (our emphasis). Such a program would be "much more practicable than the larger plan of directing the course of civilization." In short, "the bringing about of a more harmonious relationship, then, concerns certain *special fields* rather than culture or human nature as a whole" (our emphasis). The reader, by now, has a sense of the piecemeal, social-problems orientation of Ogburn's theory.

Ideological Functions of Ogburn's Theory

Ogburn's theory had hegemonic utility. The theory enabled sociologists to claim that capitalism was changing progressively. Prevailing inequities and social problems were merely considered survivals of lagging individual and cultural characteristics. Even problems introduced by technological changes could be regarded as curable by further changes in technology. The theory functioned as an apology for the status quo and justified the piecemeal, technocratic approach to social problems because the capitalist system as a whole was not considered retrogressive. The system was not the problem! Only *isolated* sections of the social system presented social problems.

Sociologists who utilized Park and Burgess' metatheory found no difficulty in integrating Ogburn's theory into their analysis; there was considerable overlap between the commonly accepted basic assumptions about the nature of social change at that time. Ogburn's theory utilized the natural-law, psychoanalytic interpretation of man. Because of this, his notion of progress was made to order for the new liberal sociology which was finally being stabilized and consolidated.

NOTES

1. According to these authors (1924:960–961), for example, "the conception which seems to be superseding the idea of progress in our day is that of control."

2. Each of these separate problems was considered a challenge to human effort and ingenuity. And even though modern man "does not blindly believe nor feel optimistically certain things will come about all right," he is "nerved to square his shoulders, to think, to contrive, and to exert himself to the foremost in his effort to conquer the difficulties ahead, and to control the forces of nature and man." Park and Burgess (1924:960–961) further declared that the new notion of control can be "quite as stimulating" to modern man as "the idea of progress was to his master."

3. Indices of this kind were also proposed by Giddings during the formative years and are now classified as "social accounting" by modern social scientists.

4. It has been noted (Duncan 1964:ix) that Ogburn worked "extensively with labor and civic groups in the cause of good government and toward the goal of social reform in the distribution of power and wealth." Ogburn himself had expressed, on his retirement from the University of Chicago in 1951, that he was interested in socialism during his youth and spent "a good deal of time in radical circles." "One of my prize possessions," he admitted, "is an edition of Karl Marx's works, inscribed to me by the Portland Unit of the Industrial Workers of the World" (quoted in Duncan [*ibid.*]). However, in spite of these titillating autobiographical references, there is nothing in Ogburn's writings to suggest that his social philosophy was ever based on anything more radical than a crude psychoanalytic and technological determinism blended with economic ideas (Ogburn 1918).

5. The fact that Ogburn's theory of cultural lag was fundamentally a psychoanalytic theory of social change is often left out of modern descriptions of the notion of cultural lag. It is also worth noting, in light of his psychoanalytic bias, that Ogburn's writings also reflected a corporate-liberal antagonism toward laissez-faire and socialist perspectives alike, although this antipathy may be obscured by his psychoanalytic jargon. For example, during the same year that his famous work *Social Change* was published, Ogburn also wrote an article entitled "Bias, Psychoanalysis and the Subjective in Relation to the Social Sciences." In that article, Ogburn claimed that laissez-faire and radical scholarship were the products of irrational and emotional thinking.

In the article, Ogburn noted that measurement is an essential condition for the development of adequate theory. However, even without measurement, a number of social scientists can be prevented from developing unscientific theories if their judgments are not biased by emotions. According to Ogburn (1964:297), "It is the emotional nature of the social sciences that has hindered their scientific development rather than their frequently mentioned complexity . . . in the absence of facts, we tend to believe what we want to believe." "We all know," Ogburn added, "how the theory of radicals tends to run into the construction of utopias, which are made of the same stuff daydreams are made of." Daydreams, Ogburn noted, are perfect examples of how emotions determine ideas.

After classifying radical thought as "emotional" constructions, Ogburn turned to an analysis of the philosophy of laissez-faire. Referring to a study by H. W. Frink, entitled *Morbid Fears and Compulsions,* Ogburn asserted that abnormal early childhood experiences can condition individuals to regard governments as symbols of hated authority. Exponents of laissez-faire theories appear to include individuals who have been so conditioned in early childhood.

While Ogburn did not go so far as to recommend psychoanalytic therapy for graduate students in sociology, he did indicate that "the study of abnormal psychology and of psychoanalysis is doing a great deal to acquaint us with the way our desires disguise themselves . . . and the part they play in forming individual opinions." In his opinion (*ibid.*:301), "a knowledge of the origins and behaviors of our prejudices and bias, while perhaps not adding to scientific output in the social sciences, might conceivably reduce the *unscientific output* by, say, over 50 percent" (our emphasis).

Considering the importance of reducing "unscientific output," it is worth noting that Burgess (1939) indicated that a research attempt *failed* to verify Ogburn's ludicrous theory of scientific bias.

CHAPTER 59

Technocratic Conceptions of Democracy

Preview

The early sociologists repeatedly used such phrases as "democratic society," "representative government," and "industrial democracy." These phrases were often repeated in the discussions of the nature of public involvement in nationwide political affairs. This involvement, as we shall see, was predicated in some cases on an interest-group model that could be used to chart an alternative to demands for grass-roots participation in political decisions. Instead of utilizing the individual community as the basis for representative government, this model particularly emphasized the role of the expert as opposed to the masses; and its advocates put their hopes for social reform on professional planners, scientific advisory boards, and governing councils.

These and other kinds of technocratic ideas introduced important changes in the conception of liberal democracy. In order to highlight these changes we will discuss, by way of contrast, the Cincinnati Social Unit Experiment in democratic participation which was described in a fascinating article by Anatole Shaffer (1971).[1] This project, like the labor of Sisyphus, was doomed from the outset because it was predicated on genuine popular control in a political economy which could not tolerate this control. Following this description, the discussion of the development of the liberal technocratic conception of democracy will be resumed.

Participant Democracy in Community Organizations

The aforementioned experiment in grass-roots participatory democracy took place in 1917. Shaffer indicates that at the time "a coalition of philanthropists, industrialists, corporate liberal ideologues and socialists" established the Cincinnati Social Unit Experiment. The liberal sponsors of the experiment felt that it would answer the threat posed by revolutionary socialist movements; by stimulating cooperation and self-determination among urban residents, the project might recapture the "idyllic" conditions of village life and thereby point the way toward overcoming the disorganizing effects of capitalist relations in urban communities. From this point of view, the social-unit plan would provide an example which would deny the "inevitability of class warfare" (Shaffer 1971:162). However, two socialists, "Mr. and Mrs. Wilber Philips," who originally conceived of the social-unit plan, regarded it as a means for developing "a cooperative commonwealth." They felt that the establishment of residential and occupational councils would provide for democratic participation in community affairs.

The social-unit plan differed from the typical ameliorative programs launched by liberals at the time because it represented an actual attempt to stimulate and build grass-roots participation and administration of organizations devoted to community needs. During the short two years of its existence, Shaffer points out, the community project was successful in meeting a number of its major goals. It developed community councils with representation from each neighborhood block. These councils were also interlocked with "occupational" councils involving labor, medical, educational, and business groups. In a relatively short time, the social-unit experiment extended public health services operating in the neighborhoods. The medical program, in particular, was highly successful. Ninety percent of the children under the age of six received free medical examinations, a considerable accomplishment for those early years. A project health center provided care for half the population of the district. A fourfold increase in the supervision of tuberculosis cases was achieved. Prenatal care was given to 45 percent of the expectant mothers in the district. And the demonstration project established the first special clinic for treatment of the terrible flu epidemic which swept the country at the time.

The increasing success of the project, however, became a threat to the political leadership of the city government. A number of demagogic politicians alleged that the social-unit plan represented "a dangerous type of socialism" which was only "a step away from Bolshevism!" (*ibid.*:168). These allegations, made in the context of an increasingly repressive political climate throughout the country, created divisiveness within the community councils and eventually destroyed the project.

In Shaffer's view, there exists an analogous relationship between the political destruction of this successful experiment in democratic participation in social reform, and the destruction of the community action efforts sponsored by the "war on poverty" initiated during the Johnson administration. Then as now, Shaffer points out, the social-unit program represented an effort to seek *participatory* rather than *technocratic* means to preserve the status quo. Shaffer (*ibid.*:170) notes that "the social unit approach, tested and shown workable, did disappear and the social work profession of the day, which had shown such great interest during the experiment, turned its community organizing interests away from such 'hare-brained schemes.'" "With a vision unique to social work," Shaffer wryly adds, "it turned its attention to the solution of the *real* problems of the time, federated financing and community chest development."

Shaffer (*ibid.*) also indicates that an evaluation of the Social Unit Experiment was made by Edward T. Devine in 1919. Devine wrote:

. . . the Social Unit conception of democracy . . . goes deeper than particular political institutions or forms of government. It penetrates to the very heart of the social order and raises the challenge as to whether the people are or are not capable of deciding with stimulated and socially *controlled expert assistance,* what their needs are and how they shall be met. This conception of democracy . . . may not be compatible with some aspects of party government or with some interpretation put upon existing constitutions . . . There is no reason to think that . . . [syndicalism, national guildism, or the soviet ideas] or any of the features which have distinguished these systems . . . are expected in connection with the Social Unit, except their democracy.

It is in other words a *political substitute* for existing political *government* and for existing voluntary social *agencies* . . . Thus the democracy which they are advocating and which they wish to extend is perhaps only another name for social progress. That its *triumph* however would make *unnecessary most of our present political machinery* . . . is hardly open to question. [our emphasis]

As both the social-unit experiment and some of the grass-roots projects during the abortive "war on poverty" demonstrated, there is never a guarantee that genuine democratic participation will remain loyal to the established political powers. Because of this, these projects are only allowed to go so far. When they become a serious threat—or have been seen as such—the local, state, and federal authorities will do everything in their power to control or destroy these organizations. This control, moreover, leads, of necessity, to the destruction of the democratic character of the community organizations.

Technocratic Conceptions of Democracy and Representative Government

Liberalism has always considered it the mark of a democratic society for each individual to be given the opportunity to compete with others for membership in the ruling groups of that society. Elitist presuppositions have been part of liberal thought for centuries. In this century, however, the liberal concept of democracy has been altered somewhat in order to cope with the democratic ideologies espoused by populist, anticolonial, and socialist movements. In the process of alteration, certain traditional tenets have been preserved; corporate liberals, for example, have retained the elitist conception that ruling groups are not only necessary in order to integrate all societies, but that these elites must be superior human beings if they are to discharge their functions successfully. However, corporate liberals have also placed great weight on the criterion of *democratic representation* of the masses. Capitalist societies, therefore, are considered democratic because their "superior" ruling elites allegedly represent the wishes of the public at large, as opposed to the earlier state of affairs when they represented only men of property. This criterion of democratic *representation* is to be distinguished nevertheless from another view positing democratic *participation,* which is predicated on whether the masses of any society themselves directly *determine* and *administer* the functions of government.

The distinction between democratic representation and democratic participation is important because of the degree to which ambiguous scholarly usages of such terms as "democratic" and "undemocratic" have obscured the developmental stages of liberal conceptions of democracy. Today, for example, Jefferson's patrician conception of democracy (i.e., a republic) is repeatedly referred to as a "democratic" conception. Le Bon's characterization of political life in industrial societies, on the other hand, is considered "undemocratic" (Bramson 1961), even though he was fervently in favor of a nineteenth-century (laissez-faire) liberal democracy. Actually, both Jefferson's and Le Bon's liberal notions were elitist conceptions representing different phases in the development of liberal conceptions of democracy related to changes in the political economy. Around the turn of the century, the agrarian relations which characterized Jefferson's colonial society had all but disappeared. The laissez-faire industrial political economy was undergoing important changes in the direction of monopoly capitalism. The liberal concept of democracy began to be modified because of the ideological consequences of these political and economic changes. In this process, the concept of democracy began to incorporate the notion of a representative but nevertheless technocratic elite.

Sociologist Albion Small's words symbolized the new technocratic orientation. He urged that the functions of the state be broadened far beyond the accepted (laissez-faire) definitions.[2] He suggested that the state could become the major arena within which social scientists would advance the development of human civilization. But his conception of the scientist's political role went beyond the mere mention of advisory or managerial functions; scientists were also seen as being capable of *representing* diverse interests in society.[3] Their expert knowledge was not useful just because it enabled prediction of social trends; it could also be employed by councils of scientists devoted to legislative tasks. In the process, it was felt that traditional democratic procedures which often intensified conflicts of interests could be replaced by the profoundly rational deliberations of social scientists.

The idea of the *expert* as a representative of the population was also expressed in the article on political democracy by Weatherly (1920). Moreover, although this article considered nonscientists to be experts in many areas of life, it nevertheless provided a clearly defined democratic rationale for the technocratic conception of political representation. The rationale itself was organized around an interesting combination of ideas mostly derived from the pluralist theory of society which was rapidly emerging out of the syndicalist perspective toward the end of the formative years. In addition, it contains elements of the positivistic utopia which was envisioned by Durkheim and which can be traced back to Comte and the Saint-Simonians.

Weatherly "democratized" the older, technocratic social vision by indicating that "intelligent" governmental regulation had become necessary because of industrial violence and war between nations. He also declared (*ibid.*:19) that "no one, in these last tragic years, has to be told that conflict breeds a biased, distorted mental attitude unfavorable to sober action." He further claimed (*ibid*:28) that an intelligent government could not be directly administered by the masses because they were not capable of ruling themselves. The average man was considered "unskilled in critical evaluation." He was alleged to be slow "to detect the trickery of virtuous or foolish leadership." Because of this, Weatherly suggested that strong and capable leaders must be encouraged to help common people "assimilate the highest truths or act for the highest ends." New means were required to select this noble leadership. These would require changing the principles of representative government to conform with pluralist conceptions of the structure of an industrial society.

Tackling the problem of democratic representation directly, Weatherly argued that traditionally, each person in a *geographical* area has been entitled to political representation. However, "no observer of current tendencies need be reminded that *interest areas* are supplanting geographical areas in social organization" (our emphasis). He claimed that individual members of geo-

467

graphical areas could not be adequately represented because of their diverse political opinions. Therefore, "what must be worked out in the near future is a system by which the *homogeneous interest-groups* shall find adequate representation as such, irrespective of [geographical] location" (our emphasis). It is apparent that pluralist principles were now being used by Weatherly to identify the necessary conditions for democratic participation by individuals in American society. And the basic terms in which the concept of democracy was defined were being reconstituted within these principles.

Weatherly *(ibid.:*30) suggested that interest groups produce leaders who become expert in group matters. These "experts who are masters of the affairs of their particular groups can be sent to legislative councils" and "must become the *rulers,* while the rest of us, so far as concerns these matters must take the positions of the governed, just as we do in private life when we require electric service or medical service" (our emphasis). The masses can become involved in this new "representative" democracy because "nearly every man is an expert in something and as such is qualified to be an intelligent voter on that thing." However, on most other matters he [the voter] is of the ignorant majority. Little can be done about this, according to Weatherly, because the majority of people will remain ignorant *"despite any conceivable improvement in education"* (our emphasis). The increase in knowledge is so great that "the number of things that any one man may adequately know will become relatively smaller." Consequently, specialization of knowledge has become the basis for "a new aristocracy." This "aristocracy," Weatherly added, "is without inherent inequality and without exploitation."

Weatherly's comments represented a marked shift from Ward's naive nineteenth-century faith in formal education, although the notion of a new aristocracy of experts was consistent with Ward's elitist viewpoint. However, it should be noted that Weatherly's technocratic views, integrated into a pluralist framework, also departed from the ideas used by Comte and by Saint-Simon and his followers. His modification of the more traditional elitist notions was the redefinition of democratic functioning in terms of interest-group participation in political life. He claimed that this kind of participation would be superior to the democratic principles which perceived each man as having an equal voice in all political issues and therefore equal representatives chosen by regional elections. Guided further by the fashionable corporate capitalist images, Weatherly noted that "when we consider how the managing bodies of *great industries* are constituted, it is surely no utopian dream to conceive of a legislative assembly composed of members, each of whom is a specialist in his field" (our emphasis). He realized, however, that since the experts are also representatives of *interest groups,* they may intensify interest-group conflict. But he was confident *(ibid.:*32) that this kind of conflict could be contained because:

If it be objected, as it often is, that such a system would destroy social solidarity, that it would give increased dominance to the class principles, the answer must be, frankly, that in the present stage of social evolution *a class society of some kind is the only possible one.* Social solidarity is still a utopian ideal; the highest that we can at present hope for is class society so well safeguarded by checks and balances that exploitation, caste control, and class conflict shall be reduced to a minimum . . . Until human nature is radically changed there is no way given under heaven or among men whereby *these conflicting interests can be adjusted* except by applying to social politics the economist's revered formula of *the higgling of the market.* [our emphasis]

NOTES

1. We would like to express our gratitude to Anatole Shaffer for the opportunity to critically discuss with him many of the ideas expressed throughout this book. Shaffer's grasp of the problems of democratic participation in the United States was extraordinary, and because of our discussions, we have been sensitized to this issue in a manner which would not have been possible without him. Our usage of such terms as "benevolence" and "humanitarianism" in describing the technocratic professional also provides evidence of his thought.

2. Small enthused (1905:197–198) in his typically Olympian manner: "We must . . . disarm the prejudice that States are merely political organizations. The modern State is both a political organization and an economic system, but it is much more. The State is a microcosm of the whole human process. The State is the co-operation of the citizens for the furtherance of all the interests of which they are conscious . . ."

3. Small suggested (1910:242–243), for example, that the state could sponsor the major planning institutions of society and stated: "The most reliable criterion of human values which science can propose would be the consensus of councils of *scientists representing the largest possible variety of human interests,* and cooperating to reduce their special judgements to a scale which would render their due to each of the interests in the total calculation" (our emphasis).

CHAPTER 60

The Professional Social Analyst and the Professional Reformer

From Rhetoric of Benevolence
to Rhetoric of Neutrality

Ogburn, Park, and Burgess insisted that the professional sociologist must be ideologically neutral. Sociological research was only justified if it was organized by a disinterested search for knowledge. These research efforts might employ the use of the concept of progress, for example, as a method but certainly not as a utopian ideal. Professional sociologists, moreover, could investigate the diverse and often antagonistic value systems in society,

469

but they should not choose between them in order to conduct their sociological activities. Professional sociologists were compared and likened to natural scientists insofar as they provided a thoroughly disinterested service to society at large.

These definitions of the role of the sociologist and the domain of the field certainly appeared to represent a marked shift from the highly ethical plane on which definitions were formulated during the first half of the formative years. Ernest Becker (1968:73–74) has illustrated this shift by contrasting the 1895 platform of the *American Journal of Sociology* (which reflected the thoughts of many sociologists) with a 1929 statement from Ogburn's presidential address to the American Sociological Society. The 1895 platform emphatically exclaimed that the journal would

. . . assist all intelligent men in taking the largest possible view of their rights and duties as citizens . . . [and] will attempt to translate sociology into the language of ordinary life, so that it will not appear to be merely a classification and explanation of fossil facts . . . to so far increase our present intelligence about social utilities that there may be much more effective combination for the promotion of the general welfare than has thus far been organized . . . and [be] an element of strength and support in every wise endeavor to insure the good of man.

Thirty-five years later, however, Ogburn declared in his presidential address:

Sociology as a science is not interested in making the world a better place in which to live, in encouraging beliefs, in spreading information [*sic*] in dispensing news, in setting forth impressions of life, in leading the multitudes, or in guiding the ship of state. Science is interested directly in one thing only, to wit, discovering new knowledge . . .

The differences between these two statements are very clear. But the *operative* significance of the differences cannot be clarified from these statements alone. In spite of the changes in rhetoric, the activities of academic social scientists remained just as firmly embedded in the same ameliorative, corporate-liberal perspective which had existed before the twenties. This perspective had previously been justified by frequent mouthings of benevolent humanitarian platitudes. By contrast with this, the new technocratic rhetoric of ideological neutrality appeared even more salient, particularly after the disappearance of Christian capitalism as a viable tradition.

Thus, if Ogburn's or Park's definitions of the role of the professional and the domain of the field were taken at face value, it would appear that they had abandoned (in the name of scientific neutrality) the so-called humanistic sociology, which had been established by the first generation of sociologists. However, there are two issues here. First, there is serious question about whether earlier sociological thought can be unambiguously classified as humanistic (i.e., democratic and libertarian) in light of its technocratic character. Second, there is even greater question about taking Ogburn's or Park's declarations of ideological neutrality at face value. After becoming familiar with the works of these men it is impossible to disregard the glaring contradictions between their professed values and their own blatant ideological biases, which were represented by their theoretical and metatheoretical writings. These contradictions become the more incredible when it is realized that it was Ogburn who spent almost his entire professional career in service as an administrative-consultant to governmental bureaus and commissions, who flatly declared in his presidential address that "Sociology as a science is not interested . . . in guiding the ship of state."

Because such sentiments had been widely shared by sociologists, it is unlikely that Ogburn was an intentional liar and hypocrite.[1] Rather, it is reasonable to assume that his comments represented a shift in styles of sociological rhetoric. In the beginning of the formative period, for example, the technocratic rhetoric of benevolence dominated the field. This rhetoric operatively justified technocratic conduct on the basis of an elitist corporate-liberal view of man and society. This style of rhetoric referred to the social good and the perfectibility of man; but the accepted standards for social well-being and human perfection were, in fact, based on the needs of established institutions and individual adjustments to the norms of these institutions.

The technocratic rhetoric of benevolence was a new view of social responsibility on the part of a number of men who considered themselves professional advisers to legislators, governing boards, political commissions, and professional managers of social institutions. It replaced the styles which had previously been established by the centuries-old conceptions of aristocratic and religious obligations. The older views had existed alongside the mercantile conceptions of responsible stewardship and the bourgeois notion of benevolent philanthropy. Although the technocratic rhetoric of benevolence did have much in common with prevailing justifications for private philanthropy, it was increasingly used to justify the expanding functions of a political state whose goal has been the promotion of the "general welfare." It evolved, because of this, into the rhetoric which is generally used to justify the role of a vast corps of bureaucratic welfare workers, social planners, and public administrators. And it is vital to note that it has been repeatedly enunciated with renewed vigor among sociologists during periods of great social instability.

Toward the end of the formative years, the technocratic rhetoric of neutrality preempted the technocratic rhetoric of benevolence. But it continued to maintain the very basic professional standards which favored the development of a corps of benevolent scientific technicians who serviced advanced capitalist political economies. The irony of this development is that a concomitant search for academic respectability also helped produce a professional who was powerless unless he or she could perform as a human instrument for stabilizing and rationalizing social and political relationships which would eventually enhance the ongoing operation of profit-making institutions.[2]

City Manager:
Illustration of Professionalized Reform

Technocratic developments were not confined in the United States to professional sociologists. They were also in evidence among practitioners such as social workers, social planners, and public administrators. Moreover, because of the pluralist and fragmented social-problems orientation of corporate liberalism, many persons who were sincerely interested in a particular *civic* reform at the time found themselves absorbed into a technocratic corps of public and social service workers. This professional corps engaged in activities which complemented the professional social analysts being produced within the basic social science disciplines, including psychology, political science, and economics as well as sociology.

While the resolution of social problems at the national level was being attempted by business leaders and spokesmen, a related development was taking place in American municipalities. The increasing magnitude and complexities of industrial cities brought into focus all the inadequacies of American party politics during the last quarter of the nineteenth century. Under relentless criticism by journalists, novelists, and reformers, municipal government was exposed as ridden with graft, vice, and other forms of political corruption. Reformers primarily laid the blame for municipal corruption at the door of crafty business practices. But the municipal reforms that eventually took place never conflicted with the primary control by business over the growth and development of American cities.

A brief glimpse at the city management reforms in municipal government can provide an illustration of technocratic developments within municipalities. In discussing the benefits that could be gained from government by experts, for example, Weatherly (1920:30) referred favorably to the city management form of local government, which had been established in a number of American cities. Reforms of this sort were being offered to cope with such persistent American urban problems as corruption and inefficiency in city government. These reforms were heralded as a means for instituting progressive changes without altering the basic foundations of the political economy. Since the reforms tackled the problems of change on a fragmented, piecemeal basis, they provided an undemocratic, technocratic alternative to the more radical proposals formulated by socialists.

By the end of the progressive period, the advocates of civic reform were comparing the city to a great corporation. As outlying areas were annexed, they were "incorporated." The city manager's office was likened to the directorship of a gigantic "stock company" (Weinstein 1968:111). These advocates declared that the daily operation of the city would be "removed from politics" through the city management plan (*ibid.*). Insofar as "politics" was equated with corruption, this implied that the city management would not be corrupt. But the stormy politics at the time also influenced the degree of participation by ordinary men in the political decisions that affected their daily lives. In this latter sense, the removal of the city management from politics meant in effect the even greater separation of the city government from its body politic. The chasm between the government and the governed became wider.

In several respects, the concept of city management was similar to Ward's and Small's technocratic vision of a society managed by experts. In such a society the technocrat would efficiently evaluate social developments, isolate the main tendencies, and engineer the control of social problems on the basis of expert knowledge and advice. The common man and especially the common woman had little to contribute to this process. Only the experts were considered competent enough to determine and manage the direction of society.

The effects of the city management plan were varied. Certain parts of the city government were run more efficiently and fairly (*ibid.*:114–115). In some cases, the city manager was less responsive to laissez-faire businessmen; however, political power was concentrated in the hands of commissioners and managers who were just as sensitive to the general needs of the business community as the older politicians had been. The "nonpartisan" ballot and other reforms, justified on the basis of encouraging democracy, actually contributed to the decrease in the growing level of participatory democracy that had developed from activities by reform, labor, socialist, and minority movements during the "progressive" era (*ibid.*:110). Furthermore, as Weinstein (*ibid.*:111) indicates, the city manager plan may have eliminated some incompetent administrators, but in practice it encouraged the appointment of a manager who "proved most often to be a man of limited social outlook, one who tended to think purely in business or, more narrowly, engineering terms." Thus, although "managers were usually proficient at increasing the efficiency of a fire department or reducing the cost of street paving . . . social and political problems were often outside their range of interest." [3]

The movements for city management, Weinstein (*ibid.*:115) notes, "fulfilled the requirements of progressivism by rationalizing city government and institutionalizing the methods and values of the corporations that had come to dominate American economic life." These movements succeeded in city after city toward the end of the progressive era. "During the First World War," while city management reforms were moving forward, "chambers of commerce and boards of trade greatly intensified their antiradical and antilabor activities, and in hundreds of small cities and towns socialist locals were destroyed by the superpatriotic business groups. Just as the war would serve to institutionalize corporation-controlled regulatory agencies on a national level . . . so on a local level the business organizations were rapidly able to press forward their political domination of American municipalities" (*ibid.*:116). By the early twenties, when Weatherly was discussing the further syndicalization of democratic participation—and Park and Burgess were outlining their piecemeal approach to social problems—leaders of local business communities had already made significant gains in reorganizing city governments.

When evaluating the treatment of social problems in American cities during the twenties and thirties, the fact that city governments were rationalized primarily in the interests of business must be kept firmly in mind. This class control established the limits to which programs aimed at amelioration of crime and delinquency could go. Advocates of recreation services for youth, or welfare for needy families, could not institute changes that would challenge the basic priorities of the business community. This meant that no long-range social planning could be instituted that would effectively cope with juvenile delinquency, or service the complex needs of the adolescent population. Instead of long-range social planning, municipal bureaucrats, social workers, clergymen, philanthropists, and civic-minded volunteers initiated programs that did not disturb the basic political and economic relationships that had created the problems of the city in the first place.

Political Repression:
Means to Professionalization of Reform

For centuries liberals have loudly proclaimed that all members of society have the right to compete for "a piece of the action." Aside from a few exceptional cases such as the Cincinnati Social Unit Experiment,[4] corporate-liberal political policies have assiduously avoided measures that would effectively stimulate the development of militant social action, particularly on the part of the most disenfranchised working people. Because of this, social welfare policies have been firmly wedded to the technocratic organizations of social reform, and corporate liberals have gone to great lengths to place the reins of social reform firmly in the hands of professional reformers in order to avoid the usurpation of ruling-class power by grass-roots working-class movements.

Economic and political movements during the progressive era stimulated a number of potentially valuable reform programs among such "helping professions" as social work. But the political oppression at the end of this era aborted any developments that could have produced an effective amelioration of modern urban problems. In describing the effects of this repression, Borenzweig (1970:15–19) states that "the red scare of the 20's made its contribution to the demise of the settlement house movement." He cites Jane Addams, who noted how the Palmer raids affected settlement-house workers: "Any proposed change was suspect," Addams indicated, "even those efforts that had been considered praiseworthy before the war." She remarked further that "social workers exhibited many symptoms of this panic and with a protective instinct carefully avoided any phraseology of social reform" (ibid.; also Chambers 1963:117). Borenzweig also points out that "the settlement house tradition of fighting for social reform became, for many of the people who financially supported the movement, synonymous with 'radicalism.' The

474

prosperity of the late 20's broke up the communities in which the settlements were located." Skilled laborers who resided in settlement areas moved to better communities and "foreigners . . . supplemented by the arrival of Negroes now inhabited the neighborhoods surrounding the settlements. The slum dwellers were viewed as 'dangerous classes.' "

Reformist goals began to change in this new repressive climate. During this period "social psychiatry" moved away from its earlier emphasis on social reform and turned en masse toward psychoanalysis. In 1926 the pioneering social worker Edward C. Lindeman observed that "no social agency would dare make an appeal to one of the large financial foundations today without including somewhere in the budget an item for individualistic mental hygiene even if orthodox family case work was the intended function. Psychiatric social work is the current fashion" *(ibid.:*22; also Lubove 1965:109).

Under the aegis of psychoanalysis and the sociological social-problems orientation, the professional role (and the limits of activity) of the social group worker and community organizer were defined. In effect, for decades since that time, any attempt of community organizers to become involved in the development of militant grass-roots movements has been seen as a blatant disregard of *professionally* defined functions. On the local level, community organization was narrowly restricted to nonpolitical spheres of community life; and community organization was primarily interpreted to mean the better integration of established social service agencies. On a citywide level, community organization primarily involved working within established political structures, or with the wealthy, white middle-class philanthropists and social service leaders who controlled the social services extended to working-class people.

NOTES

1. On the other hand, the similarities between the sentiments of ideological neutrality and the claim of impartiality by politicians and public administrators should not be overlooked. More often than not, this claim naively obscures or purposefully masks the source and differentials in power that actually determine the role of politicians and bureaucrats—as well as professional sociologists. It is more than likely that the rhetoric of neutrality opportunistically preserved the personal security of professional sociologists in the face of sharp political conflicts or the undemocratic uses of power.

2. Many examples can be provided in this regard, but no other field has been as well documented as industrial psychology. See, for example, Loren Baritz, *The Servants of Power* (1960).

3. As a result, one leader in the development of the city management plan wryly remarked in 1918, "Some day we shall have managers here who have achieved national reputation, not by . . . running their cities for a freakishly low expense per capita, but managers who have successfully led their commissions into great new enterprises of service" (Weinstein 1968:111).

4. Of course, the Cincinnati Social Unit Experiment did not involve corporate liberals only. It was based on a coalition of liberal and socialist elements.

CHAPTER 61

Technocratic Theory and Practice: A Complementary Relationship

Robert E. Park's influence on the development of urban sociology was extraordinary. In its earlier phase, this influence was highly structured by a natural-law conception of "moral regions" in urban areas. These moral regions were also called "detached milieus" and Park (1967:43) stated that "in order to understand the forces which in every large city tend to develop these detached milieus in which vagrant and suppressed impulses, passions, and ideals emancipate themselves from the *dominant* moral order, it is necessary to refer to the fact or theory of latent impulses of men" (our emphasis). Park implied that the dominant moral order was organized around established occupations and borrowed the primitivistic notion of latent impulses from Sigmund Freud (*ibid.*). Armed with these ideas of social normality and psychological functioning, he encouraged his students to conduct a series of studies which complemented the professionalization of social reform during the twenties.

The Urban Technographers

The year 1923 marked the beginning of an important series of sociological studies published by the University of Chicago Press under the editorship of Park, Burgess, and Faris. Although the sociologists who contributed the theory and research that culminated in these publications at the University of Chicago were very diverse, in certain respects they have been commonly considered members of the "Chicago School." In some circles the term "Chicago School" particularly refers to the school of ethnography which developed at the university during the twenties and thirties. Although not all of Park's students were ethnographers (even though they conducted research on urban social problems), some were followers of Park and Burgess' metatheory and were interested in ethnography; for them we prefer to use the phrase, the "school of technocratic urban ethnographers" or simply, the urban "technographers." In either form, these terms refer to scholars like Park, Anderson, Thrasher, Cressey, and others who played very concrete roles in stimulating or conducting ethnographic research at Chicago.

476

The Chicago publication series included, among other works, *The Hobo* by Nels Anderson (1923), *The Natural History of Revolution* by Lyford P. Edwards (1927), *The Gang* by Frederick M. Thrasher (1927), *The Strike* by E. T. Hiller (1928), *The Gold Coast and the Slum* by Harvey W. Zorbaugh (1929), and *The Taxi-Dance Hall* by Paul G. Cressey (1932). Other works by Park, Burgess, Ogburn, Cavan, Mowrer, Frazier, Wirth, Blumenthal, and Donovan dealt with the general principles of ecological analysis of city life, as well as the subjects of family disorganization, ethnic communities, occupational social types, and the analysis of social trends. These studies, produced mainly by third-generation sociologists, pioneered in the empirical study of urban life.

Although there are important differences between some of these studies, all of the works were within the corporate-liberal technocratic tradition. Thus, for example, Thrasher placed greater faith in neighborhood organizations for ameliorating social problems than did Zorbaugh. But both authors cast their works in the same ideological mold.

Social problems represented by the hobo and the prostitute, for example, were also categorized by the technographers as matters calling for appropriate social controls and adequate opportunities for the gratification of basic human "wishes." In *The Hobo,* Anderson (1923) proposed that individuals become tramps and hobos because of unemployment, seasonal work, discrimination, or personal crises and defects. Once committed to a migratory mode of existence, however, the hobo hungers for intimate associations and affections, even though he is "disbarred from family life." Also, in spite of the fact that his "fundamental wishes for response and status have been denied expression," the hobo (*ibid.*:149) attempts to realize these wishes by alternative means. Deprived of sexual fulfillment, for example, the hobo turns to homosexuality. Denied status in organized society, "he longs for a classless society where all inequalities shall be abolished." "In the I.W.W. and other radical organizations, he finds in association with restless men of his own kind the recognition everywhere else denied him" (*ibid.*:167).

Cressey's *The Taxi-Dance Hall* was published ten years after *The Hobo*. By that time, sociologists in the series classified an individual's behavioral regularities according to "cycles" of development. According to Cressey (1932), the first cycle in the taxi dancer began with a working girl's dissatisfaction with the type of life associated with her home and neighborhood. Driven by the frustrated desire for money, masculine contacts, or status, the girl "finds her way to the taxi-dance hall," wherein she is able to secure a satisfaction of certain wishes previously unfulfilled." At the dance hall, the girl finds herself "rushed" and "enjoys the thrill of being very popular." In time, however, she must make "a deliberate effort to maintain her status." If she fails and is no longer able to secure sufficient patronage exclusively from the white group [men], she comes eventually to accept the romantic attentions of Filipinos and other Orientals." Failure to maintain the prestige accorded by the Orientals results in frequenting the "black and tan" cabarets. If she fails to maintain her prestige in the cabarets, she finally turns to prostitution in the "black belt" (*ibid.*:89–90).

In Anderson's and Cressey's studies we find the repetitive use of the four wishes, frustrated striving, and such functionally equivalent relationships as prestigeful relations in white or Asian or "black and tan" dance halls. In later decades, the four wishes were replaced by the enculturated desires for social status or economic mobility, and functionally equivalent relationships of this kind were converted into formal categories by middle range (meta)-theorists (e.g., "legitimate" and "illegitimate *opportunity* structures").

Conceptual Structure of Thrasher's Work

Thrasher's (1927) study illustrated the degree to which researchers in the sociology of adolescence and delinquency modeled the dynamic relationships between groups on the basis of the newly systematized liberal conceptions. He utilized such concepts as social disorganization, cultural lag, and culture conflict in dealing with delinquent relationships. The political economy of the United States was seen as generally progressive and the problem of delinquency as transitional. Youthful delinquency was restricted to "intersticial areas" and considered incidental to the progressive changes in society. In these areas, the abrupt dislocation of immigrant or rural populations rendered traditional moral codes inoperative and provided a social vacuum within which the forces of uncontrolled competition prevailed. Thus, it was stated that "American industrial cities have not had time to become settled and self-controlled; they are youthful and they are experiencing the struggles and instabilities of youth. The apparent chaos in certain phases of their life may be regarded as a case of 'cultural lag' " (Thrasher 1963:337).

In this view, disorganization was considered partly a result of inadequate social controls and the gang was merely "one of the many symptoms of the more or less general *disorganization* incident to rapid economic development and the ingestion of vast numbers of alien workers" (*ibid.* our emphasis). Consequently, among the symptomatic features of disorganization was the fact that youths, or other individuals for that matter, were completely *free* to conduct themselves as they pleased without hindrance from disorganized agencies of social control.

The liberal concept of freedom was, therefore, absolutely crucial to Thrasher's theory.[1] Freedom was perceived in terms of the freedom from social constraint and was signified by the uncontrolled expression of basic individual desires. Thrasher noted, for example, that his description of "the underlying conditions of disorganization in gang areas" was simply an attempt to "explain the factors that make possible the freedom which leads to ganging." With the disorganization of the community and the loss of traditional controls, adolescent life was seen to become naturally free and wild. There was no dearth of excitement for youth under these conditions. Their play was described (*ibid.*:339) as "unhampered" and the railroad, canal, and industrial properties (which are extensive in the intersticial areas) furnished youth "a realm for adventure that is unexcelled in the playgrounds or in the more *orderly* portions of the city" (our emphasis).

Thrasher's atomistic concept of individual adolescents was captured in the phrase "lively energies." These egoistic energies were forever seeking private satisfactions. And if the family, church, school, or playground did not provide opportunities for gratification, the "lively energies" would look elsewhere unless forcibly restricted from doing so by institutions of social control. In discussing the role of the family in promoting gang life, Thrasher stated that "any condition in family life which promotes neglect or repression of its boy members, indirectly promotes the gang by stimulating the boy to find the satisfaction of his wishes outside the plan and organization of family activities." Ineffective religion and unguided recreation shared a similar responsibility insofar as they created "an opportunity for ganging or any other kind of *substitute* activity" (our emphasis). Furthermore, if the school did "not interest the boy or provide for a satisfying organization of his lively energies," then it also contributed to "an opportunity for the free life of the gang" (*ibid.*:340).

According to Thrasher, further groups come into existence among preadolescents in order to meet the basic needs of children for "new experience and recognition." Some of these groups were regulated by conventional agencies such as churches, settlement houses, and recreational institutions. Thus, the formation of youth groups was not totally an outcome of the inability of children to obtain gratification in the family, school, or recreational institution. However, it is clear that during adolescence, groups formed *outside* the adult-controlled institutions because the needs of their members could not be met inside these agencies of social control.

Although Thrasher stated that the "flowering" of adolescent gangs occurred "where other institutions are lacking or are failing to function efficiently" (*ibid.*:342), the absence of "orderly social processes" was regarded as a necessary but not sufficient condition for delinquent group behavior. In his theory, disorganized and unrewarding conventional institutions accounted for the existence of the uncontrolled peer group but not for its delinquent characteristics. This should not be surprising: the mere lack of control in corporate-liberal theorizing cannot be plausibly used to account for social change unless additional propositions and mechanisms bridge the uncontrolled group relationship with a "deviant adjustment" to this state of affairs.

Thrasher was therefore faced with the same logical difficulties encountered by other corporate-liberal "social-control" theorists. He surmounted these difficulties in an ideologically consistent fashion. He not only assumed that delinquency was related to weak and unrewarding social controls. He also proposed that under these conditions, youth *groups* were forced to use *whatever means were at their disposal* in order to successfully *compete* with each other for *survival*. It was claimed that as a result of *uncontrolled* intergroup *compe-*

tition and *conflict,* the structures and codes of gangs became gradually adapted to new conditions. Uncontrolled groups moved over the course of time from mischievous play-group forms of conduct to serious violations of the law.

Thus, it was taken for granted that delinquent gang behavior emerged out of the fierce uncontrolled competition for limited space and scarce resources that *naturally* exists under disorganized conditions. In searching for the very basic ideas underlying this assumption, however, we not only uncover the interaction processes suggested by Park and Burgess' key-concepts, competition and conflict. We also come face to face with the nineteenth-century conception of economic man and the implicit corporate-liberal criticism of laissez-faire capitalism. In addition, we encounter that very fundamental liberal assumption about the presence of the problem of *scarcity* on all levels of human existence.

Thrasher implied that the delinquent gang was a collective behavior phenomenon and that it was "integrated" through conflict. The group went through a "cycle" which involved members in "meeting face to face, milling, movement through space as a unit, conflict and planning. The result of this collective behavior was the development of tradition, unreflective internal structure, esprit de corps, solidarity, moral group awareness, and attachment to a local territory" (*ibid.:*37–38). In discussing "the cyclical process of interaction . . . in which there are alternating periods of conflict and accommodation" between delinquent gangs, Thrasher (*ibid.*) asserted that *"life is a struggle not merely for existence, but for the gratification of all human desires. Every group, as well as every person, is a self-appropriating organism attempting to wrest from its environment the fullest measure of satisfaction"* (our emphasis). In addition, "although tastes are directed toward a variety of different 'goods,' rarely is there a sufficient amount of any one of these for everybody who desires it. *The supply of any tangible or intangible thing which meets a human need . . . is limited, and struggle is the inevitable consequence"* (our emphasis). In Thrasher's (*ibid.:*128) opinion, "Society may be regarded as a complex system of accommodations in which these competitive relations are defined, standardized, and rendered stable." The corporate liberal's natural and normal "society," therefore, controls the primordial struggle for scarce goods.

In Thrasher's theory, delinquent groups were like individuals in the marketplace. They were atomistic social units which behaved like atomistic individuals. They faced a problem of scarcity and the inevitable consequences of this problem under uncontrolled conditions.

Conflict Groups, Arbiters, and Rules of Game

Park and Burgess claimed that crime came into existence because individuals refused to compete according to the rules of the game. In discussing the "struggle pattern of life," Thrasher agreed with his teachers and also pointed out that "war is carried on, partly because it is exciting and gives free play to impulses otherwise controlled." Echoing Park and Burgess' belief that warfare can be regulated by ceremonial or judicial processes, Thrasher (*ibid.:*129) noted that violent conflict can be regulated if *"the outside world, the larger group, is invited in to act as arbiter; to see fair play and to define the rules"* (our emphasis). Ceremonial forms of warfare, in this sense, can be compared to a ball game, which "may be fought with the same motives as battle" but within the framework of emerging "rules and standards." Under these conditions, "struggle tends to assume the form of regulated play in which the interests are merely subjective—superiority, prestige, etc." "This," Thrasher added, "is the point at which the outsider representing the public and community may play a role. He may function in the direction of regulation of conflict in the interest of the larger community." In these statements about the ways to *control* delinquency, Thrasher regarded adolescent groups as "interest" or "conflict groups." He used concepts related to institutional practice that were originally derived from liberal-syndicalism but were ultimately associated with pluralism, even though he was only concerned with the behavior of adolescent groups.

There is no doubt that Thrasher's work contained ideas which became central to the practice of social group work with adolescents in working-class areas. But Thrasher's analysis proposed reforms that transcended social work with either delinquent individuals or groups. He suggested more than the creation of new *social agencies* that could meet adolescent needs unmet by established institutions (*ibid.:*363). He also proposed a scheme for "community reorganization" involving the development of "local councils of social agencies." This type of council would help coordinate efforts aimed at arbitrating and regulating conflicts in the delinquency area in "the interests of the larger community." It would be capable of initiating delinquency prevention programs which, according to Thrasher, "must be based upon the social researcher rather than the superficial type of survey often employed by social agencies." [2]

It is important to note that Thrasher did not propose the creation of representative councils fashioned after the Cincinnati Social Unit plan. The councils he was talking about (*ibid.:*364–365) were to be "representative of most of the *agencies* which must co-operate in putting a [delinquency control] program into practical operation" (our emphasis). Thrasher's analysis of delinquent gangs was *not* used to justify the development of new organizational structures that would ensure democratic participation of working-class families in the administration of institutions that would enhance the quality of their community life. It was used to justify the integration and extension of *technocratically instituted* practice. This practice, needless to say, was not controlled by working-class families. Every social worker who is familiar with the history of councils of social agencies is fully aware that this practice is and always has been controlled by white middle-class families and social service administrators who live *outside* the communities they are supposed to serve.

NOTES

1. A criticism of modern delinquency theories in sociology, David Bordua's "Delinquent Subcultures: Sociological Interpretations of Gang Delinquency" (1961), stresses the role of freedom exercised by delinquents in Thrasher's work but ignores its more important liberal origins and usages.

2. Thrasher (1963:365–366) added, "No adequate program can be formulated or carried on without definite knowledge of facts regarding the children of the area and their problems and the social influences which play upon them." Thrasher did not refer to specific research efforts which epitomized this kind of research, but it is to be assumed that he meant the kind of research being developed at the University of Chicago.

CHAPTER 62

A Justification for Class Domination of City Life

American sociologists during the formative years played a significant role in constructing "scientific" theories of urban community life that were eventually used to justify the domination, by white middle- and upper-class families, of American cities.[1] The sociological theories, however, may not have appeared to fulfill this ideological function at first glance. It was only when they began to influence the empirical developments in the field of urban sociology that their pragmatic role became clearly evident. Works by Thrasher and Cressey provide illustrations of this, but the analysis of social-class modes of life among urban dwellers published in 1929 by Harvey Zorbaugh is more significant politically because it touched directly on whether working-class people were capable of organizing viable social and political movements in their own interests.

Theoretical and Political Dimensions of Zorbaugh's Study

Conducted by one of Park's students, *The Gold Coast and the Slum* has been hailed as a landmark in the development of the sociology of deviant behavior because it stimulated ethnographies of different modes of social life in urban communities (Matza 1969:48).[2] This work also serves as an example of the complementary relationship between liberal sociologists and professional reformers.

482

The Gold Coast and the Slum was a study of Chicago's "Near North Side." This area was composed of communities with marked social-class distinctions, and Zorbaugh attempted to identify the general tendencies which differentiated their unique modes of social-class life. This attempt, in his opinion, would be useful in preventing the errors made by reformers during the progressive era. (The reformer of this era was called "a fanatic who had waged an uncompromising war on reality" because he erroneously believed, among other things, that local communities could cope effectively with modern urban problems by using such antiquated methods as the democratic "discussion and vote.") Zorbaugh (1929:269–271) also felt that his scientific study was consistent with other studies offering a more "intelligent" and "realistic" conception of city life. These studies were considered to be more useful in guiding professionals who would ultimately replace the "uncompromising" and "fanatical" reformers in initiating progressive changes in the life of the city. Zorbaugh cited studies by the American Bell Telephone Company, the Russell Sage Foundation, and the Community Research Foundation in Chicago (which financed work by students at the University of Chicago) as examples. He also stated: "while reformers were vainly attempting to stem the tides of city life, however, realtors, engineers of public utilities, city-planning and zoning commissions, students in universities and others interested in predicting the future of the city were discovering much about the nature of these tides, about the ways in which the city grows."

Zorbaugh considered the Cincinnati Social Unit Experiment as an attempt at reform through local efforts. It was pointed out in a previous chapter that political repression destroyed the project. Zorbaugh (*ibid.*:267–268) recognized the fact of repression in this statement: "It is to be regretted that the failure of the social-unit experiment in Cincinnati was complicated by a political controversy, the opposition of the mayor of the city. He saw in the social-unit plan the possibility of a new political organization which might be completely subversive of party politics. And his branding of the social-unit as socialistic, even Bolshevistic, hastened its collapse." Zorbaugh added, however, "But the division of opinion which followed this controversy demonstrated that professional interest is stronger than local sentiment, and that the people who live in a given local area in the city have little in common, either of sentiment or interest that is enduring." Zorbaugh declared that ". . . a new *social politics* has grown up, consisting in the preparation of legislation by *experts of social agencies* and passed on a city-wide basis. The tendency of social politics is to take legislation *out* of the local community entirely . . . the very *nature* of city life makes community organization impossible" (our emphasis).

Thus, Zorbaugh regretted the failure of the Cincinnati Social Unit Experiment because it sought to establish the neighborliness and solidarity that was "characteristic of the town" through "a democratic organization of all persons and groups in the district." But this experiment, in his opinion, was "bound to fail" in any case. He declared that "any attempt at community organization must fail which disregards *inevitable* trends in the growth of the city" (our emphasis). These trends, according to Zorbaugh (*ibid.*:266), were in the diametrically opposed direction of *"secondary* contacts in local areas, toward *anonymity* in these areas, toward the organization of persons upon the basis of *interest* rather than of sentiment . . ." (our emphasis).

Zorbaugh organized his description of "general tendencies" in city growth around the neo-Hobbesian view of urban life developed by social disorganization theorists. In this process, his study oscillated between the analytic concepts of social change and social control developed during the formative years and systematized by Park and Burgess. Ideas associated with such key-concepts as competition, conflict, and accommodation were the symbolic reference points that structured his technographic description of social-class relationships in Chicago.

Zorbaugh felt that only technocratic and pluralistic solutions to urban social problems would be effective. He (*ibid.*:272) pointed out, for instance, that there are many new efforts which are attempting to solve the problems of the city: "The advocates of 'pluralism,' recognizing that an organization of sentiment and interest about vocational and other groups is succeeding that based on local areas, would base the vote on members in social groups rather than on residence." Zorbaugh also noted that "The commission and city manager forms of government, realizing that city government is becoming increasingly a matter of business administration rather than of crystallization and definition of opinion, attempt, with the aid of bureaus of municipal research, to introduce into city government the standardization and scientific management already found in industry." Pluralist and technocratic ideas enabled Zorbaugh to integrate his role as a *professional* social analyst and a *professional* social reformer.

Technography as Justification for Class Domination

The leading empirical notions invoked by Zorbaugh for developing his technography were derived from reform Darwinism. The natural forces of competition, according to these notions, generated higher concentrations of superior human beings toward the top of the social-class spectrum. These persons were regarded as being most capable of providing progressive leadership within the city as a whole. This leadership could not come from the poorer residential areas in the city because they were a socially disorganized "world of unconventional behavior, delinquency and crime." [3]

Zorbaugh indicated that because of the failure of democratic methods, "the attempt to control the city's problems by giving the city a voice and teaching it to act as a whole leads to a reevaluation of the city's human resources." Capable upper-class persons have become even more important to society: "The old democracy exalted 'the man in the street,' 'the doorbell vote,' 'the will of the people.' But the realistic attitude toward the city and its problems attaches a new importance to good will, vision, leadership and wealth. And these resources, we have seen, tend, in the *competition* and *selection* of city life, to become *segregated* on the city's Park Avenue or Gold Coast. Thus, the persons whose names appear in the Social Register assume a new role in the city's life" (*ibid.:*274 our emphasis).

Once his reform Darwinian precedents are specified, Zorbaugh's corporate-liberal, technographic analysis of social-class differences in community relationships takes on even more significant meaning. It provides us with possible insights into why he selected a generally upper-class community (the Gold Coast) and a working-class community (the slum) as his major references. It also provides an understanding of why he placed great emphasis on the socially disorganized characteristics of life among residents in slum areas. Zorbaugh's technographic study served as a justification for middle- and upper-class domination of the city as a whole.

In contrast to his depiction of the slums, the Gold Coast "is the only element in the city's life that sees the city as a whole, dreams dreams for it as a whole" (*ibid.:*274). "Moreover," Zorbaugh added, "the Gold Coast has the wealth to realize these dreams. It has the 'good will' to realize them; it has the leadership necessary to establish them, for, as we have seen, in the differentiation of community mentalities that takes place in the city's life, the Gold Coast comes to have a concentration of the city's expert ability and leadership." These benevolent elitist assertions were "empirically" illustrated by two maps of the Near North Side. The first map located the residences of individuals who are in *Who's Who*. The second map indicated that overlapping the first there was also a "concentration of the directors and trustees of Chicago's social agencies on the Gold Coast and along the North Shore" of Chicago. This latter assertion was interesting because other references in Zorbaugh's study suggested that this concentration resulted from the fact that directors of social agencies were handpicked (they did not rise by successful competition) by members of national upper-class families who lived in Chicago.[4]

Had Zorbaugh chosen to, he could have used the second map as proof of the effectiveness of *upper-class control* of the professional reformers and social service administrators in the city. But he did not do this. Since he was concerned with the issue of power, had he chosen to, he could have conducted an ethnographic study of working-class life in Chicago that would have been attentive to the types of grass-roots movements developed among working-class residents in Chicago, however unsuccessful these movements may have been during the twenties. He could have described the difficulties that working-class people have had in attempting to develop genuine democratic participation in American cities. Instead, his study *justified* upper-class domination of city life. Even the snobbish "social ritual" and the exclusionary practices characteristic of Gold Coast social life were regarded as contributing to "the effectiveness of the Gold Coast's leadership" and to the "fulfillment of its role in the life of the city" (*ibid.:*279). (Solidary relations

485

among working-class groups did not appear to serve this function.) It is clear that Zorbaugh's study was little more than a sociological apologetic for the upper-class political domination of Chicago.

Consequences of Technocratic Approaches to Reform

It has already been noted that the professionalization of social reform in the United States did not disturb the basic political and economic relationships that had created the problems of the city in the first place. As history has shown, the piecemeal solutions to social problems by public administrators, social workers, and other "social engineers" utterly failed to substantially ameliorate these problems in any way. Nor did the sociological interpretations of the social problems of American cities contribute to the amelioration of these problems. By 1936, for example, Howard B. Woolston (1936:364–365) noted in the *American Sociological Review:*

> Three years ago, President Hoover's Research Committee on *Recent Social Trends* published two large volumes and thirteen monographs setting forth the growing disorganization in American institutions. The introduction to this monumental work declares that it was not the function of the investigators to interpret their findings nor to outline policies based on them. The editors point to the need for such completion, and express the hope that scholars who follow them will integrate their data into larger designs for collective action. Despite this impressive admonition, our social situation today appears more confused and our ideas about what should be done seem less adequate than before we received the warning.

After almost forty years of additional urban research interpretations and outlining of policies for American cities, what can be said about urban policies at the beginning of the 1970s?

At the beginning of the 1970s, many critics contended that governmental actions aiming at amelioration of social problems such as poverty, crime, and racial inequality had provided no solutions to these problems. They also claimed that the priorities of federal, state, and municipal governments had been firmly constrained by the need to provide stable profits and protection to the privileged. This priority has always conflicted with the social and economic needs of the majority of people in the United States. The benefits enjoyed by working people have been either window dressing for the political party in office, or unplanned by-products of expanding periods in the development of the American political economy.

This view is documented by the fact that vast resources have been provided for the maintenance and growth of American businesses. Great industrial corporations are given disguised subsidies by the government in order to guarantee their "survival" in a "competitive" economy. Corporate farmers are given extraordinary payments in order to maintain high price levels for agricultural goods. In contrast, meager allocations are provided the nation's poor. Children are hungry or suffer from an inadequate diet while

486

the "natural forces of competition" are socially controlled in order to secure private profits. Urban ghetto inhabitants who suffer from high rents and rat-infested dwellings are given token job-training programs while the major resources of the government are used for implementing imperialist policies that maintain industrial and military institutions. As Galbraith (1967:228–229) indicates, "All business objection to public expenditures automatically exempts expenditures for defense or those . . . which are held to serve equivalent goals of international policy. It is these expenditures which account for by far the largest part of the increase in Federal expenditures over the past thirty-five years." In spite of the defense of these political priorities in the name of the national interest, their true aims, the defense of corporate wealth and class domination, are plain for all to see.

Benevolent Technocratic Analyst and Professionalization of Reform

The celebrated vision of a society in which no special interest group would dominate others, and the liberal-syndicalist theories which established this vision during the formative years, actually masked the class nature of political power in America. It cannot be said that these perspectives have been used to enhance the quality and degree of participation by working people in governmental affairs; coupled with a technocratic interpretation, liberal-syndicalism and pluralism generated a particular kind of approach to the concept of democratic participation. This concept justified the decision-making role of the "experts," who were represented by an army of quasi-public and public bureaucrats as well as other professional workers. Instead of control by business interests, these professionals were alleged to be the group basically in control of the daily operation of city governments.

The technocratic rhetoric of Park and Burgess, and Ogburn, is as alive today as it was during the first decades of this century. For example, in a 1965 article entitled "The Professionalization of Reform," Daniel Patrick Moynihan states that with the continuing progress of the economy, the government is likely to amass and have to dispose of large revenues. "Therefore, one of the most important tasks to which an Administration must address itself is that of devising new and responsible programs for expending public funds in the public interest." "This," Moynihan (1967:468–469) adds, "is precisely the type of decision-making that is suited to the *techniques* of modern organizations, and which ends up in the hands of persons who make a *profession* of it. They are less and less *political* decisions and more *administrative* ones. They are decisions that can be reached by *consensus* rather than *conflict*" (our emphasis). This decision-making is possible because of the professionalization of reform, which has produced an enormous number of professional and semiprofessional welfare workers in the United States. These workers, Moynihan *(ibid.:*470) declares, "are increasingly *entitled* to have their way. That is how the system works" (our emphasis).

In 1965 Moynihan *(ibid.:*470) felt that an extremely important demonstration of professional rather than lay thinking about social reform was embodied in "the provision of the Economic Opportunity Act that community action programs be carried out with the 'maximum feasible participation' of the poor themselves." According to Moynihan, this "measure was inserted in the legislation not because of any demand of the poor, but because the intellectual leaders of the social welfare profession had come to the conclusion that this was indispensable for effective social action."

By 1969, it became clear that community action programs were being emasculated by political agencies, both state and federal, from the moment they effectively stimulated political action in the interest of the poor. David Stoloff (1967) reports that antipoverty programs were diverted from their original purpose. Programs being packaged by legislators increasingly reflected the desire to avoid support of grass-roots movements. Instead, these new programs "usurped local initiative and reduced the possibilities for innovation at the local level." The trend of social welfare was toward reduction of local agencies "to mere administrative arms of national programs aimed at limited groups of people" *(ibid.:*238).

Few knowledgeable welfare workers would question that "the great promise of the antipoverty program was embodied in its community action component. This was the one program that seemed to approach the problems of poverty in a truly unique and potentially meaningful manner." But this program died. "It died," according to Stoloff *(ibid.),* "not because of the invalidity of the concept, but because the Administration had little interest in fighting for it in the local political arenas."

Moynihan's technocratic orientation anticipated the revulsion among local politicians toward militant action among the nation's poor. His 1965 article clearly indicated the degree to which militant grass-roots action was considered dispensable in achieving professional reform. He pointed out that there is little need for grass-roots political pressure when a benevolent political state could rely instead on information (i.e., technocratic intelligence) supplied by social science research and public-opinion polling. These two "systems of information," according to Moynihan (1967:474), "make it possible for a government to respond intelligently and in time to the changing needs and desires of the electorate."

Moynihan's generalizations are belied by the fact that American cities in the 1960s had to be in flames before the government responded to the "changing needs and desires of the electorate." The events following the urban rebellions indicated that social studies have never succeeded in directing the American government's attention toward the "changing needs and desires" of oppressed people in our society until these people, themselves, made a direct bid for political power.

Instead of projecting a humanistic and popular role for the professional reformer, Moynihan argued that "the *professionalization* of reform will proceed, regardless of the perils it represents" (our emphasis). He recognized that this professionalization might have its price, and in particular that "the price will be a decline in the moral exhilaration of public affairs at the domestic level" (*ibid.*). The kind of passion which the civil rights movement represents, for example, "could seep out of the life of the nation, and we would be the less for it." But, in spite of the fact that "the risk is great," Moynihan was comforted by the thought that "the potential rewards are not less great." The rewards accruing from professional rather than grass-roots reform, according to Moynihan (*ibid.*:475), include the elimination of poverty itself. From this point of view, the *expert,* not the *poor,* will create heaven on earth.

Moynihan's charitable prospectus for professional reform is heartening. Indeed, the possibility of achieving an end to poverty on the basis of professional consensus rather than fiery conflict is so appealing that one can almost imagine the pioneering American sociologists from Ward to Ogburn sitting on a cloud in heaven, nodding their heads in approval at his new but old orientation to the vital problems of our time.

NOTES

1. In cities like New York, Chicago, and Boston, some of these families were members of the national upper class.

2. David Matza (1969:48), in a work distinguished by its humanistic spirit, indicates that Zorbaugh's study recognized the diversity of urban life but nevertheless retained the orientation toward "pathological" forms of social behavior that was characteristic of work by Park and his students.

3. Zorbaugh (1929:157) states, for example, "Taking into consideration the segregated nature of the population of the cheap lodging-house, with its mobility and anonymity and its lack of group life, common social definitions and public opinion, and taking into consideration the social patterns that grew out of the cultural conflicts of the life of *the foreign colony,* it is not surprising that the slum is a world of unconventional behavior, delinquency and crime" (our emphasis).

4. Zorbaugh (1929:276) cites an autobiography by Louise de Koven Bowen whose "Astor Street home" was the scene of various meetings about social service and public agencies. One of the autobiographical references cited in this respect states:

> I remember when my friend, Mr. Alexander A. McCormick . . . was anxious to appoint good people as heads of the various county departments, such as the warden of the hospital, the head of the social service department, etc. . . . I immediately called together about twenty-five people . . . and we sat all one evening trying to think of good men and women for the various county positions. . . . There were other dinners on the question of education where matters were coming up on the school board which demanded immediate action by the citizens.
>
> Some of these plans which we formed at these dinners or meetings were sprung at large meetings held later, and I have heard people say that they wondered where the plan originated, but no one ever gave it away.

PART FIFTEEN

Academic Freedom Is a Sometime Thing

CHAPTER 63

Academic Freedom

Background and Preview

The preceding chapters have dealt with the general conditions and ideas leading to the foundations of American sociology. Little reference, however, has been made to the fact that American sociology is conspicuously an *academic* sociology. The extraordinary and uncritical identification between sociology as a body of *scientific knowledge* and the *academy* as a special kind of institution, merits very close attention. It is particularly important in this regard to ask whether American colleges and universities have actually been free marketplaces of ideas. If they have not, then the habitual association between American sociology and the academy is but another indicator of the degree to which social science is controlled in the United States.

The issue of academic freedom is so important that it will be the sole topic in this concluding part of our book. The discussion of this topic will take the reader back again to the last decade of the nineteenth century. It will describe the concern with academic freedom during the formative years and will reveal that political repression of radical scholarship within the academy has been one of the most important factors determining the nature of American sociology throughout its entire history. By examining the operative interpretations of academic freedom that have actually prevailed in the American academy, it will be concluded that it would have been virtually impossible for the field to have been dominated by Park and Burgess' metatheory—or even the modern theoretical variations in liberal-functionalism—if it were not for

490

the political repression of radical scholarship. As far as sociology in the United States is concerned, the long-term consequences of the systematic political repression of radical alternatives within the American academy cannot be overstated.

The issue of freedom for academics, as we shall presently see, was raised early in the development of the field. But this issue should be seen as coterminous with the changing definitions of the field and the standards of professional competence espoused by such men as Small and Ellwood. During the last decade of the nineteenth century, the dominating standards of professional competence in North American universities were being formulated by corporate-liberal scholars. The establishment of these standards, however, was not accomplished without conflict between the new corporate sociologists and highly conservative university trustees or reactionary politicians.

This conflict reflected far more than the competition between old and new liberal perspectives. It revealed also that the power of academic sociologists was circumscribed by trustees and administrators of the modern university, and their institutional standards of tolerance for political dissent. A brief glance at the academic freedom cases involving Edward W. Bemis, Edward A. Ross, and Richard T. Ely provides an illustration in this regard.

Bemis Dismissed by University of Chicago

In the early 1890s, Rockefeller millions transformed a small Baptist school in Chicago into a foremost symbol of the modern liberal institution of higher learning. The university officials, with President William Rainey Harper at the head, swept the nation in search for academic personnel and established the basic foundations of the university. In a short time, sociology courses were differentiated from the courses organized around the two major roots of academic sociology in the United States; namely, theology and political economy.

Albion Small was appointed as the chief academic administrator who managed the faculty responsible for the sociology courses. Edward W. Bemis, on the other hand, was one of the faculty members who taught courses in sociology and political economy in the extension program as well as the department of sociology. Bemis was an exponent of the new liberalism which called for an enlightened attitude toward "responsible" rather than radical labor organizations; a critical stance toward laissez-faire capitalists; and strong support for governmental regulation of the economy.

In 1894, when Small and Vincent published the first textbook in the field of sociology, the city of Chicago was rocked with the violent Pullman Strike. This strike was conducted by the Railway Operatives Union and led by Eugene V. Debs. Bemis, an outspoken liberal who took his convictions seriously, had attempted to "calm the troubled waters" by urging the railway employers to adopt "a conciliatory Christ-like attitude" toward their employees.

He also urged Debs and other union leaders not to strike; [1] nevertheless, when the strike did take place, Bemis made a public speech against the railway corporations and stated, "If the railroads would expect their men to be law-abiding, they must set the example. Let their open violation of the interstate commerce law and their relations to corrupt legislatures and assessors testify to their part in this regard." [2]

President Harper was outraged by Bemis' speech. He wrote Bemis a letter indicating that his own personal relations with the university trustees and other Chicago businessmen had been adversely effected by the speech. Harper implied that he was being held responsible for public utterances by his academic employees and remarked that "It is hardly safe for me to venture into any of the Chicago clubs. I am pounced upon from all sides." He then warned Bemis to exercise "very great care" in making further speeches during the remainder of his employment with the university. Bemis, however, was not actually given the opportunity to conform to Harper's mandate. He was summarily dismissed from the university at the end of the academic year in which the speech was made. He was given neither a hearing nor information about the reason for his dismissal (Metzger 1955:428). Bemis did not take the dismissal passively. He fought his firing in public, but was unsuccessful in reestablishing employment.

Albion Small Justifies Bemis' Dismissal

Small was officially involved in the administrative processes accompanying Bemis' dismissal because Bemis, although an associate professor in the University Extension Division, also taught courses in the department of sociology and had indicated a desire for a full-fledged transfer to the department. Small and Nathaniel Butler, who was director of the extension division, coauthored a statement which justified, on allegedly nonpolitical grounds, Harper's decision to discharge Bemis. This statement was originally drafted as a confidential memorandum to the university trustees, but it was stolen and publicized by an employee in the university printing office who was subsequently discharged for the theft. Harper's remarks about the theft indicate that the statement was to have been modified, after meeting the approval of the trustees, and then issued to the public. [3]

Generally, Small and Butler indicated in the stolen statement that, after three years of employment, Bemis was considered incompetent to hold his extension position because he could not systematically sustain classes large enough to defray university costs. They added that he was not competent to become a member of the sociology department because "instead of erring by teaching offensive views, the head and font of his offending was that he did not seem to present any distinct views whatever."

Small and Butler also indicated that they did not make public Bemis' incompetence at the time of his dismissal because this information would have harmed Bemis personally. They stated that their solicitous regard for Bemis' welfare was nullified by his conduct after the dismissal. Small and Butler alleged that they were forced to break silence and "advertise" Bemis' incompetency because he had misrepresented himself as "a martyr" and had become involved in "a deliberate design to misrepresent the facts." Throughout their statement Small and Butler repeatedly insisted that Bemis' dismissal did not involve issues related to "freedom of teaching." They firmly declared that Harper's decision to dismiss Bemis was not connected with any doctrine that Bemis might have espoused in his university courses. Harper's action, according to Small and Butler, only applied to conduct *outside* the university in relation to "a promiscuous audience" and that, therefore, no restraints on Bemis' academic behavior *within* the university were at issue.

Small issued a statement to the press on October 18, 1895. Upon examining the press release, Walter P. Metzger, a noted scholar who has chronicled early academic freedom violations in modern American universities, has taken issue with Small's justification of Harper's dismissal. Metzger (*ibid.*:428) properly observes that it

. . . is as damning as the action it seeks to explain. Small's exclusion of extramural utterance from the meaning of academic freedom was a truncated view of that principle and represented surrender on what to the pro-Bemis group was precisely the vital issue. His failure to grasp the intimidating overtones of Harper's letter [to Bemis] was a quibble or a deliberate evasion.

Bemis Defended by Ely, Commons, Ross, and Debs

In the controversy following his firing, Bemis was defended by Richard T. Ely, the eminent political economist, who was one of Bemis' former teachers. Ely wrote to the editor of *The Outlook,* "I will say, at once, that it is my firm conviction that Professor Bemis who is stronger than any man they now have in the department of economics, would be a member of the faculty of the University in good standing had he not held the view which he entertains." [4] In addition, other corporate liberals, including John R. Commons and Edward A. Ross, offered their support. Ross, in particular became so incensed that he wrote to Bemis on September 5, 1895:

I see that the issue between you and the Gas Trust University [5] has become a national affair. . . . I have known the tendencies there but have always tried to treat the University in a liberal spirit, but from now on I vow that I shall never recommend the economic, political or sociological departments of the University of Chicago to any student. . . . The Chicago concern has forfeited all right to the name and dignity of a University till it falls under other control.

Reference to Bemis' dismissal also appeared in the February 1896 issue of *The Adelbert,* a Western Reserve University publication in Cleveland, Ohio. This article was written by Eugene V. Debs, in response to a letter from the editor, inquiring into whether the American universities were doing anything to solve the labor problem in the United States. Debs replied emphatically that as far as American workers were concerned, the American universities were doing nothing to solve "the great labor problem." The paragraph referring to Bemis contains the reasons why Debs had come to this conclusion:

If the American university has failed in doing its share in solving the "great labor problem," no laborious research is required to find a plausible reason for its shortcomings, and recent humiliating incidents transpiring in the operation of the Chicago University, become sufficiently explanatory to satisfy the most exacting. The dismissal of Prof. Bemis proclaims the fact that the American university is not equipped to solve labor problems, but is arrogantly hostile to labor and further proof of its opposition to labor, if demanded, is found in President Harper's explanation of the dismissal of Prof. Bemis in which he is reported to have said substantially that to "express friendship for working men is well enough *but we get our money from the other side.*" [Debs 1970a:56]

Ross Forced to Leave Stanford

In the fall of 1900 and about five years after the Bemis incident, Ross was fired from Stanford University ostensibly because his criticism of capitalist exploitation, made at a San Francisco labor meeting, offended Mrs. Leland Stanford, the wife of the University's benefactor. At the time of Ross' dismissal, Leland Stanford was deceased but his wife still monitored university affairs. The university itself was officially headed by President David Starr Jordan.

In a letter to Ward, Ross (Stern 1936:184) stated, "At the beginning of last May a representative of organized labor asked Dr. Jordan to be one of the speakers at a mass meeting called to protest against coolie immigration, and to present 'the scholar's view' [of the Asian immigration question]." Ross also indicated that the meeting was sponsored by organized labor to protest the heavy "Jap immigration" and to support "the renewal of Chinese Exclusion which expires in 1902." Jordan, according to Ross, was unable to attend the meeting and asked Ross to take his place.

Ross had been at odds with those who governed Stanford over his support for Bryan and his opposition to the gold standard in favor of a bimetallic standard.[6] However, his speech at the labor meeting in San Francisco appeared to have been the straw that broke the camel's back. Ross felt that he was asked to resign because he had alleged in that speech that American capitalists had profited inordinately from the exploitation of Chinese labor. This allegation implicated Leland Stanford, who had made his fortune partly through the exploitation of Chinese workers. Ross' speech was reported in the local press and after Mrs. Stanford had read the newspaper account, "she told Jordan to discharge [Ross] immediately" (Vesey 1965:402). Jordan, however, did not ask Ross to resign immediately after the May speech. He attempted to persuade Mrs. Stanford to reconsider her decision in order to prevent the kind of public outcry which had accompanied Bemis' dismissal at the University of Chicago.

494

Ward, Small, and Ely React

When asked to resign from Stanford University, Ross wrote Ward that he was facing dismissal because he had responded to Jordan's request to speak at the labor meeting. Ross also remarked that " [Mrs. Stanford] wanted to dismiss me instantly but Dr. Jordan, who approved of everything I have done, got me reappointed for this year. He is now making a last effort to overcome her opposition." In his letter, Ross further informed Ward that he had told only two men, Small and Ely, about the situation and had enjoined them to "strict secrecy." Small was informed because Ross wanted to work at Chicago during the coming summer. Ross also communicated with Richard T. Ely, who was dean of the School of Economics at Wisconsin University, about the matter of his dismissal because he wanted to publish his essays on social control as soon as possible in light of this development. Ely was an editor for the Macmillan Company, whose publication of *Social Control* appeared a year after Ross' dismissal.

Ross (*ibid.:*185) not only asked Ely and Small to be secretive about the issue, but also told Ward: "Please keep as quiet as the grave about it for I don't want anything about it to come out before the election. A constitutional amendment is to be voted upon confirming the Stanford grant and giving the legislature the right to exempt University property from taxation. If this case of mine leaks out it will kill the amendment and thus indirectly shake the legal foundations of the University." "Moreover," Ross observed, "my case would be injured by receiving a political taint."

Ross finally informed Ward that he had become adjusted to the situation, even though he had no expectations of success. "I am serene," he wrote, and "have already had an offer from one of the strong State Universities." "If I go," he concluded, "I will at least call attention to the encroachments of wealth upon the freedom of teachers." [7]

There has been no information readily available to us indicating that Small offered Ross a position at the University of Chicago at that time; however, Small's personal correspondence with Ward reveals Small's eagerness to help Ross find work elsewhere while he was being threatened with dismissal from Stanford University. Small wrote Ward on August 22, 1900, that he "put all the State University presidents in the Miss. Valley [sic] on his [Ross'] track and wished he might be snapped up by one of them." Small also stated that he had corresponded with Jordan, and expressed his astonishment at the rumor that Ross was to leave Stanford. This letter described Ross' high "reputation among sociologists and the loss of prestige which the University will incur if he is allowed to go." Small expressed his hope to Ward that Jordan would pass the letter on to Mrs. Stanford.[8] Small's letter, however, had no effect. Jordan finally capitulated to Mrs. Stanford's demands and asked Ross to resign.

Ross left Stanford and after a few years elsewhere ultimately received a position at the University of Wisconsin. The day after his dismissal, however, he broke his silence and issued a statement to the press. The release, as Walter P. Metzger (1955:440) points out, ". . . was skillfully composed to show that there was a clear-cut violation of academic freedom. Quoting from Jordan's own letters, Ross depicted the president as a victim unwilling to become a martyr. Playing on the Westerner's fear of the "Oriental menace," he implied that his speech on coolie immigration was the primary cause of his downfall."

In the events following its public disclosure, Ross' case was hotly argued by newspapers and periodicals throughout the country. Stanford University was firmly upheld by its alumni association and sharply condemned by the American Economic Association. Also a small number of faculty members resigned in protest at Ross' dismissal.

Ideological Dimensions of the Ross Incident

The broad ideological conflict underlying the Ross incident was personified by the antagonism between Mrs. Stanford and Ross. Mrs. Stanford's ideological perspectives are quite obvious. Her attitudes toward the University and the Chinese were expressions of a benevolent and colonial ruling class mentality.[9] Moreover, her condemnation of Ross as being dangerous on the grounds that he associated with "San Francisco demagogues," excited class feelings, and played into the hands of the socialists,[10] was an expression of her laissez-faire liberalism. Ross would have had no cause for alarm if he had supported the doctrine of free labor instead of organized labor, the gold standard instead of the bimetallic standard, and McKinley's instead of Bryan's presidential candidacy. Mrs. Stanford, in fact, would not have denied his "freedom" to champion laissez-faire liberal doctrines and politicians.

Ross' ideological perspective is also quite obvious. When Ross issued his press release, he stated (1936:72) that the dismissal infringed on his "duty as an economist" to provide expert and scientific knowledge to "sober people." In this specific context, the terms "expert" and "sober people" referred, among others, to technocrats and racists like Ross himself.

Ross' dismissal may in fact have been related to a newspaper account of his criticism of capitalist exploitation. It is important, however, to also consider the racist context within which this criticism was made. Ross' speech actually appears to have been primarily an attack against Chinese immigration to the United States rather than a criticism of capitalist exploitation. According to Ross (1936:70), the speech was concerned that Chinese laborers would work for less wages because they had a lower living standard than "native" (i.e., white, Anglo-Saxon) American workers. Chinese acquiescence to a discriminatory wage standard was causally related, in his "scientific opinion," to population pressures which were developed by traditional Chinese obligations to have large families. These obligations implied more mouths to feed and ultimately lowered the standards of living for white American workers.

Ross concluded that the continued immigration of Asian workers meant not only greater competition and lower living standards for white, Anglo-Saxon workers, but also the rapid expansion and overpopulation of the West Coast with Asians. The meaning of Ross' analysis was clear: Asians should be excluded from the United States in order to protect white, Anglo-Saxon workers.

Ross felt that he had presented a "scholar's view" of the Asian immigration question. But this view, held by Ross throughout his lifetime, was organized around a corporate-liberal *neo-Malthusian* interpretation of economic relationships. His speech reinforced the racist conceptions and the pseudoscientific beliefs which had permeated the consciousness of West Coast liberals and socialists alike.

Among the socialists, however, the turn of the century marked the beginning of significant divisions over the "race question." Three years after Ross' speech, Eugene Debs denounced racial prejudice among American socialists. He argued that socialists should cleanse themselves of the notions of racial inferiority. They should also keep in mind that Marx had issued "a call to all the workers of the globe, regardless of race, sex, creed, or any other condition whatsoever" (Debs 1970b:93). In 1910, Debs labeled immigration exclusion policies as unsocialistic, reactionary and outrageous. He further suggested that if any discrimination had to be shown in the question of immigration, it should be in favor of those races which had been most exploited (Debs 1910).

NOTES

1. Bemis describes his attempts to prevent the strike in a letter to Harper (July 23, 1864, University of Chicago Archives). See also, Metzger (1955:426).

2. Letter of Bemis to Ely, in *Ely Papers,* Wisconsin State Historical Society. See also, Metzger (1955:427).

3. On October 16, 1895 (prior to Small's press release of the confidential memo) Harper wrote that Small and Butler's statement "was prepared and put in type for the purpose of submitting it to the trustees and leaving the question of its publication to their decision. The proofs of the statement were stolen from the University printing office and given to the public. The employe (sic) who committed the theft has been discovered and discharged. If it had been decided to publish the statement, the phraseology would probably have been somewhat changed, and certain additions would have been made. The statement, however, as it is published is correct."

4. Letter of Ely to Mabie, August 24, 1895, *Ely Papers,* Wisconsin State Historical Society. See also Metzger (1955:428).

5. The reference here is to the gasoline monopoly enjoyed by Rockefeller's Standard Oil Company. As indicated, a grant from Rockefeller had established the University of Chicago. Ross' statement itself is quoted in Metzger (1955:428).

6. Laissez-faire economics rested on three pillars: free trade, free labor, and *the gold standard.* Proposed as a revision of the gold standard, the bimetallic standard (silver and gold) was considered a major panacea during the post–Civil War period. First supported primarily, though not exclusively, by populist movements, "the silver issue" (as it was called) was written into the Democratic Platform of 1896, which asked for "the free and unlimited coinage of both silver and gold at the present legal ratio of 16 to 1." William Jennings Bryan's defeat, however, represented, for all practical purposes, the demise of this issue.

7. Ross' letter to Ward, October 14, 1900, in Stern (1936:184–185).

8. Small's letter to Ward, August 22, 1900, in Stern (1936:184).

9. These ideological perspectives, however, have been obscured at times by liberal historians. Vesey (1965:402), for example, claims that Mrs. Stanford's reaction to Ross was motivated by "personal feelings" toward her husband and the University rather than by "general ideas." Her condemnation of Ross alleged to be partly due to her "maternal fondness" for the Chinese who worked on her husband's railroad. The "emotional state" which was generated by the newspaper account of Ross' speech is given as an important cause of her condemnation of Ross to Jordan. These allegations and imputations, however, appear to be related to the fact that Vesey is a male who believes that a woman's political behavior makes sense when it is attributed to "personal feelings," "maternal fondness" and "emotional" states, rather than "general ideas."

10. See Vesey (1965:402) for her condemnation of Ross.

CHAPTER 64

The Liberal Magna Charta of Academic Freedom

Richard T. Ely:
Pioneer Corporate-Liberal Economist

Richard T. Ely figures importantly, although indirectly, in the development of early American sociology. After receiving his doctorate at Heidelberg in political economy, Ely returned to the United States and joined with other scholars in rejecting laissez-faire liberalism and developing a concept of Christian capitalism based, in part, on ideas developed by the German "socialists of the chair." He became a major figure in the development of the American Economic Association. Also, Ely, who favored governmental regulation of the economy at the end of the last century, noted that men like him had begun as "rebels . . . fighting for their place in the sun," but that their vision of a better society eventually became acceptable to the highest officials in the federal government (Williams 1961:401).

Upon returning from Germany around 1889, Ely joined the faculty at Johns Hopkins and became an important member of the social science community. The events and persons at Johns Hopkins provide significant reference points for understanding developments in American sociology. Among Ely's students, for example, were Ross, Bemis, and Commons.[1] Ely collaborated with Ross and Commons on a two-volume treatise on political economy.[2]

Ely also figured importantly in relation to Ward. According to Small

(1913), Ely was the only member of the Johns Hopkins faculty familiar with Ward's *Dynamic Sociology* about five years after its publication. Even though this volume did not sell well, some of Ward's later works were published by the Macmillan Company in a series edited by Ely. Both Ely and Ward objected to the twin horrors of laissez-faire anarchism and revolutionary socialism. They were also in agreement about the need for technocratic solutions to social problems. Ely, no less than Ward, conceived of the intellectual as a technocrat and declared (1902:39–55) that the nation needed a *new* "class of office holders" in order to cope with the expanding needs of the state. The universities, he stated, had become vitally important for training *experts* in "every branch of public service."

Ely, we noted previously, was on the faculty of Johns Hopkins, and was instrumental in providing Ross, one of his students, with an opportunity to develop the first courses in sociology at the university (Ely 1938:190). In 1892 Ely left Johns Hopkins for the University of Wisconsin, where he became the director of the School of Economics, Political Science, and History. In that same year, in an attempt to move the American Economic Association in a corporate-liberal direction, Ely (*ibid.:*164) nominated Ross to the secretaryship of the association. In 1906, after his dismissal from Stanford and a period of employment at the University of Nebraska, Ross was appointed by Ely to the permanent faculty at the University of Wisconsin.[3]

Richard T. Ely and Academic Freedom for Corporate Liberals

Richard T. Ely was highly instrumental in developing the corporate-liberal tradition of academic freedom. An example of the process behind this development took place just two years after Ely joined the faculty, when he personally became embattled as the main target in an academic freedom fight. At that time, the nation was being rocked by a great surge of strikes involving as many as 750,000 workers in various industries and highlighted by the great Pullman Strike. In 1894, Ely was publicly attacked by a reactionary journalist (*ibid.:*219) and an opportunistic state superintendent of education (*ibid.:*222) as being in favor of "anarchistic" socialism and trade unionism. It was specifically alleged that he advocated "Marxian socialism" in his writings (*ibid.:*218); he had entertained a union official ("a walking delegate") in his home; and he was involved in "aiding and abetting a strike in Madison" (*ibid.:*226).[4] These charges culminated in the establishment of a special investigatory committee by the regents of the university. At the committee hearings, evidence was produced (including a testimonial from Albion Small) which systematically contradicted the allegations. The United States Commissioner of Labor, Carron D. Wright (*ibid.:*231), for example, wrote the committee: "I know from my personal knowledge that Dr. Ely's views would lead men away from strikes, away from violence, and to adopt a better mode of settling their differences." One of Ely's students, Albert Shaw (*ibid.:*230), also testified, "I have a very clear impression from Dr. Ely's teaching and writing in its totality, that reverence for government and for organic institutions was inculcated by him as a great cardinal doctrine. Far from influencing his pupils in the direction of destructive socialism, Dr. Ely's economic teaching as a whole has been constructive and conservative."

Ely's direct testimony was in a similar vein. Analyzing the transcripts of the trial, for example, Metzger (1955:433–434) reports:

Replying to the charge by Regent Wells that he *had* acted on his sympathies for labor, [Ely] issued a categorical denial. This author [Ely] of a friendly history of the labor movement denied, at his trial, that he had ever entertained a walking delegate in his home, that he had ever counseled workers to strike, that he had ever threatened an anti-union firm with a boycott, or that he had ever favored the principle of a closed shop.

Indeed, it is further reported Ely wrote that if these charges were true they would "unquestionably unfit me to occupy a responsible position as an instructor of youth in a great University." [5]

Ely emerged from the sewer of accusations "smelling like a rose." The evidence clearly indicated that he had never been associated with any union official involved in the printers' union strike. It was also discovered that the witnesses to this effect had actually mistaken him for another man.[6] The testimony and testimonials provided by Ely and his attorney definitely cleansed the record of any suggestion that his beliefs might resemble anarchism or Marxian socialism. Because of these factors, the case against Ely collapsed before the planned formal investigation of his writings by the regents' committee could take place.

Commenting on this favorable outcome, Ely (*ibid.:*232) stated that "the committee, after taking the whole matter into consideration, published their decision, completely exonerating me and giving to the world that famous pronunciamento of academic freedom which has been a beacon light in higher education in this country, from that day to this." The committee's declaration (which Ely considered the Wisconsin Magna Charta) [7] is inscribed in part on a tablet, dedicated in 1915 in one of the university buildings, Bascom Hall. It reads as follows:

As regents of the university with over a hundred instructors supported by nearly two millions of people who hold a vast diversity of views regarding the great questions which at present agitate the human mind, we could not for a moment think of recommending the dismissal or even the criticism of a teacher even if some of his opinions should, in some quarters, be regarded as visionary. . . . We must, therefore, welcome from our teachers such discussions as shall suggest the means and prepare the way by which knowledge may be extended, present evils be removed, and others prevented. . . . In all lines of academic investigation it is of the utmost importance that the investigator should be absolutely free to follow the indications of truth wherever they may lead. Whatever may be the limitations which trammel inquiry elsewhere we believe that the great state University of Wisconsin should ever encourage that continual and fearless sifting and winnowing by which alone the truth can be found.

"Academic Freedom" for Whom?

The original Magna Charta did not apply to all people; it granted civil and political rights only to the barons who had been able to wrest them from King John of England at Runnymede in 1215. Who were the recipients of the Magna Charta of academic freedom? In order to answer this question, it is important to realize that this charter was granted by a benevolent governing board at the University of Wisconsin; it was *not* achieved by a *collective struggle* waged by academics in defense of their rights. Ely's defense before this governing board was successful primarily because it proved that he was not associated with leaders of a militant union. It is of no mean consequence that Ely's defense took pains to deny that he had ever advocated the use of what was alleged at the time to be a violent (strike) method for achieving better wages and working conditions.[8] Neither is it insignificant that Ely and his defense emphasized the fact that he did not advocate Marxism or any other revolutionary doctrine.[9]

It is our frank opinion that if Ely had not been cleared of these charges he would quickly have been fired from the university. After all, why did the regents' committee scrupulously investigate the charges to begin with? There was nothing in the original charges brought before the regents' committee to warrant an inquiry. If that committee had truly been committed to the principle of academic freedom, it would have rejected all the charges *at the first meeting* and *issued its statement at that time.*

The "Magna Charta of Wisconsin" made unqualified references to freedom for scholars to follow "the indications of truth wherever they may lead." It also expressed the universal mandate that "the great state University of Wisconsin should ever encourage that continual and fearless sifting and winnowing by which alone the truth can be found." But when we consider these seemingly unqualified references and this universal mandate in light of the *actual events* that produced them, it is apparent that there were sharp limits to the kinds of doctrines and truths acceptable to the men that governed the universities at that time, not only in Wisconsin, but throughout the United States. The "enlightened" regents of the University of Wisconsin enlarged the older meanings of the concept of academic freedom in the process of defending this corporate-liberal scholar at the end of the last century. However an examination can and will suggest that the *operative* interpretation of academic freedom in Wisconsin and elsewhere, then and now, would have excluded from academic life the majority of radical scholars who were considered beyond the pale of professional competence from either Small's or Ellwood's or Weatherly's or Ely's and, perhaps, even Bemis' and Ross' ideological point of view.

NOTES

1. Ross too, had been partly educated in Germany before becoming a graduate student at Johns Hopkins. He has noted that he studied under Woodrow Wilson as well as Ely. At the university, from 1890 to 1893, Ross became acquainted with Commons.

Commons was also acquainted with Small because he published seven articles on the state in the *American Journal of Sociology*. Six of these articles appeared in the 1899 volume under the general title "A Sociological View of Sovereignty" and they detailed principles of equity for the state. Another article by Commons (1907) discussed the evolution of class conflict in relation to the growth of giant business corporations. For Commons' racism and chauvinism, see Gossett (1965).

2. Ross (1936:56) stated that after finishing the articles for the treatise, the work on social control "absorbed me for six years and resulted in twenty articles in the *American Journal of Sociology*." The first of these articles appeared in 1895.

3. Ross taught at Wisconsin for thirty years and expressed his high regard for the academic freedom there by dedicating *The Principles of Sociology* to "The Good People of Wisconsin, who maintain a noble University wherein scholars in the social sciences have been protected in the same freedom of teaching and liberty of utterance that is enjoyed by their colleagues in the natural sciences."

4. The strike was sponsored by the printers' union against the Democratic Printing Company, the state printers in Madison, Wisconsin.

5. When Ely's trial came to a successful close, Edward W. Bemis wrote his former teacher and congratulated him on his "glorious victory." Bemis's letter also contained critical remarks about the vigorous denials Ely expressed before the Wisconsin regents' committee. He suggested to Ely that under certain circumstances, support of striking workers should be considered *a duty* rather than a wrong. Bemis appeared to have fulfilled his duty during the great Pullman Strike.

6. These facts should also be seen in relation to Ely's general lack of involvement in any concrete labor struggle. Metzger (1955:433–434) notes, upon comparing Bemis's activism to Ely's noninvolvement, that the latter "remained in a state of academic grace" because his "criticisms of the social order tended to be general, not specific; hortatory, not programmatic." Metzger adds, "For all his warm humanitarianism, [Ely] made no intimate contact with the multitude. 'Only twice in my life,' [Ely] once wrote, have I ever spoken to audiences of working men . . .' "

7. Ely (1938:232–233) has claimed that this "declaration on behalf of academic freedom . . . has come to be regarded as part of the *Wisconsin Magna Charter* . . . from the day these words were written to this, no responsible authority has ever succeeded in restricting freedom of research and teaching within the walls of the university . . . the tablet in Bascom Hall typifies . . . the principles that animate the university as a whole" (our emphasis).

8. In a letter dated July 22, 1894, to Amos P. Wilder, editor of the Wisconsin *State Journal*, Ely (1938:225) expressed, in his defense against the allegations, that "I am accused of believing in strikes and boycotts. . . . When and where? Quote from my books, accurately, showing justification and encouragement. Of course, no one can do it, for *the exact opposite is the truth*" (our emphasis).

9. In his statement before the regents' investigating committee, Ely denied that he advocated revolutionary doctrines. He (1938:224) ended the statement with this sentence, "In obedience to the laws and constitutional authorities of the land lies our only hope of progress."

502

CHAPTER 65

The Business Domination of University Life

Ideology, Activism, and Academic Freedom

The attacks on the freedom of Bemis, Ross, and Ely are illustrative of the repressive measures faced even by corporate-liberal social scientists who were interested in reforming laissez-faire capitalism. This repression, moreover, becomes particularly significant for the analysis of long-range academic trends when it is considered that *most* American academics have not, by any stretch of the imagination, been militant reformers to begin with.[1]

What factors have determined the overwhelmingly liberal composition of the portion of the American academic labor force devoted to the social sciences or social services? Why has militant academic political engagement outside of the established institution been infrequent or greatly muted among corporate-liberal academics? Certainly the outcomes of the early academic freedom cases mentioned previously suggest that commitment during the formative years to nonliberal ideologies, such as Marxism or anarchism, was far more likely to invite the threat of dismissal than the liberal reformism of Bemis, Ross, and Ely. But the attacks on these liberal reformers illustrate the fact that those forms of activism which opposed the *concrete* interests of powerful businessmen also placed an academic in danger, irrespective of his ideology.[2]

A significant illustration of the adverse effects of this kind of activism is provided by the events surrounding William E. B. Du Bois' decision to leave academic sociology after a brilliant fifteen-year career in American universities. The discussion of these events (which follows immediately) will also provide insight into the degree to which the black scholar's academic career was politically circumscribed by economic interests during the formative years.

W. E. B. Du Bois: Sociologist at Atlanta University

Du Bois, a black scholar, taught in American universities from 1894 to 1910, after graduating with highest honors from Harvard. Having taught elsewhere for about three years, Du Bois accepted a position at Atlanta Univer-

503

sity, where he was asked to take charge of the work in sociology and of the conferences being organized around the problems of black people in America. Du Bois plunged into the work with great energy, and in a short time Atlanta University became the most important center for scholarly research on the black American.

During his first ten years at Atlanta, Du Bois (1968:65) later reported, in spite of the fact that financial resources were meager, he optimistically laid down an ambitious research program for "a hundred years of study." Under his leadership, scholars at the university "studied . . . Negro mortality, urbanization, the effort of Negroes for their own social betterment, Negroes in business, college-bred Negroes, the Negro common school, the Negro artisan, the Negro church, and Negro crime." For a quarter of a century, Du Bois (*ibid.*) wrote, "there was no study of the race problem in America . . . which did not depend in some degree upon the investigations made at Atlanta University. . . ."

In spite of these accomplishments, Du Bois remained at Atlanta for only four more years. His opposition to the political policies of Booker T. Washington was one of the important factors resulting in his decision to leave academic sociology.

The Tuskegee Machine

"The years from 1899 to 1905," Du Bois (*ibid.:*71) observed, "marked the culmination of the career of Booker T. Washington." Washington was president of the Tuskegee Institute in Alabama and in 1903 the future of this institute was underwritten by a $600,000 gift from Andrew Carnegie. Carnegie's gift was undoubtedly motivated by the degree to which Washington had become a symbol of a gradualist solution to the problems of black people in the United States.

During the last decade of the nineteenth century, the Southern states disenfranchised their population of black voters through a series of legal and quasi-legal actions. Simultaneously, these states enacted Jim Crow laws which imposed an inferior, legal-caste status on the black population. These events further intensified the political and economic oppression of blacks in America, and in the ensuing search for solutions to this oppression, many black leaders like Washington espoused a gradualist accommodation to white political institutions as well as narrow separatist policies based on black capitalism.[3] They opposed the militant organization of black farmers and workers as well as the formation of militant political organizations among black people.

Tuskegee Institute and its president, Booker T. Washington, symbolized, as we have noted, the gradualist and accommodative approach to white institutions. Du Bois (*ibid.:*72) observed, moreover, that around the turn of the century, "There was no question of Booker T. Washington's undisputed leadership of the ten million Negroes in America, a leadership recognized gladly by the whites and conceded by most of the Negroes." Because of his political perspective, high government officials and wealthy philanthropists consulted frequently with Washington at Tuskegee. Furthermore, Tuskegee itself became "a vast information bureau and a center for advice" about the problems of black Americans (*ibid.*:73).

An increasing opposition, particularly among younger, educated blacks, arose in relation to Washington's policies. This opposition crystallized in part around the 1905 "Niagara Movement," which was led by Du Bois. This movement stimulated events which helped generate the formation of the National Association for the Advancement of Colored People in 1909. In time, however, the growth of political activism brought men like Du Bois into sharp opposition with Washington and the "Tuskegee Machine."

Du Bois pointed out that there were contradictions in the leadership Washington gave to the black people. He stated, for example,

It did not seem fair, for instance, that on the one hand Mr. Washington should decry political activities among Negroes, and on the other hand dictate Negro political objectives from Tuskegee. At a time when Negro civil rights called for organized and aggressive defense, he broke down that defense by advising acquiescence or at least no open agitation. During the period when laws disenfranchising the Negro were being passed in all the Southern states, between 1890 and 1909, and when these were being supplemented by "Jim Crow" travel laws and other enactments making color caste legal, his public speeches, while they did not entirely ignore this development, tended continually to excuse it, to emphasize the shortcomings of the Negro, and were interpreted widely as putting the chief onus for his condition upon the Negro himself.

The resources of "progressive" (corporate-liberal) capitalists became concentrated at Tuskegee. Furthermore, Du Bois (*ibid.*:73) noted,

After a time almost no Negro institution could collect funds without the recommendation or acquiescence of Mr. Washington. Few political appointments were made anywhere in the United States without his consent. Even the careers of rising young colored men were very often determined by his advice and certainly his opposition was fatal.

Upon analyzing some of the material conditions behind this development, Du Bois (*ibid.*:73–74) concluded,

. . . this Tuskegee Machine was not solely the idea and activity of black folk at Tuskegee. It was largely encouraged and given financial aid through certain white groups and individuals in the North. This Northern group had clear objectives. They were capitalists and employers . . . [who] believed that the Negro problem . . . must be a matter of business. These Negroes were not to be encouraged as voters in the new democracy, nor were they to be left at the mercy of the reactionary South. They were good laborers and they might be better. They could become a strong labor force and properly guided they would restrain the unbridled demands of white labor, born of the Northern labor unions and now spreading to the South.

Du Bois added that in order to achieve this objective, "the Negro intelligentsia was to be suppressed and hammered into conformity." This intelligentsia was to be prevented from leading "the mass of [black] laborers" and keeping "them stirred-up by ambitions" contradictory to the goals of the Northern (capitalist) group. This group, Du Bois firmly stated, "was the real force back of the Tuskegee Machine. It had money and it had opportunity, and it found in Tuskegee tools to do its bidding" (*ibid.*).

How accurate was Du Bois' estimation of the aims of the Northern corporate-liberal capitalists? Carnegie himself provides the answer to this question. In a speech before the Philosophical Institute of Edinburgh in 1907, Carnegie stated approvingly that

Booker T. Washington's influence is powerfully exerted to *keep the negroes* [*sic*] from placing *suffrage* in the front. He contends that the good *moral character* and *industrial efficiency*, resulting in the ownership of property, are the pressing needs and the sure and speedy path to recognition and enfranchisement. A few *able negroes* [*sic*] are disposed to press for the free and unrestricted vote *immediately*. We cannot but hope that the wiser policy will prevail. . . . [quoted in Ofari (1970:35), our emphasis]

Du Bois Leaves Academic Sociology

Du Bois became a socialist in later years. At the time of his employment at Atlanta, however, his approach to the solution of black problems in the United States was on the edge but, nevertheless, not outside the domain of liberal analytic thought. In spite of this, his opposition to Washington and the Tuskegee Machine had a negative influence on his opportunities for scholarly research. His biographical account of these years indicates that he found it increasingly difficult to obtain any funds for research. On one occasion, Du Bois did obtain funds for a social and economic study of Lownes County, Alabama, from the United States Department of Labor. This study, however, was suppressed and then destroyed because, according to the department, "it touched on political matters" (*ibid.:*85–86).

Du Bois also attempted to establish a monthly journal that would deal with black Americans. Attempts to obtain funds from Northern capitalists such as Jacob Schiff met with failure, for he was told that they would have to contact Tuskegee in order to obtain advice on the propriety of his enterprise (*ibid.:*83). Du Bois had had personal contact with the Northern [capitalist] group prior to his opposition to Washington. In 1902, members of this group, including, for example, such wealthy entrepreneurs as Baldwin and Schieffelin, urged him to work at Tuskegee in order to heighten the Institute's scholarly reputation among intellectuals.

In the first decade of his employment at Atlanta, moreover, Du Bois hoped to establish "a center of sociological research, in close connection and cooperation with Harvard, Columbia, Johns Hopkins and the University of Pennsylvania" (*ibid.:*62). Obviously, this plan was dependent upon the establishment of close and congenial relations with leading members of the new sociological profession. Du Bois' remarks at the second annual sociological convention, however, revealed his growing disillusionment with the possibility that these relationships could ever be established. In a response to a completely inadequate, liberal analysis of race conflict in the United States (presented by Alfred Holt Stone [1907]), Du Bois (1907:105) stated:

When we at Atlanta University say that we are the only institution in the United States that is making any serious study of the race problems in the United States, we make no great boast because it is not that we are doing so much, but rather that the rest of the nation is doing nothing, and that we can get from the rest of the nation very little encouragement, co-operation, or help for this work.

In 1910, Du Bois finally began to experience considerable political pressure at Atlanta University itself. He reported (*ibid.:*93) that "on account of my attitude toward Mr. Washington I had become *persona non grata* to powerful interests, and . . . [I became aware] that Atlanta University would not be able to get support for its general work or for its study of the Negro problem so long as I remained at the Institution." He observed that the president of the university had received promises that "under certain circumstances," increased contributions could be expected from the General Education Board. He reported that he felt sure that his disassociation from the university was one of the "circumstances" that would guarantee these contributions. With the growth of this awareness, Du Bois (*ibid.:*94) sadly realized that his work in Atlanta, and his "dream of the settlement of the Negro problem by science faded." He left the field to engage in more direct political activity. It is of no mean significance that some of the finest scholarly works on black Americans were written by Du Bois during the years *following* his employment at Atlanta, while he was engaged in political life *outside* the business-dominated institutions of higher learning.

Gatekeepers to *Academic* Sociology

Du Bois' autobiography provides many insights into the reasons why he departed from academic sociology. In contrast, Robert E. Park, who was employed as a personal secretary to Booker T. Washington for a while, went on to become one of the leading academic authorities on race relations in America. Du Bois' autobiography makes explicit some of the political dynamics that isolated him from the professional sociological society while men like Ward, Ross, Small, Ellwood, Ogburn, Chapin, Park, Burgess, Weatherly, and other corporate liberals became presidents of the American Sociological Society. These dynamics do more than influence the political composition of the academic labor force in American universities. Whoever controls the academic labor force also exerts an influence on the *dominant political composition* of the professional sociological associations because American sociology is, above all, an *academic* discipline. The same political and ideological considerations which determine the character of the academic labor force in the American colleges and universities, also exert the same influence on the professional associations and their house journals.

These hard facts suggest that very complex interrelationships are involved in the study of the ties between political repression and the development of academic sociology in the United States. These relationships also included as a factor the degree to which ideological and bureaucratic professional powers were diffused among the corporate liberals who dominated the field during the formative years. A brief glimpse at Small's career will provide a vivid contrast with that of Du Bois, and it may be helpful in clarifying the analytic importance of the *multiple* hegemonic roles performed by the men who dominated the field during the formative years.

Small: More Than a Successful Sociologist

Small's biography has been regarded as an example of "the success pattern of American life." He was a clergyman's son, studied abroad in Germany, and won scholarly distinctions at Johns Hopkins. While still young, Small became president of Colby College. Subsequently he chaired the first large university department of sociology and was appointed the dean of liberal arts at the University of Chicago. Therefore, unlike either Ward or Sumner, Small was reputed to have enjoyed "a generous salary" almost from the beginning of his academic career. As an architect of this fledgling branch of social science, Small's other "firsts," as we have seen, included coauthoring the first sociological text. He also established the first important sociological periodical: the *American Journal of Sociology*.

It has been claimed (Page 1940:113) that "sociology owes part of its 're-spectability' to Small"; that among the founders of the field, Small, in particular, "gave sociology a *'professional* status,'" and "endowed it with an *academic* vested interest" (our emphasis). Why would Small (whose major professional ties were with the academy as an administrator) contribute a sense of "respectability" to the field or enhance its status as a profession and academic discipline? There is nothing intrinsic to any *scientific* body of knowledge that forces social scientists to conduct their affairs primarily in universities. It is apparent, however, that most scholars have worked in colleges and universities simply because they have had to earn a living; and the fact that they were just as dependent upon these institutions for their livelihood at the turn of the century as they are now, is absolutely crucial for understanding the ways in which they have practiced their trade.

In this context, Small's career can be regarded as more than a simple success story. It symbolizes a set of very powerful institutional relationships that have, as far as we know, never been taken into account by historians interested in the nature of sociology during the formative years. These relations involved, in addition to Small's role as an administrator, the fact that he was editor of the *American Journal of Sociology*.

Small: Chief Editor of the Only Journal in the Field

As chief editor of the *American Journal of Sociology,* Small was responsible for providing adequate coverage of what he deemed relevant developments in the profession. The fact that his tenure as editor of this journal was *almost thirty years* is, in itself, a significant indicator of his professional prestige and power. More significant, however, is the fact that his influence was exerted through the editorship of the *only* professional journal in the field of sociology proper from 1895 to 1921.[4]

An examination of the *American Journal of Sociology* during those years reveals that the operative standards used by Small and his editorial staff not only encompassed what kind of article was considered to have greater interest to academic sociologists, but also what was considered a *sociological* article in the first place. It will be recalled that in 1894, Small took pains to place socialist ideas outside the domain of "scientific" thought. It is not surprising in light of Small's attitude toward socialist theoreticians, that although socialist writings on popular journal topics—such as crime, labor problems, public ownership, and the sovereignty of the state—were flourishing at the time, practically none of them were ever seen in black and white in the official organ of the American Sociological Society. This absence of socialist writings is the most affirmative indicator of the ideologically restricted boundaries of the field during the formative years.

On the other hand, when the *American Journal of Sociology* is evaluated in relation to later developments, it does not appear to be exceptional. The exclusion of socialist writings, for example, has been blatantly systematic in each and every professional journal in American sociology from 1895 to the *present.* Small and his editorial staff, therefore, are not solely accountable for this general state of affairs; they should be regarded instead as a symbol of a repression that *began* in their time. This repressive influence affected the development of professional circles and academic conditions that have in turn created and maintained an ideological control of academic sociology from the day of its inception. Small's career therefore exemplified the acme of the kind of effect any one man could have. However, corporate-liberal sociology was controlled, and still is, by the very men who also have had the power to determine whether their colleagues enjoy economic security, and whether or not they are regarded to be competent social scientists.

Small: As a University Administrator

Under what conditions was corporate-liberal hegemony established at the very beginning of the discipline? Small's position as an academic administrator was a contributing factor.[5] It should be recalled that in addition to serving as the president of Colby College, he was the founding chairman of the department that dominated academic sociology for many decades, and also became the dean of liberal arts at the University of Chicago. Small was an administrator for over thirty years and it is highly likely that this persistent aspect of his professional career goes far toward explaining his conservative opinions [6] and cagey rhetorical style. Further, it is very significant to American sociology that Small was an administrator in a university created on the basis of the millions Rockefeller squeezed out of such corporate entities as the Colorado Fuel and Iron Company. Nor should it be unimportant to sociologists that the funds that first launched and maintained the *American Journal of Sociology* were provided by the conservative trustees of that very same university. The kind of voluntary but nevertheless necessary indebtedness that must have been incurred for this support is suggested by Thorstein Veblen's analysis of the developments in American institutions of higher learning at that time. Veblen's analysis is especially pertinent because it was specifically predicated on his experiences at the University of Chicago.

NOTES

1. Studies of academic attitudes have not supported the claims that there are large concentrations of radical faculty members in colleges and universities. Robert M. MacIver (1955:132), for example, has indicated that generally American sociologists are not radical: the evidence indicates, on the contrary, that they "tend on the whole to the conservative side." On the other hand, survey research has indicated that sociologists are often "left of center." This finding is frequently used to justify the "socially critical" character of academic sociology. However, this volume has shown that sociologists can be both *critics* and *conservators* of capitalist relations.

2. A somewhat similar point is made by Metzger (1955) in relation to the Bemis case.

3. Some of the factors involved in this regard are discussed in Chapter 17. For a discussion of the fate of black capitalism during the formative years, see Ofari (1970).

4. Odum (1951:403) has noted that "the story of the *American Journal of Sociology* has been distinctive in the annals of sociology anywhere. For many years, from 1895 to 1921 and 1922 with the founding of *The Journal of Applied Sociology* and *The Journal of Social Forces* it stood alone in the field."

5. The political character of his administration is amply revealed by Small's role in the Bemis affair, which has been discussed in a previous chapter. It should also be noted that a token socialist, Zeublin, was employed in the department of sociology at Chicago for five years. The contrasts that have been made between Bemis and Zeublin, however, highlight the fact that the latter was *not* a political activist. *Nor* did he write about issues that touched directly on the business interests of university trustees. On the other hand, despite his also being a *non-Marxist* socialist, not a single article by Zeublin was published in the *American Journal of Sociology*. Ely's comparisons between Bemis and Zeublin also provide insight into some of the factors that enabled the latter to maintain his job until 1900 when he left to become an editor of a national publication, *The Century*. "I have no doubt," wrote Ely, "[that] Professor Zeublin is quite as brave as Dr. Bemis but the nature of the work is such that he does not feel called upon to deal specifically with the gas question, street car corporations, etc. Dr. Bemis is not by any means radical, but he happens to take an interest in one or two lines of scientific work which appear to be particularly dangerous" (quoted in Metzger [*ibid.*]).

6. Regarding Small's conservatism, Bernhard J. Stern (who collected and edited the letters written between Ward, Ross, and Small) has pointed out (1933:163) that "the frank letters of this collection [of Small's correspondence] cast Small in the role of artful diplomat, contentious with his fellow sociologists, yet ready to yield to expediency, to temper the vigor of his sociological criticism of contemporary institutions in order not to offend the sensibilities of cautious clergymen and other conservatives."

510

It seems reasonable to regard Small's contentiousness toward colleagues and his expediency toward conservatives, in part, as a function of his academic administrative position. This position afforded him a secure base from which he judged members of his discipline; but this base, itself, was notably dependent upon the sufferance of more powerful and conservative elements who influenced the academy.

CHAPTER 66

Thorstein Veblen on the Institutions of Higher Learning

Background

Although the early social scientists were primarily based in colleges and universities, they also turned their attention to consulting or lecturing in social, political, religious, and economic organizations across the nation. They became absorbed in writing textbooks and other marketable publications. As a consequence, some of these academics were receiving royalties and commissions as well as fees for their writings, consultancies, and lectureships. But even where there was frequent gainful employment as a free-lance professional, this source undoubtedly supplied but few sociologists with their basic income. For the most part, the prestigeful men who enjoyed professorial status in universities were employees of those institutions; and since we are concerned with long-term trends in sociology, the consequences of this form of economic dependency should be taken into account.

For example, the fact that the sociologist's dependence on the academy placed his scholarly work under the sanctions of university administrators, governing boards, and philanthropic foundations, was highlighted in the review of William E. B. Du Bois' experiences. His autobiography, as we have indicated, suggested that whoever controlled the academy itself as a total system also strongly influenced the long-term development of the field.

In the twentieth century, corporate liberalism became the dominant ideology within the social science disciplines and the professional schools in the North American institutions of higher learning. As indicated, this hegemonic trend was based on an extremely complex set of conditions. Fortunately, Thorstein Veblen's brilliant analysis of some of these conditions was published toward the end of the formative years.[1] Veblen's analytic work was entitled *The Higher Learning in America: A Memorandum on the Conduct of Universities by Businessmen.* Many parts of this work are as fresh and applicable to developments today as they were to the period in which they were written. Almost a half-century before Clark Kerr (1963) wrote about the modern "multiversity" for example, Veblen pointed out that academic institutions were becoming complex "aggregations" of diverse and sundry professional schools, colleges, divisions, and departments that were integrated by highly centralized administrative bodies. Veblen, however, unlike Kerr, did not apologize for this development (he subjected it instead to scathing criticism). In his opinion, the development of this "meaningless aggregation" was due to what was, for his time, a fairly recent domination of the institutions of higher learning by *business* norms.

University of Chicago: Model for Veblen's Critique

The sociology department of the University of Chicago played a crucial role in the development of American sociology as a discipline. Because of this, American sociologists today should seriously consider the implications of the fact that the University of Chicago at that time was taken as the model for Veblen's analysis. Veblen stated, of course, that the characteristics of that institution were indicative of more general developments in American institutions of higher learning. But he also pointed out that the first draft of his work was based on his experiences at Chicago.[2] His remarks were embedded in the context of more general assertions about the operating patterns of university life, which were encouraged by boards of trustees composed primarily of businessmen.

In *The Higher Learning in America,* Veblen asserted that toward the end of the last century there was agreement that universities be given over primarily to intellectual enterprises rather than to training in the vocational "arts." This took place after civilized man had finally agreed that the disinterested search for knowledge was eminently worthwhile. However, various conditions prevented this rescheduling of intellectual activities from being completed. The modern American university, for example, had emerged out of colleges and professional schools operated by the clergy for ministerial training, or they were organized primarily around "the practical arts" and hence offered other kinds of vocational learning. Universities experienced some difficulty in moving beyond these traditional objectives.

Business Domination:
Universities as Industrial Plants

Around the turn of the century, however, business domination represented the most important factor preventing the universities from reaching their cherished intellectual goals. At that time, the number of secular institutions of higher learning was expanding. Concurrently, as the college and university faculties began to realize greater freedom from clerical dogma and control, American businessmen were providing huge endowments for these institutions. The latter were also beginning to play a dominant role in the management of these institutions. This was the case with both state and private schools; boards of trustees of state colleges and universities were primarily composed of very successful businessmen.

Veblen pointed out that the systematic selection of very wealthy businessmen as university trustees was not merely due to a general belief that they possessed a great capability in administering university funds; [3] actually, their selection had been *justified* on the basis of their general competence and sagacity. However, it was just as commonly felt, Veblen argued, that American engineers, inventors, and explorers were extremely efficient, creative, and resourceful, but these latter qualities did not appear to warrant the appointment of engineers, inventors, and explorers to governing boards of colleges and universities. In fact, Veblen wryly remarked, it was much more likely that an inventor would die in poverty than sit on a board of trustees, while business success, in contrast, appeared to make a man wise in *all* ways. Great personal wealth had, as a matter of course, become sufficient for the appointment of guardians and controllers of educational institutions, which were ostensibly devoted only to intellectual learning and the disinterested search for knowledge.

Veblen asserted flatly that the business domination of governing boards had transformed institutions of higher learning into industrial organizations. In order to underscore this point, he called universities "corporations of learning" and drew analogies between institutions of higher learning and businesses engaged in retail trade. These analogies were actualized by competition between universities for prestige, greater student attendance, and private endowments. Because of the exigencies of business policy, publicity, and economy, the men who governed institutions of higher learning were transforming universities into a spectacle. Emphasis was placed on "decorative real estate, bureaucratic magnificence, elusive statistics, vocational training, genteel solemnities and sweat shop instruction" (1969:128). Even football and fraternities were considered more important than the search for knowledge.

It was also suggested that the business-type organization of the student's learning experiences had instituted a system of controls for processing the largest possible quantity of students at the least cost. According to Veblen, these controls correlated closely with those administered by houses of correction and penal settlements. Veblen felt in this regard that the limits imposed on instruction received by students, as well as the system of grading itself,[4] reflected a business approach to intellectual learning. He exclaimed, moreover, that exacting standards and systems of accountancy had little to do with the real needs of students.[5] Nor did they represent a rigorous scholarly approach to learning: they were simply a manifestation of the growing industrialization of higher learning. Universities had become *industrial plants* that processed people instead of inanimate things.

"Captains of Erudition" and Academic Blacklists

Most of Veblen's work dealt with the ways in which business policies were carried out within the university itself. He indicated, for example, that businessmen selected university presidents on the basis of their being made in the chooser's image. To be sure, the university administrators appeared to be "captains of erudition" rather than "captains of industry," but in actuality scholarship was considered unimportant.[6] A few had been promising intellectuals, as Veblen suggested, but their administrative posts prevented them from realizing their promise. Administrative control rather than intellectual enterprise had become their highest goal.

It was further noted that the increasing size of universities was generating complex systems of divisions and departments. These divisions however were primarily regarded as evidence of the need to work toward greater centralized control. Even academic committees were regarded as administrative mechanisms whose prime functions were "shifting of sawdust" rather than concern with basic policy issues. Also indicative of this trend was the degree to which academic senates had been subverted by administrators who maintained the myth of faculty independence but not its reality.[7]

Veblen (*ibid.:*69) pointed out that in order to maintain administrative control it was essential for a "captain of erudition" to exercise "the power of life and death over members of his staff." ("Otherwise," he [*ibid.*] stated, "the formally requisite 'advice and consent' would be procured only tardily and grudgingly.") The centralization of power in the universities was facilitated by the administrator's view of academics as "a species of skilled labor, to be hired at competitive wages and to turn out the largest merchantable output that can be obtained by shrewd bargaining with their employees" (*ibid.:*85). Wages for instruction were being reduced to "piece work"[8] and this indicated, in Veblen's (*ibid.:*85) opinion, "that the body of academic employees are as defenceless and unorganized as any class of the wage-earning population." He lamented the fact that academics themselves were not aware of their status as wage earners[9] even though job tenure was precarious and the great majority of academic employees were on the lower rungs of existing pay scales.[10]

The general consequence of the business control of academic life, Veblen asserted, was the development of subservient and conforming faculties. As a result, administrators were able to adhere to the *form* of democratic procedure in their relations to faculty without granting its substance. (The faculty "advice and consent," he contended, was taken as a matter of course because their servility was ensured by their powerlessness.) In fact, dissidents among the faculty, who did not perceive the world according to administrative definitions, could easily be dismissed from employment. Furthermore, dismissal was an extremely serious matter since there was an academic blacklist in existence. With regard to this, Veblen sadly declared,

So well is the academic blacklist understood, indeed, and so sensitive and trustworthy is the fearsome loyalty of the common run among academic men, that very few among them will venture openly to say a good word for any one of their colleagues who may have fallen under the displeasure of some incumbent of executive office. This work of intimidation and subordination may fairly be said to have acquired the force of an institution, and to need no current surveillance or effort. [*ibid*]

These bitter words might be attributed to Veblen's psychological "idiosyncracies" rather than his brilliant grasp of institutional trends. Sociologists who now contend that radicals threaten the *independent* inquiry, *free* discussion, and academic *self*-government in modern universities (e.g., Bendix 1970) are capable of finding many other reasons for discounting Veblen's image of academic realities. Worldly-wise academics may remark that Veblen had difficulty maintaining his position in academic institutions because he was too free in his relations with the wives of his colleagues; but it is likely that it was primarily his political and scholarly iconoclasm that accounted for many of his difficulties in sustaining his employment in business-dominated institutions.[11] Veblen's iconoclasm certainly appears to be relevant for understanding why this outstanding economist was never granted a position higher than an assistant professorship at the University of Chicago, even though he was employed by this institution for almost fourteen years (Bell 1969:7).

Distinguished Social Science versus Disciplined Worldly Wisdom

Veblen specified that business domination of university life was creating a climate of conformity among scholars in the social sciences. Although his incisive generalizations were considered applicable to all the social sciences, he reserved a few special comments for the field of economics (his own professional discipline). He condemned (*ibid*.:136) economics as a "quasi-science" because it took "the current situation for granted as a permanent state of things; to be corrected and brought back into normal routine in case of aberration, and to be safeguarded with apologetic defence at points where it is not working to the satisfaction of all parties." He also remarked that economics was a science of "complaisant interpretation, apologies, and projected remedies."

Veblen (*ibid*.:129) underscored the fact that there existed a "clamorous conformity" among social scientists. He disagreed (*ibid*.:135), however, with the claim that leading social scientists were "held under some constraint," or were "in the pay of the well-to-do conservative element"; or that these men were being prevented from following up any inquiry to its logical conclusion. It was not necessary, in his view, to regard scholars who achieved great eminence as paid Judases or to assume that they were openly coerced in order to explain why they regularly reached "conclusions innocuous to the existing law and order, particularly with respect to religion, ownership and the distribution of wealth." Veblen stated, in fact, that most academic leaders were able to conduct their research in full freedom and to the limits of their capacity. They were free to give "fullest expression to any conclusions or conventions to which their inquiries may carry them" (ibid.:136). But this freedom and its puerile results, Veblen (ibid.) noted, was due primarily to the fact that "their intellectual horizon is bound by the same limits of commonplace insight and preconceptions as are the prevailing opinions of the conservative middle class."

Thus Veblen insisted that there need be no overt signs of reward or punishment in order to maintain the conservative bias among leaders in the social sciences. All that was necessary was for the corps of leading scientists themselves to be "endowed with a large capacity for work, particularly for 'administrative' work, with a lively and enduring interest in the 'practical' questions that fall within [their] academic jurisdiction, and with a *shrewd sense of the fundamental rightness of the existing order of things,* social, economic, political, and religious" (our emphasis). Given these qualities, Veblen (ibid.:137) added, these eminent men will *voluntarily* avoid scrutiny of "those institutional facts which the conservative common sense of the elderly businessman accepts as good and final." But since their professional inquiry deals precisely with these kinds of institutional facts, Veblen implied that their so-called leadership in the social sciences was an abdication of *scientific* leadership and more conducive to maintaining established opinions than advancing scientific knowledge.

With regard to the social sciences, therefore, Veblen (ibid.:138) contended that leading scientists and their disciples applied themselves with "admirable spirit" to inquiries into "the proper, expedient and normal course of events." Their conclusions, he noted, also "shed much salutary light on what is proper, expedient and normal." But inquiries carried on in this spirit, in his opinion, should not be classified by the word "science," but rather by the term "worldly wisdom," because they are concerned primarily with the commonplace and are regulated by very "practical" and "reasonable" considerations.

In sum, Veblen's criticism of institutions of higher learning utilized the notion of business domination as the benchmark for the analysis of developmental tendencies in university relationships. In regard to the social sciences, he contended (ibid.) that the distinction between "worldly wisdom and theoretical validity" had become blurred. Because of this, academic social science had generally become "a safe and sane, if not an enthusiastic, acceptance of things as they are, without undue curiosity as to why they are such." In this climate of conformity there has emerged "a compromise between the scholar's ideals and those of business, in such a way that the ideals of scholarship are yielding ground, in an uncertain and varying degree, before the pressure of businesslike exigencies" (ibid.:139).

NOTES

1. This analysis by Thorstein Veblen suggested that social scientists should be concerned only with the disinterested pursuit of knowledge. This notion, as we have seen, was used to justify technocratic goals rather than the "disinterested" pursuit of knowledge. In spite of this limitation, Veblen's work pierced the academic myths that masked the real nature of power in university life.

2. Veblen (1969:x–ix) noted that "in its earlier formulation, the argument [expressed in his volume] necessarily drew largely on first-hand observation of the conduct of affairs at Chicago, under the administration of its first president." (William Rainey Harper, who was directly responsible for Bemis's dismissal, was the first president of the University of Chicago.) Veblen added, however, that "more than a dozen years" interceded between the period of the first draft of his work and its actual publication. In these years he became more convinced that the events witnessed at Chicago were not merely a reflection of the personal characteristics of its president. These events, Veblen stated, "belong to the impersonal essence of the case." They represented general lines of development in American universities: "Lines of policy which were once considered to be tentative and provisional have since then passed into settled usage."

3. Veblen (1969:49–50) also indicated doubt that businessmen were actually the most capable individuals for managing university funds because there were examples of the misuse of these funds by businessmen (who were members of governing boards) in order to feather their own financial nests.

4. Veblen (1969:76) stated, "So . . . there prevails a system of grading the credits allowed for the performance of these units of task-work by percentages (often carried out to decimals) or by some equivalent schemes of control of this task-work, the percentages so turned in will then be further digested and weighted by expert accountants, who revise and correct these returns by the help of statistically ascertained index numbers that express the mean average margin of error to be allowed for each individual student or instructor."

5. "It appears, then," Veblen (1969:165) stated, "that the intrusion of business principles in the universities goes to weaken and retard the pursuit of learning, and therefore to defeat the ends for which a university is maintained. This result follows, primarily, from the substitution of impersonal, mechanical relations, standards and tests, in the place of personal conference, guidance and association between teachers and students, as also from the imposition of a mechanically standardized routine upon the members of the staff, whereby any disinterested preoccupation with scholarship or academic inquiry is thrown into the background and falls into abeyance."

6. Veblen (1969:61) stated, for example, "As to the requirements of scholarly or scientific competency, a plausible speaker with a large gift of assurance, a businesslike educator or clergyman, some urbane pillar of society, some astute veteran of the scientific *demi monde,* will meet all reasonable requirements. Scholarship is not barred, of course, though it is commonly the quasi-scholarship of the popular *raconteur* that comes in evidence in these premises."

7. Veblen (1969:68) wrote, "the faculty is the keeper of the academic interests of the university and makes up a body of loosely-bound non-competitive partners." But administrators have gathered a "corps of trusted advisors and agents, whose qualifications for their peculiar work is an intelligent sympathy with their chief's ideals and methods and an unreserved subservience to his aims . . . Among these aids and advisors will be found at least a portion of the higher administrative officials, and among the number it is fairly indispensable to include one or more adroit parliamentarians, competent to procure the necessary modicum of sanction for all arbitrary acts of the executive, from a distrustful faculty convened as a deliberative body."

8. Veblen did not specify what was meant by "piece work" but he may have been talking about a practice of paying regular instructors per course of instruction.

9. Veblen (1969:86) stated, for example, "The same unadvised and unformulated persuasion that academic salaries are after all not honestly to be rated as wages, is doubtless accountable for certain other features of academic management of the payroll; notably the failure of the employees to organize anything like a trades-union, or to

fall into line on any workable basis of solidarity on such an issue as a wage bargain, as also the equivocal footing on which the matter of appointments and removals is still allowed to stand; hence also the unsettled ethics of the trade in this respect."

10. Veblen (1969:118) pointed out that on these lower rungs, the pay is "lower than any outsider appreciates."

11. It is fitting at this point to quote Arthur K. Davis (1957:291): "It has lately become fashionable to look upon Veblen as a psychological curiosity or as an outdated satirist whom we can still read pleasurably for the period flavor of his hatreds and affections—to borrow Riesman's patronizing phrase. That this view has gained a certain ready following in various intellectual circles is perhaps a better measure of these circles—and of how isolated from the workaday world they have become, 'sitting on a dry shoal upstream'—than it is of Veblen. Veblen paid his respects to such intellectuals in the *Higher Learning* . . . and there we can let the matter rest, decently interred."

CHAPTER 67

The Hired Heads

Veblen's analysis clearly indicates that businessmen and business norms controlled the modern institutions of higher learning, which had come into existence during his lifetime. (There is no question but that this is still the case.[1]) Business interests generally determined the employment policies that established and rationalized the dominant political composition of the academic labor force during the formative period. Once established, this political composition generated other hegemonic factors that involved the activities of academic administrators and faculty organizations. These factors included academic senates and faculty personnel committees, which maintained the dominant political characteristics of the academic labor force. Therefore, although business control of universities did involve such measures as academic blacklists, in most cases it was not necessary to depend on coercive means. In fact, ideological hegemony had become largely a *self-maintaining* and *self-regulating* affair.

Some Deficiencies in Veblen's Analysis

Veblen (1969:165) argued that a total commitment to scholarly or academic inquiry was thrown into the background because of the influence of business norms, which, he implied, were more closely associated with professional schools. However, it is suggested here that a similar set of priorities can and will coexist alongside the more "scholarly" approach if the institution is committed to a corporate-liberal ideology. After World War II, a number of large

518

institutions of higher learning became heavily centered around graduate training and scholarly research. Professional schools in these universities, although important, figured less significantly in the development and ongoing operation of the institution as a whole. Nevertheless, the processes of "industrialization," which were so pervasive in Veblen's time, remained just as firmly instituted among graduate students and faculty members (no matter how advanced their interest in learning or their devotion to "pure" research).[2] Even though preoccupation with the search for knowledge did become salient in graduate institutions, the quality of life in universities during the postwar period was no different, in very fundamental respects, from that produced by the more utilitarian and reformist interests shared by academics during Veblen's lifetime. If anything, the lives of graduate students and academics in modern universities were even more rationalized by political and economic considerations.[3]

Finally, it should be noted that Veblen used the doctrine of ideological neutrality in order to defend academic freedom. His belief in "the disinterested pursuit of knowledge" revealed a limited understanding of the inherent relation between ideology and social science. The doctrine of ideological neutrality was a two-edged sword. For example, in the hands of most of the early corporate-liberal scholars, it rapidly became a repressive doctrine in spite of their assertions that their "neutral" perspective was the product of the disinterested search for knowledge. According to these liberals, as we shall see in the following chapters, all other ideological points of view were shared by "fanatic," "immoral," and "incompetent" scholars.

Academy as Adjunct of Political Economy

Before we examine the corporate-liberal standards of professional competence closely, it is important to further describe some of the political and economic considerations that structure academic life in the United States. Veblen has shown that the academy is much more influenced by business than is generally realized. We will now examine the academy in relation to other political and economic realities.

Prior to the turn of the century, from approximately the 1880s onward, the national economy required a highly educated stratum of workers to be employed in governmental bureaus, museums, libraries, research institutions, public and private schools and, above all, in manufacturing and retail establishments. The men employed to educate this stratum of the labor force worked in the colleges and universities. By the opening of the twentieth century this stratum of highly educated "white collar" workers were functioning not only as professionals and teachers but also as technicians and managers. Like other members of this stratum the college and university employees were often lacking in job security. However, although they were paid low salaries on the average, and even though most were not self-employed, they denied that they were at all related to the working class. In fact, eminent sociologists like Ulysses G. Weatherly vehemently insisted that they were not "hired men."

There were, to be sure, several factors that counteracted the discordant effect of academic self-definitions on the one hand, and their probable objective status on the other.[4] We have previously indicated that one of these factors was the sense of petty bourgeois autonomy derived from the ability (on the part of a minority of academics) to publish learned works or to lecture outside of the educational institutions. Still another, however, involved the relationship inside the academy. Among these relationships were the elitist relations of authority between student and teacher, which emerged from the vital role fulfilled by academic institutions in producing the *most* highly skilled members of the labor force. Let us briefly describe the *material basis* for these elitist relations and this institutional role.

Colleges and universities are no less an adjunct to the modern political economy than the primary and secondary schools. However, a veritable mystique has veiled the rather direct relationship between 1) the necessary requirements of a modern industrial political economy and 2) both the contents of learning and the relations of authority in these institutions for advanced study. This mystique is maintained by the fact that education has been traditionally regarded as a privilege. Schools have, moreover, been considered means for transmitting the cultural heritage, or for acquiring knowledge as an end in itself. The relationships of higher learning to individual occupational advancement or monetary gain, from this naive point of view, were not the aim which institutions of higher learning were primarily geared to fulfill.

The plain fact, however, is that institutions of higher learning do prepare most individuals for their occupational roles in highly industrialized societies. Therefore, aside from all their other contributions, these institutions are, in fact, akin to industrial plants, which also produce particular kinds of commodities. But the analogy does not hold as Veblen suggested, i.e., because "mechanical systems of accountancy and scheduling" are instituted as measures of worth in place of the love of learning and the disinterested search for knowledge. The analogy holds for the more basic reason, that institutions of higher learning are producers of marketable items: they produce highly skilled workers and technical knowledge, which are useful primarily for maintaining the social, political, and economic institutions of our society.

The products of the modern university, therefore, are not primarily organized on the basis of any or all standards that happen to be entertained by academic faculties. They are primarily based on standards that eventually produce *particular* forms of labor power and technical knowledge. These specialized forms are necessary for instituting capitalist technologies, capitalist divisions of labor, and, therefore, capitalist norms of efficiency and profit. They are also necessary for regulating or repressing human relationships that are not tolerated by these norms.

The modern university is a product of developments originating in the po-

520

litical state and, above all, in the market economy of the last century. The requirements of the labor force at that time were increasingly predicated upon a small but expanding industrial technology and civil bureaucracy. Today, in highly industrialized nations, these requirements go beyond the mere institutional necessities involved in the reproduction of a small group of technicians and civil servants, or the general requirements for educating children of upper-class families. The political economies of contemporary monopoly capitalist nations require unprecedented numbers of highly skilled and educated young men and women who can institute a technology in politically sanctionable ways. It is impossible to manage and operate a modern technology and an advanced capitalist state without them.

Industrial Discipline and Relations of Authority

Training the most highly skilled members of the labor force in capitalist nations involves more than the simple transmission of capitalist standards and expert knowledge to students. It also requires the acquisition of the attitudes and disciplined work habits necessary for highly efficient participation in industrial or civil bureaucracies. These disciplined and obedient individual responses must be generalizable to a great variety of authoritative persons. Modern bureaucracies, in light of this, require a particular character-structure for efficient functioning that is extremely sensitive to invidious meritocratic rewards and punishments. They require a disciplined habit patterning that can be called a capitalist *industrial discipline*.

Although social scientists from Comte to Freud have regarded the patriarchal family as the prototypical institution for inculcating this discipline, it is the school, not the family, which has been most significant in this regard. It has been the job of the schools to condition persons to operate efficiently in modern bureaucracies. Because of this, it would not do for the relations of authority between student and teacher to be contradictory, in a generic sense, to the authority relations that characterize modern (industrial and civil) capitalist bureaucracies. Of course, family discipline is not entirely lacking from this training process.

As long as class societies continue to prevail, educative relationships will always be organized around elitist principles. Although democratic educational processes may be established on an experimental basis with very young children or in upper-middle-class institutions, for example, they will never be established on a wide scale as long as the goods of life are distributed on the basis of class privilege; and capitalist "rationalities" still prevail in social life. Like the relationships of inequality maintained by industrial discipline under these conditions, the relations between most students and teachers will continue to be reinforced by coercion as well as by hegemonic ideas.

For children and adolescents who do not fully grasp the connection between education and their future employment, the educational relations are

521

reinforced (not always successfully) by parental authority and the law. For college students, they are also buttressed by personal fear of failure to achieve desired occupational goals. In either case, the desire for knowledge, as a value in itself, has figured and will continue to figure only as a minor determinant in maintaining the elitist relations between students and teachers.

Academics as Supervisory Personnel

Academics were hired employees [5] with respect to administrators and boards of trustees during the formative years, but the previous section has suggested that their relations with students were of a diametrically different nature. With regard to most students, these instructors occupied a position of authority analogous to, but more complex than, the authority of supervisory personnel with respect to workers in industrial establishments. Students performed their tasks in a wide variety of subject-matter areas and were held accountable to a number of "supervisors" (instructors). In evaluating individual performance, these "supervisors" utilized examinations, papers, and classroom discussions. They sanctioned poor performance and by means of grading systems, initiated the discharge of students who did not function according to minimum standards. Although expelled students were not discharged from an industrial establishment per se, the consequences of their expulsion on their future occupational life increased as technical and professional employment became totally dependent upon graduation from institutions of higher learning.

It is important to note, in addition, that although the relationship between academic performance and economic life may not seem apparent for some types of students, it has always been patently obvious for students interested in *academic* careers. In graduate schools, these students bear an analogous relation to their faculties as apprentices to their masters. In these schools, the extreme subordination and extraordinary anxiety that is expressive of the highly dependent and precarious relationship occupied by these young workers-in-training is plain for all to see.

Under such general conditions, most academics who were confronted on a daily basis with dependent and conforming individuals, acquired and maintained private sets of rationalizations and illusions about their superior status. Sustained by the powerful principle that reward should be given according to competitive performance, these men perceived themselves, first and foremost, as individuals who had, in fact, achieved their own authoritative position on the basis of superior merit. Their right to dispense meritorious reward, moreover, was legitimated and reinforced, not only by their own personal academic credentials but also by the everyday responses of students who were conditioned to move through bureaucratic institutions in an obedient manner. Aware of their competitive ethos and the internecine standards that regulated their relations with others, students and teachers were locked into a mutually reinforcing system that was broken only at very rare intervals. These intervals were likely to occur during stormy political times when students and academics alike raised fundamental questions, not only about student-faculty governance but also about the general quality of life in academic institutions.

Academic Freedom and the Academic's Status as a Hired Head

Thus, it has been suggested that the academic has occupied a highly ambiguous role. On the one hand, he has had little power in the face of administrators and boards of trustees, while, on the other hand, he has occupied a commanding position in relation to students. Like others in our society who firmly believe in capitalist meritocratic principles, academics have generally opted for liberal self-definitions and rationalizations that enable them to maximize their own personal dignity in competitive terms. They have abstracted the more prestigeful and powerful relationships from all other relationships in which they are embedded, and they have utilized these relationships as the basis for their self-definitions.

In this process, academics have minimized their status as *hired* men, and in some cases *hired* women, and enhanced their status as supervisory (but nevertheless, in our view, still hired) *heads* of groups of students (who are actually workers-in-training). They have also maximized their self-definitions by stressing the intellectual character of their work and thereby acquiring the greater prestige accorded mental as opposed to manual labor in modern industrial societies. In this sense, they have organized their status around the concept of "heads" in more ways than one. In spite of this, however, it is the dual character of their activity—and therefore their ambiguous status as *hired heads*—which should be kept in mind when evaluating their *professional* and *ideological* conduct.

NOTES

1. Studies of modern American universities have consistently shown that businessmen still constitute the largest single group on governing boards. Corporation lawyers, furthermore, are usually the second largest group, indicating that business representation is not restricted to financiers, manufacturers, or business executives alone. For examples of studies in this regard, see Beck (1947), MacIver (1955), and Apthekar (1970).

2. Today, grades are as important to graduates as undergraduates; examinations and papers are even more important. Research (as an index of the "disinterested" search for knowledge) may be more salient among graduate than undergraduate faculties and students, but the "standard units of accountancy," which Veblen emphasized as examples of the influence of business norms, are no less pertinent when "publishing or perishing" is involved.

3. These considerations, of course, were different in certain respects from those existent around the turn of the century. The differences included, in particular, the relations and forces of production being generated by the state sector of the capitalist economy. For insight into these relations and forces, see O'Connor (1970a, 1970b).

4. The incongruities involved in this regard have been noted in Caplow and McGee's study of the "academic marketplace." For example, these authors observe

(1958:228–229) that, in their interviews of academics about working conditions in colleges and universities, "the typical professor, if such there be, suffers from his acceptance of an ideology which is incongruous with his situation. He tends to see himself as a free member of an autonomous company of scholars, subject to no evaluation but the judgement of his peers. But he is likely to find himself under the sway of a chairman or dean or president whose authority is personal and arbitrary . . . academic authority is exercised largely by means of the personal control which the administration has over the salary, rank and prerogatives of the working professor . . . true enough, with increasing rank and with permanent tenure some of this helplessness in the face of authority disappears, but not before habits of obediency have been formed. Even a senior professor can, as we have shown, be seriously harassed by his superiors, especially toward the end of his career, when it becomes difficult for him to seek another position."

5. Metzger (1955) points out that the employer-employee relationship in universities and colleges has been consistently upheld by the courts in the modern period.

CHAPTER 68

Changes in Class Categories

Let us broaden the discussion begun in the previous chapter by analyzing the phenomenon of the "hired heads" on the basis of general trends in social class relationships. This analysis will begin by describing some of the historical and ideological conditions influencing the subjective awareness of the class position of intellectual workers in modern institutions. This will provide the necessary background information for the following chapter concerning differences of opinion about academic freedom and how it should be defined.

Transitional States and Language of Class

Because of large-scale industrial development, the United States experienced the formation of a new stratum of highly trained "white collar" workers whose livelihood was dependent upon the fulfillment of administrative and/or technical functions in a variety of private and public institutions. Members of this stratum, in turn, generated variant conceptions of social-class relations which reflected their own unique position in the social structure. They adopted an older language of class but incorporated this language within the framework of their corporate-liberal and technocratic world views. In order to suggest the modifications made, it is necessary to touch briefly on the development of this older language of class and its categories.

During the last quarter of the eighteenth and the first half of the nineteenth century in England, the phrase *middle classes* emerged as an expression of the growing awareness of new class relationships. This perception developed in the context of a class struggle which reached a high point because of differential tax burdens imposed on owners of land and owners of capital.[1]

In the first thirty years of the nineteenth century there were illustrations of the degree to which "middle class" referred to persons who were considered superior in intelligence and industriousness. The concept of middle class also became differentiated by reference to amount and type of property.[2] By 1839, the concept of middle class further embodied, within its prevailing usages, the claim to political leadership and domination of the nation. By 1846, the association between the status and growth of middle-class groups and industrialization was also firmly established: the middle class was identified with "the progress of civilization" (Briggs 1960:56–57). During this period there arose a sharpened consciousness of the replacement of traditional notions of human relationships with what Carlyle called the "cash nexus."

It was at this time that Disraeli used the phrase "two nations" to distinguish the emerging conflicts between the working class and the bourgeoisie. Cobbet talked of the combination of different trades into a general union, "so that there is one class of society united to oppose another class." By the 1830s, the phrase *working class* came to be clearly distinguished from earlier terms like "laborers," "laboring classes," and "common people." This phrase appeared in conjunction with the development of workingmen's political and economic associations and publications. One of the earliest usages appeared in the *Gorgon,* published in London in 1818,[3] and illustrated the degree to which this term, like "middle class," was also an ideological manifestation of the class conflicts during the early industrial revolution. In these early usages, the working class was perceived as the victim of the industrial system even though its members were a majority of the population. Among an increasing number of workers this class was also identified with the interests of the society as a whole.

During the latter half of the nineteenth century, Spencer denounced the invidious rhetoric of class even though he used class categories. Until well into the twentieth century, many scholars in both England and the United States held that the development of capitalism had ushered in a classless "open society." Other scholars recognized the existence of classes but felt that they would disappear with time. However, the impact of the Great Depression during the twentieth century led to a revival of the usage of the term "class" among corporate-liberal sociologists in the United States. This usage was chiefly represented by technocratic interpretations that thoroughly obscured the significant changes in class relationships during the nineteenth and twentieth centuries.

Changes in Ownership
and in Composition of Labor Force

With the growth of monopoly capitalism, the liberal tenet that *individual* competition is the most significant relationship accounting for the reality of class differentiation became increasingly integrated into technocratic interpretations of social reality. These interpretations, however, have evolved from Ward's old fashioned theoretical emphasis on the social forces of "avarice" to Park and Burgess' concepts of "mobility," "prestige," and "accommodated statuses." Wishful visions of a harmonious society based on "functionally interdependent" occupational roles have also informed liberal analyses of class realities in the United States.

But these class realities have actually been far more dependent upon ownership and control over the means of production. In 1841, at the time of Ward's birth, about 80 percent of the work force in the United States was self-employed. A century later this proportion was reversed; 80 percent were employed by others. During Ward's lifetime the economic changes that converted the great mass of the population into a class of wage and salary earners took place at an ever-increasing pace. There is no doubt that today the American population is primarily an urban population, separated from the means of production, and employed in the competitive, the monopoly, and the state sectors of the economy.[4]

This development has been synchronized with changes in the composition of the labor force particularly during the modern period. In 1940, for instance, approximately 25 percent of the labor force was composed of white-collar workers. By 1969, this proportion increased to 46 percent (Oppenheimer 1970:28).[5] These particular changes are partially due to the expansion of distributive and service industries as well as of industries organized around electronic, chemical, and mechanical technologies; but not to these factors alone. Technological changes in traditional extractive and manufacturing industries are also contributing to the changes in the composition of the labor force. In addition, modern industrial societies are experiencing sharp pressures for the development of social, biological, oceanographic, ecological, and other well educated and highly skilled technicians and planners, in order to cope with the increasing problems engendered by the complexity and interdependence of market economies, and the general impact of these economies on the natural environment.

Among the important consequences of these changes has been the steady development of varied professional, technical, and scientific workers who have identified themselves primarily with the old middle class. In this identification, the new "white-collar workers," as they are sometimes called, have taken over, in large measure, the language of class relations which was developed during the first half of the nineteenth century. But similarities in subjective identification and language of class should not obscure the basic political

526

and economic conditions which distinguish many of these professional, technical and scientific workers from the older middle class.

These basic conditions have been created by the historical interpenetration of political and economic relationships. This interpenetration has produced a modern labor force that is largely a state-educated and, in many cases a state-regulated, force of production. The same government support is also basic to the technoscientific knowledge that operates as a vital force of production in modern societies. The production of this knowledge has become highly dependent upon state institutions and state investments. To an increasing degree, state institutions and state policies mediate the relations between (1) the persons who control the dominant economic institutions and (2) the persons who expend their labor power for the production of material wealth.

A great variety of institutions was developed in order to fulfill these mediating functions and an increasing proportion of the labor force has become absorbed into the various "service" occupations within these institutions. Members of this labor force, including teachers, technicians, scientists, and other professionals and semiprofessionals, became responsible for the reproduction of the labor force, the production of technical and scientific knowledge, and the rational organization and legitimation of capitalist relations. Private universities as well as public universities established educational curricula for training members of the labor force in the population as a whole. These institutions also developed planning and research institutes which facilitated the political mediation of economic relationships. Thus, the mediating functions of state institutions are now supported by an infrastructure which includes private as well as public institutions.

Consequently, complex institutional structures have developed in order to provide prerequisites for capital accumulation. From the beginning, however, portions of the labor force, within these evolving structures, were constituted as objects of administrative rationality and capitalist exploitation. In this process, numerous professional, scientific and technical workers have become proletarianized and subordinated to the political requirements of capital as a whole.

On the other hand, the distinctive proletarianization of these members of the intelligentsia has not occurred in isolation from the contradictory trends which preserve the characteristics that are still markedly in evidence among petty bourgeois intellectuals. These trends involve various factors. Some of these workers have high salaries, parts of which are used for investment in property. A number of intellectual workers energetically engage in a quasi-entrepreneurial form of professional activity called "grantsmanship" primarily in order to further their own careers and increase their privileges rather than to advance knowledge or develop necessary social services. Still others obtain income through royalties, lecture fees, and consultation fees for privately contracted services. Taken as a whole, these factors increase the likelihood that quite a few technical and scientific employees function more as businessmen and free-lance professionals than simply as proletarians of a new type.

The factors indicated above, along with ideological traditions that emphasize the hegemonic functions and organizational autonomy of intellectuals, have strongly contributed to the technical and scientific worker's subjective identification as unambiguous members of the middle class. Increasingly, however, among the intellectuals employed in American institutions of higher learning, the only truthful relationship being signified by this identification is the pathetic desire, on the part of those who have spent painfully long years of their lives in training for gainful employment, to also maximize, in prestige terms, what they have only recently and to a limited extent gained in salaries and working conditions.[6]

Highly Educated Labor Power Sold in the Marketplace

Instead of viewing class relations in historical and macroscopic terms, modern corporate-liberal sociologists have generally reduced class relationships to prestige relationships. Or, like Max Weber, they have preferred to think primarily in terms of atomistic definitions that regard class as a question of individual mobility (e.g., "life chances"). This selective view, which restricts the dynamics of class relations to prestige and mobility relations, has, moreover, strongly determined the scope of the analysis of subjective aspects of class relationships. Although corporate-liberal scholars have been sensitive to such subjective factors as mobility aspirations, for example, they have conspicuously avoided the subjective dimensions of situations in which highly educated workingmen and workingwomen suddenly become aware of the degree to which their labor power has become a commodity. In these situations, educated workers often discover that their occupational qualifications are bought and sold in a labor market which is only partly stabilized by state intervention.

Very highly educated workers may enjoy greater prestige than other workers. But there are situations in which this difference does little to relieve the deep personal anxieties that emerge, for example, when they are not assured adequate employment. Such situations commonly occur when public and private corporations institute the processes whereby prospective employees are selectively evaluated and rejected or hired; or when corporations confront workers with the possibility of being discharged from employment. Indeed, no situations more significantly reveal the commodity status of highly trained labor power in capitalist societies from a phenomenological point of view, than those situations in which working-class women and men in the professions are concerned about the sheer fact of being employed.

Because of this, the modern example of a rise in sectional unemployment among highly educated white-collar workers, including academics, speaks volumes about the economic position of these workers. In 1969, after almost three decades of unremitting demand for highly educated labor, there was astonishment about the increasing numbers of teachers, scientists, and technicians who were unsuccessful in finding work. At first, teachers and scholars who specialized in fields covered by the humanities were most affected by the decreasing demand for highly educated labor. Then, in 1970, at least 45,000 scientists and engineers were reportedly unemployed and even more underemployed. During the month of November, 1970, the director of the American Institute of Physics recommended that a new federal agency for unemployed scientists and engineers be established.[7] This agency was explicitly compared to the Works Progress Administration, which had provided work for the unemployed during the thirties. The call for a W.P.A. for highly educated professional employees signifies the complex class configurations of the modern period.

Subjective versus Objective Characteristics of Class

Significant changes in the composition/of class and strata relations do not occur overnight. New class relations are the product of centuries of economic and political developments. Class relations may also undergo important and complex changes after they have emerged, and many decades may pass before these changes are clearly perceived (much less understood) by intellectuals (especially when these occur under the rapidly changing conditions of industrial societies). To complicate matters further, the objective analysis of an emerging stratum, such as that of highly skilled and educated professional and technical workers, is made difficult because of the transitional characteristics that influence the intellectual perceptions of themselves.

Analytically, a transitional state simultaneously reveals a number of established plus various newly emerging properties. It also reveals modes of integration of both old and recently established relationships. Under rapidly changing conditions, for example, the kinds of social awareness among the different but neighboring strata of the population may seem to have many similarities because these parts of the population are members of the same language community in certain respects. Since the structural and phonemic characteristics of a language change slowly, the members of different classes or strata may use similar terms but invest these usages with different meanings. Thus, while the language of class adopted by the new white-collar occupations may have been in existence for a century and a half, the social awareness which organized the usages of this language may have been different from that of the traditional middle class.

To some extent, the old middle class in our society integrated its language of class within a laissez-faire liberal conception of society; they perceived their relations primarily on the basis of a mythical economy that was independent of political institutions. The new white-collar intellectuals, on the other hand, emerged in a later, politically and economically different time.

The emergence of a new type of national political economy had a profound effect on the traditional laissez-faire liberal categories of class. New divisions of labor were created by the appearance of giant corporations and the burgeoning governmental bureaucracies that are central to monopoly capitalism. At the same time, members of this new white-collar stratum made a most important departure from all the previous modes by which the major divisions in society have been conceptually integrated. In the formative years, social theorists within this new stratum began to perceive their relations to the rest of society in terms of rudimentary technocratic categories. In the modern period, American sociologists refined and elaborated these categories and theorized that American society was actually composed of innumerable overlapping organizational structures, each of which was composed of functionally interdependent roles. At the center of these structures were "authoritative positions" which integrated institutional relations throughout society. Assuming that persons were naturally competitive when there was not enough to go around, these sociologists believed that most persons were driven by such "scarce" values as wealth, income, or prestige, and freely competed with each other for the authoritative positions. Under these meritocratic conditions, the persons with superior talents and abilities generally won out and, after assuming these positions, guided the development of society in an orderly fashion.

Theories based on notions of this sort were called structural functional theories of society. It was alleged that they were faithful to social reality. Actually, these theories were derived from the technocratic categories and the technocratic utopias which were developed in the formative years. Although there are some parallels between these categories and utopias, and the functionalist conceptions of society which were developed during the medieval period, the technocratic view is an important departure from all previous modes by which major divisions in society have been integrated by social theorists.

NOTES

1. Asa Briggs (1960:53–54) points out that although the phrase "middle classes" appeared as early as 1809 in the *Monthly Review,* the *Oxford Dictionary* gives 1812 "as the first occasion on which the phrase 'middle class' was used." He adds that the instance taken as a warrant for the 1812 date (a statement in the *Examiner* during August of that year) illustrates the degree to which the expression middle class was associated with social grievances: peace and relief were being demanded for "such of the Middle Class of Society who have fallen upon evil days." Among the factors associated with early usages of the term "middle class" were the social protests against the "inequitable" taxation and other "burdens" imposed by Pitt's income tax and the Napoleonic wars.

2. Economic theories, such as the popular theory of rent developed by T. Perronet Thompson (1826), played an important role in this respect. This theory, as Briggs (1960:58) points out, was used to drive a wedge between the landowners and the rest of the community: The landowners were characterized as "selfish monopolists" who protected their own interests against the interests of the society at large. By this time, the middle class was being depicted by its members as the most representative group of society.

3. "To abridge the necessary means of subsistence of the working classes, is to degrade, consequently to demoralize them; and when the largest and most valuable portion of any community is thus degraded and demoralized, ages may pass away before society recovers its former character of virtue and happiness" (Briggs:1960:65).

4. For a sectoral analysis of the economy, see O'Connor (1970). We are indebted to James O'Connor for clarification of the characteristics of the new stratum.

5. The blue-collar portion of the work force during this time has remained approximately the same (55 percent in 1940; 47 percent in 1969).

6. It is recognized that academics have been able to command higher salaries and favorable working conditions during the fifties and sixties. However, these decades may be exceptional in certain respects when compared with previous decades. Caplow and McGee (1958:23) point out, for example, that "as late as 1953, the average annual earnings of *professors* and *associate* professors in *large state* universities compared unfavorably with the wages of railroad engineers and firemen, respectively" (our emphasis). How much lower would this average be if assistant professors and lecturers were included, or if the institutions of higher learning also alluded to smaller state institutions as well as private educational facilities?

7. This call for a new WPA was reported in the *San Francisco Chronicle* (Oct. 23, 1970, p. 5). It should be noted in passing that it is not surprising, in light of the technocratic ideology that abounds in professional associations, that the call for a WPA made no reference to the unemployed workers in the fields encompassed by the humanities.

For an excellent discussion of some of the factors involved in the overproduction of highly educated and skilled workers, see Alan Wolfe's (1970) "The PhD Glut: Hard Times on the Campus."

CHAPTER 69

Words about Academic Freedom

In their adoption of that language of class long utilized by the middle class and self-employed professionals, the early academic sociologists classified the members of the more traditional working class as "hired hands" or "hired men." But they preferred not to think of themselves in these terms, even though the long-term political and economic trends which established the new type of intellectual worker were already beginning to take shape during their lifetime.

Considering that their definitions of class were determined by their liberal ideology, it would be reasonable to expect the sociologists of the chair to have rejected the term "working class" in identifying themselves. Certainly the phrase "hired *hand*" did not reflect their functions as scholars and teachers; they engaged, for example, in mental rather than manual labor. But the term *"hired* men" might have seemed more objectively adequate for characterizing their status as employees, in spite of the fact that they received a salary instead of a wage. However, these eminent American sociologists also felt that "hired men" referred only to the powerless and subordinate relations in industrial and agricultural organizations.

531

Although these sociologists, as late as 1914, were aware of the fact that businessmen who were university trustees often regarded faculty members as their personal employees, these businessmen were considered to be "unenlightened" about the "real status" of university professors. On the other hand, it was felt that the interests of scholars and businessmen were "not necessarily antagonistic" and that "business methods" should definitely be used to make education more efficient (Weatherly 1914:140–141). Because of this, Weatherly (*ibid.*) argued that "the theory of the entrepreneur and the hired man," when it was applied directly to an examination of the work of the academic scholar, created considerable "confusion." Academics, in his opinion, should certainly not be considered "hired men."

Weatherly, who later became the president of the American Sociological Society, expressed these opinions in a paper presented at the annual sociological conference held in 1914, almost a decade and a half after Ross' dismissal. The conference session at which the paper was presented was significant because it was devoted to the topic of *academic freedom*. Statements on this topic were also presented by Henry Pritchett, Scott Nearing, Cecil North, and Edward A. Ross, among others. Weatherly and Pritchett had been asked to make extensive comments on academic freedom; the others were members of a panel that responded very briefly to these comments. A sampling of their statements will reveal some of the objective conditions of work for the academic, as well as the differences among academics regarding the issue of academic freedom.

Academic Freedom Conference

In 1914, at the sociological conference, there were a number of threads running through the discussion about academic freedom. Particularly salient was the belief that academic freedom was a pipe dream as far as most colleges and universities were concerned.[1] As one participant, Pritchett (1914:152), contended: "The mere question of existence overshadows all subtler considerations; and [under these conditions] the college teacher becomes in effect a hired man or, more often, a hired woman." In only a handful of institutions did academics feel economically *secure* enough to insist on the freedom to teach and write as they pleased.

The full implications of Pritchett's remarks about the insecurities of college professors were made explicit by another discussant, Scott Nearing. As an economist, Nearing (1914:165–166) pointed out that the issue of academic freedom was not concerned primarily with the protection of the rights of nonconforming faculty, because they were decidedly in the minority.[2] "The real issue regarding the freedom of teaching," Nearing insisted, "lies in an entirely different direction. There are in every college faculty numbers of men who are under the domination of that most rigorous of all taskmasters, the necessity for providing a living for a family. Even where they are willing and anxious to express themselves, they have this necessity constantly confronting them."

After emphasizing the significance of occupational insecurity on academic freedom, Nearing stated that most college professors are ordinary human beings "with no peculiar abilities and no special talents." "For them, the question of freedom of teaching is one involving their bread and butter. They would speak frankly if they dared, but the sacrifice involved in speaking is too great. *The name of these men is legion in American college work, and their plight is pathetic in the last degree*" (our emphasis).

Ross (1914:166) agreed with Nearing. He tersely noted that "academic asphyxiation is much more common than is generally realized." He objected to parts of Pritchett's statement (to be reviewed presently) which implied that few academics are actually dismissed by universities, much less dismissed because of political reasons. Ross commented: "President Pritchett's paper is, I think, far too optimistic. The dismissal of professors by no means gives the clue to the frequency of the gag in academic life." Ross, of course, was not without personal experience in this regard; officially Ross had voluntarily *resigned* from Stanford, although everyone knew that he was, in fact, forced to leave that institution.

The remarks made by Nearing and Ross were in *response* to the papers read by Weatherly and Pritchett, and will provide a perspective for evaluating these papers. Nearing's emphasis on occupational security, in particular, suggests that *any* standard that determines whether or not an academic will continue to hold his job, must be scrupulously examined in order to evaluate its relevance for academic freedom. This examination, as we shall presently see, will reveal operative interpretations of the principle of academic freedom that were repeatedly used to evade its practice.

Reactionary Observations and Facile Platitudes

Weatherly's presentation at the conference gave voice to the technocrat's dream of "responsible freedom" when he declared that social science will become free only when it is "intimately related to the function of government." [3] After making this incredible claim, he proposed (1914:136–137) a double standard that should be used for evaluating the freedom of "the *employed* scientist" as opposed to "the *individual* scientist" (who appears to have been a free-lance professional). According to Weatherly, "society cannot afford to hamper" the "individual" scientists who work outside of "group agencies." To the contrary, these scientists should be as free as possible. But "scientific work in the universities, on the other hand, must, in the nature of things be cooperative" because "the university involves coordination and teamwork." Weatherly concluded that since universities require "coordination and teamwork," academic scientists cannot be truly free in these institutions. [4]

After grounding his case in the "cooperative" nature of the academy, Weatherly claimed that there were additional factors that had to be considered when evaluating the issue of academic freedom. He stated (*ibid.*) that colleges where the chief function is teaching, as opposed to universities whose faculties do research, stand "for discipline in known facts rather than for the discovery of new ones." "The case for orderly conformity," Weatherly added, "is stronger here, because the college has to deal with a stage of the educational process which is preparatory to *responsible* freedom" (our emphasis). Apparently, freedom is not to be granted to students, in Weatherly's opinion, unless they have been properly socialized. College faculties must keep this socializing goal in mind before they claim the right to academic freedom for students. They must also see that there are limits to their own freedom in presenting their original thinking, as opposed to the higher value attached to contributing to the students' mastery of "a *fixed* body of knowledge" (our emphasis).

Weatherly also indicated that an academic's right to academic freedom should be curtailed if he worked for a church, a sect, or publicly funded institution. Speaking about utopian schemes, he also stated (*ibid.*:146–147) that "untrammeled license granted to irresponsible quacks who pose as scientists is as undesirable as restriction of freedom. The emotional faddist who believes that the whole process of social evolution could be finished up tomorrow morning if his pet ideas were adopted may be an admirable person in other respects, but he has *no claim* to speak in the name of science" (our emphasis). Equally troublesome is the scholar who speaks out on issues that are not related to his expertise: "Whatever practical value scientific scholarship has to society lies in its *aloofness* from partial and prejudiced judgements" (our emphasis).

After setting up the straw man of a social science riddled with irresponsible quacks and emotional faddists, Weatherly suggested further that each profession should develop methods for policing its own members. Instead of strengthening academic freedom through a professional association of college professors,[5] he declared, "The prestige of scholarship would be augmented if scholars themselves should undertake to weed out the incompetent and insist on high standards of ability and preparation for holders of academic positions." "Presidents and trustees," Weatherly added, "could then safely depend on their co-operation in the ungrateful task of clearing out of academic circles the *incompetent,* the *immoral,* and the *'impossible'* who can now be gotten rid of only at the risk of raising questions of violation of freedom where such questions have no proper place" (our emphasis).

Weatherly (*ibid.*:149) concluded his comments by sanctimoniously stating his very deep and abiding personal interest in social change, critical inquiry, and academic freedom: he proposed that the academy should find a place for the "critics, questioners, searchers-out-of-new-things"—for without them, "civilization would perish of self-contented inertia." "There is no fundamental or enduring justification for academic freedom," Weatherly finally declared, "except it lies in a steady insistence on the right to treat every question as an open question. And this is the heart of general freedom itself."

Reasonable Restrictions upon a Scholar's Freedom

Henry Pritchett's paper at the conference was entitled "Reasonable Restrictions upon a Scholar's Freedom." President Pritchett was associated with the Carnegie Foundation for the Advancement of Teaching [6] and he opened his remarks by expressing agreement with Weatherly. He also stated (1914:153) that "there is without doubt a feeling that even among our strongest universities the teacher who has radical views or strong convictions may be put under an unfair pressure." On the other hand, he noted: "So far as I know there has been *no deliberate effort* by organizations outside the colleges or by boards of trustees to control college teaching. When instances of friction have appeared, they have arisen out of differences between teachers and president and trustees in special cases, and such instances have been rare" (our emphasis). In Pritchett's magnanimous judgement, "Public opinion has in all cases so strongly condemned any exercise of pressure upon freedom of speech that such efforts have worked for freedom rather than repression."

These remarks appear to have been highly contradictory to his observations about the impossibility of maintaining any degree of academic freedom in light of the pervasiveness of occupational insecurity in academic life. But Pritchett not only ignored these blatant contradictions, he also appeared to be quite ready to doubt the veracity of those academics who claimed their freedom had been abridged.

Pritchett (*ibid.:*155) stated, for example: "When one looks over the letters which have come in the last seven years to the Carnegie Foundation from teachers who felt that their freedom of action had been unjustly limited, the most vivid impression he receives is that produced by the extraordinary egotism of these productions." "One wonders," he added, "how such absolute loss of personal perspective could come to a scholar, how such egotism could endure in the brain of an individual who has such intellectual cleverness." Since most of the letters seemed to arise out of an "unfortunate egotism," Pritchett remarked that the teachers who had written them lacked sound. judgement and were unable to distinguish between independence and freedom: "A man who accepts the obligations of a college faculty assumes certain responsibilities which limit his independence . . . Freedom may be had within the limitations of an organization. Independence can be had usually only by staying *outside* any organization" (our emphasis).

Thus, Pritchett (*ibid.:*158) felt that professional egotism is the most common cause of the friction between trustees and teachers. Another cause is the choice of trustees "for financial reasons only." He also stated (*ibid.:*156–157):

It is assumed, of course, that a professor who shows gross immorality or incompetency may with justice be removed. But how about a man who is 'impossible,' an 'agitator,' who keeps the college all the time in hot water, and generally keeps the trustees in a disturbed state of mind? About this man the college trustee in the better American college is genuinely troubled. He wants to be considered a friend of academic freedom, but his trained sense of loyalty is outraged. It is very difficult for such a trustee, generally a businessman, to excuse what he considers disloyalty in the college teacher of a sort which he would not tolerate in his business organization. The college trustee . . . fails to appreciate the differences between a business organization and a company of scholars.

Academic Freedom and Rules of the Game among Gentlemen

Frank McVey, president of the University of North Dakota, was a panel discussant who commended the "temperate and wise discussion of Professor Weatherly." He expressed (1914:162) his hope that "this program [i.e., the panel discussion] of the American Sociological Society may mark a real advance in a clearer understanding on the part of the public, of governing boards, and of university men generally of the necessity of tolerance and the wisdom of fair treatment." He also declared that academics must exercise good *judgment* and insisted that "the life of the University depends on its *withdrawal from politics*" (our emphasis). In his opinion, "academic freedom involves both a *responsibility* and a *privilege,* which can be guarded by only one thing—the *courtesy* and *honor* of a gentleman" (our emphasis).

Tact and Good Manners Make Academics "Free"

Edwin L. Earp (1914:166–167) of the Drew Theological Seminary was another brief respondent, and in his reactions to the presentations he emphasized one point that was "so ably brought to our attention by Dr. Pritchett's paper, and also by Professor Weatherly,—namely the importance of wisdom and tact in presenting new truth that may seem to be radical." He informed the members of the panel that he himself, while under consideration for a chair in sociology, had been confronted by trustees with a question about the contents of an article. Earp (*ibid.:*167) stated that the trustees mistakenly thought that he had written an irreligious article. He corrected this mistaken impression in an interview with them, and after they were satisfied that he was devoutly religious rather than irreligious, he observed, "I am glad to say that I was unanimously elected [to the office of department chairman] by the board of trustees, and in all these years there has never been at Drew any interference by the administration with the freedom of teaching in any department." He also indicated that he had knowledge of two professors who were asked to resign or who were not reappointed because of "the *manner* in which they taught," and that what was important was "the *attitude* of the person concerned when the matter was brought to their attention," rather than the subject matter inherent in their teachings. Earp's appointment to the chairmanship of the department had been threatened by the possibility that he disagreed with the trustees over substantive issues. In spite of this, he concluded his remarks by stating that "you can teach anything, no matter how radical it may be, if it is the truth, so long as you capsule it with the *proper adjectives* and present it with *wisdom* and *tact*" (our emphasis).

Brief Indications of the Real Problem

Weatherly, Pritchett, McVey, and Earp denied that there was much foundation to the general feeling regarding the frequency of violations of academic freedom. Nearing and Ross, as we have seen, differed with this conclusion. The spirit of their dissenting remarks was also expressed by E. B. Gowin of New York University. Gowin (1914:164) remarked that stimulating ideas are often called dangerous by powerful individuals or conservative newspapers.[7] He cited an instance in which two professors were hounded by a newspaper for several years and painfully concluded that "it is hard to have one's every utterance examined by hostile eyes, the worst possible interpretation put upon his every act, and harder still to avoid the awkward sentence, the garbled statement, or the misreported utterance that will give his trailers a chance to get rid of him as *incompetent*" (our emphasis).

Cecil C. North (1914:164–165) of DePauw University, another discussant, referred to Weatherly's paper and critically remarked that it did not touch on the important fact that academics had no control over their conditions of work. He declared that some limitation could be placed on college administrators' control over academic personnel without losing the "sincere respect and courtesy which should be paid the head of the institution. But when the payment of respect and courtesy must in some cases go to the extent of servility in order to surround one's department with right conditions of work then we have a right to question whether or not real freedom of teaching exists."

The final discussant, Maurice Parmelee (1914:167–168) of the College of the City of New York, also responded very briefly by expressing his agreement with both Nearing and Ross. He added that there is an even greater tragedy involved when academics "lack the strength and initiative to resist the repressive forces in their environment." In his view, the students themselves were harmed because freedom of speech and intellectual honesty were greatly undermined in the process.

NOTES

1. Pritchett (1914:152) noted, for example, that the great majority of colleges in the United States had had such limited resources that teachers were being employed from year to year. "The position of professors in such institutions," he stated, "seldom involves any question of academic freedom. *The mere question of existence overrides all others*" (our emphasis). The more mundane issues, involving the needs and whims of the job market, contributed to a situation in which "the authorities employ men as teachers and discharge them from time to time as the exigencies of the situation de-

mand." Because of the extent to which occupational insecurity permeated the entire field of higher learning, Pritchett stated that "in only a minority of institutions in the United States does the question of academic freedom present a significant issue." Pritchett indicated that these institutions included Harvard, Yale, Columbia, Johns Hopkins and the University of Chicago.

2. Nearing (1914:165) stated in this regard that "the vital issue involved in the freedom of teaching concerns itself very little with the aggressive, determined man who is constantly courting difficulties, and as constantly extricating himself from the situations which his impetuosity creates. He has something to say; he feels called upon to say it; and he answers the call with vigor and energy. Such men are in the minority in any college faculty."

3. Weatherly (1914:133–134) began his paper by indicating that progressive societies are forever at war within themselves. This is so because "innovation involves breaking 'the cake of custom' around which centers the traditional reverence." As a part of such societies, "the university, if it is to be efficient, is always on the battle line with reference to that part of its function which has to do with prompting pathbreaking knowledge." However, pointing to the areas of the physical sciences: physics, astronomy and geology, which have in the past been in conflict with prevailing conceptions of the universe, Weatherly (ibid.) informs us that "the world" has begun to perceive that it cannot afford to hamper these sciences because they "have come to be recognized as the efficient *handmaidens* of *economic* success" (our emphasis). "When social science shall have been seen to be as *intimately related to the function of government* as chemistry and physics are to the economic processes," he noted, "it will also become free, and for the same reason" (our emphasis). Hidden behind these claims is the assumption that the "handmaiden" has been free to grow and develop at will, unhampered by financial, national, and political pressures and commitments.

4. Weatherly's argument up to this point seems positively irrational. (Why should freedom be restricted because men must cooperate with each other in university life?) However, the logic of the argument may be clarified if it can be assumed that tacitly underlying Weatherly's distinctions between the "individual" and the "employed" scientist, is the old liberal dichotomy between *individualism* and *collectivism*. The scientist who is employed by the university, for example, may be regarded as working for an agency which is by nature collectivistic and, therefore, inimical to individual freedom.

5. This oblique reference to a proposed association of college professors was made when Weatherly objected to the formation of a national organization among professors. Cecil C. North (1914: 164–65) (one of the discussants on the panel), however, responded to this by stating: "This is neither the prime time nor the place to discuss the proposed association of college professors but I doubt whether the subject can be dismissed by simply referring to such an organization as a trade union."

6. Pritchett indicated that he had served sixteen years as a college professor and six years as a college president. As a foundation functionary, Pritchett received various appeals from college teachers to investigate alleged incursions into their academic freedom. Although his foundation had no commission to interfere in the affairs of institutions of higher education, these institutions were requested to provide answers to the allegations.

7. Gowin (1914:163) first made an anti-intellectual statement about "college theorists," however, by observing that it is important for sociologists "to realize from first hand experience the slow and laborious way in which mankind works toward better things." "We are less likely to have visionary schemes propounded about a proletarian revolution if one takes a healthful interest in factory legislation; it is the college theorist, not the professor who serves on a tax commission with them, who believes the men of Wall Street have hooves."

CHAPTER 70

Political Repression
and the Academic Social Sciences

The panel discussion at the 1914 annual sociological convention revealed the technocratic vocabulary that was being generated in the early controversies about academic freedom. The elements of this vocabulary have been as changeable as the social conflicts that created them. Despite the changes, certain general themes remained constant. These included technocratic (1) *definitions* of professional competency and the domain of sociology, (2) *justifications* for stripping the principles of academic freedom of all significant meaning, and (3) *mythical claims* that minimized and obscured the extent and origins of political repression in institutions of higher learning. This chapter will briefly illustrate these dimensions of this liberal technocratic vocabulary.

Corporate-Liberal Images of Dissident Academics

The notion of competency, as we have seen, became an intrinsic part of the liberal dialogue concerning the nature of academic freedom in American universities. During the early history of the discipline, eminent sociologists increasingly regarded laissez-faire liberals and socialist scholars as beyond the pale of sociological competence. During the twenties and thirties, the Christian sociologists (who felt that sociology should be grounded in religious doctrines) were added to the list of "incompetents." In time, the definition of professional competency became thoroughly "positivistic" (i.e., more precisely and perversely, *technocratic*). Some scholars, like Small, who had originally indicated that sociology should have an "ethical" (and preferably religious) foundation, eventually came to reject their earlier ideas as "old fashioned" and "opinionated" and grudgingly compromised with the newer definitions.[1]

The new definitions implied that professionals were competent only if they were ideologically neutral. Operatively, of course, the concept of ideological neutrality was usually interpreted to mean commitment to corporate-liberal interpretations and technocratic standards. Furthermore, as we have seen, ideological conformity was not only demanded in the name of competence, it was also made mandatory in the name of morality. As the 1914 session on

539

academic freedom indicated, the usage of the evaluative term "competence" was accompanied by other terms; sociologists like Weatherly added to the list, for example, that academics should be free to speak their minds as long as they were not "unreasonable," "immoral," "irresponsible," or "impossible." Pritchett, Earp, and McVey, in their remarks, expanded this catalogue of character references by proposing that a scholar should be free to write and teach as he pleased, as long as he was "a gentleman," "well-mannered," and definitely not "egotistical."

Our previous references to egotism, manners, tact, and attitudes suggested the goal of these terminological choices: its implicit object was the ouster of academics who were accused of possessing an unjustified sense of independence, a surly interest in speaking plainly, and a stubborn belief that politics and scholarship went hand in hand. Finally, Pritchett also clarified and agreed with the meaning of Weatherly's references to the omnibus word "impossible." He was using it as a pejorative label for *highly competent* scholars who repeatedly involved the college or university in political controversy.[2] Frequently academics of this genre were also referred to as "agitators." Obviously, the "defenders" of academic freedom possessed a vocabulary that covered all bets: even the *competent* but "impossible" scholars were taken into account.

Separation of University from Politics

These technocratic images of dissenting scholars were not the only conceptual tools to be utilized for restricting the scope of professional conduct and the principle of academic freedom. Another was the explicit claim that the universities should be aloof from politics. (Teaching and politics, therefore, should not be combined in the classroom.) Although the corporate-liberal ideology had finally permeated almost every facet of the educational process in American colleges and universities, it was argued that colleges, in particular, were repositories of established knowledge; academics in these institutions had no other legitimate function than to teach the "facts." If they were controversial, the personal views of the academic had no place in these institutions.[3] Tacitly underlying these arguments for political neutrality, however, were the completely fallacious assumptions that the technocratic services provided by the university to political and economic institutions were not determined essentially by political relationships; and that there was no relation between political ideology and the general understanding of man, woman, and society that was being acquired by students in institutions of higher learning.

The assumptions underlying the justifications for separating the university from politics emphasized the posited existence of the nonpolitical character of university life in general. This emphasis was also evident in the corporate-liberal images of individual dissident academics. Men like Weatherly, Pritchett, McVey, and Earp questioned the dissident academic's manners, tact, wisdom, and concern for others. These images converted political questions into issues of private morality, and dissident conduct was, therefore, considered to be predicated on essentially *non*political differences. But the justifications for separating the university from politics required, in addition, the existence of tacit agreement among liberals about a legitimate sphere for resolving politically controversial relationships. This, therefore, required a definition of the nature of legitimate politics. Legitimate relationships of this kind, as we have seen in the development of liberal-syndicalist and pluralist theories, were being defined in terms of conflicts between "interest groups" that "tolerated" each other and were, therefore, willing to play according to the "rules of the game." Toward the end of the formative years, it became impossible, with this conceptual sleight of hand, to define as legitimate, any political relationship that was not governed in the first place by *accommodation* to the basic institutions of monopoly capitalism. Obviously at this point in the real game played by corporate-liberal social scientists, the notion of politics became defined as corporate-liberal politics, and the locus of political relationships was operatively restricted to a very *limited* set of institutions in the United States (e.g., electioneering or the two-party system). This operative restriction represented, at bottom, the politically sanctioned demand that the utilization of those means for resolving conflicts that were institutionalized by the political state, constituted the only basis on which *legitimate* political relationships could be defined.

Minimizing Dirty Consequences of Political Repression

The early technocratic vocabulary centered on the role of the professional, but it had further uses. Contained within it were standards for buttressing the myth that academic freedom truly prevailed in American universities. One of these standards was incorporated in the phrase "real violation" in reference to academic freedom. After noting that some academics had been dismissed legitimately because they were "impossible," "incompetent," or "egotistical," for example, some of the discussants indicated that there were very few "real violations" of academic freedom by university officials. This claim, by implication, contradicted observations by Nearing, for example, who felt that freedom hardly existed because academics were insecure about their occupational status. It also implied that critics like Nearing were fostering an illusion because they were naive, uninformed, misled, or downright unscrupulous.

Even if the phrase "real violations" was stretched to include resignations that had been blatantly forced by the threat of outright dismissal (as in Ross' case at Stanford), there would still have been *relatively* few "real violations" of academic freedom. However, Ross' and Nearing's remarks suggested that most scholars were dreadfully afraid to express their opinions; they expressed quiet conformity rather than risk the threat of dismissal. Consequently, the actual frequency of "real violations" may have been small in proportion to the *total* number of academics in the United States. But this proportion cannot be taken as an indicator of the more insidious and pervasive form of violation referred to by Nearing.[4]

How shall we judge the significance of the proportion of "real violations" of this sort? It takes a very small amount of arsenic to kill an individual. Is the amount less significant because it is small? Nearing pointed to a general state of conformity in thought and action. Is this general state a better indicator of the quality of academic freedom than the actual frequency of unquestionably political dismissals? When we consider Veblen's remarks to the effect that business control of university life was so powerful that many faculty members did not have to be coerced into conformity, a good deal of light is shed on the actual quality of academic freedom. Those in control had generally selected faculty in *the first place* because they were conformists; or faculty members were *indoctrinated* under these conditions to the point where they gladly conformed. In general, conformity among faculties, in Veblen's view, no longer required extrinsic coercion; it had become largely self-maintaining.

Denying True Origins of Political Repression

Such categories as "egoistic," "incompetent," and "impossible" were not the sole means for concealment of the true origins of the political repression of academics. Such four-syllable metaphors were also combined with outright lies suggesting the lack of involvement of administrative officials, trustees, and nonacademic organizations in political repression. In a totally fabricated statement, Pritchett (1914:154), for example, asserted that "So far as I know there has been no deliberate effort by organizations outside the colleges or by boards of trustees to control college teaching." Pritchett's disclaimer lacked credibility, not merely because he was a foundation official who *regularly received complaints about violations of academic freedom,* but also because it appeared to be a complete falsehood in light of Nearing's, Ross', Gowin's, and Parmelee's publicly expressed observations. As a point of fact, violations emanating from administrators, trustees, and organizations had occurred repeatedly during the years prior to 1914 when the panel discussion was held on academic freedom. Indeed, the next subdivision of this chapter reports a notable violation that was instigated by leaders of a civic organization in collusion with a university trustee during the very same year in which this discussion was held. The victim of this violation, moreover, was Scott Nearing, one of the members of the panel.

Civic Federation's Conspiracy against Scott Nearing

From the period of World War I to the present, the social sciences have been shaped by political repression in one form or another. In 1914 the National Civic Federation became involved in a number of projects aimed at discrediting socialist doctrines and socialist scholars. In addition to a survey of industrial problems,[5] the federation launched a clandestine campaign to destroy socialist influence in educational institutions and the mass media. Basing his work on an examination of private memoranda and letters written by leaders of the federation, Weinstein (1968:129) reports, for example, that these men brought pressure to bear on newspaper publishers and university trustees in order to publicly expose and facilitate dismissal of socialist scholars working in institutions of higher learning.[6] Among the socialist scholars affected by this pressure was Scott Nearing, who had taken issue with Weatherly's presentation; Nearing pointing out the pathetic and servile situation existing within colleges and universities in the United States.

In 1914 Nearing was employed by the University of Pennsylvania. Ralph Easly, a leader of the National Civic Federation, wrote to John C. Bell, a trustee at that university, confiding that he would be sending him material that would be helpful in building a case against Nearing (1914:129). Easly also urged Bell to encourage his friends to become familiar with Nearing's writings and added that this would provide "plenty of reasons why he [Nearing] should have been kicked out of the university long before this." The federation's efforts paid off: Nearing was fired from the University of Pennsylvania in 1915. He eventually received employment at Toledo University; however, he was fired from that institution in 1917 (*ibid.*:244).

Government Takes Over from Federation

As early as 1912, just prior to World War I, a number of socialist leaders were becoming aware of the fact that the government was demonstrating increasing receptivity to the new reformism among liberals. Seeing this as an attempt to preempt radical demands, they urged that socialist programs not be confined to such demands as workmen's compensation, old-age pensions, and the right to organize unions; socialists should also point up the limitations of ameliorative programs and the basic inequities of the social system, which remained unaltered by these programs (*ibid.*:130–131). Men like Nearing also recognized the imperialist and repressive nature of the coming war. He castigated socialist and radical liberals [7] who were being swept up in the patriotic fervor instigated by the Wilson administration.[8]

On the other hand, there were some socialists who were not fundamentally in opposition to capitalism; they agreed with the corporate liberals that the economy could be taken in hand by governmental regulations. These socialists (who were similar in outlook to many German social democrats [9] as well as to the "socialists of the chair") were also influenced by strong nationalist sentiments. They set aside their cries for social justice and joined with militant liberals like Frank Walsh (who had chaired the Industrial Relations Commission) in supporting the preparations for war.

From 1916 onwards, national, state, and local governments in the United States made the voluntary repressive efforts of the National Civic Federation

543

superfluous. The national government actively pursued a policy of "preparedness," which culminated in American participation in the First World War. During the war, the government branded the more militant socialists as agents of the Central Powers and traitors to the nation. Socialist leaders like Eugene Debs went to jail. After the war, socialists attempted to reorganize their movements and regain their prewar strength but their efforts were smashed in 1920. During this period and afterwards, socialists were imprisoned, murdered, or deported, and socialist organizations were decimated by the infamous government raids conducted by Attorney General A. Mitchell Palmer (Preston 1963).

Repressive Rhetoric:
Saving "Democracy" in the United States

Thus, repression before and after World War I belied the platitudes about academic freedom that had been expressed by Ulysses G. Weatherly at the 1914 sociological session on academic freedom. On the other hand, Henry Pritchett's remarks did provide some indication of the degree to which academic freedom would be pushed aside by wartime considerations. Pritchett (1914:155) had called for "tolerance" and "mutual respect" between trustees and academics. But he qualified these remarks by observing that the call for tolerance was not appropriate in certain exceptional circumstances.[10] Under wartime conditions, it was noted, even mild-mannered, eighty-year-old professors are to be expected to take up arms in defense of their country and discard their tolerant attitudes toward professional colleagues with ties in opposing nations. "The professors of England, France and Germany," Pritchett concluded, "have made it clear that when war comes the fundamental human passion overrides all else." [11]

What about the academics who regarded the war with disfavor? Events proved that they were not accorded the right to dissent. Within the institutions of higher learning, the libertarian definitions of academic freedom flew out the window in the face of "patriotic," "hot-blooded" colleagues, trustees, civic organizations, and agents of the government. Even the recently formed American Association for University Professors joined the chorus of voices demanding that academics who opposed the war be dismissed from colleges and universities. Academics could be justifiably dismissed, according to the Association, if they were convicted "of disobedience to any statute or lawful executive order relating to the war." Academics could also be dismissed if they expressed any "propaganda designed, or unmistakenly tending, to cause others to resist or evade the compulsory service law or the regulations of the military authorities." Additional grounds for dismissal formulated by the Association included any action which aimed at dissuading persons "from rendering voluntary assistance to the efforts of the Government." Finally, the Association stated that professors of "Teutonic extraction and sympathy" were obligated to "refrain from public discussion of the war; and in their private intercourse with neighbors, colleagues and students, to avoid all hostile or offensive expressions concerning the United States or its government . . ." Furthermore, the post-war events demonstrated that Pritchett was *not* correct in regarding wartime conditions as exceptional circumstances.[12] Instead of initiating a tolerant period when the hostilities were over, these individuals and groups became interested in "winning the peace." They made the United States itself "safe for democracy" by continuing to suppress dissent. New justifications came to be used for this purpose; scholars like Weatherly no longer made vague comparisons between the radicals of his time and the Jacobins of the French Revolution. Nor were socialists merely called agents of the German government. The danger of socialist doctrines was soon escalated into a continuing contemporary reality made urgent by "Russian Bolshevism" and the "International Communist Conspiracy."

In 1919, the *Manufacturer's Record* and the *National Civic Federation Review* claimed that "Bolshevistic doctrines were being spread through the schools, and certain newspapers rebroadcast these assertions or ran their own exposes of radicalism in American educational circles. All of these accounts were highly colored and totally misrepresented the real situation." Murray (1955:170) indicates that the red scare permeated the secondary and elementary schools: "The classroom was regarded more and more as a holy shrine where only the goddess of 100 percent patriotism, and not truth, was to be worshiped and where no conflicting ideologies were to be either presented or discussed." From approximately 1916 until 1920, therefore, local and federal authorities initiated a wave of political repression that was highlighted by Wilson's Red Scare, the passage of the Sedition Act of 1918,[13] and the infamous Palmer raids. During this period, official sanction was accorded to bureaucratic practices that discriminated against radicals in American colleges and universities. This repression also provided official political guarantees for the corporate-liberal hegemony that had recently emerged in institutions of higher learning.

Repression: Long-term Effects on Academic Social Science

Because of the domination of corporate-liberal scholarship within the academy itself, academic researchers have never come to grips with the long-term ramifications of the periodic recurrence of political repression in the United States. There have been research observations of movements away from politically controversial ideas and activity but such efforts have been made only during recent periods of outright political repression.

Conspicuous by its omission, for example, is research by sociologists into the effects of political repression on the main historical currents in *social thought* within American institutions of higher learning. For example, Lazarsfeld and Thielens' (1958) study of the effects of the post-World War II repression contained unsystematic but nevertheless significant references to interview responses which indicated that academics acted more cautiously and conservatively during and after this repressive ("McCarthy") period. The authors noted that university men and women were withdrawing from political controversy; they were displacing their efforts toward more personally secure areas of scholarly inquiry. The study (*ibid.*:215–217) also provided a few illustrations of the marked increase in conservatism within the student body. Students, it was noted, were less interested in public affairs. Radical thought, moreover, was no longer expressed in classrooms. The advocacy of Marxism, in particular, was fraught with danger.

Another study made similar observations about the effects of the postwar repression. In spite of finding some degree of "tolerance" for senior professors who were formerly communists, Theodore Caplow and Reece J. McGee (1958:227) reported:

The net outcome of the prolonged crisis of academic freedom from 1946 to 1956 is a marked restriction of professors to engage in politics. According to some of our respondents, political activity of any kind by any faculty member is viewed unfavorably and is likely to bar or delay his advancement. Even when this is not a policy of the institution, it is likely to be construed as such by the junior faculty with the result that there is extraordinarily little participation in politics by *the rising young men of the academic generation*. [our emphasis]

There are few theoretical studies of academic repression. On the other hand, the absence of these studies is not surprising. The mystique of a free marketplace of ideas, which is maintained by the technocratic vocabulary of academic freedom [14] (as well as the subjectivism and ahistoricism that plague sociological scholarship), has prevented the majority of academic sociologists from perceiving their most cherished ways of thinking as the products of anything other than their own free choice.

The repression of academic freedom is one of the most significant factors in the development of social science in American universities. The analysis of the long-term effects of this repression, however, is complex because these effects involve relationships that are both internal and external to academic life. These repressive relationships, as we have seen, encompass the bureaucratic controls that (as exercised by university administrators and senior academics) have influenced academic working conditions and hiring practices. Furthermore, because of the identification between the academy and social science disciplines, the effects of these controls have been reinforced by the *professional* definitions of the domains of these disciplines and the *professional* criteria for evaluating scholarly competence. In academic life, moreover, both employment practices and professional standards are, to some extent, formulated, operatively interpreted, and sanctioned by the very same men.

The main trends in academic social thought also reflect the systematic effects of outright, periodic political repression in this country. Repressive attacks occurred, for example, during and after World War I, toward the end of the Great Depression, prior to and during the McCarthy period, in the later sixties, and at the present time. During these periods, overt repression, added to enduring repressive relationships, have provided multiple guarantees for the long-term domination of liberalism within the academic social sciences.

NOTES

1. The nature and enduring character of this compromise are indicated in an observation about the general opinion held by sociologists toward the end of the fifties. Paul H. Furfey (1959:526) states, "The current opinion seems to be . . . that sociology is *essentially a pure science,* but that it also partakes to some extent of the nature of an applied science."
2. Pritchett (1914:153) additionally implied similar aims when he posed this question: "How can a board of trustees which desires to maintain high ideals of university freedom get *rid* of a professor who is *able* but impossible?" (our emphasis).
3. For examples, see Weatherly (1914:137) and McVey (1914:162). It should be noted in passing that forty-four years later in a study of the attitudes of academics toward the political repression during the McCarthy period, Lazarsfeld and Thielens (1958:52) noted that some of their academic respondents felt that radical teachers should not be fired if they were being careful *not* to allow their "extremist" or "leftist" *political orientations to "color"* their classroom teaching. It should be observed, however, that Lazarsfeld and Thielens, two modern sociological researchers, did not inquire whether this rationalization had any meaning in light of the fact that no one questioned whether classroom teaching was being colored by *conservative* or *liberal* political orientations. Presumably these views were either considered unbiased or not biased enough to be included in an evaluation of unprofessional conduct in the classroom.
4. Nor can the cases encountered by the American Association of University Professors be taken as an indicator of the actual rate of violations of academic freedom. The use of these cases in this regard is as faulty as the use of *official* crime data (which grossly underrepresent the amount of crime) for estimating the actual rates of crime in the United States.
5. The federation raised fifty thousand dollars for an industrial survey that included Edward A. Ross among its sponsors. The aim of this survey was to examine industrial relationships in America and indicate reformist criteria for evaluating social progress. The federation report recommending the survey noted that the socialists had received a million votes in the previous election. (These votes were considered to have been cast in favor of "an economic program calling for a revolutionary transformation of society.") The survey, the report noted, would enable the federation to combat the growth of socialism by devising reformist alternatives to social problems (Weinstein 1968:124–127).
6. These leaders, interestingly, were conscious of the differences between socialists. They distinguished socialists who were "not necessarily in conflict with the underlying principles of the existing [capitalist] industrial order," as well as "socialists who, in their view, advocated 'proposals and direct undertakings which are socialistic and anarchistic in principle' " (Weinstein 1968:129).
7. In a letter to Walsh, Nearing (Weinstein 1968:244) wrote: "You knew about . . . Ludlow. You knew who was behind [it]. You know that the same forces are throttling democracy in America today—in the name of liberty in Europe." Nearing also declared that Walsh was making it possible for radicals to rationalize their allegiance to the war effort by lending his name to an organization that supported the government's call for preparedness. He charged Walsh with allowing "the plutocrats" to use his (Walsh's) power for their ends.
8. During the year in which the novel discussion on academic freedom was held, Wilson announced to the U.S. Senate that "the United States must be neutral in fact as well as in name . . . We must be impartial in thought as well as in action." (Message to the U.S. Senate, August 19, 1914). A year later he addressed foreign-born citizens and stated that "there is such a thing as a man being too proud to fight." In 1917 he

faced the Senate again and stated, "I am seeking only to face realities and to face them without soft concealments." The President openly charged that "a little group of wilful men reflecting no opinion but their own have rendered the great Government of the United States helpless and contemptible." Two months later he asked Congress for a declaration of war, exclaiming, "The world must be made safe for democracy."

9. On August 4, 1914, the majority of the social democratic Reichstag caucus voted to support the German government's request for a war chest to *invade* other European countries for "the *defence* of the fatherland." For a discussion of these events and the role of the social democrats in particular, see Luxemburg (1970).

10. Pritchett (1914:155) stated, "for where ought one to look for tolerance if not from the scholar—except of course in war time?"

11. Pritchett (1914:155) used a German "socialist of the chair," Professor Brentano, as an illustration in this regard. He stated, "Even Professor Brentano, whom I regarded in my student days as an elderly mild-tempered man, wields a two-edged sword. This war has at least taught us on both sides of the Atlantic that some allowance must be made for the hot blood of eighty."

12. Veblen (1969:36) also noted that the war had powerfully influenced scholarly activity. But he pointed out that its effect among German scholars, for example, was part of a "reactionary *trend*" (our emphasis). He added (*ibid.*:28, fn. 8) that "something of a correlative change has also lately come in evidence in the German universities; so that what is substantially 'cameralistic science'—training and information for prospective civil servants and police magistrates—is in some appreciable measure displacing disinterested inquiry in the field of economics and political theory."

13. The Sedition Act of 1918 was designed to intimidate and imprison socialists, pacifists, and others who were opposed, in principle, to American intervention in World War I. Many persons were arrested, prosecuted or imprisoned under the act, including Eugene V. Debs.

14. The repression during the post-World War II period predates McCarthy's demagogic utterances. In 1949, as the cold war began to reach a boiling point, six professors were fired from the University of Washington after having been accused of being members of the Communist Party. In defense of these firings, President Allen of the University invoked the technocratic vocabulary of academic freedom with the words: "Having established the nature and the characteristics of the [Communist] Party was inimical to the future welfare of *the institutions of freedom* in the United States, it follows that secret membership in such a party disqualified them for membership in the faculty of the University of Washington within the causes for dismissal listed in the Administrative Code—specifically on the grounds of *competency, dishonesty* and *neglect of duty*" (our emphasis). [quoted in Kirk, 1955:155]

It should be noted in passing that Allen's justification was based on political deception because "the institutions of freedom" in the United States were not threatened in any constitutional sense. Throughout the forties, the Communist Party had actually favored electoral politics rather than insurrection as a means for achieving political power.

PART SIXTEEN

The Age
of Accommodation

CHAPTER 71

Continuities in Liberal
Sociological Thought

Preview

Many differences separate the modern, post-World War II period from the
life and times of the men who founded American sociology. But these differences exist side by side with more significant continuities. This chapter will
briefly discuss the historical parallels between the ideas used by modern sociologists and the sociologists of the chair. It begins by describing some of the
changes in liberal metatheoretical ideas since the twenties. It points out that
sociologists today have carried forward theoretical ideas and technocratic
standards which were developed previously by classical, laissez-faire, or corporate liberals. These theoretical ideas are used separately or in combination
with each other and include egoism, the natural-law conception of scarcity,
the neo-Hobbesian problem, universal exchange, panconflictism, pluralism,
liberal-syndicalism, neo-Malthusianism, and so forth. Various illustrations of
the use of these ideas in modern liberal thought are provided in order to
demonstrate that the *dominant* theoretical assumptions today are grounded in
varied forms of the liberal world view.

Emergence of Modern Liberal Grand Theories

The sociologists of the chair, it will be recalled, were convinced that an industrial democracy was finally emerging and that such forces as the changing mores were prevailing over the anarchic effects of laissez-faire relationships. At the same time, they continued to feel that America was beset by serious problems resulting from heightened egoism and weak social controls. On the whole, they were highly optimistic about the future—a future that would be controlled, but they were realistic about the chaotic and internecine character of life at that time.

The latter twenties, the Great Depression, and the forties intervene between the modern period and the formative years. During the twenties and thirties many sociologists were still under the direct influence of the formative period; consequently they assumed the ubiquity of social conflict and disorder. By the thirties this assumption had become associated with middle-range concepts such as social disorganization which largely referred to communities, and culture-conflict which was usually applied to the study of ethnic and racial groups. During the later thirties and early forties, new developments in research and in liberal-functionalist thought began to prepare the way for the abandonment by leading sociologists of social disorganization theories. Such studies as William F. Whyte's *Street Corner Society* (1943) indicated that these theories were in error, particularly with regard to working-class modes of life.

Whyte's study was based on participant observation of an Italian working-class district in Chicago, and in certain respects was a welcome corrective to the unreal sociological interpretations of working-class life. But there are features of this study that hardly recommend it as a significant theoretical statement of human existence in urban ghettos. Whyte did not ask why this ghetto still existed in an industrial society; it was simply there; he accepted it, and he studied it. He did not clarify the relations between the local, corrupt political machine and the modern, bourgeois state; he merely took this corruption for granted and studied it. Furthermore, outside of the few references to a number of young men in the community who were unemployed, the reader was given no help in making any dynamic connection between the descriptions of life in this community and the fact that these men were living during the greatest general crisis in the history of capitalism—a crisis existing not only in the United States but in many nations of the world. The central observations and generalizations about the nature of everyday life which could have moved this work beyond the boundaries of technographic scholarship were totally missing. But the scholars who considered Whyte's study to be a major contradiction to theories of social disorganization were not interested in these limitations. They wanted evidence of order, and there was no question but that Whyte's study described a very orderly ghetto.

Whyte was a graduate student at the University of Chicago. However, during the thirties, forties, and fifties, Harvard, Columbia and other universities began to assume greater importance in the development of the field. Sociological theory and research also became increasingly diversified. Park and Burgess' classification scheme was gradually replaced by new theoretical ideas.

The rejection of the specific categories created by the grand theories of the early period, however, did not result in rejection of many of the assumptions *underlying* these theories. In the forties and fifties, the assumptions underlying the key-concepts of accommodation and conflict, and the theories of social disorganization, were reformulated and reintegrated with reference to mid-twentieth-century conditions. The socially critical liberal approach to uncontrolled and competitive relations between immigrants, delinquents, or lonely transients in slum communities changed its locale. It was replaced by a liberal criticism of alienated and internecine relations among lonely white-collar workers in large-scale bureaucracies, residents in newly formed suburban areas, or inhabitants of small towns in the post-World War II period. Students of the new approach were eventually called "mass society" theorists.

On the other hand, the single most important metatheoretical development during the postwar period was the highly conservative shift by most of the leading American sociologists toward structural functionalism. The structural functionalists continued to work with the analytic ideas that had been previously subsumed under the key-concepts of accommodation and assimilation, by refining and elaborating them. Although they moved beyond the works of the early sociologists, modern structural functionalists continued to defend historical possibilities of constructive change from a corporate-liberal point of view. During the postwar period, moreover, many structural functionalists believed that these possibilities had *finally* been realized. The stabilization of new modes of integration predicated on the rapid development of the state sector of the economy at home, and on American imperialism abroad, provided the foundations for these hegemonic beliefs.

Upon assuming an undisputed dominant position in the field during the fifties, structural functionalists undertook the task of describing life in the United States. Their technocratic doctrines and natural social-laws obfuscated the causes of war, racism, sexism, and poverty. These functionalists ignored the oppressive nature of the state and made their services useful to the Department of Defense by conducting technocratic research into military behavior. They fashioned their categories into apologetics for imperialism and neocolonialism.

During this period, structural functionalists like Daniel Bell (1956) scoffed at the "mass society" critics of cultural relations in modern capitalist societies. Capitalism, Bell claimed, was creating a new "middle-brow" mass culture. The comic book, dime adventure novel, and popular love song were being replaced by a rich and meaningful culture generated by the growing appreciation of creative arts, literature, and music. Private expenditures on these objects of consumption were even exceeding purchases of tickets to that most venerated of national pastimes: baseball. As far as the majority of the nation's population was concerned, it was argued that monopoly capitalism had brought into being a spiritual quality of life that was unprecedented in the history of mankind. The intellectual praises to the glories of advanced capitalism became so loud that C. Wright Mills, with bitter wit, referred to the 1950s as the time of the *Great American Celebration.*

By the end of the fifties and the early sixties, "conflict theory" was also distinguished as a metatheoretical perspective toward the study of social conflict and conflict resolution. Precisely because it was not Marxian, conflict theory could be generally regarded, by the beginning of the sixties, as an appropriate liberal "corrective" for the extreme emphasis on *order* in structural functionalism.[1]

Abstracted from theoretical works which had been constructed around the sociology of change, conflict theory, nonetheless, never exceeded the basic assumptions associated with Park and Burgess' key-concepts of conflict and accommodation. Although conflict metatheorists such as Coser and Dahrendorf repeatedly indicated that their analytic approach was partly dependent upon Marxian premises, it was Small's, Simmel's and Park and Burgess' panconflictism that provided the integrative categories and mechanisms for their formal approach to human relationships.

Thus, modern sociologists breathed new life into early sociological ideas by transforming them into relatively independent members of a modern liberal family of metatheoretical systems. However these early ideas were aspects of corporate liberalism. Certain metatheoretical systems in the modern period, such as "exchange theory," on the other hand, had their origins in classical liberal and laissez-faire liberal ideas rather than corporate liberalism.

Continuities: Modern Exchange Theory

Among Americans, the process of generalizing the notion of exchange (e.g., integrative exchange) began as early as 1884, in the year marking Spencer's publication of *The Man versus the State.* At that time, Albert Chavannes, an American sociologist, issued a monograph, *Studies in Sociology,* and other writings which contained a formulation of a universal law of exchange. Chavannes' monograph also described a utopian society, Socioland, whose capital city was named Spencer. From Chavannes onward, Americans have been aware of the fact that their exchange notions were generalized far beyond the limits of Adam Smith's economic analysis. Chavannes' remarks provide an almost classical statement of the wider view taken toward exchange:

. . . If Political Economy treats of material production only, Sociology cannot stop there, for its fundamental tenet is that happiness and not wealth, is the real aim of the actions of man, and that all things which help to increase happiness, whether they minister to our physical, emotional, or intellectual faculties, are fit subjects for exchange. [Chavannes 1901:57–58]

552

Homans (1958) and Blau (1964) are modern sociologists who base their natural-social-law explanations of social reality on the rationalities of exchange. Homans represents an extreme instance of the use of classical assumptions (e.g., egoism, atomism) underlying exchange theory. His writings have regarded all behavior as motivated by self-interest, including altruism: "So long as men's values are altruistic, Homans (1961:79) states, "they [self-interests] can take in altruism, too. Some of the greatest profiteers we know are altruists."

John Knox (1963) has written about the very clear parallels between Chavannes' general "law of exchange" and Homan's "exchange theory." Knox (1963:346) concludes that with regard to exchange theory, "Chavannes was ahead of his time; with Homans the wheel has come full circle. It is the *same* wheel, but now it appears to roll over a *firmer* course" (our emphasis).

Continuities: Structural Functionalists and Scarcity

Modern corporate-liberal sociologists like Parsons and Shils use specific ideas which have been largely derived from classical liberal as well as early corporate-liberal ideas. Hopkins, for instance, notes the correspondence between Hobbes' (1651) and Parsons and Shils' (1952) reliance on the concept of scarcity. The following passages by these authors are cited:

If any men desire the same thing, which nevertheless they cannot both enjoy, they become enemies; and in the way to their End, (which is principally their owne conservation, and sometimes their delectation only) endeavor to destroy, or subdue one another. [Hobbes 1651:Ch.13]

Both the facilities necessary to perform functions and the rewards which are important to the motivation of individual actors are inherently scarce. Hence their allocations cannot be left to an unregulated competitive process without great frustration and conflict ensuing. [Parsons and Shils 1952:25]

A comparison of these passages, Hopkins (1957:289) states, reveals "with equal clarity despite three centuries of intervening thought, the naturalistic [i.e., the natural law] premise usually associated with 'the scarcity postulate' when it is used to characterize the individual's situation." Thus, Hobbes may have been thinking primarily about individual landowners and merchants when he was writing, while Parsons and Shils may have been concerned with the technocratic problems posed by "unregulated competitive processes" and "motivations of individuals" who should compete with each other for authoritative positions in society. But all of these theorists wrongly assume that human beings will naturally act competitively when they are confronted with a condition of scarcity.

Numerous other parallels between the structural functionalists and the early period can easily be found by examining earlier and later writings. Parsons and Shils, for instance, identify economics with the study of exchange behavior and the economistic "allocation" of scarce resources. The identification of sociology, on the other hand, emphasizes social control (e.g., the integrative functions of "normative" relationships). Certainly Park and Burgess and other sociologists of the chair would have gone along with this technocratic view of economics and sociology.

Continuities: A Pluralist Academic Utopia

Structural functionalists are not the only sociologists who owe a debt to the formative years. Pluralists also have their roots firmly planted in the early notions about conflicting, yet potentially peaceful relations between tolerant and accommodating interest groups.

A good illustration of modern pluralist theory is contained in Friedrichs' (1970) history of American sociology. His work discounts the role of American sociologists during the formative years and indicates that modern American sociology was primarily oriented toward European scholars. Although he expresses his appreciation of some of Marx's works, Friedrichs' analysis of American sociology is liberal rather than Marxian, and is organized around two ideal-types which divide sociologists into "priests" and "prophets." The "priest" possesses specialized knowledge which has "a truth value" merely because it is based on "scientific" procedures. This knowledge is handed down in a "priestly" fashion to uninformed laymen. Consequently, the metaphor "priest," in our opinion, is used by Friedrichs to classify sociologists who have enunciated the doctrines of technocratic elitism and ideological neutrality. (The term "value free" sociology, for instance, aptly characterizes the "priestly mode" in sociological thinking.) The metaphor "prophet," on the other hand, appears to indiscriminatly symbolize as iconoclasts *all* other sociologists who are committed to reforming man's condition through the instrumentality of science. Thus, Karl Marx, who actually believed that a revolutionary praxis would change society, and the founders of American sociology, who were corporate-liberal technocratic reformers, are all regarded by Friedrichs as "prophets."

In Friedrichs' view, the ideal types, "priests" and "prophets," have been at odds with each other throughout the history of the field. He further suggests that in recent years, the development of sociology can be described as a movement away from a preoccupation with "system (i.e., structural functional) paradigms" toward "conflict paradigms." He states, "the struggle between the system and conflict paradigms may in fact be but a function of a more fundamental shift from a priestly posture back toward a prophetic stance." Among American sociologists, the lineage of the "prophetic stance" can be traced back to Ward, Small, Weatherly, and members of "the Chicago school" whose writings were, according to Friedrichs (*ibid.*:72–73), influenced by their religious backgrounds. Friedrichs, therefore, is implying sociologists are reviving reformist ways of thinking which were current during the formative years. But this revival is restricted in his work to categories associated with the "prophetic" mode.

Friedrichs, however, does not feel that the present shift from "system" to "conflict paradigms"—or from "priestly modes" to "prophetic modes" of analysis—will go so far as to make either "conflict paradigms" or "priestly modes" of analysis the supremely dominating perspectives in American sociology. He predicts, instead, an expanding "pluralist" climate in academic sociology; and he provides evidence for this prediction in a discussion of the growing acceptance of "the dialectical paradigm" among American sociologists. This paradigm, which he mistakenly identifies with Marx, is conspicuously devoid of any of the substantive references which are crucial to Marx's *revolutionary* perspective toward man, woman, and society. Indeed, Friedrichs' antipathy toward the word "revolutionary" when applied to modern conditions is so pervasive that it is even expressed in his differences with Kuhn's theory of the rise and fall of scientific paradigms.

Kuhn regarded the progressive development of science on the basis of *qualitative* transformations to be initiated by new paradigms rather than a *gradual* accretion of knowledge. His emphasis on qualitative transformations was symbolized by the use of the word "revolution" in the title of his famous work: *The Structure of Scientific Revolutions.* Friedrichs, on his part, indicates strong agreement with Kuhn's theory at the beginning of his work; but in the end, Friedrichs notes Kuhn's suggestion that in every field of science, certain paradigms are revolutionary because they *completely* preempt the ideas which previously dominated a field. Friedrichs takes issue with this aspect of Kuhn's theory, expressing the possibility that it may not apply to sociology. He concludes that new developments in the field indicate the emergence of a climate in which old and new paradigms will peacefully coexist in a pluralistic climate. Friedrichs (*ibid.:*325) states:

As a result, 'revolution' may, after a time, no longer be the appropriate image. . . . scientific communities may themselves come to accept a fundamental pluralism as an appropriate style for the life of scientific mind just as much of the larger populace of the West has come to accept pluralism in civic and religious life as an appropriate response to an awareness of the repetitive nature of revolutions in the history of the civic sphere.

It is not only clear that Friedrichs believes that pluralism is preferable to revolution in society at large, but that the present shift among sociologists toward a *"conflict* paradigm" should eventuate in an *accommodative* and *pluralistic* rather than a revolutionary state of affairs. Needless to say, Friedrichs' perspective bears a strong family resemblance to that of Park and Burgess.

Continuities: Modern Liberal-Syndicalism

Interestingly, the works by Robert Dahl, another noted pluralist, are related to the liberal-syndicalism as well as the pluralism which was developed toward the end of the formative period. This relation, however, is obscured by Dahl's limited awareness of the origins of these theoretical approaches.

Dahl's limited awareness is illustrated by his rebuttal to a criticism given by John Case (*New York Review* [June 3, 1971:40–41]). Case noted Dahl's reputation as a liberal and a pluralist who has espoused what is called "the theory of democratic elitism." Case criticized Dahl's recent "worker management plan" because it maintains private corporate property (stockholders and all) even though it ostensibly aimed at improving "industrial democracy" by providing representation for workers on management bodies. Mindful perhaps, of early radical-syndicalist ideas, Case remarked wryly that "the liberals [like Dahl] have run out of ideas, and are wondering if the old radical slogans have something to them after all." Dahl replied angrily that Case's criticism reflected an underlying and dogmatic "nineteenth century" view. This view, according to Dahl, unrealistically perceives the only viable alternatives facing Americans to be either "socialism or liberalism."

Dahl obviously regarded his own worker-management plan as an innovative proposal which had moved beyond "dogmatic" nineteenth-century frameworks. But other corporate liberals likewise perceived syndicalist alternatives to both socialism and (laissez-faire) liberalism. Durkheim, for instance, proposed a liberal-syndicalist alternative that referred to councils of employers and employees in national corporations. There are considerable grounds for regarding Dahl's worker-management plan as an updated variant of late nineteenth-century liberal ideas because it is very much in the spirit of liberal-syndicalism. Dahl, therefore, is guilty of committing the very act of nineteenth-century thinking which is attributed to Case. Furthermore, if his worker-management plan is any example, then the only viable alternatives facing Americans are *still* "socialism or liberalism."

Continuities: Technocratic Standards

Another example of the modern sociologist's debt to the assumptions and standards of the formative years is provided by a noted "conflict theorist," Lewis Coser. Coser's theory originates in the concepts associated with pan-conflictism and accommodation. Coser's works, moreover, provide an illustration of how technocratic standards, established by the early sociologists, govern evaluations of modern theoretical ideas. In a 1969 presidential address to the Society for the Study of Social Problems, Coser (1969) noted that black men are not as occupationally mobile as whites. He alleged that this lack of mobility is due to the prevalence of the so-called "mother dominated" family in black ghettos. Coser (*ibid.*:267–268) stated that, "By not providing its children with the necessary motivations and support in the struggle for occupational status, the matrifocal family and family structures with weak male role models help perpetuate the existing unequal distribution of life chances."

The concept of "mother dominated family" is a sexist category which has been used to cloud the causes and effects of racism in black ghettos. This category was used by Moynihan prior to Coser's speech, in order to justify social policy planning that avoided the macroscopic causes of racism. It did this

556

by focusing instead on the black fatherless family as an alleged cause of racial inequality in economic spheres of life. Apologetic liberal theories of this kind have been opposed by Marxist scholars like Robert Blauner, who placed greater emphasis on the repressive colonialization of black people than on family socialization, in order to explain the position of blacks in the United States.

Coser's (*ibid*.:265) speech, however, took issue with Blauner's perspective because the latter sociologist also maintained that the culture of black people has unique strengths and positive virtues. Coser felt that Blauner's view exemplified "liberal theorizing" and had "conservative consequences," because it did not take into account the adverse effects of ghetto culture or "mother dominated families," on *individual* mobility.

In the critique of Blauner, Coser implicitly and explicitly utilized some of the most significant corporate liberal standards in sociology. These standards include, among others, *individual mobility* in the labor market; successful occupational striving under *capitalist* and *racist* conditions; and *family socialization* as a means to individual mobility and racial equity. These were the normative standards used to evaluate "functions" of black culture and fatherless black families.

Finally, Coser used the criterion of *technocratic intelligence* (i.e., technical information that is useful for technocratic purposes) to judge alternative ways of thinking about racism. Blauner's theory, for instance, was regarded as deficient because it did not take "the facts" into consideration. But these "facts" were *only* significant because of technocratic priorities. Coser did not ask whether black children acquired humanistic values because of their mother's influence. He did not inquire into whether aspects of black culture were conducive to the development of a collective identity or collective solutions to racism. Only those based on successful individual striving in a highly competitive and racist society were deemed important.

Needless to say, the analytic framework and the technocratic standards, which made every one of Coser's ideas plausible and acceptable to many members of the Society for the Study of Social Problems, were laid down during the formative years of American sociology.

Continuities: Neo-Hobbesian Problem

Coser's criticism of Blauner was partly based on a confused understanding of the differences between liberal and nonliberal points of view. Bell (1956) and Bramson (1961) also overlooked these differences when they identified the origins of mass society metatheory with antiliberal modes of thought. According to Bell (1956:75), the "theory of mass society" proposes that changes in "the division of labor" and the "revolutions in transport and communication" have brought men together and made them interdependent. Despite their interdependence, they have grown estranged from each other. Traditional values have been translated into an economic rationality, and spatial and social mobility have intensified status concerns. "The old primary group ties of family and local community have been shattered; ancient parochial faiths are questioned; few unifying values have taken their place." "Most important," Bell adds in his summary of mass society theory, "the critical standards of an educated elite no longer shape opinion or taste. As a result, mores and morals are in constant flux, relations between individuals are tangential or compartmentalized rather than organic." Consequently, there "ensues a search for new faiths." The stage is set for a "charismatic leader" who can guide "the way toward solidary relationships in a world of lonely crowds seeking individual distinctions . . ."

Bell indicates that these views are central to the thinking of "the principle aristocratic, Catholic or Existentialist critics of bourgeois society today." After comparing these views to the neo-Hobbesian statements in early American sociological works, which predate any of the nonliberal critics mentioned by Bell, it is obvious that similar notions had been picked up by corporate liberals during the formative years. In the context of that period, these ideas were used to criticize American capitalism. Furthermore, the early corporate liberals borrowed ideas from antiliberals of the preceding periods, but this did not make their perspective any less liberal than, for instance, Spencer's laissez-faire perspective. The mass society theorists, David Riesman, Nathan Glazer, and Reuel Denney, who wrote *The Lonely Crowd* (1950), are undeniably liberal theorists. Their work is informed by traditional liberal assumptions: the neo-Hobbesian problem of integration; the contradiction between the individual and society; a neo-Malthusian view of the effects of population pressures; competition between atomistic entities; and "adaptive" characteristics of individuals.

Continuities: Equilibration, Natural Social-Law, and So On

Numerous other instances of the continuities in sociological thought are evident. Equilibrium mechanisms did not vanish with Ward's synergetic processes of equilibrium: they are still being used in liberal theories of political processes (e.g., Lipset 1963:8–9). Consider Kai Erikson's (1970) thought that American sociologists are only "gradually" becoming aware of "system maintaining" consequences of deviant behavior: an inspection of Erikson's theory would find that the natural-social-law tradition which underlies his functional analysis is as old as the formative years. If there is any doubt about the significance of early sociology for modern theory in adolescence and delinquency, compare Thrasher's description of adolescent "energies" with the almost identical atomistic imagery in Coleman's (1961) "The Competition for Adolescent Energies." Compare also, Travis Hirschi's (1969) "social control" theory of delinquency with W. I. Thomas' *The Unadjusted Girl*. See the notion of "territorial imperative" in Lyman and Scott's (1967) delinquency theory. For further evidence, contrast the notion of "cycling" through functionally equivalent relationships in Paul Cressey's work with Cloward and Ohlin's (1960) description of similar cycling processes between criminal and warrior or narcotics subcultures. Finally, the reductionist liberal assumptions underlying the concept of functionally equivalent relationships between "deviant" and conventional institutions, characterize every sociological theory of crime, delinquency, or "the youth culture," which has been developed by structural functionalists in the modern period (Parsons 1949, Cohen 1955, Eisenstadt 1956, Cloward and Ohlin 1960, Coleman 1961).

On the other hand, the changes in sociological vocabularies represented by modern, as opposed to early sociological writings, do mirror important variations in the evolution of liberal thought. These variations have been partly generated by academic controversy and debate. But this controversy and debate has reduced ideological and analytic issues to little more than a question of liberal choices: whether to use behaviorist or psychoanalytic mechanisms (e.g. is riot behavior "instrumental" or "irrational"); should the analysis of order emphasize voluntary consent or overt force and coercion; is the modern world best described by conflict theory or structural functionalism; which liberal approach is more appropriate to specific empirical findings or the study of particular kinds of human relationships?

An outstanding example of this "clamorous" liberal conformity is contained in the commentary and debate between John Horton, Bert N. Adams, and Robin M. Williams, Jr. In describing the differences between his insightful analytic interpretation of the "conflict" and "order" perspectives in sociology, Horton (1966:704) presents his conception of "conflict theory" which has a number of explicit Marxist dimensions. In his discussion, the "order perspective" is identified with *liberalism*. Adams (1966) and Williams (1966), however, totally disregard Horton's references to political ideology. Both make all aspects of the argument fit into a liberal mold. Adams discusses Horton's analysis as if the latter conceives of the differences between "conflict" and "order" solely from a liberal conflict theorist's or a pluralist's point of view. As a result, the differences between these perspectives are narrowly reduced to a question of whether one natural-social-law category, "force" or "coercion," plays a greater role than another natural-social-law category, "consensus," in solving the problem of social integration.

Williams, on the other hand, grounds his criticism of Horton in structural functionalism. He also ignores Horton's main argument and arrogantly implies that Horton and Adams are incompetent because they are not aware of such obvious "universals" as the "fact" that "all human populations show both coerced and voluntary authority" (Williams 1966:718). In addition to this bit of worldly (natural-social-law) wisdom, Williams rebuts Adams (and what he asumes to be the gist of Horton's argument) by indicating that both "coercion" and "consensus" play a role in solving the problem of integration as well as change. Their relative importance, Williams concludes, depends on the nature of the problem being analyzed.

In this commentary and debate, neither Adams nor Williams seems to be aware of the fact that Horton identified *his* "conflict perspective" as non-pluralistic. They ignore the fact that Horton also pointed out that "the order perspective" in sociology admitted the importance of conflict but integrated it within the notion of "ordered change." Indeed, Horton (*ibid.*:708) attempted to make this *plain* by linking liberalism, pluralism, and structural functionalism, in the capitalized title to one of the sections to his article: "The *Liberal* Society: *Structural Pluralism* within a Consensual Framework" (our emphasis). But Adams and Williams ignored the Marxist dimensions of Horton's article. In so doing, they acted no differently from the early sociologists who fought tooth and nail with each other over which liberal conception was more appropriate for describing social reality.

Continuities: Liberal Hegemony and the Academy

Academic debates among such liberal scholars as Adams and Williams objectify the analytic, methodological, and ideological issues which guide the ongoing revision of liberal ideas. This objectification, however, is also mediated by distinct liberal "translation systems" which serve to obscure certain ideological issues and certain analytic referents by redefining, vulgarizing, or discounting Marxist categories. When liberal scholars are confronted by Marxian ideas, they strip these ideas of their systematic import, and subsume their concrete referents under natural-law and natural-social-law categories.

These translation devices are imposed in social science curricula in American universities. In graduate and undergraduate schools, liberal academics generally provide students with a superficial, biased, and sketchy view of Marxian ideas. On the other hand, the student's contact with liberal writings is introduced in a very direct and very exhaustive manner. Virtually the entire curricula of the vast majority of departments in the country are organized around the writings of liberal sociologists. As a consequence, most sociologists in the United States have had neither the time, the education, nor the inclination, to deal with the complexities of Marxian thought in its own terms.

This ideological relationship, conducted in the name of academic freedom, is yet another illustration of the continuity between the modern period and the formative years.

NOTE

1. In a discussion of sociological theories of industrial relations, for instance, Edward Gross (1964:632) has stated, "although far from being a dominant approach in sociology at present, conflict theory assumes particular importance as a corrective for other approaches, especially [structural] functional theory which is criticised for its neglect of problems of social change and for ignoring conflict itself."

CHAPTER 72

The Revival
of the Formative Years

Background

Coser's criticism of Blauner, and Dahl's rebuttal to Case, mentioned in the previous chapter, are attempts by corporate liberals to represent their centrist views as being innovative, relevant and correct, in an increasingly polarized world. The sociologists of the chair had also been confronted with political polarization and a hegemonic crisis. They also held the center position from which they engaged in a battle with laissez-faire liberalism and socialism; hence, their writings and their times provide striking analogues to present-day conflicts between liberalism and socialism.

In light of this, it is not surprising to find that the conflicts during the sixties led to a massive revival of interest in corporate-liberal forms of social control and utopian thought. New corporate-liberal explanations of modern relationships organized around panconflictism, accommodation, and other natural-social-law conceptions have also appeared. Liberal scholars have resurrected the neo-Hobbesian problem and the concept of social engineering. This has been accompanied by a revival of interest in early writings which depicted sociology as being socially relevant to the social conflicts at that time.

Presidential Speeches:
High Points in Revival of Formative Years

Innumerable examples can be given of the revival of the formative years. But none of these symbolize this trend more effectively than the yearly presidential addresses that have been presented to the American Sociological Association since the middle sixties. In the stormy mid-sixties, the presidential address by Wilbert E. Moore (1966) recognized that "utopian thinking" had all but disappeared in American sociology. But he reminded sociologists that "never before in human history have so many people . . . been engaged in attempting to remodel the rules and social arrangements that govern man's interaction with others" (*ibid.*:765). Moore offered technocratic advice to so-

561

ciologists who do not want to be crowded "out of the game" by "political leaders and their antagonists." Under these conditions, they were advised to actively formulate "realistic," "deliberate," and "planful" but nevertheless non-Marxist [1] utopian conceptions [2] that would be useful for guiding *orderly* social changes.[3]

In 1967, the presidential address by Charles P. Loomis was entitled "In Praise of Conflict and Its Resolution." Loomis (1967:876) defined "the resolution of conflict" analytically, as "the process by which *mutual dependence* and/or *collaboration* of actors in conflict is, in their own thinking, increased" (our emphasis).[4]

In 1968, the presidential address by Philip Hauser pointed out that modern conflicts have been engendered by revolutionary changes that have transformed little *communities* into mass *societies*.[5] He added that *cultural lag* [6] has also created social disorder. In his opinion, a "new" approach called *"social engineering"* would go beyond "conservative" and "liberal solutions," and could stem the problems generated by this disorder.[7]

In 1969, the presidential address by Ralph H. Turner suggested that the concept of *conflict,* which was developed in the tradition of Simmel, Park and Burgess, is useful for analyzing the public perception of protest.[8]

In 1970, the presidential address by Reinhard Bendix defended the spirit of "independent inquiry, free discussion and academic self-government," which is characteristic of the academic community, against the "distrust of reason" among radical students. Bendix urged modern sociologists not to abandon the *scholarly heritage* that was created during the *formative years* by such men as Freud, Durkheim, and Weber.

In 1972, the presidential address by William J. Goode declared that sociologists have "correctly" urged that normative controls prevent a *Hobbesian war* of all against all.[9] However, Goode cautioned his colleagues also to recognize that human societies have always been integrated by *social controls* based on overt force, as well as normative consensus. Sociologists were encouraged to conduct research into the use of force.[10]

Revival of Counterattacks on Movements for Equality

The recent period has also seen a revival of *neo-Malthusian* ideas among liberal ecologists, sociologists, biologists, and psychologists. These ideas are being used to counter the movements for racial, sexual, and national equality which developed during the sixties.[11] There has been a steady stream of *social Darwinist* works about the causes of war, crime, and social inequality by Ardrey (1963,1966) and zoologists such as Lorenz (1966) and Morris (1967). These Darwinian works have been augmented by psychologists such as Jensen (1969), and Herrnstein (1971), who maintain that social class and racial differences in intelligence are based on inherited traits. The body of this research is being used to reassert the necessary relation between the meritocratic (i.e., the technocratic) distribution of material rewards and the ongoing development of "competent communities." This "necessary" relation, however, is anchored in the pseudo-scientific logics of the formative years. These logics consist of natural-laws and the natural social-law that allegedly (1) govern the behavior of naturally unequal, egoistic human beings under conditions of scarcity and (2) transform outstanding social inequalities into functional imperatives for a stable social order.

This counterattack against movements for equality has been noted by a number of scholars.[12] Miller and Ratner (1972:5), for instance, refer to the political struggles for equality during recent years as an "equality revolution." They then state that "In the pages of *Commentary,* the *New York Times, Atlantic,* and the *Public Interest,* commentators like Harvard's Nathan Glazer, Edward Banfield, Richard Herrnstein, and Daniel P. Moynihan, and N.Y.U.'s Irving Kristol and Sidney Hook demand abandonment of the liberal reformist spirit of the early sixties and the embracing of the society that the decade left us." Miller and Ratner add, significantly, that these commentators "shape the outlook of a large group who once considered themselves as *liberals* and *radicals* and now think of themselves as *moderates, centrists,* and even *conservatives"* (our emphasis).

Two observations can be added to Miller and Ratner's statements above. First, the reaction of the Glazers and the Moynihans et al., was not caused by any change in personal principles. Their commentaries were sharp reactions to the modern surge in demands for equality and democracy because these demands transcended the technocratic priorities that they had *always* supported.[13] The moment these men became aware of the revolutionary qualities of these demands, they turned against them. The reforms they once favored were rejected because these reforms had inadvertantly provided a base for radical, antitechnocratic, grassroots movements during the sixties.

Second, it is important to recognize that prior to the most recent period, there were no stable circles of Marxist sociologists in the academy that could anchor radical scholarship among left-oriented sociologists. Because of this absence, a number of liberal scholars such as Nathan Glaser, Daniel Moynihan, Lewis Coser, Dennis Wrong, Irving Horowitz, and Howard S. Becker could have been regarded as radical, without being systematically challenged on this point. In the absence of Marxist circles, their liberal criticism of sociological writings and American institutions appeared to be "left" of the highly restricted spectrum of opinions in the academic discipline. This restriction, needless to say, was the direct effect of the repression of authentically radical scholars and scholarship during the fifties.

Insurgents and Counterinsurgents

The spectrum of opinion in academic sociology was enlarged during the later sixties because of an unprecedented surge in radical developments. This surge encouraged the development of an authentic "left wing" which is being gradually anchored in Marxian thought. However, such an authentic "left wing" in American academic sociology, having a significant influence in the discipline, *never* existed before these years! And there is still great question whether a "left wing" will ever finally become established during the present period.

The surge in radical sociology after 1968 should not obscure the fact that for three quarters of a century since the 1890s, no important examples of a sustained *systematic* defense of Marxist scholarship by *circles* of academic scholars can be found in *any* subject-matter area in *any* of the sociological journals sponsored by professional associations of sociologists in the United States. Individual socialist sociologists did exist during this period; nevertheless, very few of them were Marxists and almost all of them ran the everpresent risks of being stigmatized as irrational, incompetent, and unprofessional. In 1907, for instance, Lindley M. Keasbey, a socialist who presented a short non-Marxian paper at the second annual meeting of the American Sociological Society, castigated his colleagues for their use of the term "sober" with respect to socialists. In the opening sentences of his paper, he indignantly stated:

If a sober socialist can be found, let us invite him to share in the discussion—such was someone's suggestion. I trust that I am betraying no confidence; the question is from a letter to our secretary, and the phrase appealed to me particularly: "If a sober socialist can be found!" You all know I am a socialist—professionally of the chair, personally of the floor, a sitting and standing socialist if you choose. So it's only a question of my sobriety. Individualists are never called to account—did you ever think of that? They are expected at all times to be sober, and all that goes therewith safe and sane and sound; it is only the socialists that are suspected of intellectual inebriety, unsoundness, insanity, and so forth. [Keasbey 1907:33]

Marxist circles had no significant influence on the early development of sociology when Park and Burgess' universal categories were published in 1921. This lack of influence was either because they were nonexistent, or they were generally excluded from significant deliberations at sociological association meetings.[14] Marx's ghost may have hovered over some of the critical dialogues held by academic sociologists from the twenties onwards. But it is important to keep in mind that *living* representatives, not ghosts, are required to defend, extend, and revise Marx's thought. Because of the long-term repression of Marxist scholars and scholarship, there have been no lasting circles or schools of thought among American academic social scientists representing the world view which has challenged liberalism in all its manifestations.

During the sixties, however, many graduate students as well as younger faculty members no longer took contemporary liberalism at face value. Once again in its long history, this ideology was seriously questioned on a wide scale. Flushed with their experience in civil rights and antiwar movements, armed with a contempt for liberal platitudes, and equipped with more objective understanding of American society—radical members of the new generation of American sociologists made their first significant critical assault on professional institutions at the 1968 annual conference of the American Sociological Association. At that conference, Marxist scholars like Martin Nicolaus justifiably expressed their contempt for corporate-liberal sociology and corporate-liberal institutions in very plain English. Nicolaus (1969:155–156) astonished the members of the profession by observing that,

The honored sociologist, the big-status sociologist, the fat-contract sociologist, the book-a-year sociologist, the sociologist who always wears the livery, the suit and tie of his masters—this is the type of sociologist who sets the tone of the profession, and it is this type of sociologist who is nothing more nor less than a house servant in the corporate establishment, a white intellectual Uncle Tom not only for this government and ruling class but for any government and ruling class.

Many liberal sociologists immediately responded to this assault by deriding the radicals for their "uncouth" manners, their defiant condemnation of the field, and their disrespect for the institutions that academic sociology had served so faithfully. Establishment professionals during and after the conference said that the radicals had gone too far; that American sociology had been at least ideologically neutral, or at most socially ameliorative. It was claimed, in defense of professional traditions, that American sociologists had generally served no other purpose than the "betterment" of mankind.

In subsequent years, the defenders of academic sociology began to question the competency of radical sociologists regardless of the fact that many of these radicals were addressing themselves in an increasingly sophisticated manner, to some of the most complex problems posed by the realities of American life. The radicals were engaging in analyses of ruling class relations, racial inequality, sexual inequality, colonialism, political relations, and the criminal nature of American capitalism. They were also concerned with academic sociological thought, and their exposure of class and institutional biases among established sociologists struck hard in an area where awareness of fact breeds painful knowledge. The nature of radical analyses was the very opposite of the mindless creations that they were made out to be!

During this same period, in American institutions of higher learning, radical scholars began to experience a wave of political repression. This wave was spearheaded in some instances by institutional trustees. But it was chiefly conducted by academic administrators often operating in collusion with tenured faculty members within social science departments and professional schools, or within academic senates as a whole.

By 1971, an unbroken series of articles attacking radical developments in the field began to appear in professional journals such as the *American Journal of Sociology,* the *American Sociological Review,* and the *American Sociologist.* At that time, however, the self-conscious liberal defense of sociological traditions—or the "defense of reason" as it has also been called—became more sophisticated. This defense has, in some cases, recognized the existence of scholars whose works augmented imperialist policies abroad. It has also become somewhat critical of the academic's relations with the welfare state at home. Concurrently, however, it has asserted that the radicals, including the

565

Marxists, who are criticizing sociology today, have themselves been spawned by the very professional traditions they are attacking so bitterly (Gouldner 1970). Refusing to come to grips with a developing socialist sociology, the new defense makes the following claims: (1) Radicals, including the Marxists, have exaggerated the degree to which sociology has been conservative (2) There have been "radical" schools of thought in American universities, even though these schools are either "liberal" or markedly "apolitical" [15] (3) These schools have continued to be "subversive" of established thought and established institutions. In more recent years this latter claim has been generalized: it now perceives an entity called "good sociology" or just a "sociology" that "simply" does its "cognitive job." [16] This "sociology," it is said, "unmasks vested interests" and demystifies the established order.

Park's Race Relations Theory and Good Sociology

As expected, in order to buttress their criticisms of the professional competency of radical sociologists, the defenders of academic sociology began to reach into the stockpile of ideas and standards which were grounded in the formative years. Among these ideas and standards are Ward's positivistic definitions of "pure sociology," which, in the modern parlance, have been translated as "empirical sociology," or just plain "good sociology." Good sociology, in this context, refers to an entity which is above any worldly or substantive standards, except those pertaining to the disinterested pursuit of "scientific" knowledge.

The concept of "good sociology" figured large in an article by Becker and Horowitz (1972), which has recently beckoned radical sociologists "back once again *first* to a criticism of society and only *second* to the criticism of other sociologists." In that article, Becker and Horowitz have informed radicals that "radical sociology" can be "good sociology" if it is purged of ideological bias; if it is above "parochialism" and "patriotism;" if it owes no allegiance to any social system such as capitalism or socialism; and if it engages in a "valid causal analysis" of social reality.

Radicals, of course, can take Becker and Horowitz's advice at face value and inquire into whether a "good sociology" of this kind actually exists. But an inquiry of this sort would discover that their own article presented an example of a "good" sociological analysis of the conflicts between radical and nonradical sociologists. This analysis, moreover, was structured by *interest-group* categories, based on *pluralist* and *conflict theory* assumptions, which are so formal that all of the ideological and material causes of the conflicts disappear from sight. [17]

Radicals might also inquire into the kinds of theories Becker and Horowitz recommend for the critical analysis of American society. But in this inquiry it will be discovered that these authors actually recommend an assortment of *liberal-functionalist theories,* including Park's theory of race relations. This

566

theory is recommended because "the concept of accommodation," in Becker and Horowitz's (*ibid.*:51) opinion,

> . . . can be objectionable only if we insist that its use will necessarily cause sociologists to overlook or ignore conflict, exploitation, or resistance to change where they occur. But a *full explanation of possibilities,* as in Robert Park's description of the race relations cycle (Park and Burgess 1921), applied evenhandedly, should spare sociologists such errors._[our emphasis]

Finally, radicals might inquire into the kinds of "scientific" criteria Becker and Horowitz recommend for verifying the "objective" nature of the world. But an inquiry of this kind would discover that they recommend positivistic criteria which are partly derived from the old-fashioned epistemology of classical empiricism. These authors indicate that sociologists, for various reasons, select "causes" from a "multiplicity of causes" (as one might perhaps select fruits and vegetables in a grocery store). This selection, in their view, is validated by the use of participant observation, survey questionnaires, and statistical methods. If verified, the process of choosing causal variables produces an objectively given reality which is independent of the world-view which structured the variables and research in the first place. The application of "objective" and "scientific" criteria, according to Becker and Horowitz, would help generate causal explanations which would be useful to everybody regardless of ideology. Consequently, they state (*ibid.*:60–61), "If we had a *decent* theory of consumer behavior, empirically validated, then the *radical,* knowing how advertising works, would know where to intervene so that it would not work, and the *marketing expert* would know why his techniques fail and how to improve them" (our emphasis). Both the radical and the technocrat would be the beneficiaries of a "good," "decent," that is, an ideologically free sociology.

It is on the basis of this kind of reasoning that Becker has also stated, "Good sociologists produce radical results." The meaning of his terminology is made clear in the additional comment, "What I mean by a radical result is one that rises above current orthodoxies, whether they are political, moral, institutional, scientific, or whatever. That may or may not go with political radicalism, conventionally defined" (Debro 1970:171).

NOTES

1. Moore's understanding of Marxian concepts is on the same level as Albion Small's. Instead of representing the Marxian concept of ruling class properly, Moore (1966:769) states, "The Marxists generally have been deluded into thinking of a social system as held together by a conspiratorial group wielding overt and subtle power, and barely containing the deep-seated conflicts of unwilling or unwitting participants." In this statement, Moore vulgarizes Marxian ideas which are associated with concepts of ruling class, hegemonic, and state relations.

2. Apparently, Moore considers his utopian conceptions to be more "realistic" than Marx's, because they recognize the Hobbesian nature of man. Moore (1966:771) observes that "the only effective enemy of man is man himself. . . . Given scarce resources at any given time, there is likely to be a bit of dispute . . . over their allocation, and indeed over priorities in goals." However, Moore feels that in spite of this, men

everywhere can build a better society because of their common interests in such things as long life and material well-being.

3. Since 1966, an extraordinary number of liberal utopian writings have appeared. There are now utopian periodicals and utopian "commissions" (e.g., the "Commission on the Year 2000," which is chaired by Daniel Bell). Most of these publications and "commissions" are dominated by technocratic intellectuals.

4. To his credit, Loomis criticizes the use of "bargaining" (i.e., "higgling") mechanisms in sociological analyses of conflict resolution. But his references to conflict are nevertheless liberal rather than Marxian.

5. Hauser's version of the neo-Hobbesian problem is indebted to Malthus as well as Tönnies. Hauser (1969:8) claims that *population* changes have "profoundly altered . . . the social order" because they have generated among other relationships: "secondary groups" instead of "primary groups," "rational" in comparison to "traditional behavior," "relations of utility" rather than those of "emotion and sentiment," "the nuclear family" instead of the "extended family," and "bureaucratic" rather than "small scale and informal organizations." In short, according to Hauser (*ibid.*), these changes have "transformed the little *community* which has characterized predecessor societies into the 'mass *society*' " (our emphasis).

6. Cultural lag in Hauser's explanation appears to pose the problem of integration more directly than some of the other relationships that he uses to account for social disorder and change. It appears that population changes have created cultural lag; cultural lag, in turn, has generated social disorder.

7. Hauser (1969:14) states, "The social engineering position . . . represents an utterly new approach born of the social morphological revolution to cope with the new problems engendered by it." "It is my judgment," Hauser (*ibid.:*15) continues, "that had this nation possessed a [national] Council of Social Advisors since 1947, along with the Council of Economic Advisors . . . the 'urban crisis' which surely affects us would not have reached this present acute stage."

8. Turner's speech is fascinating because it reveals the ways in which liberal analytic categories can be used to formulate a research perspective toward the phenomenon of public opinion. It is also interesting because it lacks any macroscopic and historical theory that can account for the ways in which various segments of the population perceive reformist or revolutionary movements and events. A theory, if formulated, should, at the very least, give strong consideration to the degree to which hegemonic intellectuals like Simmel, Park, and Burgess formulated ideas that were used to shape the character of public opinion, particularly among those sectors of the population that are most amenable to liberal ideas (e.g., the *technocratic* administrators and intellectuals). Park and Burgess' theory may help explain "the public perception of protest" because they may have had something to do with the creation of this perception in the first place.

9. Referring to Parsons as a case in point, Goode (1972:509) stated that "Sociologists have urged, correctly I think, that if people and groups act only with a rational view to their personal profit and with no inner normative controls, then group structures, goals, and controls would be unsupported and a war of all against all will result."

10. In urging sociologists to study uses of force, Goode pointed out: "The higher the level of management tasks to be accomplished, the less efficacious is a strong component of overt force;" and, "The greater the likelihood that force is used overtly by authorities, the more likely that it will be viewed by those authorities and outsiders as necessary and approved" (Goode 1972:517). Goode's generalizations are reminiscent of Ross' "administrative handbook."

11. Robert Chrisman (1970) describes the conservative liberal trends in the ecology movement and the movement's ties to early liberal ideas such as neo-Malthusianism. Emphasizing its racist conceptions of population control, Chrisman's analysis concludes that "White as Moby Dick, the ecology fad seems bent on creating some kind of white haven or heaven in what is left of the earth. Recognizing the fearful damage the modern military industrial complex has done to its material resources, the liberal bourgeoisie of the U.S. has come up with a solution which will not threaten the fundamental power of private industry and will guarantee that Third World peoples will not industrialize but will remain agricultural. The liberal middle class will be relieved of its burdens of conscience, and nothing will be confronted or resolved; the imperialist oppres-

sion will remain and so will the basic standard of living it enforces" (Chrisman 1970:49).

12. See, for example, the entire issue of *Social Policy* 3 (May/June) 1972.

13. Shaffer (1971:154) points out, for example, ". . . for those who are concerned with 'participatory democracy,' the failure of community action [programs] should be nothing other than expected. As Rubin Levitan and Moynihan have demonstrated, the effort was never intended to result in a restructuring of the social order. At best, participation was to be an educative device by which the *status quo* would be maintained, perhaps with a slightly broadened constituency."

14. It is recognized that there are isolated cases of individual scholars who have participated in sociological meetings or have been published infrequently in professional journals. The crux of our remarks, however, rests, as it should, on whether there were stable schools of nonliberal and radical thought in either the early or later periods. A school of thought requires the existence of stable *circles* of scholars, not token representation.

15. The identity of these schools is so varied that the only principle that seems to apply in their selection is that they are not identified with patently conservative schools of thought such as structural functionism.

16. "Simply by doing its cognitive job," Berger (1971:2) states, for example, "sociology puts the institutional order and the legitimating thought patterns under critical scrutiny . . . It unmasks vested interests and makes visible the manner in which the latter are served by social fictions." Berger claims that sociology has been "subversive" of established institutions and, therefore, radical youth have mistakenly stereotyped the academic discipline when they regard it only as a conservative force.

17. Becker and Horowitz's analysis indicates that various groups among sociologists have emerged in the wake of criticism, showing that research has furthered "the interests of the powerful" at "the expense of the powerless." The "positions" of these groups "have hardened" in a polemical process. "Radical groups" in particular have "tried to maximize their private interests" in a situation of "collective upheaval." "Conflicts of interest" have appeared among blacks, chicanos, and women's groups. Participants in these events have become "confused." The authors claim to present an ideologically free "good sociology" as a way out of this confusion.

CHAPTER 73

The Age of Accommodation

Historical Lessons:
Conservatizing Functions of Liberal Conflicts

Becker and Horowitz may not be aware of the degree to which their concept of "good sociology" is informed by the shopworn ideological ideas associated with panconflictism and pluralism of the formative years. They may also be unfamiliar with the degree to which Park and Burgess' concept of accommodation was useful in restricting the study of historical possibilities for achieving racial equality. And quite probably, they are unaware of the shallow

569

classical underpinnings of their positivistic philosophy of science. But today, radical sociologists, left-liberal and Marxists alike, are no longer naive members of a corporate-liberal academic culture. These radicals are now questioning whether it is at all possible to develop an objective as well as a liberating social science on the basis of the stockpile of liberal categories which are largely taken-for-granted in the field as a whole.

These radicals are aware that American sociologists will never develop a scientific theory of social life or a radical criticism of American society, without simultaneously engaging in a vigorous, fundamental criticism of the ruling ideas and the ruling institutions which have dominated their field for three quarters of a century. But this kind of criticism cannot emerge spontaneously on the basis of good intentions. This criticism, itself, must be informed by a materialist conception of history and a materialist philosophy of science.

Today, genuinely egalitarian and humanistic sociologists, who are alarmed by the technocratic and repressive usage of their social science, are again searching the past in order to find new ways of revitalizing their decrepit discipline. In their studies of the writings of early sociologists, however, they should be forewarned to keep in mind that corporate-liberal theory is not separable from corporate-liberal practice. Historical dynamics have based customary styles of research on abstract, universal liberal ideas and organized the roles of the professional analyst around the activities of the professional reformer. In light of this, it is not unreasonable to claim that only Marxism, not corporate liberalism, will revitalize American sociology.

The necessity for a Marxist sociology is being implicitly countered by contemporary liberal studies of American sociology. These historical studies anticipate the development of an accommodative, pluralist academic utopia, or an accommodation between Marxism and liberalism (Gouldner 1970, Friedrichs 1970). The empirical justifications for these anticipated developments are organized around ideal types which highlight the differences between analytic and reformist trends in academic sociology. But these ideal types obscure the fact that conflicts between the representatives of these trends are largely generated by contradictions between the idealistic nature of bourgeois social science and the material services this science performs for capitalist institutions.[1] The periodic resolution of these contradictions has maintained the viability of liberalism and liberal institutions. It has never transcended these ideological and institutional relationships.

Upon evaluating the recent historical studies of American sociology, it should be kept in mind that the relations between (1) the institutional practices which maintain capitalism and (2) the theories which have dominated bourgeois social science, have been contradictory as well as mutually interactive. Furthermore, the most significant changes in liberal ideas have emerged out of the conflicts among liberal intellectuals. These conflicts are related to the broader contradictions within the society at large. When liberal institutions fail to stabilize political and economic relations, a substantial crisis occurs in the American social sciences. In modern sociology, crises of this sort have emphasized the differences between the technocratic analysts and technocratic reformers. But the ensuing conflicts among these sociologists have not transcended liberalism. Instead, these conflicts have generally operated as a mechanism for revitalizing liberal-functionalism.

Consequently, the crises in American sociology are not created by "value-free" *theorizing* or the technocratic qualities of academic *ideas*. These qualities have been present from the very inception of the field. The current failure of American sociology has been generated by the fact that the fundamental instabilities in American institutions once again have come to a head. These instabilities, which are expressions of the basic contradictions in American capitalism, have never been controlled on a long-term basis. Because of this, no liberal pragmatics organized around the maintenance of order in modern capitalism has ever achieved its prime goals except for very short periods of time. But many liberal scholars in the American academy will keep trying to readjust their ideas to capitalist realities in the vain hope of solving the real problems of social integration.

Consequently, radicals should not be deluded into believing that the long-term instabilities in academic sociology, which are engendered by material and ideological contradictions in the world at large, will automatically move their field leftwards; indeed, the opposite may well be the case. Contradictory relations among liberal sociologists may resurrect the field; and repressive trends in the academy and the nation may make the establishment of an authentic left wing an impossibility in the immediate future.

Historical Lessons:
Consolidation and Extension of Radical Developments

Radical sociologists exist in a hostile environment. They are being criticized by liberal scholars who seek to affirm the existence of a "logic of science" which is independent of the struggle between materialist and idealist views of the world. Their competence is being evaluated on the basis of technocratic doctrines that obfuscate even the most blatant politically biased distribution of technical human resources in America today. They are being required to research American society without questioning the fundamental categories which underlie sociological research, as if research guided by good intentions alone will somehow "spontaneously" produce a radical sociological tradition. The academic division of labor, which is exemplified by tables of academic organization and the boundaries between academic disciplines and professional schools, operates against the development of a radical tradition.

The hostile nature of the academic environment defies any simple explanation (of academic developments) based on a conspiracy theory of history. It involves instead the most complex processes by which ideological hegemony is unceasingly generated among intellectuals in our society. But this history of repression in the American academy clearly indicates the necessity today to

571

make collective efforts to consolidate and extend radical developments in the face of the growing counterattack against radicalism in the academy, the profession, and the society at large. These efforts should be concerned with the development of radical associations.[2] In these associations, sociologists should consider the avenues and methods by which they can integrate their activities with political movements in the local communities, universities and the nation. "Tithing systems" and "defense funds" can be developed in order to provide temporary aid to sociologists who have been cut down by the ongoing repression. Radical journals should be given far more personal support than one would give to an established journal.[3] Attempts should be made to develop sociological collectives and correspondence societies among radical students and faculty members alike. Without these collective efforts, individual radicals may find the reconstruction of the analytic, methodological, and ethical foundations of the field to be an insurmountable task.

Dawning of the Age of Accommodation

Thus, collective efforts among radicals must take place independently of those institutional forms which make academic sociology what it is. The categories handed down by the sociologists of the chair were created by institutionally related activities: the category of social control, for instance, was a *socially* produced category. It cannot be explained by any epistemological model which views the production of social thought on the basis of one or two intellectuals and their objects of inquiry. This category was generated by innumerable scholars who criticized, refined, elaborated, and systematized each other's ideas. Their dialogues were carried aloft by the evolution of capitalism itself and it is this same evolutionary development which has breathed new life into the formative years.

Looking back to the formative years, sociological historians such as Robert Nisbet (1966) contend that liberal scholarship at the turn of the century represented the culmination of a golden age in social thought. Men like Durkheim, Weber, Simmel, Freud, and Tönnies are considered the foremost products of this golden age, and those who followed in their footsteps were, by implication, their scions. Our present volume, however, has presented a Marxist view of the long-term trends in social thought. It has suggested that establishment sociology, as an outcome of the most abstract ideas produced during the formative years, has been able to justify social repression in the name of freedom; to color technocratic aims with humanitarian sounding platitudes; and to mask ideological engagement with the doctrine of ideological neutrality. The formative years did not represent the culmination of a golden age; they were the dawn of an age of stone.

Modern sociologists like Reinhard Bendix (1970) have claimed that the writings of "classical" sociologists at the turn of the century were informed by the traditions of rationalism and romanticism, which emerged in the eighteenth and nineteenth centuries. But this volume has shown that works by Europeans and Americans during the formative years were not actually generated by a desire for an enlightened accommodation between rationalism and romanticism. The writings by corporate liberals operatively represented an intellectual accommodation to imperialism and monopoly capitalism. Neither the *liberating* passions nor the rational *optimism* that emerged toward the end of the Age of Reason, informed the European or American corporate liberals at the turn of this century.

It should also be recalled that modern sociology began during the formative years when the pioneering sociologists in America were preoccupied with the maintenance of capitalism, not its destruction. In their reformist zeal to achieve both order and progress, they condemned the egotistical souls of the business barons but declared that the conflict between syndicated capital and labor was reconcilable. They illuminated their sociological visions of a capitalist utopia with the shiny faces of efficient people bound together in the mythical solidarity of bygone days. The spirits of Malthus, Comte, and Darwin walked through their pages and even Christ himself was called upon in their time of need. For four stormy decades they employed the writings of the quick and the dead to revitalize the universal ideas of nineteenth-century liberalism.

In truth, the leading members of the new generation of sociologists had begun, in the 1920s, to abandon the secular and religious images of the benevolent humanitarianism that had justified their conservative reformist tradition. In a climate of political repression, men like Park, Burgess, and Ogburn consolidated the metatheoretical developments in the field and replaced the liberal *technocratic* rhetoric of benevolence with the liberal *technocratic* rhetoric of neutrality. The clarion voice of the social reformer became muted; the cautious professional tone of the "pure" academic scientist and the clean-cut image of the administrative-consultant now stood alone: the standardization of a formal ensemble of categories and the professionalization of the field finally brought the pioneering phase of sociology to an end. In 1921 and 1922—at the pinnacle of its early development—a new phase in the modern history of the field began.

Today—a half century later—the present generation of corporate-liberal sociologists is attempting to accomplish the same ends after another extraordinarily critical period in the history of our nation. Again the effort to restore the legitimacy of a decrepit ideology is being buttressed by political repression both inside and outside the academy. Whatever the degree of success obtained by this oppression, one thing is certain: corporate liberalism will not endure, because monopoly-state capitalism can never be stabilized for long. This ideology and political economy will be confronted by radical Americans time and again until both of them are consigned to the historical oblivion they so richly deserve.

NOTES

1. These contradictions are reflected in Moynihan's (1969) complaint that the war on poverty failed partly because the means for implementing this reformist policy rested on such "dubious" social science theories as the "anomie theory."

2. The Union for Radical Political Economics might be a suitable model for these associations. Associations which cut across disciplines and professional schools should also be considered.

3. Journals of this kind include, for instance, *Insurgent Sociologist* and *Socialist Revolution.*

BIBLIOGRAPHY

ADAMIC, LOUIS. 1968. *Dynamite, the Story of Class Violence in America,* New York: Chelsea House. (Originally published in 1931.)

ADAMS, BERT N. 1966. "Coercion and Consensus Theories: Some Unresolved Issues." *American Journal of Sociology* 6 (May): 714–717.

ADAMS, GRAHAM, JR. 1966. *Age of Industrial Violence, 1910–1915.* New York: Columbia University Press.

ALLEN, FREDERICK LEWIS. 1959. *Only Yesterday.* New York: Bantam Books.

ALLPORT, GORDON W. 1954. "The Historical Background of Modern Social Psychology." *Handbook of Social Psychology, I.* Gardner Lindzey, ed. Reading, Mass.: Addison-Wesley: 3–56.

AMERICAN SOCIOLOGICAL SOCIETY. 1906. "Editorial." Conference Papers and Proceedings: 1–2.

ANDERSON, NELS. 1923. *The Hobo.* Chicago: University of Chicago Press.

APTHEKAR, BETTINA. 1970. "Berkeley's Meddlesome Regents." *The Nation* 211 (September 7): 169–173.

ARDREY, ROBERT. 1963. *African Genesis.* New York: Dell Publishers.

———. 1966. *The Territorial Imperative.* New York: Dell Publishers.

ARNOLD, THURMAN W. 1937. *The Folklore of Capitalism.* New Haven: Yale University Press.

ASAKAWA, K. 1907. Response to "The Significance of the Orient for the Occident" by William I. Thomas. *Papers and Proceedings of the American Sociological Society* 2 (December): 131–134.

AUSTIN, ALEINE. 1949. *The Labor Story.* New York: Coward-McCann.

AYDELOTTE, FRANK. 1913. *Elizabethan Rogues and Vagabonds.* Oxford: Clarendon Press.

BACHOFEN, JOHANN J. 1861. *Das Mutterrecht.* Stuttgart: Krais and Hoffman.

BARAN, PAUL AND PAUL M. SWEEZY. 1966. *Monopoly Capital.* New York: Monthly Review Press.

BARITZ, LOREN. 1960. *The Servants of Power, A History of the Use of Social Science in American Industry.* Middletown, Conn.: Wesleyan University Press.

BARNES, HARRY ELMER. 1948. "Albion Woodbury Small: Promoter of American Sociology and Expositor of Social Interests." *Introduction to the History of Sociology,* Harry Elmer Barnes, ed. Chicago: University of Chicago Press: 766–792.

———. 1948. "The Social Philosophy of Ludwig Gumplowicz: The Struggle of Races and Social Groups." *Introduction to the History of Sociology,* Harry Elmer Barnes, ed. Chicago: University of Chicago Press: 191–206.

BARROWS, ISABEL C. 1908. Response to "How Does the Access of Women to Industrial Occupations React on the Family?" by Ulysses G. Weatherly. *Papers and Proceedings of the American Sociological Society* 3 (December): 147–149.

BAWDEN, H. HEATH. 1903. Review of *Pure Sociology: A Treatise on the Origin and Spontaneous Development of Society* by Lester Ward. *American Journal of Sociology* 9 (November): 408–415.

BEBEL, AUGUST. 1897. *Women in the Past, Present and Future.* San Francisco: G. B. Benham.

———. 1928. "War on the Palaces; Peace to the Cottages." (Delivered to the Reichstag on May 25, 1871). *Speeches of August Bebel.* New York: International Publishers.

BECK, HUBERT PARK. 1947. *Men Who Control Our Universities; the Economic and Social Composition of Governing Boards of Thirty Leading American Universities.* New York: King's Crown Press.

BECKER, CARL. 1936. *Progress and Power.* Stanford: Stanford University Press.

Bibliography

BECKER, ERNEST. 1968. *The Structure of Evil.* New York: George Braziller.
BECKER, HOWARD. 1950. *Through Values to Social Interpretation.* North Carolina: Duke University Press.
BECKER, HOWARD S. 1953. "Becoming a Marihuana User." *American Journal of Sociology* 59 (November): 235–242.
———— AND IRVING LOUIS HOROWITZ. 1972. "Radical Politics and Sociological Research: Observations on Methodology and Ideology." *American Journal of Sociology* 78 (July): 48–66.
BECKER, JAMES F. 1961. "Adam Smith's Theory of Social Science." *Southern Economic Journal* 28 (July): 13–21.
————. 1964. "Utilitarian Logic and the Classical Conception of Social Science." *Science and Society* 28 (Winter): 161–182.
BELL, DANIEL. 1953. "Crime as an American Way of Life." *The Antioch Review* 13 (June): 131–154.
————. 1956. "The Theory of Mass Society." *Commentary* 22 (July): 75–83.
————. 1960. *The End of Ideology.* New York: The Free Press.
————. 1969. Introduction to *The Engineers and the Price System* by Thorstein Veblen. New York: Harcourt, Brace and World: 2–35.
BENDIX, REINHARD. 1970. "Sociology and the Distrust of Reason." *American Sociological Review* 35 (October): 831–843.
BENTHAM, JEREMY. 1907. *An Introduction to the Principle of Morals and Legislation.* Oxford: Clarendon Press. (Originally published in 1789; reprinted and "corrected by the author" in 1823.)
BERGER, PETER L. 1971. "Sociology and Freedom." *The American Sociologist* 6 (February): 1–5.
———— AND THOMAS LUCKMANN. 1966. *The Social Construction of Reality, a Treatise on the Sociology of Knowledge.* New York: Doubleday.
BERLE, A. A. 1954. *The 20th Century Capitalist Revolution.* New York: Harcourt, Brace and World.
BERNARD, L. L. 1924. *Instincts: A Study in Social Psychology.* New York: Henry Holt.
———— AND JESSIE BERNARD. 1943. *Origins of American Sociology; the Social Science Movement in the United States.* New York: Thomas Y. Crowell.
BIRNBAUM, NORMAN. 1969. "On the Sociology of Current Social Research." 2 (Fall): 5–9.
BLAKE, JUDITH AND KINGSLEY DAVIS. 1964. "Norms, Values, and Sanctions." *Handbook of Modern Sociology,* Robert E. L. Faris, ed. Chicago: Rand McNally: 456–484.
BLANCHARD, PHYLLIS. 1920. "Psychoanalysis and Some Concrete Social Problems." *Publications of the American Sociological Society* 15 (December): 208–210.
BLAU, PETER. 1964. *Exchange and Power in Social Life.* New York: John Wiley.
BLUMENTHAL, ALBERT. 1938. *Small Town Stuff.* Chicago, Ill.: University of Chicago Press.
BOGGS, JAMES. 1970. "Uprooting Racism and the Racists in the United States." *Black Scholar* 2 (October): 2–10.
BORCHARD, RUTH. 1957. *John Stuart Mill, the Man.* London: C. A. Watts.
BORDUA, DAVID. 1961. "Delinquent Subcultures: Sociological Interpretations of Gang Delinquency." *The Annals of the American Academy of Political and Social Science* 338 (November): 120–136.
BORENZWEIG, HERMAN. 1970. "Social Work and Psychoanalytic Theory: A Historical Analysis." *Social Work* 16 (January): 7–16.
BRAMSON, LEON. 1961. *The Political Context of Sociology.* Princeton: Princeton University Press.
BRAUDE, LEE. 1970. "Louis Wirth and the Locus of Sociological Commitment." *American Sociologist* 5 (August): 233–239.
BREBNER, J. BARTLETT. 1947. "Laissez-Faire and State Intervention in Nineteenth Century Britain." *Journal of Economic History* 8 (Supplement VIII): 59–73.
BRIFFAULT, ROBERT. 1959. *The Mothers.* London: George Allen and Unwin. (Originally published in 1927.)
BRIGGS, ASA. 1960. "The Language of 'Class' in Early Nineteenth Century England." *Essays in Labor History,* Asa Briggs and John Saville, eds. London: Macmillan: 43–73.

BRINTON, CRANE. 1959. *A History of Western Morals.* New York: Harcourt, Brace.
————. 1963. *Ideas and Men.* 2nd Edition. Englewood Cliffs, N.J.: Prentice-Hall.
BUCKLEY, WALTER. 1967. *Sociology and Modern Systems Theory.* Englewood Cliffs, N.J.: Prentice-Hall.
BUHLE, PAUL. 1970. "The Wobblies in Perspective." *Monthly Review* 22 (June): 44–53.
BURGESS, ERNEST W. 1939. "The Influence of Sigmund Freud Upon Sociology in the United States." *American Journal of Sociology* 45 (November): 356–374.
BURKE, EDMUND. 1910. *Reflections on the French Revolution.* New York: E. P. Dutton. (Originally published in 1790.)
BURNHAM, JAMES. 1941. *The Managerial Revolution.* New York: John Day.
BURNHAM, JOHN C. 1956. "Lester Frank Ward in American Thought." *Annals of American Sociology.* Washington, D.C.: Public Affairs Press.
BYINGTON, MARGARET F. 1908. "The Family in a Typical Mill Town." *Papers and Proceedings of the American Sociological Society* 3 (December): 73–84.
CAMMETT, JOHN M. 1967. *Antonio Gramsci and the Origins of Italian Communism.* Stanford, Calif.: Stanford University Press.
CAPLOW, THEODORE AND REECE J. McGEE. 1958. *The Academic Marketplace.* New York: Basic Books.
CARLYLE, THOMAS. 1848. *The French Revolution: A History.* New York: Harper and Brothers. (Originally published in 1837.)
————. 1872. *Past and Present.* New York: Scribner, Welford and Company. (Originally published in 1843.)
CARR, WENDELL ROBERT. 1970. Introduction to *The Subjection of Women* by John Stuart Mill. Cambridge, Mass.: M.I.T. Press.
CAVAN, RUTH SHONLE AND KATHERINE HELEN RANCK. 1938. *The Family and the Depression: A Study of One Hundred Chicago Families.* Chicago, Ill.: University of Chicago Press.
CHAMBERS, CLARKE A. 1963. *Seedtime of Reform; American Social Service and Social Action, 1918–1933.* Minneapolis: University of Minnesota Press.
CHAPIN, F. STUART. 1919. "Democracy and Class Relations." *Publications of the American Sociological Society* 14: 100–110.
CHAVANNES, ALBERT. 1901. *Studies in Sociology.* 2nd Edition. Knoxville: New Thought Library. (Originally published in 1884.)
CHOMSKY, NOAM. 1967. *American Power and the New Mandarins.* New York: Pantheon Books.
CHRISMAN, ROBERT. 1970. "Ecology Is a Racist Shuck." *Scanlan's Monthly* 1 (August): 46–49.
CHUGERMAN, SAMUEL. 1965. *Lester F. Ward, the American Aristotle.* New York: Octagon Books.
CLARK, TERRY N. 1968a. "Emile Durkheim and the Institutionalization of Sociology in the French University System." *European Journal of Sociology* 9: 37–71.
————. 1968b. "The Structure and Functions of a Research Institute: The Annee Sociologique." *European Journal of Sociology* 9: 72–91.
CLOWARD, RICHARD AND LLOYD OHLIN. 1960. *Delinquency and Opportunity.* Glencoe, Ill.: Free Press.
COHEN, ALBERT. 1955. *Delinquent Boys, the Culture of the Gang.* Glencoe, Ill.: Free Press.
COLE, G. D. H. 1918. *Self Government in Industry.* London: G. Bell and Sons.
COLEMAN, JAMES. 1961. "The Competition for Adolescent Energies." *Phi Delta Kappan* 42 (March): 231–236.
COMMAGER, HENRY STEELE. 1950. *The American Mind.* New Haven, Conn.: Yale University Press.
COMMANDER, LYDIA KINGSMILL. 1908. Response to "How Does the Access of Women to Industrial Occupations React on the Family?" by Ulysses G. Weatherly. *Papers and Proceedings of the American Sociological Society* 3 (December): 136–141.
COMMONS, JOHN R. 1899–1900. "A Sociological View of Sovereignty." *American Journal of Sociology* 5 (July 1899): 1–15; 5 (September): 155–171; 5 (November): 347–366; 5 (January 1900): 544–552; 5 (March): 683–695; 5 (May): 814–825; 6 (July): 67–89.
————. 1907. "Is Class Conflict in America Growing and Is It Inevitable?" *Papers and Proceedings of the American Sociological Society* 2 (December): 138–148.

577

Bibliography

COMTE, AUGUSTE. 1877. *System of Positive Polity IV*. London: Longmans, Green. (Originally published in 1854.)

COOLEY, CHARLES H. 1902. *Human Nature and the Social Order*. New York: Charles Scribner's Sons.

————. 1909. *Social Organization*. New York: Charles Scribner's Sons.

————. 1920. "Reflections upon the Sociology of Herbert Spencer." *American Journal of Sociology* 26 (September): 129–145.

CORNFORTH, MAURICE. 1967. *Marxism and the Linguistic Analysis*. New York: International Publishers.

COSER, LEWIS A. 1967. "Response to 'Vietnam and the Liberals: a Symposium.'" *Commentary Reports*. New York: Commentary Magazine.

————. 1969. "Unanticipated Conservative Consequences of Liberal Theorizing." *Social Problems* 16 (Winter): 263–272.

————. 1971. *Masters of Sociological Thought*. New York: Harcourt Brace Jovanovich.

CRESSEY, DONALD. 1953. *Other People's Money*. New York: Free Press of Glencoe.

CRESSEY, PAUL G. 1932. *The Taxi-Dance Hall*. Chicago: University of Chicago Press.

CURTI, MERLE. 1960. "Intellectuals and the Founding Fathers." *The Intellectuals: A Controversial Portrait*, George B. de Huszar, ed. Glencoe, Illinois: The Free Press, 28–31.

DAHL, ROBERT. 1967. *Pluralist Democracy in the United States*. Chicago: Rand McNally.

DAVIS, ARTHUR K. 1957. "Thorstein Veblen and the Culture of Capitalism." *American Radicals: Some Problems and Personalities*. Harvey Goldberg, ed. New York: Monthly Review Press: 279–293.

DAVIS, KINGSLEY AND WILBERT E. MOORE. 1945. "Some Principles of Stratification." *American Sociological Review* 10 (April): 242–249.

DEALY, JAMES QUAYLE. 1927. "Lester Frank Ward." *American Masters of Social Science*. Howard Odum, ed. New York: Henry Holt: 61–96.

DEBRO, JULES. 1970. "Dialogue with Howard Becker." *Issues in Criminology* 5 (Summer): 159–179.

DEBS, EUGENE V. 1910. "A Letter from Debs on Immigration." *International Socialist Review* XI (July): 16–17.

————. 1970a. "The American University and the Labor Problem." *Eugene V. Debs Speaks*. Jean Y. Tussey, ed. New York: Pathfinder Press: 53–58.

————. 1970b. "On Race Prejudice." *Eugene V. Debs Speaks*. Jean Y. Tussey, ed. New York: Pathfinder Press: 90–104.

DEVINE, EDWARD T. 1919. "Social Unit in Cincinnati: An Experiment in Organization." *Survey* 43 (November 15): 115–126.

DIAMOND, SIGMUND. 1955. *The Reputation of the American Businessman*. Cambridge, Mass.: Harvard University Press.

DIBBLE, VERNON K. 1968. "Social Science and Political Commitments in the Young Max Weber." *European Journal of Sociology* 9: 92–110.

DICEY, ALBERT V. 1905. *Lectures on the Relation Between Law and Public Opinion in England during the Nineteenth Century*. New York: Macmillan.

DOLY, C. STEWART, ed. 1969. *The Industrial Revolution*. New York: Holt, Rinehart and Winston.

DOMHOFF, G. WILLIAM. 1969. "Where a Pluralist Goes Wrong." *Berkeley Journal of Sociology* 24: 35–57.

DONOVAN, FRANCES R. 1930. *The Saleslady*. Chicago, Ill.: University of Chicago Press.

DOUGLAS, JACK D., ED. 1970. *Deviance and Respectability*. New York: Basic Books.

DOUGLAS, DOROTHY. 1948. "The Doctrines of Guillame DeGreef's Syndicalism and Social Reform in the Guise of a Classificatory Sociology." *Introduction to the History of Sociology*. Harry E. Barnes, ed. Chicago: University of Chicago Press: 538–552.

DU BOIS, W. E. B. 1907. Response to "Is Race Friction Between Blacks and Whites in the United States Growing and Inevitable?" *Papers and Proceedings of the American Sociological Society* 2 (December): 104–108.

————. 1968. *Dusk of Dawn, An Essay Toward an Autobiography of a Race Concept*. New York: Schocken Books. (Originally published in 1940.)

DUGAN, JAMES. 1965. *The Great Mutiny*. New York: Signet Books.

DUNCAN, OTIS DUDLEY, ED. 1964. Introduction to *William F. Ogburn on Culture and Social Change*. Chicago: Phoenix Books: vii–xxii.

DUNHAM, BARROWS. 1947. *Man Against Myth*. Boston: Little, Brown.

DUNN, ERICA AND JUDY KLEIN. 1970. "Women in the Russian Revolution." *Women* 1 (Summer): 22–26.

DURKHEIM, EMILE. 1915. *The Elementary Forms of Religious Life*. J. W. Swain, tr. London: Allen and Unwin. (Originally published in 1912.)

———. 1933. *The Division of Labor in Society*. Glencoe, Ill.: Free Press. (Originally published in 1893.)

———. 1938. *Rules of Sociological Method*. 8th Edition. Sarah A. Solvay and John M. Mueller, tr. Glencoe, Ill.: Free Press. (Originally published in 1895.)

———. 1951. *Suicide*. J. Spaulding and G. Simpson, tr. New York: Free Press.

———. 1958. *Socialism and Saint-Simon*. Ed. with introduction by Alvin W. Gouldner. Tr. Charlotte Sattler from edition originally ed. by Marcel Mauss. Yellow Springs, Ohio: Antioch Press.

EARP, EDWIN L. 1914. Response to "Discussion on Freedom of Teaching in the United States" by Ulysses G. Weatherly and "Reasonable Restrictions upon the Scholar's Freedom" by Henry Pritchett. *Publications of the American Sociological Society*, Scott E. W. Bedford, ed. 9: 166–167.

EDEL, ABRAHAM. 1955. *Ethical Judgment*. Glencoe, Ill.: Free Press.

———. 1963. *Method in Ethical Theory*. New York: Bobbs-Merrill.

——— AND MARY EDEL. 1959. *Anthropology and Ethics*. Springfield, Ill.: Charles C. Thomas.

EDWARDS, LYFORD P. 1927. *The Natural History of Revolution*. Chicago: University of Chicago Press.

EISENSTADT, S. N. 1956. *From Generation to Generation, Age Groups and Social Structure*. Glencoe, Ill.: Free Press.

EISNER, HENRY. 1967. *The Technocrats, Prophets of Automation*. Syracuse, N.Y.: Syracuse University Press.

ELLWOOD, CHARLES A. 1900. "The Theory of Imitation in Social Psychology." *American Journal of Sociology* 6 (May): 721–741.

———. 1909a. "The Psychological View of Society." *American Journal of Sociology* 15 (March): 596–618.

———. 1909b. "The Science of Sociology: A Reply." *American Journal of Sociology* 15 (July): 105–116.

———. 1916. "Objectivism in Sociology." *American Journal of Sociology* 22 (November): 286–305.

ELY, RICHARD T. 1883. *French and German Socialism in Modern Times*. New York: Harper and Brothers.

———. 1902. *The Coming City*. New York: Thomas Y. Crowell.

———. 1938. *Ground Under Our Feet*. New York: Macmillan.

ENGELS, FREDERICK. 1847. Preface to First German Edition of Karl Marx's *The Poverty of Philosophy*. Moscow: Foreign Languages Publishing House: 7–24.

———. 1882. "Socialism: Utopian and Scientific." Karl Marx, *Selected Works* I, V. Adoratsky, ed. New York: International Publishers: 135–188. (The publication date of the International Publishers edition is not given. Therefore, we have only indicated the date of the original publication of Engels' essay. It should be noted that "Socialism: Utopian and Scientific" was derived from Engels' work *Herr Eugen Duhring's Revolution in Science*, 1878.)

———. 1890. Preface to 1890 German Edition of *Manifesto of the Communist Party* by Karl Marx and Frederick Engels. *Selected Works of Karl Marx*. New York: International Publishers: 193–203.

———. 1968. *The Origin of the Family, Private Property, and the State*. Moscow: Progress Publishers. (Originally published in 1884.)

ERIKSON, KAI. 1970. "Deviance and Definition." *Criminal Behavior and Social Systems: Contributions of American Sociology*, Anthony L. Guenther, ed. Chicago: Rand McNally: 32–41. (Originally published in 1962.)

FALLERS, LLOYD A. 1966. "Social Stratification and Economic Processes in Africa." *Class, Status and Power*, Second Edition. Reinhard Bendix and Seymour Martin Lipset, eds. New York: Free Press: 141–149.

Bibliography

FARIS, ELLSWORTH. 1921a. "Are Instincts Data or Hypotheses?" *American Journal of Sociology* 27 (September): 184–196.

――――. 1921b. "Ethnological Light on Psychological Problems." *Publications of the American Sociological Society* 16: 113–120.

――――. 1926. "The Nature of Human Nature." *Publications of the American Sociological Society* 20: 15–29.

FESTINGER, L. 1957. *A Theory of Cognitive Dissonance.* Evanston, Ill.: Row, Peterson.

FISHER, F. J. 1961. "Tawney's Century." *Essays in the Economic and Social History of Tudor and Stuart England,* F. J. Fisher, ed. Cambridge: The University Press.

FLEXNER, ELEANOR. 1970. *Century of Struggle, The Woman's Rights Movement in the United States.* New York: Atheneum.

FONER, PHILIP S. 1947. *History of the Labor Movement in the United States,* Volume 1. New York: International Publishers.

――――. 1955. *History of the Labor Movement in the United States,* Volume 2. New York: International Publishers.

――――. 1964. *History of the Labor Movement in the United States,* Volume 3. New York: International Publishers.

――――. 1965. *History of the Labor Movement in the United States,* Volume 4. New York: International Publishers.

FORD, HENRY J. 1909a. "The Pretensions of Sociology." *American Journal of Sociology* 15 (April): 96–103.

――――. 1909b. "The Claims of Sociology Examined." *American Journal of Sociology* 15 (September): 244–259.

FOSTER, WILLIAM Z. 1947. *American Trade Unionism.* New York: International Publishers.

FRANKENA, WILLIAM K. 1963. *Ethics.* Englewood Cliffs, N.J.: Prentice-Hall.

FRASER, JOHN. 1971. "Marxists and Intellectuals." *Science and Society* 35 (Fall): 257–285.

FRAZIER, E. FRANKLIN. 1939. *Negro Families in the United States.* Chicago, Ill.: University of Chicago Press.

――――. 1962. *The Black Bourgeoisie.* New York: Collier Books.

FREUD, SIGMUND. 1957. *Civilization and Its Discontents.* London: Hogarth Press. (Originally published in 1930.)

FRIEDRICHS, ROBERT W. 1970. *A Sociology of Sociology.* New York: Free Press.

FURFEY, PAUL H. 1959. "Social Science and the Problem of Values." *Symposium on Sociological Theory,* Llewellyn Gross, ed. Evanston, Ill.: Row, Peterson and Co.: 509–530.

GALBRAITH, JOHN K. 1967. *The New Industrial State.* Boston: Houghton Mifflin.

GEIS, GILBERT. 1964. "Sociology and Sociological Jurisprudence: Admixture of Lore and Law." *Kentucky Law Journal* 52 (Winter): 267–293.

GERTH, HANS AND C. WRIGHT MILLS. 1954. *Character and Social Structure.* London: Routledge Kegan Paul.

GETTLEMAN, MARVIN E. AND DAVID MERMELSTEIN, EDS. 1967. *The Great Society Reader.* New York: Vintage Books. (Originally published in 1965.)

GHENT, WILLIAM J. 1902. *Our Benevolent Feudalism.* New York: Macmillan.

GIDDINGS, FRANKLIN H. 1900. *Democracy and Empire, with Studies of their Psychological, Economic and Moral Foundations.* New York: Macmillan.

GILMAN, CHARLOTTE PERKINS. 1907. "How Home Conditions React upon the Family." *Papers and Proceedings of the American Sociological Society* 2 (December): 16–29.

――――. 1966. *Women and Economics.* New York: Harper Torchbooks. (Originally published in 1898.)

GIRVETZ, HARRY. 1950. *The Evolution of Liberalism.* New York: Collier Books.

GLASER, BARNEY G. AND ANSELM L. STRAUSS. 1967. *The Discovery of Grounded Theory.* Chicago: Aldine Publishing Co.

GOLDMAN, ERIC FREDERICK. 1952. *Rendezvous with Destiny.* New York: Alfred A. Knopf.

GOODE, WILLIAM J. 1972. "Presidential Address: The Place of Force in Human Society." *American Sociological Review* 37 (October): 507–519.

GOSSETT, THOMAS F. 1965. *Race: The History of an Idea.* New York: Schocken Books.

580

GOUGH, KATHLEEN. 1971. Review of *Sexual Politics* by Kate Millett. *Monthly Review* 22 (February): 47–56.

GOULDNER, ALVIN W. 1958. Introduction to *Socialism and Saint-Simon* by Emile Durkheim. Yellow Springs, Ohio: Antioch Press.

———. 1962. "Anti-Minotaur: The Myth of a Value-Free Sociology." *Social Problems* 9 (Winter): 199–213.

———. 1970. *The Coming Crisis of Western Sociology*. New York: Basic Books.

GOWIN, E. B. 1914. Response to "Freedom of Teaching in the United States" by Ulysses G. Weatherly and "Reasonable Restrictions upon the Scholar's Freedom" by Henry Pritchett. *Publications of the American Sociological Society*, Scott E. W. Bedford, ed. 9: 163–164.

GRAMSCI, ANTONIO. 1957. *The Modern Prince and Other Writings*. New York: International Publishers. (Originally published in 1919–1926.)

———. 1971. *Selections from the Prison Notebooks*. New York: International Publishers. (Edited and translated by Quintin Hoare and Geoffrey Nowell Smith.)

GRAÑA, CÉSAR. 1964. *Bohemian versus Bourgeois*. New York: Basic Books.

GREER, SCOTT. 1962. *The Emerging City*. New York: Free Press.

GROSS, EDWARD. 1964. "Industrial Relations." *Handbook of Modern Sociology*. Robert E. L. Faris, ed. Chicago: Rand McNally.

GROVES, E. R. 1920. "Sociology and Psychoanalytic Psychology." *Publications of the American Sociological Society* 15 (December): 203–205.

HALEVY, E. 1955. *The Growth of Philosophic Radicalism*. Boston: Beacon Press.

HALL, CALVIN S. AND GARDNER LINDZEY. 1954. "Psychoanalytic Theory and its Application in the Social Sciences." *Handbook of Social Psychology* I. Gardner Lindzey, ed. Reading, Mass.: Addison-Wesley: 143–180.

HANSON, NORWOOD R. 1969. "Retroduction and the Logic of Scientific Discovery." *The Nature and Scope of Social Science, a Critical Anthology*. Leonard I. Krimerman, ed. New York: Appleton Century-Crofts. (Originally published in 1961.)

HARE, NATHAN. 1970. "Black Ecology." *The Black Scholar* 1 (April): 2–8.

HARRIS, MARVIN. 1968. *The Rise of Anthropological Theory*. New York: Thomas Y. Crowell.

HAUSER, PHILIP. 1969. "The Chaotic Society: Product of the Social Morphological Revolution." *American Sociological Review* 34 (February): 1–19.

HAYEK, F. A. 1952. *The Counter Revolution of Science*. Glencoe, Ill.: Free Press.

HEIDER, FRITZ. 1958. *The Psychology of Interpersonal Relations*. New York: John Wiley.

HELVETIUS, CLAUDE. 1810. *De l'Esprit or Essays on the Mind and Its Several Faculties*. London: Printed for James Cundee, and Vernor, Hood and Sharpe. (Originally published in 1758.)

HEMPEL, CARL G. 1959. "The Logic of Functional Analysis." *Symposium on Sociological Theory*, Llewellyn Gross, ed. Evanston, Ill.: Row, Peterson and Co.: 271–307.

HENDERSON, CHARLES RICHMOND. 1908. "Are Modern Industry and City Life Unfavorable to the Family?" *Papers and Proceedings of the American Sociological Society* 3 (December): 93–105.

HERRNSTEIN, RICHARD. 1971. "I. Q." *The Atlantic Monthly* (September).

HIGHAM, JOHN. 1967. *Strangers in the Land*. New York: Atheneum.

HILLER, E. T. 1928. *The Strike*. Chicago: University of Chicago Press.

HINKLE, GISELE J. 1951. "The Role of Freudianism in American Sociology." Doctoral dissertation, University of Wisconsin.

———. 1957. "Sociology and Psychoanalysis." *Modern Sociological Theory*, Howard Becker and Alvin Boskoff, eds. New York: Holt, Rinehart and Winston.

HIRSCHI, TRAVIS. 1969. *Causes of Delinquency*. Berkeley: University of California Press.

HOBBES, THOMAS. 1969. *Leviathan*, Part I. New York: Gateway Editions. (Originally published in 1651.)

HOFSTADTER, RICHARD. 1959. *Social Darwinism in American Thought*. New York: George Braziller.

———. 1970. "The Importance of Comity in American History." *Columbia University Forum* 4 (Winter): 9–13.

HOLLINGSHEAD, AUGUST B. 1949. *Elmtown's Youth*. New York: John Wiley.

Bibliography

HOMANS, GEORGE C. 1958. "Social Behavior as Exchange." *American Journal of Sociology* 60:597–606.

——. 1961. *Social Behavior In Its Elementary Forms*. New York: Harcourt Brace and World.

HOPKINS, TERENCE K. 1957. "Sociology and the Substantive View of the Economy." *Trade and Market in the Early Empires*. Polanyi et al., eds. Glencoe, Ill.: Free Press: 271–307.

HORN, JOSHUA. 1971. *Away With All Pests*. New York: Monthly Review Press.

HOROWITZ, DAVID. 1971. *Radical Sociology; An Introduction*. San Francisco: Canfield Press.

HORTON, JOHN. 1966. "Order and Conflict Theories of Social Problems as Competing Ideologies." *American Journal of Sociology* 71 (May): 701–713.

HOWARD, GEORGE ELLIOTT. 1908. "Is the Freer Granting of Divorce an Evil?" *Papers and Proceedings of the American Sociological Society* 3 (December): 150–160.

HUME, DAVID. 1930. *An Enquiry into the Principles of Morals*. Chicago: Open Court Publishing Co. (Originally published in 1751.)

HUTCHESON, FRANCIS. 1755. *A System of Moral Philosophy*. London: F. H. Hutcheson.

IGGERS, GEORG G. 1958. *The Doctrine of Saint-Simon: An Exposition. First Year, 1828–29*. Tr. with notes and introduction by Georg G. Iggers. Boston: Beacon Press.

JACOBS, JANE. 1969. *The Economy of Our Cities*. New York: Random House.

JENSEN, ARTHUR R. 1969. "How Much Can We Boost I.Q. and Scholastic Achievement." *Harvard Educational Review* 39 (Winter).

KAPLAN, ABRAHAM. 1964. *The Conduct of Inquiry*. San Francisco: Chandler Publishing Company.

KEASBEY, LINDLEY M. 1907. "Competition." *Papers and Proceedings of the American Sociological Society* 2 (December): 33–38.

KERR, CLARK. 1963. *The Uses of the University*. Cambridge, Mass.: Harvard University Press.

——. 1969. *Marshall, Marx and Modern Times: the Multi-Dimensional Society*. London: Cambridge University Press.

KIPNIS, IRA. 1952. *The American Socialist Movement, 1897–1912*. New York: Columbia University Press.

KIRK, RUSSELL. 1955. *Academic Freedom, An Essay in Definition*. Chicago: Henry Regnery.

KNOX, JOHN B. 1963. "The Concept of Exchange in Sociological Theory: 1884 and 1961." *Social Forces* 41 (May): 341–345.

KOLKO, GABRIEL. 1967. *The Triumph of Conservatism*. Chicago: Quadrangle Books.

KROPOTKIN, PETER. 1955. *Mutual Aid*. With a foreword by Ashley Montagu, and "The Struggle for Existence" by Thomas H. Huxley. Boston: Extending Horizon Books.

LAFARGUE, PAUL. 1967. *Socialism and the Intellectuals*. New York: New York Labor News. (This address was originally presented before the "Group of Collective Students," which was attached to the Parti Ouvrier Français, March 23, 1900.)

LA FOLLETTE, ROBERT. 1960. *La Follette's Autobiography*. 2nd Edition. Madison: University of Wisconsin Press.

LAIDLER, HARRY W. 1927. *History of Socialist Thought*. New York: Thomas Y. Crowell.

LASCH, CHRISTOPHER. 1965. *The New Radicalism in America 1889–1963*. New York: Alfred A. Knopf.

LAZARSFELD, PAUL F. AND WAGNER THIELENS, JR. 1958. *The Academic Mind, Social Scientists in Times of Crisis*. With a field report by David Riesman. Glencoe, Ill.: Free Press.

LE BON, GUSTAVE. 1899. *The Psychology of Socialism*. New York: Macmillan. (Originally published in 1895.)

LEFEBVRE, HENRI. 1968. *The Sociology of Marx*. New York: Random House.

LENS, SIDNEY. 1969. *Radicalism in America*. New York: Thomas Y. Crowell.

LICHTHEIM, GEORGE. 1969. *The Origins of Socialism*. New York: Frederick A. Praeger.

LINDESMITH, ALFRED R. 1947. *Opiate Addiction*. Bloomington, Indiana: Principia Press.

LIPSET, SEYMOUR M. 1963. *The First New Nation; the United States in Historical and Comparative Perspective*. New York: Basic Books.

LONDON, JACK. 1903. *The People of the Abyss*. New York: Grosset and Dunlop.

LOOMIS, CHARLES P. AND JOHN C. MCKINNEY. 1963. Introduction to Ferdinand Tönnies' *Community and Society.* New York: Harper Torchbooks: 1–11.
———. 1967. "In Praise of Conflict and Its Resolution." *American Sociological Review* 32 (December): 875–890.
LORENZ, KONRAD. 1966. *On Aggression.* New York: Harcourt, Brace and World.
LUBOVE, ROY. 1965. *The Professional Altruist.* Cambridge, Massachusetts: Harvard University Press.
LUMLEY, FREDERICK ELMORE. 1925. *Means of Social Control.* New York and London: Century.
LUNDBERG, GEORGE. 1929. *Trends in American Sociology.* New York and London: Harper and Brothers.
LUXEMBURG, ROSA. 1970. *The Junius Pamphlet: The Crisis in the German Social Democracy.* Republished in *Rosa Luxemburg Speaks.* Mary-Alice Walters, ed. New York: Pathfinder Press. (Originally written in 1915.)
LYMAN, STANFORD M. AND MARVIN SCOTT. 1967. "Territoriality: A Neglected Sociological Dimension." *Social Problems* 15 (Fall): 236–249.
LYND, STAUGHTON, ED. 1966. "William Haywood, Testimony Before the Industrial Relations Commission, 1915." *Nonviolence in America: A Documentary History.* New York: Bobbs-Merrill: 217–241.
MAC IVER, ROBERT. 1955. *Academic Freedom in Our Time.* New York: Columbia University Press.
MCKAY, THOMAS. 1891. *A Plea for Liberty.* New York: D. Appleton and Company.
MCVEY, FRANK L. 1914. Response to "Freedom of Teaching in the United States" by Ulysses G. Weatherly and "Reasonable Restrictions upon the Scholar's Freedom" by Henry Pritchett. *Publications of the American Sociological Society,* Scott E. W. Bedford, ed. 9: 159–163.
MADISON, JAMES, JOHN JAY, AND ALEXANDER HAMILTON. 1964. *The Federalist.* New York: Modern Library.
MAGDOFF, HARRY. 1969. *The Age of Imperialism.* New York: Monthly Review Press.
MAINE, HENRY S. 1861. *Ancient Law.* London: J. Murray.
MALIA, MARTIN. 1960. "What is the Intelligentsia?" *Daedalus* 89 (Summer): 441–458.
MALTHUS, THOMAS P. 1872. *An Essay on Population.* 7th Edition. London: Reeves and Turner. (Originally published in 1826.)
———. 1914. *An Essay on Population, I.* New York: E. P. Dutton. (Originally published in 1798.)
MANDEL, ERNST. 1970. *Marxist Economic Theory,* Volumes 1 and 2. Brian Pearce, tr. New York: Monthly Review Press. (Originally published in 1962.)
MANN, GOLO. 1960. "The German Intellectuals." *The Intellectuals, A Controversial Portrait,* George B. Huszar, ed. Glencoe, Ill.: Free Press: 459–469.
MARCUSE, HERBERT. 1964. *One Dimensional Man.* Boston: Beacon Press.
MARTINDALE, DONALD. 1957. "Social Disorganization: The Conflict of Normative and Empirical Approaches." *Modern Sociological Theory in Continuity and Change,* Howard Becker and Alvin Boskoff, eds. New York: Dryden Press: 340–367.
———. 1959. "Sociological Theory and the Ideal Type." *Symposium on Sociological Theory,* Llewellyn Gross, ed. White Plains, N.Y.: Row, Peterson: 57–91.
MARX, KARL. 1847. *The Poverty of Philosophy.* Moscow: Foreign Languages Publishing House.
———. 1959. *Capital, A Critical Analysis of Capitalist Production, Vol. I.* Moscow: Foreign Languages Publishing House. (Original, 1859).
———. 1963. *The Eighteenth Brumaire of Louis Bonaparte.* New York: International Publishers. (Originally published in 1852.)
——— AND FREDERICK ENGELS. 1968. *The German Ideology.* Moscow: Progress Publishers. (Originally written in 1845–1846 and published in 1932.)
———. 1972a. *Ireland and the Irish Question: Collection of Writings by Karl Marx and Frederick Engels.* New York: International Publishers.
———. 1972b. *On Colonialism.* New York: International Publishers.
MARZANI, CARL, TR. AND ANNOTAT. 1957. *The Open Marxism of Antonio Gramsci.* New York: Cameron Assoc.
MASON, OTIS TUFTON. 1894. *Woman's Share in Primitive Culture.* New York: D. Appleton and Co.

583

Bibliography

MATZA, DAVID. 1969. *Becoming Deviant*. Englewood Cliffs, N.J.: Prentice-Hall.

MAUS, HEINZ. 1966. *A Short History of Sociology*. New York: Citadel Press.

MEAD, GEORGE H. 1899a. "The Working Hypothesis in Social Reform." *American Journal of Sociology* 5 (November): 361–371.

———. 1899b. "A Review of the Psychology of Socialism by Gustave Le Bon." *American Journal of Sociology* 5 (November): 404–412.

MEEK, RONALD. 1971. *Marx and Engels on the Population Bomb*. Berkeley, Calif.: Ramparts Press.

MERTON, ROBERT K. 1938. "Social Structure and Anomie." *American Sociological Review* 3 (October): 672–682.

———. 1957. *Social Theory and Social Structure* (revised edition). Glencoe, Ill.: Free Press. (Originally published in 1949.)

METZGER, WALTER P. AND RICHARD HOFSTADTER. 1955. *The Development of Academic Freedom in the United States*. New York: Columbia University Press.

MEYNAUD, JEAN. 1969. *Technocracy*. New York: Free Press.

MILIBAND, RALPH. 1969. *The State in Capitalist Society*. New York: Basic Books.

MILL, JOHN STUART. 1844. *Essays on Some Unsettled Questions of Political Economy*. London: John W. Parker. (Originally published in 1829–1830.)

———. 1970. *The Subjection of Women*. With introduction by Wendell Robert Carr. Cambridge, Mass.: M.I.T. Press. (Originally published in 1869.)

MILLER, S. M. AND R. S. RATNER. 1972. "The American Resignation: The New Assault on Equality." *Social Policy* 3 (May/June): 5–15.

MILLS, C. WRIGHT. 1943. "The Professional Ideology of Social Pathologists." *American Journal of Sociology* 49 (September): 165–180.

———. 1959. *The Sociological Imagination*. New York: Oxford University Press.

———. 1963. "The Labor Leaders and the Power Elite." *Power, Politics and People, The Collected Essays of C. Wright Mills*, ed. and with an introduction by Irving Louis Horowitz. New York: Ballantine Books: 97–109. (Original, 1954.)

———. 1966. *Sociology and Pragmatism*. New York: Oxford University Press.

MITCHELL, WESLEY C. 1927. *Business Cycles*. New York: National Bureau of Economic Research.

MOORE, G. E. 1903. *Principia Ethica*. Cambridge: Cambridge University Press.

MOORE, JOAN. 1970. "Colonialism: The Case of the Mexican Americans." *Social Problems* 17 (Spring): 463–472.

MOORE, WILBERT E. 1963. "Some Are More Equal than Others." *American Sociological Review* 28 (February): 13–18.

———. 1966. "The Utility of Utopias." *American Sociological Review* 31 (December): 765–772.

MORGAN, LEWIS HENRY. 1963. *Ancient Society*. With an introduction by Eleanor Burke Leacock. Cleveland: World. (Originally published in 1877.)

MORGAN, ROBIN, ED. 1970. *Sisterhood Is Powerful*. New York: Vintage Books.

MORRIS, DESMOND. 1967. *The Naked Ape*. New York: Dell Publishers.

MOWRER, ERNEST R. 1927. *Family Disorganization: An Introduction to a Sociological Analysis*. Chicago, Ill.: University of Chicago Press.

MOYNIHAN, DANIEL PATRICK. 1967. "The Professionalization of Reform." *The Great Society Reader*, Marvin E. Gettleman and David Mermelstein, eds. New York: Vintage Books: 457–475. (Originally published in 1965.)

———. 1969. *Maximum Feasible Misunderstanding*. New York: Free Press.

MURRAY, ROBERT K. 1955. *Red Scare*. New York: McGraw-Hill.

MYRDAL, JAN AND GUNNAR KESSLE. 1970. *China: The Revolution Continued*. New York: Monthly Review Press.

NAIRN, TOM. 1970. "The Faithful Meridian." *New Left Review* 60 (March/April): 3–35.

NEARING, SCOTT. 1914. Response to "Freedom of Teaching in the United States" by Ulysses G. Weatherly and "Reasonable Restrictions upon the Scholar's Freedom" by Henry Pritchett. *Publications of the American Sociological Society*, Scott E. W. Bedford, ed. 9: 165–166.

NICOLAUS, MARTIN. 1969. "Remarks at ASA Convention." *American Sociologist* 4 (May): 154–156.

NISBET, ROBERT A. 1965. *Emile Durkheim*. Englewood Cliffs, N.J.: Prentice-Hall.

———. 1966. *The Sociological Tradition*. New York: Basic Books.

584

NKRUMAH, KWAME. 1965. *Neo-Colonialism, the Last Stage of Imperialism.* New York: International Publishers.

NORTH, CECIL C. 1914. Response to "Freedom of Teaching in the United States" by Ulysses G. Weatherly and "Reasonable Restrictions Upon the Scholar's Freedom" by Henry Pritchett. *Publications of the American Sociological Society,* Scott E. W. Bedford, ed. 9: 164–165.

OBERSCHALL, ANTHONY. 1965. *Empirical Social Science Research in Germany, 1848–1914.* Paris: Mouton & Co.

O'CONNOR, JAMES. 1970a. "The Fiscal Crisis of the State: Part I." *Socialist Revolution* 1 (January–February): 12–15.

———. 1970b. "The Fiscal Crisis of the State: Part II." *Socialist Revolution* 1 (March–April): 34–94.

ODUM, HOWARD W., ED. 1927. *American Masters of Social Science.* Port Washington, N.Y.: Kennikat Press.

———. 1951. *American Sociology.* New York: Longmans, Green.

OFARI, EARL. 1970. *Black Capitalism.* New York: Monthly Review Press.

OGBURN, WILLIAM F. 1918. "The Psychological Basis for the Economic Interpretation of History." *American Economic Review* 9 (Supp. 19): 291–308.

———. 1922. *Social Change, with Respect to Culture and Human Nature.* New York: Viking Press.

———. 1964. "Bias, Psychoanalysis, and the Subjective in Relation to the Social Sciences." *William F. Ogburn on Culture and Social Change, Selected Papers,* Otis Dudley Duncan, ed. Chicago: Phoenix Books. (Originally published in 1922.)

OGDEN, C. K. 1937. *Bentham's Theory of Fictions.* London: K. Paul, Trench, Trubner.

OPPENHEIM, A. N. 1955. "Social Status and Clique Formation Among Grammar School Boys." *British Journal of Sociology* 6 (September): 228–245.

OPPENHEIMER, MARTIN. 1970. "White Collar Revisited: The Making of a New Working Class." *Social Policy* I (July / August): 27–32.

ORIGO, IRIS. 1957. *The Merchant of Prago.* New York: Alfred A. Knopf.

ORTIZ FERNANDEZ, FERNANDO. 1947. *Cuban Counterpoint; Tobacco and Sugar,* Harriet de Onis, tr. New York: Alfred A. Knopf.

OWNEN, G. 1892–1897. *The Description of Pembrokeshire. Cymmrodorian Record Series,* Part 1. (Cited in Fisher 1961:9).

PAGE, CHARLES HUNT. 1940. *Class and American Sociology: From Ward to Ross.* New York: Dial Press.

PAINE, THOMAS. 1942. *The Rights of Man, Being an Answer on Mr. Burke's Attack on the French Revolution.* New York: Willey. (Originally published in 1791–1792.)

PARENTI, MICHAEL. 1967. Introduction to *The Unadjusted Girl* by William I. Thomas. New York: Harper Torchbooks.

PARK, ROBERT E. 1918. "Education in Its Relation to the Conflict and Fusion of Cultures: With Special Reference to the Problems of the Immigrant, the Negro, and Missions." *Publications of the American Sociological Society* 13: 38–63.

——— AND ERNEST W. BURGESS. 1924. *Introduction to the Science of Sociology.* 2nd Edition. Chicago: University of Chicago Press. (Originally published in 1921.)

———. 1967. "The City: Suggestions for the Investigation of Human Behavior in Urban Environment." *The City.* Robert E. Park and Ernest W. Burgess, eds., with an introduction by Morris Janowitz. Chicago: University of Chicago Press. (Original, 1915.)

PARMELEE, MAURICE. 1914. Response to "Freedom of Teaching in the United States" by Ulysses G. Weatherly and "Reasonable Restrictions Upon the Scholar's Freedom" by Henry Pritchett. *Publications of the American Sociological Society,* Scott E. W. Bedford, ed. 9: 167–168.

PARSONS, ELSIE CLEWS. 1908. "Higher Education of Women and the Family." *Papers and Proceedings of the American Sociological Society* 3 (December): 142–147.

PARSONS, TALCOTT. 1937. *The Structure of Social Action.* New York: McGraw Hill.

———. 1949. "Age and Sex in the Social Structure of the United States." *Essays in Sociological Theory.* Glencoe, Ill.: Free Press. (Originally published in 1942.)

———. 1957. "The Distribution of Power in American Society." *World Politics* 10 (October): 123–143.

Bibliography

PARSONS, TALCOTT. 1961. Introduction to *The Study of Sociology* by Herbert Spencer. Ann Arbor: Ann Arbor Paperbacks.

———— AND EDWARD A. SHILS. 1952. *Toward a General Theory of Action.* Cambridge, Mass.: Harvard University Press.

PARSONS, TALCOTT AND NEIL SMELSER. 1956. *Economy and Society.* Glencoe, Ill.: Free Press.

PETERS, IVA L. 1920. "Psychoanalysis: Collective Behavior." *Publications of the American Sociological Society* 15 (December): 214–216.

PIERCE, CHARLES SANDERS. 1932. *Collected Papers,* Vol. 7. Cambridge, Mass.: Harvard University Press.

POLANYI, KARL. 1957. "The Economy as an Instituted Process." *Trade and Market in the Early Empires.* Glencoe, Ill.: Free Press.

POUND, ROSCOE. 1920. "A Theory of Social Interest." *Publications of the American Sociological Society* 15: 16–45.

PRESTON, WILLIAM, JR. 1963. *Aliens and Dissenters.* Cambridge, Mass.: Harvard University Press.

PRITCHETT, HENRY. 1914. "Reasonable Restrictions Upon the Scholar's Freedom." *Publications of the American Sociological Society,* Scott E. W. Bedford, ed. 9: 150–159.

PUFFER, J. ADAMS. 1912. *The Boy and His Gang.* Boston: Houghton Mifflin. (Note: Parts of this work appeared as early as 1905.)

RACZ, ELIZABETH. 1970. "The Women's Rights Movement in the French Revolution." *Women* 1 (Summer): 28–32, 64.

REDFIELD, ROBERT. 1947. "The Folk Society." *American Journal of Sociology* 52 (January): 293–308.

REED, EVELYN. 1971. "How Women Lost Control of Their Destiny and How They Can Regain It." *Problems of Women's Liberation.* New York: Pathfinder Press, 48–63.

REYNOLDS, BERTHA C. 1963. *An Uncharted Journey.* New York: Citadel Press.

RIEFF, PHILIP. 1959. *Freud: The Mind of the Moralist.* New York: Viking Press.

RIESMAN, DAVID, WITH NATHAN GLAZER AND REUEL DENNEY. 1950. *The Lonely Crowd.* New Haven: Yale University Press.

ROOSEVELT, THEODORE. 1911. "The Trusts, the People, and the Square Deal." *The Outlook* 94 (November 18): 649–656.

ROSE, ARNOLD. 1967. *The Power Structure: Political Process in American Society.* New York: Oxford University Press.

ROSS, EDWARD ALSWORTH. 1896–1901. "Social Control." *American Journal of Sociology* 1 (March 1896): 513–535; 1 (May): 743–770; 2 (July): 96–107; 2 (September): 255–263; 2 (November): 433–435; 2 (January 1897): 547–566; 2 (May): 823–838; 3 (July): 64–78; 3 (September): 236–247; 3 (November): 328–339; 3 (January 1897): 502–519; 3 (March): 649–661; 3 (May): 809–828; 5 (January 1900): 475–487; 5 (March): 604–616; 5 (May): 761–777; 6 (July): 29–41; 6 (September): 238–247; 6 (November): 381–395; 6 (January 1901): 550–562.

————. 1901. *Social Control.* New York: Macmillan.

————. 1906. Response to "Social Darwinism" by D. Colin Wells. *Publications of the American Sociological Society* 1:137–138.

————. 1907. *Sin and Society.* New York: Houghton, Mifflin.

————. 1908. Response to "Is the Freer Granting of Divorce an Evil?" by George Elliott Howard. *Papers and Proceedings of the American Sociological Society* 3 (December): 177–178.

————. 1914a. *The Old World in the New.* New York: Century.

————. 1914b. Response to "Freedom of Teaching in the United States" by Ulysses G. Weatherly and "Reasonable Restrictions Upon the Scholar's Freedom" by Henry Pritchett. *Publications of the American Sociological Society,* Scott E. W. Bedford, ed. 9: 166–167.

————. 1930. *Principles of Sociology.* New York: Century. (Originally published in 1920.)

————. 1936. *Seventy Years of It, an Autobiography.* New York: D. Appleton-Century.

ROSSI, ALICE S. 1970. "Sentiment and Intellect: The Story of John Stuart Mill and Harriet Taylor Mill." *Aphra* 2 (Winter): 24–44.

ROUSSEAU, JEAN-JACQUES. 1950. "A Discourse on Political Economy." *Social Contract and Discourses.* New York: Dutton. (Originally published in 1755, 1762.)

586

RUDNER, RICHARD S. 1966. *Philosophy of the Social Sciences.* Englewood Cliffs, N.J.: Prentice-Hall.

RUMNEY, JAY. 1966. *Herbert Spencer's Sociology.* New York: Atherton Press.

RUSKIN, JOHN. 1900. *The Crown of Wild Olives.* New York: Home Book Company. (Originally published in 1866.)

————. 1907. *Unto This Last.* London: J. M. Dent. (Originally published in 1860.)

————. 1969. *Munera Pulveris.* New York: Greenwood Press. (Originally published in 1891.)

SAINT-SIMON, CLAUDE HENRI. 1952. *Selected Writings.* F. M. Markham, ed. and tr. Oxford: Basil Blackwell.

————. 1964. *Social Organization, the Science of Man and Other Writings.* Edited and translated with an introduction by Felix Markham. New York: Harper and Row.

SARTON, GEORGE. 1962. *The History of Science and the New Humanism.* Bloomington, Indiana: Midland Books.

SCHNEIDER, DAVID AND KATHLEEN GOUGH. 1961. *Matrilineal Kinship.* Berkeley: University of California Press.

SCHUMPETER, JOSEPH A. 1942. *Capitalism, Socialism and Democracy.* New York: Harper and Brothers.

————. 1954. *History of Economic Analysis.* New York: Oxford University Press.

SHAFFER, ANATOLE. 1971. "Cincinnati Social Unit Experiment." *Social Service Review* 45 (June): 159–172.

SHAFTESBURY, ANTHONY (ASHLEY COOPER). 1714. *Characteristics of Men, Manners, Opinions, Times.* London: John Darby.

SHAW, CLIFFORD R. AND HENRY D. McKAY. 1931. "Social Factors in Juvenile Delinquency." *Publications of the National Commission on Law Observance and Enforcement,* No. 13, *Report on the Causes of Crime,* Vol. 2. Washington, D.C.: Government Printing Office.

————. 1969. *Juvenile Delinquency and Urban Areas.* Revised Edition. Chicago: University of Chicago Press. (Originally published in 1942.)

SIMMEL, GEORG. 1896. "Superiority and Subordination." Albion Small, tr. *American Journal of Sociology* 2 (September): 169–171.

————. 1904. "The Sociology of Conflict." Albion Small, tr. *American Journal of Sociology* 9 (May): 798–802.

SKLAR, MARTIN J. 1960. "Woodrow Wilson and the Political Economy of Modern United States Liberalism." *Studies on the Left* I: 17–47.

SMALL, ALBION W. 1895. "The Era of Sociology." *American Journal of Sociology* 1 (July): 1–15.

————. 1898. "The Methodology of the Social Problem." *American Journal of Sociology* 4 (September): 113–144.

————. 1900. "The Scope of Sociology." *American Journal of Sociology* 5 (January): 506–526.

————. 1905. *General Sociology.* Chicago: University of Chicago Press.

————. 1908. "The Meaning of Sociology." *American Journal of Sociology* 14 (July): 1–14.

————. 1909. *The Cameralists.* Chicago: University of Chicago Press.

————. 1910. *The Meaning of Social Science.* Chicago: University of Chicago Press.

————, ED. 1913. "Various Tributes to Lester F. Ward Upon His Death." *American Journal of Sociology* 19 (July): 61–78.

————. 1914. "A Vision of Social Efficiency." *American Journal of Sociology* 19 (January): 433–445.

————. 1917. "America and the World Crisis." *American Journal of Sociology* 23: 145–173.

————. 1925. "The Sociology of Profits." *American Journal of Sociology* 30 (January): 439–461.

————. 1967. *Origins of Sociology.* New York: Russell and Russell. (Originally published in 1924.)

———— AND GEORGE E. VINCENT. 1894. *An Introduction to the Study of Society.* New York: American Book Co.

SMELSER, NEIL J. 1962. *Theory of Collective Behavior.* New York: Free Press.

Bibliography

SMELSER, NEIL J. AND WILLIAM T. SMELSER, EDS. 1963. *Personality and Social Systems.* New York: John Wiley.

SMITH, DUSKY LEE. 1965. "Sociology and the Rise of Corporate Capitalism." *Science and Society* 29 (Fall): 401–418.

SMITH, MAPHEUS. 1943. "An Empirical Scale of Prestige Status of Occupations." *American Sociological Review* 8 (April): 185–192.

SOROKIN, PITIRIM A. 1947. *Society, Culture and Personality.* New York: Harper.

————. 1963. Foreword to *Community and Society* by Ferdinand Tönnies. New York: Harper Torchbooks: vii–viii.

SOWER, CHRISTOPHER. 1948. "Social Stratification in Suburban Communities." *Sociometry* 11 (August): 235–243.

SPENCER, HERBERT. 1851. *Social Statics.* London: John Chapman.

————. 1852. "A Theory of Population, Deduced from the General Law of Animal Fertility." *The Westminster Review* 1: 468–501. London: John Chapman.

————. 1873. *The Study of Sociology.* International Scientific Series.

————. 1894. *Principles of Sociology,* I. New York: D. Appleton. (Originally published in 1876.)

————. 1896. *Principles of Sociology,* II. New York: D. Appleton.

————. 1940. *The Man versus the State.* Caldwell, Idaho: Caxton Printers. (Originally published in 1884.)

————. 1958. *First Principles.* New York: The Dewitt Revolving Fund. (Originally published in 1862.)

STARR, HARRIS E. 1925. *William Graham Sumner.* New York: Henry Holt.

STEDMAN-JONES, GARETH. 1970. "The Specificity of U.S. Imperialism." *New Left Review* 60 (March/April): 59–86.

STERN, BERNHARD J. 1959a. *Historical Sociology, The Selected Papers of Bernhard J. Stern.* New York: Citadel Press. (Originally published in *Science and Society,* Fall 1936: 114–119.)

————. 1959b. "The Liberal Views of Lester F. Ward." *Historical Sociology:* 200–207. (Originally published in *Science Monthly* 71, August 1950: 102–104.)

————. 1959c. "Engels on the Family." *Historical Sociology:* 277–303. (Originally published in *Science and Society* 12, Winter 1948: 42–64.)

————, ED. "The Letters of Albion W. Small to Lester F. Ward." *Social Forces* 12 (December 1933): 163–173; 13 (March 1935): 323–340; 15 (September 1936): 174–186; 15 (March 1937): 305–327.

————, ED. "The Ward-Ross Correspondence 1891–1896." *American Sociological Review* 3 (June 1938): 362–401; 11 (October 1946): 593–605; 11 (December 1946): 734–748; 12 (December 1947): 703–720; 13 (February 1948): 82–94; 14 (February 1949): 88–119.

STOLOFF, DAVID. 1967. "The Short But Unhappy History of Community Action Programs." *The Great Society Reader,* Marvin E. Gettleman and David Mermelstein, eds. New York: Vintage Books: 231–239.

STRAUSS, LEO. 1969. "Natural Law." *International Encyclopedia of the Social Sciences* 15. David L. Shils, ed. New York: Macmillan and Free Press.

SUMNER, WILLIAM G. 1908. "The Family and Social Change." *Papers and Proceedings of the American Sociological Society* 3 (December): 1–15.

SUTTLES, GERALD. 1970. "Deviant Behavior as an Unanticipated Consequence of Public Housing." *Crime in the City,* Daniel Glazer, ed. New York: Harper and Row: 162–176.

SVALASTOGA, KAARE. 1965. *Social Differentiation.* New York: David McKay.

SWEEZY, PAUL M. AND HARRY MAGDOFF. 1969. "The Merger Movement: A Study in Power." *Monthly Review* 21 (June): 1–19.

TAWNEY, R. H. 1912. *The Agrarian Problem in the Sixteenth Century.* New York: Burt Franklin.

————. 1920. *The Acquisitive Society.* New York: Harcourt, Brace.

————. 1926. *Religion and the Rise of Capitalism.* New York: Harcourt, Brace.

TAYLOR, HARRIET. 1851. "The Enfranchisement of Women." *Westminster and Foreign Quarterly Review* LV (April/July): 289–311.

THEODORSON, ACHILLES G. AND GEORGE A. THEODORSON. 1969. *A Modern Dictionary of Sociology.* New York: Thomas Y. Crowell.

THOMAS AQUINAS, ST. 1938. *On the Governance of Rulers.* New York: Sheed and Ward. (Originally published in 1259.)

THOMAS, WILLIAM I. 1907. *Sex and Society.* Chicago: University of Chicago Press.

————. 1907. "The Significance of the Orient for the Occident." *Papers and Proceedings of the American Sociological Society* 2 (December): 111–124.

————. 1909. *Source Book for Social Origins.* Chicago: University of Chicago Press.

————. 1967. *The Unadjusted Girl.* New York: Harper Torchbooks. (Originally written in 1923.)

———— AND FLORIAN ZNANIECKI. 1918. *The Polish Peasant in Europe and America.* Chicago: University of Chicago Press.

THOMPSON, E. P. 1963. *The Making of the English Working Class,* New York: Vintage Books.

THORNDIKE, E. L. 1898. "Animal Intelligence: An Experimental Study of the Associative Process in Animals." *Psychological Review,* Monogr. Supplement No. 8.

————. 1907. Review of *Applied Sociology* by Lester Ward. *The Bookman* 24: 291.

THRASHER, FREDERICK M. 1963. *The Gang, a Study of 1,313 Gangs in Chicago.* Abridged and with a new introduction by James F. Short, Jr. Chicago: Phoenix Books. (Originally published in 1927.)

TÖNNIES, FERDINAND. 1963. *Community and Society.* New York: Harper Torchbooks, Harper and Row, Publishers. (Originally published as *Gemeinschaft und Gesellschaft* in 1887.)

TURNER, RALPH H. 1969. "The Public Perception of Protest." *American Sociological Review* 34 (December): 815–831.

UDRY, J. RICHARD. 1960. "The Importance of Social Class in a Suburban School." *The Journal of Educational Sociology* 33 (April): 307–310.

VEBLEN, THORSTEIN. 1899. *The Theory of the Leisure Class.* New York: Macmillan.

————. 1900. "The Preconceptions of Economic Science." *The Quarterly Journal of Economics* 14 (February): 240–269.

————. 1963. *The Engineers and the Price System.* New York: Harcourt, Brace and World. (Originally published in 1921.)

————. 1969. *The Higher Learning in America.* New York: Hill and Wang. (Originally published in 1918.)

VESEY, LAURENCE R. 1965. *The Emergence of the American University.* Chicago: University of Chicago Press.

WALLACE, WALTER L., ED. 1969. *Sociological Theory.* Chicago: Aldine.

WALLAS, GRAHAM. 1914. *The Great Society, A Psychological Analysis.* New York: Macmillan.

WARD, LESTER F. 1880. "Feeling and Function as Factors in Human Development." *Science,* original series, 1 (October 23): 211–219. (Ward 1903: 258 indicates that this paper was read on August 23, 1880, before the Section of Anthropology of the American Association for the Advancement of Science in Boston.)

————. 1883. *Dynamic Sociology,* Volumes I and II. New York: D. Appleton Co.

————. 1893. *The Psychic Factors of Civilization.* Boston: Ginn and Co.

————. 1895. "Plutocracy and Paternalism." *Forum* 20 (November): 300–310.

————. 1898. *Outlines of Sociology.* New York: Macmillan.

————. 1900. Review of *Theory of the Leisure Class* by Thorstein Veblen. *American Journal of Sociology* 5 (May): 829–837.

————. 1902a. "Contemporary Sociology." *American Journal of Sociology* 7 (May): 749–762.

————. 1902b. "Social Differentiation and Social Integration." *American Journal of Sociology* 8 (May): 721–745.

————. 1903. *Pure Sociology.* New York: Macmillan.

————. 1906a. *Applied Sociology.* New York: Ginn and Co.

————. 1906b. Response to "Social Darwinism" by D. Collin Wells. *Publications of the American Sociological Society* 1 (December): 131–132.

————. 1907. Response to "The Basis of Social Conflict" by T. N. Carver. *Papers and Proceedings of the American Sociological Society* 2 (December): 30.

————. 1913–1918. *Glimpses of the Cosmos.* 6 volumes. New York: G. P. Putnam's Sons.

————. 1935. *Young Ward's Diary.* Bernhard J. Stern, ed. New York: J. Putnam Sons.

Bibliography

WARNER, W. LLOYD. 1936. "American Caste and Class." *American Journal of Sociology* 42 (September): 234–237.

——. ED. 1949. *Democracy in Jonesville*. New York: Harper.

—— WITH MARCHIA MEEKER AND KENNETH EELS. 1949. *Social Class in America*. Chicago: Science Research Associates. (Footnoted references to this work are from first Harper Torchbook edition. New York: 1960.)

WARNOCK, MARY. 1968. *Ethics Since 1900*. New York: Oxford University Press.

WEATHERLY, ULYSSES G. 1908. "How Does the Access of Women to Industrial Occupations React on the Family?" *Papers and Proceedings of the American Sociological Society* 3 (December): 124–136.

——. 1914. "Freedom of Teaching in the United States." *Publications of the American Sociological Society*, Scott E. W. Bedford, ed. 9: 133–149.

——. 1920. "Democracy and Our Political Systems." *Publications of the American Sociological Society* 14: 23–35.

——. 1926. *Social Process: The Dynamics of Social Change*. Philadelphia: Lippincott Sociological Series.

WEBER, MAX. 1949. *The Methodology of the Social Sciences*. Edward A. Shils and Henry A. Finch, tr. Glencoe, Ill.: Free Press. (Originally published in 1904.)

WEINSTEIN, JAMES. 1968. *The Corporate Ideal in the Liberal State: 1900–1918*. Boston: Beacon Press.

WERTHMAN, CARL. 1969. "Delinquency and Moral Character." *Delinquency, Crime, and Social Process*, Donald R. Cressey and David A. Ward, eds. New York: Harper and Row: 613–632.

WHEELER, STANTON AND LEONARD S. COTTRELL, JR., WITH THE ASSISTANCE OF ANNE ROMANSCO. 1966. *Juvenile Delinquency: Its Prevention and Control*. New York: Russell Sage Foundation.

WHITE, LESLIE A. 1937. Introduction to *Extracts from the European Travel Journals* (Vol. 16) by Lewis Henry Morgan. Rochester, N.Y.: Rochester Historical Society Publications.

WHITE, MORTON G. 1947. "The Revolt Against Formalism in American Social Thought of the Twentieth Century." *Journal of the History of Ideas* 8 (April): 131–152.

WHYTE, WILLIAM A. 1920. "Some Suggestions Regarding Practical Contacts Between Sociology and Psychoanalysis." *Publications of the American Sociological Society* 15 (December): 207–208.

WHYTE, WILLIAM F. 1943. *Street Corner Society*. Chicago: University of Chicago Press.

WILD, JOHN. 1953. *Plato's Modern Enemies and the Theory of Natural Law*. Chicago: University of Chicago Press.

WILLER, DAVID. 1967. *Scientific Sociology: Theory and Method*. Englewood Cliffs, N.J.: Prentice-Hall.

WILLIAMS, GWYN A. 1960. "Gramsci's Concept of *Egemonia*." *Journal of the History of Ideas* 21 (October–December): 586–599.

WILLIAMS, ROBIN M., JR. 1966. "Some Further Comments on Chronic Controversies." *American Journal of Sociology* 6 (May): 717–721.

WILLIAMS, WILLIAM APPLEMAN. 1961. *The Contours of American History*. New York: World.

WOLFE, ALAN. 1970. "The PhD Glut: Hard Times on the Campus." *The Nation* 210 (May 25): 623–627.

WOLPE, H. 1970. "Some Problems Concerning Revolutionary Consciousness." *The Socialist Register*, Ralph Miliband and John Saville, eds. London: Merlin Press: 251–280.

WOOLSTON, HOWARD B. 1936. "American Intellectuals and Social Reform." *American Sociological Review* 1 (April): 363–372.

YOUMANS, EDWARD LIVINGSTON, ED. 1883. *Herbert Spencer on the Americans and the Americans on Herbert Spencer*. New York: D. Appleton.

ZEITLIN, IRVING M. 1968. *Ideology and Sociology*. Englewood Cliffs, N.J.: Prentice-Hall.

ZINN, HOWARD. 1970. *The Politics of History*. Boston: Beacon Press.

ZORBAUGH, HARVEY W. 1929. *The Gold Coast and the Slum, A Sociological Study of Chicago's Near North Side*. Chicago: University of Chicago Press.

ZEUBLIN, CHARLES. 1908. "The Effect on Women of Economic Dependence." *Papers and Proceedings of the American Sociological Society* 3 (December): 30–38.

INDEX

abduction, 440n

academic freedom, 503, 532; antiwar academics, 544; Bemis defended, 493; business interests, 503; case of Bemis, 491–493; case of Du Bois, 505–508; case of Ely, 499–500; case of Nearing, 542–543; case of Ross, 494–497; and Small, 492–493, 508–511; "competence," 539; double standard, 533; early conference section on, 330, 532–533; and economic security, 532–533, 537–538, 538n; general themes, 539; ideological neutrality, 519, 539–540; importance, 490; Pritchett on, 535; "real violators," 541; "reasonable restrictions" on, 535; and repression, xxiv; technocratic doctrines, 539; theory and practice, 501; Veblen, 519; Weatherly on, 533–535, 538n

academic institutions: adjustment to political economy, 520; business domination, 512–513, 518; choice of trustees, 513–514; conditions of development, 511–512; employer/employee relationship, 524n; industrial discipline, 521; as industrial organizations, 513, 517n; occupational role training, 520; politics of faculty, 518; role of instructors, 522; role of students, 522; self-definitions of academics, 523; Veblen, 512–516

academic sociology, 3, 490, 509

accommodation, xxxi, 556, 569; and assimilation, 396; as formal abstractive, 412; liberal syndicalism, 394; Park and Burgess, 386, 392–395, 484; slavery, 395; social class, 394–395; social control, 392

Adamic, Louis, 97, 120, 157

Adams, Bert N., 559

Adams, Graham, 142, 226–228, 230

Adams, John Quincy, 103

Addams, Jane, 474

"adjustment," 330; in Small, 250; in Ward, 189, 331

Africans, 105; imperialism, 105

aggression, 341, 343, 379; checked by guilt, 342; competition, 341; and egoism, 341; instincts, 341; problem of social integration, 341; social control, 343

Agnew, Spiro T., 176n

Allen, Frederick Lewis, 361

Allport, Gordon, 365, 371n

altruism, 25, 553; Freud, 348

American Indians, 102–104; Ward on, 175

American Journal of Sociology, 508–509

American Sociological Society, 361–363; 1920 annual meeting, 361–363

American sociology, 243, 444; absence of Marxism, 563; as academic sociology, 490; accounting for failures, 571; *American Journal of Sociology,* 509; attacked, 565; behaviorism, 364–365; and biologism, 165; Christian capitalism, 451; class domination of city, 482; concept of class, 530; conservative bias, 516; control of, 315, 508–509; and corporate liberalism, 3, 163, 198, 354; and corporations, 225–226; Darwinism, 241; and Durkheim, 254–260; economic dependence of sociologists, 511; Freudianism, 169, 356, 360–361, 364, 366; historical continuities, 551; historical precursors, 98, 445; human nature, 356; ideological definitions, 222ff.; ideological engagement, 415, 421, 469–471; impact of Freudianism, 336, 356; instinct theory, 356–357; laissez-faire liberalism, 445, 447–448; liberalism of, 162, 288, 445; political composition, 507–508; psychological science, 220–222, 337, 359–363; and psychologism, 165, 237, 336, 364; radicalism, 162–163, 448; recent historical studies, 570; response to Women's Movement, 329; revival of the formative years, 561; and science, 241; sexism, 290; shift to structural functionalism, 551; and socialism, 240, 447, 563; and Spencer,

Index

Metzger, Walter P., 492–493, 496, 497n, 500, 502n, 510n, 524
Mexicans, 106; imperialism, 106
Meynaud, Jean, 153, 158n
"middle-range theory," 424–426, 550
Miliband, Ralph, 151, 152n
"militaristic order" and "industrial order," 41–42; and integration, 41
Mill, Harriet Taylor, 291
Mill, James, 432–433, 438n, 439, 445
Mill, John Stuart, 26, 66–67, 182, 288, 291–298, 298n, 299n, 300, 304, 312, 318n, 326, 327n, 365, 433–435, 438, 438n, 439n
Miller, S. M., 563
Mills, C. Wright, 125, 129n, 161–162, 182, 250, 387, 431n, 438, 446n, 532
Mitchell, Wesley C., 118
mobility, 141
"modern man" (Freud), 340–344, 351
monopolies, 136; growth of in U.S., 113–114; ills accrued from, 220; Ross on, 220; Sherman Act, 135, 223; sociologists justify, 225
monopoly capitalism, 443, 526; and corporate liberalism, 97; class relationships in, 529–530; economic interest groups, 278; and liberal-syndicalism, 126; rise of, 112–115; reconstitution of liberalism, 329; Ross, 216
Montesquieu, Charles de, 308n
Moore, G. E., 423n
Moore, Joan, 110n
Moore, Wilbert E., 196n, 561–562, 567n
moral regeneration, 127, 216–217, 330, 407; Durkheim, 273; Park and Burgess, 406; problem of social integration, 127; Ross, 216–217; sexism, 29
Morgan, J. P., 135, 138, 187n
Morgan Lewis Henry, 291, 300–307, 308n, 309n, 312, 318n, 319–320, 322, 327n, 414
Morris, Desmond, 562
"mother right," 300, 305–306, 322
Moynihan, Daniel Patrick, 487–489, 556, 563, 569n, 574n
muckrakers, 145, 225
Mussolini, Benito, 151n

Nairn, Tom, 76
Napoleon, 456n
National Association for the Advancement of Colored People (N.A.A.C.P.), 505

national chauvinism, xxiv
nationalization and Ward, 179, 384
natural justice, 7
natural law, 7–14, 194–195, 315, 321, 344, 421, 462, 549; Aristotle, 9; and classical liberalism, 12, 25; Durkheim, 264; Freud, 338; Hobbes, 11; and laissez-faire liberalism, 25–26; and liberal-functionalism, 15; Locke, 12; Malthus, 33; and natural social-law, 13, 194–195; Ogburn, 461; operative interpretations of, 12; Park and Burgess, 399; Plato, 9, 14n; private property, 248–249; reductionism of, 347; Roman, 9–10; and Romanticism, 61–62; and social inequalities, 13; Spencer, 41; Stoics, 10, 14n; subjection of women, 313, 322; St. Thomas Aquinas, 8, 10–11, 14n; Ward, 172
"natural man," 205, 440–441
natural rights, 7, 12–13
natural selection, 42–43, 56, 313; Engels, 312; ideology, 312; Ross, 212; as social control, 212; subjection of women, 311–312; Thomas, 312; Ward, 312
natural social-law, 7, 13, 188–197, 197n, 387, 391, 558–559; and American sociology, 13; based on exchange, 553; competition, 388–397; elimination of social classes, 195; epitomy of ideology, 195–196; and liberalism, 195; and liberal-functionalism, 194–195; and Marxism, 196; Merton, 430n; and natural law, 13, 194–195; Park and Burgess, 388, 422; private property, 248–249
"natural society," *see* society
natural will, 199
naturalistic fallacy, 423n
Nearing, Scott, 283, 532–533, 537, 538n, 541–543, 547n
neo-Hobbesian problem, 201–202; and liberal-syndicalism, 247ff
"Niagara Movement," 505
Nicolaus, Martin, 565
Nisbet, Robert A., xxviii n, 6n, 79, 85n, 283n, 442, 572
Nizan, Paul, 255
"nondifferentiated society," *see* society
North, Cecil, 532–533, 537, 538n

Oberschall, Anthony, 94n
objectivism, 368–370; Comte, 369; Durkheim, 369; Ellwood's rejection, 369;

602